Research Handbook on Entrepreneurship and Leadership

Edited by

Richard T. Harrison

Professor of Entrepreneurship and Innovation, University of Edinburgh Business School, UK

Claire M. Leitch

Professor of Entrepreneurial Leadership, Lancaster University Management School, UK

EE Edward **Elgar**
PUBLISHING

Cheltenham, UK • Northampton, MA, USA

Published by
Edward Elgar Publishing Limited
The Lypiatts
15 Lansdown Road
Cheltenham
Glos GL50 2JA
UK

Edward Elgar Publishing, Inc.
William Pratt House
9 Dewey Court
Northampton
Massachusetts 01060
USA

Paperback edition 2019

A catalogue record for this book
is available from the British Library

Library of Congress Control Number: 2017947076

This book is available electronically in the **Elgar**online
Business subject collection
DOI 10.4337/9781783473762

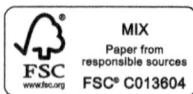

MIX
Paper from
responsible sources
FSC
www.fsc.org   FSC® C013604

ISBN 978 1 78347 375 5 (cased)
ISBN 978 1 78347 376 2 (eBook)
ISBN 978 1 78990 649 3 (paperback)

Typeset by Servis Filmsetting Ltd, Stockport, Cheshire
Printed and bound by CPI Group (UK) Ltd, Croydon, CR0 4YY

Contents

Contributors

Afsaneh Bagheri, PhD, is currently an Assistant Professor in the Department of Entrepreneurship Development, Faculty of Entrepreneurship, University of Tehran, Iran. She obtained her Doctorate in Educational Management from the Faculty of Educational Studies, University Putra Malaysia, Malaysia. She has published papers on different areas of entrepreneurship including entrepreneurial leadership, entrepreneurial self-efficacy, entrepreneurial regulation and intention, entrepreneurship education and entrepreneurial competencies. She has also presented papers on entrepreneurship and entrepreneurship education at national and international conferences. Her research interest areas are: entrepreneurial leadership, entrepreneurial competencies, entrepreneurial intention, entrepreneurship education, disabled entrepreneurship and gender and entrepreneurship.

Stewart Barnes is founder and Managing Director of QuoLux, a privately owned company specializing in leadership development of owner-managers within small and medium-sized enterprises through the delivery of the LEAD, GOLD and GAIN programmes. Stewart draws upon extensive experience of leading, growing and innovating a variety of private businesses in different markets in different countries, transforming organizations and their performance. Stewart is a Visiting Fellow at University of Gloucestershire, UK and is researching his PhD. He is co-author of *LEADing Small Business* (with Steve Kempster and Sue Smith). His work on transformational change has been featured in a number of books, articles and government best practice guidance documents.

R. Greg Bell is the Associate Dean of Faculty Affairs and Associate Professor of Management at the University of Dallas, USA. He teaches courses in Global Entrepreneurship and Corporate Social Responsibility and Sustainability. His research on corporate governance and international business has been published in leading management and entrepreneurship journals.

Malin Brännback, DSc BSc (Pharm), is Chaired Professor of International Business, and Dean at Åbo Akademi University, Finland. She was Visiting Professor in Entrepreneurship at Stockholm Business School (Stockholm University) in 2012–2014. She has 200 publications and has co-authored seven books with Alan Carsrud, including *Understanding the Entrepreneurial Mind – Opening the Black Box* (2009, Springer Verlag),

Handbook of Research Methods and Applications in Entrepreneurship and Small Businesses (2014, Edward Elgar Publishing) and *Fundamentals for becoming a Successful Entrepreneur* (2016, Pearson). She is on the review board of *Journal of Small Business Management*. Her current research interests are in entrepreneurial intentionality and cognition and entrepreneurial growth and performance.

Alan L. Carsrud, PhD, is Visiting Research Professor at Åbo Akademi University in Finland. He previously held the Rogers Chair in Entrepreneurship at Ryerson University in Toronto, Canada. He has published more than 200 papers, chapters and articles on entrepreneurship, family business and psychology.

Malcolm H. Cone, PhD, is the former Director of the Asia Institute at the University of Otago School of Business, New Zealand. He has also held positions at a number of universities including Distinguished Visiting Professor at the Management Development Institute in Delhi, India; Honorary Research Fellow at Lincoln University New Zealand; and visiting Scholar at Glasgow and Lancaster universities in the United Kingdom. He has published widely on sociological aspects of management and leadership in Islamic societies and, more recently, extensive research and publications taking a comparative approach to understanding the challenge of China especially in relation to the impact of culture on the areas of leadership, learning, creativity and strategy.

Jane Croad is a Senior Lecturer in Marketing. Before commencing her academic career, Jane enjoyed a successful corporate career and held management positions with Gwalia Housing, Johnson & Johnson and the Wicker Group. Jane is currently pursuing her Doctorate in International Marketing with Cardiff Metropolitan University, UK.

Allan A. Gibb, Professor Emeritus at Durham University, has worked extensively in the field of entrepreneurship and independent business development in more than 70 countries throughout the world. His recent work has focused on entrepreneurship education at all levels of the education field. He has for several years been advisor to the UK National Council for Graduate Entrepreneurship, and has designed and directed national entrepreneurial leadership programmes for higher education and further education senior staff development.

Eleanor Hamilton is Professor of Entrepreneurship in the Department of Entrepreneurship, Strategy and Innovation (DESI) at Lancaster University Management School, UK. She was a founder of the Institute for Entrepreneurship and Enterprise Development which undertakes research and education in entrepreneurship and innovation in dialogue with business and community. Her research focuses on family businesses and entrepreneurial learning as an inherently social rather than individual phenomenon. It also examines aspects of gender and leadership in family business and entrepreneurship. Professor Hamilton has a proven commitment to create and evidence effective forms of knowledge exchange between a university and its small and medium-sized enterprise client base.

Pegram Harrison is Senior Fellow in Entrepreneurship at Oxford University's Saïd Business School, UK. He teaches and conducts research on entrepreneurial leadership, with a focus on the Islamic world. He also runs the School's Engaging with the Humanities initiative, a programme of research, teaching and public events that connects the business school with scholars and practitioners working in the humanities.

Richard T. Harrison, PhD, is Chair of Entrepreneurship and Innovation at University of Edinburgh Business School, UK, where he is also Director of the Centre for Entrepreneurship Research and Director of the Compassionate Leadership Initiative within the Centre for Strategic Leadership. He has extensive experience in research, programme development, executive education and consultancy and advisory work in entrepreneurship (particularly early stage finance and business angels, technology transfer and business development, and entrepreneurial learning and leadership) and in strategic leadership development nationally and internationally, and is a regular speaker at national and international practitioner conferences and workshops. He is one of the world's leading scholars on business angel finance and early stage risk capital.

Gay Haskins has worked for more than 30 years in the field of management development. Now an Associate Fellow of Saïd Business School, University of Oxford, UK, she was founder, together with Professor Allan Gibb, of the Entrepreneurial University Leaders Programme (EULP), introduced at Oxford with the support of the National Centre for Entrepreneurship Education and Universities UK. Between 2006 and 2010, Gay was Dean of Executive Education at Saïd Business School, University of Oxford. She has also served as Dean of Executive Education at London Business School and the Indian School of Business. Earlier, she was Director General of the European Foundation for Management Development (EFMD), a major international association, focusing on best practice in management development.

Omaima M. Hatem, PhD, researches and lectures at the University of Edinburgh Business School, UK, in the fields of entrepreneurship, strategy and international business with specific interest in emerging markets. She is co-author of *State and Entrepreneurs in Egypt: Economic Development since 1805*. Prior to her academic career, Dr Hatem established a diversified group of companies including a number of engineering, manufacturing, consulting and international trading firms that extended services to cover more than 30 African, European and North and South American countries.

Steve Kempster is Professor of Leadership Learning and Development in the Department of Leadership and Management, Lancaster University Management School, UK. His work on owner-manager leadership learning has been published in the *International Journal of Entrepreneurial Behaviour* and the *International Journal of Management Reviews*, along with two books, *How Managers have Learnt to Lead* and *LEADing Small Business: Business Growth through Leadership Development* (with Sue Smith and Stewart Barnes). Steve is Chair of the Global Consortium of Leadership Centres, researching into responsibilities of leadership. His latest book (co-edited with Brigid Carroll) *Responsible Leadership: Realism and Romanticism*, is connected to this area.

Donald F. Kuratko, PhD, is the Jack M. Gill Distinguished Chair of Entrepreneurship and Professor of Entrepreneurship at the Kelley School of Business, Indiana University, Bloomington, USA. Professor Kuratko has been named one of the Top Entrepreneurship Scholars in the world, with more than 190 articles on entrepreneurship and corporate entrepreneurship in journals such as *Journal of Business Venturing, Entrepreneurship Theory and Practice, Strategic Management Journal, Journal of Business Ethics, Journal of Operations Management* and *Small Business Economics*. He has authored 30 books, including one of the leading entrepreneurship books in the world today, *Entrepreneurship: Theory, Process, Practice* (10th edition, 2017).

Claire M. Leitch, DPhil, holds the Chair in Entrepreneurial Leadership at Lancaster University Management School, UK. Her research interests concentrate on the development, enhancement and growth of individuals and organisations in an entrepreneurial context, with a particular focus on leadership, leadership development and learning. She is an internationally recognized scholar whose work has shaped theoretical debate and had significant industrial and policy impact. She has published in *Journal of Small Business Management, Organization Research Methods, Academy of Management Learning and Education, British Journal of Management, Regional Studies* and *Entrepreneurship Theory and Practice*. Currently she is Editor of the *International Small Business Journal*.

Adebimpe Adesua-Lincoln, PhD, has held positions in Cardiff University, University of South Wales, UK and was a Senior Lecturer in Law at

Cardiff Metropolitan University, UK before taking up a position as Assistant Professor in Saudi Arabia. She currently runs her own property development and educational consultancy business. Her research interests lie in the area of entrepreneurship, corporate governance and responsibility.

Maura McAdam, DPhil, is a Professor of Management and Director of Entrepreneurship at Dublin City University (DCU), Ireland. She is affiliated with the DCU Centre of Family Business and is a member of the Irish Successful Transgenerational Entrepreneurial Practices (STEP) team. She is an internationally recognized scholar in entrepreneurship, having a particular expertise in gender, technology entrepreneurship and family business. Accordingly, her research has been published in top-rated North American and UK journals across a range of theoretical disciplines, such as *Entrepreneurship Theory and Practice*, *Journal of Small Business Management*, *Regional Studies*, *Entrepreneurship and Regional Development* and *International Small Business Journal*.

Susan Mueller is Assistant Professor of Entrepreneurship at the University of St Gallen, Swiss Research Institute for Small Business and Entrepreneurship. In her research, Susan focuses on entrepreneurial behaviour, social entrepreneurship and entrepreneurship education. Susan holds an MBA degree from the University of Pittsburgh, USA, and received her doctoral degree from the University of St Gallen. Before she went into academia she worked as a business consultant with a focus on marketing and organization.

Zaidatol Akmaliah Lope Pihie, PhD, is a Professor at the Faculty of Educational Studies at the University Putra Malaysia. She has been involved in teaching and conducting research on various areas of entrepreneurship, entrepreneurship education and educational leadership since 1981. She has published many papers on developing entrepreneurial intentions, attributes, competencies and skills, specifically among university students. She has also published several books on educational administration, business education, educational leadership and entrepreneurial intentions.

David Rae, PhD is Professor of Enterprise, De Montfort University, Leicester, UK. He is a leading innovator and researcher in the human and social dynamics of entrepreneurship, learning and small business management. He has achieved professional and academic recognition for his contributions to entrepreneurship research, education, policy and regional development, with international connections in Europe, North America and South Asia, and is an inspirational keynote speaker at international and professional conferences. He is a Fellow of the UK Institute for Small Business and Entrepreneurship.

Maija Renko-Dolan is Associate Professor of Entrepreneurship at the University of Illinois at Chicago, USA. She studies entrepreneurship and new ventures, and her research has been published in journals such as *Journal of Management, Journal of Business Venturing* and *Entrepreneurship Theory and Practice*.

Muhammad Azam Roomi, PhD, is a Professor of Entrepreneurship and the Associate Dean of Faculty, Research and Executive Education at the Prince Mohammed bin Salman College of Business and Entrepreneurship (MBSC) in Saudi Arabia. Prior to joining MBSC, Roomi served as the Director of the Executive MBA programme and MSc Management and Entrepreneurship programme at the Cranfield School of Management, UK. He was also instrumental in setting up and developing the Centre for Women's Enterprise at the University of Bedfordshire, UK. His current research interests include entrepreneurial leadership, growth of entrepreneurial ventures, women's entrepreneurship, Islam and entrepreneurship and entrepreneurship education.

Arik Röschke is a PhD researcher at the Swiss Research Institute of Small Business and Entrepreneurship at the University of St Gallen, Switzerland. He graduated with a Master of International Affairs and Governance from the University of St Gallen, and CEMS Master in International Management. His research lies in the fields of entrepreneurship and leadership.

Leon Schjoedt, PhD, is a Professor of Entrepreneurship and Management at Mahasarakham University, Thailand. His research focuses on entrepreneurial behaviour; the intersection between entrepreneurship and organizational behavior. He has presented his research at numerous academic meetings, including the annual meeting for the Academy of Management and Babson College Entrepreneurship Research Conference. Leon has published more than 40 articles and book chapters, including in *Entrepreneurship Theory and Practice, Journal of High Technology Management Research, International Journal of Entrepreneurial Behaviour and Research, Organizational Dynamics* and *Small Business Economics.* His work has been featured in the *Wall Street Journal*.

Chrysavgi Sklaveniti is Post-doctoral Research Fellow in the Research Institute for Organizational Psychology at the University of St Gallen, Switzerland. Her research interests revolve around the relational aspects of teamwork (virtual and co-located), technological integration, entrepreneurship, creativity and leadership. Her publications pursue these themes in philosophical, conceptual and empirical formats, and the work presented here continues these developments.

Robert Smith, MA, PhD, is Professor of Enterprise and Innovation at the University of the West of Scotland, Dumfries, UK. His research interests include entrepreneurial leadership, rural and criminal entrepreneurship, entrepreneurial narrative, entrepreneurial identity, as well as small and family business. He has taught leadership at MBA level, entrepreneurial leadership at undergraduate level, and police leadership at Master's level, as well as strategy into action at DBA level. He has more than 150 peer-reviewed publications in journals and book chapters.

Sue Smith is a Professor of Innovation and Enterprise and is the Director of the Centre for SME Development at the University of Central Lancashire, UK. Sue is passionate about the interface between higher education and business, particularly small business. Her academic research and practice focuses on leadership development in small and medium-sized organizations and the relationship between universities, business and government and the impact this can have on the regional economy. Sue is co-author of *LEADing Small Business* (with Steve Kempster and Stewart Barnes). Throughout her career she has operated at the interface between higher education and business, progressing the business engagement and knowledge exchange agendas throughout different universities.

Valerie Stead, PhD, is Senior Lecturer in Leadership and Management at Lancaster University Management School, UK. Valerie's research interests are in gender, leadership and learning, adopting critical perspectives to examine women's leadership. Current projects address textual and visual representations of women's leadership in the media, and examine gender, power and leadership in entrepreneurial business. Valerie has published book chapters and in scholarly journals, including *Organization Studies, Management Learning, International Small Business Journal* and *Leadership*. Valerie has published the research monograph *Women's Leadership* (with C. Elliott, 2009), and co-edited the volume *Gender, Media, and Organization: Challenging Mis(s)Representations of Women Leaders and Managers* (with C. Elliott, S. Mavin, J. Williams, 2016).

Vicky Tzoumpa is a Doctoral researcher at the University of St Gallen, Switzerland and a Fellow of the Higher Education Academy (HEA). She has undertaken substantial research on knowledge management, organizational learning, project teams and organizational performance, strategic foresight and innovation. Her current research interests lie in the area of social innovation and entrepreneurship, strategy and management of start-ups and SMEs, and she is particularly investigating the roles of entre-preneurs, entrepreneurial action and its relational dynamics.

Vicar S. Valencia, PhD, is an Assistant Professor of Economics at the Judd Leighton School of Business and Economics, Indiana University South Bend, USA. His research interests span the fields of corporate governance, innovation, and research and development alliances. He has previously undertaken industry consultancy projects with the Australian Agency for International Development. His research has been published in the *Review of Economics and Statistics* and the *Australian Journal of Management*.

Thierry Volery holds the Chair of Entrepreneurship at the University of Western Australia. He is a Visiting Professor at the University of St Gallen, Swiss Research Institute for Small Business and Entrepreneurship. His research interests include entrepreneurs' behaviour, entrepreneurship process and entrepreneurship education.

J. Lee Whittington, PhD, is Professor of Management in the Satish and Yasmin Gupta College of Business and Co-Director of the Master of Leadership program at the University of Dallas, USA. He teaches courses on leadership and followership, organizational behavior, and complex organizations. He is the author of *Biblical Perspectives on Leadership and Organizations* and co-author of *Leading the Sustainable Organization* (with Tim Galpin and Greg Bell) and *Enhancing Employee Engagement: An Evidence-Based Approach* (with Simone Meskelis, Enoch Asare, and Sri Beldona). His research has been published in the *Leadership Quarterly*, *Journal of Management*, *Academy of Management Review* and the *Journal of Organizational Behavior.* His consulting experience includes engagements with SB International, Life.Church, Nokia, FedEx-Kinko's and Siemens.

Haina Zhang, PhD, is a Senior Lecturer at Lancaster University Management School, UK. She has extensive international research experience, and her research interest focuses on leadership, organizational behavior, international business and management, human resource management, and management in China. She has a preference to bring a philosophical and sociological perspective to these topics. She has published her research in a number of international journals, such as *Journal of Management*, *Human Resource Management*, *Journal of Vocational Behavior*, *Journal of Business Ethics*, *Asia Pacific Business Review* and *Frontiers of Business Research* in China. She is also an Associate Editor of the *European Management Journal*.

PART I

INTRODUCTION

1. The evolving field of entrepreneurial leadership: an overview
Claire M. Leitch and Richard T. Harrison

INTRODUCTION

Research into entrepreneurship and leadership is not new, but has expanded rapidly in recent years. Much of the early interest in and use of the term 'entrepreneurial leadership' was outside the field of entrepreneurship or management studies more generally. This includes, for example, research into the semi-piratical entrepreneurs of late nineteenth-century America (Destler, 1946), the transformation of American schools (Peck, 1991), the role of not-for-profit organizations in community entrepreneurship (Selsky and Smith, 1994), and political entrepreneurship (Schneider and Teske, 1992). Within the entrepreneurship and management literatures, the term has until recently been more alluded to in passing than systematically defined and explored. 'Entrepreneurial leadership' has, accordingly, been defined as a particular entrepreneurial style (Kets de Vries, 1977), as a correlate of corporate performance in different types of firms (Miller, 1983), as a missing element in entrepreneurship curricula (Hood and Young, 1993), as an identifiable trait (Satow and Rector, 1995) and as an important feature of contemporary society (Eggers and Leahy, 1994). However, there have been some salient early papers focusing specifically on entrepreneurial leadership as a prerequisite for organizational development (Lippitt, 1987), on the importance of the entrepreneur being a (visionary) leader (Cunningham and Lischeron, 1991) and on the parallels between leadership and entrepreneurship as fields of research and practice (Harrison and Leitch, 1994).

Both leadership and entrepreneurship are still to a large extent contested constructs (Harrison and Leitch, 1994; Leitch and Harrison, 2018). While there may be no agreement as to what 'leadership' is, despite more than 50 years of quantitative and qualitative research into traits, styles, contingent leadership, transactional and transformative leadership, and new post-heroic leadership, there is a widespread consensus that it is important and that it is situational. However, most leadership research has been situated in corporate contexts and there has been much less attention given to issues of leadership and leadership development in the context of entrepreneurial and small and medium-sized enterprises (SMEs). For some, this is not problematic, and entrepreneurship is simply a type of leadership that occurs in a specific setting; that is, the entrepreneurial or small business is the situation and, as such, available leadership theory can be applied to understanding it. For others, the study of entrepreneurs as leaders is a gap in both the leadership and the entrepreneurship literatures: exploring the founder or entrepreneur of small and emerging firms as a leader has yet to be a major area of study. However, as we have argued elsewhere (Leitch et al., 2013), the research that has been done suggests that the impact of leaders and leadership is a crucial factor in the success or failure of smaller entrepreneurial firms and has implications for our understanding of new venture viability and growth. Thus, we would argue, understanding leadership in the entrepreneurial context is particularly pertinent, given the importance attached to entrepreneurship as an agent of economic development and restructuring.

As a field, entrepreneurial leadership is still evolving, lacks definitional clarity and has not yet developed appropriate tools to assess its characteristics and behaviours: it is, in other words, still seeking its identity (Leitch and Harrison, 2018; Leitch et al., 2013; Renko et al., 2015). There are, however, specific issues in the entrepreneurial and SME context that suggest leadership development needs to be conceptualized differently from that in the corporate context. For instance, there is rarely a clear separation between leadership and managerial responsibilities, which is complicated by the ongoing ownership role of entrepreneurs and/or their families, and organizational structures tend to be simpler and less hierarchical. Nevertheless, entrepreneurial settings provide a venue, in terms of being characterized by highly organic, non-formalized simple structures, where the impact of leadership is likely to be most pronounced. However, the higher likely impact of leadership in this setting is matched by greater difficulty in developing that leadership. Indeed, often there may be a conflict between leadership development and the entrepreneurial situational context.

This reflects the fact that such firms tend to be influenced by dominant individuals, who are associated with a lack of flexibility, engagement, openness and responsiveness, whereas leadership development requires reflection and feedback in safe environments if lessons are to be learnt and individuals are to develop. Accordingly, we can identify five issues for debate around entrepreneurial leadership (Leitch and Harrison, 2018). First, to what extent should entrepreneurial leadership research be grounded in and shaped by theories and insights from entrepreneurship or leadership? Second, is there or can there be an overarching theory of the concept? Third, is it possible to come to a definitional consensus on what 'entrepreneurial leadership' is? Fourth, can we develop appropriate theory-grounded measurement tools to bring consistency to empirical discussions of the concept? Fifth, how can we develop and enhance entrepreneurial leadership capability?

While we do not claim to provide definitive answers to these five questions, the chapters that follow do provide new insights on each of them, and demonstrate: first, that context matters, whether this is understood as environment, organization type or culture; and second, that there remains much work to be done. In collecting together a set of conceptual and empirical chapters from a wide range of cultures and entrepreneurship and leadership ecosystems, this *Research Handbook* for the first time produces a systematic overview of the entrepreneurial leadership field, providing a state-of-the art perspective and highlighting unanswered questions and opportunities for further research. It is intended to consolidate existing theory development, stimulate new conceptual thinking and include path-breaking empirical explorations.

Elsewhere we have identified three different positions by which the parameters of the relationship between entrepreneurship and leadership can be described (Leitch and Harrison, 2018): first, entrepreneurship as a style of leadership (leadership has primacy); second, entrepreneurial leadership as an entrepreneurial mindset (entrepreneurship has primacy); and third, entrepreneurial leadership at the interface of both domains (Figure 1.1). Looking at entrepreneurial leadership as a contextualized and situated form of leadership, entrepreneurship scholars suggest that, given the absence or underdevelopment of standard operating procedures and management practices, founders initially have to lead (Hmieleski and

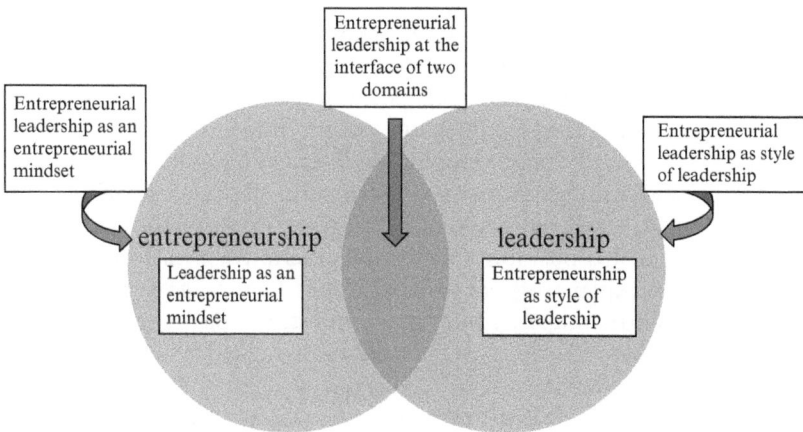

Figure 1.1   Leadership, entrepreneurship and entrepreneurial leadership

Ensley, 2007). However with growth and delegation of primary business functions the entrepreneur's role may more formally evolve to that of a leader (Jensen and Luthans, 2006). This is in keeping with the increasing formality of, and emphasis on, management and leadership practices associated with increasing organizational size (Perren and Grant, 2001). In other words, entrepreneurship is regarded as simply a type of leadership that occurs in a specific setting; that is, the entrepreneurial or small business is the situation, and available leadership theory is applied to understanding it accordingly (Vecchio, 2003). Such a perspective implies a hierarchy of leadership orientations and the unidirectional transference of ideas from the leadership domain to entrepreneurship. Further, work in this area has tended to conflate the terms 'entrepreneur' and 'leader'.

In considering entrepreneurial leadership as an entrepreneurial mindset, researchers consider that entrepreneurship is the essence of leadership, and an entrepreneurial mindset and behaviours are essential for effective leadership (Kuratko, 2007; Gupta et al., 2004). Accordingly, entrepreneurial leaders are neither entrepreneurs nor confined to operating in entrepreneurial, small SMEs, and thus this position resonates with intrapreneurship and corporate entrepreneurship. Unlike the tendency of the unidirectional transference of ideas from leadership to entrepreneurship, in this body of work no assumption is made regarding whether entrepreneurial leadership is a superior or inferior style. Instead, entrepreneurship scholars view entrepreneurs and leaders as different, and have appropriated leadership models and concepts to advance thinking in their field. Both positions, however, tend to focus on the individual over the context, and in so doing perpetuate rather than challenge leader-centric and heroic leader theories (Collinson, 2011).

Researchers at the interface of entrepreneurship and leadership are adamant that the two constructs, while similar, are not the same (McKone-Sweet et al., 2011). Work from this position is characterized by scholars identifying common themes, including vision, influence, leading innovative and creative individuals, planning, problem-solving, decision-making, risk-taking and strategic initiatives (Fernald et al., 2005; Cogliser and Brigham, 2004). However, while of value, most work on entrepreneurial leadership from this position tends to be descriptive with little analysis or advances in explanatory insights, and fails to provide guidance into how commonalities might be built on. There is, in other words, a strong disciplinary rather than interdisciplinary basis for current research into entrepreneurial leadership.

The chapters presented in this *Handbook* have been grouped into five overarching themes (Table 1.1), which are discussed below: first, theoretical perspectives on entrepreneurship and leadership; second, leadership

Table 1.1 Handbook chapter overview

Chapter/author	Focus of chapter	Conceptual/ methodological	Entrepreneurial leadership perspective	Contribution
PART II: THEORETICAL PERSPECTIVES ON ENTREPRENEURSHIP AND LEADERSHIP				
2. Röschke	Bibliometric analysis overview of field's evolution and identification of main themes and areas of debate	Methodological: bibliometric analysis	As a style of leadership	The evolution in the use of the construct term 'entrepreneurial leadership' highlighting increased cross-fertilization and convergence and the move from conceptual papers to those focused on methodology
3. Zhang and Cone	Propose an alternative understanding of entrepreneurial leadership practice based on a processual perspective	Conceptual	At the interface – leader in an entrepreneurial context	Draw on Deleuze's materialistic philosophy of immanence, complex adaptive systems (CAS) theory and the processual perspective in Chinese philosophy to illustrate a process understanding of reality where interrelatedness and relativity are emphasized and order and stability are viewed as temporary
4. Stead and Hamilton	The adoption of a reflexive critical approach to analysis to develop new conceptual frameworks to theorize about entrepreneurial leadership	Exemplar of a reflexive critical, multi-stage approach to analysis, drawing on illustrations from two empirical cases	At the interface: a leader in an entrepreneurial context	Outline and discuss the steps and value in adopting a critical perspective

Table 1.1 (continued)

Chapter/author	Focus of chapter	Conceptual/ methodological	Entrepreneurial leadership perspective	Contribution
5. Harrison and Roomi	Drawing on neo-institutional, market-based and culturally informed theory, highlight how hegemonic models and thinking are inappropriate to explain and develop Islamic entrepreneurial leadership	Conceptual	At the interface, drawing on both fields to ensure relevance	Argue that neo-institutional theory (comprising the practices and beliefs associated with the communal and societal, political and religious spheres) would provide a deeper and more nuanced appreciation of the relationships between Islamic formal and informal institutions, markets and culture

PART III: LEADERSHIP IN ENTREPRENEURIAL CONTEXTS

6. Volery and Mueller	Exploration of the strategies and behaviours adopted by entrepreneurs to preserve their entrepreneurial behaviour	Empirical: structured observation of six entrepreneurs	As a style of leadership (based on the 4 tensions or paradoxes and 10 roles identified)	Builds on strategic leadership to demonstrate that entrepreneurial leadership is an integration of visionary and managerial perspectives
7. Schjoedt and Valencia	Development of a framework to categorize entrepreneurs as either entrepreneurial leaders and/or entrepreneurial managers	Conceptual	At the interface between entrepreneurship and leadership, and entrepreneurship and management	Emphasis on the learning styles and use of knowledge between entrepreneurial leaders and managers to demonstrate that the key distinguishing feature between the two is how they engage in knowledge exploration and/or exploitation in the new venture creation process; believe that entrepreneurial leaders are similar to transformational leaders

| 8. | Bell and Whittington | Integrate the full-range model of leadership and the life-cycle approach to understand the evolution and growth of threshold firms | Conceptual | As a style of leadership: entrepreneurs operate in the role of leaders | Integrating two models and adopting a configurational perspective to identify various future research opportunities in entrepreneurial leadership focused on the efficacy of different leadership behaviours at various stages in a venture's life cycle |
| 9. | Carsrud, Renko-Dolan and Brännback | Explore the concept of entrepreneurial leadership and how it differs from other forms of leadership and why entrepreneurial leadership (EL) is critical to our understanding of new firm creation and growth, and impacts upon a firm's culture and sustainability through the leadership succession process | Conceptual | Entrepreneurial leadership is a new form of leadership applicable at multiple levels in all organizations | Entrepreneurial leadership is clearly distinguished from other leadership styles. Given the opportunity focus of entrepreneurial leaders, this can be accomplished across organizations of all types, as well as across different functional levels. As such, entrepreneurial leadership is not only the domain of new business founders but also practised by leaders in various types of organizations that are reinventing themselves. Indeed, entrepreneurial leadership can be found in leader–follower relationships anywhere in an organization |

PART IV: APPLICATIONS OF ENTREPRENEURIAL LEADERSHIP

| 10. | Kuratko | To provide enhanced understanding of the process of corporate entrepreneurial leadership | Conceptual | As an entrepreneurial mindset | Identifies four major implementation issues for corporate entrepreneurial leadership as well as six critical corporate entrepreneurial leadership responsibilities |

Table 1.1 (continued)

Chapter/author	Focus of chapter	Conceptual/methodological	Entrepreneurial leadership perspective	Contribution
11. Sklaveniti and Tzoumpa	To explore the role played by temporality, relational identity development and improvisation in entrepreneurial leadership opportunity genesis and development in social enterprises	Conceptual	As an entrepreneurial mindset: 'a perpetual and relational process of working together to mobilize business opportunities in an organizational context in pursuit of entrepreneurial goals'	Propose that practice theory is a useful analytical construct to illustrate how the performativity of practices follows the unfolding of entrepreneurship in which spontaneity, creativity and improvisation are stressed
12. Hatem	Examines the actions, processes and attributes of entrepreneurial distributed leadership in the high growth and rapid internationalization of emerging multinationals in the Middle East and North Africa (MENA) region	Empirical: 18 case study companies in the MENA region	Entrepreneurial leadership is a distinctive form of leadership	Examines how distributed leadership development can be seen as a managerial and entrepreneurial process and the role of human and social capital in its enactment in the context of high-growth, rapidly internationalizing MNEs from the emerging market MENA region; adds to the literature on business group formation through international diversification and the enactment of portfolio entrepreneurship

No.	Aim		Method	Contribution
13.	Adesua-Lincoln and Croad	To investigate the gender differences between Nigerian men and women's leadership practices and collective entrepreneurial behaviour	As a style of leadership	Empirical: survey of entrepreneurs in one Nigerian state	Taking a 'gender as variable' approach, demonstrates that on the whole women entrepreneurial leaders tend to adopt a more transformational approach to their leadership, while men entrepreneurial leaders tend to be more collective in their entrepreneurship behaviour

PART V: ENTREPRENEURIAL LEADERSHIP AND LEARNING

No.	Author	Aim	Position	Method	Contribution
14.	Kempster, Smith and Barnes	Exploration of entrepreneurial leadership learning	Interface: a leader in an entrepreneurial context	Autoethnographic account of an entrepreneurial leader's experiences of learning on an entrepreneurial leadership development programme	Draws on communities of practice (CoP) theory to illustrate how human, social and institutional capital are developed and interrelated in the context of a leadership development programme
15.	Bagheri and Pihie	To examine the motivations of student leaders of university entrepreneurship clubs and projects to develop entrepreneurial leadership competencies	As an entrepreneurial mindset: student entrepreneurial leadership is a process of social interaction and influence that develops students' entrepreneurial knowledge and competencies	Empirical: qualitative interviews of 14 student leaders in Malaysian higher education institutions	Contributes to the sparse literature on university entrepreneurial leadership development opportunities, demonstrates the potentially influential role which university entrepreneurship clubs play, and provides insights for educators on those attributes that should be developed and enhanced

Table 1.1 (continued)

Chapter/author	Focus of chapter	Conceptual/ methodological	Entrepreneurial leadership perspective	Contribution
16. Rae	Explores the ways in which entrepreneurial leaders can build a sustained culture of entrepreneurship and facilitate leadership development opportunities in their organizations	Empirical study: four case studies of leadership in different types of enterprise	Interface: a leader in an entrepreneurial context	Presents a model for leadership for sustainability in entrepreneurial organizations comprising identity, culture, community and entrepreneurial innovation
17. Smith	To understand more fully how leadership can be exercised as an abstract and abstracted concept	Single case exemplar is employed: data derived from media coverage and the organization's website which was analysed using the cultural web model	Interface: how leadership occurs in entrepreneurial settings	Entrepreneurial leadership is both a philosophy and a situated, storied practice

| 18. | Gibb and Haskins | What is the entrepreneurial university of the future, in concept and practice? | Conceptual, informed by practice | Leadership as transformational in an entrepreneurial context | Builds on a number of key concepts: entrepreneurial organization design and leadership; the definition of enterprise and entrepreneurship and their relationship to innovation; how entrepreneurship sits with the traditional 'idea' of a university |

PART VI: FUTURE DIRECTIONS

| 19. | Harrison, Leitch and McAdam | Highlight the embedded masculinity of entrepreneurial leadership domain, contending that it is gender blind, gender defensive and gender neutral | Conceptual | Interface: entrepreneurial leadership in context | Challenge prevailing gendered assumptions and conceptions to avoid the danger that entrepreneurial leadership may be co-opted into the mainstream discourse; identify recent and relevant debates and discussions, particularly within leadership studies, and develop a research agenda |

in entrepreneurial contexts; third, applications of entrepreneurial leadership; fourth, entrepreneurial leadership and learning; and fifth, future directions.

STRUCTURE OF THE BOOK

Part II Theoretical Perspectives on Entrepreneurship and Leadership

We begin with a set of chapters that advocate new perspectives on entrepreneurial leadership, based on systematic literature reviews, conceptual innovation, methodological refinement and contextual sensitivity. In Chapter 2 Röschke presents a useful bibliometric analysis of 21 representative, peer-reviewed articles published on entrepreneurial leadership research from 2003 to 2014, which highlights the evolution of entrepreneurial leadership and presents the main themes and areas of debate. While early articles separated the two, more recent articles (from 2009 to 2014) employed the term 'entrepreneurial leadership' more frequently. In addition to the core concepts of 'entrepreneurship' and 'leadership', the term 'performance' is dominant and the positive influence of leadership on venture performance is highlighted. Specifically, the analysis stressed the importance of the leadership role played by entrepreneurs and the subsequent positive outcomes achieved at an individual and organizational level. The dynamic nature of the entrepreneurial leader's role is stressed, especially the ways in which their leadership responsibilities and functions mature and crystallize as their company develops. For most of the authors in this analysis a key element of leadership effectiveness relates to a leader's style, with 'authentic', 'transformational' and 'shared' leadership dominating. Transformational leadership has shaped most of the thinking in entrepreneurial leadership which while it has provided useful insights can potentially stymie conceptual development. To prevent perpetuating the mainstream and to ensure more holistic understanding of the construct we urge scholars to embrace more recent debates and critiques in leadership theory (Leitch and Harrison, 2018).

On the basis of his research, Röschke provides a definition of entrepreneurial leadership as 'the entrepreneur's or group of entrepreneurs' ability to influence and direct the performance of an individual or a group with the aim to steer the organization in its development under uncertainty', which takes the position that entrepreneurs are leaders by virtue of their position and the context in which they work.

Zhang and Cone (Chapter 3) challenge conventional understandings of how the world works and propose that an alternative understanding of social reality is required in both leadership and entrepreneurship studies. Thus, they suggest that a move from the dominant substance perspective (Deleuze, 1994) and a focus 'away from isolated actions and activities to the recursive dynamics between external and internal complexity as new relations are created internally and as inter-organizational relations are initiated externally' (Steyaert, 2007: 457). Accordingly, their aim is to give an account of entrepreneurial leadership to prioritize flow and process over actions and decisions. Despite increasing attention being paid to a processual perspective in entrepreneurship, captured in Steyaert's (2007) phrase 'entrepreneuring', a tension remains between this and the dominant ontologies that have sustained Western culture and thinking. Zhang and Cone argue that most researchers view process to represent a change in things (phenomena) rather than an acknowledgement of epiphenomena which are transitory. In other words, flow and process are prioritized over actions and decisions to capture what they term 'the emerging now'. As an exemplar, in the context of opportunity recognition, researchers should closely attend to emerging processes and the opportunity for entrepreneurial leaders to act rather than them envisaging and creating scenarios of possible opportunities.

To provide an account of entrepreneurial leadership practice drawing on a processual understanding of social reality they build on Deleuze's materialistic philosophy of immanence, in particular his interrelating ideas of assemblage, lines of flight, desire and plateaus, complex adaptive systems (CAS) theory and the processual perspective in Chinese philosophy. To illustrate this they describe the case of China, where a process understanding of reality is normative and where interrelatedness and relativity are emphasized and order is considered to be temporary. The most radical insight of this perspective is the move away from a focus on individualism and individual agency which underpins Western social science to one which views humans as constituents of social formations or systems which are characterized by flows and flux. Thus, instead of actions and events being imposed by the will of a conscious actor, they are immanent in the flow of events and human situations. Accordingly, for Zhang and Cone to be entrepreneurial and innovative suggests having no fixed goal or particular plan so that it is possible to adapt to every twist and turn in the emerging now; in other words, engaging the emerging now.

Adopting a critical perspective that seeks to challenge hegemonic approaches and concepts, Stead and Hamilton (Chapter 4) introduce critical methodology as a means of illuminating the complexities of entrepreneurial leadership. In particular, their focus is on gender, and using illustrations from two empirical case studies they outline and discuss the steps and value in adopting a critical perspective. Their work is grounded in critical leadership studies, which questions hegemonic approaches and beliefs in mainstream literature in particular, specifically critiquing rhetoric, tradition, authority and objectivity, and addressing what is neglected, absent or deficient in mainstream research (Collinson, 2011). Accordingly, Stead and Hamilton argue that individualistic, gendered, heroic assumptions inform implicit theories of entrepreneurial leadership which are reproduced and reinforced by much of the research in this area. Therefore, the dominant masculine entrepreneurial discourse remains dominant, which stymies alternative perspectives and understandings (Ahl, 2006; Marlow and Ahl, 2012).

Building on Pullen's (2007: 316) observation that 'the gendered nature of research and researcher identity is almost always under-acknowledged', Stead and Hamilton employed different cycles of analysis to unearth and interrogate the experiences of women entrepreneurial leaders. Using data collected from a phenomenological approach the researchers were able to investigate and make explicit the micro interactions and dynamics of women leaders' social practice.

After an initial cycle of organizing the data and identifying themes, they then employed appropriate theoretical frames of reference to interrogate the data. Like Alvesson and Skoldberg (2000) they emphasize the importance of theory in allowing researchers to find meaning in the data. Such an approach requires researchers to be highly skilled, reflexive, and prepared to challenge dominant and authoritative models and frameworks to present robust analysis and interpretations which can generate useful theoretical insights. This chapter is particularly beneficial as it highlights the role critical perspectives and methodologies can play in illuminating hitherto underexplored phenomena such as power dynamics in entrepreneurial settings. In addition, the analytical approach outlined responds to calls for increased methodological pluralism in the field (Leitch et al., 2009; Neergaard and Ulhoi, 2007).

Extending Gupta et al.'s (2004: 7) view that there is an increasing need for entrepreneurial leadership that is not confined to the US or even the so-called Anglo cultures, Harrison and Roomi (Chapter 5) draw on neo-institutional, market-based and culturally informed theory to highlight the ways in which current models and theories are inappropriate to explain and develop Islamic entrepreneurial leadership. In challenging the hegemonic Euro-American understandings of entrepreneurial leadership, their work can be located in more critical perspectives. In aiming to understand how entrepreneurial leadership is comprehended and manifested in the Muslim world, they stress that they do not assume a unitary conceptualization of Islam. Like other major religions, Islam is a multivalent and multi-vocal counterpoint of forms, purposes, meanings and aspects practised in different ways and to differing degrees in a wide variety of socio-cultural environments with multiple influences. Despite the challenges this poses they argue that Islam, conceptualized as a set of socio-cultural phenomena, provides a lens through which to conceptualize entrepreneurial leadership.

The starting point for Harrison and Roomi's contextual analysis is to critique Kuran's (2008) interpretation that the effect of Islam on entrepreneurship in the Middle East has been inhibitive rather than developmental. Accordingly, they suggest that current interpretations of institutions, markets and cultures all hamper how we understand Islamic entrepreneurship and leadership. Thus, they suggest that neo-institutional theory, which takes cognizance of the practices and beliefs associated with the communal and societal, political and religious spheres (Mair et al., 2012), would provide a deeper and more nuanced appreciation of the relationships between Islamic formal and informal institutions, including legal and financial systems, markets and culture. Harrison and Roomi conclude that as diffuse cultural forces determine sustainable and systematic attempts to encourage entrepreneurship in general and to develop entrepreneurial leadership more specifically, practice-led, empirical research is required to enable more comprehensive insights into how Islamic entrepreneurial leadership might be conceptualized and enacted. In so doing, they by implication call for more research in this area which is grounded outside the dominant Anglo-American consensus.

Part III Leadership in Entrepreneurial Contexts

Turning the focus to the entrepreneurial context specifically, this section contains four chapters that address the nature and role of entrepreneurship, leadership and management in a range of organizational contexts. Volery and Mueller (Chapter 6) draw on strategic leadership theory to augment the transformational approach to understanding entrepreneurial leadership. Specifically, they explore the behaviours displayed and roles filled by six entrepreneurs when confronted with the leadership paradoxes and tensions in business creation and growth. They view entrepreneurs as strategic leaders who have to navigate the conflicts arising from the operational, day-to-day pressures, and strategic and longer-term demands, which can be simultaneous and contradictory.

Employing structured observation, different 'units of action' or examples of a specific behaviour displayed by the entrepreneur were recorded and analysed. After analysis it emerged that entrepreneurial leaders face four paradoxes: the exploration and exploitation of opportunities; balancing short-term and long-term perspectives and actions; maintaining stability and adaption; and managing internal and external orientations.

In addressing these, ten main roles were performed by entrepreneurial leaders, three of which were future-oriented, focusing on discovering and shaping entrepreneurial opportunity (the visionary, the discoverer, the steersman), three oriented to operational issues (the frontline worker, the trouble-shooter, the controller) and the remaining four relating to their ability to balance the two, that is, the business's day-to-day activities and its longer-term needs (the information broker, the decision-maker, the salesman, the networker). On the basis of these they identified four strategies which entrepreneurial leaders could employ to overcome the tensions they faced. In building on strategic leadership this research draws attention to the fact that entrepreneurial leadership is a synergistic combination of managerial and visionary leadership.

Like Volery and Mueller, Schjoedt and Valencia in Chapter 7 focus on the distinction between operational and strategic issues by arguing that preferred learning styles and use of knowledge will differ between entrepreneurial leaders, who they suggest will favour knowledge exploration, and entrepreneurial managers, who instead will emphasize exploitation. Specifically, they base their differentiation between entrepreneurial leaders and managers according to a distinction between process and function: while leadership and entrepreneurship are processes, management is a function comprising a number of roles (Penrose, 1959).

To explain the distinction between entrepreneurial leaders and managers they draw on three theories. First, March's (1991) concepts of knowledge and exploitation, to illustrate that entrepreneurial leaders' exploratory learning involves searching, risk-taking, discovery and innovation; while learning exploitations comprises for entrepreneurial managers choice, refinement, efficiency and implementation. Second, Lumpkin et al.'s (2004) creativity-based model of opportunity recognition, which provides a two-phase, five-stage approach to illustrate how creativity influences opportunity recognition and the initial venture creation process. In the first phase of discovery the focus is on exploring knowledge through preparation, incubation and insight, while in the second phase of formation learning is centred on knowledge exploitation through evaluation and elaboration. Third, in common with others who have explored entrepreneurial learning (Corbett, 2005; Harrison and Leitch, 2005; Lumpkin and Lichtenstein, 2005), Kolb's (1984) learning cycle helps to identify an entrepreneur's preferred learning style.

Schjoedt and Valencia argue that as entrepreneurs disrupt the market through opportunity recognition and innovation, the entrepreneurial leader is more adept at envisioning future possibilities and transformations and accordingly is more focused on the discovery phase. On the other hand, the entrepreneurial manager's role is much more transactional, focusing on the efficient and effective execution of ideas and innovations and on maintaining control and order, which is more apt in the formation phase. Schjoedt and Valencia acknowledge that this is a very blunt distinction and that much overlap exists between the activities in which entrepreneurs, leaders and managers engage. Nevertheless, the value of this work is that it draws attention to the complexity in new venture creation and the importance of a team-based approach.

The distinctions highlighted by Schjoedt and Valencia mirror debate among leadership scholars, which ranges from an extreme position of essential difference between leaders and managers (Zaleznik, 1977; Bennis and Nanus, 1985) to one of complementarity (Kotter, 1990) and interdependence (Yukl and Lepsinger, 2005). A common thread running through all of these positions is that they are essentialist, assuming that actors will have particular traits and behaviours influencing their approaches in different settings. However, from a social constructionist perspective, Grint (2005) argues that the relationship between leadership and management is a more complex intersection of self, social and contextual constructions. Accordingly, leadership and management are constituted by social actors' preferences and comfort with regard to power and uncertainty as opposed purely to anything innate. While psychological approaches are important, we argue that entrepreneurial leadership would benefit from the inclusion of social perspectives to provide a more holistic understanding of the construct.

The focus of Bell and Whittington's research (Chapter 8) is to explore, from a leadership perspective, the skills, capabilities and knowledge required to scale and grow a venture, which to date few researchers have explored. Like the majority of scholars in entrepreneurship, their perspective of entrepreneurial leaders is that it is a style of leadership. They draw on the full-range model of leadership developed by Avolio (2010), comprising five transformational and three transactional factors of leadership, and the life-cycle approach, to understand the evolution and growth of threshold firms. Drawing on configurational logic, Bell and Whittington argue that Avolio's (2010) model is appropriate as the different mixtures of leadership behaviours identified can be drawn on at any stage of an organization's growth. For them this acknowledges the importance of a dynamic approach to leading to reflect the complex, constantly evolving environments in which organizations operate. In integrating two models and adopting a configurational perspective, Bell and Whittington propose that various combinations of transformational and transactional leadership behaviours may have differential effects across the variety of scenarios faced by a growing venture. Accordingly, entrepreneurial leaders have to possess the cognitive capability, insight and willingness to adapt their leadership behaviours, with those who do so likely to be more successful. Helpfully, Bell and Whittington propose a number of research opportunities to advance our thinking in this area.

Carsrud, Renko-Dolan and Brännback (Chapter 9) explore the concept of entrepreneurial leadership (EL) and how it differs from other forms of leadership and why EL is critical to our understanding of new firm creation and growth. Specifically, they discuss how EL impacts upon a firm's culture and sustainability through the leadership succession process. This chapter builds on their more extensive review of the literature associated with the measurement of entrepreneurial leadership (Renko et al., 2015). As such, the entrepreneur as a leader is the focus of this chapter, and they explore in some depth the relationship between being an entrepreneur and being a leader. Based on a review of relevant entrepreneurship and leadership literatures they conclude that, given the changing economic climate, the more traditional styles of leadership are becoming less important. Accordingly, firms should focus on being entrepreneurial in their leadership style and in so doing focus on discovery, development and growth as well as on coordination-focused administrative tasks. For Carsrud et al., the changing economic landscape and increasingly multicultural context means that in order to thrive organizations must constantly innovate and learn. This means encouraging and maintaining entrepreneurial behaviours at all levels of the firm, from senior management to the newest employee. To compete effectively on a global and a local level, all ventures must become entrepreneurial organizations with entrepreneurial leaders.

Carsrud et al. argue that entrepreneurship and leadership share similarities (the early search for characteristics and traits, the more recent emphasis on transformational leaders, the attention given to vision and organizational alignment). Despite these similarities their definition of what entrepreneurial leadership stands for clearly distinguishes it from other leadership styles. Specifically, they argue that the opportunity focus of entrepreneurial leaders is evident in leaders' own actions as well as in the expectations from their followers. The recognition and pursuit of opportunities can be accomplished across organizations of all types, as well as across different functional levels. As such, entrepreneurial leadership is not only the domain of new business founders but also practised by leaders in various types of organizations that are reinventing themselves. Indeed, entrepreneurial leadership can be found in leader–follower relationships anywhere in an organization, while strategic constructs, such as entrepreneurial orientation, only reflect the decisions of those at the top of an organization.

Part IV Applications of Entrepreneurial Leadership

Carsrud et al.'s argument is taken a stage further by Kuratko (Chapter 10). Underpinned by a belief that the current global entrepreneurial revolution is more impactful than the industrial revolution (Kuratko and Morris, 2013), Kuratko suggests that corporate entrepreneurial leadership is a vital component in the modern global economy. The capacity to take entrepreneurial action through leading, taking risks and causing disruption is characteristic of the entrepreneurial mindset perspective. However, while few would necessarily disagree that the contributions made and the role played by corporate entrepreneurial leaders is important, there is little understanding of the process of corporate entrepreneurial leadership. He draws on four literatures to identify four major implementation issues for corporate entrepreneurial leadership, as well as six critical corporate entrepreneurial leadership responsibilities. First, he reviews current understandings of corporate entrepreneurship, specifically the focus on businesses establishing sustainable competitive advantage as a foundation for profitable growth; second, he examines the concept of entrepreneurial intensity, the degree and frequency of entrepreneurial actions undertaken by an organization or individual which he considers to be the cornerstone of entrepreneurial leadership (Morris et al., 2011); third, he highlights the importance of a conducive organizational climate for corporate entrepreneurial activity and the role it plays in the development of appropriate entrepreneurial leadership behaviours; and fourth, he identifies critical leadership responsibilities at all organizational levels. For Kuratko, the identification of the six corporate entrepreneurial leadership responsibilities, while not necessarily definitive, are necessary to enable the shift in focus from traditional product and service innovations to pioneering innovations across a range of organizational functions including processes, value chains and business models, necessary for companies to flourish.

Adopting a processual understanding of entrepreneurship and its relational dynamics, embedded in social constructionism, Sklaveniti and Tzoumpa (Chapter 11) develop a conceptualization of entrepreneurial leadership and highlight the ever-changing idea of becoming by drawing on ideas of temporality, relational identity and improvisation. Following a meta-theoretical summary of common theoretical developments within the fields of both entrepreneurship and leadership, they argue that the individualistic, essentialist and deterministic perspective which underpins the majority of research in both domains does not capture sufficiently the dynamic and relational nature of the entrepreneurial leadership process. For them entrepreneurial leadership can be defined as 'a perpetual and relational process of working together to mobilize business opportunities in an organizational context in pursuit of entrepreneurial goals'.

They ground their argument in the specific context of social enterprises, which they view as building on the Schumpeterian (1934) concept of contributing to change through innovative combinations, albeit in relation to a social mission. Emphasizing the relational aspect of social entrepreneurship, Sklaveniti and Tzoumpa explore the concepts of change, inclusiveness and uncertainty. With specific reference to change they draw on Orlikowski and Yates's (2002) work to illustrate the temporal unfolding of change from a *kairotic* perspective, that moment of coming into being of, for example, an opportunity, instead of it being something that can be discovered. This emphasis on temporality and emergence is also evident in their conceptualization of the ways in which entrepreneurial leadership is enacted: not as a series of stable practices and actions, but through a process of continual revitalization and revision. Accordingly, in social enterprises characterized by change, uncertainty and multiple interpretations, entrepreneurial leaders need to coordinate actions, synchronize meanings and adapt to contextual particularities. In the context of opportunity genesis and development, Sklaveniti and Tzoumpa suggest that practice theory is a useful analytical construct to illustrate how the performativity of practices follows the unfolding of entrepreneurship in which spontaneity, creativity and improvisation are stressed.

Hatem (Chapter 12) picks up on Harrison and Roomi's plea for more socially and culturally grounded research (Chapter 5). She uses a detailed case study approach to examine the actions, processes and attributes of entrepreneurial distributed leadership in the high growth and rapid internationalization of emerging multinationals in the Middle East and North Africa (MENA) region. For Hatem, entrepreneurial leadership is a distinctive style of leadership that can be present in an organization of any size, type or age (Renko et al., 2015). Although leadership is the resource most distinctive to a specific organization, effective leadership processes are fundamental to the development and growth of new international ventures, and to the provision of entrepreneurial leadership in established corporations. Based on insights drawn from a series of detailed case studies, Hatem argues that her respondents, as leaders of entrepreneurial firms, highlighted the importance of 'distributed leadership'; this meant that as founders they drove, encouraged, motivated and worked with entrepreneurial team members to initiate viable initiatives for the future of their internationally diversified companies. As a result, the development of entrepreneurial teams for distributed leadership was what these leaders concluded to be an exceptional element in their respective diversified firms' superior performances as they rapidly internationalized.

This research makes a contribution to the concept of distributed leadership as it connects in a meaningful way with the experiences and aspirations of leadership teams in high-growth firms in the MENA region. However, Hatem concludes that the key contribution of distributed leadership is not in offering a replacement for other accounts, but in enabling the recognition of a variety of forms of leadership in a more integrated and systemic manner, recognizing the inherently political nature of leadership within organizations. In so doing she has demonstrated its applicability during the different stages of growth of the rapid internationalizing multinational firms from the emerging markets of the MENA region. The challenge arising from this work is to explore this in further empirical research in a wider range of entrepreneurial contexts.

Taking a 'gender as variable' approach, Adesua-Lincoln and Croad (Chapter 13) examine the gender differences between Nigerian men and women's leadership practices and collective entrepreneurial behaviour. To overcome poverty and unemployment in Nigeria, increasing numbers of women are engaged in entrepreneurial activity (GEM, 2012). This is despite the twin hurdles of an unfavourable business environment (infrastructural deficiencies, weak institutions, low access and high cost of finance, corruption, lack of diversification, an inability to compete with imported goods, low productivity) and discriminatory practices and biases rooted in traditional socio-cultural values and practices. Adesua-Lincoln and Croad's research builds on calls for greater insights into gender-based leadership practices across cultures, especially in terms of fostering work teams and collective entrepreneurship. They build on work by Eagly et al. (2003) and Park (1996) to argue that gender is related to leadership behaviour, with women tending towards more transformational and collaborative approaches underpinned by compassion, sensitivity and empathy.

A convenient sampling strategy was adopted to administer a survey to men and women entrepreneurs in Lagos state. Regarding leadership behaviours the findings, while mixed, suggest that on the whole women entrepreneurs tend to adopt a transformational style of leadership behaviour. Despite this, in order to achieve set targets they can be task-oriented. However, in the case of collective entrepreneurship the findings show a more stark distinction, with men leaders being more likely to communicate effectively with their employees, enhancing collaboration and increased team interaction. In line with De la Rey (2005), Adesua-Lincoln and Croad suggest that in a patriarchal society such as Nigeria, women due to their isolation and lack of exposure to entrepreneurship are less likely to encourage team-based approaches, or possess entrepreneurial vision or effective communication skills. In essence, male dominance is endemic in the socio-cultural system and determines the entrepreneurship practices adopted by women as they interact across different societal and cultural lines.

Part V Entrepreneurial Leadership and Learning

In Part V of the book we explore a number of dimensions of the interface between entrepreneurship, leadership and learning, reflecting an emphasis highlighted in some of the early work on entrepreneurship and leadership (Harrison and Leitch, 1994). Kempster, Smith and Barnes (Chapter 14) use communities of practice (CoP) theory, from Lave and Wenger's (1991) model of situated learning, a social learning theory involving engagement in a 'community of practice', to explore entrepreneurial leadership learning. Their work takes a relational ontological perspective and they position entrepreneurial leadership as socially constructed, whereby relational practices, context and identity are important and where leadership is an outcome of a process. In the context of learning they argue that entrepreneurial leaders learn through participating in everyday activities, conversations and interactions. Using their experiences of a leadership development programme targeted at entrepreneurial leaders they use CoP to provide the analytical tool for analysing entrepreneurial leadership learning processes and their relationship between identity and context for an entrepreneurial leader. Specifically, they conceptualize the leadership development programme as a CoP where delegates are co-learners who apply and refine their learning in the context of their own businesses. They also draw on Leitch et al.'s (2013) research on the importance of developing institutional capital in such entrepreneurial leadership programmes to enhance both human and social capital. With specific reference to a single case, Kempster et al. illustrate how human, social and institutional capital are developed and interrelated within a community of practice. Like entrepreneurial leadership, our knowledge and understanding of entrepreneurial leadership learning is limited. Kempster et al. outline a social learning dynamic of entrepreneurial leadership learning incorporating the three capitals of human, social and institutional capital, which underpin the creation and enhancement of a fourth, that of economic capital.

Like Kempster et al., the focus of Bagheri and Pihie's work (Chapter 15) is to explore entrepreneurial leadership learning. Atypically, they do this by examining the motivations of student leaders, of university entrepreneurship clubs and projects, to develop their entrepreneurial leadership competencies. They argue that while entrepreneurship education is one of the most significant environmental factors in motivating students to learn and enhance their entrepreneurial capability (Guerrero et al., 2008; Pittaway and Cope, 2007a, 2007b), compulsory and ineffective education can also reduce students' motivations and ambitions to become entrepreneurs.

Building on Leitch et al.'s (2013) definition of entrepreneurial leadership, they advance a definition of student entrepreneurial leadership as 'a process of social interaction and influence that develops students' entrepreneurial knowledge and competencies as well as their capabilities to successfully perform the tasks and roles of the leader in university entrepreneurship clubs and projects'. To understand better those factors motivating students to acquire entrepreneurial leadership skills and capabilities, they examined the everyday leadership experiences, practices and reflections of 14 student leaders of university entrepreneurship clubs in private and public higher education institutions in Malaysia. Specifically, they focused on investigating the challenges the students faced in creating ideas, recognizing opportunities, marshalling essential resources and mobilizing a group to successfully fulfil a project's objectives.

Their findings revealed that two types of competency are necessary in the development of student entrepreneurial leadership: first, personal competencies, including entrepreneurial leadership self-efficacy and love of challenges; and second, leadership competencies, comprising the creation of caring interpersonal relationships, the ability to delegate, and building self-efficacy among group members. The student entrepreneurial leaders were driven to learn and develop these competencies through a combination of intrinsic factors (personal interest and self-development) and extrinsic factors (learning opportunities, entrepreneurial leadership development courses, and entrepreneurial tasks and demands). Bagheri and Pihie's research contributes to the lack of literature in the context of university entrepreneurial leadership development opportunities, demonstrates the potentially influential role which university entrepreneurship clubs play, and provides insights for educators of those attributes that should be developed and enhanced.

In the context of achieving long-term organizational sustainability, Rae (Chapter 16) explores the ways in which entrepreneurial leaders can build a sustained culture of entrepreneurship and facilitate leadership development opportunities in their organizations. His research draws on the points of convergence between ideas of sustainable entrepreneurship as a social movement, and leadership as a distributed concept. The application of ideas and innovations in a sustainability context differ from a free-enterprise model as social, environmental, ecological, technological, cultural, heritage and aesthetic dimensions are important in addition to financial and economic dimensions. To succeed, Rae suggests that sustainable entrepreneurship is dependent on entrepreneurial leadership, entrepreneurial learning, and a supportive cultural, political and economic context. Like Kempster et al. (Chapter 14), Rae views entrepreneurial leadership as a social and connected practice involving trust, shared values and reciprocity. Learning, for entrepreneurial leaders, is a process of social emergence and identity construction by which an individual's full potential can be achieved.

Adopting an interpretive and inductive approach Rae presents four in-depth cases comprising entrepreneurial organizations facing ongoing sustainability challenges. In each case the venture's founder was the key informant about a range of organizational issues including its strategy, culture, developmental opportunities, approaches to leadership development and governance. After analysis he presents a model for leadership for sustainability in entrepreneurial organizations comprising four interrelated aspects: identity (co-constructed between individuals, the organization and the community), culture, community (the active engagement and participation of the organization's staff and stakeholders) and entrepreneurial innovation. While much of the work investigating entrepreneurial leadership development has tended to be conducted in the context of formal and structured programmes, much less work has been centred on the development of distributed leadership opportunities within the more informal context of organizations.

Smith (Chapter 17) takes the perspective that while entrepreneurs and small business owners might well perform many different types of leadership actions and activities, not all of these can necessarily be classified as being entrepreneurial leadership. Instead, he believes that for the term 'entrepreneurial leadership' to be used, specific characteristics or qualities relating to newness, novelty or difference must be evident. In particular, his concern in this chapter is to better appreciate how leadership can be exercised as an abstract and abstracted concept. Accordingly, he employs a single case study, BrewDog, and applies leadership theories to better understand the two founders' style of entrepreneurial leadership. To do this he identifies stories and scenarios from media coverage and the company's website which he considers to be examples of entrepreneurial leadership, and employs the cultural web model as an analytical tool to identify patterns of organizing. In this instance, Smith employs the model to demonstrate the shared semiotics between entrepreneurship, leadership and entrepreneurial leadership. On the basis of his analysis he stresses that the case study demonstrates not only situated entrepreneurial leadership, but also examples of entrepreneur and leader stories too; in other words, at different times the founders behave and act as entrepreneurs, and at others as leaders. Of particular interest is that through examining the nature and role of leadership in a rapidly expanding entrepreneurial firm it is possible to operate separately or simultaneously as an entrepreneur and as a leader, which demonstrates a lack of rigidity between the two constructs in practice. For Smith, this indicates that entrepreneurial leadership is both a philosophy and a situated, storied practice.

Gibb and Haskins (Chapter 18) focus on the entrepreneurial leadership role of one particular organization type: the university. The overall objective of this chapter is to explore key issues in the design and development of the entrepreneurial university in both concept and practice. Their intent, reflecting an emphasis in the other chapters in this section, is to be of value not only to members of the academic community who wish to explore this issue but also to policy-makers and the wide range of international stakeholders, public and private, who are demonstrating a growing interest in this development. In terms of purpose, they seek to capture the not inconsiderable experiment in organizational design of universities, across the world, as they attempt to adjust to an environment growing in complexity and uncertainty. In so doing, the discourse moves beyond a focus upon entrepreneurship and enterprise education in universities, which has been the subject of considerable practical development and academic publication over the past decade or so, and beyond what has almost become a 'traditional' entrepreneurial focus upon the technology transfer role of universities.

In developing their vision for what the entrepreneurial university of the future might look like, they identify the leadership role in universities as crucial. Leadership in managing change under conditions of uncertainty and complexity is of critical, transformational importance in several key respects: presenting a strong intellectual and passionate vision of the entrepreneurial role for the university and the rationale for entrepreneurial behaviours; establishing a culture of supporting innovation and some risk-taking across the university; building a team of shared values; presenting a clear and convincing vision of organization design aimed at bottom-up empowerment across the university; identifying, supporting and rewarding the key change agents at the faculty and departmental level; demonstrating strong network and relationship management skills both externally and internally; and demonstrating a strong strategic orientation, allowing flexibility for initiative-taking across the university via a process of informal culture trust-based development. In clearly articulating their vision for the entrepreneurial university, Gibb and Haskins provide an illuminating account of what (transformational) entrepreneurial leadership in practice might look like.

Part VI Future Directions

In their conceptual chapter, Harrison, Leitch and McAdam (Chapter 19) offer a new direction for entrepreneurial leadership research. They highlight the embedded masculinity of the entrepreneurial leadership domain, contending that it is gender blind, gender defensive and gender neutral. They argue that it is important to challenge prevailing gendered assumptions and conceptions, not least to avoid the danger that entrepreneurial leadership may be co-opted into the mainstream discourse without taking account of recent and relevant debates and discussions, particularly within leadership studies.

Specifically, they argue that neglecting the role of gender in entrepreneurial leadership is at odds with the considerable and growing attention to gender in leadership studies. There are two dimensions to this. First, the difficulty in separating the terms 'leadership' and 'men', as the languages of masculinity, leadership and entrepreneurship have effectively become synonymous. Second, this has been compounded by most research being conducted in Western industrialized cultures that expound these masculine ideals. As a result, in entrepreneurial leadership the male/masculine is regarded as the universal, neutral subject against which the woman/female is judged. In leadership research, however, two emerging literatures offer the possibility of a more nuanced treatment of gender. First, post-heroic models of leadership that emphasize leadership as a collaborative, relational process and are often presented as gender neutral. Second, the notion of feminine leadership highlights apparently feminine attributes, attitudes and behaviours such as an interpersonal orientation, collaboration, empathy, kindness, and more participatory and relational leadership styles.

Elaborating on Metcalfe and Woodhams's (2012) recent review of new directions in gender, diversity and organization theorizing, Harrison et al. develop a research agenda for the gendered analysis of entrepreneurial leadership, which is undertaken at three levels. At the micro level, they extend current gender research on social constructionism, critical management studies and intersectionality to contemporary entrepreneurial leadership research. Specifically, three themes are highlighted: the (in)visibility of women leaders negotiating their in-group/out-group status; the role of glass walls and ceilings in attenuating women's experience-building and career progression; and the role of gender fatigue in reinforcing masculinist conceptions of leadership. At the meso level, building on the critical social science literature on men's studies and race studies, they highlight the importance of understanding intersectionality and the dangers of simply treating gender, ethnicity, and so on as variables to be analysed in an essentialist manner. At the macro level, they propose that post-colonial feminist studies, transnationalism and the geographies of place and space can provide a foundation for theoretically advancing the knowledge domain of a context-aware and situationally grounded entrepreneurial leadership research. This research agenda, incorporating new frameworks and perspectives, presents an opportunity for entrepreneurial leadership scholars to address wider issues concerning diversity, the generalizability of their findings and the inclusivity of the theories they develop.

CONCLUSION

In compiling this *Handbook* we have sought to reflect the current diversity of research on entrepreneurship and leadership. Our own position is that entrepreneurial leadership sits at the intersection of both leadership and entrepreneurship, and we see that there is significant opportunity for theories and constructs in both to inform its development. As a number of our contributors indicate, explicitly or by implication, transformational leadership has been a particularly influential influence, despite (or perhaps because of, given the ideological baggage accompanying much of the advocacy of entrepreneurship) the danger that the language employed in the theory tends towards the evangelical and idealistic, in that transforming leaders are considered to provide a positive moral guide of working for the benefit of the team, organization and/or community (Tourish, 2013). However, in the wider entrepreneurial leadership literature there has been little discussion of or reaction to critiques of this, and more recent developments in leadership theory are for the most part not reflected in current discussions. This is despite the recognition that the domains of entrepreneurship and leadership continue to share similarities, not least an increasing awareness of the importance of context, a move away from the 'Great Man', charismatic individualistic understanding of leader and entrepreneur as hero, and a greater sensitivity to the processes used to develop and revise processes in organizations to build leadership or entrepreneurial capability and capacity in an organization. Fundamentally, and reflected throughout this *Handbook*, contemporary research in both fields sees leadership and entrepreneurship as relational, based on the importance of interactions with others, benefiting from a critical approach (including acknowledgement of a social constructionist approach) in which separation of the individual (leader/entrepreneur) from the process (leadership/entrepreneurship) becomes an important issue in determining the appropriate object of study.

Common to both the entrepreneurship and leadership literatures is a widespread neglect of the importance of power relations and unethical behaviour (Howell and Avolio, 1992); an under emphasis of the pursuit of self-serving, self-interested behaviour at the expense of followers' interests (Christie et al., 2011); a continuing lack of clarity and agreement on conceptual definitions and models linking influences on mediating processes and outcomes (van Knippenberg and Sitkin, 2013); and an implicit contextless universalism. Further, much current theorizing is still leader-centric and based on highly gendered, heroic images of the Great Man. This is problematic for two reasons. First, as Stead and Hamilton (Chapter 4) and Harrison et al. (Chapter 19) in this *Handbook* make clear, it perpetuates a patriarchal view of leadership at odds with the emerging post-heroic schools of leadership. Second, this plays down the role of followers in defining the leadership condition (Crossman and Crossman, 2011). A number of our contributors have followed Renko et al. (2015) in highlighting the role of followers in entrepreneurial leadership, but it remains the case that in leadership studies more generally there has been relatively little consideration of the role of the follower and the dynamics of follower–leader interaction as a process of social and relational interaction (Kelley, 1992; Uhl-Bien et al., 2014; Grint, 2001).

Central to the contributions to this *Handbook* are a number of themes which point to a fruitful agenda for future research at the interface between entrepreneurship and leadership. First, there is a widespread concern with context – organizationally, socially, culturally and geographically – which belies the implicit universalism of much of the extant research in both domains. Second, there is growing interest in a more critical perspective that questions hegemonic approaches and beliefs in mainstream literature; critiques rhetoric, tradition, authority and objectivity; and addresses what is neglected, absent or deficient in mainstream research (Collinson, 2011). Third, increased attention to leader–follower dynamics points to a renewed interest in power (and the way it is reproduced in particular structures, relationships and practices) and identity constructions (through which leadership dynamics are reproduced, rationalized, sometimes resisted and occasionally transformed) (Collinson, 2005).

Fourth, a more nuanced understanding of leader–follower and other relationships recognizes entrepreneurship and leadership as socially constructed, given shape by their social, political and cultural context. This emphasis on the relationship between the entrepreneurial leader and the entrepreneurial system in which they and their business operate, shapes and influences how they exercise power and authority. Fifth, there is growing interest in exploring the relations between macro social relations and meso organizational practices and processes as well as the micro dynamics of entrepreneurial leaders and others in a variety of entrepreneurial settings, drawing on more relational and collective approaches to leadership such as shared leadership and distributed leadership. Sixth, many of our contributors reflect the view that leadership is a firm-wide phenomenon, which throws light on the importance of developing entrepreneurial leadership capability throughout an organization instead of focusing on one or a handful of individuals in senior positions. Seventh, this has implications for entrepreneurial leadership education and development that parallels the distinction between 'leader' and 'leadership' as the focus shifts from individualistic to more relational understandings of leadership, and from leader development (developing an individual leader's human capital, knowledge, skills and abilities) to leadership development (expanding an organization's collective capacity so that all of its members can engage in leadership processes) (Day, 2000; Day et al., 2014). Research on entrepreneurial leadership is still in its infancy but, as the contributions to this *Handbook* make clear, offers fertile ground for exploration and innovation and an opportunity to shape thinking in both its parent disciplines.

REFERENCES

Ahl, H.J. (2006) Why research on women entrepreneurs needs new directions. *Entrepreneurship Theory and Practice*, 30 (5), 595–621.

Alvesson, M. and Sköldberg, K. (2000) *Reflexive Methodology: New Vistas for Qualitative Research*. London: SAGE.

Avolio, B. (2010) *Full Range Leadership Development*, 2nd edition. Thousand Oaks, CA: SAGE.

Bennis, W.G. and Nanus, B. (1985) *Leaders: The Strategies for Taking Charge*. New York, NY: Harper & Row.

Christie, A., Barling, J. and Turner, N. (2011) Pseudo-transformational leadership: model specification and outcomes. *Journal of Applied Social Psychology*, 41 (1), 2943–84.

Cogliser, C.C. and Brigham, K.H. (2004) The intersection of leadership and entrepreneurship: mutual lessons to be learnt. *Leadership Quarterly*, 15, 771–99.

Collinson, D. (2005) Dialectics of leadership. *Human Relations*, 58, 1419–42.

Collinson, D.L. (2011) Critical leadership studies. In A. Bryman, D.L. Collinson, K. Grint, B. Jackson and M. Uhl-Bien (eds), *The SAGE Handbook of Leadership*. London: SAGE, pp. 179–92.

Corbett, A.C. (2005) Experiential learning within the process of opportunity identification and exploitation. *Entrepreneurship Theory and Practice*, 29, 473–91.

Crossman, B. and Crossman, J. (2011) Conceptualising followership: a review of literature. *Leadership*, 7 (4), 481–97.

Cunningham, J.B. and Lischeron, J. (1991) Defining entrepreneurship. *Journal of Small Business Management*, 29, 45–61.

Day, D. (2000) Leadership development: a review in context. *Leadership Quarterly*, 11 (4), 581–611.

Day, D.V., Fleenor, J.W., Atwater, L.E., Strum, R.E. and McKee, R.A. (2014) Advances in leader and leadership development: a review of 25 years of research and theory. *Leadership Quarterly*, 25, 63–82.

de la Rey, C. (2005) Gender, women and leadership. *Agenda: Empowering Women for Gender Equity*, 65, 4–11.

Deleuze, G. (1994) *Difference and Repetition*. London: Athlone Press.

Destler, C.M. (1946) Entrepreneurial leadership among the 'robber barons': a trial balance. *Journal of Economic History*, 6 (S1), 28–49.

Eagly, A.H., Johannesen-Schmidt, M.C. and Van Engen, M.L. (2003) Transformational, transactional and laissez-faire leadership styles: a meta-analysis comparing men and women. *Psychological Bulletin*, 129 (4), 569–91.

Eggers, J.H. and Leahy, K.T. (1994) Entrepreneurial leadership in the US. *Leadership in Action*, 14, 1–5.

Fernald, L.W. Jr., Solomon, G.T. and El Tarabisby, A. (2005) A new paradigm: entrepreneurial leadership. *Southern Business Review*, 30 (2), 1–10.

GEM (2012) *Global Entrepreneurship Monitor Women's Report*. Global Entrepreneurship Research Association. Available at http://www.babson.edu/Academics/centers/blank-center/global-research/gem/Documents/GEM%202012%20Womens%20Report.pdf.

Grint, K. (2001) *The Art of Leadership*. Oxford: Oxford University Press.

Grint, K. (2005) *Leadership: Limits and Possibilities*. Hampshire, UK: Palgrave Macmillan.

Guerrero, M., Rialp, J. and Urbano, D. (2008) The impact of desirability and feasibility on entrepreneurial intentions: a structural equation model. *International Entrepreneurship Management Journal*, 4, 35–50.

Gupta, V., McMillan, I. and Surie, G. (2004) Entrepreneurial leadership: developing and measuring a cross-cultural construct. *Journal of Business Venturing*, 19, 241–60.

Harrison, R.T. and Leitch, C.M. (1994) Entrepreneurship and leadership: implications for education and development. *Entrepreneurship and Regional Development*, 6, 111–25.

Harrison, R.T. and Leitch, C.M. (2005) Entrepreneurial learning: researching the interface between learning and the entrepreneurial context. *Entrepreneurship Theory and Practice*, 29 (4), 351–71.

Hmieleski, K.M. and Ensley, M.D. (2007) A contextual examination of new venture performance: entrepreneur leadership behaviour, top management team heterogeneity and environmental dynamism. *Journal of Organizational Behaviour*, 28 (7), 865–89.

Hood, J.N. and Young, J.E. (1993) Entrepreneurship's requisite areas of development: a survey of top executives in successful entrepreneurial firms. *Journal of Business Venturing*, 8, 115–35.

Howell, J.M. and Avolio, B.J. (1992) The ethics of charismatic leadership: submission or liberation. *Academy of Management Executive*, 6, 43–54.

Jensen, S.M. and Luthans, F. (2006) Entrepreneurs as authentic leaders: impact on employees' attitudes. *Leadership and Organisation Development Journal*, 27, 646–66.

Kelley, R.E. (1988) In Praise of Followers. *Harvard Business Review*, 66 (6), 142–8.

Kelley, R.E. (1992) *The Power of Followership: How to Create Leaders People Want to Follow and Followers who Lead Themselves*. New York, NY: Doubleday.

Kelley, R.E. (2008) Rethinking followership. *The Art of Followership: How Great Followers Create Great Leaders and Organizations*, 1st edition. San Francisco, CA: Jossey-Bass.

Kets De Vries, M. (1977) The entrepreneurial personality: a person at the crossroads. *Journal of Management Studies*, 14, 34–57.

Kolb, D.A. (1984) *Experiential Learning: Experience as the Source of Learning and Development*. Englewood Cliffs, NJ: Prentice Hall.

Kotter, J. (1990) What leaders really do. *Harvard Business Review*, 68 (3), 103–12.

Kuran, T. (2008) The scale of entrepreneurship in Middle Eastern history: inhibitive roles of Islamic institutions. Duke University Working Paper, Duke University.

Kuratko, D.F. (2007) Entrepreneurial leadership in the 21st century. *Journal of Leadership and Organizational Studies*, 13, 1–12.

Kuratko, D.F. and Morris, M.H. (2013) *Entrepreneurship and Leadership*. Cheltenham, UK and Northampton, MA: Edward Elgar Publishing.

Lave, J. and Wenger, E. (1991) *Situated Learning: Legitimate Peripheral Participation*. Cambridge: Cambridge University Press.

Leitch, C.M. and Harrison, R.T. (2018) Entrepreneurial leadership: a critical review and research agenda. In R. Blackburn, D. De Clercq, and J. Heinonen (eds), *The SAGE Handbook of Small Business and Entrepreneurship*. London: SAGE, pp. 15–37.

Leitch, C.M., Hill, F.M. and Harrison, R.T. (2009) The philosophy and practice of interpretivist research in entrepreneurship: quality, validation and trust. *Organizational Research Methods*, 13 (1), 67–84.

Leitch, C., McMullan, C. and Harrison, R. (2013) The development of entrepreneurial leadership: the role of human, social and institutional capital. *British Journal of Management*, 24, 347–66.

Lippitt, G.L. (1987) Entrepreneurial leadership: a performing art. *Journal of Creative Behavior*, 21, 264–70.

Lumpkin, G.T. and Lichtenstein, B.B. (2005) The role of organizational learning in the opportunity-recognition process. *Entrepreneurship Theory and Practice*, 29 (4), 451–72.

Lumpkin, G.T., Hills, G. and Shrader, R. (2004) Opportunity recognition. In H.P. Welsch (ed.), *Entrepreneurship: The Way Ahead*. New York, NY: Routledge, pp. 73–90.

Mair, J., Martí, I. and Ventresca, M. (2012) Building inclusive markets in rural Bangladesh: how intermediaries work institutional voids. *Academy of Management Journal*, 55 (4), 819–50.

March, J.G. (1991) Exploration and exploitation in organizational learning. *Organization Science*, 2, 71–87.

Marlow, S. and Ahl, H. (2012) Exploring the dynamics of gender, feminism and entrepreneurship: advancing debate to escape a dead end. *Organization*, 19 (5), 543–62.

McKone-Sweet, K., Greenberg, D. and Wilson, H.J. (2011) Giving voice to a values approach to educating entrepreneurial leaders. *Journal of Business Ethics*, 8, 337–42.

Metcalfe, B.D. and Woodhams, C. (2012) Introduction: new directions in gender, diversity and organization theorizing – re-imagining feminist post-colonialism, transnationalism and geographies of power. *International Journal of Management Review*, 14, 123–40.

Miller, D. (1983) The correlates of entrepreneurship in three types of firms. *Management Science*, 29, 770–791.

Morris, M.H., Kuratko, D.F. and Covin, J.G. (2011) *Corporate Entrepreneurship and Innovation*, 3rd edition. Mason, OH: South-Western/Thomson Publishers.

Neergaard, H. and Parm Ulhøi, J. (eds) (2007) *Handbook for Qualitative Research Methods in Entrepreneurship*. Cheltenham, UK and Northampton, MA: Edward Elgar Publishing.

Orlikowski, W.J. and Yates, J. (2002) It's about time: temporal structuring in organizations. *Organization Science*, 13, 684–700.

Park, D. (1996) Gender role, decision style and leadership style. *Women in Management Review*, 11 (8), 13–17.

Peck, K.L. (1991) Before looking for the gas pedal: a call for entrepreneurial leadership in American schools. *Education*, 111 (4), 516–20.

Penrose, E.T. (1959) *The Theory of the Growth of the Firm*. New York, NY: Wiley.

Perren, L. and Grant, P. (2001) *Management and Leadership in UK SMEs*. Council for Excellence in Management and Leadership.

Pittaway, L. and Cope, J. (2007a) Entrepreneurship education: a systematic review of the evidence. *International Small Business Journal*, 25 (5), 479–510.

Pittaway, L. and Cope, J. (2007b) Simulating entrepreneurial learning: integrating experiential and collaborative approaches to learning. *Management Learning*, 38 (2), 211–33.

Pullen, A. (2007) Becoming a researcher: gendering the research self. In A. Pullen, N. Beech and D. Sims (eds), *Exploring Identity: Concepts and Methods*. Basingstoke: Palgrave Macmillan, pp. 316–33.

Rae, D. (2000) Understanding entrepreneurial learning: a question of how?. *International Journal of Entrepreneurial Behavior & Research*, 6 (3), 145–59.

Renko, M., El Tarabishy, A., Carsrud, A.L. and Brännback, M. (2015) Understanding and measuring entrepreneurial leadership. *Journal of Small Business Management*, 53 (1), 54–74.

Satow, R. and Rector, J. (1995) Using Gestalt graphology to identify entrepreneurial leadership. *Perceptual and Motor Skills*, 81, 263–70.

Schneider, M. and Teske, P. (1992) Toward a theory of the political entrepreneur: evidence from local government. *American Political Science Review*, 86, 737–47.

Schumpeter, J.A. (1934) *The Theory of Economic Development: An Inquiry into Profits, Capital, Credit, Interest and the Business Cycle* (transl. Redvers Opie). Cambridge, MA: Harvard University Press.

Selsky, J.W. and Smith, A.E. (1994) Community entrepreneurship: a framework for social change leadership. *Leadership Quarterly*, 5, 277–96.

Steyaert, C. (2007) Entrepreneuring as a conceptual attractor? A review of process theories in 20 years of entrepreneurship studies. *Entrepreneurship and Regional Development*, 19 (6), 453–77.

Tourish, D. (2013) *The Dark Side of Transformational Leadership: A Critical Perspective.* London: Routledge.

Uhl-Bien, M., Riggio, R.E., Lowe, K.B. and Carsten, M.K. (2014) Followership theory: a review and research agenda. *Leadership Quarterly*, 25, 83–104.

Van Knippenberg, D. and Sitkin, S.B. (2013) A critical assessment of charismatic-transformational leadership research: back to the drawing board?. *Academy of Management Annals*, 7 (1), 1–60.

Vecchio, R.P. (2003) Entrepreneurship and leadership: common trends and common threads. *Human Resources Management Review*, 13, 303–27.

Yukl, G. and Lepsinger, R. (2005) Issues and observations: improving performance through flexible leadership. *Leadership in Action*, 25 (4), 23–4.

Zaleznik, A. (1977) Managers and leaders: are they different?. *Harvard Business Review*, 55, 67–78.

PART II

THEORETICAL PERSPECTIVES ON ENTREPRENEURSHIP AND LEADERSHIP

2. The concept and evolution of entrepreneurial leadership: a bibliometric analysis
Arik Röschke

INTRODUCTION

Leadership has been a major research topic in psychology and management for almost a century and has spawned thousands of empirical and conceptual studies (Cogliser and Brigham, 2004). However, only a few parts of this literature have permeated the field of entrepreneurship and small business (e.g., Ensley et al., 2006a; Jensen and Luthans, 2006; Soriano and Martínez, 2007). The intersection of these two fields under the label 'entrepreneurial leadership' is of great importance because entrepreneurs must rely on people to exploit opportunities and reach their objectives. In addition, entrepreneurs need to motivate, direct and lead employees, all of which suggests that leadership capabilities are necessary in entrepreneurship (Renko et al., 2012). As such, the entrepreneur as someone who makes decisions that impact employees and their behavior can be considered a leader par excellence.

However, within the emerging domain of entrepreneurial leadership there exists no agreed-upon definition and conceptualization of the term. According to Harrison et al. (2015), 'entrepreneurial leadership as an emerging field remains atheoretical, lacks definitional clarity and appropriate tools to assess its characteristics and behaviors', although '20 years have passed since commentators first advocated integrating the two domains entrepreneurship and leadership' (ibid.: 694).

Once a discipline matures, its scholars commonly review the literature to assess the discipline's general state (Ramos-Rodríguez and Ruíz-Navarro, 2004). Although there has been a continuing emergence of entrepreneurial leadership in both research and practice (e.g., Gupta et al., 2004; Kuratko, 2007; Leitch et al., 2013; Renko et al., 2015; Harrison et al., 2015), studies have presented little evidence of a theoretical and conceptual convergence in this area of inquiry. Thus, this chapter includes a thematic analysis under the broad field of bibliometrics (White and McCain, 1989) to quantitatively analyse the academic literature in entrepreneurial leadership and the evolution of the field through a bibliometric examination of articles.

Using the text-analytic software Leximancer provides results from an associational analysis of textual data in a language-independent manner (e.g., Liesch et al., 2011; Smith and Humphreys, 2006).

The first key motivation to carry out this study was to reveal the evolution of research in the field of entrepreneurial leadership. According to Culnan et al. (1990: 453), 'understanding the intellectual roots of a field identifies the basic intellectual commitments that serve as the field's foundation as it matures'. Because research on entrepreneurial leadership is a maturing field of investigation, understanding its roots is vitally important. This study aimed to illustrate the evolution in this field of research, which was best conducted by using data that offered a comprehensive overview of activities within the scientific process.

The second motivation was to map the literature on entrepreneurial leadership comprehensibly and at different stages. Thereafter, the emerging paradigms can be observed empirically as the field matures and advances theories.

The third motivation was the high relevancy of entrepreneurial leadership for both new start-ups and established businesses, because entrepreneurs cannot successfully develop new ventures without displaying effective leadership behaviors (Baumol, 1968; Cogliser and Brigham, 2004; Leitch et al., 2013). New ventures have no standard operating procedures, management practices or organizational structures to fall back on, so it is left to the founders to lead (Hmieleski and Ensley, 2007).

Finally, comprehensive insight into the development of entrepreneurial leadership offers great promise for research, particularly given the increase in the volume of articles published in this area – especially since 2012. This was a very timely opportunity to present a thorough and detailed analysis that sheds new light on the field.

This chapter contributes to the discussion on entrepreneurial leadership and investigates the evolution of the field by considering the work of numerous researchers over an extended period. More specifically, the chapter addresses the following questions:

1.   How has the research field of entrepreneurial leadership evolved?
2.   Which concepts in entrepreneurial leadership occur with the greatest frequency?
3.   What is the epistemological orientation of the articles?
4.   Which words occur with the greatest frequency?
5.   Which journals are represented in this domain?
6.   Which authors publish in this domain?
7.   What possibilities are there for scholars to investigate in the future?

DIFFERENT VIEWS ON ENTREPRENEURIAL LEADERSHIP

The field of entrepreneurial leadership is in an early stage of conceptual and theoretical development. Its exposure to sometimes contradictory views has led to definitional challenges. Therefore, this section first describes the research fields 'entrepreneurship' and 'leadership', followed by an overview of approaches to defining 'entrepreneurial leadership'.

Entrepreneurship

The research field 'entrepreneurship' is rather unsettled and its focus varies greatly. It has been characterized as a diverse field of inquiry that is fragmented, in ferment (Aldrich, 2012; Gartner, 2001) and difficult to define because it is a multifaceted phenomenon that spans many disciplinary boundaries (Busenitz et al., 2003). For instance, studies have focused on entrepreneurial persons, traits or social networks; new venture, product or service offering creation; and even country-specific framework conditions (Schildt et al., 2006).

According to Frese and Gielnik (2014):

> The most important drivers of entrepreneurship research came from economics, psychology, and sociology. The scholars credited to be the fathers of the field of entrepreneurship research, Schumpeter (1934) and later McClelland (1967), took a psychological perspective, with individuals being the major objects of entrepreneurship research. This changed in mainstream entrepreneurship research around the years 1980-2005. The approach during this time period was to explain entrepreneurship by using economic and strategy theories (Kirchhoff, 1991). More recently, scholars have once again acknowledged the importance of a psychological perspective because entrepreneurship is fundamentally personal (Baum, Frese, and Baron, 2007). (Frese and Gielnik, 2014: 414)

The non-existence of a generic definition of entrepreneurship arises mainly from the fact that, until the late 1990s, most researchers defined it only in terms of who the entrepreneurs were and what they did (Bruyat and Julien, 2001). However, defining the field only in terms of the individual generated incomplete definitions of entrepreneurship that did not withstand scrutiny (Venkataraman, 1997). Additionally, that approach disregarded two entrepreneurship conditions: the presence of viable opportunities, and enterprising individuals, which Shane (2003) described as the 'individual–opportunity nexus'. Along these lines, Wickham (2006) suggested that an individual, a market opportunity, adequate resources, a business organization and a favorable environment must be present in order for entrepreneurship to take place, and the entrepreneur is responsible for bringing these contingencies together to create new value.

Leadership

Reviewing publications on leadership showed the same theory evolution highlighted in the entrepreneurship section, and many constructs used in entrepreneurship were found in mainstream leadership theory (Vecchio, 2003). Scholarly interest in leadership has spawned various fields, such as traits, situational interaction, function, behavior, power, vision and charisma, and produced various definitions. Researchers have suggested that leadership is a source of competitive advantage in a complex, ambiguous and dynamic business environment (Küpers and Weibler, 2008; Yukl, 2008). They have assumed that leaders will make a difference, that their behaviors are important, and that they produce positive group and organizational effects (Pierce and Newstrom, 2011). On a general level, the quintessence of leadership revolves around 'influencing and facilitating individual and collective efforts to accomplish shared objectives' (Yukl, 2012: 66). Increasingly, researchers have shifted their focus away from only the individual leader to followers, peers, supervisors, context and culture, including a broader domain of individuals, and the field of leadership is therefore perceived 'as dyadic, shared, relational, strategic, global, and a complex social dynamic' (Avolio et al., 2009: 423).

Entrepreneurial Leadership

The term 'entrepreneurial leadership' is characterized by opposing positions and understandings. According to Vecchio (2003), research on leadership can extend to entrepreneurship, in the sense that entrepreneurship is a form of leadership. Contrarily, Kuratko (2007) has argued that leadership should be perceived as a constituent of entrepreneurship, in the sense that 'an entrepreneurial mind-set and behaviors are essential for effective leadership: entrepreneurship becomes the essence of leadership' (Harrison et al., 2015: 7). Cogliser and Brigham (2004) adopt an approach in the middle and argue that this field of study emerged from the theoretical overlap between the fields of entrepreneurship and leadership due to historical and conceptual parallels in the two domains. Following this approach, Roomi and Harrison (2011: 2) have suggested that entrepreneurial leadership is 'a fusion of these two constructs: having and communicating the vision to engage teams to identify, develop and take advantage of opportunity in order to gain competitive advantage'. According to Harrison et al. (2015: 694), 'A common thread running through these definitions is their focus on the traits, characteristics, and behaviors of entrepreneurial leaders and leadership in terms that are very clearly rooted in the entrepreneurial literature'. This is also reflected in the cluster generated by Renko et al. (2012), who divided the research on entrepreneurial leadership into studies of entrepreneurial behaviors and attitudes of high-level corporate executive leaders (e.g., Covin and Slevin, 2002; Gupta et al., 2004; Ireland et al., 2003; McGrath and MacMillan, 2000; Thornberry, 2006), engagement with new business owners who had to adopt leadership roles in order for their companies to grow (e.g., Baum et al., 1998; Ensley et al., 2006a; Ensley et al., 2006b; Jensen and Luthans, 2006; Peterson et al., 2008; Soriano and Martínez, 2007; Swiercz and Lydon, 2002) and distinctions and similarities between leaders and entrepreneurs (Baumol, 1968; Ensley et al., 2006b; Vecchio, 2003).

A common thread running through the majority of these definitions is their focus on the traits, characteristics and behaviors of entrepreneurial leaders and leadership in terms that are very clearly rooted in the entrepreneurial literature. The attempt to categorize the literature showed similarities in some entrepreneurial leadership works, but also indicated the diversity within the field. Nevertheless, the focus of these definitions on traits, characteristics and behaviors is apparent. Only a few studies take an integrated disciplinary basis for research on entrepreneurial leadership. However, according to Harrison et al. (2015), this is beginning to change, so that holistic approaches emerge.

METHODOLOGY

This section thoroughly documents the data search and collection process to establish the database. In addition, it methodically presents the analytical process used and introduces the analytical software Leximancer, with which the data was analysed.

Data Collection Strategy

The objective of the data collection phase was to compile and sort journal articles published from 2003 to 2014 in the research field of entrepreneurial leadership in small and medium-sized enterprises (SMEs). As such, a database comprising all relevant articles in the research field had to be constructed, applying a systematic collection strategy. The separation from large enterprises and focus on SMEs arises from the importance of context, given that 'in the study of entrepreneurial leadership and concepts, frameworks, and modes of analysis that are appropriate and effective in one domain may not be so in another' (Harrison et al., 2015: 697).

In the first step, all meta-information of articles in the journals implied in the Google Scholar categories 'Entrepreneurship and Innovation' and 'Human Resources and Organizations', plus seven additional journals highly ranked in the domain and published by Elsevier, were downloaded in April 2014 via a proxy. This search led to an Excel file with 45 876 articles. The sorting included the author(s), publication title, year, journal name, issue, volume and abstract.

In the second step, journals that could not be downloaded via the proxy were browsed through an EBSCO metasearch using the search terms 'leader*' OR 'manage*' AND 'entrepreneur' in 'Abstract', which led to another 1372 articles (without limitation for publication year). The search term was tested and developed with a second researcher, leading to the most satisfactory and constructive results. The search results then were exported into Excel via Endnote.

In the third step, to ensure all relevant publications were included, another EBSCO metasearch was conducted using the search terms 'leader*' OR 'manage*' AND 'entrepreneur' in 'Abstract', but limited to peer-reviewed journal articles published in English. This resulted in 2484 additional publications (without limitation for publication year). Again, the results were exported into Excel via Endnote.

In Excel, the FIND() function was used to search for the keywords 'small-firm manager', 'small business manager', 'SME manager', 'leader' and 'entrepreneur'. Since FIND() is sensitive to capital letters, all possibilities of spelling were included. Whenever a keyword was included, the value '1' was assigned. This led to an Excel file with 2042 potential articles for analysis. Because only articles published in the selected journals were used for further analysis, the number of articles significantly decreased to 170. Those results were then limited to the period 2003–2014, resulting in 78 articles.

In addition to the systematic article search in the first three steps, an unsystematic article search was conducted in step four. Specifically, backward tracking of references identified an additional ten articles for inclusion in the review (for a total of 88 articles).

This approach made it necessary to establish guidelines for relevancy and accuracy. For a publication to be included in this study, it had to discuss entrepreneurial leadership in SMEs or deal with entrepreneurial leadership on a conceptual level. As such, entrepreneurial leadership in large companies or multinational corporations, as well as corporate entrepreneurship, were excluded. Furthermore, following previous state-of-the-art and bibliometric analyses (e.g., Gardner et al., 2011; Volery and Mazzarol, 2015), this study focused solely on scholarly publications published in English. All conference papers, dissertations, working papers, book reviews, editorials and comments were removed from the collection in order to retain a focus on peer-reviewed publications. The reason for limiting this study to scholarly publications arose from the belief that these publications were peer-reviewed, fully developed and based on sound theory and empirical methods. Including in this analysis any theories or findings generated from excluded works could potentially undermine the study results and development of the field. Thus, to limit the data set to publications that dealt only with entrepreneurial leadership in SMEs, two coders (the author and a master's student) read all abstracts of the 88 articles and assigned the value '1' to those that met the previously determined guidelines.

In the abstracts, some authors used the term 'entrepreneur' and 'small firm manager' interchangeably. For instance, some studies interviewed small firm managers who did not show evident innovation or growth attributes. Similarly, the term 'entrepreneurial' was used at times to fashionably position an article without actually delving into entrepreneurship. Consequently, few articles met the predetermined guidelines and were assigned the value '1'.

After this first reading of the abstracts, an interrater reliability analysis using the Kappa statistic was performed to determine consistency between the two raters. This led to a value of 0.833 ($p < 0.000$), 95% CI [0.695, 0.945]. According to Landis and Koch (1977), values above 0.810 show almost perfect strength of agreement. The two coders then discussed differences until they reached consensus on final classification of the data. This final screening reduced to 21 the number of articles considered for analysis. After 'cleaning' the papers by removing headings, footnotes, page numbers, reference lists, tables and figures, the entire article content was included in the analysis via Leximancer.

Data Analysis

The following section thoroughly describes the data analysis process, in particular how the analytical tool Leximancer analyses text and how the keyword analysis and the epistemological orientation of the articles was executed. Reasoning that 'a word can be defined by its context in usage' (Smith and Humphreys, 2006: 262), the information for a narrative inquiry on a subject can be uncovered by analysing the co-occurrence of words used in texts. Co-occurring words replicate concepts in the investigated articles that address the application of entrepreneurial leadership in SMEs. To detect these concepts, Leximancer – a software text analytic tool that can be used to represent the main concepts within a text and how those concepts relate – was deployed (Leximancer, 2011). Leximancer weights terms within a text according to how frequently they occur in sentences containing the concept, compared with how frequently they occur elsewhere. It tags sentences as containing a concept if it finds enough accumulated evidence. This approach identifies which concepts exist in a set of texts and allows the concepts to be coded automatically in a grounded fashion. This method therefore differs from standard content analysis in that particular word strings are not required (Cretchley et al., 2010). According to Angus et al. (2013: 262), 'The advantage of generating the concept list automatically is that the list is statistically reliable and reproducible, being generated from the input text itself, whereas manual lists require checks for coding reliability and validity'. Therefore, the use of Leximancer increases the objectivity, hence decreasing the preconceptions of manual content analysis (Smith and Humphreys, 2006). Additionally, subtle or unusual relationships may be more likely to emerge using automated concept list creation.

Smith and Humphreys (2006) also demonstrated the software's face validity, stability and reproducibility; however, they used in-progress research for testing functional validity and outlined minor issues in the area of correlative validity. Nevertheless, the software is only a tool; the researcher must explore other avenues of analysis and bring intellectual rigor to the task of interpretation.

Another advantage of Leximancer is the highly consistent way in which it classifies text and identifies relationships among concepts; the same result is produced no matter how often a data set is coded and recoded. However, the analysis is stochastic, and initially the concepts are strewn randomly in multidimensional space. Thus, a map must be developed several times in reduced dimensions to check for a stable concept configuration (Cretchley et al., 2010). For this study, Leximancer produced stable maps.

Leximancer has previously been used to analyse the content of selected articles (Thomas, 2014) and even entire scientific journals such as *Long Range Planning* (Cummings and Daellenbach, 2009), the *Journal of International Business Studies* (Liesch et al., 2011) and the *International Small Business Journal* (Volery and Mazzarol, 2015). More examples of research using Leximancer as an analytic tool are available on its corporate website (Leximancer, 2014).

For the content analysis, the appropriate selected articles were uploaded into Leximancer. Common function words (for example, 'and', 'not' and 'of') that comprised a standard set of excluded words in Leximancer were also excluded from the analysis. In addition, the total number of concepts was set at 90 because Leximancer (2011) recommended using fewer than 100, and general terms (for example, 'common', 'example', 'others', 'table', 'used' and 'using') that did not add meaning to the concept map were deleted. For the 2003–2009 and 2010–2014 maps, the percentage of theme size was set to 50 per cent in order to decrease the numbers of themes on the map.

The keyword analysis was confusing, going in multiple directions. The EBSCO metasearch provided 78 keywords (subject terms); most appeared only once. Specifically, except for leadership (ten times), entrepreneurship (eight times), shared leadership and industrial management (three times each), SMEs, innovations in business, organizational behavior and employees' attitudes (two times each), all other 70 keywords appeared only once. Additionally, author-provided keywords were too widespread among the articles for analysis. Therefore, to enable a meaningful analysis, consolidation was necessary.

This consolidation was best achieved by aggregating and generating self-developed keywords. To do so, two researchers who separately developed keywords undertook the initial classification by examining the article's title and reviewing its abstract and, to some extent, the article itself. Subsequently, the researchers' separate keyword lists were compared and discrepancies discussed until reaching consensus on final classification by reviewing the articles again. This process resulted in six meta-keywords, with each article represented by a maximum of three keywords. The two researchers then coded each article according to the self-developed keywords. Again, discrepancies were discussed until consensus was reached, so that the remaining articles could be classified unequivocally.

In order to determine the epistemological orientation of the articles, each article was coded using the classification scheme of De Bakker et al. (2005), a systematic and parsimonious examination of the epistemological evolution of the academic field of entrepreneurial leadership. Table 2.1 represents the classification scheme.

This classification system suggests that articles generally can have a theoretical, prescriptive or descriptive orientation. According to De Bakker et al. (2005: 294), 'Papers make a theoretical contribution if they enhance the systematic understanding of some phenomenon at an abstract level'. Note that a theoretical contribution may or may not involve collection of new empirical data. Further, the theoretical orientation may be subdivided into three categories: first, conceptual articles that do not rely on empirical data and typically aim to advance theory or the theory development process; second, theoretical articles that can be classified as predictive if they use data to confirm or refute hypotheses; and third, exploratory

Table 2.1   Classification scheme for epistemological orientation of articles

Classification		Description
Theoretical	Conceptual	Major focus is on developing propositions, hypotheses or (cor)relations between theoretical constructs, based on a discussion of state-of-the-art literature; no new empirical material has been collected for this work
	Exploratory	Major focus is on developing propositions, hypotheses and (cor)relations among theoretical constructs, based on examination of extensive, new empirical data
	Predictive	Major focus is on testing (refutation, confirmation) of propositions, hypotheses or (cor)relations among theoretical constructs, based on examination of extensive, new empirical data
Prescriptive	Instrumental	Major focus is on providing prescription (means, ideas, recipes for action) to practitioners and professionals, which are instrumental in the realization of some desired end, such as improved performance along some dimension
	Normative	Major focus is on providing prescription (means, ideas, recipes for action) to practitioners and professionals, which are valuable in themselves when considered from some ethical, moral or religious point of view
Descriptive	Descriptive	Major focus is on reporting fact or opinion; no intention of a theoretical or prescriptive contribution

Source: De Bakker et al. (2005: 294).

articles that typically develop expectations about relationships between constructs. Articles make a prescriptive contribution if they provide action, means, ideas and recipes on how practitioners could realize some desired end. Descriptive articles report data or opinion as interesting in themselves, without the author noticeably attempting to contribute to either theory or practice.

In order to ensure consistency, the two researchers separately coded the same articles with the classification scheme. An interrater reliability analysis using the Kappa statistic was performed to determine consistency between the raters. The Kappa was found to be 0.756 ($p < 0.001$) 95%

CI [0.397, 1.000]. Kappas from 0.61 to 0.80 were interpreted as substantial agreement (Landis and Koch, 1977). The only disagreement was the classification of abstracts as descriptive as opposed to exploratory. The disagreement can be ascribed to differences in the length and clarity of the provided abstracts. Afterward, the two researchers compared notes and discussed discrepancies until reaching consensus about the final classification.

RESULTS

This section provides a descriptive overview of the field of entrepreneurial leadership to produce insights into and observations on the current state in this field. To do so, all 21 articles that remained for analysis were extracted and placed into MS Word documents before undertaking the three-stage data Leximancer analysis. First, all 21 articles across the 2003–2014 period were examined together to provide an overall picture of the field. Next, the years 2003–2009 (14 articles) were examined separately, followed by an examination of the years 2012–2014 (seven articles). These two latter examinations were chosen in order to show the evolution of the field with bundles of publications at the beginning and at the end of the examined timeframe.

2003–2014: Overall Concept Map

Figure 2.1 depicts the themes within the data set. These themes (circles) contain clusters of concepts; those that appear together often in the data set are represented close to one another on the map. The themes summarize the main ideas in particular clusters, and the cluster size denotes the number of concepts found within each cluster. The most prominent concept in each theme is represented by the largest dot in the scheme and named after it (Leximancer, 2011).

Referring to Figure 2.1, the overall concept map shows that across the analysed period, the articles contained a core set of concepts, namely 'performance', 'leadership' and 'entrepreneurial'. However, it is obvious that the last two mentioned appear prominent because they were used as search terms during the data collection phase and naturally would be heavily represented in the data. Therefore, their presence confirms the prevalence of entrepreneurship and leadership as a focal point of the articles studied; especially 'leadership', where its central location on the map indicates its prominence throughout all articles.

Going deeper into the Leximancer analysis, 'leadership' came first in a

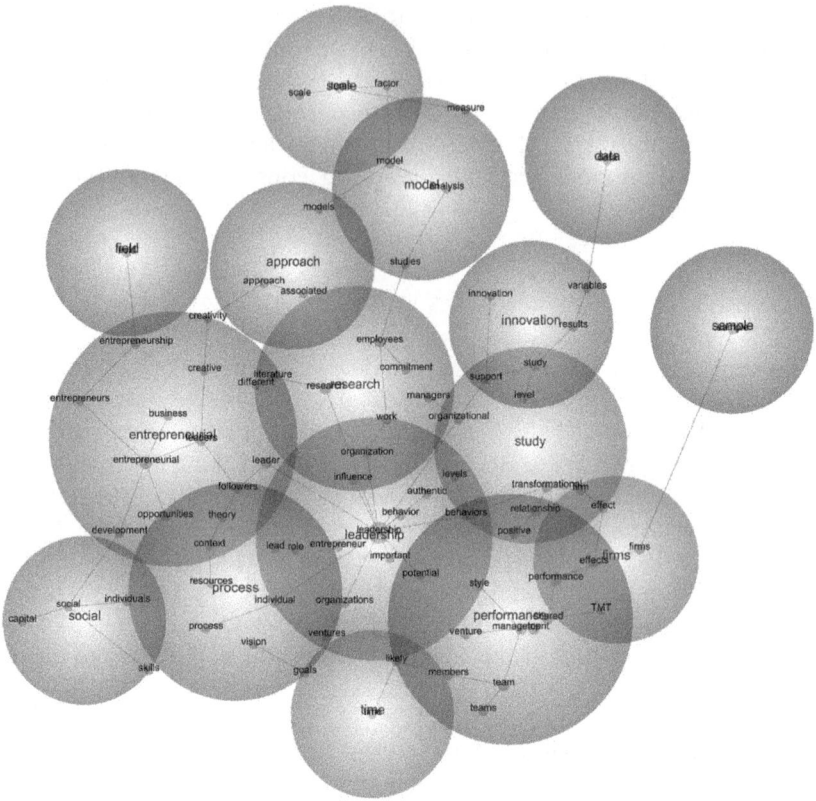

Figure 2.1   Leximancer overall concept map

ranked list based on the number of times the concepts occurred in the set of articles. The rankings were then converted into a relevance score, computed as the frequency percentage of text segments coded with that concept and relative to the most frequent concept in the list (Thomas, 2014). The most frequent concepts encountered in this study were 'leadership', 'entrepreneurial', 'performance', 'team', 'research', 'study', 'employees', 'management' and 'top', with 'leadership' co-occurring in the text. 'Leadership' co-occurred particularly in the context of leadership styles, such as authentic (e.g., Jensen and Luthans, 2006; Hmieleski et al., 2012), transformational (e.g., Gumusluoglu and İlsev, 2009) and shared (e.g., Hmieleski et al., 2012; Mihalache et al., 2014; Zhou et al., 2013), indicating the relevance of these styles in the context of entrepreneurial leadership. Renko et al. (2012) even described entrepreneurial leadership as a particular leadership style.

The overlap of 'leadership' and 'performance' and the analysis of corresponding text segments uncovered the positive influence of leadership on venture performance (e.g., Ensley et al., 2006a; Ensley et al., 2006b; Zhou et al., 2013). Interestingly, the knowledge pathway within Leximancer also revealed a linkage between 'entrepreneurial' and 'performance'. Analysing corresponding text segments uncovered that individual entrepreneurs have a strong leadership role, as their passion and behavior influence the employees and team members and therefore enhance venture performance (e.g., Breugst et al., 2012; Engelen et al., 2012).

The theme 'leadership' also overlaps with the themes 'entrepreneurial' and 'process'. This reflects the dynamics in leadership development – in particular the enhancement of human capital, such as knowledge, skills and capabilities, in a setting where any kind of change is needed – by individuals who must lead people and therefore also must change their role as the company further develops (e.g., Chen, 2007; Cogliser and Brigham, 2004; Leitch et al., 2013).

Interestingly, the theme 'entrepreneurial' consists of concepts strongly associated, on one hand, with the characteristics and traits of the entrepreneur, and on the other hand, with leading followers and inspiring creativity. This intersection emphasizes the importance of the entrepreneur as a person who must identify and fill a need. This identification and need are important to the entrepreneurs' characteristics and traits. Without the individual, there would be nobody to follow or to inspire and encourage creative action that advances the business (e.g., Chen, 2007; Renko et al., 2012; Wu et al., 2008).

In relation to methodology, the most common across all time periods were theoretical articles (e.g., Becherer et al., 2008; Cogliser and Brigham, 2004; Fernald et al., 2005; Kuratko, 2007; Vecchio, 2003). Empirical articles often applied large-scale samples to measure a specific leadership style in the context of entrepreneurial leadership (e.g., Jensen and Luthans, 2006; Zhou et al., 2013) or its influence on performance (e.g., Ensley et al., 2006b; Hmieleski and Ensley, 2007). The latter outcome is also represented in lesser themes found in the overall concept map that focused on methods, such as 'research', 'data', 'sample', 'factor', 'scale', 'model', 'measure', 'approach', 'variable' and 'effect', and referred to the research methods that were applied in the empirical articles.

2003–2009

The analysis incorporated 14 articles for the 2003–2009 period. The cluster map for this period (Figure 2.2) has the first-order theme 'leadership' as its most prominent and 'characteristics' as its least prominent (ranked

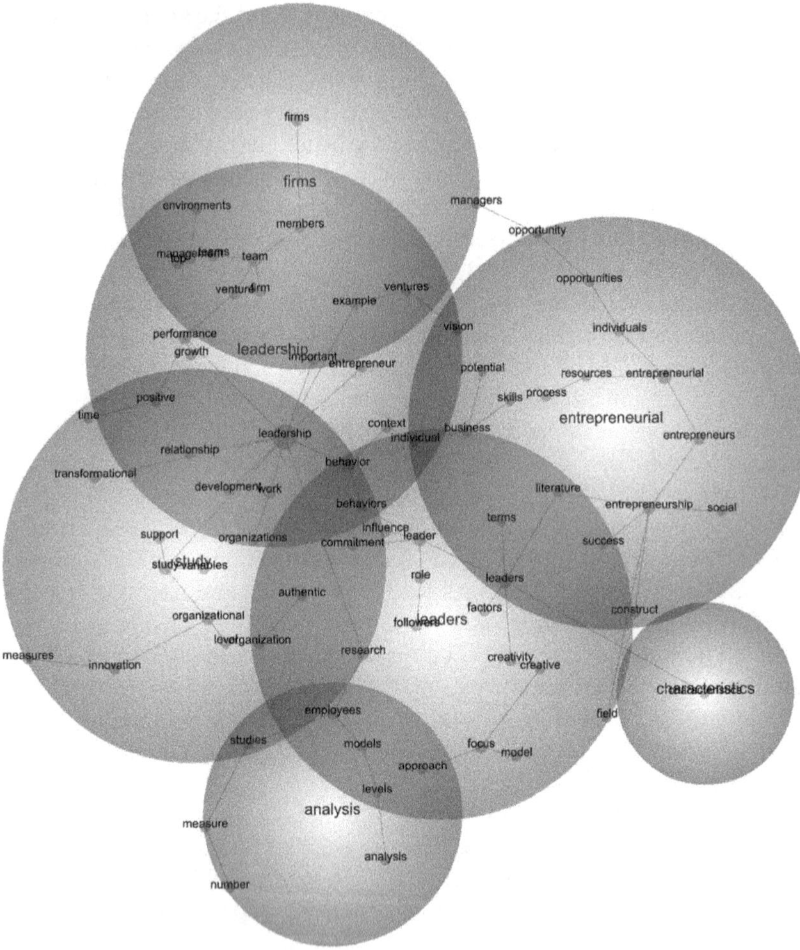

Figure 2.2   Leximancer concept map, 2003–2009

seventh). The most frequent concepts within 'leadership' were 'authentic', 'transformational' and 'behavior', which refer to leadership styles. The articles reflected the prominence of leadership styles, discussed the various styles that best described entrepreneurial leaders, and used studies of these styles to define entrepreneurial leadership (e.g., Ensley et al., 2006a; Gumusluoglu and İlsev, 2009; Jensen and Luthans, 2006). 'Entrepreneur' was also an important theme within leadership concepts but was not a solid theme in the whole 2003–2009 data set. However, 'entrepreneurial' was the fourth most frequent theme on the map, intersecting with the themes 'leaders', 'leadership' and 'characteristics'. On the surface, that primarily confirmed the strong alignment of entrepreneurship and leadership within the articles investigated.

Looking deeper into the articles, the data indicated that entrepreneurial skills, resources, opportunities and success were heavily studied in articles discussing 'entrepreneurial'. This was because venture performance was of great interest in the various articles that strongly associated the entrepreneur person with the entrepreneur's skills and resources, as well as the context (e.g., Ensley et al., 2006b; Hmieleski and Ensley, 2007).

Regarding leaders, the articles focused on leaders' creativity (e.g., Chen, 2007) and leadership approach, as well as their possibility to influence the work team (e.g., Jensen and Luthans, 2006; Soriano and Martínez, 2007). Due to the fact that 'entrepreneur' was one of the search terms in the data collection process, it also appeared in the leadership theme.

2012–2014

The analysis of the 2012–2014 period was based on seven articles (Figure 2.3), with 'leadership' being the most prominent theme (636 hits). Its prominence had stood out when looking at the titles of the papers: 85 per cent included 'leadership' in the title, with an emphasis on shared leadership (e.g., Hmieleski et al., 2012; Mihalache et al., 2014; Zhou et al., 2013). Within the leadership theme, the most frequent concepts were 'shared', 'TMT' (top management team), 'performance', 'team', 'management', 'members', 'effect', 'study', 'organizational', 'role', 'ambidexterity', 'levels', 'style', 'authentic', 'organization', 'diversity', 'processes', 'information' and 'innovation'. Besides 'shared leadership', the prominence of 'teams' and 'TMT' in relation to leadership is striking. An article by Mihalache et al. (2014) proposed that 'top management team' shared 'leadership' as an important enabler of organizational ambidexterity. A closer look into the Leximancer analysis showed the overlap of 'leadership' with the theme 'development', which indicated that leadership skills must be developed within the leading teams and roles need to be newly defined (e.g., Leitch et al., 2013).

'Authentic leadership' is also relevant in the analysed articles, again showing the importance of a specific leadership style. For example, the results of a study by Hmieleski et al. (2012) demonstrated a positive indirect effect of shared authentic leadership behavior on firm performance.

The large overlap of the two most prominent themes, 'leadership' and 'entrepreneurial', is particularly striking but not surprising, as those two terms were used as search terms and built the centerpiece of this study. Additionally, 'transformational leadership style' is a concept within

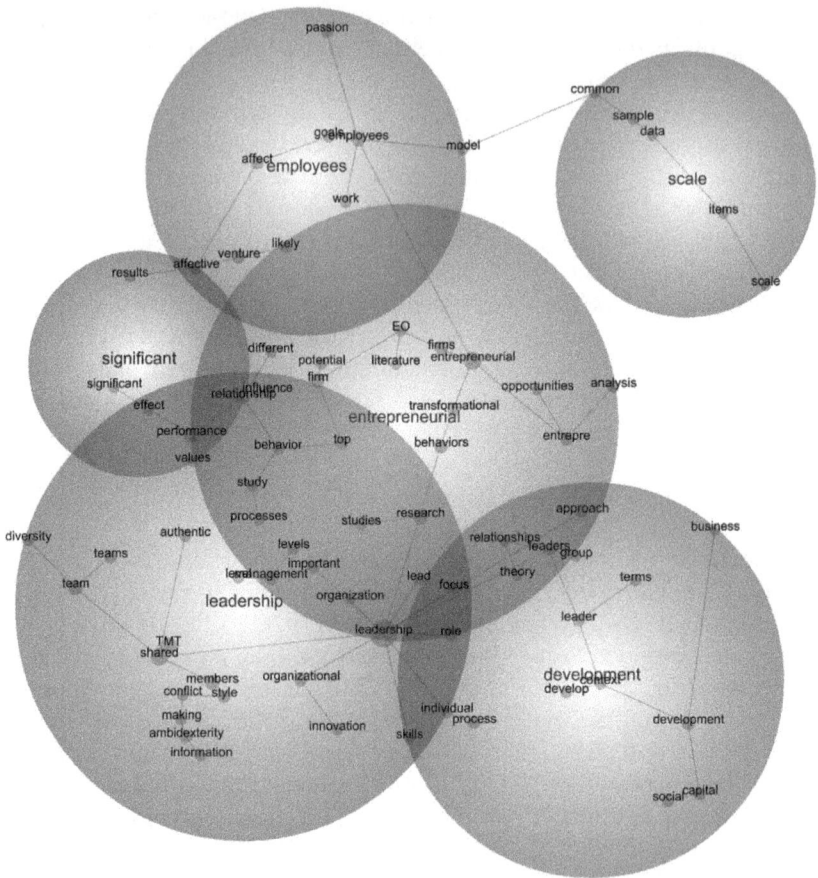

Figure 2.3   Leximancer concept map, 2012–2014

'leadership', reinforcing the intersection of entrepreneurship and leadership (e.g., Engelen et al., 2012; Renko et al., 2012). Within 'entrepreneurial', the construct of entrepreneurial orientation appeared in reference to firms' entrepreneurial behavior such as risk-taking, innovativeness and proactiveness. Various authors addressed these behaviors when discussing entrepreneurship as a construct (e.g., Mihalache et al., 2014; Zhou et al., 2013).

The important role of 'employees' also appears in this concept map (Figure 2.3), overlapping with the 'entrepreneurial' theme because perceived entrepreneurial passion influences the employees of entrepreneurial ventures, according to Renko et al. (2012). The two themes 'scale' and

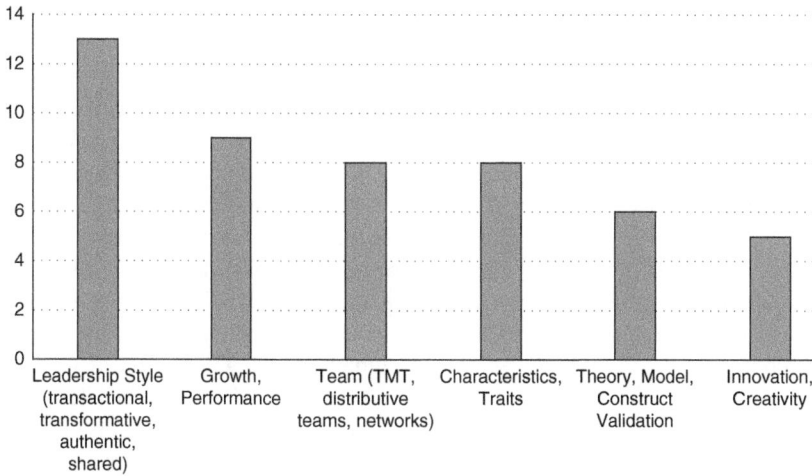

Figure 2.4   Keyword frequencies

'significant' highlighted empirical methods that the articles applied to entrepreneurial leadership, with concepts such as 'items', 'data', 'sample', 'results' and 'significant' (e.g., Breugst et al., 2012; Engelen et al., 2012; Leitch et al., 2013).

Keyword Frequencies

Keyword analysis drew upon the assumption that an article's keywords constitute an adequate description of its content or the links the articles established between problems. Therefore, in this section, the self-developed keywords are presented (see Figure 2.4). Keywords such as 'entrepreneurship', 'entrepreneurial' and 'leadership' were not incorporated in Figure 2.4 because they were already represented in the applied search terms. As such, they already had built the principal items for all articles used in this analysis and would not have added meaning. However, their overall relevance should be kept in mind.

That a majority of the articles examined the topic of 'leadership style' can be explained by the fact that providing direction, implementing plans and motivating people are important in an entrepreneurial setting, especially in association with the growth of a company. Ensley et al. (2006a), for example, found that both vertical and shared leadership were highly significant predictors of new venture performance. Therefore, 'growth' and 'performance' could be retrieved as the second most frequent keywords (e.g., Ensley et al., 2006a and b; Hmieleski and Ensley, 2007; Zhou et al., 2013). These keywords also covered articles regarding employee satisfaction because performance is not limited to monetary fields, but can also come from high employee satisfaction rates (e.g., Breugst et al., 2012). Also the importance of 'teams' in entrepreneurial leadership settings was represented in the keywords, which implies that entrepreneurial opportunities might be detected within a team, or that entrepreneurial leaders need to influence employees in order to stay in the market (e.g., Ensley et al., 2006a; Soriano and Martínez, 2007; Zhou et al., 2013). In addition to considering a group of people, various articles focused on the individual entrepreneur's 'characteristics' and 'traits' (e.g., Becherer et al., 2008; Cogliser and Brigham, 2004; Fernald et al., 2005; Gupta et al., 2004; Renko et al., 2012; Vecchio, 2003). A few articles also covered 'innovation' and 'creativity' when discussing entrepreneurial leadership (e.g., Chen, 2007; Gumusluoglu and İlsev, 2009; Soriano and Martínez, 2007; Wu et al., 2008).

Represented Journals, Authors and Timely Distribution of Articles

Of 53 journals (38 represented in the Google Scholar catego- ries 'Entrepreneurship and Innovation' and 'Human Resources and Organizations', seven highly ranked in the domain, plus eight from back- ward tracking of references), 17 journals contained the 21 articles remain- ing for analysis. In most of the journals, only one article was relevant for this study (see Table 2.2).

The *Journal of Business Venturing* was most frequently represented, supporting its aim to cover a multiplicity of disciplines and methodologies in entrepreneurship research. Three empirical articles were represented in this journal: Gupta et al. (2004), Ensley et al. (2006b) and Wu et al. (2008). Next most frequently represented were two journals, each with two publications focused on leadership and management. One, the *Leadership Quarterly*, focused on leadership topics of interest to scholars, consultants, practicing managers, executives, administrators and university faculty members. Thus, both of its selected articles focused on entrepreneurial leadership. The first article, by Cogliser and Brigham (2004), was a review article that looked at the intersection of entrepreneurship and leadership. The second article, by Ensley et al. (2006a), focused on shared leadership within top management teams and its influence on venture performance. The other journal, the *Journal of Management*, focused on scholarly empirical and theoretical research articles with strong impact on the management field, which applies to research on entrepreneurial leader- ship. Interestingly, both articles within the *Journal of Management* were

Table 2.2   Represented journals

Journal	Articles (#)	Author(s) and year
Journal of Business Venturing	3	Gupta et al. (2004)
		Ensley et al. (2006b)
		Wu et al. (2008)
Leadership Quarterly	2	Cogliser and Brigham (2004)
		Ensley et al. (2006a)
Journal of Management	2	Hmieleski et al. (2012)
		Engelen et al. (2012)
British Journal of Management	1	Leitch et al. (2013)
Creativity and Innovation Management	1	Chen (2007)
Entrepreneurship Theory and Practice	1	Breugst et al. (2012)
Human Resource Management Review	1	Vecchio (2003)
International Entrepreneurship and Management Journal	1	Zhou et al. (2013)
Journal of Leadership and Organizational Studies	1	Kuratko (2007)
Journal of Organizational Behavior	1	Hmieleski and Ensley (2007)
Journal of Product Innovation Management	1	Gumusluoglu and İlsev (2009)
Journal of Small Business Management	1	Renko et al. (2012)
Leadership and Organization Development Journal	1	Jensen and Luthans (2006)
Management Decision	1	Soriano and Martínez (2007)
New England Journal of Entrepreneurship	1	Becherer et al. (2008)
Southern Business Review	1	Fernald et al. (2005)
Strategic Entrepreneurship Journal	1	Mihalache et al. (2014)

of an empirical nature and focused on performance (Engelen et al., 2012; Hmieleski et al., 2012).

Most of the other represented journals can be considered as typically suitable for articles on entrepreneurial leadership. However, two journals stood out. The first, the *Southern Business Review*, a magazine published by Georgia Southern University's College of Business Administration, did not appear on the VHB-Jourqual or ABS ranking lists. However, it published the article, 'A new paradigm: entrepreneurial leadership' by Fernald et al. (2005), which almost every other article on entrepreneurial leadership used as a reference, although the journal did not have an international reputation. The second stand-out, the *New England Journal of*

Entrepreneurship, was published by Sacred Heart University's John F. Welch College of Business (2014) with the objective, 'To be an invaluable forum for exchange of scholarly ideas, practices and policies in the field of entrepreneurship and small business management', this journal also was not listed in the VHB-Jourqual or ABS ranking lists. Nevertheless, it published the article, 'Separated at birth: an inquiry on the conceptual independence of the entrepreneurship and the leadership constructs' by Becherer et al. (2008), which was also used as a reference in almost every other article on entrepreneurial leadership.

Table 2.2 also indicates a certain fragmentation. Specifically, in total, 50 authors published in 17 journals that were anchored in different disciplines, such as entrepreneurship, leadership, human resources and organizational behavior. A few authors were represented more frequently than others. For example, Hmieleski was represented with four articles (twice as first author and once each as second and third author); followed by Ensley, represented with three articles (once as first author, twice as second author); and El Tarabishy and Pearce were both represented twice (each as second and third author). (As an aside, there was also an accumulation of Anglo-American authors, and male authors outnumbered female authors.)

Figure 2.5 illustrates the chronological distribution of the publications. The publications were concentrated in the years 2006–2008, with a total of nine articles (three publications in 2006, four in 2007, and two in 2008) and in the years 2012–2014, with a total of seven articles (three publica-

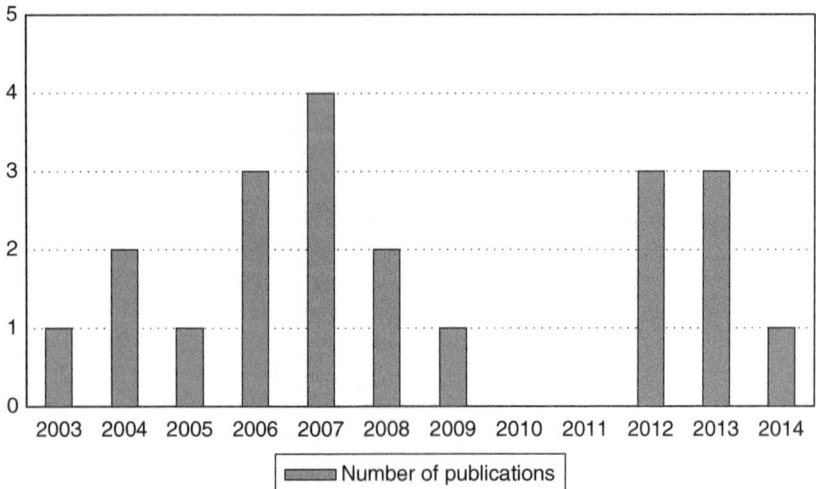

Figure 2.5   Number of publications

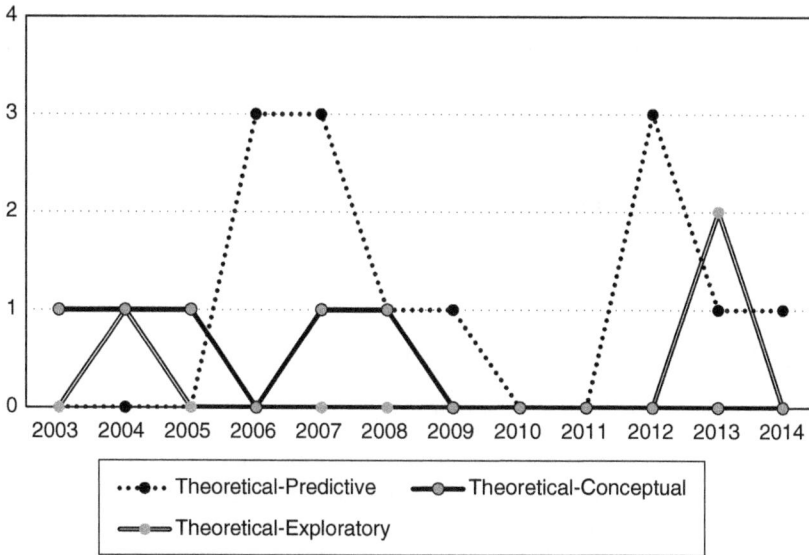

Figure 2.6   Epistemological orientation of articles

tions each in 2012 and 2013). Only one article was published in each of the years 2003, 2005, 2009 and 2014, and no articles were published in 2004, 2010 and 2011.

Epistemological Orientation of Articles

Figure 2.6 illustrates that all of the articles were of a theoretical nature. According to De Bakker et al. (2005: 294), 'Papers make a theoretical contribution if they enhance the systematic understanding of some phenomenon at an abstract level [that] may or may not involve the collection of new empirical data'. Further, Figure 2.6 shows that the majority (13) of the articles were of a predictive nature, which implies testing hypotheses or propositions using extensive empirical data (e.g., Breugst et al., 2012; Cogliser and Brigham, 2004; Ensley et al., 2006a). Most predictive articles in this study were published in 2006, 2007 and 2012.

Conceptual articles account for the second largest share of publications (five) used in this article (e.g., Cogliser and Brigham, 2004; Fernald et al., 2005; Vecchio, 2003). Conceptual articles focus on developing propositions and hypotheses based on a discussion of state-of-the-art literature. They dominated over predictive and exploratory papers in the beginning time frame of this analysis, before the increase of predictive publications in 2006 and 2007. The larger amount of conceptual articles during the emergence of entrepreneurial leadership represents the field's early stage (2003), when conceptual articles were based upon broadly accepted facts or moved from factual assumptions to developing an evolving research field without the use of new empirical data. Fernald et al. (2005), Leitch et al. (2013) and Renko et al. (2012) wrote the rare exploratory articles that focused on developing propositions and hypotheses based on examination of new empirical data of a qualitative nature to develop expectations about relationships among constructs.

DISCUSSION AND CONCLUSION

Analysing research on entrepreneurial leadership is of great importance because the body of literature in this field has increased and, despite certain fragmentation and definitional disagreements, a convergence between entrepreneurship and leadership underpinned the development of the field. To address this issue in this chapter, a systematic bibliometric study of the field of entrepreneurial leadership, analysing 21 peer-reviewed academic journal articles published from 2003 to 2014, was conducted. This review provided a systematic and comprehensive analysis and helped to visualize the development of the research field to its current state.

This analysis suggested that the dominant themes within the research field were 'entrepreneurial' and 'leadership', which was to be expected in an analysis focused on entrepreneurial leadership. However, the analysis revealed important changes in how research has been conducted in this field in the time frame 2003–2014. In the first concept map (2003–2009), the articles often separated the terms 'entrepreneurship' and 'leadership' when describing the construct of entrepreneurial leadership. The later concept map (2009–2014) indicated the merger of these two constructs, resulting in 'entrepreneurial leadership'. However, the various definitions represented considerable diversity in approach, which is reflected in the absence of an agreed-upon definition (Harrison et al., 2015).

Also interesting is the relevance of leadership styles, traits, characteristics and behaviors in both periods 2003–2009 and 2012–2014, as was displayed in the keyword analysis. The relevance of leadership styles particularly stands out in the keyword analysis. Most authors referred to leadership styles such as 'authentic', 'transformational' or 'shared' to indicate their relevance in this context. The relevance of leadership styles in entrepreneurial settings was generally striking as a key element of leader effectiveness. The variety and extensive discussion of leadership styles in the investigated articles reflected the many leadership styles from which to choose. The prominent presence of leadership styles in the articles can also be explained by the fact that providing direction, implementing plans and motivating people are important in entrepreneurial settings, particularly when it regards company growth and innovation. More recently, Renko et al. (2012) vividly described the unique entrepreneurial leadership style and differentiated it in particular from transformational leadership. That shows a disengagement from studies that are primarily descriptive and separated the fields 'entrepreneurial' and 'leadership', to emerge into a single field of inquiry where 'entrepreneurial leadership' is now described as a distinct construct.

During the second studied time frame (2012–2014), the focus of the articles shifted, giving greater attention to 'scale', 'items', 'sample' and 'data'. This change reflected the increasing trend toward a more exploratory or predictive epistemological orientation of the articles, whereas conceptual articles were more frequent in earlier years. In addition, the role of employees was emphasized in the second time frame. These articles identified the importance of employees as a source of innovation and entrepreneurial activities, instead of surrendering the field solely to the individual entrepreneur or leader (e.g., Breugst et al., 2012; Mihalache et al., 2014).

This study showed that a number of journals had published articles on the topic of 'entrepreneurial leadership'. Only three journals (*Journal of Business Venturing, Leadership Quarterly* and *Journal of Management*) were represented more than once, and the focal points of the represented journals varied greatly. Again, that variation indicated the diverse topics within entrepreneurial leadership and their complexity; however, the variation also indicated a lack of convergence.

Variation also applied to the authors who published in this research domain. Fifty authors participated in writing the analysed articles, but only a few authors appeared with high frequency. This suggests that no luminary author or expert exists within this field of research (unlike other disciplines). It likewise underpins the foregoing perception that the field is still evolving, lacks definitional clarity and appropriate tools to assess its characteristics and behaviors, and is still seeking its identity (Leitch et al., 2013; Renko et al., 2012).

This analysis also reveals increased cross-fertilization of the fields of entrepreneurship and leadership, and convergence between the fields in the sense that more holistic approaches are pursued. That is also indicated in the merger of these two constructs in the later concept map, resulting in 'entrepreneurial leadership'. However, the various definitions represented considerable diversity in approach, which is reflected in the absence of an agreed-upon definition. Therefore, this section closes with an attempt at a definition, incorporating the considerations of the analysed articles:

'entrepreneurial leadership' can be defined as: the entrepreneur's or group of entrepreneurs' ability to influence and direct the performance of an individual or a group with the aim to steer the organization in its development under uncertainty.

LIMITATIONS AND FUTURE RESEARCH

Among the limitations of this analysis, some resulted from the search design and others as a direct consequence of the applied technique. Among the main search design shortcomings was the concentration on peer-reviewed scientific journal articles. This concentration inevitably limited the potential scope of the results, because the analysed articles represent a mere fraction of all research papers and book chapters discussing entrepreneurial leadership. However, the included articles represented the major research efforts that have been made in this research domain. In addition, the present study primarily followed a descriptive approach and therefore owes a deeper explanation of the detected phenomena. This leaves room for further research, such as a follow-up examination of why the described observations existed and what the findings imply.

This analysis was also subject to limitations inherent in bibliometric techniques in general and text mining in particular. Although Leximancer cannot provide detailed conceptual insights by shifting the analysis level from the researcher to the actual content, it simplifies (but does not interpret) the concepts. A researcher must still interpret the output, which comes with biases because interpreting the resulting maps is inevitably subjective. Therefore, this study should be regarded neither as offering definitive results with respect to the issues under study nor as the only potential application of bibliometric analysis on entrepreneurial leadership. Nevertheless, Leximancer provides a great advantage in disclosing related concepts and themes and in visualizing relationships in a meaningful way.

Another shortcoming lay in the data collection sources, but although there were other sources for retrieving the data, each would have had its own inaccuracies and biases. However, the limitations could be minimized and provide an incentive to improve on the techniques applied in this study. For example, future research samples could be enlarged to a broader journal base in order to gain valuable insights from other authors and geographical areas and to cover international aspects. Conference papers, dissertations, working papers, book chapters, book reviews, editorials and comments could be incorporated into the analysis to comprise a larger spectrum and further identify knowledge claims.

Due to the wide proliferation of authors, journals and competing definitions in this field of inquiry, it would be of utmost interest to further define, measure and rigorously investigate the construct of entrepreneurial leadership. This could be done with a study of literature focused on analysing the applied methodologies, research methods and underlying theoretical foundations. In so doing, shifts in research directions and articles that are likely to alter topic and methodological trends could be identified. In addition, conceptual convergence could be furthered by focusing on the patterns and relationships of co-citations (for example, the most frequently cited references) used by entrepreneurial leadership scholars. Finally, future research could investigate if and how entrepreneurial leadership can be learned and then focus on developing a reliable measurement instrument. Addressing the study's limitations and incorporating the foregoing suggestions could provide a more comprehensive analysis of the evolution of the entrepreneurial leadership discipline over time and further advance the field.

REFERENCES

Aldrich, H.E. (2012), 'The emergence of entrepreneurship as an academic field: a personal essay on institutional entrepreneurship', *Research Policy*, 41 (7), 1240–1248.

Angus, D., S. Rintel and J. Wiles (2013), 'Making sense of big text: a visual-first approach for analysing text data using Leximancer and Discursis', *International Journal of Social Research Methodology*, 16 (3), 261–7.

Avolio, B.J., F.O. Walumbwa and T.J. Weber (2009), 'Leadership: current theories, research, and future directions', *Annual Review of Psychology*, 60, 421–49.

Baum, J. Robert, Michael Frese and Robert Baron (2007), *The Psychology of Entrepreneurship*, Mahwah, NJ: Lawrence Erlbaum Associates.

Baum, J.R., E.A. Locke and S.A. Kirkpatrick (1998), 'A longitudinal study of the relation of vision and vision communication to venture growth in entrepreneurial firms', *Journal of Applied Psychology*, 83 (1), 43–54.

Baumol, W.J. (1968), 'Entrepreneurship in economic theory', *American Economic Review*, 58 (2), 64–71.

Becherer, R.C., M.E. Mendenhall and K.F. Eickhoff (2008), 'Separated at birth: an inquiry on the conceptual independence of the entrepreneurship and the leadership constructs', *New England Journal of Entrepreneurship*, 11 (2), 13–27.

Breugst, N., A. Domurath, H. Patzelt and A. Klaukien (2012), 'Perceptions of entrepreneurial passion and employees' commitment to entrepreneurial ventures', *Entrepreneurship Theory and Practice*, 36 (1), 171–92.

Bruyat, C. and P.A. Julien (2001), 'Defining the field of research in entrepreneurship', *Journal of Business Venturing*, 16 (2), 165–80.

Busenitz, L.W., G. Page West, D. Shepherd, T. Nelson, G.N. Chandler and A. Zacharakis (2003), 'Entrepreneurship research in emergence: past trends and future directions', *Journal of Management*, 29 (3), 285–308.

Chen, M.H. (2007), 'Entrepreneurial leadership and new ventures: creativity in entrepreneurial teams', *Creativity and Innovation Management*, 16 (3), 239–49.

Cogliser, C.C. and K.H. Brigham (2004), 'The intersection of leadership and entrepreneurship: mutual lessons to be learned', *Leadership Quarterly*, 15 (6), 771–99.

Covin, Jeffrey G. and Dennis Slevin (2002), 'The entrepreneurial imperatives of strategic leadership', in Michael A. Hitt, R. Duane Ireland, S. Michael Camp, and Donald L. Sexton (eds), *Strategic Entrepreneurship: Creating a New Mindset*, Oxford: Blackwell Publishers, pp. 309–27.

Cretchley, J., D. Rooney and C. Gallois (2010), 'Mapping a 40-year history with Leximancer: themes and concepts in the Journal of Cross-Cultural Psychology', *Journal of Cross-Cultural Psychology*, 41 (3), 318–28.

Culnan, M.J., C.A. O'Reilly III and J.A. Chatman (1990), 'Intellectual structure of research in organizational behaviour, 1972–1984: a co-citation analysis', *Journal of the American Society for Information Science*, 41 (6), 453–8.

Cummings, S. and U. Daellenbach (2009), 'A guide to the future of strategy? The history of long range planning', *Long Range Planning*, 42 (2), 234–63.

De Bakker, F.G.A., P. Groenewegen and F. Den Hond (2005), 'A bibliometric analysis of 30 years of research and theory on corporate social responsibility and corporate social performance', *Business and Society*, 44 (3), 283–317.

Engelen, A., V. Gupta, L. Strenger and M. Brettel (2012), 'Entrepreneurial orientation, firm performance, and the moderating role of transformational leadership behaviors', *Journal of Management*, 41 (4), 1069–97.

Ensley, M.D., K.M. Hmieleski and C.L. Pearce (2006a), 'The importance of vertical and shared leadership within new venture top management teams: implications for the performance of startups', *Leadership Quarterly*, 17 (3), 217–31.

Ensley, M.D., C.L. Pearce and K.M. Hmieleski (2006b), 'The moderating effect of environmental dynamism on the relationship between entrepreneur leadership behavior and new venture performance', *Journal of Business Venturing*, 21 (2), 243–63.

Fernald, L.W., G.T. Solomon and A. Tarabishy (2005), 'A new paradigm: entrepreneurial leadership', *Southern Business Review*, 30 (2), 1–10.

Frese, M. and M.M. Gielnik (2014), 'The psychology of entrepreneurship', *Annual Review of Organizational Psychology and Organizational Behavior*, 1 (1), 413–38.

Gardner, W.L., C.C. Cogliser, K.M. Davis and M.P. Dickens (2011), 'Authentic leadership: a review of the literature and research agenda', *Leadership Quarterly*, 22 (6), 1120–45.

Gartner, W.B. (2001), 'Is there an elephant in entrepreneurship? Blind assumptions in theory development', *Entrepreneurship Theory and Practice*, 25 (4), 27–39.

Gumusluoglu, L. and A. İlsev (2009), 'Transformational leadership and organizational innovation: the roles of internal and external support for innovation', *Journal of Product Innovation Management*, 26, 264–77.

Gupta, V., I.C. MacMillan and G. Surie (2004), 'Entrepreneurial leadership: developing and measuring a cross-cultural construct', *Journal of Business Venturing*, 19 (2), 241–60.

Harrison, R.T., C.M. Leitch and M. McAdam (2015), 'Breaking glass: toward a gendered analysis of entrepreneurial leadership', *Journal of Small Business Management*, 53 (3), 693–713.

Hmieleski, K.M., M.S. Cole and R.A. Baron (2012), 'Shared authentic leadership and new venture performance', *Journal of Management*, 38 (5), 1476–99.

Hmieleski, K.M. and M.D. Ensley (2007), 'A contextual examination of new venture performance: entrepreneur leadership behavior, top management team heterogeneity, and environmental dynamism', *Journal of Organizational Behavior*, 28, 865–89.

Ireland, R.D., M.A. Hitt and D.G. Sirmon (2003), 'A model of strategic entrepreneurship: the construct and its dimensions', *Journal of Management*, 29 (6), 963–89.

Jensen, S.M. and F. Luthans (2006), 'Entrepreneurs as authentic leaders: impact on employees' attitudes', *Leadership and Organization Development Journal*, 27 (8), 646–66.

John F. Welch College of Business (2014), New England Journal of Entrepreneurship website, accessed 28 December 2014 at http://www.sacredheart.edu/academics/johnfwelchcollegeofbusiness/aboutthecollege/newenglandjournalofentrepreneurship/.

Kirchhoff, B. (1991), 'Entrepreneurship's contribution to economics', *Entrepreneurship Theory and Practice*, 16 (2), 93–112.

Küpers, W. and J. Weibler (2008), 'Inter-leadership: why and how should we think of leadership and followership integrally?', *Leadership*, 4 (4), 443–75.

Kuratko, D.F. (2007), 'Entrepreneurial leadership in the 21st century', *Journal of Leadership and Organizational Studies*, 13 (4), 1–11.

Landis, J.R. and G.G. Koch (1977), 'The measurement of observer agreement for categorical data', *Biometrics*, 33 (1), 159–74.

Leitch, C.M., C. McMullan and R.T. Harrison (2013), 'The development of entrepreneurial leadership: the role of human, social and institutional capital', *British Journal of Management*, 24 (3), 347–66.

Leximancer (2011), Leximancer Manual Version 4, https://www.leximancer.com/site-media/lm/science/Leximancer_Manual_Version_4_0.pdf.

Leximancer (2014), 'Leximancer', accessed 20 May 2014 at https://www.leximancer.com/science/.

Liesch, W., L. Håkanson, S.L. McGaughey, S. Middleton and J. Cretchley (2011), 'The evolution of the international business field: a scientometric investigation of articles published in its premier journal', *Scientometrics*, 88 (1), 17–42.

McClelland, David C. (1967), *The Achieving Society*, London: Free Press.

McGrath, Rita Gunther and Ian C. MacMillan (2000), *The Entrepreneurial Mindset: Strategies for Continuously Creating Opportunity in an Age of Uncertainty*, Boston, MA: Harvard Business School Press.

Mihalache, O.R., J.J.P. Jansen, F.A.J. van den Bosch and H.W. Volberda (2014), 'Top management team shared leadership and organizational ambidexterity: a moderated mediation framework', *Strategic Entrepreneurship Journal*, 8 (2), 128–48.

Peterson, S.J., F.O. Walumbwa, K. Byron and J. Myrowitz (2008), 'CEO positive psychological traits, transformational leadership, and firm performance in high-technology start-up and established firms', *Journal of Management*, 35 (2), 348–68.

Pierce, Jon and John W. Newstrom (2011), *Leaders and the Leadership Process*, 6th edn, Boston, MA: McGraw-Hill.

Ramos-Rodríguez, A.R. and J. Ruíz-Navarro (2004), 'Changes in the intellectual structure of strategic management research: a bibliometric study of the Strategic Management Journal, 1980–2000', *Strategic Management Journal*, 25 (10), 981–1004.

Renko, M., A. El Tarabishy, A.L. Carsrud and M. Brännback (2012), 'Understanding and measuring entrepreneurial leadership style', *Journal of Small Business Management*, 53 (1), 54–74.

Roomi, M.A. and P. Harrison (2011), 'Entrepreneurial leadership: what is it and how should it be taught?', *International Review of Entrepreneurship*, 9 (3), 1–43.

Schildt, H.A., S.A. Zahra and A. Sillanpää (2006), 'Scholarly communities in entrepreneurship research: a co-citation analysis', *Entrepreneurship Theory and Practice*, 30 (3), 399–415.

Schumpeter, Joseph A. (1934), *The Theory of Economic Development*, Cambridge, MA: Harvard University Press.

Shane, Scott A. (2003), *A General Theory of Entrepreneurship: The Individual–Opportunity Nexus*, Cheltenham, UK and Northampton, MA: Edward Elgar Publishing.

Smith, A.E. and M.S. Humphreys (2006), 'Evaluation of unsupervised semantic mapping of natural language with Leximancer concept mapping', *Behavior Research Methods*, 38 (2), 262–79.

Soriano, D.R. and J.M.C. Martínez (2007), 'Transmitting the entrepreneurial spirit to the work team in SMEs: the importance of leadership', *Management Decision*, 45 (7), 1102–22.

Swiercz, M. and S.R. Lydon (2002), 'Entrepreneurial leadership in high-tech firms: a field study', *Leadership and Organization Development Journal*, 23 (7), 380–389.

Thomas, D.A. (2014), 'Searching for significance in unstructured data: text mining with Leximancer', *European Educational Research Journal*, 13 (2), 235–56.

Thornberry, Neal (2006), *Lead Like an Entrepreneur: Keeping the Entrepreneurial Spirit Alive within the Corporation*, New York, NY: McGraw-Hill.

Vecchio, R.P. (2003), 'Entrepreneurship and leadership: common trends and common threads', *Human Resource Management Review*, 13 (2), 303–27.

Venkataraman, S. (1997), 'The distinctive domain of entrepreneurship research', in Jerome A. Katz (ed.), *Advances in Entrepreneurship: Firm Emergence and Growth*, volume 3, Greenwich, CT: JAI Press, pp. 119–38.

Volery, T. and T. Mazzarol (2015), 'The evolution of the small business and entrepreneurship field: a bibliometric investigation of the articles published in the International Small Business Journal', *International Small Business Journal*, 33 (4), 374–96.

White, H.D. and K.W. McCain (1989), 'Bibliometrics', *Annual Review of Information Science and Technology*, 24, 119–86.

Wickham, Philip (2006), *Strategic Entrepreneurship*, 4th edn, Harlow: Prentice Hall.

Wu, C., J.S. McMullen, M.J. Neubert and X. Yi (2008), 'The influence of leader regulatory focus on employee creativity', *Journal of Business Venturing*, 23 (5), 587–602.

Yukl, G. (2008), 'How leaders influence organizational effectiveness', *Leadership Quarterly*, 19 (6), 708–22.

Yukl, G. (2012), 'Effective leadership behavior: what we know and what questions need more attention', *Academy of Management Perspectives*, 26 (4), 66–85.

Zhou, W., D. Vredenburgh and E.G. Rogoff (2013), 'Informational diversity and entrepreneurial team performance: moderating effect of shared leadership', *International Entrepreneurship and Management Journal*, 11 (1), 39–55.

3. Engaging 'the emerging now': an alternative ontology of entrepreneurial leadership practice

Haina Zhang and Malcolm H. Cone

INTRODUCTION

In the recent past, leading researchers have noted the escalating ineffectiveness of traditional approaches to organizational strategy and entrepreneurial practice (Bettis and Hitt, 1995; Brown and Eisenhardt, 1997). Designed during a period of relative tranquility, the dominant paradigms in organizational theory are based on stability-seeking and uncertainty avoidance through structure and processes. These paradigms are inadequate for global, hypercompetitive environments (Ilinitch et al., 1996). Corporate decision-makers have tried various strategic alternatives such as structural change (from traditional hierarchical efficiency-oriented forms to flatter, decentralized and flexible designs) (Whittington et al., 1999), process change (for example, interactive processes and horizontal flows that promote co-adaptive exploitation) (Brown and Eisenhardt, 1997), and changing boundaries (Prahalad and Hamel, 1999).

Recently scholars have argued that a more integrative understanding of entrepreneurship is required to take into account the realization that innovation is embedded in a social matrix, which was previously identified with individual creativity and flair (McMullen and Shepherd, 2006; Murphy et al., 2006; Bruton et al., 2008; Zahra and Wright, 2011). A critical review of entrepreneurship and leadership literature reveals the same process of theory evolution. This process of historical evolution begins with a focus on the innate and exceptional characteristics of successful leaders and entrepreneurs in traits theories and the effects of followers and contextual factors on entrepreneurship and leadership activities in later theories (e.g., Fiedler, 1967, 1986; Dansereau et al., 1975; Wofford, 1982; Graen and Uhl-Bien, 1995; McGrath and MacMillan, 2000). Within this background, entrepreneurial leadership is constructed as a model of leadership that exhibits both entrepreneurial and strategic leadership characteristics and behaviors (Ireland and Hitt, 1999; McGrath and MacMillan, 2000; Meyer and Heppard, 2000). As Kamm et al. (1990) argue, entrepreneurial leadership necessarily embodies the characteristics of both successful entrepreneurs and successful leaders, because success is often the result of entrepreneurial teams motivated by a leader who is able to instil an entrepreneurial vision and influence onto others in the pursuit of an opportunity.

In this chapter we adopt the challenge made by Steyaert (2007: 457), when he argues that entrepreneurial leadership involves activities that evolve 'in a non-linear and interdependent way'; therefore 'the focus turns away from isolated actions and activities to the recursive dynamics between external and internal complexity as new relations are created internally and as new inter-organizational relations are initiated externally'. Following this argument, we suggest that an alternative understanding of social reality is required in entrepreneurship and leadership studies. This alternative perspective liberates us from the conventional understanding of how the world works, which is from a substance perspective that has been dominant in our way of thinking about the natural world and the actions of human agents in that world.

The turbulent and fast-growing market environment in China is challenging entrepreneurial leaders to find ways to innovate and convert their technological ideas into viable commercial products (Li et al., 2008). The proliferation of new ventures in China presents a new research environment for researchers to explore the evolution and practice of the entrepreneurial leadership process. It has been suggested that researchers should not assume that findings in a developed economy will be equally applicable in an emerging economy such as China (Li and Tsui, 2002; Wang, 2003; Tsui, 2004, 2006, 2007; Tsui et al., 2007; Chen, 2008; Zhang et al., 2011). Therefore, management research with recognition and application of alternative perspectives is welcomed when studying business practice in the international avenue.

In this chapter, we seek to give an account of entrepreneurial leadership practice in a way that prioritizes flow and process over actions and decisions. We adopt Hitt et al.'s (2011) position that we should see the practice of entrepreneurship as a process. To achieve this we will develop an account of practice that draws on a processual understanding of social reality. In pursuit of this objective we will be arguing for a perspective on practice radically different from that found in the contemporary entrepreneurship literature. This alternative perspective will be developed by drawing from ideas and concepts that emerge from the work of the French philosopher Gilles Deleuze (1993, 1994) and Deleuze and Guattari (1988), the theory of complex adaptive systems (CAS) (Holland, 1995; Boisot and Child, 1999; Urry, 2005), and the processual perspective in Chinese philosophy (Cheng, 1991; Mair, 1991; Jullien, 1999; Shen, 2003; Zhang et al., 2011; Zhang and Cone, 2014). Having developed an account of a processual understanding of entrepreneurial practice in theory, we will conclude by describing the case of China where a process understanding of reality is normative. We have chosen to do this because by giving an account of an existing practice it is easier to comprehend how a processual world view leads to particular forms of practice.

We follow Lawley (2005: 43) when he suggests that Deleuze's philosophy 'resonates with a process ontology which conceptualizes the organization in terms of movement and becoming', thus 'organizational "reality" is seen in terms of a "becoming-realism" rather than a static, reified "being-realism"' (see Chia, 1996). Complexity theory also provides a processual way of thinking about reality. Since its emergence as a new science, it has become the normative paradigm for understanding processes in the natural world (Beynon, 2007). We argue that both Deleuze's (1993, 1994) philosophy and CAS theory (Holland, 1995; Boisot and Child, 1999; Urry, 2005) emphasize a process-oriented and materialist view of reality. Recent work by Proveti (2001) and Styhre (2002) has established a clear connection between them. Therefore, by bringing the insights together and combining these two theories we will enrich our perspective and provide a critique of the existing assumptions about what constitutes entrepreneurial practice. By rethinking of what constitutes practice and applying these insights, we seek to outline an understanding of creativity, inspiration, learning and innovation that can be considered as an alternative account of the guiding principles of entrepreneurial leadership practice.

THE ONTOLOGY OF ENTREPRENEURIAL PRACTICE IN THE LITERATURE

A process perspective has had a respectable position in European scholarship since the early decades of the twentieth century (for example, Simmel, 1907 [1978]; Bergson, 1911; Elias, 1939 [2000]); therefore it is unsurprising that the scholars who develop theories of entrepreneurship in Europe are exposed to these ideas. We note that in the work of early pioneering theorists of entrepreneurial practice (for example, Knight, 1921; Schumpeter, 1934, 1942; Von Mises, 1949; Shackle, 1972; Kirzner, 1973, 1979, 1985; Schultz, 1975, 1980) there was an apparent openness to a dynamic processual perspective that unfortunately has not been taken up and co-opted into the rational management paradigm in recent management research. In this early work we see an openness which is transient and emergent.

In reading the early writers' work, we find that entrepreneurial thinking and practice were linked to uncertainty, to risk-taking, as well as to the efforts on the part of the individual (entrepreneur) who ventures to transform visions into business activities. Hébert and Link (1989) identify three intellectual traditions in the development of entrepreneurial research: the German Tradition developed by Schumpeter and Von Thuenen; the Chicago Tradition by Knight and Schultz; and the Austrian Tradition based on Von Mises, Kirzner and Shackle. Schumpeterian (1934, 1942) theory views entrepreneurship as a disequilibrating phenomenon, rather than an equilibrating force, hence his theory of creative destruction where new firms with entrepreneurial characteristics displace less innovative competitors, thus leading to a higher degree of economic growth. Knight (1921) identifies risk as core for the entrepreneur; Kirzner (1979) focuses on opportunities, arguing that the entrepreneurial spirit enables the entrepreneur to see new opportunities, thus suggesting that alertness is a key behavior to ensure entrepreneurial success.

From these perspectives, we agree with the following as the common characteristics that constitute entrepreneurship as a process. Risk-taking as entrepreneurial action is always associated with uncertainty (Knight, 1921; von Mises, 1949), innovation and creativity (Schumpeter, 1934), the creation of value (Ireland et al., 2003), plus exploration and alertness (Kirzner, 1979) and innovative use of resources (Schumpeter, 1934; Shane and Venkataraman, 2000). Therefore, we follow Katsikis and Kyrgidou's (2009) and Kyrgidou and Hughes's (2010) suggestion that the study of entrepreneurial practice needs to be directed towards developing an understanding of the internal environment that includes such factors as corporate culture, strategic intent, organizational focus and the internal process that serve to ensure the functioning of the organization in such a way that embodies the entrepreneurial spirit to encourage entrepreneurial practice.

However, the ontological perspective that tacitly informs research into organizations and organizational practice in traditions is dominated by the view of objective realism, which is that the social world is made of things in which processes represent change in things. This perspective leads decision-makers to assume a position outside the structures, rules and practices that shape an organization's ongoing existence, in the belief that it is possible to make decisions independent of the ongoing flow of time that will effectively adapt the organization to changing circumstances (Schindehutte and Morris, 2009). These habits of thought are deeply ingrained, prioritizing 'permanence, stability, organization, and control over transience, flux, transformation, and uncertainty' (Schindehutte and Morris, 2009: 249). Therefore, we find that many or most theorists who have striven to elucidate the potential of a process view of reality have themselves fallen prey to what Whitehead (1967) called the 'fallacy of misplaced concreteness', the concept he used to describe what is called by

Deleuze (1994) 'the substantivist approach' which is blind to the effects of process (Wood, 2005). This stems to a large degree from the normative language position of the Indo/European languages which invariably privilege nouns over verbs (Elias, 1992). We find recognition of this problem is perceived by Steyaert (2007) when he notes that a process view of entrepreneurship means that what we call 'entrepreneurship' would be better understood if we substitute a verb for the noun; thus 'entrepreneuring' better expresses a process approach to entrepreneurial practice, as a flow of action that captures what we seek to develop here.

The problem is that if we can set aside this cultural preference for a substance view of reality, can we at the same time set aside the dominant ontologies that sustain Western culture and social science? If we continue to base our research and theory-building on the same assumptions as those we inherited from the scholarship in the twentieth century, we will be facing the same risk noted above. We argue that these assumptions serve to limit the potential for understanding of processes in which processes represent change in things (e.g., Downing, 2005; Schindehutte and Morris, 2009; Morris et al., 2012) rather than the alternative view, that is, a processual perspective that this research tries to develop, in which things are epiphenomenal, dependent for their transitory existence on flows of energy. This is a critical distinction regarding the nature of organizations, one that challenges us to move past the traditional view of organization as a noun, and adopt an alternative view of organizing as a verb in a world of continuous change and flux (Van de Ven and Poole, 1995; Schindehutte and Morris, 2009). In this alternate view entrepreneurial leadership roles are associated with closely attending to the emerging process and taking the opportunity to act (Schindehutte and Morris, 2009; Morris et al., 2012) rather than envisaging and creating scenarios of possible opportunities (Gupta et al., 2004). Thus we follow Hitt et al.'s (2011) suggestion that more research should be required to understand the interaction of both individual and organizational capabilities and the predispositions that embody their relationship to entrepreneurial activities. It is time to make a much more critical evaluation of our basic assumptions.

This realization provides an opportunity to review the current ontologies that inform our understanding of entrepreneurial leadership. One common theme is that current leadership research is built on a taken-for-granted individualism that must be articulated and challenged. For example, Carroll et al. (2008) and Bolden and Gosling (2006) suggest an urgency to study leadership as practices rather than as competencies held by individual managers. Gronn (2009) suggests the study of leadership activities rather than leaders as the unit of analysis; and Drath et al. (2008)

propose an ontology based on the definition of leadership as activities with certain outcomes.

ENGAGING THE EMERGING NOW

In this chapter we seek to give an account of entrepreneurial leadership practice as process; to take a further step, we intend to give an account of practice in a way that prioritizes flow and process over actions and decisions. This can be illustrated by Chia and MacKay's (2007: 225) term 'weak ontology'; this 'weak' ontological view 'emphasizes a transient, ephemeral and emergent reality'. By contrast, contemporary understandings of entrepreneurial practice are founded on what Chia and MacKay (2007: 225) call a 'strong ontology (the study of the nature and essence of things)'. This 'process reducibility' approach (Rescher, 1996) deems all processes and practices to be the result of the intentional actions of agents interacting with other agents and objects. In this way, the individual entrepreneur or entrepreneurial leader is the agent who initiates action, thus being the cause of events. Hence human agency is given ontological 'primacy over activities, processes and practices', in which the individual is assumed to be the initiator of innovative activities, processes and practices; therefore, from this perspective in normative thinking, 'changes are only brought about through the active, deliberate intentions and actions of individuals' (Chia and MacKay, 2007: 225). For example, Wood (2005) suggests that most practical notions of 'ontology' in contemporary leadership literature commit the 'fallacy of misplaced concreteness' (the condition described above) where the processual character of practice is neglected in favor of definitions, delimited courses of action and static accounts. In contrast, Chia (1995) argues that business studies should be guided by the process 'ontology of becoming' (cf. Wood, 2005).

We follow this lead and propose that this is about 'wiping away the clichés and the ready-mades of the doxa' (Boundas, 2009: 2) and offering solutions through rethinking existing orthodoxy in a way that allows us to experience the real as process, a flow of resonating correlations, like music, blending together in creative fusion. In such a view of entrepreneurial leadership practice, processes cannot be managed so as to reverse what has already happened, neither can management control their effects, because the interactions of entrepreneurs and their organizations are constantly evolving in continuous response to the flow of time and events (Chia, 1995; Hernes, 2007). As noted earlier, there are two strands to our argument: first we draw on theories emerging from the insights generated in the literature on complexity as it applies to an understanding of complex adaptive systems; second, we draw upon the work of Deleuze. The key supposition of the complexity perspective is that the world is constituted by flows of events, in which there is a precarious balance between order and chaos, between stasis and change; this is the ultimate principle underlying all processes. We bring these two paradigms together in this chapter as they constitute the ingredients we believe are necessary to develop an understanding of entrepreneurial practice as engaging 'the emerging now', and later in this chapter to describe the entrepreneurial field in China.

Complex Adaptive Systems

We turn now to give a brief account of the nature of complexity theory as it is applied to the study of complex adaptive systems. The following discussion is drawn from a treatise on traditional Chinese medicine which relates the functions of the body to a system formed by a particular constellation of energy fields and flows. From a complexity science perspective the world is like a river: 'As the river flows, waves, eddies, currents, rapids, pools, etc. emerge' (Herfel et al., 2007: 59). These eddies and currents cannot exist independently of the river. Their existence is dependent on river flow; they are what is called dissipative structures (Herfel et al., 2007), dependent on the flow for their existence; and at the same time they are entities in their own right insofar as their inner dynamics can be studied independently of the constituting flow. However, these dynamics whilst being intrinsic to the entity being studied are entirely dependent on the context in which the entity exists. This can be extended to all living phenomena: an organism is not a separate object existing independently; instead it is an identifiable pattern within the myriad of flows that constitute the world, as all organisms are also dissipative structures. Just like a river, the flow of food and energy through an organism is utilized to sustain their internal structures and maintain their internal processes (Herfel et al., 2007).

For our purposes from a CAS perspective we can understand entrepreneurial practice as a dissipative structure, depending on a flow of energy, which for humans and organizations includes information, for its existence. The existence of a dissipative structure (entrepreneurial practice) depends on energy/information flow; for the practice to be maintained there has to be a flow of energy/information through the system. If one removes the energy/information (that is, removes the water flow in a river or inputs into an organization or into a person), the structure (the standing wave, the organization or the entrepreneur) disappears. Thus, we can say that its systemic properties (the entrepreneurial drive) are emergent, arising from the relationships and interaction of the parts; the whole can be said to be 'greater than the sum of its parts' and the 'dissection of a system into its components, either physically or theoretically, destroys that system and precludes a full understanding of its dynamics and properties' (Capra, 1996: 29). Therefore, complexity 'promotes a relational and processual style of thinking, stressing organizational patterns, networked relationships and historical context' (Bousquet and Curtis, 2011: 45). From this discussion we identify the term that will enable a refocusing of the debates about entrepreneurial leadership practice: engaging 'the emerging now'.

This account of complex adaptive systems is in our view a useful way of thinking about how the world works. Yet when confronted with the dominant ontologies of human practice reviewed earlier, the question must be how we translate these insights drawn from the natural sciences and apply them to entrepreneurial practice, innovation and learning in an organizational context. The problem, as we have already noted, is that the dominant way of thinking simply makes the implementation of insights from the natural sciences into the applied social sciences difficult for the ontological reasons discussed earlier.

The argument that we put forward here is that employing a CAS perspective supported by the application of some Deleuzian concepts (which we discuss in the following section) and the accompanying processual understanding of the linkage between human subjectivity and the natural world gives us a way to transfer the wisdom of the natural sciences to the social sciences. In this case this chapter is an attempt to develop an alternative understanding of practice and an insight into creativity, innovation and learning from an entrepreneurial perspective.

Deleuze's Philosophy of Process

We argue that CAS can be fruitfully applied to the social sciences by employing a Deleuzian (1988, 1993, 1994) ontology of process. This will enhance our ability to apply insights drawn from CAS with the concepts that Deleuze develops to move away from a reliance on conventional terminology. We employ four concepts to achieve this. First is 'difference', which we illustrate with reference to a river, which flows because of the energy differential (the gradient) that exists. In Deleuzian terminology this would be described as the 'difference' between its source and estuary. Second, his concept of 'line of flight' is developed to describe the flow of events and of human thoughts, desires and imagination, where thought and action are about 'difference' moving in new ways (Goodchild, 1996). This, we argue, fosters creativity and a movement away from conventional ways of thinking. In Deleuze's terms this movement is known as 'deterritorializing', that is, establishing a line of flight to somewhere else. Such lines of flight have 'the potential to create the conditions wherein new connections and combinations can be drawn socially, linguistically, perceptually, economically, conceptually and historically' (Parr, 2005: 146).

Third is Deleuze's concept of 'assemblage', which has some resonance with the idea of bricolage as it is discussed in the entrepreneurship literature, by which heterogeneous ingredients and factors formerly unrelated are brought together to create something new (Baker and Nelson, 2005; Domenico et al., 2010). However, there is a clear distinction between bricolage and assemblage. Bricolage is an agglomeration of heterogeneous objects, whilst an assemblage contains states of events that are material and immaterial processes rather than objects; these processes are dissipative structures and include bodies, technologies, raw materials and immaterial processes, that is, ideas, relationships, conventions, power differentials and territories (Parr, 2005). These immaterial processes are driven by 'desire' (Parr, 2005; Deleuze and Parnet, 2006). For Deleuze, desire is a flow of aspirations, contexts, memories and hopes. Rather than seeing desire as a lack of something, he sees it as being a necessary condition for creativity. In his view, in order to be creative, a person needs to become aware of opportunity; for an event to occur, there has to be a difference of potential: two levels are required, and there has to be a flash, a stream that is the domain of desire (Deleuze and Parnet, 2006).

Fourth, we use the idea of 'plateau': a Deleuzian plateau is 'a continuous vibrating region of intensities that do not have a point of culmination or an external goal' (Goodchild, 1996: 81). This has strong resonance with the Chinese world view which sees the world as being entirely constituted by flows and nodes of intensity. The art of leading, the emergence of innovation and the development of strategy are about harnessing these flows and constellations of energy to the service of human objectives. Therefore, we can say that a Deleuzian plateau provides the necessary conditions to foster and sustain a passion or desire for a certain state of being; in other words, a passion for continuous innovation. We contend that these concepts suggest a sense of movement and flow, thus providing an evocative concept to understand and describe a processual perspective of social reality.

Engaging 'the Emerging Now'

Using the insights from Deleuze and CAS we suggest that the role of a leader depends on their success in retaining balance and focusing on the complex factors that stimulate the flow of 'desire'/energy (that is, 'a line of flight') that forms a dissipative structure (that is, 'an assemblage'). The 'assemblage' is constituted by bringing together desire, bodies, technologies and materials on to a vibrating 'plateau' (that is, 'a strange attractor') that fosters a flow of creativity and innovation.

In the processual perspective developed by Deleuze, an assemblage emerges when a function – that is, an opportunity – materializes; ideally it is innovative and productive. The result of a productive assemblage is a new way of thinking and new means of expression, a new behavior, a new realization and a new organization. The concept of assemblage allows us to think about change and adaptation to changing circumstances by making new connections. A key aspect of this formulation is that it allows us to think how creativity and environmental change can be thought of from the perspective described in CAS where the world is constituted by flows. Deleuze's philosophy brings CAS insights into social reality as flows of energy, both human creativity and effort, and political and social change. These concepts also allow us to think about the attendant fact from a processual view of reality: an assemblage is a constellation of productive forces that, if they retain their dynamic relationship with the context in which they operate, will thrive via a process of continuous change, adaptation and renewal.

Thus, a new assemblage is emergent, in that the forces that cause its appearance are immanent in its configuration, which is in turn a response to a particular flow of forces. This corresponds with the key point of CAS. The assemblage has a natural tendency toward self-organization, a tendency that can be captured in the image of a surfer riding on a wave (Holmdahl, 2005; Schindehutte and Morris, 2009), being continuously engaged in the moment, balancing, weaving, harnessing the power of the natural process to achieve an objective. We argue that in adopting this perspective, and as a consequence placing less reliance on the notion of 'laws' and the concept of 'cause and effect', we are in a better position to understand and adapt to complex phenomena.

To complete the analogy between CAS and Deleuzian ontology we can see that the Deleuzian 'vibrating plateau' – to use a term from CAS, a 'strange attractor' (Berressem, 2005) – is the context in which an assemblage emerges; its emergence depends on 'difference' (that is, its energy differential). In the case of CAS it is difference in gradient, density or energy; in the Deleuzian account of social reality, it is human desire that recognizes difference or, to use the Chinese concept, 'the propensity of things' (Jullien, 1999). Following this perspective we can say that objects do not populate the world, but 'the world consists of interrelating processes' (Herfel et al., 2007: 59). Therefore, what are referred to in substantive terms as 'objects' are from a processual perspective better understood as 'stabilized patterns of a flow' (Herfel et al., 2007); that is, Deleuze's terminology 'a line of flight' on a particular plateau. From this perspective, the world including humans and organizations is a process within a process, flows within flows, and within each entity are processes that constitute it. Nothing exists in the absence of the flow of energy/information.

From both a Deleuzian perspective and a CAS understanding of reality we can recognize the pervasiveness of emergent 'un-owned' processes, which suggests that to be entrepreneurial is to be continuously conscious of the underlying 'propensity of things' (Jullien, 1999), and how that underlying propensity plays a key role in shaping eventual outcomes; something successful entrepreneurs are particularly attuned to. The consequence of abiding by this process view of reality is that timing and timeliness, emotional resonance and situational appropriateness feature pre-eminently in the process of 'entrepreneuring' (Steyaert, 2007). We therefore also suggest that entrepreneurial practice needs to be understood as a learning process (Minniti and Bygrave, 2001). Learning is a vital aspect in entrepreneurship, since it consists in the acquisition or alteration of business skills, knowledge, habits and attitudes. As such, an entrepreneur is defined as a permanent learner (Gibb, 1997). Learning for the entrepreneur is being alert to economic opportunities and making use of information advantages. Indeed, we agree with Kirzner's (1979) observation that entrepreneurship is based on spontaneous learning. This learning allows the entrepreneur to recombine disparate items of information and to determine new relations between them, thus retaining a balance in a constantly changing environment. Accordingly, we suggest that in the study of entrepreneurial practice we can expect to see a dual process of 'feed-forward' and feedback of flows of information within organizations. This gives us a fresh understanding of all aspects of entrepreneurial practice from the ideas of creativity, innovation, timing, ownership, competition, cooperation and ethics. It allows us to avoid the pitfall that stems from taking a causal model of planned behavior. We can more clearly see that entrepreneurial activities are best described as having a learning focus that utilizes environmental feedback (Sarasvathy, 2001; Goldstein et al., 2010). Because outcomes are frequently impossible to predict and represent, decisions are impossible to anticipate. Again, to use the concepts from Deleuze, we need to see the organization that is driven by an entrepreneurial spirit as an assemblage driven by desire. These arguments lead us to suggest that we need to re-examine the way in which entrepreneurial practice relates to leadership in terms of creating and sustaining the complex flows of ideas, beliefs and desires that constitute an entrepreneurial organization (an assemblage).

In summary, we suggest that the dynamic business environment which confronts all firms domestically and internationally means that there is a need for entrepreneurial leadership to be adapted to different contexts, where there can be no one best way for effective entrepreneurial leadership. Our perspective is in agreement with the suggestion that the relationship between leadership and the context in which it operates is critical (Boal and Hooijberg, 2001; Osborn and Hunt, 2007; Porter and McLaughlin, 2006). In other words, leadership depends on the situation (Vroom and Jago, 2007), and a degree of consistency or fit is needed among leaders' behaviors and the leadership context (Fiedler, 1967).

We suggest that the much used and misused term 'culture' is of key importance here. We see it as an essential component of understanding entrepreneurial practice so that we need to take into account the culture of the organization (assemblage). Thus, we choose to define culture as the flows of information that are a constituent of stable interrelations and exist inside an organization. A process of feedback and feed-forward, this information provides the energy that constitutes the system, which to be sustainable must be 'self-organizing' (Jantsch, 1980). The behavior is not directed by an outside intelligence, but results from what agents 'know'; a complex adaptive system learns as 'interacting agents adapt by changing their rules as experience accumulates' (Holland, 1995: 10). Again, we can use the concepts from Deleuze to more graphically provide a description that signals all of these things, in concepts such as 'difference', 'assemblage', 'plateaus' of potential energy that emerge in a 'line of flight'. We suggest that organizational becoming can be understood as a process in which an 'assemblage' of disparate strands and fragments, a bricolage of motives and motivations, are brought into alignment by a superordinate goal.

Following these discussions we can see that CAS is particularly sensitive to properties and relationships, which means that such a system cannot be understood by the analysis of its constituent parts. The behavior of systems is determined more by the nature of the interactions than by what is contained in the components (Cilliers, 1998). For example, as Polanyi (1963: 47) argued, 'take a watch to pieces and examine however carefully its separate parts in turn, and you will never come across the principles by which a watch keeps time'. Thus we need to accept the idea that it is neither some innate personality characteristics that are determinative of entrepreneurial behavior, nor can entrepreneurial activity (that takes place in one time and place) be replicated as if there was a blueprint available. Such a perspective calls into question the idea that entrepreneurship can only be taught or learned outside the context in which the creative activity takes place.

PROCESS ONTOLOGY IN CHINESE PHILOSOPHY

> In China the real, thus, is not understandable as a series of individual entities, but instead as flows of energy or chi; constellated in various patterns of transitory relations, in a co-evolutionary interdependent manner. (Mair, 1991: 376)

In this correlative world view we find a perspective that sees the world and all that is in it as being a dynamic creative process driven by the interaction of complementary processes in the natural cycles that exist in every part of nature (Hall and Ames, 1987; Cheng, 1991; Shen, 2003). There is no need for theory. Let things evolve. 'Allow the propensity of things to operate outside you as their own disposition dictates; do not project values or desires but adapt constantly to the necessity of their evolution' (Jullien, 1999: 39). There is always tentativeness-in-action at play. Therefore, for the Chinese, 'activity' is processual, relational, less goal-oriented, and more path-dependent than the Western notion of 'action' as something individually initiated, purposeful and goal-driven (Hall and Ames, 1987; Jullien, 1999; Miller, 2010).

The consequence of abiding by this process view of reality is that in the approach to entrepreneurial leadership practice in China is to pay close attention to timing and timeliness, emotional resonance, situational appropriateness and indirectness in communication; these attentions to the detail of personal relationships feature pre-eminently in the behavioral repertoire of the Chinese (Zhang and Cone, 2014). These findings suggest that for the Chinese, every human situation is perceived 'as a particular deployment or arrangement . . . to be relied on and worked to one's advantage' (Jullien, 1999: 15; cf. Cheng, 1991; Tan, 2004). This has close affinities to the ideas discussed earlier, particularly those of lines of flight, desire and assemblage, which means that in China many aspects of what we have described from a CAS or Deleuzian process perspective are normative. In other words, in practice an entrepreneur is always looking for the natural flow and the underlying process which leads to an appreciation of the underlying 'propensity of things' (Hall and Ames, 1987, 1995; Jullien, 1999; Shen, 2003) and how propensity plays a key role in shaping eventual outcomes. We see this as modelling the patterns and flow that can be readily understood in the Deleuzian concepts discussed above, where indeterminacy, immanence, time, and a sense of the flow of time and events are the ever-present and only reality. 'Nothing exists in isolation or individually . . . One functions only in relation to the other; it is the relationship itself which is constitutive and which has an intrinsic existence' (Mair, 1991: 376; cf. Hall and Ames, 1987; Tu, 1989; Tan, 2004; Stephens, 2009). Events unfold by means of the interplay of opposition and simultaneous association. These have an operative value through the efficacy by which an outcome is revealed. 'Reality is apprehended in its becoming, and it is this perspective that one finds at the bottom of the most ancient Chinese thought' (Mair, 1991: 377; cf. Hall and Ames, 1987; Ames, 2003). Processes are 'unowned' (Rescher, 1996: 27) in that they are not the 'doings' of active agents. Rather, situations contain their own internal dynamics ('lines of flight') so that outcomes emerge not through the actions of identifiable agents, but because of the ongoing reconfiguration of spontaneous self-generating processes, independently of human intentions (Aligica, 2007; Sim, 2009).

These insights suggest that the processual view in China favors an approach that is readily understood from a Deleuzian or CAS perspective: that is, a dissipative structure dependent entirely on the flows of energy in the system for its continued existence. Therefore, we find some interesting correspondences between these ideas and some aspects of the ontological assumptions that form Chinese understandings of social reality. As we choose to discuss them here they provide a hint of where to look to see some (but not all) aspects of a CAS perspective in a modern, highly productive economy. Thus Chinese entrepreneurs seeking new inspiration for their enterprises have turned to their own philosophical traditions for inspiration. In China entrepreneurial practice is pragmatic; that is, letting situations unfold so that the potentials present can be identified before acting, tending to conserve resources rather than attempting to alter what is seen as a fragile entity. Further, as research in Chinese and Korean business contexts has indicated, the potentially coercive power of organizational hierarchies which can stifle creativity and entrepreneurial behavior are overcome by affective networks that arise spontaneously and cut across organizational hierarchies that are irrelevant to the functioning of a network. As long as each member of the affective network contributes to the welfare of others, this indirectly 'allows all boats to rise together' (Lew et al., 2011). This behavioral pattern can be seen as an example of engaging 'the emerging now', as it reduces the negative effects of hierarchies, especially in inhibiting innovation and creativity in the workplace (Yu and Lee, 2008). This suggests that in Chinese culture these affective networks foster a way of thinking that allows for the development of multiple, non-hierarchical ways of organizing information (DeLanda et al., 2005). As a result, we propose that an alternative way to understand entrepreneurial process in Chinese organizations is to adopt the concepts of 'difference' and 'desire' (Deleuze and Guattari, 1988).

Chinese thinking is focused around two ideas: that of a situation (*xing*) as it evolves before our eyes as a field of energy; and that of potential (*shi*), which is a potential in that situation and can be made to work to one's benefit (Jullien, 1999). Chinese thought, as in Deleuzian philosophy, is immanentist and vitalistic; thus attention is focused on the moment as the only reality. In this view inspiration and motivation come from the natural world and relationships, contexts, memories and hopes. The concepts of *xing* and *shi* focus on the potential in a similar way to Deleuze's understanding of desire; that is, not as a lack of something but as the necessary condition for creativity. In order to be creative, a person needs to become aware of opportunity; for an event to occur there has to be a difference of potential (two levels are required) and there has to be a flash, a stream that is the domain of desire (Deleuze and Parnet, 2006). As noted earlier, the application of the 'difference' and 'desire' is evidenced in Chinese entrepreneurial practice, for example bypassing hierarchical strata (bureaucracies) through spontaneously arising affective networks, self-organizing and self-consistent aggregates (social groups) (Lew et al., 2011). As a result, entrepreneurial practice emerges when the alienating effects of hierarchy and power are overcome by affective connection. This is further confirmed in Wang et al.'s (2012) work on Chinese contingent entrepreneurial leadership practice.

In summary, we argue that in China the consequences of the characteristics of timing and appropriateness (such as *shi*), emotional resonance (such as an affective network), context (such as *xing* and *shi*), and a deeply ingrained empiricism (such as pragmatic practice) mean that a process view of reality is normative. This is because the current circumstance is all one can be confident of, each situation is pregnant with opportunity and risk; thus the way to succeed is to emotionally engage with reality in such a way as to open to the emerging now, the unfolding present.

CONCLUSION

In this chapter we have attempted to develop a processual understanding of the practice of entrepreneurial leadership that provides an alternative explanation for the emergence of the energy and creativity that fosters innovation. The concepts we use to achieve this objective are drawn from the work of Deleuze, who in the period from 1960 to 1992 developed the concepts of 'lines of flight', 'difference', 'assemblage', 'desire' and 'plateaus' to better explain his vitalistic, materialist philosophy of immanence as they embody the feeling of movement and flow, bifurcation and continuous transformation. We see his work as having a natural association with the account of reality developed in CAS theory, which describes it as a process (Holland, 1995; Boisot and Child, 1999; Urry, 2005). We acknowledge that other approaches to understanding entrepreneurship as a process (e.g., Sarasvathy, 2001; Schneider and Somers, 2006; Steyaert,

2007; Schindehutte and Morris, 2009; Goldstein et al., 2010) share some commonalities with what we are advocating here. However, these works have mainly drawn upon CAS theory rather than confronting the difficulty of translating the full implications of adopting dynamic approaches and iterative processes into practice, due to the Western ontological tendency of transforming their meaning in practice to the substantivist perspective discussed previously (Chia, 1995; Jullien, 1999; Aligica, 2007). Our work contributes to further developing a process perspective by aligning CAS and Deleuzian theories with a Chinese processual ontology.

The most radical insight in this view is the recognition that the limitations placed on human agency, individual autonomy, the notion of a person being independent of the flows by which they are constituted, are in some way problematic. Our understanding is limited because these are based on assumptions made about the status of the individual that underpins the 'strong ontology' of Western social science (Chia and MacKay, 2007). The alternative to the pervasive individualism that exists in most of the developed world is being challenged by one in which there is no presupposition of the prior existence of already constituted individuals; rather, the individual is in themself a secondary phenomenon, the product or the 'effect' of more primary sets of flows or processes (Linstead and Thanem, 2007). Thus, humans are seen as the subjects of social formations that are physical systems, constituted by a coalescence of energy in the genetic form of a human that is itself defined in terms of their processes (Ames, 2008) or, more precisely, in terms of a generalized theory of flows and flux: flows of matter, flows of population and commodities, flows of capital and labor, flows of traffic and flows of knowledge (Smith, 2011). We believe that these characteristics are a necessary component of a construct of 'engaging the emerging now' that are to varying degrees (that is, depending on the situation) constitutive of an entrepreneur from a processual perspective. These are in addition to the requirement that an entrepreneur needs to create and implement an entrepreneurial strategy, as well as demonstrate the behaviors of proactiveness, innovation and risk-taking. 'Entrepreneuring' (Steyaert, 2007) entails a natural tendency to 'look only at the movements' (Hillier and Cao, 2013: 395), that is, continuous variation, which inspires the entrepreneurial response; the antithesis of autonomous inspiration and self-directed practice. From this perspective, it is suggested that to be entrepreneurial and innovative it is more appropriate to have no fixed goal, no particular plan, so that one can adapt to every twist and turn in 'the emerging now'.

To this end we argue in this chapter that the forces of change are immanent in the flow of events and human situations, rather than being externally imposed by the will of a conscious actor. We also suggest that we need to adopt an alternative mode of thinking that avoids seeing the world as an object (that is, the world as a noun), but instead understands it as a process (that is, the world as a verb) (Nayak, 2008; Hitt et al., 2011). For example, we should see entrepreneurship as 'entrepreneuring' (Steyaert, 2007) instead of as 'entrepreneur' or 'entrepreneurial'. To achieve this, we need to avoid the practice or habit of using words in noun form to describe reality – such as 'organizations', 'individuals', 'environment', 'structure' and 'culture' – as these terms reinforce the thinking that sees them as social entities with intrinsic attributes separate from each other. From a process perspective, we need to think instead of contexts, coherences, confluences and constellations of energy, flows and nested hierarchies (Schneider and Somers, 2006; Schindehutte and Morris, 2009).

Our discussion of entrepreneurial practice in China demonstrates the attributes that we are describing in this chapter. Chinese philosophy emphasizes the interrelatedness and relativity of everything in the world, in which any perceived order is essentially temporary and may be accomplished in any number of ways depending on context and circumstances. In this correlative world view we find a perspective that regards the world and all that is in it as being a dynamic creative process driven by the interaction of complementary processes in the natural cycles that exist in every part of nature. This account of Chinese culture brings into view a processual perspective on experience, one that is characterized by flows, connections and becomings whose functioning logic is more about 'flow than structures, more complex than linear, more recursive than dialectical, more emergent than totalizing' (Linstead and Thanem, 2007: 1483).

Therefore, theorizing on Deleuze's philosophy, the Chinese philosophy of process and the CAS model, we argue for a way of understanding practice, especially entrepreneurial practice, as engaging 'the emerging now'; that is, a configuration of productive forces that coalesce into a processual flow that entails the arranging, organizing and coming together of hitherto unrelated concepts, qualities and practices in a new way. When a constellation of potentials come together to constitute a plateau, the flows of energy that constitute it will provide the conditions for the emergence of an assemblage which focuses the creative desire of the entrepreneurial spirit, thus permitting creativity and innovation to occur.

REFERENCES

Aligica, P.D. (2007), 'Efficacy, East and West: François Jullien's explorations in strategy', *Comparative Strategy*, 26 (4), 325–37.

82   *Research handbook on entrepreneurship and leadership*

Ames, R. (2003), 'Confucianism and Deweyan pragmatism: A dialogue', *Journal of Chinese Philosophy*, 30 (3/4), 403–17.
Ames, R. (2008), *Confucian Role Ethics: A Vocabulary*, Honolulu, HI: University of Hawai'i Press.
Baker, T. and R.E. Nelson (2005), 'Creating something from nothing: Resource construction through entrepreneurial bricolage', *Administrative Science Quarterly*, 50 (3), 329–66.
Bergson, H. (1911), *The Philosophy of Change*, Edinburgh: T.C. & E.C.
Berressem, H. (2005), 'Multiplicity: Foldings in architectural and literary landscapes', *Space in America: Theory, History, Culture*, 1, 91–105.
Bettis, R.A. and M.A. Hitt (1995), 'The new competitive landscape', *Strategic Management Journal*, 16 (S1), 7–19.
Beynon, M. (2007), 'Radical empiricism, empirical modelling and the nature of knowing', in I.E. Dror (ed.), *Cognitive Technologies and the Pragmatics of Cognition*, Amsterdam: John Benjamins Publishing Co., pp. 155–84.
Boal, K.B. and R. Hooijberg (2000), 'Strategic leadership research: Moving on', *Leadership Quarterly*, 11 (4), 515–49.
Boisot, M. and J. Child (1999), 'Organizations as adaptive systems in complex environments: The case of China', *Organization Science*, 10 (3), 237–52.
Bolden, R. and J. Gosling (2006), 'Leadership competencies: Time to change the tune?', *Leadership*, 2 (2), 147–63.
Boundas, C.V. (2009), 'Introduction', in C.V. Boundas (ed.), *Gilles Deleuze: The Intensive Reduction*, London: Continuum International Publishing Group, pp. 1–6.
Bousquet, A. and S. Curtis (2011), 'Beyond models and metaphors: Complexity theory, systems thinking and international relations', *Cambridge Review of International Affairs*, 24 (1), 43–62.
Brown, S.L. and K.M. Eisenhardt (1997), 'The art of continuous change: Linking complexity theory and time-paced evolution in relentlessly shifting organizations', *Administrative Science Quarterly*, 42 (1), 1–34.
Bruton, G.D., D. Ahlstrom and K. Obloj (2008), 'Entrepreneurship in emerging economies: Where are we today and where should the research go in the future?', *Entrepreneurship Theory and Practice*, 32 (1), 1–14.
Capra, F. (1996), *The Web of Life: A New Synthesis of Mind and Matter*, London: Harper Collins.
Carroll, B., L. Levy and D. Richmond (2008), 'Leadership as practice: Challenging the competency paradigm', *Leadership*, 4 (4), 363–79.
Chen, X.P. (2008), 'Independent thinking: A path to outstanding scholarship', *Management and Organization Review*, 4 (3), 337–48.
Cheng, C.Y. (1991), *New Dimensions of Confucian and Neo-Confucian Philosophy*, Albany, NY: State University of New York Press.
Chia, R. (1995), 'From modern to postmodern organizational analysis', *Organization Studies*, 16 (4), 579–604.
Chia, R. (1996), 'The problem of reflexivity in organizational research: Towards a postmodern science of organization', *Organization*, 3 (1), 31–59.
Chia, R. and B. MacKay (2007), 'Post-processual challenges for the emerging strategy-as-practice perspective: Discovering strategy in the logic of practice', *Human Relations*, 60 (1), 217–42.
Cilliers, P. (1998), *Complexity and Postmodernism: Understanding Complex Systems*, New York, NY: Psychology Press.
Dansereau, F., G.B. Graen and W. Haga (1975), 'A vertical dyad linkage approach to leadership in formal organizations', *Organizational Behavior and Human Performance*, 13 (1), 46–78.
DeLanda, M., J. Protevi and T. Thanem (2005), 'Deleuzian interrogations: A conversation with Manuel DeLanda and John Protevi', *Tamara Journal for Critical Organization Inquiry*, 3 (4), 65–88.
Deleuze, G. (1993), *The Fold: Leibniz and the Baroque*, Minneapolis, MN: University of Minnesota Press.

Deleuze, G. (1994), *Difference and Repetition*, London: Athlone Press.
Deleuze, G. and F. Guattari (1988), *A Thousand Plateaus: Capitalism and Schizophrenia*, London: Anthlone Press.
Deleuze, G. and C. Parnet (2006), *Dialogues II*, New York, NY: Continuum.
Domenico, M., H. Haugh and P. Tracey (2010), 'Social bricolage: Theorizing social value creation in social enterprises', *Entrepreneurship Theory and Practice*, 34 (4), 681–703.
Downing, S. (2005), 'The social construction of entrepreneurship: Narrative and dramatic processes in the coproduction of organizations and identities', *Entrepreneurship Theory and Practice*, 29 (2), 185–204.
Drath, W.H., C.D. McCauley, C.J. Palus, E. Van Velsor, P.M. O'Connor and J.B. McGuire (2008), 'Direction, alignment, commitment: Toward a more integrative ontology of leadership', *Leadership Quarterly*, 19 (6), 635–53.
Elias, N. (1939 [2000]), *The Civilizing Process: Sociogenetic and Psychogenetic Investigations*, Oxford: Basil Blackwell.
Elias, N. (1992), *Time: An Essay*, Oxford: Blackwell.
Fiedler, F.E. (1967), *A Theory of Leadership Effectiveness*, New York, NY: McGraw-Hill Education.
Fiedler, F.E. (1986), 'The contribution of cognitive resources and leader behavior to organizational performance', *Journal of Applied Social Psychology*, 16 (6), 532–48.
Gibb, A.A. (1997), 'Small firms' training and competitiveness: Building upon the small business as a learning organisation', *International Small Business Journal*, 15 (3), 13–29.
Goldstein, J., J.K. Hazy and J. Silberstang (2010), 'Complexity science and social entrepreneurship: Adding social value through systems thinking', *Journal of Social Entrepreneurship*, 1 (1), 101–25.
Goodchild, P. (1996), *Deleuze and Guattari: An Introduction to the Politics of Desire*, London: SAGE.
Graen, G.B. and M. Uhl-Bien (1995), 'Relationship-based approach to leadership: Development of leader–member exchange (LMX) theory of leadership over 25 years: Applying a multi-level multi-domain perspective', *Leadership Quarterly*, 6 (2), 219–47.
Gronn, P. (2009), 'Leadership configurations', *Leadership*, 5 (3), 381–94.
Gupta, V., I.C. MacMillan and D. Surie (2004), 'Entrepreneurial leadership: Developing and measuring a cross-cultural construct', *Journal of Business Venturing*, 19 (2), 241–60.
Hall, D. and R.T. Ames (1987), *Thinking Through Confucius*, Albany, NY: State University of New York Press.
Hall, D. and R.T. Ames (1995), *Anticipating China: Thinking though the Narratives of Chinese and Western Culture*, Albany, NY: State University of New York Press.
Hébert, R.F. and A.N. Link (1989), 'In search of the meaning of entrepreneurship', *Small Business Economics*, 1 (1), 39–49.
Herfel, W., D. Rodrigues and Y. Gao (2007), 'Chinese medicine and the dynamic conceptions of health and disease', *Journal of Chinese Philosophy*, 34 (S1), 57–79.
Hernes, T. (2007), *Understanding Organizations as Process: Theory for a Tangled World*, London: Routledge.
Hillier, J. and K. Cao (2013), 'Deleuzian dragons: Thinking Chinese strategic spatial planning with Gilles Deleuze', *Deleuze Studies*, 7 (3), 390–405.
Hitt, M.A., R.D. Ireland, D.G. Sirmon and C.A. Trahms (2011), 'Strategic entrepreneurship: Creating value for individuals, organizations, and society', *Academy of Management Perspectives*, 25 (2), 57–75.
Holland, J.H. (1995), *Hidden Order: How Adaptation Builds Complexity*, Reading, MA: Addison-Wesley.
Holmdahl, L. (2005), 'Complexity theory and strategy, a basis for product development', accessed 22 July 2014 at http://www.complexityforum.com/articles/complexity-strategy.pdf.
Ilinitch, A.Y., R.A. D'Aveni and A.Y. Lewin (1996), 'New organizational forms and strategies for managing in hypercompetitive environments', *Organization Science*, 7 (3), 211–20.
Ireland, R.D. and M.A. Hitt (1999), 'Achieving and maintaining strategic competitiveness

in the 21st century: The role of strategic leadership', *Academy of Management Executive*, 13 (1), 43–57.

Ireland, R.D., M.A. Hitt and D.G. Sirmon (2003), 'A model of strategic entrepreneurship: The construct and its dimensions', *Journal of Management*, 29 (6), 963–89.

Jantsch, E. (1980), *The Self-Organizing Universe: Scientific and Human Implications of the Emerging Paradigm of Evolution*, New York, NY: Butterworth-Heinemann.

Jullien, F. (1999), *The Propensity of Things: Toward A History of Efficacy in China*, New York, NY: Zone Papers.

Kamm, J.B., J.C. Shuman, J.A. Seeger and A.J. Nurick (1990), 'Entrepreneurial teams in new venture creation: A research agenda', *Entrepreneurship Theory and Practice*, 14 (4), 7–17.

Katsikis, I.N. and L.P. Kyrgidou (2009), 'Entrepreneurship in teleology: The variety of the forms', *International Journal of Entrepreneurial Behavior and Research*, 15 (2), 209–31.

Kirzner, I.M. (1973), *Competition and Entrepreneurship*, Chicago, IL: University of Chicago Press.

Kirzner, I.M. (1979), *Perception, Opportunity, and Profit: Studies in the Theory of Entrepreneurship*, Chicago, IL: University of Chicago Press.

Kirzner, I.M. (1985), *Discovery and the Capitalist Process*, Chicago, IL: University of Chicago Press.

Knight, F. (1921), *'Risk', Uncertainty and Profit*, Boston, MA: Houghton Mifflin.

Kyrgidou, L.P. and M. Hughes (2010), 'Strategic entrepreneurship: Origins, core elements and research directions', *European Business Review*, 22 (1), 43–63.

Lawley, S. (2005), 'Deleuze's rhizome and the study of organization: Conceptual movement and an open future', *Tamara Journal for Critical Organization Inquiry*, 3 (4), 36–49.

Lew, S.-C., W.-Y. Choi and H.S. Wang (2011), 'Confucian ethics and the spirit of capitalism in Korea: The significance of filial piety', *Journal of East Asian Studies*, 11 (2), 171–96.

Li, J. and A.S. Tsui (2002), 'A citation analysis of management and organization research in the Chinese context: 1984–1999', *Asia Pacific Journal of Management*, 19 (1), 87–107.

Li, Y., H. Guo, Y. Liu and M. Li (2008), 'Incentive mechanisms, entrepreneurial orientation, and technology commercialization: Evidence from China's transitional economy', *Journal of Product Innovation Management*, 25 (1), 63–78.

Linstead, S. and T. Thanem (2007), 'Multiplicity, virtuality and organization: The contribution of Gilles Deleuze', *Organization Studies*, 28 (10), 1483–501.

Mair, V.H. (1991), 'The language of Chinese thought', *Philosophy East and West*, 41 (3), 373–86.

McGrath, R.G. and I.C. MacMillan (2000), *The Entrepreneurial Mindset: Strategies for Continuously Creating Opportunity in an Age of Uncertainty*, Boston, MA: Harvard Business Press.

McMullen, J.S. and D.A. Shepherd (2006), 'Entrepreneurial action and the role of uncertainty in the theory of the entrepreneur', *Academy of Management Review*, 31 (1), 132–52.

Meyer, G.D. and K.A. Heppard (2000), 'Entrepreneurial strategies: The dominant logic of entrepreneurship', in G.D. Meyer and K.A. Heppard (eds), *Entrepreneurship as Strategy: Competing on the Entrepreneurial Edge*, Thousand Oaks, CA: SAGE, pp. 1–23.

Miller, D. (2010), 'Exchange: West meets East towards an ambicultural approach to management', *Academy of Management Perspectives*, 24 (4), 17–24.

Minniti, M. and W. Bygrave (2001), 'A dynamic model of entrepreneurial learning', *Entrepreneurship Theory and Practice*, 25 (3), 5–16.

Morris, M.H., D.F. Kuratko, M. Schindehutte and A.J. Spivack (2012), 'Framing the entrepreneurial experience', *Entrepreneurship Theory and Practice*, 36 (1), 11–40.

Murphy, P.J., J. Liao and H.P. Welsch (2006), 'A conceptual history of entrepreneurial thought', *Journal of Management History*, 12 (1), 12–35.

Nayak, A. (2008), 'On the way to theory: A processual approach', *Organization Studies*, 29 (2), 173–90.

Osborn, R.N. and J.G.J. Hunt (2007), 'Leadership and the choice of order: Complexity and hierarchical perspectives near the edge of chaos', *Leadership Quarterly*, 18 (4), 319–40.

Parr, A. (2005), *The Deleuze Dictionary*, Edinburgh: Edinburgh University Press.
Polanyi, M. (1963), *The Study of Man*, Chicago, IL: University of Chicago Press.
Porter, L.W. and G.B. McLaughlin (2006), 'Leadership and the organizational context: Like the weather?', *Leadership Quarterly*, 17 (6), 559–76.
Prahalad, C. and G. Hamel (1999), 'The core competence of the corporation', in M.H. Zack (ed.), *Knowledge and Strategy*, Boston, MA: Butterworth-Heinemann, pp. 41–62.
Proveti, J. (2001), *Political Physics, Deleuze Derrida and the Body Politic*, London: Athlone Press.
Rescher, N. (1996), *Process Metaphysics: An Introduction to Process Philosophy*, Albany, NY: State University of New York Press.
Sarasvathy, S.D. (2001), 'Causation and effectuation: Toward a theoretical shift from economic inevitability to entrepreneurial contingency', *Academy of Management Review*, 26 (2), 243–63.
Schindehutte, M. and M.H. Morris (2009), 'Advancing strategic entrepreneurship research: The role of complexity science in shifting the paradigm', *Entrepreneurship Theory and Practice*, 33 (1), 241–76.
Schneider, M. and M. Somers (2006), 'Organizations as complex adaptive systems: Implications of complexity theory for leadership research', *Leadership Quarterly*, 17 (4), 351–65.
Schultz, T.W. (1975), 'The value of the ability to deal with disequilibria', *Journal of Economic Literature*, 13, 827–46.
Schultz, T.W. (1980), 'Investment in entrepreneurial ability', *Scandinavian Journal of Economics*, 82, 437–48.
Schumpeter, J.A. (1934), *The Theory of Economic Development*, Cambridge, MA: Harvard Economic Studies.
Schumpeter, J.A. (1942), *Capitalism, Socialism, and Democracy*, New York, NY: Harper & Row.
Shackle, L.S. (1972), *Epistemics and Economics: A Critique of Economic Doctrine*, Cambridge: Cambridge University Press.
Shane, S. and S. Venkataraman (2000), 'The promise of entrepreneurship as a field of research', *Academy of Management Review*, 25 (1), 217–26.
Shen, V. (2003), 'Some thoughts on intercultural philosophy and Chinese philosophy', *Journal of Chinese Philosophy*, 30 (3/4), 357–72.
Sim, M. (2009), 'Introduction: American pragmatism and Chinese philosophy', *Journal of Chinese Philosophy*, 36 (1), 3–8.
Simmel, G. (1907 [1978]), *The Philosophy of Money*, London: Routledge & Kegan Paul.
Smith, D.W. (2011), 'Flow, code and stock: A note on Deleuze's political philosophy', *Deleuze Studies*, 5 (S), 36–55.
Stephens, D.J. (2009), 'Confucianism, pragmatism, and socially beneficial philosophy', *Journal of Chinese Philosophy*, 36 (1), 53–67.
Steyaert, C. (2007), '"Entrepreneuring" as a conceptual attractor? A review of process theories in 20 years of entrepreneurship studies', *Entrepreneurship and Regional Development*, 19 (6), 453–77.
Styhre, A. (2002), 'Nonlinear change in organizations: Organization change management informed by complexity theory', *Leadership and Organization Development Journal*, 23 (6), 343–51.
Tan, S. (2004), *Confucian Democracy: A Deweyan Reconstruction*, Albany, NY: State University of New York Press.
Tsui, A.S. (2004), 'Contributing to global management knowledge: A case for high quality indigenous research', *Asia Pacific Journal of Management*, 21 (4), 491–513.
Tsui, A.S. (2006), 'Contextualization in Chinese management research', *Management and Organization Review*, 2 (1), 1–13.
Tsui, A.S. (2007), 'From homogenization to pluralism: International management research in the Academy and beyond', *Academy of Management Journal*, 50 (6), 1353–64.
Tsui, A.S., S. Zhao and E. Abrahamson (2007), 'What to study in China? Choosing and

crafting important research questions', *Management and Organization Review*, 3 (2), 171–81.

Tu, W.M. (1989), 'The rise of industrial East Asia: The role of Confucian values', *Copenhagen Journal of Asian Studies*, 4 (1), 81–96.

Urry, J. (2005), 'The complexities of the global', *Theory, Culture and Society*, 22 (5), 235–54.

Van de Ven, A.H. and M.S. Poole (1995), 'Explaining development and change in organizations', *Academy of Management Review*, 20 (3), 510–540.

Von Mises, L. (1949), *Human Action: A Treatise on Economics*, New Haven, CT: Yale University Press.

Vroom, V.H. and A.G. Jago (2007), 'The role of the situation in leadership', *American Psychologist*, 62 (1), 17–24.

Wang, C.L., D.D. Tee and P.K. Ahmed (2012), 'Entrepreneurial leadership and context in Chinese firms: A tale of two Chinese private enterprises', *Asia Pacific Business Review*, 18 (4), 505–30.

Wang, Z.M. (2003), 'Managerial competency modelling and the development of organizational psychology: A Chinese approach', *International Journal of Psychology*, 38 (5), 323–34.

Whitehead, A.N. (1967), *Science and Modern World*, Cambridge: Cambridge University Press.

Whittington, R., A. Pettigrew, S. Peck, E. Fenton and M. Conyon (1999), 'Change and complementarities in the new competitive landscape: A European panel study, 1992–1996', *Organization Science*, 10 (5), 583–600.

Wofford, J.C. (1982), 'An integrative theory of leadership', *Journal of Management*, 8 (1), 27–47.

Wood, M. (2005), 'The fallacy of misplaced leadership', *Journal of Management Studies*, 42 (6), 1101–21.

Yu, J.E. and J.W. Lee (2008), 'Creating rhizomatic networks and ethics for the marginalized group', *Systemic Practice and Action Research*, 21 (4), 253–66.

Zahra, S.A. and M. Wright (2011), 'Entrepreneurship's next act', *Academy of Management Perspectives*, 25 (4), 67–83.

Zhang, H. and M.H. Cone (2014), 'Strategies for success in China: A case study of HSBC', paper presented at International Association for Chinese Management Research Conference, Beijing, China, June.

Zhang, H., M.H. Cone, A.M. Everett and G. Elkin (2011), 'Aesthetic leadership in Chinese business: A philosophical perspective', *Journal of Business Ethics*, 101 (3), 475–91.

4. Using critical methodologies to examine entrepreneurial leadership
Valerie Stead and Eleanor Hamilton

This chapter examines how employing critical methodologies can develop new conceptual frameworks to theorize entrepreneurial leadership. In this chapter we draw on Leitch et al. (2012: 2) to understand entrepreneurial leadership as 'the leadership role performed in entrepreneurial ventures'. Taking this view focuses less on the style of leaders within entrepreneurial ventures and more on their everyday practice, and interactions with others, so offering opportunity to examine more closely the micro social practices and dynamics of what it is to be an entrepreneurial leader. The term 'critical' is somewhat loaded and subject to different meanings. In this chapter we use the term to signal a view that leadership and entrepreneurial research is not objective. To be critical is to challenge taken-for-granted norms and to question the basis upon which knowledge is claimed to be valid, whose views it represents and whose voices are absent (Alvesson and Deetz, 2000; Collinson, 2011; Tedmanson et al., 2012).

We draw on critical perspectives from leadership and entrepreneurship research. Critical theory contributes 'awareness of the political-ideological character of research' (Alvesson and Sköldberg, 2000: 8). Social science exists within a political and ethical context, and what is researched, and how, serves either to support or to challenge existing social conditions. How reality is represented supports or challenges different social interests. Thus the underlying theoretical assumptions and subsequent interpretations are not neutral but are part of, and help to construct, ideological conditions. Introducing the use of critical methodology is a means to illuminate the complexities of leadership in the small entrepreneurial business context. In this chapter our critical focus is on gender. Using illustrations from two empirical studies of the co-construction of gendered identities in small businesses, we outline and discuss the steps and value involved in adopting a critical stance. Deeply ingrained historical ideas and practices are reflected in the research process itself; 'the gendered nature of research and researcher identity is almost always under-acknowledged' (Pullen, 2007: 316). This discussion contributes a critical methodological framework for the study of entrepreneurial leadership using different cycles of analysis, cycles that unearth and interrogate critical issues.

Post-heroic understandings of leadership emerged in the academic literature in the late 1990s to challenge individualistic, heroic notions of leadership (Fletcher, 2004). Conceiving of leadership as a social, relational and shared practice, post-heroic understandings draw attention to the dynamic and distributed nature of leadership (Crevani et al., 2007; Cunliffe and Eriksen, 2011). Leadership is understood as developed 'over time through the interaction, interpretation and sense-making of people' (Jepson, 2009: 68) rather than as an individual trait or characteristic. Fletcher (2004: 648) argues, however, that although post-heroic models 'emphasize leadership as a collaborative, relational process dependent on social networks of influence, the concepts are often presented as gender and, to a lesser degree, power neutral'. This paradox, she warns us, has the effect of obscuring important gender–power relations that are fundamental to the social construction of leadership. Greater attention is therefore called for to adopt critical perspectives and methodologies that illuminate gender–power dynamics (Fletcher, 2004; Stead and Elliott, 2009). Furthermore, in the entrepreneurship literature scholars have called for the adoption of critical approaches (Ahl, 2006; Calas et al., 2009; Marlow and McAdam, 2013) and more methodological pluralism (Gartner and Birley, 2002; Neergard and Ulhoi, 2007; Anderson and Starnawska, 2008). In this chapter we argue that employing critical methodologies can begin to address these calls, by offering fresh perspectives for theorizing and practising leadership in the entrepreneurial context.

CRITICAL METHODOLOGIES

In their introduction to critical management research, Alvesson and Deetz (2000) argue that critical research methods are based upon a relationship between critical theory and postmodernism which allows us to question prevalent and dominant orders, norms, practices, ideologies, discourse and institutions. United in their concern to challenge traditional and dominant ways of thinking and being, critical studies of management and leadership draw on multiple theoretical perspectives, ontologies and epistemologies including critical realism, feminism and post-structuralism (Collinson, 2011). Alvesson and Deetz (2000) draw attention to two aspects of critical research. First, where critical studies are concerned to examine an object or phenomenon in relation to its broader social, cultural, economic and political context as a means to illuminate the development of asymmetrical social relations. For instance, they point to examples of class and late capitalism. Second, they observe an interest in 'micro-oriented forms' (ibid.: 1) of critical study. They encourage interpretive research that is concerned with examining 'the micro-practices of everyday life' (ibid.: 1). These studies focus more particularly on practices that reproduce asymmetries, and that result in the construction of particular social understandings and realities.

What constitutes critical studies could be accused of adopting a narrow band of definition. For example, they are often seen to either outline critical theory methodological principles that are broadly relevant but that have little connection to empirical studies or to employ broadly traditional forms of qualitative research, and add in aspects of critical theory (Alvesson and Deetz, 2000). A broad spectrum of methodologies might be included, however: for instance, a semiotic tradition of textual and visual analyses that draw attention to dominant discourses in leadership practice (Hellgren et al., 2002), and persistent imagery in the portrayal of entrepreneurs (Achtenhagen and Welter, 2011; Hamilton, 2013a). Further, a developing stream of narrative identity literature, such as Nicholson and Carroll's (2013) work, examines how identity and power relations interweave in leaders' development; while Down (2006) uses ethnographic research to examine entrepreneurial identity. There is a gap, therefore, in thinking about how perspectives of critical theory such as post-structuralism and feminism can stimulate fresh approaches to qualitative research and 'how methodology can benefit from an ambitious incorporation of critical-philosophical insights' (Alvesson and Deetz, 2000: 2). This chapter considers how we might develop greater appreciation of critical methodological approaches to advance empirical research and interpretive studies of entrepreneurial leadership.

Our subject focus is entrepreneurial leadership and our scholarly concern is how we can access and illuminate the complexity of what it is to be a leader in an entrepreneurial context. Located at the intersection of entrepreneurial and leadership literatures, we therefore begin our discussion of critical methodology by exploring how critical methodology is employed within the leadership and entrepreneurial literatures.

CRITICAL METHODOLOGIES IN LEADERSHIP RESEARCH

Understanding leadership within the small entrepreneurial business context is becoming increasingly significant. It has been pointed out that despite the variety and scale of small businesses – for example, family businesses, partnerships, social enterprises – relatively little attention has been paid to leadership within the context of the entrepreneurial firm (Leitch et al., 2012: 2). One aspect is clear: stereotypical assumptions about an individualistic, gendered, heroic leader inform implicit theories of entrepreneurial leadership. The dominant entrepreneurial discourse remains exemplified by an archetypical white male (Essers and Benschop, 2009). These assumptions are reproduced and reinforced by both the academic literature and the media (Hamilton, 2013a). Critical entrepreneurial studies observe this dominant masculine entrepreneurial discourse (Ahl, 2006; Essers and Benschop, 2009; Hamilton, 2013a, 2013b), and call for more nuanced understandings of gendered entrepreneurial identities (Bruni et al., 2005; Hamilton, 2006, 2013b; Ahl, 2006; Pullen, 2007; Marlow and McAdam, 2012).

These entrepreneurial studies also encourage the use of critical approaches to illuminate hitherto hidden assumptions in how we research and theorize entrepreneurship. For instance, Calas et al. (2009) draw attention to how adopting a critical lens can offer opportunity to extend the boundaries of how we understand and theorize entrepreneurship. They suggest that calling into question a dominant view of entrepreneurship as a positive economic activity alerts us to how entrepreneurial studies are limited by locating entrepreneurship as 'economic phenomena in market societies' (ibid.: 552). They argue that this positioning promotes and frames research to focus on the individual entrepreneur's actions in relation to the market. Framing entrepreneurship in this way as 'a universal market-based phenomenon' presupposes a particular (realist) ontology and can neglect 'contextual dynamics' (ibid.: 553). Critical approaches that challenge normative understandings can enable 'reframing', allowing for plurality of ontological perspectives and fresh directions for how we think about and research entrepreneurship. Adopting critical perspectives provides opportunities to re-examine assumptions, particularly around issues of gender, and calls for greater reflexivity from researchers in approaching leadership research in the entrepreneurial context.

Critical leadership studies, in common with an emerging critical literature in entrepreneurship and drawing on critical management studies, aim to question traditional orthodoxies and to examine what is neglected or underexplored in mainstream leadership research (Collinson, 2011). In both entrepreneurship and leadership studies assumptions persist concerning who a leader or entrepreneur is and what leadership or entrepreneurship involves (Ogbor, 2000; Ahl, 2004; Fletcher, 2004; Stead, 2013). Critical leadership studies should 'critique the power relations and identity constructions through which leadership dynamics are often reproduced, frequently rationalized, sometimes resisted and occasionally transformed' (Collinson, 2011: 181). Thus, critical studies draw on a plurality of approaches with diverse theoretical roots to stimulate alternative directions for considering how we think about and organize leaders and leadership (Collinson, 2011). For example, critical leadership scholars invite us to challenge idealized images of leadership (Tourish, 2013) and to 'rethink' it as a set of dynamic, shifting and often contradictory dialectical relationships often riven with tension and contradiction (Collinson, 2005: 1419).

Collinson (2011) alerts us to how the problematization of power and authority as a point of departure encourages scholars to look beyond mainstream leadership theorizing, towards philosophy, politics, and social and cultural theories. Fletcher's (2004) research, for example, adopts a feminist theoretical perspective to challenge mainstream theorizing of leadership. A move from understandings of leadership as invested in individuals to post-heroic ideas promotes leadership as a social process dependent on social networks of influence. In this chapter we use the term 'feminist theory' in its broad sense, as encompassing intellectual traditions that seek to make explicit the female experience, and to draw attention to gender as socially constructed rather than defined in relation to biological sex (Donovan, 2012). A historical tendency for leadership and entrepreneurial research to focus on male experience results in theory and models that favour the male perspective and neglect the female view (Jennings and Brush, 2013; Stead and Elliott, 2009). This research, however, is often presented as gender neutral, assuming that it reflects both male and female experience. A central concern of feminist methodologies is to challenge the presentation of social practices such as leadership and learning as gender neutral; that is, a lack of attention to the influence of dominant gender discourses on the ways in which individuals behave (Acker, 1995; Fletcher, 2004).

Feminist methodologies emphasize gender as socially constructed, (re) created through processes and practices that maintain difference (Ashcraft and Mumby, 2004; Gatrell and Swan, 2008; Wharton, 2005). This view alerts us to the 'doing' of gender; that is, how gender is embedded in everyday practice (West and Zimmerman, 1987) and (re)produced in particular social or organizational contexts (Broadbridge and Simpson, 2011). Thus, drawing on social ideas of gender, Fletcher (2004) critiques the extent to which leadership invokes the 'social'. In spite of theorizing leadership as a social process, Fletcher believes that leadership often continues to be presented as gender neutral, thereby neglecting important power relations that shape and influence leadership and leaders. Feminist perspectives can then enable an interrogation of whose voices are heard, whose knowledge is taken as valid and whose experiences are deemed authoritative in different social and organizational settings. Entrepreneurial studies also alert us to the utility of feminist theory as a means to provide more nuanced analyses of entrepreneurial processes and how they create and recreate gendered normative practices (Hughes et al., 2012; Marlow et al., 2009).

In their concern to extend the boundaries of entrepreneurship theory and research, Calas et al. (2009) draw attention to how feminist theorizing is associated with social change. Based on the premise that gender is a fundamental structuring element of society, feminist theorizing aims to analyse and theorize with a view to illuminating how women are historically disadvantaged and how this might be changed (ibid.). This 'critical position', Calas et al. (2009: 554) suggest, illustrates how knowledge will necessarily promote the interests of some above others.

Another critical approach utilized in critical leadership studies is the adoption of post-structural methodologies that help to surface issues of power and gender and illuminate how leadership practices and processes such as promotion and recruitment, decision-making and networking can reinforce the leadership norm as male, thereby positioning women as 'other' (Ford, 2006). The aim of post-structuralism is to deconstruct taken-for-granted knowledge and challenge dualistic tendencies that 'separate individual from society, mind from body, rationality from emotion' (Collinson, 2003: 527). Individuals, therefore, are embedded within their social world (ibid.). Post-structural perspectives endorse leadership as emerging from and situated in everyday leadership activity and practice and draw attention to experience as 'culturally framed and shaped' (Swan, 2007: 204). Such a perspective recognizes that leaders and leadership are influenced by social conditions such as class, gender, race and ethnicity. Leadership and management discourses then reflect and are constituted by their social and cultural context, 'giving form to reality' (Cunliffe, 2001: 352). In particular, post-structural studies of leadership aim to identify and interrogate prevalent discourses and social structures, drawing attention to their performative effect, how they bring into being and reproduce dominant ways of thinking and being (Ford et al., 2008).

Within the tradition of feminist theorizing outlined above, scholars adopting feminist post-structuralist approaches foreground gender and are concerned with social change (Grogan, 1996). For example, research by Stead and Elliott (2013) examines their leadership teaching experiences from a feminist post-structuralist perspective to explore how the use of leadership models in the classroom can reproduce and 'fix' particular ideas that can serve to exclude some above others. Using their reflections, they suggest a more critical and reflexive approach to the use of epistemic objects in leadership teaching.

Entrepreneurial studies that draw on post-structuralist approaches also draw attention to the importance of examining prevalent discourses. Research by Bruni et al. (2004) has suggested adopting 'a deconstructive gaze' to examine the subtext of entrepreneurial discourse that shapes understandings of entrepreneurship and what it is to be an entrepreneur

(Bruni et al., 2004). This gaze highlights a dominant male entrepreneurial discourse where 'to think entrepreneur' is 'to think male' (Marlow et al., 2009). Feminist and post-structuralist methodologies highlight not only the sex of actors or research participants but also 'the cultural production of their subjectivities and the material production of their social lives' (Calas et al., 2009: 555). A key feature of leadership and entrepreneurial studies adopting feminist theorizing and feminist and post-structuralist methodologies is their call for research that offers detailed understanding of the contexts within which leadership and entrepreneurship is located, including cultural, social, economic and political contexts (Collinson, 2011; Hughes et al., 2012; Marlow et al., 2009).

ADOPTING A CRITICAL APPROACH: TWO ILLUSTRATIONS

In this chapter we present illustrations from two studies to outline what is involved in taking a critical approach to entrepreneurial leadership. These studies were selected for three reasons. First, they focus on the experiences of entrepreneurial leaders, those who hold leadership roles in entrepreneurial ventures (Leitch et al., 2012), paying attention to the micro interactions and dynamics of their social practice. This emphasis is helpful in making explicit power relations, a central concern of critical studies as defined earlier. Second, they fit a critical agenda in their aim to draw attention to those who may not necessarily fit the traditional understanding of entrepreneurial leader, including women who take on leadership in family businesses (Studies 1 and 2) and in social enterprises (Study 1). Third, by adopting a feminist theoretical approach they are intended to be helpful illustrations of critical methodologies. The first study examines gendered power relations in action, learning from the experiences of women owner-managers of small entrepreneurial businesses (Stead, 2014); and the second explores how entrepreneurial identities are constructed socially in relation to others, shaped by multiple discourses (Hamilton, 2013b). We explore how both of these employ phenomenological approaches to data collection as a means to focus on the view of the 'experiencer' (Giorgi and Giorgi, 2008: 167). Reflexive cycles of analysis reveal critical issues of power and gender.

Study 1: Gendered Power Relations and Action Learning

This study takes a critical approach to provide insight into gendered power relations in action learning. It draws on reflections from six women who participated in action learning sets that were part of a ten-month leadership development programme for owner-managers of small businesses. Action learning was a core component of the programme, which also included one-to-one coaching, lectures from business practitioners, exchanges with other participants and a residential workshop. Action learning sets consisted of a group of five to seven participants and were based on Revans's (1980) principles of offering a supportive and challenging environment in which individuals can discuss business issues, share experiences and identify strategies and actions to resolve issues. Interviews with the women were guided by a phenomenological approach that stressed the view of the 'experiencer' (Giorgi and Giorgi, 2008: 167) and which were concerned with perception and emotion (Giorgi, 1977). Attention was also paid to the situated person and the individual's socio-cultural context. This was pertinent to this study, as its aim was to understand leadership and leadership development as situated within and given shape by socio-cultural contexts.

In order to gain insights into gendered power relations the study adopted a feminist perspective as a means to draw attention to the female experience and to provide a critical frame that would guide the design of the study and the analysis of the women's reflections. Framing the enquiry within feminist theory rejected essentialist views of gender that understand gender as biological difference. Rather, it supported conceptions of gender as socially constructed, produced and reproduced through social activities and processes (Gatrell and Swan, 2008). This framing enabled the study to draw attention to the 'doing' of gender (West and Zimmerman, 1987) and how it is (re)created, negotiated and maintained in particular social or organizational contexts (Broadbridge and Simpson, 2011). In viewing gender as socially constructed, as 'something that is *done*', the study aimed to illuminate important power relations by examining how gender is produced and reproduced through social interaction (Ahl, 2006: 612). Concerned both to showcase women's experiences and to explore gendered power relations, two different cycles of analysis were employed.

First, drawing on the phenomenological interest in the women's views and perceptions, and with reference to qualitative analysis techniques (e.g., Ritchie and Lewis, 2003) often adopted by phenomenological researchers, the initial cycle of analysis sought to organize the data and to elicit key themes (Eatough and Smith, 2008). Phenomenological approaches are concerned with 'lived experience', and recognize that lived experience embraces 'the embodied and socio-culturally and historically situated person' (Eatough and Smith, 2008: 181). In this study, such a perspective enabled exploration of how action learning is understood within the women's socio-cultural context as represented by their reflections. This cycle involved close reading of the interview transcripts to form an initial set of categories (Amernic et al., 2007). These were further developed and refined by moving back and forth between the transcripts and the categories to establish relationships between categories. The final two broad categories 'action learning environment' and 'looking like a leader' then encompassed a number of subcategories that provided detail and description. For example, the broad category of 'action learning environment' included subcategories of action learning structure, set atmosphere, set culture, feeling isolated and feeling excluded. This first cycle of analysis was important in providing a broad overview and description of the key elements relating to gender and the women's experiences of action learning. Explaining and describing offered a means to highlight the richness of the data and to showcase what the women said, to depict in their words how they felt about their experiences.

The second cycle of analysis aimed to offer a critical interpretation of the findings and to examine more deeply the gendered power relations in action learning. This drew on feminist post-structuralist ideas as a means to interrogate the women's reflections more closely. Post-structuralist ideas understand discourse as constituted by its social and cultural context, and also as constitutive in producing and reproducing social and cultural norms (Fairclough and Wodak, 1997). Discourse, through the women's spoken reflections, is then dynamic, actively producing ideas and bringing them into being (Ford et al., 2008). Feminist post-structuralist ideas promote the examination of gender (Baxter, 2003), which in this study enabled critique of the women's reflections to examine how they reflected on the ways in which gender operates in the educational context of action learning to privilege particular knowledge or certain ideas (Metcalfe, 2008). This cycle of analysis, therefore, was concerned to bring to light the 'doing' of gender; in other words, how gender is produced and reproduced in the women's reflections and to examine how these representations connect to wider socio-cultural and historical contexts.

The critical intent of this cycle offered a chance to explore beyond the surface of the women's feelings, illuminated by the first cycle of analysis, to how gender is accomplished in educational and developmental activities such as action learning. For example, a focus on the 'doing of gender' revealed how power relations in the action learning sets were reinforced by the language used to describe action learning as a 'circle of trust'. The women's reflections showed that this had the effect of silencing concerns, making it difficult for them to raise issues such as feeling marginalized or isolated, calling into question levels of trust. In this study, taking a feminist post-structuralist perspective drew attention to how leadership development interventions such as action learning for entrepreneurial leaders might affirm gendered power relations that disadvantage women. These insights are helpful in understanding the operation of gendered power relations, their effects and how learning development programmes for entrepreneurial leaders might take gender into account.

Study 2: Family Business and Gendered Entrepreneurial Identities

This was a study of five family businesses based in the north of England, drawing on interviews with two generations, the founders and their successors in the second generation. Sixteen individuals from the five families participated in the research. An interview research technique originally presented by Thompson et al. (1989) was purposely adopted. They proposed existential phenomenology as an alternative paradigm for theorizing consumer behaviour, and provided the philosophical assumptions of the approach designed to elicit descriptions of lived experience in relation to a particular phenomenon. By adopting an existential-phenomenological world view they contend that we assume that human experience can be seen as a pattern emerging from a context. The research goal is to give a thematic description of experience. Thompson et al. (1989) describe in some detail existential phenomenology as a method, and provide guidelines for conducting a phenomenological interview. The in-depth interview should obtain a first-person description of some specified domain of experience. Interviewers are advised that since the topic is the respondent's experience, they should not begin the interview by assuming that they know more about the subject than the respondent. They advise that apart from an opening question the interviewer should ask no other set questions: 'the interview is intended to yield a conversation, not a question and answer session'. In essence, 'the interviewer should aim to be non-directive listener' (ibid.: 138). The phenomenological approach, its advantages and its dilemmas, is discussed in detail in Cope (2005).

Interviews with the founding generation began with an open conversational device: 'Tell me about the family and the business'. The succeeding generations were asked the question: 'When did you first become aware of the business?' By engaging in non-directive conversation the aim was to encourage and support participants to feel at ease and be able to respond freely, to tell their own story. Holstein and Gubrium (2003) point out that with increased interest in representational issues characteristic of postmodern, post-structuralist, constructionist and ethnomethodological studies, interviewing is treated 'as a social encounter in which knowledge is constructed ... a site of, and an occasion for, producing reportable knowledge itself' (ibid.: 68). In eliciting these accounts which are socially and culturally embedded, we ask, 'what is it that we can responsibly do with them?' (Davies and Davies, 2007: 1140).

The first cycle of organizing data and identifying themes was illuminating, and required a suspension of preconceptions that were both personal and theoretical. This initial cycle of interaction with the empirical material was followed by cycles of interpretation at different levels. Alvesson and Sköldberg (2000: 249) say that reflexivity occurs at the interface of the different levels of interpretation. They talk of moving from data collecting to preliminary interpretation, guided by theory and other frames of reference (cultural and implicit), and the researcher allowing the empirical material to 'inspire, develop and reshape theoretical ideas'. But crucially they make the point that it is the theory that allows the researcher to find meaning in the empirical material, and that the researcher's 'repertoire of interpretation' determines what is possible in terms of interpretation. They believe that the 'formula' for reflection is rich data plus breadth and depth in the repertoire of interpretation, enhancing the chance of 'empirically grounded imagination' (Alvesson and Sköldberg, 2000: 251). Thus, in engaging with critical methodology, it is important to have to hand an appropriate repertoire of critical to enhance the interpretive possibilities. At the same time, we have to position ourselves as researchers to challenge 'authoritative frameworks which suppress difference and multiplicity' (Pullen, 2007: 316).

The second cycle of interpretation involved a deliberate attempt to understand gendered identities and their construction in family business. Masculine and feminine identities have been researched in the workplace (Collinson and Hearn, 1996; Whitehead and Barrett, 2001; Gatrell and Swan, 2008; Stead and Elliott, 2009; Gatrell et al., 2013). Family relationships, however, 'represent an important site where people do gender' (Morgan, 2001: 232). In this study the construction of gender identities crafted in the narratives of family business were examined. These gender identities were complicated, shifting and negotiated within narrative discourse (Hamilton, 2013a). We can recognize the 'coercive and creative effects of cultural discourses' (Kondo, 1990: 140). Feminist researchers have long recognized that language plays an important part in social practice and institutions 'in reflecting, creating and sustaining gender divisions in society' (Talbot, 1998: 15).

This study adopted an interdisciplinary approach, taking the work of Mulholland (1996a, 1996b) combined with Kondo's (1990) study to create fresh understanding of gender relations and identity in family business, underpinned by Ricoeur's (1980) narrative theory of identity. In the interpretative process it was possible to identify patriarchal forces in family businesses, the conditions under which patriarchy is challenged, and the nature of those challenges, material and discursive (Hamilton, 2006). McNay (2000: 92) reminds us, however, that 'identity is contingent upon a particular set of social relations; it is not fixed, but neither is it purely arbitrary in that some narratives have deep historical resonance and durability'. Patriarchal discourse and practice is dominant but gender relations in family business are not so simply determined. This study revealed gendered identities are constantly negotiated and renegotiated. They are enmeshed in relationships of duty, love and conflict (Kondo, 1990), and embedded in wider discourses determined by historical and cultural context.

A REFLEXIVE CRITICAL METHODOLOGY

The approaches taken by these empirical studies have in common two key features: first, a concern to access accounts of people's experiences in the micro-practice of the everyday; and second, a broad critical intent. This critical intent is significant in its concern to take into account the experiences and views of those who do not fit the dominant form. In particular, Calas et al. (2009) highlight the significance of developing 'a more complete picture of the world' by exploring the relationship of those who are non-dominant in relation to those who occupy a dominant posi- tioning. An analytical focus is therefore placed on micro social practices, for instance the ways in which people interact and the language they use and how this reflects and contributes to broader macro social processes, including how gender is (re)produced (Calas et al., 2009).

To develop this analytical focus both studies employed phenomeno- logical techniques as a means to elicit people's experience and to organize the data (ibid.: 561). Phenomenological philosophy is concerned with the experiential underpinnings of knowledge. It argues that the relation between our perception and the objects we perceive is not passive, that human consciousness actively constitutes the objects of experience, and that we all actively constitute and reconstitute the world of everyday life because our experience is mediated by our perceptions. We must be alert to the subjectivist nature of the phenomenological approach and acknowl- edge its philosophical roots. However, in adopting a particular interview technique we do not assume that we are directly accessing lived experi- ence in some way. Such an assumption would 'falsely separate discourse and experience' (Summerfield, 2004: 67). We have to acknowledge ques- tions about the way we use discursive accounts of experience as empirical material without 'attempting to fix and limit their meanings' (Davies and Davies, 2007: 1139). Phenomenological philosophy offers an important foundation for qualitative interviewers to develop techniques to elicit empirical data about complex phenomena.

These techniques therefore enable the researcher to present data in a form that is descriptive and rich, and positioned clearly as the interviewee's subjective experience, with interview accounts then offering different potential representations of social reality (Silverman, 2011). The presentation of phenomenological data typically uses an interviewee's words or phrases to capture feelings and reflections. This offers closeness to the data, grounded within what was actually said, that is not always explicit or easily accessible in critical interpretive texts. Thus, utilizing phenomenological techniques emphasizes the view of the 'experiencer' and so necessarily embraces the interviewee's socio-cultural context (Giorgi and Giorgi, 2008: 167). In this respect phenomenological techniques have resonance with critical approaches that acknowledge the situated and relational nature of leadership (Collinson, 2005). In these exemplars the researchers adopt phenomenological techniques as part of a broad critical intent to challenge dominant theoretical understandings by unearthing critical issues, particularly gendered power relations. This intent, signalled in the aims of the studies and in their intended contribution, provided the context for the design and development of both studies.

The approaches drawn upon by these studies to advance understandings of leadership in the small entrepreneurial business context support a critically reflexive methodology that is informed by and builds on Alvesson and Sköldberg's (2009) reflexive methodological approach. They propose an initial explanation and exploration of data, followed by critical interpretation and reflection. In their model criticality is applied as a later part of an interpretive process. We propose, however, a model where the process is framed by critical intent. Figure 4.1 brings together ideas from critical thinking, reflexive methodology and phenomenological approaches to suggest a critically reflexive approach that emphasises the importance of critical intent from the outset. Research methods, analytical techniques and interpretive lenses must work within a critical frame and towards critical insights connecting critical theory to empirical data. This critical intent is important in signalling a challenge to the normative, and an adherence to enquiry that will examine issues of power and identity. Adopting a critically reflexive methodology involves identifying theory, process and method that enable the realization of a critical intent. The studies outlined above demonstrate this by taking a critical theory such as feminism to frame their research objectives, such as the interrogation of gendered power relations. The process to do this follows cycles of interpretation that first present and organize the data, illuminating reflections and

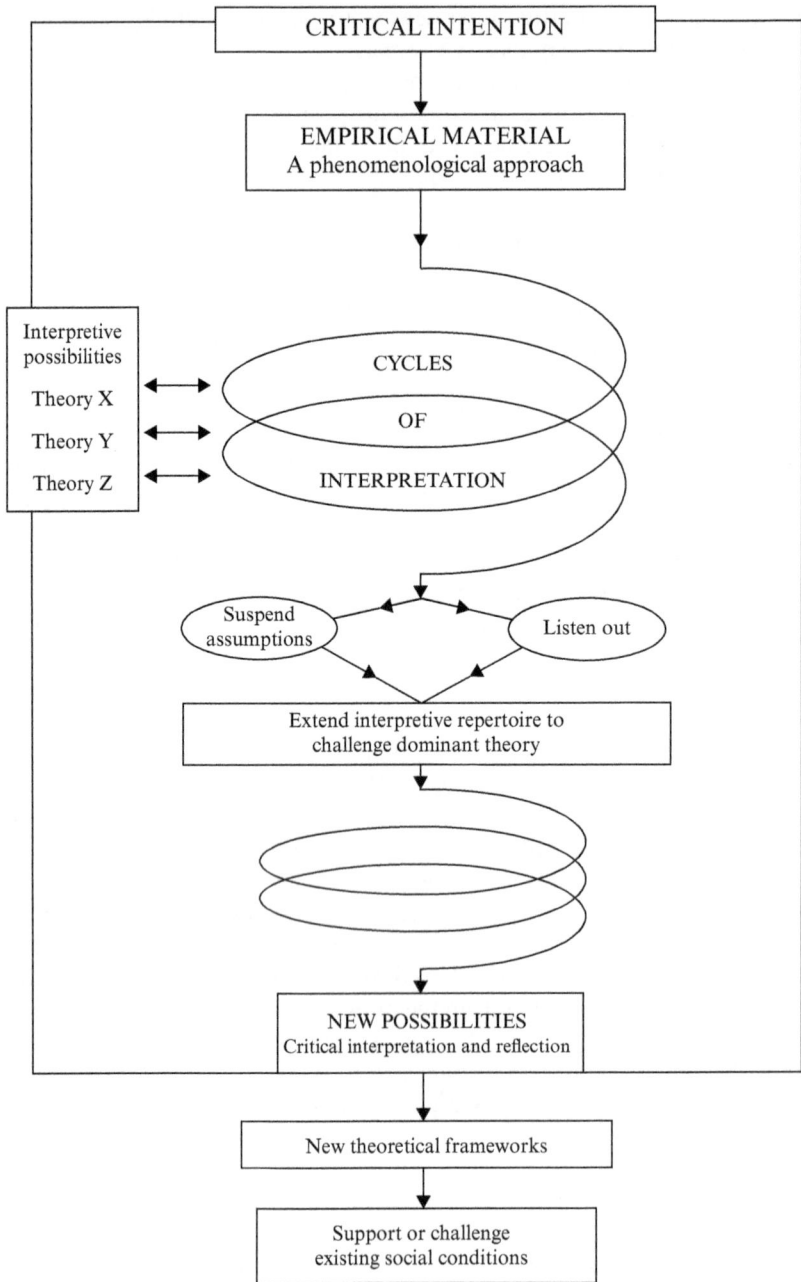

Figure 4.1   Critically reflexive methodological approach

experiences and simultaneously pointing to their interpretive potential; and second, offer a critical interpretation that enables a more nuanced appreciation of relational power dynamics. Connected by critical intent, this critically reflexive methodology promotes new possibilities for the ways we can explain, describe and interpret phenomena. This can lead to the development of new theoretical frameworks that may support or challenge existing social conditions.

Both studies engaged in critical cycles of analysis drawing on feminist post-structuralist approaches to develop a more nuanced appreciation of the dynamics of gendered power relations in relation to entrepreneurial leaders. Viewing discourse as both conditioned by its social and cultural context and constitutive in its production and reproduction of social norms (Fairclough and Wodak, 1997), we have shown how taking a feminist post-structuralist perspective provides a means to interrogate the connection between individual reflections of micro social practices and the broader social context. This leads to greater understanding of the macro social; how gender is reproduced in broader socio-cultural contexts, and how gendered power relations influence the ways in which entrepreneurs present themselves, perceive themselves and are perceived as leaders.

In this chapter we have pointed to the need for greater reflexivity in research design and practice as a means to interrogate the social complexity of entrepreneurial leadership (Alvesson and Sköldberg, 2009; Stead and Elliott, 2013). In writing about our research methodologies we need to adopt a reflexive stance in order to challenge 'authoritative frameworks which suppress difference and multiplicity' (Pullen, 2007: 316). As critical researchers we need to reflect on our research practice 'as a first step in making the commonsensical and self-evident precarious and problematic' (Johnson and Duberley, 2000: 2). In proposing a critical framework that comprises cycles of analysis, we offer a conceptual framework for theory-building that invites reflexivity and more profound ways of understanding, yet also reveals unanswered questions and opportunities for research in entrepreneurial leadership.

REFERENCES

Achtenhagen, L. and F. Welter (2011), '"Surfing on the ironing board" – the representation of women's entrepreneurship in German newspapers', *Entrepreneurship and Regional Development*, 23 (9/10), 763–86.

Acker, J. (1995), 'Feminist goals and organizing processes', in M.M. Ferree and P.Y. Martin (eds), *Feminist Organizations: Harvest of the New Women's Movement*, Philadelphia, PA: Temple University Press, pp. 137–44.

Ahl, H. (2004), *The Scientific Reproduction of Gender Inequality: A Discourse Analysis of Research Texts on Women's Entrepreneurship*, Libor: Copenhagen Business School Press.

Ahl, H. (2006), 'Why research on women entrepreneurs needs new directions', *Entrepreneurship Theory and Practice*, 30, 595–621.

Alvesson, M. and S. Deetz (2000), *Doing Critical Management Research*, London: SAGE.

Alvesson, M. and K. Sköldberg (2000), *Reflexive Methodology: New Vistas for Qualitative Research*, London: SAGE.

Alvesson, M. and K. Sköldberg (2009), *Reflexive Methodology: New Vistas for Qualitative Research*, 2nd edition, London: SAGE.

Amernic, J., R. Craig, and D. Tourish (2007), 'The transformational leader as pedagogue, physician, architect, commander, and saint: Five root metaphors in Jack Welch's letters to stockholders of General Electric', *Human Relations*, 60 (12), 1839–72.

Anderson, A.R. and M. Starnawska (2008), 'Research practices in entrepreneurship: Problems of definition, description and meaning', *International Journal of Entrepreneurship and Innovation*, 9 (4), 221–30.

Ashcraft, K.L. and D.K. Mumby (2004), *Reworking Gender: A Feminist Communicology of Organization*, Thousand Oaks, CA: SAGE.

Baxter, J. (2003), *Positioning Gender in Discourse: A Feminist Research Methodology*, Basingstoke: Palgrave Macmillan.

Broadbridge, A. and R. Simpson (2011), '25 years on: Reflecting on the past and looking to the future in gender and management research', *British Journal of Management*, 22 (3), 470–83.

Bruni, A., S. Gherardi and B. Poggio (2004), 'Entrepreneur-mentality, gender and the study of women entrepreneurs', *Journal of Organizational Change Management*, 17 (3), 256–68.

Bruni, A., S. Gherardi and B. Poggio (2005), *Gender and Entrepreneurship: An Ethnographical Approach*, Abingdon: Routledge.

Calas, M.B., L. Smircich and K.A. Bourne (2009), 'Extending the boundaries: Reframing "entrepreneurship as social change" through feminist perspectives', *Academy of Management Review*, 34 (3), 552–69.

Collinson, D.L. (2003), 'Identities and insecurities: Selves at work', *Organization*, 10 (3), 527–47.

Collinson, D. (2005), 'Dialectics of leadership', *Human Relations*, 58 (11), 1419–42.

Collinson, D. (2011), 'Critical leadership studies', in A. Bryman (ed.), *The SAGE Handbook of Leadership*, London: SAGE, pp. 181–94.

Collinson, D.L. and J. Hearn (eds) (1996), *Men as Managers, Managers as Men: Critical Perspectives on Men, Masculinities and Managements*, London: SAGE.

Cope, J. (2005), 'Towards a dynamic learning perspective of entrepreneurship', *Entrepreneurship: Theory and Practice*, 29 (4), 373–97.

Crevani, L., M. Lindgren and J. Packendorff (2007), 'Shared leadership: A postheroic perspective on leadership as a collective construction', *International Journal of Leadership Studies*, 3 (1), 40–67.

Cunliffe, A.L. (2001), 'Managers as practical authors: Reconstructing our understanding of management practice', *Journal of Management Studies*, 38 (3), 351–71.

Cunliffe, A.L. and M. Eriksen (2011), 'Relational leadership', *Human Relations*, 64 (11), 1425–49.

Davies, B. and C. Davies (2007), 'Having, and being had by, "experience"', *Qualitative Inquiry*, 13 (8), 1139–68.

Donovan, J. (2012), *Feminist Theory: The Intellectual Traditions*, New York, NY: Bloomsbury Publishing USA.

Down, S. (2006), *Narratives of Enterprise: Crafting Entrepreneurial Self-identity in a Small Firm*, Cheltenham, UK and Northampton, MA: Edward Elgar Publishing.

Eatough, V. and J.A. Smith (2008), 'Interpretative phenomenological analysis', in C. Willig, and W. Stainton-Rogers (eds), *The SAGE Handbook of Qualitative Research in Psychology*, London: SAGE, pp. 179–95.

Essers, C. and Y. Benschop (2009), 'Muslim businesswomen doing boundary work: The negotiation of Islam, gender and ethnicity within entrepreneurial contexts', *Human Relations*, 62 (3), 403–23.

Fairclough, N. and R. Wodak (1997), 'Critical discourse analysis', in T. Van Dijk (ed.), *Discourse Studies: A Multidisciplinary Introduction*, Vol. 2, London: SAGE, pp.258–84.

Fletcher, J.K. (2004), 'The paradox of postheroic leadership: An essay on gender, power, and transformational change', *Leadership Quarterly*, 15, 647–61.

Ford, J. (2006), 'Discourses of leadership: Gender, identity and contradiction in a UK public sector organization', *Leadership*, 2 (1), 77–99.

Ford, J., N. Harding and M. Learmonth (2008), *Leadership as Identity: Constructions and Deconstructions*, Aldershot: Palgrave Macmillan.

Gartner, W.B. and S. Birley (2002), 'Introduction to the special issue on qualitative methods in entrepreneurship research', *Journal of Business Venturing*, 17 (5), 387–95.

Gatrell, C. and Swan, E. (2008), *Gender and Diversity Management: A Concise Introduction*, London: SAGE.

Gatrell, C.J., S.B. Burnett, C.L. Cooper and P. Sparrow (2013), 'Work–life balance and parenthood: A comparative review of definitions, equity and enrichment', *International Journal of Management Reviews*, 15 (3), 300–316.

Giorgi, A. (1977), 'Phenomenological psychology', in B.J. Wolman (ed.), *International Encyclopaedia of Psychiatry, Psychology and Psychoanalysis*, New York, NY: Aesculapius Publishers.

Giorgi, A.P. and B. Giorgi (2008), 'Phenomenological psychology', in C. Willig and W. Stainton-Rogers (eds), *The SAGE Handbook of Qualitative Research in Psychology*, London: SAGE, pp.165–78.

Grogan, M. (1996), *Voices of Women Aspiring to the Superintendency*, Albany, NY: State University of New York Press.

Hamilton, E. (2006), 'Whose story is it anyway? Narrative accounts of the role of women in founding and establishing family businesses', *International Small Business Journal*, 24, 253–71.

Hamilton, E. (2013a), 'The discourse of entrepreneurial masculinities (and femininities)', *Entrepreneurship and Regional Development*, 25 (1/2), 90–99.

Hamilton, E. (2013b), *Entrepreneurship Across Generations: Narrative, Gender and Learning in Family Business*, Cheltenham, UK and Northampton, MA: Edward Elgar Publishing.

Hellgren, B., J. Löwstedt, L. Puttonen, J. Tienari, E. Vaara and A. Werr (2002), 'Discursive practices in the AstraZeneca merger', *British Journal of Management*, 13 (2), 123–40.

Holstein, J.A. and J.F. Gubrium (2003), 'Active interviewing', in J. Gubrium and J. Holstein (eds), *Postmodern Interviewing*, London: SAGE, pp.67–80.

Hughes, K.D., J.E. Jennings, C. Brush, S. Carter and F. Welter (2012), 'Extending women's entrepreneurship research in new directions', *Entrepreneurship Theory and Practice*, 36 (3), 429–42.

Jennings, J.E. and C.G. Brush (2013), 'Research on women entrepreneurs: Challenges to (and from) the broader entrepreneurship literature?', *Academy of Management Annals*, 7 (1), 663–715.

Jepson, D. (2009), 'Studying leadership at cross-country level: A critical analysis', *Leadership*, 5 (1), 61–80.

Johnson, P. and J. Duberley (2000), *Understanding Management Research: An Introduction to Epistemology*, London: SAGE.

Kondo, D.K. (1990), *Crafting Selves: Power, Gender, and Discourses of Identity in a Japanese Workplace*, Chicago, IL: University of Chicago Press.

Leitch, C., C. McMullen and R.T. Harrison (2012), 'The development of entrepreneurial leadership: The role of human, social and institutional capital', *British Journal of Management*, 2 February, DOI: 10.1111/j.1467-8551.2011.00808.

McNay, L. (2000), *Gender and Agency: Reconfiguring the Subject in Feminist and Social Theory*, Malden, MA: Polity Press.

Marlow, S., C. Henry and S.L. Carter (2009), 'Exploring the impact of gender upon women's business ownership', *International Small Business Journal*, 27 (2), 139−48.

Marlow, S. and M. McAdam (2012), 'Analyzing the influence of gender upon high-technology venturing within the context of business incubation', *Entrepreneurship Theory and Practice*, 36 (4), 655−76.

Marlow, S. and M. McAdam (2013), 'Gender and entrepreneurship: Advancing debate and challenging myths; exploring the mystery of the under-performing female entrepreneur', *International Journal of Entrepreneurial Behaviour and Research*, 19 (1), 114−24.

Metcalfe, B.D. (2008), 'A feminist poststructuralist analysis of HRD: Why bodies, power and reflexivity matter', *Human Resource Development International*, 11 (5), 447−63.

Morgan, D.H.J. (2001), 'Family, gender and masculinities', in S.M. Whitehead and F.J. Barrett (eds), *The Masculinities Reader*, Cambridge: Polity / Blackwell Publishers, pp. 223−32.

Mulholland, K. (1996a), 'Gender and property relations within entrepreneurial wealthy families', *Gender, Work and Organisation*, 3 (2), 78−102.

Mulholland, K. (1996b), 'Entrepreneurialism, masculinities and the self-made man', in D.L. Collinson and J. Hearn (eds), *Men as Managers, Managers as Men, Critical Perspectives on Men, Masculinities and Managements*, London: SAGE, pp. 123−49.

Neergard, H. and J.P. Ulhoi (2007), 'Introduction: methodological variety in entrepreneurship research', in H. Neergard and J.P. Ulhoi (eds), *Handbook of Qualitative Research Methods in Entrepreneurship*, Cheltenham, UK and Northampton, MA: Edward Elgar Publishing, pp. 1−16.

Nicholson, H. and B. Carroll (2013), 'Identity undoing and power relations in leadership development', *Human Relations*, 66 (9), 1225−48.

Ogbor, J.O. (2000), 'Mythicizing and reification in entrepreneurial discourse: Ideology-critique of entrepreneurial studies', *Journal of Management Studies*, 37 (5), 605−35.

Pullen, A. (2007), 'Becoming a researcher: Gendering the research self', in A. Pullen, N. Beech and D. Sims (eds), *Exploring Identity: Concepts and Methods*, Basingstoke: Palgrave Macmillan, pp. 316−33.

Revans, R.W. (1980), *Action Learning: New Techniques for Management*, London: Blond & Briggs.

Ricoeur, P. (1980), 'On narrative', *Critical Inquiry*, 7 (1), 169−90.

Ritchie, J. and J. Lewis (2003), *Qualitative Research Practice: A Guide for Social Science Students and Researchers*, London: SAGE.

Silverman, D. (2011), *Interpreting Qualitative Data*, 4th edition, London: SAGE.

Stead, V. (2013), 'Learning to deploy (in)visibility: an examination of women leaders' lived experiences', *Management Learning*, 44 (1), 63−79.

Stead, V. (2014), 'The gendered power relations of action learning: A critical analysis of women's reflections on a leadership development programme', *Human Resource Development International*, 17 (4), 416−37.

Stead, V. and C. Elliott (2009), *Women's Leadership*, Basingstoke: Palgrave Macmillan.

Stead, V. and C. Elliott (2013), 'Women's leadership learning: A reflexive review of representations and leadership teaching', *Management Learning*, 44 (4), 373−94.

Summerfield, P. (2004), 'Culture and composure: Creating narratives of the gendered self in oral history interviews', *Cultural and Social History*, 1 (1), 65−93.

Swan, E. (2007), 'Blue-eyed girl? Jane Elliott's experiential learning and anti-racism', in M. Reynolds and R. Vince (eds), *The Handbook of Experiential Learning and Management Education*, Oxford: Oxford University Press, pp. 202−20.

Talbot, M.M. (1998), *Language and Gender: An Introduction*, Cambridge: Polity Press.

Tedmanson, D., K. Verduyn, C. Essers and W.B. Gartner (2012), 'Critical perspectives in entrepreneurship research', *Organization*, 19 (5), 531−41.

Thompson, C.J., W.B. Locander and H.R. Pollio (1989), 'Putting consumer experience back into consumer research: The philosophy and method of existential phenomenology', *Journal of Consumer Research*, 16, 33−146.

Tourish, D. (2013), *The Dark Side of Transformational Leadership: A Critical Perspective*, London: Routledge.

West, C. and D.H. Zimmerman (1987), 'Doing gender', *Gender and Society*, 1 (2), 125−51.

Wharton, A.S. (2005), *The Sociology of Gender: An Introduction to Theory and Research*, Malden, MA: Blackwell Publishing.

Whitehead, S.M. and F.J. Barrett (eds) (2001), *The Masculinities Reader*, Cambridge: Polity / Blackwell Publishers.

5. Islamic insights on entrepreneurial leadership
Pegram Harrison and Muhammad Azam Roomi

INTRODUCTION

In previous research (Roomi and Harrison, 2011) we asked how leaders learn to be entrepreneurial, and how entrepreneurs learn leadership. After reviewing the literature and conducting a fairly simple survey, we concluded that the current constructs for understanding these processes, and the current methods for teaching entrepreneurial leadership, are not quite adequate to the task. We made some recommendations for improving the situation, consisting largely of a number of teaching techniques for stimulating critical debate about the two topics, with the practical outcome of enhancing students' ability to lead in an entrepreneurial context.

Encouraging more critical debate, we feel, is crucial. This is a challenge of relevance: of making leadership relevant to entrepreneurship and entrepreneurship relevant to leadership. However, we laid out this challenge within a fairly specific educational context: a conventional, high-education, social science, classroom-based, developed-world and gender-neutral context. The experiential learning methods that we recommended for enhancing critical engagement with the topic, while tried and tested in that conventional context, are not necessarily applicable in other contexts. As we have learned in other work (Roomi and Harrison, 2010), many people and environments engaged in entrepreneurial leadership, and in need of entrepreneurial leadership development, operate in different contexts: women in Pakistan, for example, have very different considerations from white male students in the USA.

Thus, restating and recombining the research questions of our earlier work, this chapter will ask: what is entrepreneurial leadership, and how should it be promoted in a much broader compass of contexts? How should it be understood in specific socio-cultural contexts? Can we observe how it is conceptualised and conveyed in non-formal educational environments such as non-literate social groups, disenfranchised populations or otherwise marginalised categories? What can be learned from the observation that entrepreneurship and entrepreneurial leadership manifestly occur, and are learned, in contexts far outside most entrepreneurship and leadership research? To approach these questions, we will look specifically at insights into entrepreneurial leadership from the Muslim world, in both scholarship and practice.

EMPIRICAL CHALLENGES AND THEORETICAL SUGGESTIONS

There are many things in the world that are true but not provable. The idea that Muslim entrepreneurs learn how to be leaders in ways that will also be instructive for others is probably just such a thing. But can we prove it? If there is an insight in asking the question, in debating it, then there is value. It will be a challenge to add a higher degree of certainty about the enquiry through empirical engagement, and we enthusiastically invite that sort of research from others. Prior to that, we believe that there are additional, and equally important, ways of approaching valuable insights.

Certainly some excellent scholars are beginning to do so: Zelekha et al. (2014) focus on the impact of religious institutions generally on entrepreneurship through a quantitative analysis, and find clear evidence that different religious institutions have a significantly different impact on the tendency to become an entrepreneur. They propose empirical evidence in which a country's main religion significantly influences its level of entrepreneurship at the macro level, in addition to theorising about the mechanisms that characterise the effects of religion on entrepreneurship. However, when they suggest that such large-scale effects of religion underpin a country's dominant culture and institutions, as well as the logics of the dominant cultural artefacts within it, they do not greatly enhance what thinkers of many sorts have known from time immemorial. It is not new to observe that religious institutions affect social behaviour, including economic and entrepreneurial activity; neither is it sufficient to explain this through social science methods using statistical analysis. We have always known that religion affects economic behaviour; Zelekha et al. take us no closer to knowing why this is true.

Other work presses further. Gümüşay (2014) offers a different conceptualisation and approach. Here, entrepreneurship from an Islamic perspective is framed in ways specifically different from other entrepreneurial contexts, and rests on three pillars: entrepreneurial, socio-economic and ethical, and religio-spiritual. Again, the idea is that Islam 'shapes' entrepreneurship at all levels; although here no overly intricate attempt is made to prove this. Instead, Islam is said to be 'an entrepreneurial religion' insofar as 'it enables and encourages entrepreneurial activity' (ibid.: 5). However, we do not know how it does this, and why it works; in other words, by considering Islamic examples, how it can become a model for learning how to become entrepreneurial and learning how to be more self-aware as a leader is an intriguing and fresh notion. Gümüşay concludes that entrepreneurship from an Islamic perspective is 'a core activity within a global entrepreneurial landscape, a multi-dynamic concept transforming as context changes' (ibid.: 8). The further research required to confront the challenges Gümüşay raises is necessarily interdisciplinary; pushing beyond the tools and techniques of most entrepreneurship research, rooted as that has been in mono-disciplinary methods, is an appropriately entrepreneurial turn.

These two recent sources, Zelekha et al. (2014) on the one hand and Gümüşay (2014) on the other, represent the twin poles of research into entrepreneurial leadership within an Islamic perspective: one attempts to be highly scientific and empirical, the other more ethics-oriented and conceptual. Is there some value in combining the two perspectives? How might we complement a still rigorous proof process with a more interdisciplinary and humanistic conceptualisation?

Gümüşay's framework suggests that an approach which is less oriented around the individual entrepreneur, or on how they learn to be entrepreneurial, and more oriented to a social-cultural perspective, might be more valid. This is also suggested by the idea that context at its most broad is the dominant influence on shaping everything within it; so we should examine and understand that broad context first. Some attention has been paid in the anthropology literature to the influence of contemporary Muslim subjectivities on economic practice (Hefner, 1998; Osella and Osella, 2009; Rudnyckyj, 2009; Sloane, 1999; Soares, 2005). Osella and Osella (2009) particularly look at the intersection of Islam, entrepreneurship and leadership, and stress that current modes of enquiry into this intersection are inadequate to explain how it works, and why it is significant:

> By promoting modern education among Muslims, entrepreneurs seek to promote economic development while also embedding economic practices within a framework of ethics and moral responsibilities deemed to be 'Islamic'. Inscribing business into the rhetoric of the 'common good' also legitimizes claims to leadership and political influence. Orientations towards self-transformation through education, adoption of a 'systematic' lifestyle, and a generalized rationalization of practices have acquired wider currency amongst Muslims following the rise of reformist influence and are now mobilized to sustain novel forms of capital accumulation. At the same time, Islam is called upon to set moral and ethical boundaries for engagement with the neoliberal economy. Instrumentalist analyses cannot adequately explain the vast amounts of time and money which Muslim entrepreneurs put into innumerable 'social' projects. (Osella and Osella, 2009: s202)

While it is very interesting to note that 'instrumentalist analyses' cannot explain why Muslim entrepreneurs do what they do, this more anthropological enquiry attempts to explain it as an 'economic calculation' that will bring increased prosperity and power. We find this conceptualisation of entrepreneurial leadership somewhat cynical, highlighting as it does the accumulation of economic and social capital by harnessing religious custom and authority. Nonetheless, it points to the validity of taking a broad view of the topic, and of enquiring into what an Islamic social context might have to say about entrepreneurial leadership generally.

Also, it is important to stress that 'Islam' is no one thing. It is an enormously multivalent, multi-vocal counterpoint of forms, purposes, meanings, aspects, practices, and so on, widely varied around the world, practised in different ways and to differing degrees by 2 billion Muslims in a hugely varying set of socio-cultural environments and influences. Of course Muslims everywhere are affected by these other contextual forces as well as by Islam, and also by numerous factors such as education, physical environment, ethnicity, gender, and so on. This chapter in no way assumes a unitary conceptualisation of Islam, except to indicate that as a lens through which to conceptualise entrepreneurial leadership it has been inappropriately neglected, and that there is considerable relevance in exploring how Islamic perspectives can help to widen our insights.

THEORIES ABOUT THE SOCIAL CONTEXT OF ENTREPRENEURSHIP

At its most basic, entrepreneurship is 'the pursuit of opportunity without regard to the resources currently controlled' (Stevenson, 1983, p. 1). In slightly more detail, entrepreneurship concerns the environment conditioning opportunity, the process of discovering opportunity, the evaluation and exploitation of opportunity, and the individual decision-makers who do these things (Shane and Venkataraman, 2000). In an inherently resource-constrained context such as that in which most entrepreneurs are (almost by definition) operating, manifold obstacles prevent other actors from perceiving and pursuing opportunities, because of obstructed access to resources and the presence of social risks; whereas entrepreneurs perceive these conditions not as constraints but as opportunities.

Do these theoretical models appropriately accommodate the social context of entrepreneurship? An early enquiry into this raised questions (Shapero and Sokol, 1982) but encouraged other scholars. For instance, the theory of embeddedness concerns the role of entrepreneurs within society and its informal institutions such as family and gender. For

Granovetter (1985) almost any research, of any sort, underplays the social context of human actions despite being inextricably embedded in it. For Aldrich and Cliff (2003: 573), 'transformations in the institution of the family have implications for the emergence of new business opportunities, opportunity recognition, business start-up decisions, and the resource mobilisation process'. Similarly, Jack and Anderson (2002: 476) note that 'being embedded in the social structure creates opportunity and improves performance', and that 'embedding enabled the entrepreneurs to use the specifics of the environment. Thus, both recognition and realisation of opportunity are conditioned by the entrepreneur's role in the social structure.'

Building on the notion that the social context conditions the development of competencies, our research in Pakistan takes up the theoretical challenge of investigating entrepreneurial competencies within a specific social context that is constrained by aspects of Islamic tradition (Roomi and Harrison, 2010). The findings point to the importance of culturally conditioned networks as a means of pursuing and accessing resources not currently controlled. Empirical work from Sri Lanka demonstrates that an ability to mobilise scarce resources is more important to success in new venturing than innovative ideas, and that most important of all is an ability to extract value from social networks (Kodithuwakku and Rosa, 2002). This might have negative implications for entrepreneurs in Islamic societies insofar as their access to networks of social capital can be impeded by certain Islamic socio-cultural norms, which in turn limits their access to other forms of capital; or it might have positive implications if social capital is conceived and appropriately identified actually to enable access to capital. Either way, can we deduce from this theoretical debate that entrepreneurs anywhere are equally embedded within their social structures? Are these models theoretically relevant in the context of Islamic societies?

WHY STUDY ISLAMIC ENTREPRENEURIAL LEADERSHIP?

Currently, there are about 2 billion Muslims on the planet, out of a total of about 7.125 billion people (World Bank, 2014); thus Muslims represent more than a quarter of the world's population, and are more numerous than the populations of China and Brazil combined.[1] Also, this number is growing at 2.5 per cent per annum: 43 per cent of Muslims are currently under 25; by 2050, 53 per cent will be under 18; so the growth and the rate will continue to accelerate. Even earlier, by 2025, the UK will be one-third

Muslim (for other demographic indicators about the global Muslim population, see Pew Research Center (2009, 2011, 2012)).

Globally, Muslim industry comprises over $2 trillion. The *halal* food sector alone in 2011 was $800 billion: comparable to the $900 billion global automotive industry, bigger than either India or China (Temporal, 2011). Adding in other sectors such as Islamic finance increases the figure considerably, and it will continue to rise as some areas of Islamic business grow at double-digit rates. Whatever its exact size, Muslim industry comprises a 'vertical segment' in which there are no dominant corporate models, no easy means or points of entry for Western corporations, and no clear understanding of how the numerous, disaggregated entities that constitute the economies in most Muslim regions, nations and societies even operate, much less get started as entrepreneurial ventures. The implications of this ignorance are considerable. Imagine not sufficiently understanding how Japanese businesses or socio-economic patterns work? Had scholars and practitioners missed the opportunity to learn from them in the 1960s and 1970s, and to improve operations, manufacturing, supply chain management, and so on, the world would be very different today. Moreover, in contrast to the comparatively coherent example of Japan, 'Islam' is a vastly complex set of categories that must also be understood in the context of other concurrent cultural patterns; the warp to many wefts.

Generally we need better insights, theoretical and methodological, to pursue our understanding of the enabling environment for entrepreneurship in Islamic regions which are themselves widely diverse. The basic foundations of management and entrepreneurship theory seem ill equipped for this task, and will require contributions from other disciplines such as history, sociology, anthropology and political science to proceed (Goody, 1996). The tenets of the religion, moreover, are less at issue than the many varieties of cultural context represented by the full spectrum of Islamic social values and traditions (Carswell and Rolland, 2004; Goody, 1996; Greenblatt, 2010), and by those with which it interacts. Thus, when we speak about Islamic entrepreneurship, we are speaking not only about a religious or spiritually determined view of entrepreneurship, but also about a dynamic network of social contexts for the understanding of entrepreneurial activity. Islam comprises a major set of social forces – even if only for reasons of sheer demographic quantity – and we need to consider how this will alter our understanding of other, major intersecting social forces such as entrepreneurship and leadership.

More specifically, most research on entrepreneurship looks at the phenomenon without much respect for cultural context. As we will see below, especially in the section on 'cultural approaches', there are only limited means of accommodating cultural perspectives in entrepreneurship research and, by extension, entrepreneurial development efforts. Whether we are talking about Islamic or Japanese or gay or youth 'culture', or anything comparable, current theory and research dispute how these concepts help to explain, and shape, entrepreneurial activity. Again, entrepreneurial theory is not quite up to the task of shaping entrepreneurial development in cultural environments substantially different from that in which such theory has been evolving, and we feel it is important – given the rapid expansion of highly varied Muslim cultural impacts in the world – to contribute this new dimension to entrepreneurship research.

Another good reason to study Islamic entrepreneurship in general, in addition to the fact that it is not properly conceptualised in current research, is that it is also not properly quantified. Most work creates the impression, or states, that there is less entrepreneurship (both relatively and absolutely) in certain regions dominated by Islamic societies, for example the Middle East (Essers and Benschop, 2009; GEM, 2014). Despite this, it is possible to argue that the great bulk of economic activity in the Muslim world is in fact entrepreneurial, at least in a broad sense of the term. The contribution of small firms to the gross domestic product (GDP) of most Muslim-dominated countries is above 50 per cent, and is even as high as 76 per cent in Egypt. Admittedly, in some significant countries the opposite is true: Saudi Arabia, for example, scores only an approximate 29 per cent (SRCC, 2003, cited in Kayed and Hassan, 2013: 266). Oil accounts for this difference. In countries without oil, there are few other dominant industries and the bulk of economic activity consists of disaggregated small or 'factor-driven' micro-enterprises, dominated by subsistence agriculture and extraction businesses, with a heavy reliance on labour and natural resources (WEF, 2014). Moreover, the Global Entrepreneurship Monitor (GEM) notes that 'unregistered businesses, in fact, can compose as much as 80 per cent of economic activity in developing countries' (GEM, 2014). An earlier GEM report stresses that even in Saudi Arabia with its low entrepreneurial contribution to GDP, over 75 per cent of the population perceive significant entrepreneurial opportunity (GEM, 2010: 19). As in Egypt and Iran, the potential for job creation from entrepreneurial activity is very high in the kingdom because the pressure to diversify the economy is mounting (GEM Home Page, 2014).

From a leadership perspective, there have been calls from the more rigorous voices in the research community to deal with issues of universal relevance. Gupta et al. (2004) state that 'there has emerged an increasing need for entrepreneurial leaders', and thus an increasing need to understand what they are and how they emerge. However, they go on to say that the cultural referent for existing theory is too narrow:

We feel that this increasing need for entrepreneurial leadership is not confined to the US, or even the so-called Anglo cultures, but is something which pervades all economies in our increasingly global society. We need to explore the extent to which the underlying concepts are similar and where they differ from culture to culture. (Gupta et al., 2004: 7)

They give some examples of research pointing in promising directions:

For instance Hartog et al. (1999, p. 225) find evidence to the effect that universal endorsement of a leadership prototype does not preclude cultural differences of such a prototype . . . The environmental perceptions are moderated by the values and beliefs of the respondents, as well as situational conditions, as is suggested by the information processing perspective. (Shaw, 1990: 631)

Gupta et al. (2004: 7) strongly imply that without a wider span of reference, the validity of such research is limited: 'therefore in the development and validation of the entrepreneurial leadership construct, an important issue is the extent to which it operates across contexts like culture, industry, geography and circumstances'.

Building on Hofstede's (1980) explorations of cultural difference, much work has been done with Project GLOBE (Global Leadership and Organizational Behavior Effectiveness Research) (House et al., 2002; Javidan et al., 2010; Javidan and Dastmalchian, 2009; Javidan et al., 2006), including some testing of its ideas and findings by other researchers specifically concentrating on Islamic societal clusters, especially in Arabian and Southern Asian cultures (see, especially, Kennedy, 2002; Mansor and Kennedy, 2000; Dastmalchian et al., 2001; Neal et al., 2005). One problem with this body of work is that its societal clusters mingle Islamic and non-Islamic cultures: for example, 'Southern Asia' includes Iran together with Malaysia, Thailand and the Philippines; 'sub-Saharan Africa' includes Nigeria and South Africa, both of which are highly syncretic societies; and even the 'Middle East' cluster includes relatively liberal and multicultural societies such as Turkey and Egypt, but not Saudi Arabia. Also, none of this work includes Islamic social groups embedded in other dominant cultures, such as Muslims in the United Kingdom, France or Germany, for example. So with its emphasis on these clusters, and on countries, this work on leadership and culture is of limited relevance when trying to understand the contextual influence of a specifically Islamic identity on entrepreneurial leadership. Furthermore, in all of these cases and others (and there are relatively few of them), the extent to which a model of entrepreneurial leadership is varied by any version of an Islamic cultural context is not explicitly discussed. For example, Gerstener and Day (1994), who specifically set out to engage in cross-cultural comparison, do not consider at all the countries where

Islam is prevalent (the only approximation is India, but its Islamic sub-cultures are not acknowledged). Beekun and Badawi (1999) do take a specifically Islamic perspective on leadership, but a very theological one, and do not discuss the entrepreneurial context. Generally speaking, the leadership literature, even the strands dealing with culture, do not accommodate Islam and engage even less with the project of understanding Islamic entrepreneurial leadership.

So, why study Islamic entrepreneurial leadership? Reasons include the number of Muslims worldwide; the amount of entrepreneurial activity in the Muslim world; and the lack of understanding of how it is led. Research on how to create and sustain an appropriately Islamic entrepreneurial environment is of vital importance for the continuing development of many world regions. Though we do not propose our own model of Islamic entrepreneurial leadership here, we do argue strongly that one is needed. We offer a critique of the inadequate few that have been proposed by others, in order properly to understand entrepreneurial leadership in an Islamic context and to determine the best means of promoting more of it.

HOW TO STUDY ISLAMIC ENTREPRENEURSHIP?

One way to consider how to study Islamic entrepreneurship is to consider history. Kuran (2008, 2012), reviewing the differing interpretations of the role of entrepreneurship in Middle East history, points out that some sources see Islam as inhibitive because it fosters fatalism, conservatism and conformity (Lewis, 2002; Patai, 1983; Sayigh, 1958). However, he also demonstrates that other sources see the opposite: that Islam promotes shared risk-taking; creative experimentation in science, technology and economics; and that its scriptures and commentaries actively encourage trade as a religious and social responsibility (Sadeq, 1990; Siddiqui, 1979). As Kuran notes, each of these readings is selective and incomplete. On balance, though, he inclines to the view that the effect of Islam on entrepreneurship – at least in the Middle East – is more inhibitive than developmental. His reasoning is that 'decisions to innovate depend on institutions', and that 'no matter how motivated people are to take chances, if they cannot raise capital, or their entrepreneurial rewards are insecure, they will turn their energies elsewhere' (Kuran, 2008: 2). This seems debateable. Three points that are central to Kuran's argument – namely institutions, markets and culture – are often defined and represented rather differently in much entrepreneurship literature, so Kuran's approach is worth questioning.

In what follows we try to look deeper at each point separately and to situate them better in entrepreneurship and leadership research. Kuran (2008: 2) has stated that 'the supply of entrepreneurship depends on the suitability of the prevailing institutions to the challenges at hand'. Again, this is heavily interpretative. It seems to imply that economic activity in the Islamic Middle East is well suited to small-scale entrepreneurial activity but incapable of scaling up to an industrial level. Since this definition of entrepreneurship is somewhat limited, Kuran's explanation of the effects of Islam upon entrepreneurial development seems incomplete. Kuran (2008: 4) cites Casson (2003) on entrepreneurs as people who 'create new markets . . . enhance their productivity in existing ones . . . generate new forms of organizations, find novel ways to deploy the new forms, and initiate refinements'. This is a reasonable definition of entrepreneurship but it is not the only one, and it is itself quite limited. It concentrates on the person, for example, not the personality or the process or the context or, indeed, anything else. Entrepreneurs can also be defined by what they do, not necessarily who they are or why they are that way. Moreover, the idea of entrepreneurship is not defined, but instead is derived from the identity of entrepreneurs. The argument seems to be that if there are few entrepreneurs, there is little entrepreneurship. This is circular, and one could equally argue it the other way around: with little entrepreneurship there will be fewer entrepreneurs. It is in any case descriptive, and not explanatory, of the nature of entrepreneurship. Thus, it is unfair to jump to the idea that Middle Eastern Islamic institutions have historically and systematically suppressed entrepreneurial activity and the population of entrepreneurs, insofar as commercial practices and contract law did not evolve significantly between the tenth and seventeenth centuries (CE). From evidence about the lack of development in contract law, Kuran (2012; see also Lewis, 2002) deduces 'institutional stagnation' as an inhibitive factor on entrepreneurship, without extensively exploring whether some other shared constraint has inhibited both entrepreneurship and the evolution of institutions. There is no proof of causality here. In any case, explaining the lack of entrepreneurial activity through the paucity of change in contract law as a proxy for the entire Islamic institutional environment is a very specific approach, based on a tight definition of entrepreneurship. This general critique of work such as Kuran's has been levelled elsewhere, for example Ul-Haq and Westwood (2012), arguing that it repeats orientalist tropes of the backwardness of Muslim societies and institutions.

ALTERNATE THEORETICAL APPROACHES TO ENTREPRENEURIAL LEADERSHIP

We suggest that Kuran's work does not offer sufficiently specific recommendations for stimulating entrepreneurship in the Middle East, largely because of his conceptualisation of entrepreneurship and of how it relates to Islam. We propose to strengthen this analysis by examining three alternate bodies of theory about entrepreneurial leadership: institutional, market-oriented and cultural.

Neo-institutional theory derived from North (1990) has been exceedingly influential in thinking about organisations and their leadership in a broader context. It has also given rise to the idea that the role of institutions is limited, as outlined by Khanna and colleagues in the notion of institutional 'voids' (Khanna and Rivkin, 2006; Khanna and Palepu, 2000, 1997; Khanna et al., 2005). Other sources posit a more nuanced understanding of how markets form without, or around, institutions (Mair et al., 2012; Dorado and Ventresca, 2013). Thinking about the connections between these perspectives allows us to situate analysis specifically in cultures infused with Islam whose observable entrepreneurship activity is not explained by dominant models.

Institutional Approaches

Northian neo-institutional theory has for some time strongly influenced development economics (Grief, 2006; Ogilvie, 2011; Rodrik, 2008; Sen, 1999; Toye, 1995), as well as management and leadership studies (DiMaggio and Powell, 1991). There are also some fairly recent studies connecting it to entrepreneurial leadership, including Veciana and Urbano's (2008) research. The questions approached by neo-institutional theory are fundamental: why in the long term do some countries grow while others stagnate? Inefficient outcomes persist in economic activity because all economic agents must act on incomplete information; where formal or informal institutions exist to render that asymmetry a benefit rather than a deficit, growth occurs. Entrepreneurial leaders, for example, can be construed as the sort of agents that benefit from economic inefficiency – being able to profit from conditions of uncertainty and risk – and thus represent (informal) institutional drivers of growth.

Some writers, following North's work, look less at institutions themselves and more at the spaces around them, or replacing them. The term 'institutional void' has acquired a degree of currency; it can be defined as a situation where institutional arrangements that support markets are absent, weak or lack meaning, or do not accomplish the role expected of them. This is derived to some extent from the work of Polanyi and followers (Hann and Hart, 2009; Polanyi, 1944). The idea of the institutional void has been identified as both a barrier to entrepreneurship (without supporting institutions, entrepreneurship cannot flourish) and an enabler (without supporting institutions, entrepreneurs find ways to flourish while others flounder). The relationship between institutions and entrepreneurship is either 'because of' or 'in spite of', and debate continues about which interpretation is best.

Obviously, neo-institutional theory is enormously more complex than this, but connecting it to entrepreneurial leadership theory in this way allows us to return to the line of enquiry into whether Islamic institutions drive growth or inhibit it. Is this influence mutable at different times, and in different places? Does neo-institutional theory help to explain entrepreneurial activity in an Islamic cultural context, and can this be the basis for a systematic understanding of entrepreneurial leadership?

For a start, does it allow us to look at the right institutions? Does Islamic 'culture' constitute of a set of formal and informal institutions? Concepts such as *musharakah* (مشاركة†) and *mudarabah* (مضاربة†), for example, betoken radically different conceptualisations of risk and venturing, in which risk is shared more or less equally, and complications of agency that so affect the relationship between investor and entrepreneur are diffused. Even the word '*rizk*' – which might be etymologically related to the English word 'risk', and can be translated loosely as 'sustenance' or 'provision' or even 'adventure' – emphasises that everything someone has or does comes not from their own effort, but from God; this is a very different notion of 'risk' as it more familiarly applies to the practice of entrepreneurial venturing and leadership. Moreover, all of these notions are very much enshrined in Islamic law and practice, albeit to widely differing degrees in many countries. In Sudan and Saudi Arabia, an Islamic regulatory environment is explicit; while in the Gulf and South East Asia it runs in parallel with other systems; and in countries such as Egypt and Jordan it is neither supported nor opposed (Sherbiny, 1986). It is worth enquiring into how these notions, formally or informally, explicitly or implicitly, condition the structure of entrepreneurial ventures as well as the practice of leadership within them. It behoves us all, as such conceptualisations disseminate more broadly and variously around the globe, to understand them, how they work and how they define entrepreneurial leadership.

In light of this, it is dispiriting to see Kuran state that some Islamic institutions inhibit entrepreneurial activity. Islamic entrepreneurs do raise capital (often from family and tribal networks, at times on a large scale), and their rewards are secure and balance risk (albeit in ways different from non-Islamic ones, according to the notions of *musharakah* and *mudarabah* and *rizk*; see, for example, Rodinson (1966 [1978])). Capital and security happen; if not in the same manner as in Silicon Valley, then in ways and through channels that look perhaps less specifically 'institutional' and more 'cultural' if one stands outside of the cultural context of those institutions. In any case, it will take more thought and research to explore this issue properly.

A bottom-up approach of practice-led research in an institutional context is certainly emerging as an appropriate and rigorous methodology. Smets et al. (2011) observe that change originates in the everyday work of individuals, which then results in a shift of field-level logic. By concentrating on the earliest moments of change that extant research neglects, and by contesting existing accounts that focus on 'active entrepreneurship', they highlight the importance of observing what is happening right before our eyes, but not currently part of our understanding. Their study is 'the first empirical multi-level account of the reciprocal relationships between micro-level practices and field-level logics' (ibid.: 880) and is a suggestive model for confronting the challenge of accommodating the increasingly unavoidable Islamic context into the field-level logic of entrepreneurial leadership.

Another methodological model is research conducted by Armour and Cumming (2006), who explore options available to policy-makers seeking to replicate the success of Silicon Valley and question whether establishing institutions, such as deep and liquid stock markets, is the right approach to enabling innovation. They use rigorous empirical means to show that government programmes more often hinder rather than help the development of private equity; that liberal bankruptcy laws stimulate entrepreneurial demand for venture capital; and that the legal environment matters as much as the strength of stock markets. These comprehensive results suggest that although institutional conditions might be necessary for enabling entrepreneurship, they are not sufficient; and also suggest that similar rigour applied to the analysis of comparable environmental factors, such as cultural factors, might reveal similarly stimulating effects (see also Casson, 2003; De la Costa and Coulson, 1965). We cannot know until we test it, but certainly the legal 'culture' of Islam is highly distinct from that of Silicon Valley in any variety or expression. Further, the formal Islamic laws governing entrepreneurial finance, and the informal narratives of leadership as well as the more formal Islamic cultures and institutions themselves, vary enormously around the world, especially in the extent to which financial systems and banking policy are incorporated in a country's legal system (Sherbiny, 1986). However, these variations as a whole, as much as any individual instance, remain understudied. A specifically Islamic environment, in whatever form it takes, matters as much as other institutional factors, formal and informal, to the development of entrepreneurial leadership capacity. Moving in this direction, the findings of recent work looking specifically at the Middle East and North Africa (MENA) region suggest that 'the pattern of internationalisation into antagonistic environments with scarce infrastructure' demonstrates how entrepreneurial leaders specifically target markets with weak institutions to identify, evaluate and exploit opportunities (Hatem, 2012). This is an important new data set, unique in being a compilation of rapidly internationalising MENA enterprises, and although it does not explicitly explore how entrepreneurial leadership itself is influenced by Islam, will provide a basis for further study of entrepreneurial leadership that is informed by both institutionalism and Islam.

Neo-institutional theory suggests other angles on Islamic entrepreneurial leadership worth exploring empirically. Friedland and Alford (1991) include Christianity in their assessment of the institutional logics governing organisational activity in society. Organisations include and respond to multiple institutional logics, including religion (Greenwood et al., 2010; Greenwood et al., 2011), and institutions themselves change as multiple logics recombine in ways determined by evolving practice (Smets et al., 2011; Pache and Santos, 2010), including the 'practice' of faith-based logics. Inside this swirl of institutional complexity, the entrepreneurial leader, with a generally high tolerance for uncertainty, sits perhaps more comfortably than another sort of actor. And within Islamic institutions, deriving as they do from a context denoted by the very name 'submission', is the Islamic entrepreneurial leader essentially empowered where others might be confounded? An institutional approach, more nuanced and practice-led and grounded in an understanding of the Islamic context, suggests this might be so.

Market Approaches

Some recent work has reframed this debate by looking at the complexity of institutions, and how their origins can be 'traced back to a complex knitting together of practices and beliefs that are associated with the communal/societal, political, and religious spheres' (Mair et al., 2012; see also Dorado and Ventresca, 2013). This approach offers insights into how entrepreneurial activity actually occurs within cultural contexts that do not readily fit Western notions of market economies. The findings go beyond the formation, infrastructure and role of institutions, by highlighting the activity and work involved in market building. In other words, they help to explain how entrepreneurship develops within specific social-cultural contexts, without presuming that Western-derived models of entrepreneurial development necessarily apply in non-Western environments. This work suggests that the development of entrepreneurial leadership capacity will need to prioritise cultural factors over institutional ones, including those derived from or operating with Islam.

How does this work on market formation apply to the challenge of entrepreneurial leadership development in an Islamic context? As market architecture is reinterpreted, and indeed remade, as new actors are legitimated and enter the market, the resulting activity is essentially entrepreneurial and determined by the deep, thick complexity of cultural factors including Islam. Islamic entrepreneurship can be better explained by this sort of market-oriented, culturally rooted theorising than by traditional entrepreneurship research or classical institutional and development theory, not least because it acknowledges the myriad different influences of cultural context on entrepreneurial activity in an integrated way. It will be important, when feasible, to test this market model of entrepreneurial leadership development in a specifically Islamic empirical context.

Cultural Approaches

We want to stress again that we are treating Islam as a set of socio-cultural phenomena, although other scholars consider religion and management generally (Chan-Serafin et al., 2013; Gundolf and Filser, 2013; King, 2008; Tracey, 2012; El Garah et al., 2012). While some focus on religion and entrepreneurship directly (Dana, 2010; Dodd and Gotsis, 2007; Dodd and Seaman, 1998; Kayed and Hassan, 2013; Audretsch and Bönte, 2007), they do so by regarding entrepreneurship through lenses such as spirituality, theology, ethics, and the like. Very few engage holistically with the intersection of Islam and entrepreneurship (Adas, 2006; Gümüşay, 2014; Kayed and Hassan, 2013; Sloane, 1999), or take the view, with Adas (2006: 113), that 'a new synthesis between religion and capitalism is unfolding where culture has not been outdone but is creatively transformed and integrated to capitalism'.

In the case of Islam, there are many reasons why we feel that a different approach is appropriate, not least because Islam represents itself in a more holistic way as more than spirituality, more than religion, but as 'a complete way of life':

> not only concerned with the spiritual upliftment of human beings, it is equally concerned about their material and physical well-being. Islam guides its followers in financial and economic matters, in social and political affairs, and also in moral and personal spheres of human life . . . Islam is a compact system of life in which all its aspects (religious, ideological, social, political and ethical) are well synchronized. (Rizvi, 1993)

Other Islamic thinkers make this same point in various ways: Muhammad Iqbal, for example, poet-philosopher and political hero in Pakistan, wrote on Islam as a political and legal philosophy as well as a religion; different from Christianity and Hinduism, Islam consisted integrally of legal and civic concepts that are integral to the spiritual ones (Iqbal, 1934).

In a special issue of *Entrepreneurship Theory and Practice* exploring the relationship between entrepreneurship and culture, the editors point to 'substantial gaps in our knowledge of this relationship' and adopt broad definitions: 'culture is . . . the enduring set of values of a nation, a region, or an organization' (George and Zahra, 2002: 5). This, like most other research on culture and entrepreneurship, looks comparatively at behavioural indicators for certain traits (locus of control, need for achievement, and so on), thereby reading culture rather differently as an aggregation of personality characteristics in a population, assessed and analysed through psychometrics. Even George and Zahra themselves (George et al., 2002) concentrate on behavioural research, rather than on models of cultural analysis, and point out that in any case, twenty-one previous studies of entrepreneurial culture have mainly relied on the problematic conceptualisation of national culture advanced by Hofstede (1980). Looking beyond behaviour at an organisational level, Edgar Schein's (1985) work on culture, though enormously influential, cannot easily be extrapolated above the organisation to larger units of analysis; the same is true for other organisational researchers whom he influenced (Altman and Baruch, 1998; O'Reilly et al., 1991; Smircich, 1983).

It is worth enquiring whether more analytical models for studying culture and entrepreneurship than the behavioural and organisational ones highlighted above can be applied in a cultural landscape infused by Islam. Little has been written in English, and while there is much that is interesting and suggestive in Adas (2006), the range of reference is largely confined to Turkey and a Turkish form of Islamism. A recent review of entrepreneurship training literature by Saudi Arabian authors does not mention an Islamic social context at all (Azim and Al-Kahtani, 2014). One other, bigger study pushes further and considers Islamic entrepreneurship directly, and it is to this that we now turn. Though mainly focused on Saudi Arabia, Kayed and Hassan (2013) develop the idea that there is a specifically Islamic form of entrepreneurial leadership, and that Islamic approaches to economic activity are coming into greater prominence and stability. A values-based argument, rather than a behavioural one, their work is methodologically less rigorous. Also, as it deliberately sets out to raise the profile of a Saudi understanding of Islamic entrepreneurship and to promote economic alternatives for Islamic nations that are overdependent upon extractive or manufacturing industries, it pursues a fairly strong social development agenda. Nonetheless, it suggests that a model of entrepreneurship inflected by Islamic perspectives might be possible and beneficial to improving our understanding of entrepreneurial leadership in general.

A general theme of 'modernisation without Westernisation' governs this enquiry, as it seeks a source in the tenets of a specific sort of Islam for the observable entrepreneurial activity in certain societies, and for the developmental trajectory of future economic well-being. In other words, if Japan and South Korea, for example, can innovate in ways that are uniquely Japanese and Korean, but still compete head-to-head with Western innovation systems (Dore and Whittaker, 2001; Freeman, 1995; Friedland and Alford, 1991), can we find this potential in the wide variety of Islamic societies as well? In addition, where we find economic potential in Islamic countries being under-realised, as in Malaysia for example, how can we explain the problem (Yusuf & Nabeshima, 2011)? In approaching such questions, Kayed and Hassan separate themselves from much main-stream entrepreneurship and leadership literatures. Instead of discussing economic empowerment, or related concepts, they embed the culminating sections of their analysis in the Islamic concepts of *falah* (حالف) and *tawhid* (ديحوت), which they translate as human well-being and the unity of God, and which derive to some extent from the work of Islamic economic writers (Chapra, 1993, 2000; Sardar, 1997; Siddiqui, 1979). Even without discussing the spiritual dimension (which is evidently important in their analysis), it is possible to see alignment between the work of Kayed and Hassan and that of socio-economists attempting to reconnect economic theory with humanistic values (Backhouse, 2011; Bronk, 2011; Easterlin, 1995; Geroski, 2003; Kagan, 2011; Nelson, 2006). Though these sections of their book are less well argued than others, being grounded less in research or theory and more on theological interpretation, nonetheless they point toward a structured 'model' of entrepreneurial leadership that is notably different from ones not rooted in Islamic religious and cultural values.

Kayed and Hassan's specific model for Islamic entrepreneurship is interesting, if rather too intricate. Its key element appears to be the notion of balance between common obligation and self-interest. This is nothing new, and hardly unique to Islam in general; and it could apply equally to Weber's conceptualisation of the Protestant work ethic, for example, which has been intensively analysed (Furnham, 1984), empirically (Furnham, 1990; Furnham et al., 1993; Miller et al., 2002) and even in a few old cases with reference to a Muslim context (Bellah, 1963; De la Costa and Coulson, 1965; Furnham and Muhiudeen, 1984). All this work observes that where inputs are informed by Islamic social forces as opposed to others, their outputs will be distinctive. That basic understanding is absent from, or at best only implied in, other models of entrepreneurial development.

Kayed and Hassan root their model of entrepreneurship in Islamic culture by filtering two strands of entrepreneurial theory – behaviour and attitude – through a lens of specifically Saudi Islamic values, traditions and customs, and look for consistencies and inconsistencies. Entrepreneurs who can be seen to behave in certain ways inconsistent with these particular Islamic values are not Islamic entrepreneurs, even if they happen to be Muslims living and working in a Muslim society. This is somewhat tautological, but it is interesting as a mode of analysis in its difference from other models that seek to explain entrepreneurship by other means, including personality, behaviour, institutions, markets, and so on. More specifically, Kayed and Hassan denote two 'pro-entrepreneurship' institutions – religion and family – as generative, and not just tolerant, of entrepreneurial activity. Because of these factors, Islam is for them, too, 'an entrepreneurial religion' (Kayed and Hassan, 2013: 299). Similarly, they see the family-based, tribal structure of society as conducive to a notion of shared risk and reward, and to certain notions of return and value that are consistent with (and perhaps even derived from) *halal* parameters (ibid.: 300). This is indicative, or at least suggestive, of a specifically Islamic entrepreneurship.

Why might (or might not) a culturally informed model of entrepreneurial leadership development be more valid than other approaches, such as those informed by institutions and markets? Essentially, for all their limitations, Kayed and Hassan helpfully suggest that classical varieties of entrepreneurship theory do not readily explain entrepreneurial leadership activity in any Islamic cultural context. Behavioural and organisational analysis conceptualise both entrepreneurship and leadership in ways inconsistent with Islam, and fail to offer the field-level logics to explain the entrepreneurial leadership we see in Islamic societies. Similarly, theory that explains entrepreneurial activity mainly through institutions cannot easily identify ways to move beyond comparatively low levels of development and competitiveness in most Islamic nations. In reality there is plenty of entrepreneurial leadership in Islamic societies, if we can but adjust our lenses for detecting and explaining it. While the institutional barriers seem not to pose as much of a problem as they are supposed to, we do not know why this is the case. This leads us to ask two questions. First, how can we explain what we see? And second, how can we harness this unsystematic activity and channel it into a more comprehensive understanding of Islamic entrepreneurial leadership?

CONCLUSION

Gümüşay (2014: 8) observes, that 'religion matters in practice – it should also in theory'. Our review of theory suggests that diffuse cultural forces are highly determinant of the sustainability of any systematic attempt to encourage entrepreneurship and to develop entrepreneurial leadership. Essentially, the challenge faced in many Islamic environments is to enable an appropriate environment for entrepreneurial leadership; and for those interacting with or in those socio-cultural contexts, the challenge is to understand how they adapt dominant models of entrepreneurial leadership. Until there is more empirical research of the practice-led sort represented by Smets et al. (2011) that will change the field-level logic of entrepreneurial leadership in general, we do not feel ready to propose a model of Islamic entrepreneurial leadership ourselves. For now, we feel that it is important to suggest that current direction in research and policy could be based on richer and stronger theoretical grounds, and that the few models proposed in the literature could be improved. Traditional models of entrepreneurship are inappropriate to an Islamic cultural context, and the emerging models are not yet fit for purpose. Until we understand why this is, and how these models might be adjusted, efforts to promote entrepreneurial leadership in Islamic environments will have limited success.

NOTE

1. Brazil: 200 361 925; China: 1 357 380 000; India: 1 252 139 596.

REFERENCES

Adas, E. (2006). The making of entrepreneurial Islam and the Islamic spirit of capitalism. *Journal for Cultural Research* 10 (2), 113–37.
Aldrich, H. and Cliff, J. (2003). The pervasive effects of family on entrepreneurship: towards a family embeddedness perspective. *Journal of Business Venturing* 19 (5), 573–96.
Altman, Y. and Baruch, Y. (1998). Cultural theory and organizations: analytical method and cases. *Organization Studies* 19 (5), 769–85.
Armour, J. and Cumming, D. (2006). The legislative road to Silicon Valley. *Oxford Economic Papers* 58 (4), 596–635.
Audretsch, D. and Bönte, W. (2007). Religion and entrepreneurship. CEPR Discussion Paper, 6378.
Azim, M. and Al-Kahtani, A. (2014). Entrepreneurship education and training: a survey of the literature. *Life Science Journal* 11 (1), 127–35.
Backhouse, R. (2011). *The Puzzle of Modern Economics: Science or Ideology.* Cambridge: Cambridge University Press.
Beekun, R. and Badawi, J. (1999). *Leadership: An Islamic perspective.* Beltsville, MD: Amana Publications.

Bellah, R. (1963). Reflections on the Protestant Ethic analogy in Asia. *Journal of Social Issues* 19(1), 52–60.

Bronk, R. (2011). *The Romantic Economist: Imagination in Economics.* Cambridge: Cambridge University Press.

Carswell, P. and Rolland, D. (2004). The role of religion in entrepreneurship participation and peception. *International Journal of Entrepreneurship and Small Business* 1 (3/4), 280–286.

Casson, M. (2003). *The Entrepreneur: An Economic Theory.* Cheltenham, UK and Northampton, MA: Edward Elgar Publishing.

Chan-Serafin, S., Brief, A. and George, J. (2013). How does religion matter and why? Religion and the organizational sciences. *Organization Science* 24 (5), 1585–600.

Chapra, M. (1993). *Islam and Economic Development: A Strategy for Development with Justice and Stability.* Islamabad: International Institute of Islamic Thought and Islamic Research Institute.

Chapra, M. (2000). Is it necessary to have Islamic economics?. *Journal of Socio-Economics* 29 (1), 21–37.

Dana, L. (2010). *Entrepreneurship and Religion.* Cheltenham, UK and Northampton, MA: Edward Elgar Publishing.

Dastmalchian, A., Javidan, M. and Alam, K. (2001). Effective leadership and culture in Iran: An empirical study. *Applied Psychology* 50 (4), 532–58.

De la Costa, H. and Coulson, N. (1965). Religion and progress in modern Asia. In R. Bellah (ed.), *Religion and Progress in Modern Asia.* New York, NY: Free Press, pp. 489–533.

DiMaggio, P. and Powell, W. (1991). *The New Institutionalism in Organizational Analysis.* Chicago, IL: University of Chicago Press.

Dodd, S.D. and Gotsis, G. (2007). The interrelationships between religions and entrepreneurship. *International Journal of Entrepreneurship and Innovation* 8 (29), 93–112.

Dodd, S.D. and Seaman, P. (1998). Religion and enterprise: an introductory exploration. *Entrepreneurship Theory and Practice* 23 (1), 71–7.

Dorado, S. and Ventresca, M. (2013). Crescive entrepreneurship in complex social problems: institutional conditions for entrepreneurial engagement. *Journal of Business Venturing* 28 (1), 69–82.

Dore, R. and Whittaker, H. (2001). *Social Evolution, Economic Development and Culture: What It Means to Take Japan Seriously.* Cheltenham, UK and Northampton, MA: Edward Elgar Publishing.

Easterlin, R. (1995). Will raising the incomes of all increase the happiness of all?. *Journal of Economic Behavior and Organization* 27 (June), 35–8.

El Garah, W., Beekun, R., Habisch, A., Lenssen, G. and Adaui, C. (2012). Practical wisdom for management from the Islamic tradition. *Journal of Management Development* 31 (10), 991–1000.

Essers, C. and Benschop, Y. (2009). Muslim businesswomen doing boundary work: The negotiation of Islam, gender, and ethnicity in entrepreneurial contexts. *Human Relations* 62 (3), 403–23.

Freeman, C. (1995). The 'National Systems of Innovation' in historical perspective. *Cambridge Journal of Economics* 19 (1), 5–24.

Friedland, R. and Alford, R. (1991). Bringing society back in: Symbols, practices, and institutional contradictions. In P.J. DiMaggio and W. Powell (eds), *The New Institutionalism in Organizational Analysis.* Chicago, IL: University of Chicago Press, pp. 232–63.

Furnham, A. (1984). The Protestant Work Ethic: a review of the psychological literature. *European Journal of Social Psychology* 14 (1), 87–104.

Furnham, A. (1990). A content, correlational, and factor analytic study of seven questionnaire measures of the Protestant Work Ethic. *Human Relations* 43 (4), 383–99.

Furnham, A., Bond, M., Heaven, P., Hilton, D., Lobel, T., Masters, J., Payne, M., Rajamanikam, R., Stacey, B. and Van Daalen, H. (1993). A comparison of Protestant Work Ethic beliefs in thirteen nations. *Journal of Social Psychology* 133 (2), 185–97.

Furnham, A. and Muhiudeen, C. (1984). The Protestant Work Ethic in Britain and Malaysia. *Journal of Social Psychology* 122 (2), 157–61.

GEM (2010). *Global Entrepreneurship Monitor: Global Report 2010*. Wellesley, MA: Babson College and Universidad del Desarollo.
GEM (2014). *Global Entrepreneurship Monitor: Global Report 2013*. Wellesley, MA: Babson College.
GEM Home Page (2014). *Global Entrepreneurship Monitor*. Retrieved 31 July 2014 from http://m.gemconsortium.org/what-is-gem/.
George, G. and Zahra, S. (2002). Culture and its consequences for entrepreneurship. *Entrepreneurial Theory and Practice* 26 (4), 5–9.
George, G., Zahra, S. and Hayton, C. (2002). Culture and entrepreneurship: a review of behavioural research. *Entrepreneurship Theory and Practice* 26 (4), 33–53.
Geroski, P. (2003). *The Evolution of New Markets*. Oxford: Oxford University Press.
Gerstener, C. and Day, D. (1994). Cross-cultural comparison of leadership prototypes. *Leadership Quarterly* 5 (2), 121–34.
Goody, J. (1996). *The East in the West*. Cambridge: Cambridge University Press.
Granovetter, M. (1985). Economic action and social structure: the problem of embeddedness. *American Journal of Sociology* 91 (3), 481–510.
Greenblatt, S. (ed.) (2010). *Cultural Mobility*. Cambridge: Cambridge University Press.
Greenwood, R., Diaz, A., Li, S. and Lorente, J. (2010). The multiplicity of institutional logics and the heterogeneity of organizational responses. *Organization Science* 21 (2), 521–39.
Greenwood, R., Raynard, M., Kodeih, F., Micelotta, E. and Lounsbury, M. (2011). Insitutional complexity and organizational responses. *Academy of Management Annals* 5 (1), 317–71.
Grief, A. (2006). *Institutions and the Path to the Modern Economy: Lessons from Medieval Trade*. Cambridge: Cambridge University Press.
Gümüşay, A. (2015). Entrepreneurship from an Islamic perspective. *Journal of Business Ethics* 24 (4), 371–93.
Gundolf, K. and Filser, M. (2013). Management research and religion: a citation analysis. *Journal of Business Ethics* 112 (1), 177–85.
Gupta, V., MacMillan, I. and Surie, G. (2004). Entrepreneurial leadership: developing and measuring a cross-cultural construct. *Journal of Business Venturing* 19 (2), 241–60.
Hann, C. and Hart, K. (eds) (2009). *Market and Society*. Cambridge: Cambridge University Press.
Hartog, D., House, R., Hanges, P., Ruiz-Quintanilla, S. and Dorfman, P. (1999). Culture specific and cross-culturally generalizable implicit leadership theories: are attributes of charismatic/transformational leadership universally endorsed?. *Leadership Quarterly* 10 (2), 219–56.
Hatem, O. (2012). High growth and rapid internationalisation of firms from emerging markets: the case of the Middle East and North Africa (MENA) Region. 27 November. Retrieved 1 December 2014 from Edinburgh Research Archive, https://www.era.lib.ed.ac.uk/handle/1842/9894.
Hefner, R. (1998). *Market Cultures: Society and Morality in the New Asian Capitalisms*. Boulder, CO: Westview.
Hofstede, G. (1980). *Culture's Consequences: International Differences in Work-Related Values*. Beverly Hills, CA: SAGE Publications.
House, R., Javidan, M., Hanges, P. and Dorfman, P. (2002). Understanding cultures and implicit leadership theories across the globe: an introduction to project GLOBE. *Journal of World Business* 37 (1), 3–10.
Iqbal, M. (1934). *The Reconstruction of Relgious Thought in Islam*. Oxford: Oxford University Press.
Jack, S. and Anderson, A. (2002). The effects of embeddedness on the entrepreneurial process. *Journal of Business Venturing* 17 (5), 467–87.
Javidan, M. and Dastmalchian, A. (2009). Managerial implications of the GLOBE project: a study of 62 societies. *Asia Pacific Journal of Human Resources* 47 (1), 41–58.
Javidan, M., Dorfman, P., De Luque, M. and House, R. (2006). In the eye of the beholder:

cross cultural lessons in leadership from Project GLOBE. *Academy of Management Perspectives* 20 (1), 67–90.

Javidan, M., Dorfman, P., Howell, J. and Hanges, P. (2010). Leadership and cultural context: a theoretical and empirical examination based on Project GLOBE. In N. Nohria and R. Khurana (eds), *Handbook of Leadership Theory and Practice*. Cambridge, MA: Harvard Business Press, pp. 335–76.

Kagan, J. (2011). *The Three Cultures: Natural Sciences, Social Sciences, and the Humanities.* Cambridge: Cambridge University Press.

Kayed, R. and Hassan, K. (2013). *Islamic Entrepreneurship.* London: Routledge.

Kennedy, J. (2002). Leadership in Malaysia: traditional values, international outlook. *Academy of Management Executive* 16 (3), 15–26.

Khanna, T. and Palepu, K. (1997). Why focused strategies may be wrong for emerging markets. *Harvard Business Review* 75 (4), 41–51.

Khanna, T. and Palepu, K. (2000). The future of business groups in emerging markets: long-run evidence from Chile. *Academy of Management Journal* 43, 268–85.

Khanna, T., Palepu, K. and Sinha, J. (2005). Strategies that fit emerging market. *Harvard Business Review* June, 4–19.

Khanna, T. and Rivkin, J. (2006). Inter-organizational ties and business group boundaries: evidence from an emerging economy. *Organization Science* 17, 333–52.

King, J. (2008). (Dis)missing the obvious: will mainstream management research ever take religion seriously?. *Journal of Management Inquiry* 17 (2), 214–24.

Kodithuwakku, S. and Rosa, P. (2002). The entrepreneurial process and economic success in a constrained environment. *Journal of Business Venturing* 17 (5), 431–65.

Kuran, T. (2008). The scale of entrepreneurship in Middle Eastern history: inhibitive roles of Islamic institutions. Duke University Working Paper.

Kuran, T. (2012). *The Long Divergence: How Islamic Law Held Back the Middle East.* Princeton, NJ: Princeton University Press.

Lewis, B. (2002). *What Went Wrong?: Western Impact and Middle Eastern Response.* New York, NY: Oxford University Press.

Mair, J., Martí, I. and Ventresca, M. (2012). Building inclusive markets in rural Bangladesh: how intermediaries work institutional voids. *Academy of Management Journal* 55 (4), 819–50.

Mansor, N. and Kennedy, J. (2000). Malaysian culture and the leadership of organizations: a GLOBE study. *Malaysian Management Review* 35 (2), 44–53.

Miller, M.J., Woehr, D.J. and Hudspeth, N. (2002). The meaning and measurement of work ethic: construction and initial validation of a multidimensional inventory. *Journal of Vocational Behavior* 60 (3), 451–89.

Neal, M., Finlay, J. and Tansey, R. (2005). 'My father knows the minister': a comparative study of Arab women's attitudes towards leadership authority. *Women in Management Review* 20 (7), 478–97.

Nelson, J. (2006). *Economics for Humans.* Chicago, IL: University of Chicago Press.

North, D. (1990). *Institutions, Institutional Change, and Economic Performance.* Cambridge: Cambridge University Press.

Ogilvie, S. (2011). *Institutions and European Trade: Merchant Guilds, 1000–1800.* Cambridge: Cambridge University Press.

O'Reilly, C., Chatman, J. and Caldwell, D. (1991). People and organizational culture: a profile comparison approach to assessing person–organization fit. *Academy of Management Journal* 34 (3), 487–516.

Osella, F. and Osella, C. (2009). Muslim entrepreneurs in public life between India and the Gulf: making good and doing good. *Journal of the Royal Anthropological Institute* 15 (s1), s202–s221.

Pache, A. and Santos, F. (2010). When worlds collide: the internal dynamics of organizational responses to conflicting institutional demands. *Academy of Management Review* 16 (1), 145–79.

Patai, R. (1983). *The Arab World.* New York: Charles Scribner & Sons.

Pew Research Center (2009). *Mapping the Global Muslim Population.* Pew Forum on Religion and Public Life. Washington, DC: Pew Research Centre.
Pew Research Center (2011). *The Future of the Global Muslim Population: Projections for 2010–2030.* Washington, DC: Pew Research Center.
Pew Research Center (2012). *The World's Muslims: Unity and Diversity.* Washington, DC: Pew Research Center.
Polanyi, K. (1944). *The Great Transformation: The Political and Economic Orgins of Our Time.* Boston, MA: Beacon Press.
Rizvi, S. (1993). *Khums: An Islamic Tax.* Qom: Ansariyan Publications.
Rodinson, M. (1966 [1978]). *Islam and Capitalism.* B. Pearce (trans.). Austin, TX: University of Texas Press.
Rodrik, D. (2008). *One Economics, Many Recipes.* Princeton, NJ: Princeton University Press.
Roomi, M. and Harrison, P. (2010). Behind the veil: women-only entrepreneurship training in Pakistan. *International Journal of Gender and Entrepreneurship* 2 (2), 150–172.
Roomi, M. and Harrison, P. (2011). Entrepreneurial leadership: what is it and how should it be taught?. *International Review of Entrepreneurship* 9 (3), 1–44.
Rudnyckyj, D. (2009). Spiritual economies: Islam and neoliberalism in contemporary Indonesia. *Cultural Anthropology* 24, 104–41.
Sadeq, A. (1990). *Economic Development in Islam.* Petaling Jaya, Malaysia: Pelanduk Publications.
Sardar, Z. (1997). Beyond development: an Islamic persepctive. *European Journal of Development Research* 8 (2), 36–55.
Sayigh, Y. (1958). Toward a theory of entrepreneurship for the Arab East. *Explorations in Entrepreneurial History* 10, 123–7.
Schein, E. (1985). *Organizational Culture and Leadership.* San Francisco, CA: Jossey-Bass.
Sen, A. (1999). *Development as Freedom.* Oxford: Oxford University Press.
Shane, S. and Venkataraman, S. (2000). The promise of entrepreneurship as a field of research. *Academy of Management Review* 25, 217–36.
Shapero, A. and Sokol, L. (1982). The social dimensions of entrepreneurship. In C. Kent, D. Sexton and K. Vesper (eds), *The Encyclopedia of Entrepreneurship.* Englewood Cliffs, NJ: Prentice-Hall, pp. 72–90.
Shaw, J. (1990). A cognitive categorization model for the study of intercultural management. *Academy of Management Review* 15 (4), 626–45.
Sherbiny, N. (1986). *Arab Financial Institutions and Developing Countries.* Washington, D.C.: World Bank.
Siddiqui, M. (1979). *The Economic Enterprise in Islam.* Lahore: Islamic Publications.
Sloane, P. (1999). *Islam, Modernity and Entrepreneurship among the Malays.* London: Macmillan Press.
Smets, M., Morris, T. and Greenwood, R. (2011). From practice to field: a multi-level model of practice-driven institutional change. *Academy of Management Journal* 55 (4), 877–904.
Smircich, L. (1983). Concepts of culture and organizational analysis. *Administrative Science Quarterly* 28 (3), 339–58.
Soares, B. (2005). *Islam and the Prayer Economy: History and Authority in a Malian Town.* Edinburgh: Edinburgh University Press.
SRCC (2003). Small enterprises are main engines for economic development. Riyadh: Riyadh Economic Forum Towards Sustainable Economic Development.
Stevenson, H. (1983). *A Perspective on Entrepreneurship.* Cambridge, MA: Harvard Business School Press.
Temporal, P. (2011). *Islamic Branding and Marketing.* Asia: Wiley & Sons.
Toye, J. (1995). The new institutional economics and its implications for development theory. In J. Harriss, J. Hunter, and C. Lewis (eds), *The New Insitutional Economics and Third World Development.* Burr Ridge, IL: Irwin Press, pp. 17–26.
Tracey, P. (2012). Religion and organization: a critical view of the current trends and future directions. *Academy of Management Annals* 6 (1), 87–134.

Ul-Haq, S. and Westwood, R. (2012). The politics of knowledge, epistemological occlusion and Islamic management and organization knowledge. *Organization* 19 (2), 229–57.

Veciana, J. and Urbano, D. (2008). The institutional approach to entrepreneurship research. *International Entrepreneurship and Management Journal* 4 (4), 365–79.

WEF (2014). *The Global Competitiveness Report: 2013⊠2014*. Geneva: World Economic Forum.

World Bank (2014). data.worldbank.org. Retrieved 30 July 2014 from http://data.worldbank.org/indicator/SP.POP.TOTL?cid=GPD_1.

Yusuf, S. and Nabeshima, K. (2011). *Can Malaysia Escape the Middle-Income Trap?: A Strategy for Penang*. Washington, D.C.: World Bank Development Research Group.

Zelekha, Y., Avnimelech, G. and Sharabi, E. (2014). Religious institutions and entrepreneurship. *Small Business Economics* 42 (4), 747–67.

PART III

LEADERSHIP IN ENTREPRENEURIAL CONTEXTS

6. Managing paradoxes and tensions: a key element of entrepreneurs' leadership behaviour

Thierry Volery and Susan Mueller

INTRODUCTION

At a macro level, entrepreneurship is a process of creative destruction. By this, Schumpeter (1934) referred to the simultaneously destructive and constructive consequences of innovation. The new destroys the old. Entrepreneurs are central to the process of creative destruction; they identify opportunities and bring the new technologies and new concepts into active commercial use. Entrepreneurs, therefore, can upset the status quo, disrupt accepted ways of doing things, and alter traditional patterns of behaviours. As Eggers and Smilor (1996) noted:

> perhaps the most compelling aspect of the entrepreneurship process is its paradoxical nature. Only by recognizing the range of paradoxes that exists for entrepreneurs and their ventures is it possible to appreciate the dynamism and unpredictability of the entrepreneurial process as well to appreciate the tremendous energy required to move a venture along the entrepreneurial continuum. (ibid.: 17)

Paradoxes denote contradictory yet interrelated elements that seem logical in isolation but absurd and irrational when appearing simultaneously (Andriopoulos and Lewis, 2009). The emergence of new business ventures and the management of entrepreneurial firms raise multiple tensions such as effectuation–causation, exploration–exploitation, delegation–control, tradition–innovation, flexibility–efficiency, growth–stability, regional–global and emotional–rational. As the business venture grows and becomes more complex, contradictory demands are likely to intensify.

By drawing on the strategic leadership theory (Adair, 2002; Rowe, 2001), we posit that a central role of the entrepreneur is to navigate the conflicting demands arising from these paradoxes. As strategic leaders, entrepreneurs must ideally have the ability to consider the long-term future of their business ventures, seeing the big picture, as well as understanding the current contextual setting and pressing operative issues. They must, therefore, facilitate stakeholders' efforts to accomplish shared objectives in the business venture while constantly 'doing the splits' by undertaking operative (day-to-day) and strategic (long-term) responsibilities.

The objectives of this chapter are threefold: (1) to investigate the paradoxical tensions facing entrepreneurs in growth-oriented ventures while observing their behaviours; (2) to outline the main roles that entrepreneurs perform to address these tensions; and (3) to identify the patterns of behaviour which help to sustain entrepreneurial leadership over time. This is an exploratory study which builds on a recent stream of research on entrepreneurs' behaviour conducted by the authors (Mueller et al., 2012; Volery et al., 2013; Volery et al., 2009).

REVIEW OF THE LITERATURE

Entrepreneurship Behaviour and Leadership

In essence, entrepreneurship can be viewed as an organizational phenomenon due to its connection to the creation and growth of organizations. However, the goals, problems and behaviours of entrepreneurs differ substantially from those of managers in established organizations. The launch of a business venture is an 'enacted' phenomenon (Weick, 1979) and constitutes a form of constructed reality characterized by equivocality. 'Entrepreneurs talk and act "as if" equivocal events were non-equivocal by offering plausible explanations of current and future events' (Gartner et al., 1992: 17). The entrepreneur is the central actor in the creation of a new venture. While economic circumstances, social networks and even public agency assistance can play an important role, it is ultimately the entrepreneur who identifies and shapes a business opportunity, and who has the motivation to persist until the job is done (Shaver and Scott, 1991).

Therefore, entrepreneurs' behaviour is ultimately rooted in human volition and actions such as developing a prototype, registering a business, lodging a patent, acquiring resources, selling, and so forth. More broadly, Bird and Schjoedt (2009: 328) defined entrepreneurs' behaviour as 'the concrete enactment of an individual task or activity required to initiate, grow, or transform a business venture'. This approach implies that the overt or covert actions of individuals who perform the social function of the entrepreneur will reflect entrepreneurial behaviours. In line with this definition, Gartner et al. (2010) propose that:

> entrepreneurship is fundamentally about organizing and that the entrepreneurs take the centre stage in this process. They act both as the mind and the chief

conductor behind the enactment processes leading to the initiation and growth of a business venture. Organizing involves the coordination and establishment of routines, structures, and systems. (ibid.: 10)

From an organizational perspective, entrepreneurs are assuming roles which lead to the creation, maintenance, direction and coordination of certain subsystems to ensure that goals are appropriately defined and, eventually, attained (Fleishman et al., 1991). Organizational leadership is reflected in the behaviour – the actions taken by the individual – in view of goal definition and attainment. Consequently, we suggest that organization leadership theory (Stogdill, 1974; Yukl, 2012) is an adequate theoretical anchor for entrepreneurs' behaviour. More specifically, the organization systems stream (Katz and Kahn, 1978) in the leadership research tradition provides a framework to analyse entrepreneurs' behaviour. This approach focuses on the boundary-spanning and internal coordination responsibilities of leaders within open social systems. In other words, this perspective 'emphasizes the role of the leader in coordinating and maintaining system interconnectedness and promoting system adaptiveness to external change' (Zaccaro and Klimoski, 2001: 21).

Since organizational leadership is reflected in the behaviour in view of goal definition and attainment, this perspective will help us to understand the essential and critical things entrepreneurs do when they build an organization. In particular, this perspective can shed some light on the key activities performed by entrepreneurs as leaders, to what extent these activities are related to typical organizational functions, and how the role of the entrepreneur evolves as the business venture expands.

In the specific context of entrepreneurship, McGrath and MacMillan (2000) defined leadership as the ability to create visionary scenarios that are used to build a cast of competent and committed supporters to accomplish the objectives underlying the scenario. Thus, entrepreneurial leaders envision and enact a proactive transformation of the firm's transaction set (Venkataraman and Van de Ven, 1998). Using data from an international research project, Gupta et al. (2004) identified attributes associated with five entrepreneurial leadership roles dealing with, on the one hand, envisaging and creating scenarios of possible opportunities (scenario enactment), and on the other hand, convincing potential followers and the firm's stakeholders to accomplish the objectives underlying the scenario (cast enactment).

Along these lines, a central capacity of the entrepreneur as a leader is to simultaneously anticipate and envision, and to work with others to implement the vision and create a viable future for the business venture. This fits the concept of strategic leadership defined by Rowe (2001: 83) as 'the ability to work with others to voluntarily make day-to-day decisions that enhance the long-term viability of the organization, while maintaining its short-term stability'. We find a similar temporal tension during the enactment process pertaining to the launch and growth of a business venture: entrepreneurs operate in both the (short-term) here and now and the long-term future. In addition, one crucial task of entrepreneurs is to marshal resources to transform their vision into reality; this invariably requires enlisting the aid and support of stakeholders (employees, customers, suppliers, investors).

The Evolution of Entrepreneurial Leadership Research

Leadership, as defined by Yukl (2012: 66), 'revolves around influencing and facilitating individual and collective efforts to accomplish shared objectives'. Leadership has been a major topic of research in psychology and management for almost a century and has spawned thousands of empirical and conceptual studies. Despite this level of effort, various parts of this literature have yet to permeate the field of entrepreneurship and small business management. In fact, both the leadership and entrepreneurship field would benefit from mutual cross-fertilization. Cogliser and Brigham (2004: 789) remarked in this respect: 'There are numerous potential areas where entrepreneurship researchers might benefit from observing the challenges, continuing struggles, and successes of leadership researchers.' On closer inspection, entrepreneurs are, more often than not, expected to be leaders as they rely on people to realize their vision and accomplish their objectives. Successful entrepreneurs are generally effective 'people managers' and mentors who play a major role in motivating, directing and leading co-workers.

In a pioneer paper, Cunningham and Lischeron (1991) identified two streams of writings concerning entrepreneurial leadership. The first stream of development has been grouped within the 'great person' school, and describes the numerous initial studies which researched the personal traits and characteristics that are more often present in leaders than in followers or subordinates. The 'great person' school followed early leadership research which suggested that traits such as adaptability to situations, cooperativeness, energy and willingness to take responsibility are important aspects of success (Stogdill, 1974; Bass, 1985). This stream of research is often associated with a heroic view of entrepreneurs: these are individuals launching a business, taking necessary risks, battling against adversity and 'making it happen'. The entrepreneur, often with limited experience of leadership (Kempster and Cope, 2010), reflects heroic notions of individual leadership.

The second, more pervasive, stream of the entrepreneurial leadership school is concerned with how a leader gets tasks accomplished and responds to the needs of people. A promising avenue in this stream has been followership: the ability to inspire and motivate subordinates, especially in light of the riskiness inherent in early start-up conditions (Baum et al., 1998). In addition to the personal inducements that the entrepreneur-leader can offer, there is a need to consider the attributes and expectations of followers in such a social process. For example, Vecchio (2003: 316) noted that, for many people in small firms, 'the opportunity to interact with the top person in a firm represents a significant opportunity to receive approval or affirmation from an authority figure'. Entrepreneurs are often perceived as charismatic and authentic leaders because of their ability to captivate employees' interest and to create a transparent, future-oriented and associate-building organization. For example, Jensen and Luthans (2006: 658) found that 'employees who perceived their entrepreneur-leader to be more authentic had correspondingly higher levels of organizational commitment, job satisfaction, and work happiness'.

Another avenue drawing on followership can be found in the theory and research related to leader–member exchange theory (see Schriesheim et al., 1999 for a review). This theory, in essence, argues that 'leaders and followers negotiate specific social exchange relationships wherein leaders offer such inducements as salary and opportunities for input on decision-making, and followers offer effort and loyalty' (Vecchio, 2003: 316). According to this school of thought, entrepreneurs fulfil the role of 'social architects', promoting and protecting values, preserving organizational intimacy, empowering people and developing a human resource system.

This perspective fits the transformational leadership style, which is considered an appropriate model for an entrepreneurial context, particularly in opposition to the transactional style (Roomi and Harrison, 2011). Transformational leadership typically portrays leaders as charismatics or visionaries who are able to inspire and energize workers into following them; such leaders thereby transcend self-interest in order to alter an organization (Robbins, 1984). 'By using their ability to empower and to encourage others to achieve a shared vision and by leading through example, they are able to influence and motivate their followers to do' (Roomi and Harrison, 2011: 7). Transactional leadership, on the other hand, is based on the legitimate power given to the leader within the bureaucratic structure of the organization (Kotter, 1990), and primarily considers end-results such as work tasks and outcomes, rewards and punishments (Mullins, 2002). It is also concerned with managing workers under strict rules and regulations to avoid change as far as possible and to avoid making decisions that could alter the status quo of the organization.

In the specific context of growth-oriented small and medium-sized enterprises (SMEs), one of the main challenges for the entrepreneur is to move from a 'one-man show', individualist leader–led relationship to a distributed leadership system by transferring responsibility and control to others. As Leitch et al. (2009) have observed, there is often a conflict between leadership development and the SME context, as small businesses 'tend to be influenced by dominant individual(s), who are associated with a lack of flexibility, engagement, openness and responsiveness' (ibid.: 243). Therefore, as suggested by Cope et al. (2011), there is a need to adopt a distributed leadership based on an entrepreneurial team – rather than a single individual – as the business grows in order to mitigate a possible 'crisis of leadership'. In essence, distributed leadership draws on multiple leaders taking multiple decisions and multiple, coordinated actions.

Overall, there is a broad convergence between the strategic leadership and transformational leadership perspectives in relation to the key abilities and skills that entrepreneurs should perform in the dynamic process of business creation and growth. Entrepreneurs typically act as strategic leaders who can recognize and exploit opportunities, thereby adding considerable business value; and, by the same token, behave as transformational leaders who are always looking for ways to overturn the status quo of their organization through major change. As highlighted at the beginning of this chapter, the dynamic nature of entrepreneurship generates a wide range of paradoxes that entrepreneurs have to deal with. These paradoxes have been defined by Eggers and Smilor (1996: 17) as 'contradictory or diametrically opposed elements, both of which are real and true, that exist side by side in the same environment at the same time'. This chapter contributes to the field of entrepreneurial leadership by shedding some light on how entrepreneurs deal with such paradoxical tensions and what constitutes their behaviour in such situations.

Method

This chapter draws on a data set that was originally generated to investigate how entrepreneurs spend their time; in other words, we wanted to better understand 'the entrepreneur's job' (Mueller et al., 2012; Volery et al., 2009). To collect this original set of data, we used the sociological method of structured observation, a method that 'couples the flexibility of open-ended observation with the discipline of seeking certain types of structured data' (Mintzberg, 1973: 231).

Sample
The sample group of six entrepreneurs was selected according to a pre-

defined set of criteria. These criteria required the entrepreneurs to be experienced (the ventures were between five to nine years old at the time of the observation), to be the founder or co-founder of the company, and to be growth-oriented. We used three types of indicators to determine the growth orientation, namely new products launched in the last four years, the compound annual growth rate of the past four years, and the entrepreneur's growth intentions.

All owner-managers were recipients of the Entrepreneur of the Year award from Ernst & Young (an established award for entrepreneurs at the helm of successful high-growth and innovative businesses). The SMEs were located in Switzerland, Germany and Austria, and they were operating in different industries, including robotic rehabilitation, pharmacy retail, software development, internet services, fencing franchise and clean technology. Table 6.1 provides a descriptive overview of the sample.

Each entrepreneur was observed over four working days between January and June 2009, totalling 260 hours of observation. A team of three researchers conducted the observations, albeit only one researcher observed each entrepreneur concurrently. In total, we identified over 2000 'units of action' performed by the entrepreneurs. A unit of action captures a single, basic behaviour of the entrepreneur and can span from a few seconds (for example, writing a two-line email to an employee) to an hour or more (for example, doing a sales pitch for a client). Typically, we defined behaviour as a new action if the location, the communication medium or the people involved in the action changed.

Data analysis
All recorded actions were entered into a database, and an iterative process involving three researchers and measures to ensure inter-rater reliability was initiated. During this process, we developed a series of categories to aggregate the data in a meaningful way. We identified six relevant categories: three of them captured the actions' content (that is, strategic versus operative actions, activities and functions), and three captured their communication aspects (that is, communication status, communication partner and media). We then defined subcategories for all of the categories (e.g., marketing, sales and PR as constitutive elements of the category 'function') and assigned these to each of the recorded actions. To reach a better understanding about the entrepreneurs' engagement in exploration versus exploitation activities (for patterns of how entrepreneurs deal with ambidexterity see Volery et al., 2013) we revisited the data and assigned each unit of action to one of the two subcategories 'exploration' and 'exploitation'. Again, we engaged in a process that ensured inter-rater reliability.

Table 6.1 *Sample overview*

	Entrepreneur #1 Internet services	Entrepreneur #2 Pharmacy retail	Entrepreneur #3 Software	Entrepreneur #4 Robotic rehabilitation	Entrepreneur #5 Fencing franchise	Entrepreneur #6 Clean technology
Founding year	2001	2004	2000	2000	2003	2004
Size (employees in 2009)	165	20	65	104	13/300*	60
Turnover (2009, in million €)	47	2.5	n/a	21	25.5	4.8
New products						
New products launched in last 4 years	6	15	5	5	3	3
Sales growth						
Average sales growth past 4 years**	5%	36%	2.5%	22%	27%	59%
Growth intention						
Importance of future sales growth (1=not important at all; 5=highly important)	5	5	5	4	5	4

Notes: * 13 employees (franchisor); 300 employees (franchise network). ** Compound annual growth rate.

For this chapter, we report on tensions underpinning the job of the entrepreneur and the strategies employed by entrepreneurs to ensure entrepreneurial leadership behaviour over time. These patterns and strategies emerged through engagement with the data. Additionally, to carve out key tensions of the entrepreneurs' job and strategies used to ensure entrepreneurial leadership behaviour, literature on paradoxical tensions in organizational studies was consulted (Andriopoulos and Lewis, 2009; Groen et al., 2008; Lewis, 2000). We propose that the patterns and roles described below help to explain how entrepreneurs deal with conflicting demands or opposing perspectives.

We conducted post-observation interviews with all entrepreneurs to better understand the tensions and roles that we identified throughout the process.

RESULTS

Four Key Tensions Underpinning the Job of the Entrepreneur

First, we identified four tensions inherent to the job of entrepreneurs, requiring them to maintain a subtle balance between exploration and exploitation, short-term and long-term perspectives, dealing with employees and outsiders, and stability and adaption.

Exploration versus exploitation
In line with March (1991: 71), we considered exploitation as 'refinement, choice, production, efficiency, selection, implementation and execution', contrasting it with exploration, which involves 'search, variation, risk-taking, experimentation, discovery and innovation'. In this vein, we categorized actions taken to run or improve existing business operations through choice, execution and variance reduction as 'exploitation'. Such actions included, for example, time spent on administrative tasks, actions taken to increase efficiency, selling products to existing customers or maintaining relationships with employees. In contrast, we categorized actions related to searching, recognizing, exploring and enacting opportunities as 'exploration'. These actions are linked to learning and experimentation, and they are typically open-ended and contain an element of risk. They include, among others, environment monitoring, product development, the evaluation of new business options and changes of the existing business structure.

Entrepreneurs are doers. Not surprisingly, exploitation appears to be the default activity for all of them. Once they arrive on the business premises, they invariably tend to get bogged down in solving pressing problems and answering queries from their employees. Therefore, exploitation is the 'default mode of action'. However, the entrepreneurs saw the benefit of stepping back and not getting stuck in the immediate in order to explore, reflect and engage in strategic projects. A key challenge was to preserve 'free' time for exploration. In five out of six cases, the entrepreneurs engaged in creating time windows for themselves, and sometimes others, to engage in exploration activities.

Another source of tension stems from the personal preferences of the entrepreneurs. The post-observation interviews revealed that five out of six observed entrepreneurs are more inclined to enact exploration activities. Nevertheless, they recognize that it is important to engage in exploitation activities to secure and grow the current business. In terms of the distribution of time, entrepreneurs allocate more time to exploitation activities than they would like to. Thus, they need to balance the tension between what they really enjoy doing and the perceived requirements of the business. Entrepreneur #3 remarked in this respect: 'As an "innovator", I would prefer 100% exploration, 0% exploitation. Ideally, as an entrepreneur: 30% exploration and 70% exploitation would be better.' Similarly, entrepreneur #5 said: 'I would rather only do exploration, because that suits me better because it is much more exciting. I like to try out things and pioneer work . . . the implementation afterwards can be cumbersome at times.'

Time span: short-term versus long-term
Strongly interconnected with the exploration versus exploitation tension was the time span of attention paid to activities. Typically, entrepreneurs had to take short-term actions while maintaining long-term vision. Behaviours related to exploitation often encompasses immediate or pressing issues which appear to be more urgent than exploration activities, even though the latter might be more relevant to the company's success in the long-term. One entrepreneur mentioned the following story with regard to trouble-shooting issues: 'If a [franchising] partner, who has some kind of problem or request, then of course, I try to find a solution or give him a quick hint, and then I am right in the middle of sorting problems' (entrepreneur #5, fencing franchise).

Therefore, entrepreneurial behaviour is characterized by the ability to make quick, incremental decisions to adapt the evolving environment (markets, government, competitors, and so on). This behaviour pattern is consistent with Bird's (1989) notion that entrepreneurs operate both in the here-and-now and in the long-term future, and as a result experience greater temporal tension than most managers. Our observations indicate that the entrepreneurs' actions contributed to the daily business operations as well as to the future development of their companies. For example, while the function 'production and service delivery' is clearly associated with the daily business, 'product development' and 'organizational development' are associated with the future development of the company. These entrepreneurs constantly managed a tension between shaping the future of their organization and running it on a daily basis.

External versus internal orientation
Another potential source of exploration–exploitation tension lies in the orientation of the actions performed by the entrepreneurs. Should the entrepreneur focus their attention on the discovery and evaluation of new opportunities in the market, or rather scale up existing production and increase efficiency? One entrepreneur expressed the tension as follows:

> We are always confronted with new business opportunities. Sometimes customers ask us for a specific product or service, which is not in our offering. We have the competence to provide these services and this could help us to generate the cash flow we need to finance other promising projects. However, we all too often get side-tracked by fulfilling specific customers' needs. (entrepreneur #1)

The requirement to stay competitive in terms of current product offerings and technology is another source of tension between exploitation and exploration behaviours. One example given by one of the entrepreneurs was related to the refinement of technologies and the leveraging of existing competencies rather than to developing new skills and capacities. Entrepreneur #4 summarized this dilemma as follows:

> We recognised that we have to consolidate our technological base so that everyone in the company is up-to-date with the technology we incorporated in our product. In addition, this will increase the reliability of our product. But at the same time, I always let a couple of people from R&D [Research and Development] pursue their pet projects without making much publicity about it. In this way, we can do some technological scouting and this mitigates the risk that our technology will become obsolete.

Organizational requirements: stability versus adaptability
Another aspect of the trade-off between exploration and exploitation behaviours concerned the choice between stability and adaptability. Whereas flexibility and change are associated with exploration, stability and inertia are associated with exploitation that confines adaption to things already known (Lavie et al., 2010). This was particularly apparent in the product offering and organizational structure of the SMEs

observed. Many of the owner-managers indicated that there was a need to find a balance between new and old products in the offering. 'You need to keep products for a while in the catalogue in order that they get a chance to establish themselves in the marketplace, while at the same time offer a few novelties that have the greatest potential', said entrepreneur #5 from the fencing industry. 'Of course, if you leave it to the sales guys, they would rather change the entire offering every year. But if you listen to the finance manager, he would make only cosmetic change and keep the same products on our catalogue.'

Adjusting the organizational structure of the firm as it adds new lines of products or expands in international markets, while at the same time keeping a certain stability so that everyone in the organization knows 'who's doing what', presents a similar challenge. Entrepreneur #4 remarked:

> It must be the fifth organisational chart we adopt [*sic*] since we started our business. We have to adjust our organisation to our international expansion and to recognise that we have been very good at selling our products. But once the sale was done we tended to forget about our customers. We now need to develop an after-sales service.

He added a few rules of thumb about organizational change: 'We focus on one department at a time, and we don't change our organisational chart more than once a year, otherwise our staff and our clients would find it hard to cope with continuous changes.'

In some cases, entrepreneurs were able to concentrate on exploration activities to the extent they wanted because they had employees able to take care of the exploitation activities; while others felt they had to take care of these themselves in order to get the job done 'properly'. The following two statements show this contrast: 'At the moment I can say that my job is 70% exploration, 30% exploitation. Because for the exploitation part, there are people here who are at least as capable as I am, if not better, to do it' (entrepreneur #1, internet services). 'Well, I know that I have to take care of a certain part of exploitation myself, for ensuring it goes well' (entrepreneur #5, fencing franchise).

The Roles of the Entrepreneurs

To a large extent, the four tensions we observed illustrate a more general dilemma between shaping the future of the organization and the day-to-day running of it. This tension forms the root of the quandary between exploitation and exploration in organizations. As mentioned above, March (1991: 71) defined exploitation as 'refinement, choice, production,

Shaping the Future   Running the Daily Business

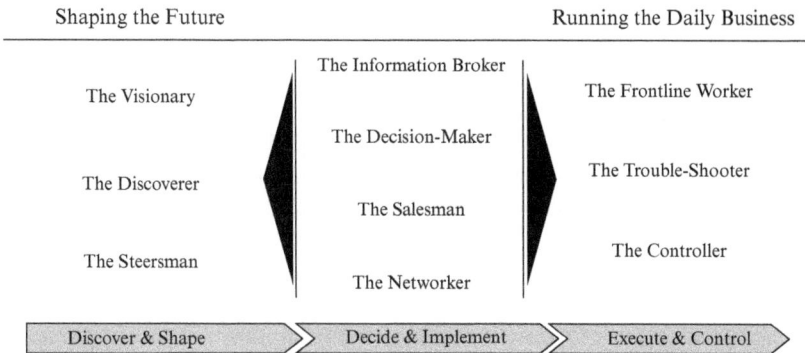

The Visionary   The Information Broker   The Frontline Worker

The Decision-Maker

The Discoverer   The Trouble-Shooter

The Salesman

The Steersman   The Controller

The Networker

Discover & Shape   Decide & Implement   Execute & Control

Figure 6.1   The roles of entrepreneurs

efficiency, selection, implementation and execution', contrasting it with exploration, which involves 'search, variation, risk-taking, experimentation, discovery and innovation'. Consequently, entrepreneurial behaviour has a somewhat ambiguous nature, in that it is both one which generates a discontinuity in economic order by creating new ways of realizing value (exploration, shaping the future), while at the same time it ensures continuity in economic order by combining different economic resources which existed before (exploitation, running the daily business).

To reach a clearer and more accessible view on this phenomenon, we identified ten main roles that entrepreneurs perform (depicted in Figure 6.1). Three roles (the visionary, the discoverer, the steersman) are oriented towards the future and focus on discovering and shaping entrepreneurial opportunities. Another three roles (the frontline worker, the trouble-shooter, the controller) revolve around the execution and control of activities related to the management of the daily business. Between these two poles, entrepreneurs perform four other roles (the information broker, the decision-maker, the salesman, the networker) where they demonstrate their ability to make day-to-day decisions that enhance the long-term viability of the organization, while maintaining its short-term financial stability.

The visionary
Most observed behaviours were proactive, shaping ideas and changing the way employees think about what is desirable, possible and necessary. As visionary leaders, entrepreneurs were concerned with shaping the future of their organization and articulating a strategy. Due to the novelty and unique nature of their ventures, the observed entrepreneurs often relied on

stories in order to provide the necessary accounts to explain, rationalize and promote an idea. In fact, they often shared their vision to rally key stakeholders (employees, investors, clients) toward a big and daring goal. Once articulated, understood and repeated, we found that entrepreneurial stories became institutionalized accounts that provided both explanations of and rationales for entrepreneurial behaviour. Thus, these stories contributed to reduce the uncertainty typically associated with the entrepreneurial process.

The discoverer

As a discoverer, entrepreneurs actively search for new business opportunities and show alertness: a propensity to notice and be sensitive to information about objects, incidents and patterns of behaviour. The entrepreneurs we observed displayed a particular sensitivity to maker and user problems, unmet needs and novel combinations of resources in order to develop new products or services. They used their wealth of knowledge and their creative thinking to find patterns that suggested ideas for new products or services; ideas that could potentially serve as the basis for growth initiatives.

The steersman

Although entrepreneurs may have significant plans and visions for their ventures, they usually provide a framework (for example, a set of rules, commonly held norms and beliefs) that channels the fantasy and creative energy of their employees. Therefore, while entrepreneurs might initially identify and welcome a wide variety of opportunities, they will quickly perform an initial evaluation of the idea. As a steersman, the entrepreneur must, on the one hand, be open-minded and receptive to new ideas; and on the other hand, steer the venture and the employees toward a common goal.

Entrepreneur #2 used the expression 'freedom within boundaries' to outline the importance of the steersman's role in a fast-growing business venture. 'There are so many entrepreneurial opportunities you pursue,' he said. 'However, you have to consider what makes sense for your business very early on, and not forget that you have limited resources. It's therefore essential that you give a direction to the organization while you remain open for new ideas at the same time. This is a delicate balance.' In addition to a set of rules that would rally employees toward clear objectives and a goal, the entrepreneurs we observed relied on heuristics – simplifying strategies – to make judgements quickly and efficiently. The strategies allowed them to evaluate emerging opportunities quickly and to stay focused.

The information broker
The acquisition, processing and dissemination of information are a central role of the entrepreneur. In fact, three-quarters of the actions we recorded entailed a form of communication (one-to-one, one-to-many or many-to-many). The entrepreneurs we observed spent just over 50 per cent of their working time communicating with internal communication partners, and 24 per cent communicating with external communication partners. An example of this role is an entrepreneur who was designing and implementing a new organizational chart during the observation. The information collected during an event with prospective and current customers revealed that the company was neglecting its existing clients (a software update for the product had not been delivered, and there was no regular contact with the client once the product was sold). This confirmed the entrepreneur's suspicion that 'we are good at developing, manufacturing and selling products, but weak in maintaining contacts with clients and retain them'. It was therefore clear that an after-sales department had to be created, and that the company's organizational chart had to be adapted. The entrepreneur spent a significant amount of time explaining and convincing other executives and employees about this issue, and informing people as to the necessity for change.

The decision-maker
Entrepreneurs have to make difficult decisions with incomplete information, and often they must do so quickly. Entrepreneurial decision-making can be operative in nature (for example, a leaflet for a new product, the allocation of office space or the programme for the yearly company outing) or have a more strategic dimension (for example, the recruitment of a manager, the development of a new product line or the opening of a subsidiary overseas). Our observations indicate that entrepreneurs are often involved in operative decision-making because of the relatively small size of their organizations, and because they are the owners of the business. While the time invested in a single operative decision was usually very short, a strategic decision requires significantly more time on average in order to 'build a solid case' for action. As such, the entrepreneurs followed a disciplined process that balanced rigour with speed, considered the trade-offs involved, and took both short- and long-term goals into account.

The salesman
Behaviours relating to sales were observed amongst all entrepreneurs. Some entrepreneurs directly engaged in selling to customers. For expensive, complex products or services, this often involved preparing an offer

and negotiating the terms and conditions of the sale. Other entrepreneurs were indirectly engaged in selling by attending exhibitions or visiting potential customers. For entrepreneurs, selling often goes far beyond 'making a one-off deal'. They know that it is easier and more cost-effective to generate sales through repeat orders from existing customers. The entrepreneurs, therefore, dedicated particular attention to after-sales and customer satisfaction. Contact with existing customers and attending to their feedback were recurrent behaviours.

The networker
Our observations provided a unique opportunity to observe the entrepreneurs interacting with people both inside and outside the organization. In their role as 'networker', the entrepreneur connects with a variety of social contacts ranging from casual acquaintances to close family in order to identify opportunities, marshal resources and develop the organization. The entrepreneurs we observed had 'open' networks with many weak ties and social connections. They recognized that their personal network was the bedrock which was essential to obtain resources that may otherwise have been unavailable to them. One key pattern that emerged from the observations was the external (boundary-spanning) behaviours with a wide range of actors, including customers, suppliers, professionals and even competitors. The entrepreneurs would often meet or communicate repeatedly with these actors, which over time became part of the entrepreneurs' network. All observed entrepreneurs were able to create and maintain networks outside the company that they used for exploitation and exploration purposes.

The frontline worker
As a frontline worker the entrepreneur is personally involved in creating products or providing services to current customers. We found that when performing operative activities, entrepreneurs obtain information about the state of the business whilst maintaining their original knowledge and training. The entrepreneurs derived personal satisfaction in producing goods or delivering a service. At times, customers expected to deal with the entrepreneur, and assumed that they would be directly involved in the planning, production and/or delivery process.

The trouble-shooter
We observed that all entrepreneurs were engaged in short, sporadic activities which change in an abrupt, uncontrolled and unpredictable manner. These activities are characterized by brevity and fragmentation. Entrepreneurs are constantly solicited by their employees and busi-

ness partners in order to get information, ask for permission or arrange appointments. Invariably, entrepreneurs have to deal with the chaos arising from the dynamic process of entrepreneurship: the innovative nature of the products and processes often create teething problems, the organization is expanding and the structure and processes must adapt, and new markets are prospected, all of which require the attention of a trouble-shooter when unforeseen events and circumstances arise. Our observation records revealed interruptions as well as uncontrolled and unpredictable changes of activity. For example, two minutes of desk work may be interrupted by a one-minute phone call which is followed by a thirty-second unscheduled meeting then a three-minute tour. Even if our sample comprised established business ventures with clear organizational structures and processes, the founder often had no other choice but to 'roll up his sleeves' and resolve the problem at hand.

The controller
The observed entrepreneurs had all developed formal control mechanisms (for example, operating metrics in a dashboard, monthly meetings, performance evaluations). They realize that, with the onset of delegation, they can no longer control the behaviour of individuals within the organization; the focus of control must shift from behaviour to performance. The control activities allow the entrepreneur to review situations and to learn everything possible in order to apply the knowledge to the next round of events. Additionally, control activities such as performance evaluations allow employees to be rewarded according to their effort. In addition to these formal control mechanisms, the entrepreneurs often rely on 'soft control' mechanisms such as informal discussions with their employees and existing customers.

Overall, the roles which emerged from our findings fit the concept of strategic leadership defined by Rowe (2001, p. 83) as 'the ability to work with others to voluntarily make day-to-day decisions that enhance the long-term viability of the organization, while maintaining its short-term stability'. As strategic leaders, entrepreneurs constantly deal with paradoxes to simultaneously recognize and exploit opportunities.

Sustaining Entrepreneurial Leadership Behaviour over Time

In a third stage, we sought to identify patterns of entrepreneurial leadership behaviour which the established entrepreneurs were able to preserve. According to Gupta et al. (2004: 242), 'entrepreneurial leadership creates visionary scenarios that are used to assemble and mobilize a "supporting cast" of participants who become committed by the vision to the discovery and exploitation of strategic value creation'. Mobilizing resources and gaining commitment to create value can be regarded as abilities of an entrepreneurial leader who is able to enact an opportunity, shape a vision, foster a culture of innovation and convince people to take part in value creation. We found four key behaviours illustrating entrepreneurial leadership.

Allocating sufficient time to exploration activities

Entrepreneurial leadership behaviour requires the ability to search and enact opportunities. We captured this notion with the differentiation between exploitation and exploration activities. Quoting directly from March (1991: 71): 'Exploration includes things understood in terms like research, variation, risk-taking, experimentation, play, flexibility, discovery, innovation. Exploitation includes things like improvement, choice, production, efficiency, implementation, execution.' In other words, 'exploration engages individuals and organisations in search, experimentation, and variation, whereas exploitation enhances productivity and efficiency though choice, execution, and variance reduction' (Lavie et al., 2010: 110). In this vein, we categorized actions taken to run or improve existing business operations as 'exploitation'. Such actions included time spent on administrative tasks, actions taken to increase efficiency, or maintaining relationships with employees. In contrast, we categorized actions taken to explore or develop new business options as 'exploration'; for example, product development, meetings to discuss new business options, changes to existing business structure.

All entrepreneurs allocated a comparable amount of time for exploitation (about 80 per cent of the working time) and exploration (about 20 per cent of the working time). Thus, although the majority of the time was spent on exploitation, the entrepreneurs still kept developing new business opportunities. Such actions included time spent on projects to enter new markets, the development of new products, or meetings with potential business partners. The entrepreneurs were able to keep in balance the explorative dimension (for example, long-term perspective, adaptation, future orientation) and the exploitative dimension (for example, short-term perspective, stability, here and now) of their job.

In line with Andriopoulos and Lewis (2009), we suggest passion (personal expression, challenge and pride) and discipline (explicit roles and dutifulness) as interwoven requirements for managing the tension between exploration and exploitation in growing business ventures. Product development challenges – clients seeking exciting new products in short time frames with limited budgets – demand both sides of the coin.

Enabling organizational change

Entrepreneurial leadership behaviour entails envisioning future opportunities and enabling organizations to transform their transactions sets (Venkataraman and Van de Ven, 1998). Thus, the task of an entrepreneur is not only to add new products to the portfolio but also to adapt the organization's structure in order to respond to internal constraints (for example, a growing number of employees, span of control) and external constraints (for example, meeting customer demand, entering a new market). We propose that fostering the transformation of the company is an important element of entrepreneurial behaviour. The entrepreneurs dedicated 8 per cent of their time to 'business and organizational development'. Underlying actions include exploring possibilities to cooperate with others, establishing new branches, restructuring the value proposition or changing the organizational chart of the company. Here again, the entrepreneurs had to balance exploration and exploitation. Adjusting the organizational structure of the firm as it adds new lines of products or expands on international markets, while at the same time keeping a certain stability so that everyone in the organization knows 'who's doing what', illustrates this challenge.

Eliciting participation and involvement from others

Entrepreneurial leadership aims to facilitate participation and the involvement of the team. Thus interaction and communication processes with the team play an important role. This behaviour was reflected in the communication patterns of the entrepreneurs: our entrepreneurs spent more than half of their time in communication with other people within their company. Communication can be described as the means to reveal and use the innovation potential of the employees, and thus use the human resources for the company's survival and future development.

During the start-up phase, ideas for new products and services mainly come from the founders. In later stages, entrepreneurs remain an important source of ideas, but each new employee constitutes an additional source of ideas. To utilize this potential, communication behaviour eliciting involvement and participation becomes crucial. Thus, we state that successful entrepreneurial leadership behaviour reaches participation and involvement of the people in the company.

Focus on near-to-market and near-to-people activities

While managers tend to be specialists, entrepreneurs tend to be generalists (Bird, 1989). This predication is supported by our observations. During the four-day observation period, the entrepreneurs were involved in a variety of organizational aspects. With regards to the category of 'function', all entrepreneurs were involved in at least seven (out of the nine) different attributes. Despite the variety of performed actions, we found two near-to-market and near-to-people functions that were important: 'marketing and sales' and 'human resources' (HR). The entrepreneurs in our sample dedicated 18 per cent of their time to marketing and sales, and 20 per cent to HR/employee relation issues. Both functions are critical to the development of the company. Engaging in marketing and sales actions helps the entrepreneur to be aware of what is happening in the market and recognize potential shifts in customer needs and market trends early on. Also, actions related to marketing and sales are important for start-up ventures since they generate the necessary cash flow to support all other activities. The employees are needed to actually reshape and fulfil the value proposition. Thus, both activities are crucial entrepreneurial leadership behaviour.

CONCLUSION

In this chapter, we draw on data gathered through the sociological method of structured observation to capture the behaviour of entrepreneurs during growth stages. This behaviour is anchored in the volition and actions of the entrepreneurs. By proposing that leadership is also a property of individuals occupying the social function of entrepreneurs, we implied that effective leadership behaviour will be reflected in those overt actions taken by entrepreneurs as they interact with stakeholders to realize their vision. Because the goals and problems confronting entrepreneurs vary across organizations, one might expect substantial variability in leader behaviour. However, as Fleishman et al. (1991: 259) remarked, 'the effective generation, selection, and implementation of problem solutions will always be conditioned by certain basic, requisite activities'.

We identified a series of three key findings, which provided insights into the behavioural characteristics of entrepreneurs at the helm of growth-oriented SMEs. First, our results suggest that entrepreneurial behaviour has a somewhat paradoxical nature, in that it both generates a discontinuity in the economic order by creating new ways of realizing value (exploration, shaping the future), while at the same time it ensures continuity in the economic order by combining different economic resources which existed before (exploitation, running the daily business). Our chapter provides an insight into the paradoxes and tensions underpinning the work of entrepreneurs. Specifically, we identified four inherent tensions in the job of entrepreneurs, requiring them to maintain a subtle balance between discipline and passion, short-term and long-term perspectives, dealing with employees and outsiders, and stability and adaption.

Second, we identified ten different roles played by the entrepreneurs in order to deal with the paradoxes and tensions underpinning their work. Three roles (the visionary, the discoverer, the steersman) are oriented towards the future and focus on discovering and shaping entrepreneurial opportunities. Another three roles (the frontline worker, the trouble-shooter, the controller) revolve around the execution and control of activities related to the management of the daily business. Between these two poles, entrepreneurs perform four other roles (the information broker, the decision-maker, the salesman, the networker) where they demonstrate their ability to make day-to-day decisions that enhance the long-term viability of the organization, while maintaining its short-term financial stability.

Third, we identified strategies adopted by the entrepreneurs to preserve entrepreneurial leadership behaviour. These strategies essentially revolve around allocating sufficient time to exploration activities, enabling organizational change, eliciting participation and involvement from others, and focusing on near-to-market and near-to-people activities.

Overall, our findings support Rowe's (2001) approach of strategic leadership as a synergistic combination of managerial and visionary leadership. The entrepreneurs we observed behaved as visionaries as they were concerned with ensuring the future of their venture; they were proactive, shaped ideas, changed the way people think; and they influenced the attitudes and opinions of others within the organization. In parallel, they got involved in situations and contexts related to day-to-day activities; they considered necessities, not desires and dreams; and they influenced the actions and decisions of those they worked with. One of the key advantages of entrepreneurs is that they have the control of their business. Thus, they are uniquely positioned to integrate the visionary and managerial perspectives of leadership and to reap the rewards, which 'will often be wealth creation and above-normal performance whether an organization is entrepreneurial or established' (Rowe, 2001: 92).

One limitation of this contribution is related to the small sample size of six entrepreneurs and the exploratory nature of the study. The heterogeneity of the sample might also constitute another issue. Since the entrepreneurs were engaged in very different industries, we could not trace whether the variance in time allocation originated from the individuals' preferences or the environment. A second limitation is the limited duration of the observations we conducted. Although we collected our data over several – not necessarily consecutive – days, our study gives minor consideration to the influence of time. An entrepreneur in a given environment does not continually engage in the same activities. Their job varies according to many situational factors such as adjustments to the business plan, new financing rounds, periodic expansion programmes or periods of crisis.

We hope that our research will be followed by more empirical studies focusing on entrepreneurial activities, and we call for observational studies with larger sample sizes and research designs comparing the behaviour of different entrepreneur cohorts. Future research should take into account the cognitive, interpersonal and social richness of leadership in SMEs and come to grips with processes that would account for outcome. Finally, more research is needed to learn how entrepreneurs as leaders adapt their behaviour to changing situations and contexts (for example, regional environment, business life cycle, market turbulence).

REFERENCES

Adair, J. (2002), *Effective Strategic Leadership*. London: Macmillan.

Andriopoulos, C. and Lewis, M. (2009), 'Exploitation–exploration tensions and organizational ambidexterity: managing paradoxes of innovation', *Organization Science*, 20(4), 696–717.

Bass, B.M. (1985), *Leadership and Performance Beyond Expectation*. New York, NY: Free Press.

Baum, J.R., Locke, E.A. and Kirkpatrick, S.A. (1998), 'A longitudinal study of the relation of vision and vision communication to venture growth in entrepreneurial firms', *Journal of Applied Psychology*, 83(1), 43–54.

Bird, B.J. (1989), *Entrepreneurial Behaviour*. Glenview, IL: Scott Foresman.

Bird, B.J. and Schjoedt, L. (2009), 'Entrepreneurial behaviour: its nature, scope, recent research, and agenda for future research', in A.L. Carsrud and M. Brännback (eds), *Understanding the Entrepreneurial Mind*, International Studies in Entrepreneurship series. New York, NY: Springer Science & Business Media, pp. 327–58.

Cogliser, C. and Brigham, K. (2004), 'The intersection of leadership and entrepreneurship: mutual lessons to be learned', *Leadership Quarterly*, 15(6), 771–99.

Cope, J., Kempster, S. and Perry, K. (2011), 'Exploring distributed leadership in the small business context', *International Journal of Management Reviews*, 13(3), 270–285.

Cunningham, B. and Lischeron, J. (1991), 'Defining entrepreneurship', *Journal of Small Business Management*, 29(1), 45–58.

Eggers, J.H. and Smilor, R.W. (1996), 'Leadership skills of entrepreneurs', in R. Smilor, and D. Sexton (eds), *Leadership and Entrepreneurship*. Westport, CT: Quorum Books, pp. 15–38.

Fleishman, E.A., Mumford, M.D., Zaccaro, S.J., Levin, K.Y., Korotkin, A.L. and Hein, M.B. (1991), 'Taxonomic efforts in the description of leader behaviour: a synthesis and functional interpretation', *Leadership Quarterly*, 2(4), 245–87.

Gartner, W.B., Bird, B. and Starr, J. (1992), 'Acting as if: differentiating entrepreneurial from organizational behaviour', *Entrepreneurship Theory and Practice*, 16(3), 13–31.

Gartner, W.B., Carter, N.M. and Reynolds, P.D. (2010), 'Entrepreneurial behaviour: firm organizing processes', in Z. Acs and D. Audretsch (eds), *International Handbook Series on Entrepreneurship*, Vol. 5. New York, NY: Springer, pp. 99–127.

Groen, A., Wakkee, I. and de Weerd-Nederhof, P. (2008), 'Managing tensions in a high tech startup: an innovation journey in social system perspective'. *International Small Business Journal*, 26(1), 57–81.

Gupta, V., MacMillan, I.C. and Surie, G. (2004), 'Entrepreneurial leadership: developing and measuring a cross-cultural construct', *Journal of Business Venturing*, 19(2), 241–260.

Jensen, S.M. and Luthans, F. (2006), 'Entrepreneurs as authentic leaders: impact on employees' attitudes', *Leadership and Organization Development Journal*, 27(8), 646–666.

Katz, D. and Kahn, R.L. (1978), *The Social Psychology of Organizations*, 2nd edn. New York, NY: Wiley.

Kempster, S. and Cope, J. (2010), 'Learning to lead in the entrepreneurial context', *International Journal of Entrepreneurial Behaviour and Research*, 16(1), 6–35.

Kotter, J. (1990), 'What leaders really do', *Harvard Business Review*, 68(3), 103–12.

Lavie, D., Stettner, U. and Tushman, M. (2010), 'Exploration and exploitation within and across organizations', *Academy of Management Annals*, 4(1), 109–55.

Leitch, C.M., McMullan, C. and Harrison, R. (2009), 'Leadership development in SMEs: an action learning approach', *Action Learning: Research and Practice*, 6(3), 243–63.

Lewis, M.W. (2000), 'Exploring paradox: toward a more comprehensive guide', *Academy of Management Review*, 25(4), 760–776.

March, J.G. (1991), 'Exploration and exploitation in organizational learning', *Organization Science*, 2(1), 71–87.

McGrath, R.G. and MacMillan, I.C. (2000), *The Entrepreneurial Mindset: Strategies for Continuously Creating Opportunity in an Age of Uncertainty*. Boston, MA: Harvard Business Press.

Mintzberg, H. (1973), *The Nature of Managerial Work*. New York, NY: Harper & Row.

Mueller, S., Volery, T. and von Siemens, B. (2012), 'What do entrepreneurs actually do? An observational study of entrepreneurs' everyday behaviour in the start-up and growth stages', *Entrepreneurship Theory and Practice*, 36(5), 995–1017.

Mullins, L. (2002), *Management and Organisational Behaviour*. Harlow: Pearson Education.

Robbins, S. (1984), *Essentials of Organisational Behaviour*. Englewood Cliffs, NJ: Prentice Hall.

Roomi, M. and Harrison, P. (2011), 'Entrepreneurial leadership: what is it and how should it be taught?', *International Review of Entrepreneurship*, 9(3), 1–44.

Rowe, W. (2001), 'Creating wealth in organizations: the role of strategic leadership', *Academy of Management Executive*, 15(1), 81–94.

Schriesheim, C.A., Castro, S.L. and Cogliser, C.C. (1999), 'Leader–member exchange (LMX) research: a comprehensive review of theory, measurement, and data-analytic practices', *Leadership Quarterly*, 10(1), 63–113.

Schumpeter, J. (1934), *The Theory of Economic Development*. Cambridge, MA: Harvard University Press.

Shaver, K.G. and Scott, L.R. (1991), 'Person, process, choice: the psychology of new venture creation', *Entrepreneurship Theory and Practice*, 16(2), 23–45.

Stogdill, R.M. (1974), *Handbook of Leadership: A Survey of the Literature*. New York, NY: Free Press.

Vecchio, R.P. (2003), 'Entrepreneurship and leadership: common trends and common threads', *Human Resource Management Review*, 13(2), 303–27.

Venkataraman, S. and Van de Ven, A.H. (1998), 'Hostile environmental jolts, transaction sets and new business development', *Journal of Business Venturing*, 13(3), 231–55.

Volery, T., Mueller, S. and von Siemens, B. (2009), *The Entrepreneur's Job*. Bericht Ernst & Young – Agenda Mittelstand. Zürich: Ernst & Young.

Volery, T., Mueller, S. and von Siemens, B. (2013), 'Entrepreneurs' ambidexterity: a study of entrepreneurs' behaviours and competencies in growth-oriented SMEs', *International Small Business Journal*, 33(2), 109–29.

Weick, K.E. (1979), *The Social Psychology of Organizing*. Reading, MA: Addison-Wesley.

Yukl, G. (2012), 'Effective leadership behaviour: what we know and what questions need more attention', *Academy of Management Perspectives*, 26(4), 66–85.

Zaccaro, S.J. and Klimoski, R.J. (2001), *The Nature of Organizational Leadership*. San Francisco, CA: Jossey-Bass.

7. Entrepreneurial leaders and entrepreneurial managers: differences and similarities in their learning approach
Leon Schjoedt and Vicar S. Valencia

INTRODUCTION

Some scholars have considered entrepreneurs, leaders and managers as archetypes (see Czariawska-Joerges and Wolff, 1991), while others observe that the roles overlap. As such, they have important roles to play at different times and various situations in the new venture creation process and, in turn, venture performance. But are they archetypes? The literatures on leadership and entrepreneurship contain many definitions but offer little help in terms of clear definitions (Cogliser and Brigham, 2004; Gartner, 1990) and in terms of distinguishing between leadership and entrepreneur as archetypes. As the title of this chapter announces, we contribute to both strands of the literature on leadership and entrepreneurship by providing a holistic perspective on the differences and similarities between entrepreneurial leaders and entrepreneurial managers. This distinction is important as it provides a framework to distinguish between entrepreneurs and their strategic priorities in new venture creation.

As some scholars note, there are distinct differences among entrepreneurs, leaders and managers. Penrose (1959) posits that there are entrepreneurial and managerial activities that distinguish entrepreneurs and managers and are of central importance in new venture creation and to venture performance. Specifically, she points out that managerial activities involve the execution of entrepreneurial activities, while the entrepreneurial activities are focused on opportunity recognition in the form of identification of a new product, location or important change in technology. Even though Penrose (1959) implies that there are important overlaps among entrepreneurs, leaders and managers, other prominent authors are more explicit: Schumpeter (1934) points out that entrepreneurs and leaders overlap when he notes that entrepreneurs are a special kind of leader, and Mintzberg (1989) observes that entrepreneurs and leaders are managers taking on specific roles depending on the situation.

While some researchers posit that entrepreneurs, leaders and managers are archetypes (Czariawska-Joerges and Wolff, 1991), others argue that they overlap (Mintzberg, 1989; Penrose, 1959; Schumpeter, 1934). Among the reasons for these different points of view may be that research on entrepreneurs and on leaders and managers has, for the most part, taken place in distinct types of organization (unlike most research on entrepreneurs, research on managers and leaders has mostly taken place in established organizations), and has been published in separate bodies of literature. A small but growing body of research is aimed at integrating these research streams to gain insights into entrepreneurship and leadership, which includes this current volume.

In this chapter, we elucidate the overlap between entrepreneurs and leaders, forming what we refer to as 'entrepreneurial leaders' and, by the same token, the overlap between entrepreneurs and managers, creating another distinct type which we call 'entrepreneurial managers'. We define entrepreneurial leaders as individuals who create new-to-the-world businesses via new venture creation, independently or as what is referred to as corporate entrepreneurship; and we define entrepreneurial managers as those who launch businesses similar to those that already exist (for example, franchisees). Specifically, based on March's (1991) concepts of knowledge exploration and exploitation, we illustrate that entrepreneurial leaders' exploratory learning takes place in the form of search, risk-taking, experimentation, discovery and innovation; and entrepreneurial managers' learning exploitation involves choice, refinement, efficiency and implementation. Learning is a complex and multidimensional process; as such, to facilitate our explanation, we follow Kolb's (1984) assertion that individuals are predisposed to have a preferred learning style. Hence, in this chapter we will explain that the extent to which entrepreneurs tend to be entrepreneurial leaders or entrepreneurial managers depends on how they learn and how they employ their knowledge in the venture creation process. By explaining the similarities and differences among entrepreneurial leaders and entrepreneurial managers, we emphasize the importance of the entrepreneur in the process of venture creation, and illustrate that the distinguishing feature between entrepreneurial leaders and entrepreneurial managers is how they engage in knowledge exploration or knowledge exploitation in the new venture creation process.

ENTREPRENEURSHIP: THE PROCESS OF VENTURE CREATION

Entrepreneurship is a process in which a person – the entrepreneur, as an individual or part of a group – creates radical changes in the market by introducing new products, combinations, methods of production, markets

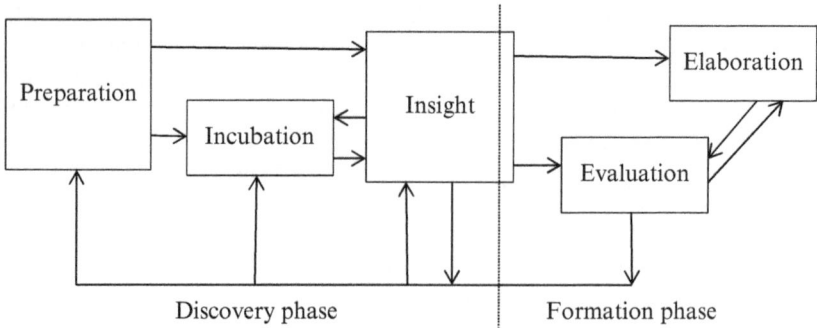

Source: Adapted from Lumpkin et al. (2004).

Figure 7.1   Creativity-based model of opportunity recognition

or organizations (Schumpeter, 1934). It is in this aspect that Schumpeter (1934) laid the foundations for the importance of entrepreneurship in the pursuit of innovation, be it the radical redesign of the management structure and implementation of cost-cutting measures (process innovation), or the introduction of new products and services (product innovation). More recently, and in addition to a focus on opportunity recognition, scholars have pointed out that the questions driving entrepreneurship research include: (1) what factors contribute to entrepreneurs' success? and (2) why are some persons adept in new venture creation? (Baron, 2002; Shane and Venkataraman, 2000).

One model of the venture creation process is the creativity-based model of opportunity recognition provided by Lumpkin et al. (2004), which is shown in Figure 7.1. These scholars provide a two-phase, five-stage model that illustrates how creativity influences opportunity recognition and the initial venture creation process. The five stages are grouped into two phases: discovery and formation. The discovery phase consists of preparation, incubation and insight, and the formation phase consists of evaluation and elaboration. If considered in the context of learning and knowledge exploration or exploitation (March, 1991; Kolb, 1984), the discovery phase is focused on learning from exploring knowledge, whereas the formation phase is centered on learning from knowledge exploitation. In the first stage of the creativity-based model of opportunity recognition (Lumpkin et al., 2004), the preparation stage, people count on their prior knowledge. Fiet et al. (2004) observed that entrepreneurs use specific prior knowledge in recognizing opportunities. In the second stage, incubation, people subconsciously process knowledge (Csikszentmihalyi, 1996) and combine knowledge via bisociation (Ko, 2004) pertaining to an idea or a problem. In the third stage, insight, people discover a breakthrough of the idea or a solution to the problem. These three stages, the discovery phase, are what most scholars refer to as opportunity recognition (Shane and Venkataraman, 2000). During the fourth stage, evaluation, people continuously investigate the identified opportunity. This typically includes marketability, financial considerations, and resource availability and requirements. The entrepreneurs also use their networks to assess the feasibility of the opportunity recognized. Finally, during the fifth stage, elaboration, the business planning begins or the new venture is launched. As different as these stages and the two phases are, entrepreneurs will need to employ different learning styles depending upon whether the new venture is in the discovery or formation phase.

EXPERIENTIAL LEARNING THEORY

Kolb (1984) informs us that the acquisition and transformation of experiences are fundamental to learning, and learning depends on previous knowledge, perception, cognition and experience. Considering this in the context of the two phases of the creativity-based model of opportunity recognition (Lumpkin et al., 2004), and in line with Hayek's (1945) observation of inherent problem in entrepreneurship – the problem of the dispersion and utilization of knowledge – it appears that the new venture creation process is about knowledge exploration and exploitation (March, 1991).

As part of his experiential learning theory, Kolb (1984) observes that experiential learning is a process of transforming experiences into knowledge. His model illustrates how people learn from experience, reflection, thought and experimentation in a cyclical manner, as shown in Figure 7.2. This cycle is based on four modes of learning from concrete experience, reflective observation, abstract conceptualization and active experimentation. He also observes how people acquire and transform information, both of which feed into the circular process of experiential learning. Kolb (1984) notes that the circular learning process may be initiated by people acquiring information through either a direct experience (apprehension) or a reaction to experience (comprehension). Then, people transform their experiences via either extension – actively testing ideas and experiences – or intention: reflecting upon attributes of their experiences and ideas. If initiated by apprehension of concrete experiences, the circle of learning process continues as follows: a person reflects upon the experience to transform the experience into knowledge (intention) before the person

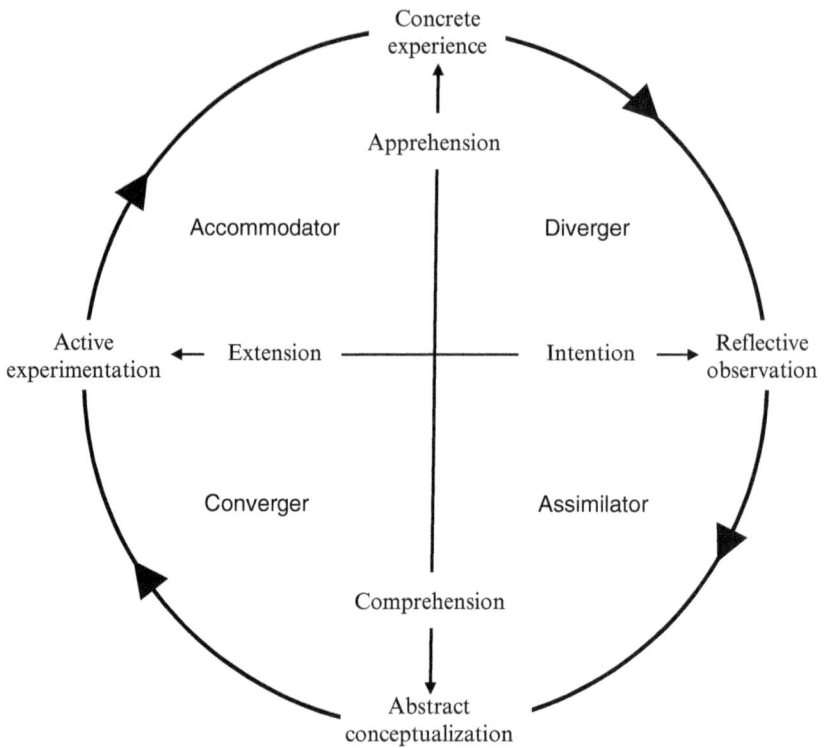

Source: Adapted from Kolb (1984).

Figure 7.2   Kolb's circular learning process

comprehends by engaging in abstract conceptualization; the person then experiments actively using extension; finally having a concrete experience that is transformed via apprehension, which completes the circle (Kolb, 1984).

The type of knowledge created by the person depends on whether the person understands via apprehension or comprehension, and transforms information via reflection or experimentation. As Kolb (1984) posits, a person who acquires information from concrete experience (apprehension), and transforms the experience via intention, creates divergent knowledge. When a person acquires information via concrete experience and transforms the experience by extension, the person creates accommodative knowledge. If experience is obtained from comprehension of abstract conceptualization and transformed via intention, the person creates assimilative knowledge. Finally, a person creates convergent knowledge when the person acquires information via a reaction to experience (comprehension) and transforms the experience through extension.

Together, the dimensions of information acquisition and of transformation of experience provide four learning styles: converger, diverger, assimilator and accommodator:

- The converger learns from transforming thinking and theorizing by doing and applying.
- The diverger learns from transforming feeling and doing by watching and reflecting.
- The assimilator learns by transforming thinking and theorizing through watching and reflecting.
- The accommodator learns by transforming feeling and doing through doing and applying.

Scholars (e.g., Kolb, 1984; Kolb et al., 2000; Mainemelis et al., 2002) point out that people learn best when they engage in the full circular process of learning by using all four forms of learning: concrete experience, reflective observation, abstract conceptualization and active experimentation. Yet, Kolb (1984) observes that people tend to rely on one preferred learning style across situations, but may engage temporarily in a learning style that is not their preferred one to adapt to a situation.

LEARNING STYLES AND THE VENTURE CREATION PROCESS

Learning theories may be grouped into behavioral, cognitive and situational (Greeno et al., 1996). Behavioral learning theories tend to emphasize proper responses to a stimulus and outcomes. As such, they may be appropriate for established organizations seeking to improve routines, operational processes and efficiency, and are appropriate for situations in which there are clear goals and feedback. Consequently, behavioral learning theories may have limited explanatory value in the new venture creation process, which is characterized by risks and uncertainties associated with the initiation, design and creation of new ventures that do not easily lend themselves to quantifiable and controllable outcomes. A learning theory that is both cognitive and situational is better suited for explaining the new venture creation process in which the situation changes from discovery to formation, and eventually to the management of an established organization. This conceptualization harkens back to Lumpkin et al.'s

(2004) creativity-based model of opportunity recognition. The experiential learning theory (Kolb, 1984) is focused on the process of how people use cognition to transform situational experiences into new knowledge. Also, experiential learning theory is not confined by clear goals and routines as behavioral learning theories since it allows for people to develop new knowledge. This particular aspect of learning and knowledge creation echoes well with Schumpeter's (1934) emphasis on the importance of innovation in entrepreneurship, which includes the discovery of new products, combinations, methods of production, markets or organizations.

To illustrate Kolb's learning styles and their relevance to entrepreneurship, Corbett (2005) augmented the creativity-based model of opportunity recognition provided by Lumpkin et al. (2004). He argued that the convergent learning style is most appropriate in the preparation stage, and the assimilative learning style is most relevant in the incubation stage of opportunity recognition. This means that the learning that takes part in the opportunity recognition – the preparation and incubation phases – is characterized by transforming thinking and theorizing into new knowledge. While Corbett (2005) does not consider learning to take place in the insight phase because it is the '*eureka*' experience – a moment in time that is a reaction to learning – he does note that the learning style most useful in the evaluation phase is divergent learning, and the most appropriate learning style for the elaboration phase is accommodative learning. This means that the formation phase is based on transforming feeling and doing by watching and reflecting in the evaluation stage, and by doing and applying in the elaboration stage.

EXPLORATION AND EXPLOITATION IN THE VENTURE CREATION PROCESS

Considering that opportunity discovery is based on transforming thinking and theorizing, and opportunity formation is based on transforming feeling and doing, and also considering that people tend to have a preferred learning style (Kolb, 1984), Corbett (2005) suggests that people are better at some parts of the new venture creation process due to their preferred learning style.

Baron and Ensley (2006) compare novice and repeat entrepreneurs – novice entrepreneurs have started one new venture, whereas repeat entrepreneurs have launched more than one new venture – in terms of how they recognize opportunities. Their findings show that both types of entrepreneurs employ prototypes in recognizing opportunities; in effect, entrepreneurs use prototypes to recognize opportunities, and these prototypes differ substantially. Baron and Ensley (2006) also find that repeat entrepreneurs show more agreement than novice entrepreneurs regarding the attributes of an opportunity, such as clarity of the opportunity, factors pertaining to launching and managing the new venture, solving a customer problem, speed of revenue generation, positive cash flow and manageable risks. In effect, Baron and Ensley (2006) find that repeat entrepreneurs use pattern recognition to identify opportunities. Placing the findings by Baron and Ensley (2006) in the context of learning, it appears that repeat entrepreneurs employ past learning from feeling and doing in recognizing opportunities; whereas novice entrepreneurs, being more concerned with innovativeness of the opportunity and intuition, base their opportunity recognition upon thinking and theorizing.

While the novice entrepreneurs employ thinking and theorizing, and repeat entrepreneurs use feeling and doing predominantly in recognizing opportunities, the adaptive process plays an important role in transitioning from opportunity discovery to opportunity formation in the creativity-based model of opportunity recognition provided by Lumpkin et al. (2004). The adaptive process pertains to the relation between exploration and exploitation of knowledge (Holland, 1975; March, 1991). 'Exploration' refers to learning in terms of Kolb's (1984) four modes: thinking, theorizing, feeling and doing. 'Exploitation' pertains to refinement, choice, production, implementation, execution and efficiency (March, 1991). In the context of entrepreneurship, entrepreneurs explore when they engage in the opportunity recognition process – both the opportunity discovery and formation phases – and in exploitation when they have formed the opportunity and begin to pursue it by exploiting their learning from the opportunity recognition phase of discovery and formation. The transition between exploration and exploitation – the adaption process (March, 1991) – seems to occur during the formation phases of the opportunity recognition process.

Based on March's (1991) considerations with respect to the adaptation process, entrepreneurs who engage in exploration at the exclusion of exploitation are unlikely to launch a new venture based upon the recognized opportunity; they will experience the costs of exploration without the benefits of exploitation. Also, entrepreneurs who engage in exploitation at the exclusion of exploration are not likely to identify the best opportunity for them to pursue. These entrepreneurs may launch new ventures, but they are based upon existing knowledge. This means, as March (1991) advocates, that maintaining an appropriate balance between exploration and exploitation – the adaption process – is critical in the new venture creation process and in the continued management of the new venture.

March (1991) observes that keeping an appropriate balance between exploration and exploitation is complicated. Consider the adaption process and its complexity in the context of the new venture creation process and learning. The opportunity recognition process is dependent upon knowledge exploration, especially in the discovery phase, character-ized by exploring ideas by thinking and theorizing. The formation phase of opportunity recognition, with its emphasis on feeling and doing, is where entrepreneurs begin to adopt knowledge exploitation. As the opportunity recognition moves from discovery to formation and beyond, the entre-preneur needs to adapt from one learning style to another as they move from predominantly exploration to, increasingly, exploitation. Thus, entrepreneurs' ability to adapt to an appropriate balance between knowl-edge exploration and exploitation during the new venture creation process and, later, management of the new venture, is critical to the survival and success of the new venture. Also, considering that people have one pre-ferred learning style (Kolb, 1984), maintaining an appropriate balance between exploration and exploitation is a critical issue in entrepreneurship and may explain why some entrepreneurs depart from the new venture when it has emerged.

Even after an opportunity is recognized and the venture creation becomes mostly about knowledge exploitation, March (1991) observes that the adaptive process may be self-destructive because the effects of exploitation, such as focusing on more efficient use of existing knowledge, limit exploration. Consequently, for entrepreneurs there is a need to revert back to exploration, in order to balance exploration and exploitation for the venture to remain competitive. Balancing exploration and exploitation is complicated because entrepreneurs will have to employ different learn-ing styles – thinking, theorizing, feeling, and doing (Kolb, 1984) – on a continuous basis to balance exploration and exploitation.

LEADERSHIP, MANAGEMENT AND ENTREPRENEURSHIP

As noted in the introduction, the activities that entrepreneurs, leaders and managers engage in overlap. Schumpeter (1934) distinguishes between entrepreneurs and managers, pointing out that entrepreneurs are a special kind of leaders who create new ventures, whereas managers maintain dis-cipline and introduce order. Penrose (1959) differentiates the activities of entrepreneurs and managers, noting that managerial activities are focused on the execution of entrepreneurial activities, and entrepreneurial activi-ties are centered on innovations to solve problems. She also notes that managerial activities are short-term in orientation whereas entrepreneurial activities are long-term in nature. Mintzberg (1989) observes that managers engage in both leadership and entrepreneurial roles depending on the situation.

Leadership may be defined as the process of influencing others toward a goal (Bryman, 1996; Chemers, 1997). As noted earlier, entrepreneurship is the process of new venture creation. Unlike leadership and entrepreneurship, management is not a process. It is a function that comprises of ten roles, according to Mintzberg (1989), including roles as leader and entrepreneur. According to Mintzberg, in the leader role, the manager influences a group, department or organization toward a goal; whereas in the entrepreneurial role, the manager creates and manages change by solving problems, generating new ideas and solutions, and implementing them. Thus, a manager may engage in a leadership or entrepreneurship role by leading others towards a goal, or by creating change or new solutions. Yet, a manager's time horizon is short-term compared to that of leaders (Kotter, 1990; Penrose, 1959; Zaleznik, 1977), and the manager is focused on maintaining control and order, whereas the entrepreneur is focused on innovation (Penrose, 1959; Schumpeter, 1934; Stevenson, 1983). These considerations illustrate the lack of clarity that exists in distinguishing among entrepreneurs, leaders and managers.

In the next section, we expand our understanding of the combined literature on entrepreneurs, leaders and managers by explaining the distinction between entrepreneurial leaders and entrepreneurial managers in their pursuit of new ventures. In particular, we posit the dependency of new ventures on the entrepreneur's preferred learning style and the propensity to engage in knowledge exploration and knowledge exploitation.

ENTREPRENEURIAL LEADERS

Entrepreneurial leadership may be considered as the process of influencing others toward creating a new venture over time by engaging in innovation (Bryman, 1996; Chemers, 1997; Penrose, 1959; Schumpeter, 1934). As such, entrepreneurial leadership is a process in which the entrepreneurial leader develops a vision for a better future, at least implicitly, by pursuing an opportunity. Consequently, entrepreneurial leaders create new ventures that do not presently exist.

Entrepreneurial leaders are similar to transformational leaders: people who form a vision of a better future, motivate and inspire others to pursue this vision, and create change via innovation (Baum et al., 1998; Bennis and Nanus, 1985; Burns, 1978; Carsrud et al., Chapter 9 in this volume;

Gupta et al., 2004; Harrison and Leitch, 1994). In effect, entrepreneurial leaders envision future possibilities and transform the present to achieve the vision by framing, absorbing uncertainty, path-clearing, specify limits and building commitment to the vision (McGrath and MacMillan, 2000). As this implies, the critical phase of the new venture creation process for entrepreneurial leaders is the opportunity recognition – the discovery phase (Lumpkin et al., 2004) – with exploration being central to their learning (March, 1991); and long-term time orientation, which is unlike entrepreneurial managers (Kotter, 1990; Penrose, 1959; Zaleznik, 1977). Entrepreneurial leaders are less concerned with knowledge exploitation, which is preferred by entrepreneurial managers.

ENTREPRENEURIAL MANAGERS

Unlike entrepreneurial leadership, entrepreneurial management is a function. Entrepreneurial management may be defined as the efficient and effective execution, coordination and control of activities to create a new venture (Kotter, 1990; Penrose, 1959; Schumpeter, 1934; Zaleznik, 1977). This means that the entrepreneurial manager focuses on transactions (Bennis and Nanus, 1985; Burns, 1978) and knowledge exploitation (March, 1991) to achieve the effective and efficient execution, coordination and control of venture creation activities (Penrose, 1959). An example of entrepreneurial managers is franchisees, who create new outlets by following set guidelines provided by the franchisor.

Considering that adaptive processes tend to increase exploitation and reduce exploration over time, as the new venture creation process moves from opportunity recognition to the creation of the venture – the formation phase – the entrepreneurial leader may adapt to the venture creation process by engaging in knowledge exploitation and, thereby, assume the role of entrepreneurial manager. Because people tend to prefer one learning mode over another (Kolb, 1984), people preferring exploration over exploitation may opt out of the new venture creation process to pursue venture creation at an earlier stage of the process (for example, the discovery phase), to again engage in knowledge exploration. For the entrepreneurial leader who stays with the new venture, and for the entrepreneurial manager, there is a need to continuously balance exploration and exploitation to maintain the venture's survival and success (March, 1991).

DISCUSSION

How entrepreneurs create new ventures is a central issue in entrepreneur-ship research (Shane and Venkataraman, 2000; Venkataraman, 1997). Despite studies showing the importance of entrepreneurs in creating new ventures, there has been a paucity of research examining entrepreneurial behavior (Bird and Schjoedt, 2009; Bird et al., 2012). In this chapter, we put forward a framework for explaining the process of new venture creation from the perspective of not only entrepreneurs' behavior but also, importantly, entrepreneurs' learning.

Learning may be defined as the acquisition of new knowledge, or the modification or reinforcement of existing knowledge or behaviors through experience (Kolb, 1984). The distinction between new and existing knowl-edge in learning is critical in the new venture creation process because it includes two distinct phases: opportunity recognition and new venture creation. This is illustrated in the creativity-based model of opportunity recognition (Lumpkin et al., 2004).

We employed this model of the new venture creation process provided by Lumpkin et al. (2004) to illustrate how entrepreneurs transition from a discovery phase in which an opportunity is recognized, to a formation phase in which the opportunity is refined and a new venture is launched. We also employed Kolb's (1984) experiential learning theory to illustrate how entrepreneurs transition from learning new knowledge in the dis-covery phase, to learning from modification or reinforcement of existing knowledge in the formation phase in the new venture creation process, and, later, in management of the new venture. This approach is consistent with Hayek's (1945) observation that the 'economic problem' inherent in the evolution of economic markets is a problem of dispersion and utili-zation of knowledge, and the considerations provided by March (1991) regarding knowledge exploration, knowledge exploitation and the adap-tion process.

Employing these models, we showed that the discovery phase of new venture creation, the preparation and incubation stages, is facilitated by entrepreneurs who create new knowledge by engaging in knowledge exploration by transforming existing knowledge and experiences via thinking and theorizing (Hayek, 1945; Kolb, 1984; Lumpkin et al., 2004; March, 1991). Also, in concert with Corbett (2005), we illustrated that the formation phase, the stages of evaluation and elaboration that emphasize new venture planning and launch, is enabled by entrepreneurs' knowledge exploitation by doing and by applying existing knowledge (Hayek, 1945; Kolb, 1984; Lumpkin et al., 2004; March, 1991).

Kolb (1984) points out that people have one preferred learning style across all situations, even though they can engage in other learning styles. This may explain why some people perform better in some situations than in others. Considering that entrepreneurs have been defined as people who discover, evaluate and exploit opportunities (Shane and Venkataraman, 2000; Venkataraman, 1997) and the transition necessary from knowledge exploration to knowledge exploitation as the new venture creation process moves from the discovery phase to the formation phase (Lumpkin et al., 2004), and in turn to management of an existing venture, it becomes clear why many new ventures are created by an entrepreneurial team. While the two phases of the new venture creation process, discovery and formation, favor knowledge exploration and knowledge exploitation, it is important to observe that entrepreneurs need to adapt to the new venture creation process as it progresses (Holland, 1975; March, 1991; Schumpeter, 1934), and also to observe that entrepreneurs will continuously need to engage in the adaption process between knowledge exploration and exploitation to keep innovating to maintain competitiveness in the marketplace. These considerations may provide, at least in part, an explanation why some entrepreneurs depart the new venture in favor of pursuing another new venture: their learning style facilitates knowledge exploration, not knowledge exploitation. It may also be indicative of why some entrepreneurs are replaced by professional managers whose learning style is based upon knowledge exploitation.

As an alternative to placing entrepreneurs' learning from knowledge exploration and knowledge exploitation, we could have employed a causation–effectuation framework. In her seminal work on effectuation, Sarasvathy (2001) observes that one aspect of knowledge exploration is the effectuation process, while knowledge exploitation is predominately about causation. She notes that causation and effectuation may be complementary, similarly to knowledge exploration and exploitation in Kolb's (1984) circular process of learning. The distinguishing feature between the approaches we took in this chapter and Sarasvathy's is that she argues that the adaptive process may be better explained by effectuation than causation.

While we acknowledged the need for the adaptive process in the new venture creation process and, later, in the continued management of the venture and its success, we used learning from knowledge exploration and knowledge exploitation as the distinguishing feature between entrepreneurial leaders and entrepreneurial managers. We also noted that entrepreneurial leaders focus on the discovery phase (Lumpkin et al., 2004), which is typically referred to as opportunity recognition in the entrepreneurship literature (Shane and Venkataraman, 2000; Venkataraman, 1997), and entrepreneurial managers focus on knowledge exploitation.

We did so because entrepreneurs disrupt the market by recognition of opportunities and creation of innovations that stem from exploration of knowledge and experiences (Kolb, 1984; Sarasvathy, 2001; Schumpeter, 1934; Shane and Venkataraman, 2000; Venkataraman, 1997). The key distinguishing feature between entrepreneurial leaders and entrepreneurial managers is, thus, the degree to which they employ knowledge exploration or knowledge exploitation as part of the new venture creation process, specifically in the discovery phase. In the discovery phase, the entrepreneurial leaders recognize opportunities for new products that may disrupt the market and, in turn, become new brands; whereas entrepreneurial managers further existing products and brand names (da Silva Lopes and Casson, 2007). The entrepreneurial leaders use knowledge exploration to develop a vision and innovate despite the vicissitudes, risks and uncertainties of success and failure in the pursuit of this vision; whereas the entrepreneurial managers exploit knowledge to maintain order and control risk. This distinction is not in line with Mintzberg's (1989) ten roles of managers; however, it is consistent with the distinctions Penrose (1959) made regarding the activities of entrepreneurs and managers.

CONCLUDING REMARKS

In this chapter, we have argued that Kolb's (1984) learning styles can be used as a framework for distinguishing entrepreneurs as either entrepreneurial leaders or entrepreneurial managers in the context of new venture creation. Entrepreneurial leaders prefer to engage in knowledge exploration in order to innovate and to create new products and market niches; whereas entrepreneurial managers tend to engage in knowledge exploitation in line with the administration of tasks and duties and the containment of risks and uncertainties.

Research shows that the functional background of the chief executive officer (CEO) influences the CEO's attitude towards risks, tolerance of ambiguity and choice of venture strategy (Beal and Yasai-Ardekani, 2000; Entrialgo, 2002; Gupta and Govindarajan, 1984). This is perhaps best illustrated by labeling famous entrepreneurs as either entrepreneurial leaders or entrepreneurial managers. Recall that entrepreneurial managers emphasize efficient execution, coordination and control (Kotter, 1990; Penrose, 1959; Schumpeter, 1934; Zaleznik, 1977). This means that entrepreneurial managers tend to pursue a low-cost strategy over a differentiation strategy; and vice versa for entrepreneurial leaders who favor knowledge exploration and have a higher tolerance of risk and ambiguity. It also means that famous entrepreneurs such as Henry Ford, Bill Gates and Sam Walton may be classified as entrepreneurial managers; while Walt Disney, Steve Jobs and Thomas Edison may be classified as entrepreneurial leaders. Considering these entrepreneurs as either entrepreneurial leaders or entrepreneurial managers, it seems that entrepreneurial leaders' learning from knowledge exploration results in a vision of a different world, in which product innovations change the world in a radical manner; whereas entrepreneurial managers' learning from knowledge exploitation results in incremental innovation providing more efficient products, delivery, processes, and so on.

The considerations we have presented in this chapter are not without limitations. We did not consider the speed of learning. March (1991) notes that speed of learning complicates the learning process, as it influences the adaptive process and the balance between knowledge exploration and exploitation. Future empirical research will benefit from the inclusion of speed of learning to clarify how and where speed of learning has the most impact in the learning process, adaptive process and new venture creation process. Another limitation to our considerations pertains to the adaptive process. The literature on how and when people balance exploration and exploitation of knowledge, as either a person or a group, holds potential for development. This also pertains to the adaptive process in the new venture creation process. Research on effectuation may inform us, at least implicitly, about the adaptive process. Yet, future research that directly examines the adaptive process will be beneficial to our understanding of entrepreneurship. Considering that Bill Gates is known as a ferocious reader and Steve Jobs as a visionary, future research may benefit from the development of measurements to assess entrepreneurs as either entrepreneurial leaders or entrepreneurial managers, based on their preferred learning style of either exploration or exploitation of knowledge. While the literature on learning in the new venture process is limited (Hamel and Prahalad, 1996), the potential for future research to shed light on the impact of learning in entrepreneurship seems to be a fruitful avenue to better understand entrepreneurship. We have taken one step along this avenue by using learning to distinguish entrepreneurs as either entrepreneurial leaders or entrepreneurial managers, based on their preferred learning style.

REFERENCES

Baron, R.A. (2002). OB and entrepreneurship: The reciprocal benefits of closer conceptual links. *Research in Organizational Behavior*, 24, 225–69.
Baron, R.A. and Ensley, M.D. (2006). Opportunity recognition as the detection of meaningful patterns: Evidence from comparisons of novice and experienced entrepreneurs. *Management Science*, 52, 1331–44.

Baum, J.R., Locke, E.A. and Kirkpatrick, S.A. (1998). A longitudinal study of the relation of vision and vision communication to venture growth in entrepreneurial firms. *Journal of Applied Psychology*, 83, 43–54.

Beal, R.M. and Yasai-Ardekani, M. (2000). Performance implications of aligning CEO functional experiences with competitive strategies. *Journal of Management*, 26, 733–62.

Bennis, W.G. and Nanus, B. (1985). *Leaders: The Strategies for Taking Charge*. New York, NY: Harper & Row.

Bird, B. and Schjoedt, L. (2009). Entrepreneurial behavior: Its nature, scope, recent research and future research. In A.L. Carsrud and M.E. Brännback (eds), *Understanding the Entrepreneurial Mind: Opening the Black Box* (pp. 327–58). Dordrecht: Springer AG.

Bird, B.J., Schjoedt, L. and Baum, J.R. (2012). Entrepreneurs' behavior: Elucidation and measurement. *Entrepreneurship Theory and Practice*, 36(5), 889–913.

Bryman, A. (1996). Leadership in organizations. In S.R. Clegg, C. Hardy and W.R. Nord (eds), *Handbook of Organization Studies* (pp. 276–84). Thousand Oaks, CA: SAGE.

Burns, J.M. (1978). *Leadership*. New York, NY: Harper & Row.

Chemers, M.M. (1997). *An Integrative Theory of Leadership*. Mahwah, NJ: Lawrence Erlbaum Associates.

Cogliser, C.C. and Brigham, K.H. (2004). The intersection of leadership and entrepreneurship: Mutual lessons to be learned. *Leadership Quarterly*, 15, 771–99.

Corbett, A.C. (2005). Experiential learning within the process of opportunity identification and exploitation. *Entrepreneurship Theory and Practice*, 29, 473–91.

Csikszentmihalyi, M. (1996). *Creativity*. New York, NY: HarperCollins.

Czariawska-Joerges, B. and Wolff, R. (1991). Leaders, managers, entrepreneurs on and off the organizational stage. *Organizational Studies*, 12, 529–46.

da Silva Lopes, T. and Casson, M. (2007). Entrepreneurship and the development of global brands. *Business History Review*, 81, 651–80.

Entrialgo, M. (2002). The impact of the alignment of strategy and managerial characteristics on Spanish SMEs. *Journal of Small Business Management*, 40, 260–270.

Fiet, J.O., Clouse, V.G.H. and Norton, W.I. (2004). Systematic search by repeat entrepreneurs. In J.E. Butler (ed.), *Opportunity Identification and Entrepreneurial Behavior* (pp. 1–27). Grenwich, CT: Information Age Publishing.

Gartner, W.B. (1988). 'Who is an entrepreneur?' Is the wrong question. *American Journal of Small Business*, 12, 11–32.

Gartner, W.B. (1990). What are we talking about when we talk about entrepreneurship? *Journal of Business Venturing*, 5, 15–28.

Greeno, J.G., Collins, A.M. and Resnick, L.B. (1996). Cognition and learning. In D.C. Berliner and R.C. Calfee (eds), *Handbook of Educational Psychology* (pp. 15–46). New York, NY: Macmillan.

Gupta, A.K. and Govindarajan, V. (1984). Business unit strategy, managerial characteristics, and business-unit effectiveness at strategy implementation. *Academy of Management Journal*, 27, 25–41.

Gupta, V., MacMillan, I.C. and Surie, G. (2004). Entrepreneurial leadership: Developing and measuring a cross-cultural construct. *Journal of Business Venturing*, 19, 241–60.

Hamel, G. and Prahalad, C.K. (1996). Competing in the new economy: Managing out of bounds. *Strategic Management Journal*, 17, 237–42.

Harrison, R.T. and Leitch, C.M. (1994). Entrepreneurship and leadership: The implications for education and development. *Entrepreneurship and Regional Development*, 6, 111–25.

Hayek, F.A. (1945). The use of knowledge in society. *American Economic Review*, 35, 519–30.

Holland, J.H. (1975). *Adaption in Natural and Artificial Systems*. Ann Arbor, MI: University of Michigan Press.

Ko, S. (2004). Bisociation and opportunity. In J.E. Butler (ed.), *Opportunity Identification and Entrepreneurial Behavior* (pp. 99–114). Greenwich, CT: Information Age Publishing.

Kolb, D.A. (1984). *Experiential Learning: Experience as the Source of Learning and Development*. Englewood Cliffs, NJ: Prentice Hall.

Kolb, D.A., Boyatzis, R.E. and Mainemelis, C. (2000). Experiential learning theory: Previous research and new directions. In R.J. Sternberg and L.F. Zhang (eds), *Perspectives on Cognitive, Learning and Thinking Styles* (pp. 227–47). Mahwah, NJ: Lawrence Erlbaum.

Kotter, J.P. (1990). *A Force for Change: How Leadership Differs from Management*. New York, NY: Free Press.

Lumpkin, G.T., Hills, G. and Shrader, R. (2004). Opportunity recognition. In H.P. Welsch (ed.), *Entrepreneurship: The Way Ahead* (pp. 73–90). New York, NY: Routledge.

Mainemelis, C., Boyatzis, R. and Kolb, D.A. (2002). Learning styles and adaptive flexibility: Testing the experiential theory of development. *Management Learning*, 33, 5–33.

March, J.G. (1991). Exploration and exploitation in organizational learning. *Organization Science*, 2, 71–87.

McGrath, R.G. and MacMillan, I.C. (2000). *The Entrepreneurial Mindset: Strategies for Continuously Creating Opportunity in an Age of Uncertainty*. Boston, MA: Harvard Business Press.

Mintzberg, H. (1989). *Mintzberg on Management: Inside our Strange World of Organizations*. New York, NY: Free Press.

Penrose, E.T. (1959). *The Theory of the Growth of the Firm*. New York, NY: Wiley.

Sarasvathy, S.D. (2001). Causation and effectuation: Toward a theoretical shift from economic inevitability to entrepreneurial contingency. *Academy of Management Review*, 26, 243–63.

Schumpeter, J.A. (1934). Fundamentals of economic development. *The Theory of Economic Development* (pp. 65–94). Cambridge, MA: Harvard University Press.

Shane, S. and Venkataraman, S. (2000). The promise of entrepreneurship as a field of research. *Academy of Management Review*, 25, 217–26.

Stevenson, H. (1983). A perspective on entrepreneurship. Harvard Business School Working Paper 9-384-131.

Venkataraman, S. (1997). The distinctive domain of entrepreneurship research. *Advances in Entrepreneurship, Firm Emergence and Growth*, 3, 119–38.

Zaleznik, A. (1977). Managers and leaders: Are they different? *Harvard Business Review*, 55, 67–78.

8. Exploring the full range of leadership across the organizational life cycle and growth states of entrepreneurial firms
R. Greg Bell and J. Lee Whittington

Entrepreneurship and leadership are often treated as distinct constructs. However, there is some common ground between them that is important to explore. For instance, if we think of leaders as change agents who challenge the status quo (Maritz et al., 2011), then we can certainly see entrepreneurs as change agents who seek to identify market niches and change the status quo by providing new products and services to fill the perceived gap. We can also see entrepreneurs acting as leaders who inspire investors and employees to commit to the adventure of creating something that does not exist.

Entrepreneurship scholars recognize that the skills needed to begin a new venture are different from those needed to scale and grow. However, few have endeavored to look at the requisite skills needed to make this transition from a leadership perspective. In this chapter we view entrepreneurs as operating in the role of leaders. Specifically, we explore how the specific leadership behaviors that are helpful for getting new ventures started are not necessarily the ones needed to grow and sustain the enterprise. However, we recognize that it is a rare individual who has the full set of skills required to both create and grow a sustainable organization. Both entrepreneurship and leadership researchers and practitioners agree that organizations often reach a critical stage when there is a need to bring in others who have skills that can advance the firm beyond its current state.

In this chapter we evaluate the link between entrepreneurship and leadership by utilizing the 'full range of leadership model' (FRLM) (Avolio, 2010). The FRLM is one of the most consistent, researched and comprehensive models to conceptualize and measure leadership (Bass and Avolio, 1994). The model encompasses both transformational elements of leadership (such as building trust, acting with principle and integrity, inspiring others, innovating and developing others), and transactional elements (including contingent reward and management by exception) and avoidant or laissez-faire leadership behaviors. No leadership model has received as much support over the past three decades as has the 'full range of leadership' paradigm. The full-range model has its roots in the pioneering work of Burns (1978), who defined leadership as: 'leaders inducing follow-ers to act for certain goals that represent the values and the motivations – the wants and needs, the aspirations and expectations – *of both leaders and followers*' (ibid.: 19).

After outlining the FRLM, we take a 'life-cycle' approach by examin-ing which aspects of the full-range model are most appropriate at the different stages of the firm's development. Despite their popularity and intuitive appeal, a growing criticism to life-cycle models is that they are overly sequential and linear (Levie and Lichtenstein, 2010; Phelps et al., 2007). Yet, we agree with Phelps et al. (2007) that stage models are useful metaphors that appreciate how structural and contextual factors change as organizations evolve. We suggest that as the organization evolves, lead-ership becomes increasingly important. For example, at the earliest stage the entrepreneur performs many roles simultaneously, such as financial controller, marketing, product development, and many others. However, as the venture grows in both size and complexity, entrepreneurs can del-egate certain functions. Yet, the entrepreneur should concentrate their efforts on the leadership role.

Later in the chapter we draw upon Short et al. (2008), who suggest that 'the use of configurational logic is noticeably absent in leadership research to date' (ibid.: 17). Building upon recent empirical studies demonstrating the usefulness of a configurational perspective in evaluating leadership substitutes (Whittington et al., 2013), we suggest that together the life-cycle perspective of firm growth and the FRLM, when evaluated through a configurational lens, can be useful in understanding how various com-binations of transformational and transactional leadership behaviors may have differential effects across the variety of states of growth that a venture may experience.

Our chapter adds to the growing body of research focused on the major changes and transitions that occur within entrepreneurial firms as they mature. For instance, one example is the transition from the emergence stage to being professionally managed (Zahra and Filatotchev, 2004). As they grow, entrepreneurial firms often hit a juncture whereby the private resources of the founders will no longer be sufficient to support growth opportunities. In order to surmount this 'threshold' (Zahra and Filatotchev, 2004), firms often look to public equity markets to overcome resource constraints and finance their growth strategies. Likewise, profes-sionalization often occurs through the adoption of boards of directors.

The FRLM provides us a valuable lens through which we can explore several under-researched areas associated with the leadership of small and medium-sized enterprises (SMEs), and specifically organizations that have survived the early growth stages. For example, much of the current emphasis in both entrepreneurship research and entrepreneurship education deals almost exclusively with initial staffing decisions. No doubt, these are very important decisions, as inattention to the initial talent mix can limit the growth potential of new ventures. In these early phases of an organization's life the entrepreneur must simultaneously challenge the status quo and paint a vision that will not only attract investors, but also appeal to the key talent needed to launch the firm. However, as the organization grows the entrepreneurial leader is often confronted with multiple decisions and tasks associated with attracting, developing and retaining employees.

We agree with Kempster and Cope (2010) who state that entrepreneurship becomes a distinct form of leadership during the growth process. Scholars suggest that 'developing the people-management skills to encourage delegation (participation and empowerment), communication and teamwork is a primary need for firms that need to make the transition from owner micromanagement to larger-scale professional structures' (Phelps et al., 2007: 8). Our conceptualization of leadership emphasizes the interdependencies that entrepreneurs face in forging a vision together with building a cast of competent supporters who are not only capable, but also committed and engaged in the day-to-day tasks necessary to help the firm grow (Gupta et al., 2004). Moreover, the needs and challenges associated with both developing individual employees and designing appropriate rewards are certainly important to firms that have survived the initial growth stages.

Our chapter begins with a detailed discussion of the full-range model of leadership. Then, we present an overview of the stages of the life cycle of an entrepreneurial firm. As we discuss the stages of the life cycle, we integrate a discussion of the aspects of leadership that are most crucial to that stage. We then explore how the FRLM can be evaluated from a configurational perspective. We conclude the chapter by offering several potential future research directions related to the FRLM and the growth states of entrepreneurial firms.

THE FULL-RANGE MODEL OF LEADERSHIP

No leadership model has received as much support over the past three decades as has the 'full range of leadership model' (FRLM). The full range of leadership theory postulates a spectrum of five transformational and three transactional factors of leadership. The set of transformational leadership behaviors include idealized vision, inspirational motivation, intellectual stimulation, individualized consideration, and implicit contingent reward, while the transactional behaviors include explicit contingent rewards, active management by exception, and passive management by exception, all of which we explore below. These behaviors are not mutually exclusive. Indeed, Avolio's (2010) FRLM suggests that effective leaders engage in a full range of behaviors that encompass elements of both transactional and transformational leadership, with transactional leadership as the basis for the subsequent development of transformational leadership. The FRLM suggests that different combinations of leadership traits may be effective, given the organizational situation (Bass and Avolio, 1994). We rely upon the full-range leadership perspective because it uniquely reflects the fact that different mixtures of transformational and transactional leadership behaviors can be utilized during any stage of growth. Bass and Riggio (2006) observe that leaders tend to tailor their behavior to achieve group objectives, suggesting that there are times when the transformational leadership behaviors are more salient, and other times when transactional behaviors are required.

The full-range model has its roots in the pioneering work of Burns (1978: 19), who defined leadership as: 'leaders inducing followers to act for certain goals that represent the values and the motivations – the wants and needs, the aspirations and expectations – *of both leaders and followers*'. We discuss below how the interaction between a leader and their followers could take either transactional or transforming forms, as well as involve a combination of the forms. While our emphasis here is centered on the behaviors of leaders during different growth stages, we recognize that there is a growing body of knowledge devoted to understanding followership in leadership research (Baker, 2007; Bligh, 2011; Carsten et al., 2010; Kelley, 1988). In response to this growing interest, we highlight several potential research directions related to followership and the FRLM later in the chapter.

Transactional leadership occurs when a leader exchanges something of economic, political or psychological value with a follower. These exchanges are based on the leader identifying performance requirements and clarifying the conditions under which rewards are available for meeting these requirements. The goal is to enter into a mutually beneficial exchange, but not necessarily to develop an enduring relationship. Although a leadership act transpires, it is not one that binds the leader and follower together in a mutual and continuing pursuit of a higher purpose.

Transactional leadership emphasizes two factors: management-by-exception and contingent reward (Bass, 1985). Management-by-exception is a less active approach to leadership than contingent reward that essentially informs followers of job expectations, but resists further involvement with the follower unless the follower's actual performance varies significantly from those expectations. Contingent reward refers to the efforts made by the leader to clarify expectations so that followers will understand what they need to do in order to receive rewards. Hence, contingent reward shows the degree to which the leader lets others know what they need to do in order to be rewarded, emphasizing what is expected from them, and that their accomplishments will be recognized.

When used correctly, transactional behaviors can accomplish the leader's goals and also satisfy the interests of the followers. These behaviors can take either of two forms. 'Constructive transactions' are those that are used to clarify expectations and identify the linkages between performance and rewards. If done properly, these exchanges form a compact of expectations (Avolio, 2010) by which followers will evaluate the consistency and trustworthiness of their leader. In contrast, 'corrective transactions' focus on creating a desired change in behavior, cooperation or attitude. These transactions are somewhat negative in that they clarify what must be done to avoid censorship, reproof, punishment or other disciplinary actions (Avolio, 2010).

Both constructive and corrective transactions are important to the effectiveness of transactional leaders. As they honor constructive agreements and consistently apply corrective measures, their followers are able to develop perceptions about the consistency of their behavior and the likelihood that they will meet their leaders' expectations. As such, the recognition of transactional behaviors by followers is important to the establishment of a productive, trusting relationship between the leader and their followers (Whittington et al., 2009).

Transactional leadership is generally easily identifiable because the behaviors revolve around key issues of employment such as wages and salaries, performance feedback, rewards for performance such as promotions, and so on, and are centered on relatively concrete acts. Although transactional leadership is not enough to develop the full potential of followers, it is a necessary transitional step in developing the trust between a leader and follower that is required for transformational leadership to be implemented and become effective (Avolio, 2010).

Transforming leadership augments transactional leadership by moving beyond a merely exchange-based relationship and engaging individuals with each other in such a way that the leader and follower raise one another to higher levels of motivation and morality (Burns, 1978). Effective transformational leadership includes one or more of the following characteristics: idealized vision, inspirational motivation, intellectual stimulation and individualized consideration (Bass, 1985; Bass and Avolio, 1994). These behaviors describe leaders with strong social skills who are capable of communicating effectively in order 'to arouse, inspire, and motivate followers' (Riggio et al., 2003: 85). This transformation occurs by raising the followers' awareness of the significance of designated outcomes, getting followers to transcend their self-interests for the good of the organization, or augmenting followers' needs on Maslow's (1954) hierarchy of needs (Bass, 1985).

Idealized influence refers to the role-modeling behavior of transformational leaders. These leaders consider the needs of others over their own, share risk with their followers and demonstrate high standards of moral conduct. Leaders demonstrate faith in others by empowering followers and creating a joint sense of mission (Avolio, 2010). Consequently, their followers identify with and attempt to emulate them (Bass and Avolio, 1994; Bass and Riggio, 2006). Therefore, idealized influence indicates the extent to which a leader maintains their followers' trust and respect. This is achieved by the leader appealing to the followers' hopes and dreams and then demonstrating dedication to seeing those hopes realized.

Transformational leaders use inspirational motivation to build emotional commitment to the organization's vision or goal. They do this by articulating a vision that portrays an attractive future which provides meaning and challenge for followers (Bass, 1985). Clear expectations are communicated, with a demonstrated commitment to goals and the shared vision. Inspirational motivation entails the degree to which the leader provides a compelling vision that will appeal to the head and the heart of followers (Kotter, 2012). This requires the use of appropriate symbols and images to help others focus on the significant contribution their work makes toward achieving that vision.

Transformational leaders are change agents who use intellectual stimulation to question assumptions, reframe problems and approach existing situations from a fresh perspective (Bass, 1985). This behavior encourages innovation and creativity. Participation and creative risk-taking are encouraged without the fear of public criticism or penalty for departure from the leader's ideas (Bass and Riggio, 2006). Intellectual stimulation shows the degree to which the leader invites others to be creative in looking at old problems in new ways. By challenging the status quo (Kotter, 2012), these leaders create an environment that is tolerant of seemingly extreme positions, and encourage people to question existing values and beliefs of the organization. Rather than seeing this as a threat, transformational leaders see this as a healthy exercise that is vital for continued growth and sustainability.

In terms of garnering research attention, transformational leadership is the most popular leadership theory (Bass and Riggio, 2006). Unfortunately, though, the theory is generally regarded as suffering from an inattention to the characteristics or initiative of the followers. While there is a focus on improving the quality of the leader–follower relationship, critics contend that transformational leadership is leader-centric in that it falls short of viewing followers in a broader manner (Uhl-Bien et al., 2014). However, in response to these critics we point to individualized consideration, which refers to the transformational leader's mentoring role in which the leader pays special attention to each individual's need for well-being, personal growth and achievement (Bass, 1985). We suggest that individualized consideration does devote attention to followers, in that it indicates the degree to which a leader shows interest in others' well-being. Transformational leaders are intentional about creating learning opportunities and a supportive environment to facilitate the development of followers. They use delegation as a developmental tool and assign projects individually to advance followers to successively higher levels of potential.

Leaders who fail to provide the solid foundation associated with transactional leadership are often likely to leave their employees' role expectations unclear. This results in an ill-defined sense of direction and ambiguous task assignments. However, when these role expectations have been appropriately clarified through the use of transactional leadership behavior, the stage is set for more mature relationships between a leader and their followers to evolve over time. Thus, the clarification of role expectations provides a crucial basis for building a more general framework of mutual expectations between the leader and the follower. Furthermore, when leaders honor their various transactional arrangements with their followers, trust begins to develop, creating the foundation for a sustained relationship that enables the effective utilization of the full-range of leadership behaviors (Avolio, 2010).

Consistent with the full-range model, others in the field of leadership have shown that differences in leadership behaviors can be traced to cognitive processes that underlie those behaviors. For example, Wofford and his associates (Wofford and Goodwin, 1994; Wofford et al., 1998) used an information processing framework (Lord and Maher, 1991) to understand the cognitive structures that underlie both transactional and transformational leadership behavior. They found that different cognitive processes did in fact underlie both transactional and transformational leadership.

Effective leaders supplement transactional leadership behavior with one or more of the transformational behaviors (Bass and Avolio, 1994; Avolio, 2010). However, not all leaders have the capacity (Wofford et al., 1998) or willingness to do this. In fact, some lean hard into the transactional behaviors and ignore the transformational aspects of the full-range model. Transformational leaders also have within their cognitive repertoire elements pertaining to transactional leadership behavior (Wofford et al., 1998). That is, individuals who are able to engage in transformational leadership behavior may revert to the more concrete level of *quid pro quo* agreements and engage in transactional leadership behavior as needed. Yet, leaders who were identified by their followers as transactional did not have the same level of cognitively complexity found in leaders who were identified as transformational (Wofford et al., 1998). In this study, leaders who were identified as transactional focused on the immediate needs of the organization by emphasizing the efficient implementation of policies and operational procedures. The transformational leaders were also capable of providing this operational focus, but they supplemented this by emphasizing the broader concerns of the organization and a more strategic, long-term perspective. These results argue for a hierarchical framework, progressing upward from concrete to more abstract representations in memory, wherein transactional leadership provides the more concrete and pragmatic foundation upon which transformational leadership rests (Wofford et al., 1998).

In the following section we review the characteristics of the various stages of organizational development. Our discussion of each stage will be supplemented with a discussion of the leadership requirements associated with the stage. This discussion is normative or ideal. As we have said, not every entrepreneur will possess a full range of leadership skills, or be comfortable relinquishing control by bringing others into the leadership team who can enhance the organization by augmenting the existing leadership capacity. We explore these issues in the following sections.

STAGES OF DEVELOPMENT IN ENTREPRENEURIAL FIRMS

In this section we discuss a model of organizational development that is based on an integration of the organizational life-cycle frameworks of Adizes (1979) and Greiner (1972). Both are illustrated in Figures 8.1 and 8.2. Multi-stage models imply that organizations go through predictable patterns of growth (Greiner, 1972; Kazanjian and Drazin, 1989; McMahon, 2001). The underlying premise shared by these models is that organizations evolve on the basis of solutions to problems (Kazanjian and Drazin, 1989; Scott and Bruce, 1987), while others suggest that organizations move through periods of evolution and steady growth to the next stage (Greiner, 1972). Each stage has unique characteristics and challenges that must be met with an appropriate leadership response. In addition to the challenges faced within a phase of the organizational life cycle, the transition from one stage to another requires additional leadership competencies.

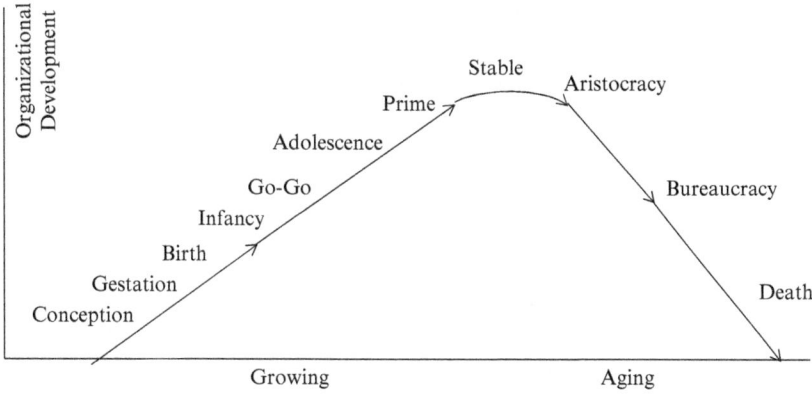

Figure 8.1   Adizes corporate life cycle

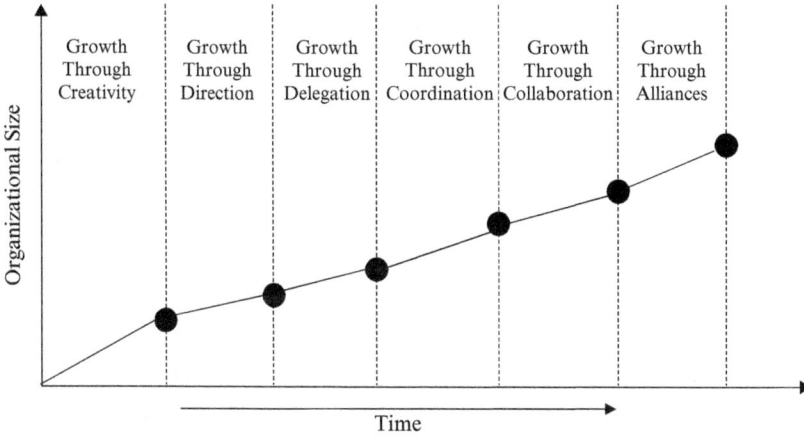

Figure 8.2   Greiner growth model

Critics suggest that life-cycle models are overly sequential and linear (Levie and Lichtenstein, 2010; Phelps et al., 2007). These models have also been criticized for being overly descriptive, and neglectful of a thorough analysis of the factors that actually drive growth. A growing body of research suggests that the sequence of growth stages can be heterogeneous (Aislabie, 1992; Levie and Hay, 1998; Rutherford et al., 2003; Phelps et al., 2007). Bridge et al. (2003) suggest that firms can grow, stagnate and decline, in any order. Moreover, firms may experience these phases more than once. Firms can even reverse their steps, and the timing in which firms progress through growth phases can vary considerably (Blundel and Hingley, 2001). Levie and Lichtenstein (2010) found in their review of more than 100 studies centered on stage models of growth that firms do in fact go through different stages at different points in their life. However, there is little consensus on basic constructs, nor agreement on defining the stages of enterprise growth.

Despite the criticisms levied against the salience life-cycle models, we agree with Phelps et al. (2007) that stage models are useful as metaphors in that they appreciate how structural and contextual factors change as organizations grow in size and age. Indeed, as the organization evolves, leadership becomes increasingly important. For example, at the earliest stage the entrepreneur performs many roles simultaneously, such as financial control, marketing, product development, and many others. However, as the venture grows in both size and complexity, entrepreneurs can delegate certain functions. Yet, the entrepreneur should concentrate their efforts on the leadership role. Developing the requisite people and administrative skills necessary for delegation, to communicate effectively and to achieve teamwork, is critical if ventures are to successfully move from owner micromanagement to larger-scale professionalized organizations. Hence, our conceptualization of the FRLM supports the interdependencies that entrepreneurs face in forging a vision together with building a cast of competent supporters who are not only capable, but are also committed and engaged in the day-to-day tasks necessary to help the firm grow (Gupta et al., 2004).

Greiner (1972) (Figure 8.2) suggested that firms grow through five distinct stages. Each growth phase includes a calm period and ends with a management crisis. Greiner characterizes these five stages as creativity, direction, delegation, coordination and collaboration. He suggests that firms go through both evolution and revolution crises, and that these can be solved by introducing new structures and programs enabling employees to revitalize the firm. Adizes (1979) (Figure 8.1) is another significant contributor to the life-cycle perspective, and suggests that a leader, through their attitude and style, has considerable influence on the effectiveness of a firm as it evolves across the organizational life cycle. More recently, Chaston (2009) suggests that organizational growth is a function of crossing five types of chasms, which are: launch capacity, expansion, organizational formalization, success and long-term growth. The ability to cross each chasm depends upon entrepreneurs acquiring new skills and prioritizing managerial tasks inside the organization.

Leadership across the Life Cycles

Leadership is a key element in the effectiveness of small businesses (Longenecker et al., 2013), and in small firms incorporates many behaviors, including communicating a vision that reflects a long-term orientation. Within entrepreneurship research, the question of leadership remains understudied, and research emphasis has shifted from a trait approach to a behavioral approach (Ensley et al., 2006). The life-cycle model presents a valuable lens through which we can critically evaluate leadership challenges facing entrepreneurs, and how internal and external environmental factors influence leadership behaviors. Just as the organizational form must adapt to the environment (Duncan, 1972), so the requirements of management and leadership must also be adapted to the unique challenges faced by the organization in each phase of development. In this section, we discuss the importance of various dimensions of the full-range model at the various stages of the firm's development.

The early stages of the life-cycle model make up what Greiner (1972) refers to as the creativity phase (Figure 8.2). Using a metaphor of childbirth, Adizes suggests that this phase involves conception, gestation and birth. In the context of an entrepreneurial firm, conception implies the inception of a product or organizational idea. Gestation refers to the pre-launch testing of the idea with potential customers and investors. This phase would also involve the attraction of the necessary capital. This phase ends with the birth of the new organization. During the pre-birth and early life of the organization, the entrepreneur must attract investors who are willing to capitalize the effort. In addition to attracting investors, the entrepreneur must also attract the key talent that will help to launch the firm.

In the creativity period it is particularly important for the leader to make a compelling case for the need of new products and the markets that will be served. Hence, the entrepreneur as leader will need to combine intellectual stimulation alongside inspirational motivation. Intellectual stimulation provides the challenge to the status quo, and the identification of significant gaps in the current offerings of the market. Through inspirational motivation, the entrepreneur paints a vision of how new products can satisfy this gap. The vision appeals to the 'heads' of investors who are seeking an opportunity to invest in projects that promise a return. This vision also appeals to the 'hearts' of potential employees who are seeking opportunities to invest themselves in an exciting and meaningful future (Kotter, 2012). The entrepreneurial leader should also engage in the idealized influence that demonstrates their personal commitment to the endeavor. This display of willingness to accept personal risk provides the tangible evidence that others need in order to join the endeavor as investors or employees.

As the organization grows, the entrepreneur as leader will need to become more balanced in their efforts. They must continue to emphasize the need for growth, while providing the discipline needed for execution. The need for inspirational motivation continues; the growth of the workforce requires the ongoing commitment to role clarification provided by the disciplined application of contingent reward behavior. There is also now a simultaneous need for leaders to focus their efforts on the development as well as the retention of key talent. To date, much of the current emphasis in both entrepreneurship research and entrepreneurship education deals almost exclusively with initial staffing decisions. However, as the organization advances through the go-go phase the entrepreneurial leader is often confronted with multiple decisions and tasks associated with both attracting and retaining employees. Moreover, the needs and challenges associated with both developing individual employees and designing appropriate rewards are certainly important to firms that have survived the initial growth stages. This requires the leader to engage in the mentoring and coaching associated with the individualized consideration facet of the full-range model. During this phase, growth continues in an environment of more formal communications, budgets, and focus on separate activities such as marketing and production. Incentive schemes replace stock as a financial reward. However, there comes a point when the products and processes become so numerous that there are not enough hours in the day for one person to manage them all, and they cannot possibly know as much about all these products or services as those lower down the hierarchy.

According to Greiner (1972), the creativity phase ends with an autonomy crisis where additional structures based on delegation are called for. Professional management that provides focus on day-to-day operating efficiency is now needed, to supplement the leadership focus. Although some founders may change their style and take on this role, resolution of the crisis often requires that someone new is brought in. Successfully transitioning through this crisis leads to a new phase of growth through direction (Greiner, 1972). This may create a 'founder's trap', because the founder remains closely identified with the company (Adizes, 1990). However, as the organization matures, their leadership will very often become more diffused. Founders will often attempt to decentralize by delegating authority and responsibility, yet this is often hampered by the founder's need for control and the employees' inability to accept the distance from the leader that such delegation creates (Adizes, 1990).

Working through the issues associated with the autonomy crisis requires a more complex approach to leading that incorporates the full range of transactional and transformational leadership behaviors. The leadership team must challenge the emerging culture of conflict. This requires intellectual stimulation that explicitly identifies a lack of acceptance with the emerging culture. This challenge must also be supplemented with a return to goals and vision that transcend functional and individual goals. Thus the leader must engage in inspirational motivation. It is critical that the leader models the way by engaging in the type of behavior they wish to see demonstrated among the employees. Finally, in a rather negative application of contingent reward, the leader must use corrective transactions to clarify the consequences for those who refuse to embrace the need to eliminate any infighting and refocus on the needs of the organization and its customers.

Organizations in the stability and aristocracy phases begin to experience the 'architecture of simplicity' (Miller, 1993). Many researchers claim that organizations which were once successful fail because they have lost their edge; however, Miller offers a contrary thesis. He defines simplicity as an overwhelming preoccupation with a single goal, strategic activity, department or world view; one that increasingly precludes consideration of any others. Accordingly, many outstanding organizations lapse into decline precisely because they have developed too sharp an edge. They amplify and extend a single strength or function while neglecting most others. Ultimately, a rich and complex organization becomes excessively simple; it turns into a monolithic, narrowly focused version of its former self, converting a formula for success into a path toward failure.

As simplicity overtakes an organization, secondary issues are forgotten and the parties responsible for them lose influence. The organization becomes more monolithic, with its members and subunits having fewer and increasingly similar preoccupations, and its systems becoming more specialized. There are both objective and subjective varieties of organizational simplicity, and most of these are interdependent. The objective varieties include dominance of a single goal or subunit; information systems and routines that reflect only a narrow range of skills and concerns; and a lion's share of resources going to one central tactic or activity. But simplicity may also be reflected subjectively by the narrowing and increasingly homogenous 'lenses' or world views that often underlie the more objective forms of simplicity (Miller, 1993).

Confronting the architecture of simplicity requires a heavy dose of intellectual stimulation that forces the organization to confront what Drucker (1994) calls the 'theory of the business'. The theory of the business is a set of three assumptions that are often implicit, yet have a powerful influence on the organization. First, there are assumptions about the environment of the organization: society and its structure, the market, the customer and technology. Second, there are assumptions about the specific mission of the organization. Third, there are assumptions about the core competencies needed to accomplish the organization's mission. The assumptions about environment define what an organization is paid for. The assumptions about mission define what an organization considers to be meaningful results; in other words, they point to how it envisions itself making a difference in the economy and in the society at large. Finally, the assumptions about core competencies define where an organization must excel in order to maintain leadership. Through intellectual stimulation the leader forces the organization to make these implicit assumptions explicit, and thus challenges the validity of the assumptions. While these assumptions may have been valid when the firm was founded, market dynamics may deem them inappropriate for the present reality. The result of such an exercise is often a new vision that resets the direction of the organization. This may result in diversification of the organization's portfolio through product development and innovation, as well as divesture of business units that no longer fit the reconstituted theory of the business.

Full-Range Leadership across Growth States

Along with the life-cycle perspective of firm growth, we suggest that the FRLM when evaluated through a configurational lens can be useful in helping to explain how certain aspects of leadership may have differential effects across the variety of states of growth a venture may experience. Despite its growing use in organizational research, Short et al. (2008: 17) suggest that 'the use of configurational logic is noticeably absent in leadership research to date'. There is a growing recognition among organizational researchers that many factors contribute to performance in complementary ways, and should not be evaluated in isolation from each other. As we mentioned earlier, the FRLM suggests that different combinations of leadership traits may be effective, given the organizational situation (Bass and Avolio, 1994). Viewing the entire range of transformational and transactional leadership behaviors as 'bundles' presents a rich opportunity for the identification of the manner in which both transformational and transactional leadership behaviors may complement or substitute for one another at different points during an organization's life.

Evaluating entrepreneurial leadership from a configurational perspective using the FRLM could begin, first, by reviewing the variety of classifications authors have used to categorize firms. For example, O'Farrell and Hitchens (1988) suggest that ventures could be fast growers, satisfiers, and those that attempt fast growth but fail. Similarly, Storey (1994) classified ventures as failures, trundlers (ventures that survive over time, yet do not create jobs) and flyers. Others categorize firms as lifestyle, comfort zone (providing its owner with sufficient returns for the level of comfort they want in life) and growth (Bridge et al., 2003).

Second, a configurational approach with the FRLM can be useful in answering several important related questions. How do transformational and transactional entrepreneurial leadership behaviors combine in ways that are supportive of fast-growing firms? Alternatively, and perhaps more importantly, what combinations of transformational and transactional leadership behaviors are detrimental to fast-growing ventures? Also, we believe a configuration perspective would be useful to understanding what combinations of transformational and transactional entrepreneurial leadership behaviors are supportive of firms that Storey (1994) describes as 'trundlers' (ventures that survive over time, yet do not experience a growing number of employees).

Davidsson et al. (2009) recently developed a framework that categorizes firms as either above or below their industry average both in terms of growth and in terms of profit. Their framework (see Figure 8.3) yields four cases, labeled 'star' (high on both), 'profit' (high profitability, low growth), 'growth' (high growth, low profitability) and 'poor' (low on both). We believe this categorization has potential to be helpful in understanding what combinations of transformational and transactional leadership behaviors would be supportive of firms that are both high-growth and highly profitable, as well as the bundles that are found in low-growth and low-profit ventures. Further, this categorization framework provides opportunities to address Levie and Lichtenstein's (2010) call for research investigating how firms make transitions between different growth states.

	Growth	
	Low	High
Profit		
Low	*Poor*	*Growth*
High	*Profit*	*Star*

Source: Davidsson et al. (2009).

Figure 8.3   Categorization schema of firms by growth and profitability

Indeed, the salient transformational and transactional leadership bundle 'recipe' for moving from growth to profit states will likely be different from the transformational and transactional leadership bundle 'recipe' that guides firms from either the growth or the profit states to the star state. Further, there are likely to be differences based upon age and industry context.

The 'full range of leadership model' has the ingredients to serve entrepreneurs well over the life cycle of the organization. As we have suggested, effective leadership is not based on a universal set of behaviors that apply equally in all contexts. Indeed, even in the context of one organization that evolves over time, effective leadership requires a full range of behaviors. The need for a dynamic approach to leading, and organizing, is based on the fact that entrepreneurial organizations operate in dynamic and complex environments. If these environments were constantly stable and simple, the requirements of leadership would not be as great, and a focus on operational efficiencies through transactional leadership would be sufficient. However, the increasing complexity of dynamic markets requires constant adaptation, and calls for the challenge and inspiration provided by a transformational leader. Some entrepreneurs are able to embrace this need for adaptation, while others are not. The founding entrepreneur's willingness to change, or to create a leadership team of individuals with complementary skill sets, may be a deciding factor in the ultimate survival of the firm.

Along with attracting, engaging and rewarding employees, both the life-cycle and configurational perspectives enable a closer inspection into the leadership challenges associated with growing new ventures. In Box 8.1 we highlight several research possibilities. For example, the barriers that can prevent entrepreneurs from appointing others to leadership roles include how their ego may blind them from embracing the value that someone else would add. As Maccoby (2000) has shown, the narcissism of an entrepreneurial leader has both tremendous benefits and costs. In addition, efforts to formalize and professionalize may actually disguise and perhaps even complicate the actual functioning of the business. Bennis and Nanus (2003) describe this as a conflict between the 'manifest organization' and the 'extant organization'. Quite often, the danger for smaller entrepreneurial ventures in advancing beyond the initial growth stages is that too often they remain leader-centric, even though formal organization charts might suggest otherwise.

It is quite possible that the entrepreneur's personal preferences may direct them to emphasize either transformational or transactional behaviors, at the expense of the other behaviors. This can lead to a misalignment between the leadership style being employed and the particular needs of

---

BOX 8.1   FUTURE RESEARCH OPPORTUNITIES IN ENTREPRENEURSHIP LEADERSHIP

In what ways do the cognitive processes and structures that are primed by the feedback and the leader's environment differ between serial entrepreneurs and nascent entrepreneurs?

How do organizational and new venture team characteristics impact the entrepreneur's emphasis on either transformational or transactional behaviors?

How does an entrepreneur's prior experience impact his/her emphasis on either transformational or transactional behaviors?

In what ways do boards of directors, angel investors, and venture capitalists influence the entrepreneur's emphasis on either transformational or transactional behaviors?

What is the relationship between misalignment in entrepreneur leadership style and organizational failure?

What is the relationship between accurate alignment and organizational success?

What organizational and extra-organizational factors mitigate the effects of misalignment between the entrepreneurial leadership style being employed and the particular needs of the organization?

In what ways does the use of transformational and transactional behaviors differ between social entrepreneurial leaders and market-based ventures?

What is the role that institutions and country level factors play in the entrepreneur's emphasis on either transformational or transactional behaviors?

Are there multiple combinations (both strong and weak) of intellectual stimulation, inspirational motivation, and idealized influence?

What is the role of networks on entrepreneurs' leadership styles and behaviors?

What bundle of factors prompt entrepreneurs to recognize the need to retain key talent?

What combinations of factors enable entrepreneurs to successfully challenge emerging cultures of conflict?

What evaluation processes do entrepreneurial leaders follow in selecting collaboration partners?

---

the organization at that time. This misalignment indicates the need for an individual leader to expand their repertoire of leadership behaviors, or to supplement their personal leadership by hiring an individual, or individuals, who will complement their leadership style by supplying those behaviors that are needed. This step is complicated by the fact that recognizing such a limitation may be threatening to the ego of a narcissistic leader. Even when the entrepreneur as leader recognizes this need and hires additional leadership talent, relinquishing control may still provide an insurmountable threat to the founder.

There are several additional research opportunities that entrepreneurship scholars should consider. Studies have identified the unique importance of a leader's use of intellectual stimulation, inspirational motivation and idealized influenced to the creativity phase. Yet, research has not explored the role of these factors from a configurational perspective. Specifically, the question remains whether there are multiple strong and weak combinations of intellectual stimulation, inspirational motivation and idealized influence which can influence the success of new ventures. For example, there might be differences between nascent and serial entrepreneurs, such as in their opportunity-seeking behaviors. Yet there is little known of the cognitive schemata of nascent and serial entrepreneurs, and how environmental factors influence them.

Research is also needed that focuses on leader and team dynamics. For example, research has yet to explain how prior experience influences the entrepreneur's choice of transactional or transformational leader behaviors. Similarly, little is known about how new venture team dynamics influence the use of transactional and transformational behaviors among new venture leadership teams. Also, while studies have shown that angels, venture capitalists and boards all influence entrepreneurial ventures, research has yet to explore how these groups influence an entrepreneur's cognitive processes and their utilization of transactional and transformational leadership behaviors. There is a growing body of research on entrepreneurial firms going through transition stages in institutionally distant countries. The influence of institutions and culture on the cognitive processes and structures of entrepreneurial leaders has yet to be examined, along with how home- and host-country factors influence the entrepreneur's use of transactional or transformational leader behaviors.

We suggest that there are considerable opportunities for further research on founders within the go-go phase. Founders are the initial architects of the organization's structure and strategy. In this role they hold a vision of what they want the organization to be and do, and they are generally unconstrained by previous ways of doing things (Robbins, 2000), and can leave a lasting imprint on organizational processes. Much of the body of work on organizational founding exists in both organizational theory (Hannan and Freeman, 1989) and entrepreneurship (e.g., Bhave, 1994; Carter et al., 1996). Interestingly, studies evaluating founder succession tend to be confined to firms transitioning to public company status (see Nelson, 2003). However, founders will often exit with the advent of angel and venture capital investment. There are potentially numerous reasons why they exit during the go-go stage that qualitative analysis could help identify. Unfortunately, founders are the research focus in only a handful of qualitative studies (see Chandler, 1962; Mintzberg and Waters, 1982; Kimberly, 1980).

Finally, another potentially fruitful area of investigation could come from applying the full-range leadership or life-cycle approach to social entrepreneurs. For example, Zahra et al. (2009) suggest that social entrepreneurs are not all the same. They identify social bricoleurs as social entrepreneurs who usually focus on discovering and addressing small-scale local social needs (Zahra et al., 2009). On the other hand, social constructionists will often exploit opportunities and market failures by filling gaps to underserved clients in order to present reforms and innovative solutions to the broader social system (Zahra et al., 2009). Finally, social engineers recognize systemic problems within existing social structures and address them by introducing revolutionary change. These entrepreneurs often destroy outdated systems, and replace them with newer and more suitable ones (Zahra et al., 2009). While each of these are, in fact, social entrepreneurs, they differ in terms of how they define and interpret opportunities, how they view their missions, the manner in which they seek and acquire resources and the way they address social ills. These differences will very likely manifest themselves in unique leadership challenges as ventures of each of these types advance through their respective life cycles, and especially as these ventures advance through the adolescent stage.

CONCLUSION

This chapter evaluates the link between entrepreneurship and leadership by utilizing the 'full range of leadership model' (FRLM) (Avolio, 2010). We take a 'life-cycle' approach and also a configurational perspective to suggest how various combinations of transformational and transactional leadership behaviors may have differential effects across the variety of states of growth a venture may experience. As firms grow, the challenges of leadership evolve. Indeed, founders and leaders of entrepreneurial firms struggle with developing new skills and adapting their strategy to match the opportunities and threats they might encounter as they move to the next stage (Daily and Dalton, 1992). Also, there are leadership challenges associated with obtaining external financing, as well as those in guiding the firm from sole-proprietor to professionally managed, and finally in balancing the revenue-enhancement and wealth-protection roles. The growth of the organization also requires increased leader attention to attracting and retaining quality employees (Galpin and Whittington,

2012). In light of different organizational and environment demands, the salience of certain leadership behaviors will vary among firms that are at different stages of growth.

In this chapter we have examined this problem by integrating the full-range model of leadership with a life-cycle approach to understanding the evolution and growth of threshold firms. The full-range model identifies several dimensions of both transactional and transformational leadership behavior that are generally associated with effective leadership. However, we contend that some of these behaviors are more important at certain junctures of an organization's development than others. Thus, successful entrepreneurial leaders need both the cognitive complexity and the willingness to adapt their leadership style to the particular needs of the organization during that particular phase. Those who can expand and use a full range of leadership behaviors will be more successful.

We believe there are considerable opportunities for additional research by leveraging the full-range model of leadership to the study of entrepreneurial firm growth, because of the array of substantive transitions entrepreneurial firms experience as they mature. Moreover, this is because the leadership behaviors needed to launch a new firm are different from those required to grow and sustain the firm over time.

REFERENCES

Adizes, I. (1979). Organizational passages – diagnosing and treating lifecycle problems of organizations. *Organizational Dynamics*, 8(1), 3–25.

Adizes, I. (1990). *Corporate Life Cycles: How and Why Corporations Grow and Die and What to Do About It*. Carpenteria, CA: Adizes Institute of Publishing.

Aislabie, C. (1992). Sudden change in a model of small firm growth. *Small Business Economics*, 4, 307–14.

Avolio, B. (2010). *Full Range Leadership Development*, 2nd edition. Thousand Oaks, CA: SAGE.

Baker, S.D. (2007). Followership: Theoretical foundation for a contemporary construct. *Journal of Leadership and Organizational Studies*, 14(1), 50–60.

Bass, B. (1985). *Leadership and Performance Beyond Expectations*. New York, NY: Free Press.

Bass, B. and Avolio, B. (1994). *Improving Organizational Effectiveness through Transformational Leadership*. Thousand Oaks, CA: SAGE.

Bass, B. and Riggio, R. (2006). *Transformational Leadership*, 2nd edition. Mahwah, NJ: Lawrence Erlbaum and Associates.

Bennis, W. and Nanus, B. (2003). *Leaders: The Strategies for Taking Charge*. New York, NY: Harper Row.

Bhave, M.P. (1994). A process model of entrepreneurial venture creation. *Journal of Business Venturing*, 9, 223–42.

Bligh, M. (2011). Followership and follower-centered approaches. In A. Bryman, D. Collinson, K. Grint, B. Jackson and M. Uhl-Bien (eds), *The SAGE Handbook of Leadership* (pp. 425–36). London: SAGE.

Blundel, R.K. and Hingley, M. (2001). Exploring growth in vertical inter-firm relationships: Small–medium firms supplying multiple food retailers. *Journal of Small Business and Enterprise Development*, 8(3), 245–65.

Bridge, S., O'Neill, K. and Cromie, S. (2003). *Understanding Enterprise, Entrepreneurship and Small Business*. London: Palgrave Macmillan.

Burns, J.M. (1978). *Leadership*. New York, NY: Harper & Row.

Carsten, M.K., Uhl-Bien, M., West, B.J., Patera, J.L., and McGregor, R. (2010). Exploring social constructs of followership: A qualitative study. *Leadership Quarterly*, 21(3), 543–62.

Carter, N.M., Gartner, W.B. and Reynolds, P.D. (1996). Exploring start-up event sequences. *Journal of Business Venturing*, 11, 151–66.

Chandler, A. (1962). *Strategy and Structure: Chapters in the History of the Industrial Enterprise*. Cambridge, MA: MIT Press.

Chaston, I. (2009). *Entrepreneurial Management in Small Firms*. London: SAGE Publications.

Daily, C.M. and Dalton, D.R. (1992). The relationship between governance structure and corporate performance in entrepreneurial firms. *Journal of Business Venturing*, 7(5), 375–86.

Davidsson, P., Steffens, P. and Fitzsimmons, J. (2009). Growing profitable or growing from profits: Putting the horse in front of the cart?. *Journal of Business Venturing*, 24(4), 388–406.

Drucker, P. (1994). The theory of the business. *Harvard Business Review*, 72(5), 95–104.

Duncan, R.B. (1972). Characteristics of organizational environments and perceived environmental uncertainty. *Administrative Science Quarterly*, 17(3), 313–27.

Ensley, M.D., Pearce, C.L. and Hmieleski, K.M. (2006). The moderating effect of environmental dynamism on the relationship between entrepreneur leadership behavior and new venture performance. *Journal of Business Venturing*, 21(2), 243–63.

Galpin, T.J. and Whittington, J.L. (2012). Creating a culture of sustainability in entrepreneurial enterprises. In M. Wagner (ed.), *Entrepreneurship, Innovation and Sustainability* (pp. 68–87). Sheffield: Greenleaf Publishing.

Greiner, L.E. (1972). Evolution and revolution as organizations grow. *Harvard Business Review*, 50(4), 37–46.

Gupta, V., MacMillan, I.C. and Surie, G. (2004). Entrepreneurial leadership: Developing and measuring a cross-cultural construct. *Journal of Business Venturing*, 19(2), 241–60.

Hannan, M.T. and Freeman, J. (1989). *Organizational Ecology*. Cambridge, MA: Harvard University Press.

Kazanjian, R.K. and Drazin, R. (1989). An empirical test of a stage of growth progression model. *Management Science*, 35(12), 1489–503.

Kelley, R.E. (1988). In praise of followers. *Harvard Business Review*, 66(6), 141–8.

Kempster, S. and Cope, J. (2010). Learning to lead in the entrepreneurial context. *International Journal of Entrepreneurial Behaviour and Research*, 16, 6–35.

Kimberly, J. (1980). Initiation, innovation, and institutionalization in the creation process. In J. Kimberly and R. Miles (eds), *Organizational Life Cycle* (pp. 134–60). San Francisco, CA: Jossey-Bass.

Kotter, J. (2012). *Leading Change*. Harvard Business Review Press.

Levie, J. and Hay, M. (1998). Progress or just proliferation? A historical review of stages models of early corporate growth. Working paper: London Business School.

Levie, J. and Lichtenstein, B.B. (2010). A terminal assessment of stages theory: Introducing a dynamic states approach to entrepreneurship. *Entrepreneurship Theory and Practice*, 34(2), 317–50.

Longenecker, J., Petty, J., Palich, L. and Hoy, F. (2013). *Small Business Management*. Boston, MA: Cengage Learning.

Lord, R.G. and Maher, K.J. (1991). Cognitive theory in industrial and organizational psychology. *Handbook of Industrial and Organizational Psychology*, 2, 1–62.

Maccoby, M. (2000). Narcissistic leaders: The incredible pros, the inevitable cons. *Harvard Business Review*, 78(1), 68–78.

Maritz, R., Pretorius, M. and Plant, K. (2011). Exploring the interface between strategy-making and responsible leadership. *Journal of Business Ethics*, 98(1), 101–13.

Maslow, A.H. (1954). The instinctoid nature of basic needs. *Journal of Personality*, 22(3), 326–47.

McMahon, R.G.P. (2001). Deriving an empirical development taxonomy for manufacturing SMEs using data from Australia's business longitudinal survey. *Small Business Economics*, 17(3), 197–213.

Miller, D. (1993). The architecture of simplicity. *Academy of Management Review*, 18(1), 116–38.

Mintzberg, H. and Waters, J. (1982). Tracking strategy in an entrepreneurial firm. *Academy of Management Journal*, 25, 465–99.

Nelson, T. (2003). The persistence of founder influence: Management, ownership, and performance effects at initial public offering. *Strategic Management Journal*, 24, 707–24.

O'Farrell, P.N. and Hitchens, D.M.W.N. (1988). Alternative theories of small-firm growth: A critical review. *Environment and Planning*, 20(10), 1365–83.

Phelps, R., Adams, R. and Bessant, J. (2007). Life cycles of growing organizations: A review with implications for knowledge and learning. *International Journal of Management Reviews*, 9(1), 1–30.

Riggio, R.E., Riggio, H.R., Salinas, C. and Cole, E.J. (2003). The role of social and emotional communication skills in leader emergence and effectiveness. *Group Dynamics: Theory, Research, and Practice*, 7(2), 83.

Robbins, S.P. (2000). *The Essentials of Organizational Behavior*. Upper Saddle River, NJ: Prentice-Hall.

Rutherford, M.W., Buller, P.F. and Mcmullen, P.R. (2003). Human resource management problems over the life-cycle of small to medium-sized firms. *Human Resource Management*, 42, 321–35.

Scott, M. and Bruce, R. (1987). Five stages of growth in small business. *Long Range Planning*, 20(3), 45–52.

Short, J.S., Payne, G.T. and Ketchen, D.J. (2008). Research on organizational configurations: Past accomplishments and future challenges. *Journal of Management*, 34(6), 1053–79.

Storey, D. (1994). *Understanding the Small Business Sector*. London: Routledge.

Uhl-Bien, M., Riggio, R.E., Lowe, K.B. and Carsten, M.K. (2014). Followership theory: A review and research agenda. *Leadership Quarterly*, 25(1), 83–104.

Whittington, J.L., Coker, R.H., Goodwin, V.L., Ickes, W. and Murray, B. (2009). Transactional leadership revisited: Self–other agreement and its consequences. *Journal of Applied Social Psychology*, 39(8), 1860–1886.

Whittington, J.L., McKee, V., Goodwin, V.L. and Bell, R.G. (2013). Applying fuzzy set methodology to evaluate substitutes for leadership. *Research in the Sociology of Organizations*, 38, 279–302.

Wofford, J.C. and V.L. Goodwin (1994). A cognitive interpretation of transactional and transformational leadership theories. *Leadership Quarterly*, 5(2), 161–86.

Wofford, J.C., V.L. Goodwin and J.L. Whittington (1998). A field study of a cognitive approach to understanding transformational and transactional leadership. *Leadership Quarterly*, 9(1), 55–84.

Zahra, S.A. and Filatotchev, I. (2004). Governance of the entrepreneurial threshold firm: A knowledge-based perspective. *Journal of Management Studies*, 41(5), 885–97.

Zahra, S.A., Gedajlovic, E., Neubaum, D.O. and Shulman, J.M. (2009). A typology of social entrepreneurs: Motives, search processes and ethical challenges. *Journal of Business Venturing*, 24(5), 519–32.

9. Understanding entrepreneurial leadership: who leads a venture does matter

Alan L. Carsrud, Maija Renko-Dolan and Malin Brännback

INTRODUCTION

The entrepreneur as a leader is the focus of this chapter. We explore in some depth the relationship between being an entrepreneur and being a leader. One might assume that an entrepreneur who starts a new venture is by definition also the leader of that new firm. While the founder of a new firm is undoubtedly the leader at its inception, that individual may not fulfill the necessary functions of leadership as the firm grows and becomes established, assuming the firm does not fail in the early stages.

Entrepreneurial leadership is an area that has engaged us before (Renko et al., 2015; Renko et al., 2012). This is a topic that Schumpeter (1934) must have assumed was true when discussing the entrepreneur. Early writers on the topic made similar assumptions. Cantillon (1755 [1931]) defined the economic role of the entrepreneur as bearing the risk of buying at certain prices and selling at uncertain prices. Economists, such as Kirzner (1973, 1979), often imply the entrepreneur has aspects of a leader, but rarely overtly define what are the characteristics, situational constraints and behaviors impacting entrepreneurial leadership. These factors are usually in the purview of psychologists. For example, Sashkin (1987, 1988) called for a new vision of leadership that tied together personality traits, situational context and behaviors. This approach preceded the study of entrepreneurial leadership, yet fits nicely into our view of it and its measurement (Renko et al., 2015).

The term 'entrepreneurial leadership' appears frequently in the popular press and is used in various contexts such as describing the leadership style of the US Navy in the future (Allen, 2001), the leadership of the Apostle Paul (Hybels, 1998), as well as the behavior of a chief executive officer (CEO) suspected of criminal behavior (Gow, 2008). Despite the popular use of this term, there has been little guidance from the academic literature on what entrepreneurial leadership really means and how it is manifested in an organization. Based on our research, there are few published articles in top tier journals clearly defining this term. Schulz (1993), in his dissertation, explores through field research methods how entrepreneurial leaders and strategists conceptualize, identify, invest in, develop and protect skills and competencies within the organization. He raised the notion of the importance of entrepreneurial leadership; however, he never attempted to operationalize the term. His dissertation was one of the first to use the term 'entrepreneurial leader' as a type of leader needed in today's business world.

Even without this underpinning research, universities are establishing chairs in entrepreneurial leadership and, in addition, entrepreneurial leadership centers and institutes are starting to flourish. As we have noted previously (Renko et al., 2015; Renko et al., 2012), entrepreneurial leadership can be measured and is critical not only to the growth of new ventures, but also to the survival of established family owned and managed firms.

It should be noted that this chapter is not focused on entrepreneurial orientation (EO), which has been widely studied as a firm-level construct, although some use the term as a cognitive schema at the individual level. In our view, entrepreneurial leadership (EL) can appear anywhere in the firm, while EO is usually associated with strategic choices at the firm level by senior management who may or may not have any degree of EL. We do believe that EL at the early stages of a new venture impacts a firm's culture, strategy and values and can become engrained in the social values of the business and its management.

Students of entrepreneurship are well acquainted with the serial entrepreneur, who has no interest in long-term leadership activities in a single firm. Such individuals commonly divest themselves of their successful entrepreneurial ventures (or abandon their failed ones) and promptly begin others. One might be content with the study of such entrepreneurship if one accepts the flawed assumption that further innovation in the successful established firm is unnecessary or does not require leadership skills to manage a changing organization within changing markets. It is also clear that managing a start-up is different from managing an established firm. It is possible that the leadership skills required differ at various stages of firm development. While this is consistent with the views held by Sashkin (1987, 1988), it also does not preclude entrepreneurial leadership from being adaptive to various situations because of the traits of the entrepreneur and the behaviors they exhibit.

In this chapter we start by examining the nature of leadership and entrepreneurship in organizations. We then focus on the issue of entrepreneurial leaders in comparison to managers, recognizing that both effective leadership and successful management are necessary for long-term organizational success and survival. Finally, we provide a brief overview of the two relevant research domains – entrepreneurship and leadership – with particular attention to the areas of overlap between the two.

While both the entrepreneurship and leadership constructs have been studied extensively there remain a number of differences among scholars and researchers as to their underlying nature and operation. We try in this chapter to succinctly present that which is generally accepted about entrepreneurship and about leadership, without attempting to tie down every remaining difference and disagreement. We then look at the interaction of leadership and entrepreneurial roles of those who create new firms. We also note that many new ventures become family owned and managed firms and maintain the 'flavor' of the family in terms of the values of the leader who founded the venture and initiated the firm's 'culture'.

Certainly the roles of entrepreneurs and leaders develop and change over time and context as the firm matures. That is, effective leaders of successful new entrepreneurial ventures also must realize that they have to develop additional leadership capacity within themselves and others in the firm. To do so enables new leaders within the venture, who are able to seize new opportunities for innovation, meet new challenges and deal with new threats. This is the case in succession within a family business (Renko et al., 2012) as well as changes in technology or markets that face any established firm.

The issue of entrepreneurial leaders versus managers requires recognition that both effective leadership and successful management are necessary for long-term organizational success, and that this survival is complex in its nature. McGrath and MacMillan (2000: 1) emphasize the need for an entrepreneurial mindset in today's fast-changing organizations, which they define as a 'way of thinking about your business that captures the benefits of uncertainty'. Fernald et al. (2005), as well as Cogliser and Brigham (2004), suggest that we can better understand the domain of entrepreneurial leadership if we first compare the characteristics of entrepreneurs and leaders.

More specifically, Fernald et al. (2005) suggest that this approach can lead to the development of a model that specifies the personal characteristics reflected in those who practice entrepreneurial leadership, which subsequently has led to the development of a tool to measure it (Renko et al., 2015) that captures the behaviors and attributes that typify entrepreneurial leaders (for a detailed understanding of how that scale was developed, the reader is referred to that article). In this chapter, we build on these previous studies of entrepreneurship and leadership and address the following question: What are the critical components of entrepreneurial leadership, and how can entrepreneurs and managers develop their entrepreneurial leadership skills?

Entrepreneurship and leadership are very distinct concepts, yet they intersect at various points. Thus, our overview of the two relevant research domains (entrepreneurship and leadership) pays particular attention to the areas of overlap between the two. We then move on to discuss entrepreneurial leadership as it manifests itself in relation to organizational culture, especially in the contexts of innovative, growing and family-led enterprises. Finally, we provide a rationale for why entrepreneurial leadership is needed at all levels of a venture and in any type of organization.

OVERVIEW OF ENTREPRENEURSHIP

'Who is an entrepreneur?' and 'What is entrepreneurial?' have been the key questions in academic entrepreneurship for decades. Gartner (1988) challenged the assumption that there is a stereotype of the entrepreneur. However, the question persists despite his claim that it is the wrong question, and despite many researchers reaching the same conclusion as Gartner. Policy-makers, venture capitalists, researchers and practitioners have not stopped searching for the prototypical entrepreneur. At the same time, the field has spent more than three decades attempting to find a commonly accepted definition of entrepreneurship. As Carsrud and Brännback (2007) have noted, this was not achieved, since the definition is dependent upon the specific perspective of each researcher: whether they are interested in what happens when an entrepreneur acts, why they act, how they act, or who this actor is – as if there was a specific type of human who is equipped with certain unique, entrepreneurial characteristics.

Also, Carsrud and Brännback (2007, 2011) have observed that many people assume we could identify would-be entrepreneurs provided we first know what 'it' is, by listing the specific entrepreneurial characteristics to look for in an individual and then finding such persons. The reality is that entrepreneurship is very contextually driven and thus any specific set of characteristics may not be generalizable across all situations. This has certainly been seen as the case in leadership as well. The popular press still continues to ask questions like, 'Why did X start a venture?' and 'What makes Y such a great leader?' The answers tend to be along the lines of, 'Because they have certain inner qualities or experiences.' Humans look for role models to mimic, effectively generating new entrepreneurs and leaders that look alike.

Schumpeter (1934) defined entrepreneurship as innovation. Entrepreneurs carried out new combinations, often considered to be 'purposeful innovation', implying that they led the innovation. However, as Carsrud and Brännback (2007) have pointed out, this definition can take at least five different forms of innovation: (1) a new product or service, or a new quality of a service or product; (2) a new method of production not previously tested, that does not need to be founded upon scientific discovery; (3) a new market, regardless of whether it has existed before; (4) new sources of supply, regardless of whether they already exist or have to be created; and (5) the carrying out of new organization. It is the last of these that implies leadership. We suggest that Schumpeter implies that creating a new organization is an act of leadership. The role of leadership in entrepreneurship is explicitly found in Baumol (1968), who sees the entrepreneur as an individual who exercises leadership. Thus the act of creating any organization requires an individual to lead themselves and others in forming this new entity. Baumol argues that managers do not exercise this type of leadership, of leading into the creation of the new entity, and therefore it sets them apart from entrepreneurs.

OVERVIEW OF LEADERSHIP

Leadership research started by identifying personal characteristics of leaders, not unlike the approach taken in the early study of entrepreneurship (Carsrud and Brännback, 2011), and by the 1940s enough sound research had accumulated to make possible an integrative review (Stogdill, 1948). Examining more than 100 studies, Stogdill concluded that there were no general personality characteristics or traits associated with leadership, not unlike the result for entrepreneurial traits and motivations (Gartner, 1988; Carsrud et al., 2009; Carsrud and Brännback, 2011). This led to a refocusing of research to a more behavioral approach to leadership. Over the past decades, the trend has been towards a focus on empowering and creativity-enhancing leadership styles with a view to establishing how leadership can contribute to organizational success. However, Renko et al. (2015) note that the leader, as an individual, often remains the focus of leadership research.

Entrepreneurship and leadership researchers have explored the traits and behaviors that distinguish an individual leader (or entrepreneur) from a non-leader (or non-entrepreneur). However, leadership is more than a combination of certain individual traits or attributes: leadership is concerned with using influence (Hunt, 2004). It represents a more complex and dynamic phenomenon than that of an individual actor. In a similar way, 'the entrepreneur' is not equal to 'entrepreneurship'. Entrepreneurship focuses not only on the entrepreneur, but also on the intersection of that enterprising person and business opportunities (Shane and Venkataraman, 2000). Combining ideas from leadership and entrepreneurship, then, entrepreneurial leadership concerns the process of influence in an organization that promotes all organizational members to identify and pursue entrepreneurial opportunities. We do know that leadership style can affect employee morale, grievances, turnover and absenteeism. However, the impact on performance depends on the task orientation of the leader, which we believe is a critical part of the skill set of the entrepreneurial leader who is more action-oriented and transformational in their approach.

Over the past 20 years, a new genre of leadership theories, variously termed charismatic, inspirational or transformational leadership, has been developed to emphasize exceptional leadership that has profound effects on followers and organizations, as well as societies. When referring to transformational leadership in the following sections, it is recognized that some authors have employed the terms charismatic or inspirational leadership instead to talk about the same kinds of leaders.

Weber first integrated the concept of charisma with leadership (Weber, 1924 [1947]), but it did not gain noteworthy attention in the organizational sciences until work by Bass (1985), Burns (1978) and House (1977) drew attention to the construct (Cogliser and Brigham, 2004). Bass (1985) developed a taxonomy of transformational, transactional and laissez-faire leadership styles, which have been widely adopted in subsequent leadership research. Avolio and Bass (1995) further developed this line of theory, grounding transactional leadership on the idea that leader–follower relationships are based on a series of exchanges or implicit bargains in which followers receive certain valued outcomes on the condition that they act according to their leaders' wishes. Transformational leadership, however, centers on the identification of what might be termed the 'moral' dimension of leadership, with the aims of motivating others to perform well for their organization while doing good in moral terms, and thus transforming them and the organization by functioning at higher levels of both performance and ethics.

Transformational leadership approaches argue that organizational leaders do not focus directly on subordinates' task performance. Instead, they use personal charisma to arouse and focus followers' motivation to attain organizational goals. Bass (1985) identified four primary ways in which leaders do this. Leaders act as ideal models, explicitly aiming to get followers to want to be like them. They communicate in ways that inspire followers; and, in addition, they engage followers with intellectually stimulating – and goal-relevant – ideas. Finally, they demonstrate to individual followers their personal consideration for them. In these ways leaders 'transform' followers by getting them to recognize the importance and value of their work, to focus on team and organizational goals that go beyond their own self-interest, and to seek to satisfy what Maslow (1943) referred to as 'higher order needs', such as belonging to the team and achieving their own potential. Research on these types of leadership approaches has generally shown positive results in terms of being more productive and successful than organizations whose top leaders are less transformational (Judge and Piccolo, 2004). The benefits of transformational leadership in start-up firms have also been demonstrated (Baum et al., 1998; Covin and Slevin, 2002; Gupta et al., 2004).

TRANSFORMATIONAL VERSUS ENTREPRENEURIAL LEADERSHIP

Clearly there are characteristics of transformational leadership that many people also would consider to be characteristics of entrepreneurial leadership. For example, transformational leaders always seek new ways of working and are not likely to support the status quo. In addition, previous research has shown that a CEO's transformational leadership shapes the characteristics of the top management team, which in turn impact the firm's engagement in corporate entrepreneurship (Ling et al., 2008). While transformational leadership can have such beneficial outcomes in terms of corporate-level entrepreneurship, we propose that entrepreneurial leadership is different in that it directly contributes to enhanced opportunity recognition and exploitation by an organization through both leaders' and employees' very engagement in opportunity-focused behaviors. While the benefits of transformational leadership have been widely documented in existing research, and span from military leadership (Dvir et al., 2002) to group creativity (Sosik et al., 1998, 1999) and individual creativity in the workplace (Shin and Zhou, 2003), we believe that distinguishing entrepreneurial leadership as a specific, opportunity-focused form of leadership is important, especially in the venture creation process.

Entrepreneurial leadership guides attention to those very parts of leadership that can enhance entrepreneurial behaviors among followers. It also provides academics with a conceptual model that is more focused on the inherently entrepreneurial aspects of leadership than is the case with transformational leadership. The requirements of transformational leadership, such as 'a leader with vision, self-confidence, and inner strength to argue successfully for what he sees is right or good, not for what is popular or is acceptable according to established wisdom of the time' (Bass, 1985: 17), describe overall exceptional leadership. However, the mere assessment of what is 'right or good' can encompass any variety of domains (from human resource management to product-market strategies, and from new product development decisions to stakeholder management), making transformational leadership a very generalized concept. One of the benefits of entrepreneurial leadership is that it provides a greater concentration on what truly matters for entrepreneurial action.

ENTREPRENEURIAL VERSUS OTHER LEADERSHIP STYLES

In addition to transformational leadership, there are other leadership styles (including paternalism and participative leadership), that are relevant for the understanding of entrepreneurial leadership. For example, Koiranen (2003) observes a connection between entrepreneurship and paternalism (emotionality). Emotionality is a strong psychological force behind any affective reaction, such as commitment to a new business. Entrepreneurs themselves and those involved in entrepreneurial businesses are inspired, excited, passionate and devoted. At times they are almost obsessive, and protective of their new venture. The prevalence of paternalistic leadership practices in both new ventures and family businesses may be closely related to the strong emotional connections prevalent in such firms, and the need to behave entrepreneurially. Participative leadership is characterized by the leader involving organizational members in decision-making. Such participation can provide an important mechanism for interpersonal processes for adaptation and change in the business. Other benefits of participative leadership include conflict resolution, increased decision acceptance, increased job satisfaction and work enrichment (Bass, 1990; Yukl, 1998). Overall, there are multiple examples of how leadership style is related to employee and organizational creativity. Leader behavior that is expressly intended to encourage subordinate problem-finding and problem construction has a marked impact on the originality of their problem solutions (Redmond et al., 1993). Since creativity is an essential component of entrepreneurial opportunity recognition and exploitation, leadership approaches that enhance creativity can be considered entrepreneurial in nature.

LEADERSHIP AND CULTURE

Another set of approaches sees the central role of leaders as building or constructing their organizations' culture. In practice, organizational leadership and culture are interrelated (Ward, 1987). Both influence the long-term success of the venture; and while the leader's behaviors shape the culture of the enterprise, the underlying values and assumptions (culture) of the enterprise also influence the leadership styles adopted, especially as the organization ages and grows.

Schein (1983) points out that it is the founder's assumptions, often unstated and perhaps even unconscious, that are the basis for the values that drive actions and patterns (or norms) of behavior that can be observed and are typically identified as 'how we do things around here'. He also states that the only really important function of leaders is to construct organizational culture, a view echoed by Denison (1990) and by Hatch (2013), who developed models of organizational culture that relate to leadership. All of these models argue that organizations have four underlying functions that must be fulfilled if the organization is to survive: (1) they must adapt to external conditions and pressures; (2) they must attain goals that satisfy clients or customers; (3) they must achieve internal coordination of work processes, involving individuals and teams; and (4) they must define how these functions are carried out and provide stability for all operations including adaptation, goal attainment and integration (or coordination). This fourth function may be guided by what is called a 'culture', consisting of the underlying assumptions, beliefs and values that are shared by an organization's members. This culture provides them with guidance as to how they should act with regard to the other three functions.

Leadership in an entrepreneurial context is, however, more often about creating change and cultures that can embrace change. If you want to make change then you must look at the crucial fourth function, the set of assumptions, beliefs and values held by individuals within an organization. Schein argues that leaders achieve this by constructing the organization's culture, and do so by defining the basic assumptions and values that direct and drive the actions of organization members. Leaders do not necessarily do this explicitly through making speeches and statements; but, more importantly, by establishing and enforcing organizational policies and practices that embody the values they want the organization's culture to be based on. This position is similar to that presented by current management theorists who argue that top management teams define the strategy of their organizations (Westley and Mintzberg, 1989).

When the leader is seen as a culture-builder, as an organizational architect, the similarities with an organization's entrepreneurial orientation (EO) become clear. The three aspects of EO – innovativeness, proactiveness and risk-taking – can be expressed as values and as patterns of action (Lumpkin and Dess, 1996). An organizational strategic orientation that promotes the entrepreneurial values of taking risks and staying innovative and proactive in moves against competitors is a logical outcome of leadership that promotes such ideals. However, as we have discussed before (Renko et al., 2015), there are also important differences between entrepreneurial leadership and the organizational entrepreneurial orientation. Importantly, one can consider the view that leadership is a process of influence that is present in the interactions between individuals at all levels of an organization on a daily basis. The strategic orientation of an organization directly concerns the decision-making at the top management level.

DEFINING ENTREPRENEURIAL LEADERSHIP

Our view of entrepreneurial leadership spawns from the entrepreneurship, leadership and cultural perspectives described above (see Figure 9.1). On the one hand, there are studies of new business owners who have to adopt leadership roles in order for their companies to prosper and grow (e.g., Baum et al., 1998; Ensley et al., 2006; Hmieleski and Ensley, 2007). On the other hand, entrepreneurial leadership has also been studied as the culture (value system) of a firm that reflects the entrepreneurial values and vision of its leader(s) (e.g., Covin and Slevin, 2002; Gupta et al., 2004; McGrath and MacMillan, 2000; Thornberry, 2006). For example, Covin and Slevin

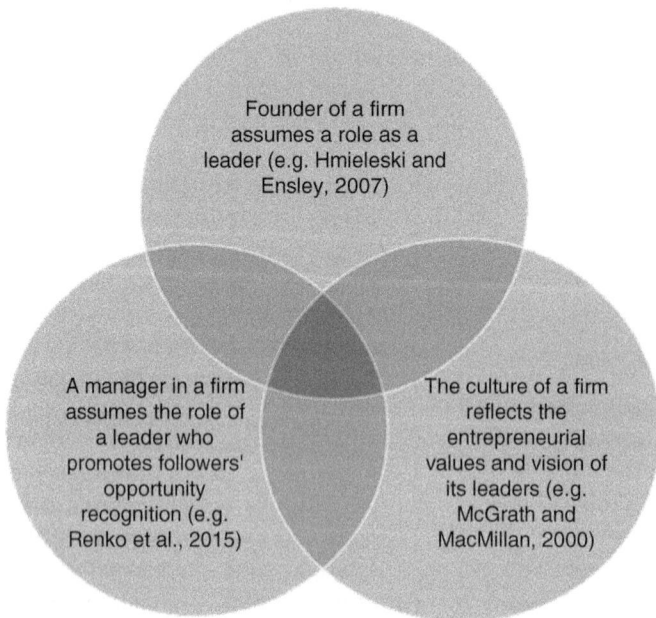

Figure 9.1   Perspectives of entrepreneurial leadership

(2002) argue that entrepreneurial leadership is characterized by the following six imperatives: (1) nourishing an entrepreneurial capability; (2) protecting innovations that might threaten the current business model; (3) making sense of opportunities; (4) questioning the dominant logic; (5) revisiting the 'deceptively simple questions'; and (6) linking entrepreneurship and strategic management.

Building on these perspectives, we see entrepreneurial leadership as a leadership style that can exist in organizations of any age, size and focus. To understand entrepreneurial leadership this way, it is important to start from the commonly accepted definition of entrepreneurship as: 'a process by which individuals – either on their own or inside organizations – pursue opportunities without regard to the resources they currently control' (Stevenson and Jarillo, 1990: 23). Indeed, the basis of our definition of entrepreneurial leadership is the pursuit of entrepreneurial opportunities, which distinguishes entrepreneurial firms from other forms of enterprise (Shane and Venkataraman, 2000). Building on these two definitions we argue that entrepreneurial leadership is not limited just to small firms, but can exist in large complex organizations. It exists anywhere it is possible to pursue entrepreneurial opportunities. The concept of corporate entrepreneurship carries this notion as well, as does social entrepreneurship, which also means that entrepreneurial leadership is not another subclass of leadership. To be precise, we should point out that an individual pursuing an entrepreneurial opportunity truly on their own would engage in self-employment, which refers to a sense of an individual's financial self-sustainability. The nature of being a leader when one is the only employee is not the subject of this chapter; frankly, to lead requires someone to follow. That follower does not have to be an employee, but could be external to the venture, such as a stakeholder. In this chapter we are concerned with a firm that has multiple employees and has some level of sustainable growth (Brännback et al., 2014).

The notion of opportunity is central to most contemporary definitions of entrepreneurship. While Schumpeter (1934) saw the entrepreneur as a change-maker, disrupting the socio-economic equilibrium through innovation, Drucker (1985) emphasized the view that the entrepreneur exploited opportunities that create change. Indeed, entrepreneurship relies upon both creative destruction and opportunity recognition (Baron and Ensley, 2006). The entrepreneur may create or may simply discover a potentially disruptive innovative opportunity, but the decision to exploit this entrepreneurial opportunity is the central activity of entrepreneurship (Shane and Venkataraman, 2000). Inherent in the above discussion is a form of leadership behavior, although it is not expressed overtly.

Building on this opportunity focus, we define entrepreneurial leadership as 'influencing and directing the performance of group members toward the achievement of organizational goals that involve recognizing and exploiting entrepreneurial opportunities' (Renko et al., 2015). As such, entrepreneurial leadership is a distinctive style of leadership in that it involves influencing the activities of an organized group toward a goal or set of goals. As a leadership style it differs from management, which is focused on coordination and planning (Michael et al., 2002). An entrepreneur pursues opportunities, while an entrepreneurial leader inspires followers to do the same. As Renko et al. (2015) note, entrepreneurial leadership is at the intersection of entrepreneurial behaviors and good leadership practices. It concerns the process of influence in an organization that promotes all organizational members to identify and pursue entrepreneurial opportunities.

A vision for the future is a central element in entrepreneurial leadership regardless of whether the focus is on organizational culture or a leadership style. Indeed, being a visionary emerges as common to both leaders and entrepreneurs when doing a review of both literatures (Renko et al., 2015; Fernald et al., 2005). Similarly, Cogliser and Brigham (2004) conclude that vision is an important area of thematic overlap across leadership and entrepreneurship. Reflecting a vision for the future, Thornberry's (2006) entrepreneurial leaders possess a strong desire to create, build or change things. In sum, a characteristic of entrepreneurial leadership is a vision for the future of the firm based on continuous recognition of new entrepreneurial opportunities, and pursuing this vision through creative, innovative and sometimes risky tactics.

DIFFERENT TYPES OF ENTREPRENEURIAL LEADERS AND THEIR DEVELOPMENT

The opportunity focus of entrepreneurial leadership can manifest itself in various areas of business operations. For example, Thornberry (2006) identifies different types of entrepreneurial leaders, such as explorers and miners. Demonstrating an opportunity focus in external relationships, market-focused 'explorers' concentrate on developing new markets, services and products; that is, exhibit highly innovative and proactive behaviors. Leaders like the late Steve Jobs of Apple, who became known for his inspiring and visionary approach to new product development, exemplify this type of entrepreneurial leadership. Focusing on opportunities inside their firms, 'miners' are more concerned with operational issues and making the company run more efficiently while serving customers better. For example, Jim Case, the founder of UPS, was known for this leadership style (Niemann, 2007). In the case of miners, entrepreneurship is demonstrated in processes rather than in products, which is the case with explorers (Thornberry, 2006).

Regardless of the operational focus of entrepreneurial leadership, this type of leadership is exhibited by a leader guiding employees to pursue goals that are driven by entrepreneurial opportunities. The dual roles of the entrepreneurial leader include serving as an example for followers through the leader's own identification and pursuit of entrepreneurial opportunities, as well as directly influencing followers' actions by providing encouragement, resources and incentives (Gupta et al., 2004; Thornberry, 2006). There is a contingent relationship between a leader's personal characteristics and the situational needs of the organization (Rubenson and Gupta, 1996), and an entrepreneurial leader is able to view changing environments, markets and competitive conditions as opportunities for entrepreneurial initiatives. Such a leadership style sets an example for others in the organization to follow.

Besides varying in their areas of operational focus, the types of entrepreneurial leadership also vary depending on the type of organization being led. For example, in a family business – more so than in any other form of business – entrepreneurial opportunities that are being pursued have to be lucrative in an economic (market) sense, and they also have to be aligned with those values and standards that are at the core of the family which owns the firm (Renko et al., 2012). The leadership culture of family firms is most often paternalistic (autocratic leadership), where relationships are arranged hierarchically; managers retain key information and decision-making authority, and closely supervise employees (Dyer, 1986; Fiegener et al., 1996; Sorenson, 2000). For such family owned and managed firms to succeed in the turbulence of today's economic conditions, they should adopt a more entrepreneurial approach to leadership. Direction, organizational renewal and innovativeness enabled by entrepreneurial leadership are particularly important for family owned and managed businesses for three reasons, as summarized in Renko et al. (2012).

First, leadership can be helpful in dealing with misunderstandings and conflict, which often arise from the embeddedness of both the family and business systems when looking at family owned and managed firms (Sharma, 2006; Carsrud and Brännback, 2012). Second, entrepreneurial leadership can help in developing, communicating and reinforcing desired vision and organizational culture over extended tenures of different leaders. Third, entrepreneurial leadership directs attention to the entrepreneurial role of all in the firm, including mid-level management and employees. There is a need to devote more attention to understanding the perspective of employees – not just family members – in wanting a firm to succeed, and entrepreneurial leadership can be employed in trying to understand issues that are important to them. Thus it can lead to superior performance of these individuals along various dimensions.

Another type of organizational context where entrepreneurial leadership is particularly important – and also challenging – is a growth-stage start-up firm. While there has been research on the start-up teams, much of the work focuses on the networks involved and the founder's intentions, and little on the leadership behaviors of the founder(s) with respect to the rest of the start-up team. The alignment of members of the start-up team is most likely greatest during the initial stages of the venture, suggesting that collective leadership and venture governance are less affected by agency problems than is leadership as the firm matures and grows. The separation of ownership and control – the key condition giving rise to agency cost in large business settings – is muted in the founding team that shares ownership (Eisenhardt, 1989; Randøy and Goel, 2003) or in many family owned and managed firms, regardless of size.

As the firm grows, effective leadership reflects the entrepreneurial team's ability to convey their vision to others, especially younger family members, as well as subsequent employees of the firm. A new venture is governed and managed with the intention to shape and pursue the vision of the business held by a dominant coalition of the founders in a manner that is potentially sustainable across decades (Chua et al., 1999). Problems occur when the founder(s) fail to articulate a compelling vision, particularly when new employees enter the firm and the leadership group. Because of the ever-changing business environment and resulting managerial challenges, there is a need for constant innovation as well as adaption to multicultural settings. This requires the development of an entrepreneurial organization that can deal with globalization and the emergence of new economic powers. Thus policy-makers, practitioners and academics have started to embrace entrepreneurial leadership (Renko et al., 2015).

ENTREPRENEURIAL LEADERSHIP: INSPIRING FOLLOWERS

Not all individuals are equally susceptible to similar leadership influences (Shin and Zhou, 2003). The opportunity-oriented outcomes of entrepreneurial leadership depend not only on the level of entrepreneurial leadership demonstrated by the leader, but also on the characteristics and receptivity of the followers. For example, when followers believe in their entrepreneurial skills (that is, have higher levels of entrepreneurial self-efficacy), when they are passionate about their entrepreneurial pursuits, and when they feel empowered in the organization, they are more suscep-tible to entrepreneurial leadership influences (Renko et al., 2015).

The benefits of entrepreneurial leadership to the organization are likely to materialize through those new opportunities that are brought about through entrepreneurial behaviors by many within the venture. Even if these effects are only likely to occur over time, entrepreneurial leader-ship may also have a more immediate effect on the organization through employees' satisfaction with their work as well as with the overall organi-zation (Hollander and Webb, 1955). Leadership has long been identified as a key factor in the goal achievement of groups and organizations. For example, leader–member exchange theory (Graen and Scandura, 1987) suggests that the quality of the relationship between a leader and a sub-ordinate is the key to understanding how leaders influence those subordi-nates. One of the consistent findings in the leadership literature is that the quality of the relationship between a leader and a subordinate is related to job satisfaction (Gerstner and Day, 1997). Positive relationships with leaders provide benefits to members, such as decision influence, empower-ment and career advancement (Erdogan and Enders, 2007; Liden et al., 2000). These create a positive environment for members, leading to higher job satisfaction (Erdogan and Enders, 2007).

Entrepreneurial leadership should be positively related to employees' satisfaction with their job as well as their perception of the positive quali-ties of their organization, and should create conditions for a meaningful job requiring challenge and opportunity for recognition, which allows one therefore to derive satisfaction from work (Herzberg et al., 1959). Individuals who perceive their jobs to be significant and worthwhile feel higher levels of work satisfaction than those who perceive their jobs as having little value (Hackman and Oldham, 1976). Individuals should derive a sense of satisfaction with the work itself when they feel that they have been directly involved in outcomes that affect the organization, which is the very case of entrepreneurial leadership.

Entrepreneurial leaders encourage their employees to take on entrepre-neurial roles through encouragement, guidance and resource allocations (Renko et al., 2015). Providing access to resources is an integral part of entrepreneurial leadership in that it is necessary for creativity-supportive behaviors (Tierney and Farmer, 2004) as well as opportunity recognition and exploitation. This resource access is yet another key aspect where entrepreneurial leadership clearly differs from transformational leader-ship. According to McGrath and MacMillan (2000), entrepreneurial leaders emphasize the need to allocate top organizational talent as well as budget and operating capacity for entrepreneurial initiatives. From the perspective of employees, pursuing entrepreneurial opportunities cannot proceed beyond initial ideas unless concrete resources are available to them to do so. They also need encouragement, flexibility and patience from entrepreneurial leaders in order for their opportunity-focused behaviors to flourish. Encouragement, advocacy and goals specific to creative behaviors are essential elements of entrepreneurial leadership and necessary for inspiring followers.

A challenge for entrepreneurial leaders is to find a balance between the managerial and administrative requirements of their everyday work on one hand, and the future-oriented and opportunity-focused behaviors of their leadership role on the other. Firms will increasingly need to rely on their leaders for discovery, development and growth as well as coordination-focused administrative tasks. In this business environment, leaders will need to guide their followers to take advantage of the opportunities that arise, and avoid the traps of simply focusing on administrative activities. Such leaders are using technological advances where possible to keep up with market changes and the increasingly global competition (Michael et al., 2002). To the extent that entrepreneurial leadership can empower employees and promote an appropriate level of autonomy, it may direct existing firms' attention to new entrepreneurial opportunities. These are some of the benefits of entrepreneurial leadership.

It is obvious that one part of entrepreneurial leadership is to motivate others to behave in entrepreneurial ways. Much still needs to be researched to understand this process, as highlighted by Carsrud et al. (2009) and Carsrud and Brännback (2011), who have called for a renewed study of the role of motivation in entrepreneurial behaviors. One of the behaviors of an entrepreneurial leader is to set both incremental and end goals for subordinates and for themselves. While the study of goal-setting by entrepreneurs has been a focus of some study, what still needs to be examined is how EL impacts goal-setting, and how those goal-oriented behaviors impact firm performance.

CONCLUSIONS

Given the changing economic climate, the more traditional styles of leadership are becoming less important. We have tried to show that firms should focus on being entrepreneurial in their leadership style. It seems likely that to both survive and thrive, firms will need to focus on discovery, development and growth as well as on coordination-focused administrative tasks. Entrepreneurs, despite the pressures to be managers, need to avoid the traps of simply focusing on administrative activities.

They are going to have to be experts in traditional business areas, but also lead their organizations to take advantage of technological advances where possible, and to pioneer market changes and be proactive given increased global competition. This is where the flexibility of EL can be most useful. As we mentioned earlier, the changing economic landscape and increasingly multicultural context means that in order to thrive, organizations must constantly innovate and learn. This means encouraging and maintaining entrepreneurial behaviors at all levels of the firm from senior management to the newest employee. To compete effectively on a global and a local level, all ventures must become entrepreneurial organizations with entrepreneurial leaders.

We hope that we have demonstrated in this chapter how entrepreneurship and leadership share similarities in how their early study was focused on the search for characteristics and traits that 'make' a leader or an entrepreneur. More recently, the leadership field's focus on transformational leaders has been reflected in the study of entrepreneurs as well. Indeed, the roles of transformational leaders and entrepreneurs as leaders overlap, particularly when it comes to having and articulating a vision for the future. Also, leaders and entrepreneurs are concerned with building organizational cultures that allow their firms to survive and prosper.

Despite these similarities between entrepreneurship and leadership, our definition of what entrepreneurial leadership stands for clearly distinguishes it from other leadership styles. Specifically, the opportunity focus of entrepreneurial leaders is evident in leaders' own actions as well as in their expectations from their followers. The recognition and pursuit of opportunities can be accomplished across organizations of all types, as well as across different functional levels. As such, entrepreneurial leadership is not only the domain of new business founders but is also practiced by leaders in various types of organizations that are reinventing themselves. Indeed, entrepreneurial leadership can be found in leader–follower relationships anywhere in an organization; while strategic constructs, such as entrepreneurial orientation, only reflect the decisions of those at the top of an organization. We do believe that EL at the early stages of a new venture impacts a firm's culture and values and can become engrained in the social values of the business and its management.

Constant changes in various contextual factors, such as globalization and the emergence of new economic powers, means that entrepreneurial leadership will become even more important. To the extent that entrepreneurial leadership can empower employees and promote an appropriate level of autonomy, it may help existing organizations to focus on new entrepreneurial opportunities. These are some of the benefits of entrepreneurial leadership.

REFERENCES

Allen, M. (2001). Bush foresees more open-minded military. *Washington Post*, 26 May.

Avolio, B.J. and Bass, B.M. (1995). Individual consideration viewed at multiple levels of analysis: A multi-level framework for examining the diffusion of transformational leadership. *Leadership Quarterly*, 6(2), 199–218.

Baron, R.A. and Ensley, M.D. (2006). Opportunity recognition as the detection of meaningful patterns: Evidence from comparisons of novice and experienced entrepreneurs. *Management Science*, 52(9), 1331–44.

Bass, B.M. (1985). *Leadership and Performance beyond Expectation*. Free Press, New York, NY.

Bass, B.M. (1990). *Bass and Stogdill's Handbook of Leadership*. Free Press, New York, NY.

Baum, J.R., Locke, E.A. and Kirkpatrick, S.A. (1998). A longitudinal study of the relation of vision and vision communication to venture growth in entrepreneurial firms. *Journal of Applied Psychology*, 83(1), 43.

Baumol, W.J. (1968). Entrepreneurship in economic theory. *American Economic Review*, 58(1), 64–71.

Brännback, M., Carsrud, A. and Kiviluoto, N. (2014). *Understanding the Myth of High Growth Firms, the Theory of the Greater Fool*. SpringerBriefs, New York, NY.

Burns, J.M. (1978). *Leadership*. Free Press, New York, NY.

Cantillon, R. (1755 [1931]). *Essai sur la nature du commerce en général*. Edited and with an English translation by Henry Higgs for the Royal Economic Society. Macmillan & Co., London.

Carsrud, A.L. and Brännback, M. (2007). *Entrepreneurship*. Greenwood Press, Westport, CT.

Carsrud, A.L. and Brännback, M. (2011). Entrepreneurial motivations: What do we still need to know?. *Journal of Small Business Management*, 49(1), 9–26.

Carsrud, A.L. and Brännback, M. (2012). *Understanding Family Businesses: Undiscovered Approaches, Unique Perspectives, and Neglected Topics*. Springer Verlag, New York, NY.

Carsrud, A.L. Brännback, E., Elfving, J. and Brandt, K. (2009). Motivations: The entrepreneurial mind and behavior. In A. Carsrud and M. Brännback (eds), *Understanding the Entrepreneurial Mind: Opening the Black Box*. Springer Verlag, New York, NY, pp. 141–66.

Chua, J.H., Chrisman, J.J. and Sharma, P. (1999). Defining the family business by behavior. *Entrepreneurship Theory and Practice*, 23(4), 19–39.

Cogliser, C.C. and Brigham, K.H. (2004). The intersection of leadership and entrepreneurship: Mutual lessons to be learned. *Leadership Quarterly*, 15(6), 771–99.

Covin, J.G. and Slevin, D.P. (2002). The entrepreneurial imperatives of strategic leadership. In M.A. Hitt, R.D. Ireland, S.M. Camp and D.L. Sexton (eds), *Strategic Entrepreneurship: Creating a New Mindset*. Blackwell Publishers, Oxford, pp. 309–27.

Denison, D.R. (1990). *Corporate Culture and Organizational Effectiveness*. Wiley, New York, NY.

Drucker, P.F. (1985). *Innovation and Entrepreneurship*. Harper Business, New York, NY.

Dvir, T., Eden, D., Avolio, B.J. and Shamir, B. (2002). Impact of transformational leadership on follower development and performance: A field experiment. *Academy of Management Journal*, 45(4), 735–44.

Dyer, J.W.G. (1986). *Cultural Change in Family Firms: Anticipating and Managing Business and Family Transitions*. Jossey-Bass, San Francisco, CA.

Eisenhardt, K.M. (1989). Agency theory: An assessment and review. *Academy of Management Review*, 14(1), 57–74.

Ensley, M.D., Hmieleski, K.M. and Pearce, C.L. (2006). The importance of vertical and shared leadership within new venture top management teams: Implications for the performance of startups. *Leadership Quarterly*, 17(3), 217–31.

Erdogan, B. and Enders, J. (2007). Support from the top: supervisors' perceived organizational support as a moderator of leader–member exchange to satisfaction and performance relationships. *Journal of Applied Psychology*, 92(2), 321.

Fernald, L.W., Solomon, G.T. and El Tarabishy, A. (2005). A new paradigm: Entrepreneurial leadership. *Southern Business Review*, 30(2), 1–10.

Fiegener, M.K., Brown, B.M., Prince, R.A. and File, K.M. (1996). Passing on strategic vision: Favored modes of successor preparation by CEOs of family and nonfamily firms. *Journal of Small Business Management*, 34(3), 15–27.

Gartner, W.B. (1988). 'Who is an entrepreneur?' Is the wrong question. *American Journal of Small Business*, 12(1), 11–32.

Gerstner, C.R. and Day, D.V. (1997). Meta-analytic review of leader–member exchange theory: Correlates and construct issues. *Journal of Applied Psychology*, 82(6), 827.

Gow, D. (2008). Financial: Deutsche Post boss resigns after tax inquiry. *Guardian*, 15 February.

Graen, G.B. and Scandura, T.A. (1987). Toward a psychology of dyadic organizing. *Research in Organizational Behavior*, 9(1), 175–208.

Gupta, V., MacMillan, I. and Surie, G. (2004). Entrepreneurial leadership: Developing a cross-cultural construct. *Journal of Business Venturing*, 19(3), 241–60.

Hackman, J.R. and Oldham, G.R. (1976). Motivation through the design of work: Test of a theory. *Organizational Behavior and Human Performance*, 16(2), 250–279.

Hatch, M.J. (2013). *Organization Theory*, 3rd edn., Oxford University Press, New York, NY.

Herzberg, F., Mausner, B. and Snyderman, B. (1959). *The Motivation to Work*. Wiley, New York, NY.

Hmieleski, K.M. and Ensley, M.D. (2007). A contextual examination of new venture performance: Entrepreneur leadership behavior, top management team heterogeneity, and environmental dynamism. *Journal of Organizational Behavior*, 28(7), 865–89.

Hollander, E.P. and Webb, W.B. (1955). Leadership, followership, and friendship: An analysis of peer nominations. *Journal of Abnormal and Social Psychology*, 50(2), 163.

House, R.J. (1977). A 1976 theory of charismatic leadership. In J.G. Hunt and L.L. Larson (eds), *Leadership: The Cutting Edge*. Southern Illinois University Press, Carbondale, IL, pp. 189–207.

Hunt, J.G. (2004). What is leadership?. In J. Antonakis, A.T. Cianciolo and R.J. Sternberg (eds), *The Nature of Leadership*. SAGE, Thousand Oaks, CA, pp. 19–47.

Hybels, B. (1998). Finding your leadership style. *ChristianityToday.com*, The Pastor's Soul, 1 January.

Judge, T.A. and Piccolo, R.F. (2004). Transformational and transactional leadership: A meta-analytic test of their relative validity. *Journal of Applied Psychology*, 89(5), 755–68.

Kirzner, I.M. (1973). *Competition and Entrepreneurship*. Chicago University Press, Chicago, IL.

Kirzner, I.M. (1979). *Perception, Opportunity, and Profit*. Chicago University Press, Chicago, IL.

Koiranen, M. (2003). Understanding the contesting ideologies of family business: Challenge for leadership and professional services. *Family Business Review*, 16(4), 241–51.

Liden, R.C., Wayne, S.J. and Sparrowe, R.T. (2000). An examination of the mediating role of psychological empowerment on the relations between the job, interpersonal relationships, and work outcomes. *Journal of Applied Psychology*, 85(3), 407.

Ling, Y.A.N., Simsek, Z., Lubatkin, M.H. and Veiga, J.F. (2008). Transformational leadership's role in promoting corporate entrepreneurship: Examining the CEO–TMT interface. *Academy of Management Journal*, 51(3), 557–76.

Lumpkin, G.T. and Dess, G.G. (1996). Clarifying the entrepreneurial orientation construct and linking it to performance. *Academy of Management Review*, 21(1), 135–72.

Maslow, A.H. (1943). A theory of human motivation. *Psychological Review*, 50, 370–396.

McGrath, R.G. and MacMillan, I.C. (2000). *The Entrepreneurial Mindset*. Harvard Business School Publishing, Boston, MA.

Michael, S., Storey, D. and Thomas, H. (2002). Discovery and coordination in strategic management and entrepreneurship. In M.A. Hitt, D.R. Ireland, M.S. Camp and D.L.

Sexton (eds), *Strategic Entrepreneurship: Creating a New Mindset*. Blackwell Publishing, London, pp. 45–65.

Niemann, G. (2007). *Big Brown: The Untold Story of UPS*. Jossey-Bass, San Francisco, CA.

Randøy, T. and Goel, S. (2003). Ownership structure, founder leadership, and performance in Norwegian SMEs: Implications for financing entrepreneurial opportunities. *Journal of Business Venturing*, 18(5), 619–37.

Redmond, M.R., Mumford, M.D. and Teach, R. (1993). Putting creativity to work: Effects of leader behavior on subordinate creativity. *Organizational Behavior and Human Decision Processes*, 55(1), 120–151.

Renko, M., El Tarabishy, A., Carsrud, A. and Brännback, M. (2012). Entrepreneurial leadership in family business. In A. Carsrud and M. Brännback (eds), *Understanding Family Businesses: Undiscovered Approaches, Unique Perspectives, and Neglected Topics*. Springer Verlag, New York, NY, pp. 169–84.

Renko, M., El Tarabishy, A., Carsrud, A. and Brännback, M. (2015). Understanding and measuring entrepreneurial leadership style. *Journal of Small Business Management*, 53(1), 54–74.

Rubenson, G.C. and Gupta, A.K. (1996). The initial succession: A contingency model of founder tenure. *Entrepreneurship Theory and Practice*, 21(2), 21–36.

Sashkin, M. (1987). A new vision of leadership. *Journal of Management Development*, 6(4), 19–28.

Sashkin, M. (1988). The visionary leader: A new theory of organizational leadership. In J.A. Conger and R.N. Kanungo (eds), *Charismatic Leadership: The Elusive Factor in Organizational Effectiveness*. Jossey-Bass, San Francisco, CA, pp. 120–160.

Schein, E.H. (1983). The role of the founder in creating organizational culture. *Organizational Dynamics*, 12(1), 13–28.

Schulz, W. (1993). Skill-based strategy and entrepreneurial leadership: How individual and corporate entrepreneurs create value. Dissertation Abstracts International, AAT 9329840.

Schumpeter, J.A. (1934). *The Theory of Economic Development*. Oxford University Press, Oxford.

Shane, S. and Venkataraman, S. (2000). The promise of entrepreneurship as a field of research. *Academy of Management Review*, 25(1), 217–26.

Sharma, P. (2006). An overview of the field of family business studies: Current status and directions for the future. In P. Poutziouris, K. Smyrnios and S. Klein (eds), *The Handbook of Research on Family Business*. Edward Elgar Publishing, Cheltenham, UK and Northampton, MA, pp. 25–55.

Shin, S.J. and Zhou, J. (2003). Transformational leadership, conservation, and creativity: Evidence from Korea. *Academy of Management Journal*, 46(6), 703–14.

Sorenson, R.L. (2000). The contribution of leadership style and practices to family and business success. *Family Business Review*, 13(3), 183.

Sosik, J.J., Kahai, S.S. and Avolio, B.J. (1998). Transformational leadership and dimensions of creativity: Motivating idea generation in computer-mediated groups. *Creativity Research Journal*, 11(2), 111–21.

Sosik, J.J., Kahai, S.S. and Avolio, B.J. (1999). Leadership style, anonymity, and creativity in group decision support systems: The mediating role of optimal flow. *Journal of Creative Behavior*, 33(4), 227–56.

Stevenson, H.H. and Jarillo, J.C. (1990). A paradigm of entrepreneurship as a field of research. *Strategic Management Journal*, 11(1), 17–27.

Stogdill, R.M. (1948). Personal factors associated with leadership: A survey of the literature. *Journal of Psychology*, 25(1), 35–71.

Thornberry, N. (2006). *Lead Like an Entrepreneur: Keeping the Entrepreneurial Spirit Alive within the Corporation*. McGraw Hill, New York, NY.

Tierney, P. and Farmer, S.M. (2004). The Pygmalion process and employee creativity. *Journal of Management*, 30(3), 413–42.

Ward, J.L. (1987). *Keeping the Family Business Healthy: How to Plan for Continuing Growth, Profitability, and Family Leadership*. Jossey-Bass, San Francisco, CA.

Weber, M. (1924 [1947]). *The Theory of Social and Economic Organization*. T. Parsons (trans.). Free Press, New York, NY.

Westley, F. and Mintzberg, H. (1989). Visionary leadership and strategic management. *Strategic Management Journal*, 10(S1), 17–32.

Yukl, G.A. (1998). *Leadership in Organizations*. Prentice Hall, Englewood Cliffs, NJ.

PART IV

APPLICATIONS OF ENTREPRENEURIAL LEADERSHIP

10. The challenge of corporate entrepreneurial leadership
Donald F. Kuratko

INTRODUCTION

The challenge of leadership today has more to do with entrepreneurial thinking than ever before. As Kuratko (2014) points out, entrepreneurship is more than the mere creation of business. The characteristics of seeking opportunities, taking risks beyond security, and having the tenacity to push an idea through to reality combine into a special perspective known as an entrepreneurial mindset which has become the standard by which true leadership is now measured. The entrepreneurial revolution has taken hold in a global economic sense, and the entrepreneurial mindset is the dominant force.

If leadership means the capacity to lead and entrepreneurship means assuming risks beyond security, then entrepreneurial leadership combines the capacity to lead and the capacity to take risks. The combination of these two terms may be one of the most significant phrases in the twenty-first century because the current global 'entrepreneurial revolution' is more impactful than the industrial revolution was for earlier centuries (Kuratko and Morris, 2013). As entrepreneurial thinking is about searching for opportunities and driving innovation, it has become the standard by which true leadership is now measured. It is leadership in discovering new possibilities, opening up new horizons, promulgating a new vision, combining resources in new ways, and inspiring others to create new venture concepts (Kuratko and Morris, 2013). The ability to trigger entrepreneurial action is a cornerstone of entrepreneurial leadership (McMullen and Shepherd, 2006). However, because it is essentially disruptive, as it introduces change to organizations, markets, industries and individuals, it may also be considered threatening. Thus, there are numerous obstacles to the implementation of such action. The willingness to take on the risks associated with entrepreneurial action and the courage to address the obstacles and sources of resistance represent the essence of entrepreneurial leadership.

As corporations seek out innovation as the key competitive advantage, corporate entrepreneurial leaders must be critical contributors to economic growth through their innovations, research and development effectiveness, job creation, competitiveness, productivity and formation of new industry. It is clear that large firms existing in mature industries will have to restructure and reinvent themselves, learning to become more entrepreneurial (Morris et al., 2011), if they hope to sustain themselves for the future. To understand corporate entrepreneurial leadership one must first understand the concept of corporate entrepreneurship.

UNDERSTANDING THE CONCEPT OF CORPORATE ENTREPRENEURSHIP

The concept of corporate entrepreneurship has evolved over the last four decades and the definitions have varied considerably over time. The early research in the 1970s focused on venture teams and how entrepreneurship inside existing organizations could be developed (Hill and Hlavacek, 1972; Peterson and Berger, 1972; Hanan, 1976). In the 1980s, researchers conceptualized corporate entrepreneurship as entrepreneurial behavior requiring organizational sanctions and resource commitments for the purpose of developing different types of value-creating innovations. In other words, it was a process of organizational renewal (Alterowitz, 1988; Burgelman, 1983a, 1983b, 1984; Pinchott, 1985; Kanter, 1985; Schollhammer, 1982; Sathe, 1989; Sykes and Block, 1989).

By the 1990s researchers had adjusted their focus on corporate entrepreneurship to re-energizing and enhancing the firm's ability to develop the skills through which innovations could be created (Jennings and Young, 1990; Merrifield, 1993; Zahra, 1991; Birkinshaw, 1997; Borch et al., 1999; Barringer and Bluedorn, 1999; Zahra et al., 1999). More comprehensive definitions began to take shape during the 1990s, such as Guth and Ginsberg's (1990) approach that outlined two major types of phenomena: new venture creation within existing organizations and the transformation of ongoing organizations through strategic renewal. Then, Zahra (1991: 261) observed that:

> corporate entrepreneurship may be formal or informal activities aimed at creating new businesses in established companies through product and process innovations and market developments. These activities may take place at the corporate, division (business), functional or project levels, with the unifying objective of improving a company's competitive position and financial performance.

By the end of the decade Sharma and Chrisman (1999: 18) suggested that corporate entrepreneurship 'is the process where by an individual or a group of individuals, in association with an existing organization, create a new organization or instigate renewal or innovation within that organization'. With all of these various definitions taking shape, the twenty-first-century approach to corporate entrepreneurship evolved into a firm's efforts to establish sustainable competitive advantages as the foundation for profitable growth. Recent research efforts have suggested particular domains into which these corporate entrepreneurial activities can be categorized.

THE CURRENT DOMAINS OF CORPORATE ENTREPRENEURSHIP

Many of the elements essential to constructing a theoretically grounded understanding of the domains of corporate entrepreneurship can now be identified. Kuratko and Audretsch (2013) attempted to provide a clear understanding of what comprises the concept of corporate entrepreneurship. Outlining the depiction used by Morris et al. (2011), corporate entrepreneurship can be manifested in companies through either 'corporate venturing' or 'strategic entrepreneurship'.

Corporate venturing activities have generally been categorized in two main activities. The first activity incorporates any innovation that is created within the firm, referred to as internal corporate ventures (ICVs). With internal corporate venturing, new businesses are created and owned by the corporation and typically reside within the current corporate structure. The second activity would be any innovation that is created outside of the firm, referred to as external corporate ventures (ECVs). External corporate venturing involves new businesses that are created by parties outside the corporation and subsequently invested in or acquired by the corporation. These external businesses are typically very young ventures or early-growth-stage firms (Covin and Miles, 2007; Morris et al., 2011). Miles and Covin (2002) reported that firms pursue corporate venturing for three primary reasons: (1) to build an innovative capability as the basis for making the overall firm more entrepreneurial and accepting of change; (2) to appropriate greater value from current organizational competencies or to expand the firm's scope of operations and knowledge into areas of possible strategic importance; and (3) to generate quick financial returns.

Strategic entrepreneurship approaches refer to a broad array of significant entrepreneurial activities or innovations that are adopted in the firm's pursuit of competitive advantage which usually do not result in new businesses for the corporation. With reference to strategic entrepreneurship approaches, innovation can be found within any of five areas: the firm's strategy, product offerings, served markets, internal organization (that is, structure, processes and capabilities) or business model (Kuratko and Audretsch, 2013). These innovations can also represent a firm's fundamental differentiation from its industry rivals. Hence, there are two possible reference points that can be considered when a firm exhibits strategic entrepreneurship: (1) how much the firm is transforming itself relative to where it was before (for example, transforming its products, markets, internal processes, and so on); and (2) how much the firm is transforming itself relative to industry conventions or standards (again, in terms of product offerings, market definitions, internal processes, and so forth). Strategic entrepreneurship can take one of five forms: strategic renewal (adoption of a new strategy), sustained regeneration (introduction of a new product into an existing category), domain redefinition (reconfiguration of existing product or market categories), organizational rejuvenation (internally focused innovation for strategy improvement) and business model reconstruction (redesign of existing business model) (Covin and Miles, 1999; Hitt et al., 2001; Ireland et al., 2003; Ireland and Webb, 2007; Morris et al., 2011).

ENTREPRENEURIAL INTENSITY OF AN ORGANIZATION

Entrepreneurial ability is a variable that each individual possesses at some level. The challenge becomes one of determining the level of each particular entrepreneurial individual or action. This assessment may be done through identifying the 'degree' and 'frequency' of entrepreneurial actions. The work of Covin and Slevin (1991) and Morris et al. (2011) is drawn on to examine how such an assessment could be accomplished. Covin and Slevin introduced the concept of entrepreneurial orientation (EO), which consisted of three underlying dimensions – innovativeness, risk-taking and proactiveness – with different combinations of these dimensions possible. Morris et al. (2011) employed this distinction to suggest that each entrepreneurial action could be regarded as highly or only nominally innovative, risky and proactive. Accordingly, the 'degree' of entrepreneurial action refers to the extent to which events are innovative, risky and proactive. The 'frequency' of entrepreneurial actions refers to the number of actions pursued by an individual or organization over a given period of time. It may vary, from those companies that produce a steady stream of new products, services or processes, to other companies that rarely introduce something new.

The overall level of the degree and frequency of entrepreneurial actions demonstrated by an individual or organization is known as 'entrepreneurial intensity'. Morris et al. (2011) have created a two-dimensional matrix ('entrepreneurial grid') with the frequency (number of entrepreneurial events) on the vertical axis, and the degree (extent of innovativeness, risk and proactiveness) on the horizontal axis. As there are no absolute standards for degree or frequency of entrepreneurial actions, the results are relative, meaning that different points on the grid at different periods in time could be applied to the same organization or person depending on their activity. However, a firm's entrepreneurial intensity does provide some measure of an organization's entrepreneurial activity at any point in time that could then form the basis for what constitutes a corporate entrepreneurial strategy.

Specifically defined, a corporate entrepreneurial strategy is 'a vision-directed, organization-wide reliance on entrepreneurial behavior that purposefully and continuously rejuvenates the organization and shapes the scope of its operations through the recognition and exploitation of entrepreneurial opportunity' (Ireland et al., 2009: 21). As companies have found themselves continually redefining their markets, restructuring their operations and modifying their business models, learning the skills to think and act entrepreneurially has become a major source of competitive advantage.

Initiating entrepreneurial actions is not something that management can simply decide to do. Corporate entrepreneurship does not produce instant success. It requires considerable time and investment, and there must be continual reinforcement. By their nature, organizations impose constraints on entrepreneurial behavior. To be sustainable, the entrepreneurial spirit must be integrated into the mission, goals, strategies, structure, processes and values of the organization. Flexibility, speed, innovation and entrepreneurial leadership are the cornerstones. The leadership mindset must become an opportunity-driven mindset, where actions are never constrained by the resources currently controlled (Morris et al., 2011). This entrepreneurial mindset becomes the essence of corporate entrepreneurship. The true challenge embedded within corporate entrepreneurial leadership is to create or maintain an entrepreneurial mindset within an organization, which requires that a corporate culture of innovation must be established. The creation of that culture is examined in the next section.

AN ORGANIZATIONAL CLIMATE FOR CORPORATE ENTREPRENEURIAL ACTIVITY

The internal work environment usually indicates the perceived costs and benefits associated with taking personal risks, and whether it allows for the ambiguity and stress that entrepreneurial behavior can create. Therefore, corporate entrepreneurial activity is more likely in companies where all individuals' entrepreneurial potential is nurtured. Leadership's challenge is to develop an innovation-friendly internal environment. Employee perception of an innovative environment is critical for stressing the importance of the leadership's commitment to potential innovative projects (Hornsby et al., 2009).

A firm's internal entrepreneurial climate should be assessed to evaluate in what manner it is supportive for entrepreneurial behavior to exist and how that is perceived by the leaders. When attempting to inventory the firm's current situation regarding the readiness for innovation, leaders need to identify parts of the firm's structure, control systems, human resource management systems and culture that inhibit, and parts that facilitate, entrepreneurial behavior as the foundation for successfully implementing corporate innovation (Ireland et al., 2006a, 2006b).

In order to understand the most effective internal environment for corporate entrepreneurial activity, an examination of antecedents for individual entrepreneurial behavior is critical. Most of the research dealing with the impact of organizational antecedents on individual-level entrepreneurial behavior is based on the empirical work of Kuratko and his colleagues (Kuratko et al., 1990; Hornsby et al., 1999; Hornsby et al., 2002; Kuratko et al., 2004; Kuratko et al., 2005b; Hornsby et al., 2009). In the Kuratko et al. (1990) study, results from factor analysis showed that what had been theoretically argued to be five conceptually distinct factors that would elicit and support entrepreneurial behavior on the part of first- and middle-level managers (top management support for corporate entrepreneurship (CE), reward and resource availability, organizational structure and boundaries, risk-taking and time availability) were actually only three in number. Based on how items loaded, they concluded that three factors – management support, organizational structure, and reward and resource availability – were important influences on the development of an organizational climate in which entrepreneurial behavior on the part of first- and middle-level managers could be expected.

In extending this early study, Hornsby et al. (1999) conducted empirical research to explore the effect of organizational culture on entrepreneurial behavior in a sample of Canadian and US firms. In particular, they sought to determine whether organizational culture creates variance in entrepreneurial behavior on the part of managers. The results, based on data collected from all levels of management, showed no significant differences between Canadian and US managers' perceptions of the importance of five factors – management support, work discretion, rewards/reinforcement, time availability and organizational boundaries – as antecedents to their entrepreneurial behavior. These findings partially validated those reported by Kuratko et al. (1990) and extended the importance of organizational antecedents of managers' entrepreneurial behavior into companies based in a second national culture.

Hornsby et al. (2002) then developed the corporate entrepreneurship assessment instrument (CEAI) to partially replicate the previous studies and provide a sound instrument for analyzing employee perceptions of the antecedents to an organizational climate conducive for entrepreneurial activity. The instrument featured 48 Likert-style questions that were used to assess antecedents of entrepreneurial behavior. Results from factor analyses supported the five stable antecedents of middle-level managers' entrepreneurial behavior. The five antecedents are: (1) management support (the willingness of top-level managers to facilitate and promote entrepreneurial behavior, including the championing of innovative ideas and providing the resources people require to behave entrepreneurially); (2) work discretion/autonomy (top-level managers' commitment to tolerate failure, provide decision-making latitude and freedom from excessive oversight, and delegate authority and responsibility to middle- and lower-level managers); (3) rewards/reinforcement (developing and using systems that reinforce entrepreneurial behavior, highlight significant achievements and encourage pursuit of challenging work); (4) time availability (evaluating workloads to ensure that individuals and groups have the time needed to pursue innovations, and that their jobs are structured in ways that support efforts to achieve short- and long-term organizational goals); and (5) organizational boundaries (precise explanations of outcomes expected from organizational work, and development of mechanisms for evaluating, selecting and using innovations). This instrument measures the degree to which individuals within a firm perceive these five elements to be critical to an internal environment conducive for individual entrepreneurial activity (Kuratko et al., 2014b). Through the results of this instrument, corporate entrepreneurial leaders are better able to assess, evaluate and manage the firm's internal work environment in ways that support entrepreneurial behavior, which becomes the foundation for successfully implementing a corporate innovation strategy. Yet there are critical roles that must be fulfilled by the different levels of leadership.

IDENTIFYING THE CRITICAL LEADERSHIP RESPONSIBILITIES

Leaders at all organizational levels have critical strategic roles to fulfill for the organization to be successful (Ireland et al., 2002). According to Floyd and Lane (2000), senior-, middle- and first-level managers (leaders) have distinct responsibilities which are then associated with particular managerial actions.

In examining the role of senior-level managers, Burgelman (1984) contends that in successful corporate entrepreneurship senior-level management's principal involvement takes place within the strategic and structural context determination processes. In particular, senior-level managers are responsible for 'retroactively rationalizing' certain new businesses into the firm's portfolio and concept of strategy, based on their evaluations of those businesses' prospects as desirable, value-creating components of the firm. They are also responsible for structuring the organization in ways that accommodate and reinforce the business ventures embraced as part of the firm's strategic context. Overall, Burgelman (1984) sees such managers as having a 'selecting' role in the corporate venturing form of CE.

Ling et al. (2008) examined 152 firms in regard to how 'transformational' chief executive officers impacted on corporate entrepreneurship. Their research demonstrated that they had a significant role in directly shaping four salient characteristics of top management teams: behavioral integration, risk-taking propensity, decentralization of responsibilities, and long-term compensation. This study provided impetus to the importance of the directing role that top management must embrace. Thus, senior-level managers have critical roles in CE activity in the articulation of an entrepreneurial strategic vision and instigating the emergence of an organizational climate conducive to entrepreneurial activity. In addition, senior-level managers are also centrally involved in the defining processes of both the corporate venturing and strategic entrepreneurship forms of CE, as they provide leadership to various entrepreneurial initiatives.

Evidence shows that middle-level managers are the hub through which most organizational knowledge flows (Floyd and Wooldridge, 1992, 1994; King et al., 2001). To interact effectively with first-level managers, middle-level managers must possess the technical competence required to understand the firm's core competencies, and simultaneously, interacting effectively with senior-level executives, middle-level managers must understand the firm's strategic intent and goals. Through interactions with senior- and first-level managers, those operating in the middle of an organization's leadership structure influence and shape their firms' corporate entrepreneurial strategies. Kuratko et al. (2005b) argue that middle-level managers' work as change agents and promoters of innovation is facilitated by their position in the organization hierarchy. They contend that middle-level managers endorse, refine and shepherd entrepreneurial initiatives and identify, acquire and deploy resources needed to pursue those initiatives.

The work of Kuratko et al. (2005b) further described each of the roles for middle-level managers. In the endorsement role, middle-level managers often find themselves in evaluative positions with entrepreneurial initiatives emerging from lower organizational levels. Then middle-level managers must endorse those valued initiatives to the top level of the organization. They must also endorse the top-level initiatives and 'sell' their value-creating potential to the primary implementers: first-level managers. In the refinement role, middle-level managers are molding the entrepreneurial opportunity into one that makes sense for the organization, given the organization's strategy, resources and structure. Middle-level managers must convert potential entrepreneurial opportunities into initiatives that fit the organization. The shepherding role is where middle-level managers champion and guide the entrepreneurial initiative to assure that entrepreneurial initiatives originating at lower organizational levels are not abandoned once their continued development requires higher-level support. With their identification role, middle-level managers must know which resources will be needed to convert the entrepreneurial initiative into a business reality, as these initiatives tend to evolve in their scope, content and focus as they develop (McGrath and MacMillan, 1995). Finally, the acquisition and deployment roles involve middle-level managers being responsible for redirecting resources away from existing operations and deploying them into entrepreneurial initiatives appearing to have greater strategic value for the firm (Burgelman, 1984). In short, it might be argued that the middle management level is where entrepreneurial opportunities are given the best chance to flourish, based on the resources likely to be deployed in their pursuit.

According to Floyd and Lane (2000), first-level managers have experimenting, adjusting and conforming roles. The experimenting role is expressed through the initiating of entrepreneurial projects. The adjusting role is expressed through, for example, first-level managers responding to recognized and unplanned entrepreneurial challenges. Finally, the conforming role is expressed through first-level managers' adaptation of operating policies and procedures to the strategic initiatives endorsed at higher organizational levels.

In one empirical examination of managers' relation to employees in the corporate entrepreneurship process, Brundin et al. (2008) examined the entrepreneurial behavior of employees in entrepreneurially oriented firms and found a direct relation to managers' emotions and displays. The employees' willingness to act entrepreneurially increased when managers displayed confidence and satisfaction about an entrepreneurial project. It was also shown that the employees' willingness to act entrepreneurially decreased when managers displayed frustration, worry or bewilderment about an entrepreneurial project.

In an effort to study entrepreneurial actions within the context of CE at different levels of management (leadership), Hornsby et al. (2009) conducted an empirical study of 458 managers at different levels in their firms. They found that the relationship between perceived internal antecedents (as measured by the corporate entrepreneurship assessment instrument mentioned earlier) and corporate entrepreneurial actions (measured by the number of new ideas implemented), differed depending on managerial level. Specifically, the positive relationship between managerial support and entrepreneurial action was more positive for senior- and middle-level managers than it was for first-level (lower-level) managers, and the positive relationship between work discretion and entrepreneurial action was more positive for senior- and middle-level managers than it was for first-level managers. The few studies that have explored managerial level (primarily conceptual studies) have emphasized the role of first-level managers in a 'bottom-up' process of corporate entrepreneurship (Burgelman, 1983a, 1983b, 1984). This study offered a counterweight to this 'bottom-up' process with arguments and empirical support for the notion that, given a specific organizational environment, more senior managers have greater structural ability to 'make more of' the conditions and thus implement more entrepreneurial ideas than do first-level managers.

Even with the differences found with levels of management in the Hornsby et al. (2009) study, it reinforced the belief that working jointly, senior-, middle- and first-level managers (leaders) are responsible for developing the entrepreneurial behaviors that could be used to form the core competencies through which future competitive success can be pursued (Kuratko et al., 2005a). Thus, organizations developing an environment conducive to entrepreneurial activity must recognize that there is an integrated set of roles at the senior, middle and first levels of management (leadership). Research continues to examine the impact of these differing levels. Even with all managerial responsibilities acknowledged, the ultimate challenge is in the implementation of corporate entrepreneurial leadership.

IMPLEMENTING ENTREPRENEURIAL LEADERSHIP IN THE CORPORATE SETTING

It is clear that corporate entrepreneurial leadership is a critical component in the modern global economy. However, the exhibition and implementation is not so easy. As Kuratko et al. (2014a) demonstrate, there are four major elements that must be addressed by today's leaders if corporate entrepreneurial activity is to become a reality in organizations. Summarized in Box 10.1, the four major elements are delved into here.

The first is understanding the type of innovation that a firm seeks. There are numerous definitions of innovation, so any discussion of corporate entrepreneurship must first address the matter of how we categorize innovation; specifically, by basic type or trajectory. The basic types of innovation include: product innovation – changes to physical products; process innovation – changes to the processes that produce products or services; and service innovation – changes to services that customers use. The basic trajectory for innovation may be radical – the launching of inaugural breakthroughs; incremental – the systematic evolution of a product or service into newer or larger markets; and disruptive – transforms business practice to rewrite the rules of an industry. Disruptive innovation often occurs because new sciences and technology are introduced or applied to a new market that offers the potential to exceed the existing limits of technology.

BOX 10.1   MAJOR IMPLEMENTATION ISSUES FOR
            CORPORATE ENTREPRENEURIAL LEADERSHIP

1. *Understanding the type of innovation that a firm seeks*: product innovation, process innovation, service innovation, radical, incremental, disruptive.
2. *Coordination of managerial roles*: senior, middle, first-line.
3. *Effective use of operating controls*: operations control processes and mechanisms.
4. *Proper individual training and preparation*: training program that includes:

   ● overview of corporate entrepreneurship;
   ● a process of entrepreneurial thinking;
   ● idea acceleration process;
   ● barriers and facilitators to entrepreneurial activity;
   ● failure recognition;
   ● innovation teams;
   ● innovation action plan.

The second major element is coordination of managerial (leadership) roles. Successful implementation of corporate innovation faces another impediment in the lack of managerial coordination at all levels throughout the organization. As pointed out earlier in this chapter, an innovation strategy can only work with the integrated efforts of all levels of management to ensure a sustaining innovative strategy (Kuratko et al., 2005a). Congruence needs to be achieved at the individual and organizational levels (Hornsby et al., 2009). Corporate entrepreneurship must 'run deep' within organizations and every level of management must be coordinated to carry out their specific roles. Senior-level managers set the vision increasingly for the innovative imperatives created by their competitive landscapes, while middle- and first-level managers of an organization have significant roles within innovative and strategic processes (Hornsby et al., 2009). Without sustained and strong commitment from all levels of the organization, innovative behavior will never be a defining characteristic of the organization.

The third major implementation issue is effective use of operating controls. Without proper operating control mechanisms, corporate entrepreneurial activity may 'tend to generate an incoherent mass of interesting but unrelated opportunities that may have profit potential, but that don't move [those] firms toward a desirable future' (Getz and Tuttle, 2001: 277). Therefore, successful corporate entrepreneurial activity is contingent upon a firm's ability to align operations control processes and mechanisms that select, guide and possibly terminate innovative actions and initiatives (Morris et al., 2006). Leaders have come to realize that a mixture of formality and discretion is a key to providing both high effectiveness and high efficiency (Naveh, 2007). In a study of 177 firms operating in a wide variety of industries, Goodale et al. (2011) investigated the effect on innovation performance of several recognized determinants of corporate innovation, namely, management support, work discretion/autonomy, rewards/reinforcements, time availability and organizational boundaries (Kuratko et al., 2014b). Their results indicated that each of the five innovation determinants significantly interacted with one or both of the operations control variables, thereby influencing innovation performance. This is a significant finding that supports the importance of effectively using control systems with innovation. In the Goodale et al. (2011) study, innovation performance was greatest when corporate entrepreneurship was combined with operating control.

The fourth major issue is proper individual training and preparation. Success with corporate entrepreneurship requires that those within the firm be educated and trained as to what constitutes the concept of a corporate entrepreneurship (Kuratko et al., 2001). Leaders must create an understanding of the entrepreneurial process for their employees. Having assessed whether the firm's internal work environment supports innovative activity (see Kuratko et al., 2014b), senior leaders should also determine whether corporate innovation and entrepreneurial behavior are understood by the firm's employees. Experience demonstrates that executives need to develop a program with the purpose of helping all parties who will be affected by corporate innovation to understand the value of the entrepreneurial behavior the firm is requesting of them (Kuratko et al., 2014a). As a way for organizations to develop understanding of the need for innovation and entrepreneurial activity, corporate entrepreneurship or innovation training programs are often employed, such as one example of a corporate entrepreneurship training program with seven modules:

1. Corporate Entrepreneurship: an overview of the corporate entrepreneurship experience, in which participants are introduced to the entrepreneurial revolution that has taken place throughout the world over the last three decades.
2. Entrepreneurial Thinking: the process of thinking innovatively is discussed within an organization, with the misconceptions about thinking innovatively reviewed.
3. Idea Acceleration Process: participants generate a set of specific ideas which they would like to work on, while examining a number of aspects of the corporation, including structural barriers and facilitators.
4. Barriers and Facilitators to Entrepreneurial Activity: the most common barriers to innovative behavior are reviewed and discussed. Participants complete several exercises that will help them to deal with barriers in the workplace.
5. Failure Recognition: project failure is a common occurrence, and organizational routines and rituals are likely to influence the grief recovery of those involved in the failed project. To the extent that a social support system could be offered by the organizational environment for individuals' negative emotions, there will likely be greater learning and motivational outcomes (Shepherd and Kuratko, 2009).
6. Innovation Teams (I-Teams): the concept of forming I-Teams to focus on specific innovations is examined (Kuratko et al., 2012). Participants work together to form teams based on the ideas that have been circulating among the entire group.
7. Innovation Action Plan: teams are asked to begin the process of completing an action plan that includes setting goals, establishing an I-Team, assessing current conditions, developing a step-by-step timetable for project completion, and project evaluation.

While this is only one example of a training format, the outline at least depicts the type of education and preparation needed within an organization so that a general understanding of corporate entrepreneurship can be accomplished.

If these four major implementation issues are understood and appropriately addressed, the creation of an effective innovative ecosystem within the organization is certainly enhanced. In addressing these issues, executives are attempting to provide 'entrepreneurial leadership' for their organization (Kuratko, 2007; Ling et al., 2008), yet they must also accept certain responsibilities in this leadership role.

CONCLUSION: THE RESPONSIBILITIES OF CORPORATE ENTREPRENEURIAL LEADERSHIP

As part of the corporate entrepreneurial leadership role, the first responsibility involves providing a clear definition of the specified duties or challenges involved with innovative projects that every team member should accomplish. In so doing, an effective 'framing' of the innovative challenge is accomplished.

The second responsibility for entrepreneurial leaders is to make uncertainty less daunting in the eyes of team members. Corporate entrepreneurial activity contains inherent risks, and many people lack the self-confidence to implement such activity in an organization. If leaders can create the self-confidence within individuals by 'reducing the uncertainty' to act on opportunities without seeking managerial permission, then employees will not be overwhelmed by the complexity inherent in many innovative situations.

A third responsibility is to define acceptability; that is, what will be accepted and what cannot be accepted as actions within the firm. In other words, to outline the limiting conditions or control mechanisms that are in place within the organization (Goodale et al., 2011). Once individuals understand and accept the parameters, then far more entrepreneurial activity can be accomplished. This is what the entrepreneurial mindset is all about: seeing the opportunities amidst the barriers and controls.

A fourth responsibility of entrepreneurial leadership involves 'clearing obstacles' that arise as a result of internal competition for resources. This can be a problem, especially when the entrepreneurial innovation is beginning to undergo significant growth. A growing venture will often find itself pitted squarely against other (often established) aspects of the firm in a fierce internal competition for funds and staff. Creative tactics, political skills, and an ability to regroup, reorganize and attack from another angle become invaluable.

The fifth responsibility is for entrepreneurial leaders to understand the 'grief' that may be associated with project failures (Shepherd et al., 2009). As was noted in the corporate entrepreneurship training program (outlined earlier in this section), failure can be an important source of information for learning, yet this learning is not automatic. The emotions generated by failure, such as grief, can interfere with the learning process, and grief recovery may be an important component for individual innovation to continue. Recognizing the grief process and providing assistance to manage it for individuals and organizations will be critical to the recovery process and lead to enhanced learning (Shepherd and Kuratko, 2009; Shepherd et al., 2009). Thus, having failed, innovators recover more quickly from the emotions of grief; being able to learn more from their project failures and remain committed to future innovative endeavors will likely enhance the organization's sustained innovative output. A sixth and final responsibility for entrepreneurial leaders is to keep their 'finger on the pulse' of the project. This involves constructive monitoring and control of the developing opportunity (Morris et al., 2011). Box 10.2 summarizes these responsibilities.

Continuous innovation (in terms of products, processes, and administrative routines and structures) and an ability to compete effectively in the global markets are among the skills that increasingly are expected to influence corporate performance in the twenty-first century. Today's executives agree that innovation is the most important pathway for companies to accelerate their pace of change in the global environment. Corporate entrepreneurship is envisioned as a process that can facilitate firms' efforts to innovate constantly and cope effectively with the competitive realities that companies encounter when competing in world markets. Corporate entrepreneurship is risky, but it has to start somewhere, perhaps on a small scale and under corporate control. However, if it starts, there is

---

BOX 10.2   KEY RESPONSIBILITIES OF CORPORATE ENTREPRENEURIAL LEADERSHIP

Frame the innovative challenge.
Reduce the uncertainty to act on innovation.
Define the parameters of entrepreneurial activity.
Clear the obstacles of internal competition.
Understand the 'grief' associated with project failures.
Monitor developing opportunities.

the likelihood of greater success. Leaders become more comfortable with the idea, confidence builds, results occur, and soon the first corporate assigned projects evolve into more autonomous ventures that reach farther out before being required to report into administrative structure.

Corporate entrepreneurial leadership is considered as moving beyond the traditional product and service innovations to pioneering innovation in processes, value chains, business models and all functions of management. The major thrust behind corporate entrepreneurship is a revitalization of innovation, creativity and leadership in today's organizations. It appears that corporate entrepreneurship may possess the critical components needed for the future productivity of all organizations. If so, then corporate entrepreneurial leadership is necessary for firms of all sizes to prosper and flourish in competitive environments (Kuratko, 2014; Kuratko et al., 2012).

REFERENCES

Alterowitz, R. (1988), *New Corporate Ventures.* New York, NY: Wiley.
Barringer, B.R. and Bluedorn, A.C. (1999), Corporate entrepreneurship and strategic management. *Strategic Management Journal*, 20: 421–44.
Birkinshaw, J. (1997), Entrepreneurship in multinational corporations: The characteristics of subsidiary initiatives. *Strategic Management Journal,* 18: 207–29.
Borch, O.J., Huse, M. and Senneseth, K. (1999), Resource configuration, competitive strategies, and corporate entrepreneurship: An empirical examination of small firms. *Entrepreneurship Theory and Practice*, 24 (1): 49–70.
Brundin, E., Patzelt, H. and Shepherd, D.A. (2008), Managers' emotional displays and employees' willingness to act entrepreneurially. *Journal of Business Venturing*, 23 (2): 221–43.
Burgelman, R.A. (1983a), A process model of internal corporate venturing in the major diversified firm. *Administrative Science Quarterly*, 28 (2): 223–44.
Burgelman, R.A. (1983b), Corporate entrepreneurship and strategic management: Insights from a process study. *Management Science*, 23: 1349–63.
Burgelman, R.A. (1984), Designs for corporate entrepreneurship in established firms. *California Management Review*, 26 (3): 154–66.
Covin, J.G. and Miles, M.P. (1999), Corporate entrepreneurship and the pursuit of competitive advantage. *Entrepreneurship Theory and Practice*, 23 (3): 47–64.
Covin, J.G. and Miles, M.P. (2007), Strategic use of corporate venturing. *Entrepreneurship Theory and Practice*, 31 (2): 183–207.
Covin, J.G. and Slevin, D.P. (1991), A conceptual model of entrepreneurship as firm behavior. *Entrepreneurship Theory and Practice*, 16 (1): 7–25.
Floyd, S.W. and Lane, P.J. (2000), Strategizing throughout the organization: Managing role conflict in strategic renewal. *Academy of Management Review*, 25: 154–77.
Floyd, S.W. and Wooldridge, B. (1992), Middle management involvement in strategy and its association with strategic type. *Strategic Management Journal*, 13: 53–168.
Floyd, S.W. and Wooldridge, B. (1994), Dinosaurs or dynamos? Recognizing middle management's strategic role. *Academy of Management Executive*, 8 (4): 47–57.
Getz, G. and Tuttle, E.G. (2001), A comprehensive approach to corporate venturing. *Handbook of Business Strategy*, 2 (1): 277–9.
Goodale, J.C., Kuratko, D.F., Hornsby, J.S. and Covin, J.G. (2011), Operations management and corporate entrepreneurship: The moderating effect of operations control on the

antecedents of corporate entrepreneurial activity in relation to innovation performance. *Journal of Operations Management*, 29 (2): 116–27.

Guth, W.D. and Ginsberg, A. (1990), Corporate entrepreneurship. *Strategic Management Journal*, 11 (Special Issue): 5–15.

Hanan, M. (1976), Venturing corporations: Think small to stay strong. *Harvard Business Review*, 54 (3): 139–48.

Hill, R.M. and Hlavacek, J.D. (1972), The venture team: A new concept in marketing organizations. *Journal of Marketing*, 36: 44–50.

Hitt, M.A., Ireland, R.D., Camp, S.M. and Sexton, D.L. (2001), Strategic entrepreneurship: Entrepreneurial strategies for wealth creation. *Strategic Management Journal*, 22 (Special Issue): 479–91.

Hornsby, J.S., Kuratko, D.F. and Montagno, R.V. (1999), Perception of internal factors for corporate entrepreneurship: A comparison of Canadian and US managers. *Entrepreneurship Theory and Practice*, 24 (2): 9–24.

Hornsby, J.S., Kuratko, D.F., Shepherd, D.A. and Bott, J.P. (2009), Managers' corporate entrepreneurial actions: Examining perception and position. *Journal of Business Venturing*, 24 (3): 236–47.

Hornsby, J.S., Kuratko, D.F. and Zahra, S.A. (2002), Middle managers' perception of the internal environment for corporate entrepreneurship: Assessing a measurement scale. *Journal of Business Venturing*, 17: 49–63.

Ireland, R.D., Covin, J.G. and Kuratko, D.F. (2009), Conceptualizing corporate entrepreneurship strategy. *Entrepreneurship Theory and Practice*, 33 (1): 19–46.

Ireland, R.D., Hitt, M.A. and Sirmon, D.G. (2003), A model of strategic entrepreneurship: The construct and its dimensions. *Journal of Management*, 29 (6): 963–89.

Ireland, R.D., Hitt, M.A. and Vaidyanath, D. (2002), Strategic alliances as a pathway to competitive success. *Journal of Management*, 28: 413–46.

Ireland, R.D., Kuratko, D.F. and Morris, M.H. (2006a), A health audit for corporate entrepreneurship: Innovation at all levels – Part I. *Journal of Business Strategy*, 27 (1): 10–17.

Ireland, R.D., Kuratko, D.F. and Morris, M.H. (2006b), A health audit for corporate entrepreneurship: Innovation at all levels – Part 2. *Journal of Business Strategy*, 27 (2): 21–30.

Ireland, R.D. and Webb, J.W. (2007), Strategic entrepreneurship: Creating competitive advantage through streams of innovation. *Business Horizons*, 50: 49–59.

Jennings, D.F. and Young, D.M. (1990), An empirical comparison between objective and subjective measures of the product innovation domain of corporate entrepreneurship. *Entrepreneurship Theory and Practice*, 15 (1): 53–66.

Kanter, R.M. (1985), Supporting innovation and venture development in established companies. *Journal of Business Venturing*, 1: 47–60.

King, A.W., Fowler, S.W. and Zeithaml, C.P. (2001), Managing organizational competencies for competitive advantage: The middle-management edge. *Academy of Management Executive*, 15 (2): 95–106.

Kuratko, D.F. (2007), Entrepreneurial leadership for the 21st century. *Journal of Leadership and Organizational Studies*, 14 (1): 1–11.

Kuratko, D.F. (2014), *Entrepreneurship: Theory, Process, Practice*, 9th edn. Mason, OH: Cengage Publishing.

Kuratko, D.F. and Audretsch, D.B. (2013), Clarifying the domains of corporate entrepreneurship. *International Entrepreneurship and Management Journal*, 9 (3): 323–35.

Kuratko, D.F., Covin, J.G. and Hornsby, J.S. (2014a), Why implementing corporate innovation is so difficult. *Business Horizons*, 57 (5): 647–55.

Kuratko, D.F., Goldsby, M.G. and Hornsby, J.S. (2012), *Innovation Acceleration: Transforming Organizational Thinking*. Upper Saddle River, NJ: Pearson/Prentice Hall.

Kuratko, D.F., Hornsby, J.S. and Bishop, J.W. (2005a), Managers' corporate entrepreneurial actions and job satisfaction. *International Entrepreneurship and Management Journal*, 1 (3): 275–91.

Kuratko, D.F., Hornsby, J.S. and Covin, J.G. (2014b), Diagnosing a firm's internal environment for corporate entrepreneurship. *Business Horizons*, 57 (1): 37–47.

Kuratko, D.F., Hornsby, J.S. and Goldsby, M.G. (2004), Sustaining corporate entrepreneurship: A proposed model of perceived implementation/outcome comparisons at the organizational and individual levels. *International Journal of Entrepreneurship and Innovation*, 5 (2): 77–89.

Kuratko, D.F., Ireland, R.D., Covin, J.G. and Hornsby, J.S. (2005b), A model of middle level managers' entrepreneurial behavior. *Entrepreneurship Theory and Practice*, 29 (6): 699–716.

Kuratko, D.F, Ireland, R.D. and Hornsby, J.S. (2001), The power of entrepreneurial outcomes: Insights from Acordia, Inc. *Academy of Management Executive*, 15 (4): 60–71.

Kuratko, D.F., Montagno, R.V. and Hornsby, J.S. (1990), Developing an entrepreneurial assessment instrument for an effective corporate entrepreneurial environment. *Strategic Management Journal*, 11 (Special Issue): 49–58.

Kuratko, D.F. and Morris, M.H. (2013), *Entrepreneurship and Leadership*. Cheltenham, UK and Northampton, MA: Edward Elgar Publishing.

Ling, Y., Simsek, Z., Lubatkin, M.H. and Veiga, J.F. (2008), Transformational leadership's role in promoting corporate entrepreneurship: Examining the CEO–TMT interface. *Academy of Management Journal*, 51 (3): 557–76.

McGrath, R.G. and MacMillan, I.C. (1995), Discovery-driven planning. *Harvard Business Review*, 73 (4): 4–12.

McMullen, J.S. and Shepherd, D.A. (2006), Entrepreneurial action and the role of uncertainty in the theory of the entrepreneur. *Academy of Management Review*, 31 (1): 132–52.

Merrifield, D.B. (1993), Intrapreneurial corporate renewal. *Journal of Business Venturing*, 8: 383–9.

Miles, M.P. and Covin, J.G. (2002), Exploring the practice of corporate venturing: Some common forms and their organizational implications. *Entrepreneurship Theory and Practice*, 26 (3): 21–40.

Morris, M.H., Allen, J., Schindehutte, M. and Avila, R. (2006), Balanced management control systems as a mechanism for achieving corporate entrepreneurship. *Journal of Managerial Issues*, 18 (4): 468–93.

Morris, M.H., Kuratko, D.F. and Covin, J.G. (2011), *Corporate Entrepreneurship and Innovation*, 3rd edn. Mason, OH: Cengage/South-Western Publishers.

Naveh, E. (2007), Formality and discretion in successful R&D projects. *Journal of Operations Management*, 25 (1): 110–125.

Peterson, R. and Berger D. (1972), Entrepreneurship in organizations. *Administrative Science Quarterly*, 16: 97–106.

Pinchott, G. (1985), *Intrapreneurship*. New York, NY: Harper & Row.

Sathe, V. (1989), Fostering entrepreneurship in large diversified firm. *Organizational Dynamics*, 18 (1): 20–32.

Schollhammer, H. (1982), Internal corporate entrepreneurship. In C. Kent, D. Sexton and K. Vesper (eds), *Encyclopedia of Entrepreneurship*. Englewood Cliffs, NJ: Prentice-Hall.

Sharma, P. and Chrisman, J.J. (1999), Toward a reconciliation of the definitional issues in the field of corporate entrepreneurship. *Entrepreneurship Theory and Practice*, 23 (3): 11–28.

Shepherd, D.A., Covin, J.G. and Kuratko, D.F. (2009), Project failure from corporate entrepreneurship: Managing the grief process. *Journal of Business Venturing*, 24 (6): 588–600.

Shepherd, D.A. and Kuratko, D.F. (2009), The death of an innovative project: How grief recovery enhances learning. *Business Horizons*, 52 (5): 451–8.

Sykes, H.B. and Block, Z. (1989), Corporate venturing obstacles: Sources and solutions. *Journal of Business Venturing*, 4: 159–67.

Zahra, S.A. (1991), Predictors and financial outcomes of corporate entrepreneurship: An exploratory study. *Journal of Business Venturing*, 6: 259–86.

Zahra, S.A., Kuratko, D.F. and Jennings, D.F. (1999), Entrepreneurship and the acquisition of dynamic organizational capabilities. *Entrepreneurship Theory and Practice*, 23 (3): 5–10.

11. Weaving together entrepreneurial leadership in social enterprises: a collective achievement towards social purpose
Chrysavgi Sklaveniti and Vicky Tzoumpa

INTRODUCTION

Arguably, the ongoing implications of the recent economic crisis call for a revision of market capitalism to moral capitalism, moving from corporate value to social value (Munro, 2014; Weiskopf and Willmott, 2013). Social value is central to our chapter and we seek to address it through illustrating entrepreneurial leadership in social enterprises. Our chapter aims to appraise, provoke and shape the discussion towards a processual understanding of entrepreneurship and its relational dynamics. Specifically, we focus on the creative processes of entrepreneurial practice in the context of social organizations.

Our proposed conceptualization begins by recognizing that entrepreneurship has been principally conceptualized in a fixed manner, idealizing the individual entrepreneur or the appropriate contingencies that give rise to entrepreneurship (Shane, 2012). Our key argument is that fixedness does not fully reveal the highly dynamic phenomenon of entrepreneurship (McMullen and Dimov, 2013; Zahra and Dess, 2001). It is not sufficient to study nascent entrepreneurship and the concurrent process of value creation at the individual (entrepreneur) or situational (configuration between entrepreneur and others) levels of analysis. Entrepreneurship might be better understood by its relational aspects, which encapsulate the dynamics of such a processual phenomenon (Busenitz et al., 2003; Uhl-Bien, 2006).

This chapter illustrates the processual dynamics of entrepreneurship, by presenting the notion of entrepreneurial leadership from a relational perspective. In doing so, we draw attention to the process of opportunity genesis and development, introducing temporality, relational identity development and improvisation in the study of entrepreneurship. We seek to address these, first, by demonstrating the current state of literature in the fields of entrepreneurship and leadership; second, by presenting the special case of social enterprises and their contextual particularities; and third, by illustrating the dynamics of entrepreneurial leadership therein. In line with our aims and questions, we conclude by offering implications of our work for the academic and practitioner communities, aligning with Lewin's (1945) timeless contention that there is nothing as practical as good theory.

We structure our chapter as follows. First, we take apart the notion of entrepreneurial leadership, which has emerged as an area of study addressing commonalities between the two subfields of entrepreneurship and leadership (Leitch et al., 2013). In doing so, we follow the thinking of individualism which has developed in parallel in the two domains. Our immediate observations are that individuals or relationships between entities are in the spotlight, as if organizing happens in isolation. Contradicting this romantic attachment to entities (Meindl et al., 1985), our conceptualization treats entrepreneurship as an ongoing process of becoming (Tsoukas and Chia, 2002), and entrepreneurial leadership reveals the interactive process through which entrepreneurship and entrepreneurial opportunities are created, developed and sustained in an ecological fashion. We conclude by offering the indicative definition of entrepreneurial leadership as a perpetual and relational process of working together to mobilize business opportunities in an organizational context in pursuit of entrepreneurial goals.

Next, we focus the development of entrepreneurial leadership in social enterprises (Peredo and McLean, 2006; Sullivan Mort et al., 2003), since we anticipate that these types of organizations carry increasing weight in societal welfare. Our interest is in entrepreneurial activity that creates social value by catalysing social change or meeting social needs. Putting our understanding about social entrepreneurship into perspective, we identify four streams of thinking that, respectively, deal with the individual entrepreneur (Zahra et al., 2009), the limited nature of resources available to social enterprises (Sharir and Lerner, 2006), the role of institutions (Mair and Marti, 2009; Urbano et al., 2010) and the performance of social enterprises (Darby and Jenkins, 2006). Individualism prevails in all of these streams, so it is important to move into more dynamic realms of understanding (Langley et al., 2013). For our analysis, social entrepreneurship is a process of creating social change by means of entrepreneurial leadership, leading to collaborative forms of organizing (Hosking, 1988). To understand this, it is vital to explore the special context of social enterprises (Pettigrew, 1997), which we do by attending to the concepts of change, inclusiveness and uncertainty. First, we note the temporal unfolding of change from a *kairotic* perspective (Orlikowski and Yates, 2002), which refers to timely occurrence over chronological events. Second, we highlight the inclusive nature of organizing in social enterprises, where both the organization and society participate in the happenings (Mair and Marti, 2006) which change their circumstances. Third, uncertainty is evident in the emergence of social enterprises as they seek to provide answers to multiple interpretations (Weick, 1995).

We suggest that responding to these contextual challenges requires entrepreneurial leadership to ensure the endurance of momentum. With the specific context in the background, we then present the dynamics of relational leadership, expressed by the notion of temporality, relational identity development and improvisation. Temporality can be approached by examining the relational connections that enable the coordination of efforts, producing societal impact and generating commitment to the mission. We draw on practice theory as an analytical construct, where performativity of practices follows the unfolding of entrepreneurship in social enterprises. Next, we present relational identity development, which captures temporary expressions of connections between participants and shapes the ongoing process of entrepreneurial leadership. Boundary conditions seem to be important in understanding how entrepreneurial leadership expresses different forms of relating, and how these forms interpret the composition of boundaries. We argue that such an understanding arises not from a sketch of boundary structures, but from apprehending how the latter emerge. This takes us to the emergence of novelty, which we propose viewing through the lens of improvisation that includes simultaneous and continuous mixing of the established with the novel, under conditions of uncertainty. We end our chapter by offering our parting thoughts about how our propositions can be followed in both research and practice. This includes attending to the tenets of processual philosophy that call for attention to emergence and spontaneity.

ENTREPRENEURIAL LEADERSHIP

Entrepreneurial leadership has emerged as an area of study that seeks to address analogous themes and links between the notions of entrepreneurship and leadership (Cogliser and Brigham, 2004). Indeed, it is a dynamic domain that can prove critical in our understanding of turbulent environments and can offer promising insights into entrepreneurial ventures (Leitch et al., 2013). Still in its infancy, the notion is relatively new and open for exploration, both theoretical and empirical. In this vein, we move the discussion forward by taking entrepreneurial leadership to a processual stance of relating, embedded in social constructionism (Dachler and Hosking, 1995; Gergen, 1994, 2009, 2010; Hosking, 2011).

Our proposed conceptualization describes leadership enacted in an entrepreneurial context (Leitch et al., 2013), recognizing its dynamic and emergent nature. To introduce our arguments, we proceed with a meta-theoretical (Tsoukas and Knudsen, 2003) summary of common developments within the two respective fields. Specifically, our synopsis examines the theme of individualism and proposes relationality (Gergen, 2009) as a promising counterpart in an ever-changing world of organizing (Tsoukas and Chia, 2002).

Underpinning both fields of entrepreneurship and leadership is an attractive attachment to individualism, whereby both phenomena are determined by individual acts (Drath, 2008; Drath et al., 2008). Charting the literature on entrepreneurship, the dominant line of thinking reduces the phenomenon to the individual entrepreneur who successfully exploits opportunities (Busenitz et al., 2003; Choi and Shepherd, 2004; Keupp and Gassmann, 2009; Low and MacMillan, 1988; Morris et al., 1993; Short et al., 2010). As such, theories are concerned with identifying the unique characteristics that set some individuals apart from the rest and render them capable of recognizing and pursuing these opportunities (Shane and Nicolaou, 2013). Following the hegemony of competent entrepreneurs, failure in a venture is attributed to non-existent opportunities (Alvarez et al., 2014; Eckhardt and Ciuchta, 2008). In such a manner, entrepreneurship is regarded as a path-dependant product of entrepreneurs, who recognize the right opportunities (Garud et al., 2010; Gruber, 2010; McMullen et al., 2007; Short et al., 2010).

The principal point of critique lies in the fixedness such thinking assumes, specifically when compared to the turbulent nature of organizing (Nayak and Chia, 2011). The idealization of the individual assumes that opportunities are objective things 'out there', ready to be successfully exploited. Success and opportunity can only be recognized retrospectively and backwards, at the end of entrepreneurial action. In addition to this epistemological gap, empirical material is also critical. It seems that traits are not adequate predictors of entrepreneurship, since a definite skill set cannot be identified (Gartner, 1988; Gartner and Shane, 1995), especially since 'entrepreneurs come in every shape, size, colour, and from all backgrounds' (Hatten, 2011: 32).

Building on individualism, other views of entrepreneurship describe it as a phenomenon starting from the individual and extending out to highlight the prominence of surroundings (Eckhardt and Shane, 2003; Gartner, 2007). Emphasis is not solely on entrepreneurs, but also on the relationships that they develop. Similar to the previous stream of theories, entrepreneurship is again reduced to individuals. The novel addition here is the inclusion of surrounding conditions (Ramoglou, 2013), which are objectively evaluated by entrepreneurs. Therefore, analytical focus lies in the nature of intrinsic attributes that permits entrepreneurs to engage in entrepreneurship, establishing a dichotomy between them and their environment (Koppl and Minniti, 2008). Under such an analysis, it becomes apparent that a lack of entrepreneurship can be attributed to a dearth of appropriate contingencies.

These streams of thinking around individualism run in parallel in the leadership domain. On one hand, there are theories that reduce the complex phenomenon of leadership to the leadership of the individual; the impact of the leader is so pervasive that leadership is the property of the leader. Examples of this stream are Great Man, traits, behavioural, situational, contingency, constitutive, transformational, charismatic and servant theories (Northouse, 2004), which prescribe what leadership should be and propose that the route to achieving effectiveness is an ideal leader exerting influence on external variables (Gemmill and Oakley, 1992; Hernandez et al., 2011; Rost, 1993; Wood, 2005). Presenting leadership as property and product of the leader implies that only certain individuals express leadership, specifically those who hold formal hierarchical positions (Metcalf and Benn, 2013; Wood, 2005). It also implies that researching about leadership means examining the competencies and qualities of the leader (Bryman, 2004; Crevani et al., 2010).

The second stream of theories in leadership view it as starting from individuals and extending into collaboration between one or more. Examples in this stream include leader–member exchange (LMX), shared and distributed theories (Bolden, 2011; Graen and Uhl-Bien, 1995; Northouse, 2004; Pearce and Conger, 2003), whereby leadership is considered to exist between leader–follower relationships. Accordingly, the theories are concerned with examining how individuals evaluate the relationships they have with each other. The quality and engagement of these relationships varies significantly from LMX (Graen and Uhl-Bien, 1995) to distributed theories (Bolden, 2011); still, it is important to acknowledge that it is assumed that participants objectively decide about the nature of these relationships (Contractor et al., 2012; Uhl-Bien, 2006). Therefore, since individuals and relationships are assumed to be distinct entities (Uhl-Bien, 2006), there is no reason to look into the social elements of leadership; it is enough to study individual acts present in organized relationships.

Our review has uncovered the parallel progression of individualistic thinking in the fields of entrepreneurship and leadership. Although we have previously stated that the notion of entrepreneurial leadership is in its infancy, it is worth noting that the crossroads between the two fields is not a new development (Cogliser and Brigham, 2004; Ruvio et al., 2010; Vecchio, 2003). Leadership has been treated as a predictor of entrepreneurial achievements, with studies examining leadership traits pertinent to success (Jensen and Luthans, 2006). Such a mix of the two fields highlights the romance of individualism and mystifies the entrepreneur as a heroic figure (Bligh et al., 2011; Bligh and Schyns, 2007; Meindl, 1995; Meindl et al., 1985). For our part, in weaving together entrepreneurial leadership, we intend to tackle a number of resonant ideas, but we wish to distinguish ourselves from individualist perspectives. The romance of individualism tends to dramatize the impact of leadership on organizational success, in both theoretical and empirical developments (Meindl et al., 1985). In particular, performance is attributed to the individual, as if organizing happens in a void and in a strictly prognostic manner (Meindl, 1995; Wood, 2005; Wood and Case, 2006). Moreover, leadership is glorified as a causal category, imposing a much-needed desire to make sense of organizational phenomena (Bligh et al., 2011; Bligh and Schyns, 2007). We understand this romantic attachment to leadership as it expresses a facet of human nature that looks for an exemplary figure to offer the way out of uncertainty (Grint, 2011). However, we wish to eschew individualism and introduce a processual approach to entrepreneurial leadership. In doing so, we hope to stimulate discussion about relational processes that give rise to entrepreneurial action towards the attainment of social value (Brown and Hosking, 1986; Gergen, 2009; Hosking, 1988; Ladkin, 2010).

BEYOND INDIVIDUALISM: A RELATIONAL VIEW OF ENTREPRENEURIAL LEADERSHIP

First, we conceptualize entrepreneurship as an ongoing process of becoming (Nayak and Chia, 2011; Tsoukas, 2008; Tsoukas and Chia, 2002), which differs from the individualistic representation of an attribute that develops in a stepwise manner. We approach and describe the interactive process through which entrepreneurship and entrepreneurial opportunities are created, developed and sustained in an ecological fashion, which means accepting complexity and recognizing the weight of the contextual and the timely, which are both fundamental in process theory. Langley and Tsoukas (2010: 5) note that process thinking is 'sensitive to context, interactive experience, and time; and it acknowledges non-linearity, emergence and recursivity'. These processual underpinnings guide our exploration of change in the context of social enterprises, described by entrepreneurial leadership.

Second, our perspective challenges path-dependency approaches, by suggesting that the success of an entrepreneurial venture cannot be bound by past developments (Chia and Holt, 2009). Such a conceptual basis suggests that opportunities are not independent from the individuals making them, but rather emerge in relating and in pursuit of change (Alvarez and Barney, 2013; Garud and Karnoe, 2001; Mintzberg and Waters, 1985). That is, there can be no such thing as an entrepreneurial opportunity in solitude; relating to one another leads to the process of entrepreneurship (Gergen, 2009). Moving beyond individualism, there is a definite break from the deterministic dualism between path-dependency and success (Alvarez and Barney, 2013; Alvarez et al., 2013). Analysis here focuses on the process of creativity, where opportunities evolve constantly and success cannot be anticipated (Alvarez and Barney, 2007; McMullen et al., 2007).

To elaborate further, a relational perspective of entrepreneurial leadership brings about deep insights about the interactive processes through which entrepreneurship is realized and constructed. Taking such a stance in our work means that we endeavour to provide interpretive routes for different kinds of questions. For example, instead of asking how competent entrepreneurs discover opportunities, we now ask how entrepreneurship arises in the process of interacting with others in the quest of emerging opportunities. To be precise, we may use the term 'opportunity', but we refrain from the deterministic connotation it carries: opportunities are simultaneously made in the process of relating and it would be hasty to separate the two. Rather, the use of the term in the context of the question aims to answer how relating dynamics develop the appropriate decisions as the process of opportunity unfolds (Shotter, 2005).

To conclude this section, we reckon that it is appropriate to offer a working description of our conceptualization of entrepreneurial leadership, anchored in processual orientations of relating (Dachler and Hosking, 1995; Gergen, 1994, 1999, 2009; Nayak, 2008; Nayak and Chia, 2011; Shotter, 2005). We do not suggest that it encompasses all possible dimensions; it may even be more limiting as to what it does not include. Still, we believe there is some value in offering a tentative definition so that we can proceed relationally with our readers to the rest of the chapter. In this respect, synthesizing the above, we suggest that entrepreneurial leadership is a perpetual and relational process of working together to mobilize business opportunities in an organizational context in pursuit of entrepreneurial goals.

SOCIAL ENTERPRISES

Social enterprises as a form of entrepreneurship have been long present in business, but have gained particular prominence in the past few years, owing to greater demands on societal welfare, and in the light of the recent economic crisis (Nicholls and Cho, 2006). Given these developments, social enterprises appear to offer a promising form of organizing aimed at addressing societal concerns. Therefore, we theoretically explore the process of social value that social enterprises bring, as we believe that these types of organizations have increasing weight on societal welfare.

Still at an early stage of theoretical and empirical development, social entrepreneurship draws from an interdisciplinary synthesis of literatures including not-for-profit and charitable organizations (Ruvio et al., 2010), social responsibility (Wartick and Cochran, 1985), cross-section collaborations (Austin et al., 2006) and entrepreneurship (Shane and Venkataraman, 2000). In these broad interpretations, we note that the distinction of social entrepreneurship is rather blurry, and seems to span across a continuum of both commercial and social value orientations. We believe it is important to clarify this position, and offer an overarching definition blending the ideas of social change in a sustainable manner. This understanding of social entrepreneurship builds on the Schumpeterian (1934) concept of contributing to change through innovative combinations. Specifically, we suggest that social entrepreneurship extends this concept by conceiving innovation in relation to a social mission. In doing so, we review the relevant literatures and, similarly to the previous sections, we offer a meta-theoretical appreciation (Tsoukas and Knudsen, 2003) about where four identified streams of thinking can assist our understanding about social entrepreneurship.

The first stream of thinking focuses on the individual entrepreneur and the nature of opportunities, whereby innovative approaches are utilized to cater for social concerns and produce social change (Barendsen and Gardner, 2004; Perrini and Vurro, 2006). Motivation and personal attributes are also examined, with positive characteristics such as empathy, fairness or nobleness being highlighted (Hemingway, 2005; Sullivan Mort et al., 2003). The second stream of thinking deals with the limited nature of resources available to social enterprises (Sharir and Lerner, 2006). Largely descriptive, studies in this stream emphasize a constrained environment and discuss how social enterprises access and use resources to meet their social goals. Underpinned by principles of resource-dependency and resource-based views, the debate here suggests ways of manipulating resources to serve the social mission (Pastakia, 1998). The third stream of research introduces the role of institutions in two ways (Urbano et al., 2010): first, related theories have developed around existing institutions and their mediating role for the emergence and success of social entrepreneurship (Korosec and Berman, 2006); and second, related theories have coalesced around the lack of institutions that trigger the genesis of social enterprises as a response to lack or failure of supporting schemas (Mair and Marti, 2009). Finally, in the fourth stream of research, social entrepreneurship is approached through an evaluative dimension, which examines the performance of social enterprises (Flockhart, 2005; Millar and Hall, 2013; Ryan and Lyne, 2008) and addresses benchmarking of best practices, investment in a socially responsible manner or social return on investment. From a theoretical perspective, this stream aims to address the outcomes of social entrepreneurship and its societal impact in addition to social change.

Despite the diverse lenses in the identified streams, social advancement is an underlying point of reference, with key themes such as change, inclusiveness and complex context evident. Our analysis suggests that the process of creating social change remains rather overlooked since all four bodies of literature have, yet again, an individualistic focus either on the sole entrepreneur or on the configuration between the entrepreneur and others. Consistent with our processual orientation (Gergen, 2009; Nayak and Chia, 2011; Tsoukas and Chia, 2002), we address the process of creating social change by means of entrepreneurial leadership with the purpose of highlighting the creative aspects, leading to collaborative forms of organizing.

CONTEXT PARTICULARITIES OF SOCIAL ENTERPRISES

Our philosophical orientation is grounded in processual thinking, which implicates that our analysis of entrepreneurial leadership in social enterprises is framed by its context (Pettigrew, 1997). In this section, we wish to outline and describe the prominent themes underlying the discussion about social entrepreneurship as a relational process. These are the concepts of change, inclusiveness and uncertainty. In doing so, we illustrate that social enterprises provide the ideal platform for exploring entrepreneurial leadership and the creative dynamics of relating.

The concept of change in social entrepreneurship refers to meaningful interventions in society that promote the common good, at least in principle (Bryson and Crosby, 1992; Chetkovich and Kunreuther, 2006). The pervasive impact of change is strongly characterized by temporality, in the sense that change is represented in sequences of different occurrences that happen over time, one after the other (Mitchell and James, 2001). When change is conceptualized as such, by means of chronological time, it becomes mechanical (Bergson, 1949). Although significant events frame change, their chronology is neither the 'central organising principle'

(Pentland, 1999: 712), nor necessary for organizing (Langley et al., 2013). Indeed, chronological time only allows us to see snapshots of static entities (Bluedorn and Standifer, 2006; Chia, 1999), returning entrepreneurship back to fixed representations.

We wish to follow the temporal unfolding of change, but we will do so from a different type of time. We conceptualize time as *kairotic*, carrying the interpretation of the Greek word *kairos* which means the propitious moment for coming into being (*OED Online*, 2014). *Kairos* concentrates on the fullness of time and the context of what is included in the unfolding (Orlikowski and Yates, 2002). We find that *kairotic* time is relevant to entrepreneurship, as it refers to the appropriate time rather than the discovery of opportunities. On these grounds, we discuss how entrepreneurial leadership drives the process of change, incorporating its temporality. The relational aspects of entrepreneurial leadership reveal continuity and persistence in time (Chiles et al., 2007), so that direction is accomplished in participants' interactions, not in the discrete actions of individuals (Hosking, 2011).

Next, we wish to address the inclusive nature of organizing in social enterprises. The unique nature of social enterprises embodies inclusiveness, as they go beyond offering to the 'deprived' (Shane and Venkataraman, 2000). The organizational mission of achieving social change implies that the so-called 'deprived' participate in the happenings which change their circumstances. This novel diffusion of participation uncovers the creative dynamics of entrepreneurship and highlights the relational expression of leadership (Drath et al., 2008; Hosking, 2007). Yet, this model of organizing in social enterprises cannot be captured when considering the ideal traits of the entrepreneurs or the ideal combinations of contingencies. We suggest that relationality can provide insight into how social enterprise participants come together to take up work that produces direction, endorses commitment and allows alignment to the social mission (Drath et al., 2008). These perpetual processes express the relational dynamics of leadership, described by Hosking (1988) as the organizing demands of collective action.

Finally, we wish to address the intense uncertainty which dominates entrepreneurial action in social enterprises (Weerawardena and Mort, 2006), arising from resource constraints, market idiosyncrasy and anxiety about future survival (McMullen and Shepherd, 2006; Weerawardena and Mort, 2006). To be clear, we do not suggest that uncertainty is a stimulus for social entrepreneurship, as it can neither define nor cause it. Rather, we suggest that uncertainty creates the conditions in which social entrepreneurship may be the response. We follow Weick's (1995) interpretation of uncertainty as shock, where participants act to handle multiple available interpretations. Linked to the previous two dimensions, our processual perspective deals with suspending time and relevant uncertainty, which we deem crucial for understanding the creative practices that generate change in social enterprises (Mainemelis, 2001).

Together, these characteristics determine a hostile environment for entrepreneurship to emerge and develop (Dacin et al., 2011). We suggest that responding to these challenges requires entrepreneurial leadership to ensure momentum and to benefit from each unique contribution to relating (Gergen, 2009, 2010; Hosking, 1988, 2011). In the remainder of the chapter, we develop the relational dynamics of entrepreneurial leadership, expressed with the themes of temporality, relational identity development and improvisation.

RELATIONAL DYNAMICS OF ENTREPRENEURIAL LEADERSHIP

This section introduces our conceptualization of entrepreneurial leadership in social enterprises with the purpose of exploring the genesis, development and sustainment of social change. We argue that the attainment of such a virtuous purpose from a working collective is critically dependant on the guiding dynamics of leadership, with particular reference to temporality, relational identity development and improvisation towards the attainment of the social value.

Temporality

We wish to address the emergence of social entrepreneurship from the temporal perspective of relational leadership. Social enterprises seek to create change, readjusting previously created institutions or organizations or even correcting market failure. Central to the process of change is the relationship between the new and the old system (Sandberg and Tsoukas, 2011), demonstrating how the two systems are connected (Lok and De Rond, 2012). That means that it is possible to participate in more than one system at any time by sharing not only different contexts, but also different temporal orientations (McMullen and Dimov, 2013). Switching between the different systems means that it is vital to renew the temporal relationships in the different contexts, illustrating the centrality of relating. Approaching social entrepreneurship from such a temporal perspective, we are able to consider the notion of opportunity, and how it is linked to social ventures. We noted previously that opportunity has been conceptualized as a 'thing' to be discovered, associated with the entrepreneur's skill-set (Eckhardt and Shane, 2003). We now wish to suggest the notion of temporal opportunity, as expressed by conditions of relationality when intersecting across different relations and moments in time.

Describing opportunities as 'out there' to be discovered assumes causality that is ascribed rather than inferred, as the attribution of opportunity occurs when placing meaning on the past and projecting it into the future (Weick, 1995). We argue, instead, that the temporal involvement of participants compels them to mould continually the past and the future into the present, as they proceed in the flow of opportunities (Bergson, 1949; Shotter, 2008). In the passage across time, relational dynamics can cast light onto the critical encounters that lead to the emergence of new perspectives, reinventing both past and future. Thus, this may be an interesting lens through which to study the emergence of social entrepreneurship, by examining the relational connections that enable the coordination of efforts.

To achieve this, we suggest drawing on practice theory (Schatzki et al., 2001) as an analytical construct that is consistent with our conceptual basis. The notion of practice refers to situated activities that are established jointly through collective meaning-making, and are temporally and contextually specific (Orlikowski and Yates, 2002; Wenger, 2000). As such, emergence can be seen as a collective accomplishment from the organizing demands of social change (Hosking, 1988). Adding to this, de Certeau (1988) clarifies that social action is created out of dialectical relationships between participants and their world, capturing the very essence of practice as the unit of analysis (Schatzki et al., 2001). Following this, it transpires that practices are not stable, but need to be continually revitalized. Hence, the performativity of practices through relating can allow us to follow the unfolding of entrepreneurship in social enterprises.

Relational Identity Development

To address the context of inclusiveness in social enterprises, we develop the notion of relational identity by means of entrepreneurial leadership. In developing our argument we focus on aspects of identity work that can provide an explanatory vehicle for the change dimension that we have identified as worthy of attention for the study of social enterprises. We turn to the appreciation of identity as central, enduring and distinctive (Gioia et al., 2000), where core associations distinguish the self or the group from others (Albert et al., 2000), while simultaneously framing the paradox of uniqueness and distinctiveness (Fiol, 2001). As such, identity is well developed in social sciences and has been explored from both individualistic and relational perspectives (Cerulo, 1997; Somers, 1994). On the one hand, individualistic traditions assume that identity is stable and can, therefore, predict individuals' behaviours. On the other hand, relational representations argue that, rather than fixed, identity is continuously created and re-created in a social context.

In our domain of inquiry, we note that identity developments are still devised with reference to Schumpeter's (1934) iconic descriptions of the entrepreneur. The attributes that constitute an entrepreneurial identity are innovativeness, opportunity discovery, risk propensity and self-motivation. The dominant voices in the literature present an extraordinary image of the individual entrepreneur (Anderson and Warren, 2011; Shane and Nicolaou, 2013), who has a strong sense of self. Interestingly, self-identities vary in how they fit different entrepreneurial profiles, but research and dominant perceptions converge to the attributes of the typical entrepreneur (Sharir and Lerner, 2006). Complementing the ideal profile of the entrepreneur is a view of identity focusing on the activities that are associated with the role of the entrepreneur (Cardon et al., 2009). Adding to the convergent image of the prototypical entrepreneur, identity also encompasses the activities of founding the organization, exhibiting innovative practices, managing risk and rationally exploiting opportunities (Alvarez and Barney, 2013; Shane and Venkataraman, 2000).

These models suggest that identity is an outcome at any given time (Albert et al., 2000). Therefore, identity can be considered as an intentional procedure of holding expectations and perceptions about membership in the organization. To clarify this, we may offer the example of Weaver and Agle's (2002) work, which noted that a religious identity implies covert ethical behaviour, such as helping others. In similar vein, identity defines the sphere of action and lends itself to predictions about the circumstances under which certain behaviours are more likely to occur (Ashforth et al., 2000).

For the sake of our analysis, we narrow our critique to the concept of group identity to illustrate a meaningful suggestion for dealing with inclusiveness in social enterprises. As we remarked earlier, identity work infers endurance over time. However, organizations are in flux, constantly experiencing change (Weick, 2000). Correspondingly, the above-mentioned models of identity do not seem to fit with the notion of change, which implies that identity should change too (Ashforth et al., 2011; Gioia et al., 2010). Such models hinder flexibility and promote change as a threat to the status quo. More recent work in entrepreneurship has focused on constructionist perspectives, which suggest that selves are formed through social relationships that shift considerably (e.g., da Costa and Silva Saraiva, 2012; Warren, 2004). We complement these approaches by considering a processual orientation to identity construction.

From our conceptualization of entrepreneurial leadership, we propose that identity is developed by an ongoing process of relational interactions, which captures temporary expressions of connections between participants (Nayak, 2008). Identity development as a process of relating reflects the special context of social enterprises, where multiple participants come together to fulfil a social mission. This way of thinking offers compelling advantages in examining the dynamic organizational work of social enterprises, accounting for flexibility, coherence and continuity (Weick, 1995), as well as ambiguity (Chia, 1999). Thus, we propose examining identity development through processes of relating that reveal how participants in social enterprises coordinate actions, synchronize meanings and adapt to contextual particularities. This focus displays unique leadership dynamics: identity development is fluid, while continuing the entrepreneurial endeavour. The entrepreneurial self is constantly in the making as venture participants pursue social mission.

To understand identity development, we should specifically look at how relating reproduces and sustains meanings within and between participants. Since primacy is given to relationships, the nexus of possibilities is multilayered and comprises of temporal and spatial considerations (Nayak and Chia, 2011; Weick et al., 1999). We have extensively developed temporal considerations in the previous sections, and we now offer an early overview of space in relational terms. Inclusiveness in social enterprises involves extra-organizational influences, such that organizational boundaries are composite and ever changing in both impact and substance (Daft and Weick, 1984; Orton and Weick, 1990). In pursuit of a social mission, organizational boundaries are created, relocated and compounded. Hence, the very essence of spatiality for the organization is not given, but open to change. From an analytical point of view, it would be intriguing to explore the boundary properties of social enterprises in search of temporal stability and aptness to flexibility.

From a relational stance, this means that boundaries are neither intentional nor incidental for social enterprises (Luhmann, 1995). Rather, the emergence of spatiality takes place through entrepreneurial leadership, where boundaries are created and re-created in relational interactions. Such conceptualization is certainly helpful for understanding the dynamic nature of social enterprises. However, it also poses an important challenge, as it demands studying impermanence, which cannot be captured by searching for visible or tangible structures, such as office buildings (Hernes, 2004). It is more meaningful to look for relational bonding amongst participants, which determines the scope of boundaries at any given point (Dachler and Hosking, 1995; Gergen, 2010). By attending to the relational bonding that shapes organizational boundaries, spatiality also explains temporality in the sense that boundaries are likely to change during different stages of enterprise growth and maturity (Hernes, 2004). The insights we hope to gain from addressing relational identity and boundary conditions in social enterprises relate to how entrepreneurial leadership finds expression in different forms of relational interactions, and how these interpret the composition of boundaries. Therefore, relational identity represents an analytical lens that helps to illuminate how social enterprises act together with society for the fulfilment of social missions (Polletta and Jasper, 2001). This understanding does not come from studying individuals or a group of individuals; rather, it comes from studying the relational interactions among them.

Improvisation

Reviewing identity development is often associated with structuralist perspectives that address patterns of relationships. Ranging in their focus on individuality from depreciation to rejection (Emirbayer and Goodwin, 1994), structuration theory places emphasis on the links with one another. In its authentic form, structuration theory is an explanatory vehicle of discursive explanations for organizational change, under the founding assumption that individuals and structure are interwoven with each other (Giddens, 1991). Although this theorizing has gained popularity in the literature, we question the degree to which structuration has offered empirical insights (Barley and Tolbert, 1997).

In particular, we call into doubt the tendency to separate levels of analysis, which maintains individualism and overlooks the temporal nature of change (e.g., Heracleous and Barrett, 2001). Similarly, we query causality between action and pre-established structures, since it privileges boundaries at the expense of emergence (Putnam and Nicotera, 2008). Lastly, we contest predominance of the past as predictive of structuring patterns, since it presents snapshots rather than the whole of change (Pozzebon and Pinsonneault, 2005). Specifically, there is the tendency to consider social structures and resulting network configurations as a platform for resources exploitation, hinting to individualistic traditions which leaves the process of change unexamined (Hoang and Antoncic, 2003).

On the basis of this questioning, we propose that change emerges through the relationships underlying the structures, which has remained underdeveloped in research (Hite, 2005). Drawing on the previous section about temporality, we suggest that change arises in the present when the retained past meets the projected future (Tsoukas and Chia, 2002). Therefore, composition of boundaries does not rest solely on their structures, but rather on how these structures emerge. Reinstating attention to entrepreneurship in social enterprises, our interest lies in sustainability for the future. To a certain extent, there is agreement that creativity is prerequisite for present successful performance (Schumpeter, 1947). What is underexplored, though, is how creativity arises and how contextual pressures mediate the emergence of novelty in social enterprises (Mainemelis, 2010). Drawing on Weick (1998), we propose improvisation as a lens for exploring the practices with which entrepreneurial leadership is expressed in social enterprises.

Improvisation describes the process from which change occurs through 'reworking precomposed material and designs in relation to unanticipated ideas conceived, shaped, and transformed under the special conditions of performance, thereby adding unique features to every creation' (Berliner, 1994: 220). It is closely associated with Lévi-Strauss's (1966) concept of bricolage, which refers to finding creative uses for available material. Coined as such, improvisation triggers different aspects of spontaneity, each of which corresponds to appropriate responses to different situations (Montuori, 2003; Peplowski, 1998). To elaborate further, improvisation helps us to uncover how relating develops in pursuit of a social mission, as it addresses the temporal mobilization of resources to deal with specific issues. In this sense, improvisational relating occurs randomly, following a certain predetermined rhythm in unprecedented ways (Hatch, 1999). Extending from the previous section on identity development, in order for improvisation to take place, it needs to rely on existing patterns that guide action before, during and after. This is crucial, as there needs to be a collective basis for improvisation to delineate from the rhythm, create the unexpected and return back to the rhythm. Thus, when bringing identity in the discussion, it becomes plausible to argue that improvisation may not be possible in the absence of relational identity.

From our analysis, it appears that improvisation can be regarded as an organizational response, which is 'either a last resort or an established way of evoking creativity' (Bateson, 2001: 4). For our purpose of demonstrating entrepreneurial leadership in social enterprises, we emphasize the aspects of limited resources and novelty, by attending to the spontaneous and creative dimensions of improvisation, best summarized as dealing 'with circumstances for which no script appears to be immediately at hand' (Mangham and Pye, 1991: 4). The spontaneous dimension deals with the unplanned, while the creative dimension develops something useful to the context. To restate our processual focus, we view improvisation as a process, not as an output of creative aspects. It is important to clarify this distinction, as we are building on a processual view of creativity, meaning that improvisation brings about creative acts regardless of anticipated outcomes (Drazin et al., 1999). Respectively, improvisation may bring about creative acts that may or may not lead to success.

To be clear, there is an element of 'intentionality' in improvisational relating, but it is not teleological. For example, let us consider how social enterprises improvise to promote their noble mission. They engage in spontaneous and creative processes of relating and strive to achieve their goals in a new way, responding to the identified problem with novelty (Steyaert and Hjorth, 2008). In this respect, improvisation is a relational concept in the sense that social enterprises create something new to them, which has been previously done by others in a different way or in a different context. Therefore, 'intentionality' is not attached to an end-point, but is rather tied in with responsiveness, which is consistent with Weick's (1998) portrayal of the 'unexpected'. In such a manner, we feature entrepreneurial leadership as describing improvisational interaction, which requires creative processes to meet the social mission without the privilege of predictability, but within the constraints of contextual environment.

This oxymoron seems to ideally describe action in social enterprises as it is coupled with a context that combines action with reflection (Leybourne, 2007), where both processes are done at the same time, revoking our previous accounts about temporality. Entrepreneurial leadership unfolds against the backdrop of pre-established rules (local culture), which are defined by relational identity development around a social mission and serve as the basis for improvisation. These rules form the essence of improvisation for entrepreneurial leadership in social enterprises as they epitomize simultaneous and continuous mixing of the established with the novel, under conditions of uncertainty.

IMPLICATIONS AND FUTURE DIRECTIONS

In conclusion, we have developed a conceptualization of entrepreneurial leadership under conditions of temporal complexity that underpin organizing in social enterprises. Our goal has been to offer the prospects of processual philosophy to include in our theorizing the ever-changing idea of becoming. Thereupon, we have contributed to entrepreneurial scholarship by introducing new understandings of relational leadership and specifically, with the dimensions of temporality, relational identity and improvisation. Looking ahead, we acknowledge that our theoretical proposition is broad in nature and still at an early stage of development, as are processual perspectives. There are a plethora of directions that could be pursued, but we prioritize and develop those areas that we think are more relevant to practitioners, given the complexity and uncertainty of their work.

Our proposed conceptualization of entrepreneurial leadership represents a dialectical concept, in the sense that it seeks to transcend dichotomies, such as individual versus group, planning versus emerging, or predictability versus spontaneity. Because entrepreneurial leadership in social enterprises involves the management of constraints, such organizations can explore current practices and allow room for improvisation that would bring about renewal. Researchers could follow our line of thinking and examine improvisational practices that account for flexibility. Furthermore, it would be beneficial to explore how relational dynamics build up and mediates between established and spontaneous action.

Another intriguing theme for future research is to explore how the present discussion about entrepreneurial leadership deals with unexpected events. Arguably, improvisation seems to be an ideal response to the unexpected. However, research needs to shed light onto how improvisational action develops and how participants engage in taking initiatives that exceed established ways of acting. Such a research orientation could provide useful feedback to organizations about error tolerance and risk-handling. Additionally, a culture of improvisation revisits training and performance evaluation, which should include principles of relationality and creativity. These insights can be developed not only in the arena of social enterprises, but also in the greater field of entrepreneurship and organizing.

Finally, our conceptualization offers a novel appreciation of time as a relational concept. Our work raises awareness about the temporality of practice and the unfolding process of change. This consequently calls for different research orientations that capture emergence in real time, rather than fixed representations, or effects after change has happened. A research focus on emergence could consider how organizational members interpret and perform action, rather than propose predictive models that work *ceteris paribus*. We value this as the most important contribution, as it offers fresh observations about flexibility to act at the right time and in response to the vast array of relationships that make up organizations.

We conclude by hoping that our chapter has enabled us to make a contribution to entrepreneurship by studying the underdeveloped concept of entrepreneurial leadership in the unique setting of social enterprises, and by offering our processual conceptualization of relationships. Ultimately, we hope to stimulate the discussions further with fellow academics as well as practitioners, both of whom are engaged with the complex ideas we have tried to unravel.

REFERENCES

Albert, S., Ashforth, B.E. and Dutton, J.E. (2000). Organizational identity and identification: Charting new waters and building new bridges. *Academy of Management Review*, 25, 13–17.

Alvarez, S.A. and Barney, J.B. (2007). Discovery and creation: Alternative theories of entrepreneurial action. *Strategic Entrepreneurship Journal*, 1, 11–26.

Alvarez, S.A. and Barney, J.B. (2013). Epistemology, opportunities, and entrepreneurship: Comments on Venkataraman et al. (2012) and Shane (2012). *Academy of Management Review*, 38, 154–7.

Alvarez, S.A., Barney, J.B. and Anderson, P. (2013). Forming and exploiting opportunities: The implications of discovery and creation processes for entrepreneurial and organizational research. *Organization Science*, 24, 301–17.

Alvarez, S.A., Barney, J.B., McBride, R. and Wuebker, R. (2014). Realism in the study of entrepreneurship. *Academy of Management Review*, 39, 227–31.

Anderson, A.R. and Warren, L. (2011). The entrepreneur as hero and jester: Enacting the entrepreneurial discourse. *International Small Business Journal*, 29, 589–609.

Ashforth, B.E., Kreiner, G.E. and Fugate, M. (2000). All in a day's work: Boundaries and micro role transitions. *Academy of Management Review*, 25, 472–91.

Ashforth, B.E., Rogers, K.M. and Corley, K.G. (2011). Identity in organizations: Exploring cross-level dynamics. *Organization Science*, 22, 1144–56.

Austin, J., Stevenson, H. and Wei-Skillern, J. (2006). Social and commercial entrepreneurship: Same, different, or both?. *Entrepreneurship Theory and Practice*, 30, 1–22.

Barendsen, L. and Gardner, H. (2004). Is the social entrepreneur a new type of leader? *Leader to Leader*, 2004, 43–50.

Barley, S.R. and Tolbert, P.S. (1997). Institutionalization and structuration: Studying the links between action and institution. *Organization Studies*, 18, 93–117.

Bateson, M.C. (2001). *Composing a Life*. New York, NY: Grove Press.

Bergson, H. (1949). *An Introduction to Metaphysics*. Indianapolis, IN: Hackett Publishing.

Berliner, P.F. (1994). *Thinking in Jazz: The Infinite Art of Improvisation*. Chicago, IL: University of Chicago Press.

Bligh, M.C., Kohles, J.C. and Pillai, R. (2011). Romancing leadership: Past, present, and future. *Leadership Quarterly*, 22, 1058–77.

Bligh, M.C. and Schyns, B. (2007). Leading question: The romance lives on: Contemporary issues surrounding the romance of leadership. *Leadership*, 3, 343–60.

Bluedorn, A.C. and Standifer, R.L. (2006). Time and the temporal imagination. *Academy of Management Learning and Education*, 5, 196–206.

Bolden, R. (2011). Distributed leadership in organizations: A review of theory and research. *International Journal of Management Reviews*, 13, 251–69.

Brown, M.H. and Hosking, D.M. (1986). Distributed leadership and skilled performance as successful organization in social movements. *Human Relations*, 39, 65–79.

Bryman, A. (2004). Qualitative research on leadership: A critical but appreciative review. *Leadership Quarterly*, 15, 729–69.

Bryson, J.M. and Crosby, B.C. (1992). *Leadership for the Common Good: Tackling Public Problems in a Shared-Power World*. San Francisco, CA: Jossey-Bass.

Busenitz, L.W., West, G.P., Shepherd, D., Nelson, T., Chandler, G.N. and Zacharakis, A. (2003). Entrepreneurship research in emergence: Past trends and future directions. *Journal of Management*, 29, 285–308.

Cardon, M.S., Wincent, J., Singh, J. and Drnovsek, M. (2009). The nature and experience of entrepreneurial passion. *Academy of Management Review*, 34, 511–32.

Cerulo, K.A. (1997). Identity construction: New issues, new directions. *Annual Review of Sociology*, 23, 385–409.

Chetkovich, C.A. and Kunreuther, F. (2006). *From the Ground Up: Grassroots Organizations Making Social Change*. Ithaca, NY: Cornell University Press.

Chia, R. (1999). A 'rhizomic' model of organizational change and transformation: Perspective from a metaphysics of change. *British Journal of Management*, 10, 209–27.

Chia, R. and Holt, R. (2009). *Strategy without Design: The Silent Efficacy of Indirect Action.* Cambridge: Cambridge University Press.

Chiles, T.H., Bluedorn, A.C. and Gupta, V.K. (2007). Beyond creative destruction and entrepreneurial discovery: A radical Austrian approach to entrepreneurship. *Organization Studies,* 28, 467–93.

Choi, Y.R. and Shepherd, D.A. (2004). Entrepreneurs' decisions to exploit opportunities. *Journal of Management,* 30, 377–95.

Cogliser, C.C. and Brigham, K.H. (2004). The intersection of leadership and entrepreneurship: Mutual lessons to be learned. *Leadership Quarterly,* 15, 771–99.

Contractor, N.S., DeChurch, L.A., Carson, J., Carter, D.R. and Keegan, B. (2012). The topology of collective leadership. *Leadership Quarterly,* 23, 994–1011.

Crevani, L., Lindgren, M. and Packendorff, J. (2010). Leadership, not leaders: On the study of leadership as practices and interactions. *Scandinavian Journal of Management,* 26, 77–86.

da Costa, A.d.S.M. and Silva Saraiva, L.A. (2012). Hegemonic discourses on entrepreneurship as an ideological mechanism for the reproduction of capital. *Organization,* 19, 587–614.

Dachler, H.P. and Hosking, D.M. (1995). The primacy of relations in socially constructing organizational realities. In D.M. Hosking, H.P. Dachler and K.J. Gergen (eds), *Management and Organization: Relational Alternatives to Individualism* (pp. 1–28). Aldershot: Avebury.

Dacin, M.T., Dacin, P.A. and Tracey, P. (2011). Social entrepreneurship: A critique and future directions. *Organization Science,* 22, 1203–13.

Daft, R.L. and Weick, K.E. (1984). Toward a model of organizations as interpretation systems. *Academy of Management Review,* 9, 284–95.

Darby, L. and Jenkins, H. (2006). Applying sustainability indicators to the social enterprise business model: The development and application of an indicator set for Newport Wastesavers, Wales. *International Journal of Social Economics,* 33, 411–31.

de Certeau, M. (1988). *The Practice of Everyday Life.* Berkeley, CA: University of California Press.

Drath, W.H. (2008). Leadership beyond leaders and followers. *Leadership in Action,* 28, 20.

Drath, W.H., McCauley, C.D., Palus, C., Van Velsor, E., O'Connor, P.M.G. and McGuire, J.B. (2008). Direction, alignment, commitment: Toward a more integrative ontology of leadership. *Leadership Quarterly,* 19, 635–53.

Drazin, R., Glynn, M.A. and Kazanjian, R.K. (1999). Multilevel theorizing about creativity in organizations: A sensemaking perspective. *Academy of Management Review,* 24, 286–307.

Eckhardt, J.T. and Ciuchta, M.P. (2008). Selected variation: The population-level implications of multistage selection in entrepreneurship. *Strategic Entrepreneurship Journal,* 2, 209–24.

Eckhardt, J.T. and Shane, S.A. (2003). Opportunities and entrepreneurship. *Journal of Management,* 29, 333–49.

Emirbayer, M. and Goodwin, J. (1994). Network analysis, culture, and the problem of agency. *American Journal of Sociology,* 99 (6), 1411–54.

Fiol, C.M. (2001). Revisiting an identity-based view of sustainable competitive advantage. *Journal of Management,* 27, 691–9.

Flockhart, A. (2005). Raising the profile of social enterprises: The use of social return on investment (SROI) and investment ready tools (IRT) to bridge the financial credibility gap. *Social Enterprise Journal,* 1, 29–42.

Gartner, W.B. (1988). 'Who is an entrepreneur?' is the wrong question. *American Journal of Small Business,* 12, 11–32.

Gartner, W.B. (2007). Is there an elephant in entrepreneurship? Blind assumptions in theory development. In A. Cuervo, D. Ribeira and S. Roig (eds), *Entrepreneurship: Concepts, Theory and Perspective* (pp. 229–242). New York, NY: Springer.

Gartner, W.B. and Shane, S.A. (1995). Measuring entrepreneurship over time. *Journal of Business Venturing*, 10, 283–301.
Garud, R. and Karnoe, P. (2001). *Path Dependence and Creation*. New York, NY: Psychology Press.
Garud, R., Kumaraswamy, A. and Karnoe, P. (2010). Path dependence or path creation?. *Journal of Management Studies*, 47, 760–774.
Gemmill, G. and Oakley, J. (1992). Leadership: An alienating social myth?. *Human Relations*, 45, 113–29.
Gergen, K.J. (1994). *Realities and Relationships: Soundings in Social Construction*. Cambridge, MA: Harvard University Press.
Gergen, K.J. (1999). Agency: Social construction and relational action. *Theory and Psychology*, 9, 113–15.
Gergen, K.J. (2009). *Relational Being: Beyond Self and Community*. Oxford, UK and New York, USA: Oxford University Press.
Gergen, K.J. (2010). Co-constitution, causality, and confluence: Organizing in a world without entities. In T. Hernes and S. Maitlis (eds), *Process, Sensemaking and Organization* (pp. 55–69). Oxford: Oxford University Press.
Giddens, A. (1991). Structuration theory: Past, present and future. In C.G.A. Bryant and D. Jary (eds), *Giddens' Theory of Structuration. A Critical Appreciation* (pp. 210–221). London: Routledge.
Gioia, D.A., Price, K.N., Hamilton, A.L. and Thomas, J.B. (2010). Forging an identity: An insider–outsider study of processes involved in the formation of organizational identity. *Administrative Science Quarterly*, 55, 1–46.
Gioia, D.A., Schultz, M. and Corley, K.G. (2000). Organizational identity, image, and adaptive instability. *Academy of Management Review*, 25, 63–81.
Graen, G.B. and Uhl-Bien, M. (1995). Relationship-based approach to leadership: development of leader–member exchange (LMX) theory of leadership over 25 years: applying a multilevel multidomain perspective. *Leadership Quarterly*, 6, 219–47.
Grint, K. (2011). A history of leadership. In A. Bryman, D. Collinson, K. Grint, B. Jackson and M. Uhl-Bien (eds), *The SAGE Handbook of Leadership* (pp. 3–14). London: SAGE Publications.
Gruber, M. (2010). Exploring the origins of organizational paths: Empirical evidence from newly founded firms. *Journal of Management*, 36, 1143–67.
Hatch, M.J. (1999). Exploring the empty spaces of organizing: How improvisational jazz helps redescribe organizational structure. *Organization Studies*, 20, 75–100.
Hatten, T.S. (2011). *Small Business Management: Entrepreneurship and Beyond*. Boston, MA: Cengage Learning.
Hemingway, C.A. (2005). Personal values as a catalyst for corporate social entrepreneurship. *Journal of Business Ethics*, 60, 233–49.
Heracleous, L. and Barrett, M. (2001). Organizational change as discourse: Communicative actions and deep structures in the context of information technology implementation. *Academy of Management Journal*, 44, 755–78.
Hernandez, M., Eberly, M.B., Avolio, B.J. and Johnson, M.D. (2011). The loci and mechanisms of leadership: Exploring a more comprehensive view of leadership theory. *Leadership Quarterly*, 22, 1165–85.
Hernes, T. (2004). Studying composite boundaries: A framework of analysis. *Human Relations*, 57, 9–29.
Hite, J.M. (2005). Evolutionary processes and paths of relationally embedded network ties in emerging entrepreneurial firms. *Entrepreneurship Theory and Practice*, 29, 113–44.
Hoang, H. and Antoncic, B. (2003). Network-based research in entrepreneurship: A critical review. *Journal of Business Venturing*, 18, 165–87.
Hosking, D.M. (1988). Organizing, leadership and skilful process. *Journal of Management Studies*, 25, 147–66.
Hosking, D.M. (2007). Not leaders, not followers: A post-modern discourse of leadership processes. In B. Shamir, R. Pillai, M.C. Bligh and M. Uhl-Bien (eds), *Follower-Centred*

Perspectives on Leadership: A Tribute to the Memory of James R. Meindl, Information Age (pp. 243–63). Charlotte, NC: Information Age Publishing.

Hosking, D.M. (2011). Moving relationality: Meditations on relational approach to leadership. In A. Bryman, D. Collinson, K. Grint, B. Jackson and M. Uhl-Bien (eds), *The SAGE Handbook of Leadership* (pp. 455–67). London: SAGE Publications.

Jensen, S.M. and Luthans, F. (2006). Entrepreneurs as authentic leaders: Impact on employees' attitudes. *Leadership and Organization Development Journal*, 27, 646–66.

Keupp, M.M. and Gassmann, O. (2009). The past and the future of international entrepreneurship: A review and suggestions for developing the field. *Journal of Management*, 35, 600–633.

Koppl, R. and Minniti, M. (2008). Entrepreneurship and human action. In G.E. Schockley, P.M. Frank and R.R. Stough (eds), *Non-Market Entrepreneurship: Interdisciplinary Approaches* (pp. 10–27). Cheltenham, UK and Northampton, MA: Edward Elgar Publishing.

Korosec, R.L. and Berman, E.M. (2006). Municipal support for social entrepreneurship. *Public Administration Review*, 66, 448–62.

Ladkin, D. (2010). *Rethinking Leadership: A New Look at Old Leadership Questions*. Cheltenham, UK and Northampton, MA: Edward Elgar Publishing.

Langley, A., Smallman, C., Tsoukas, H. and Van De Ven, A.H. (2013). Process studies of change in organization and management: Unveiling temporality, activity, and flow. *Academy of Management Journal*, 56, 1–13.

Langley, A. and Tsoukas, H. (2010). Introducing perspectives on process organization studies. In A. Langley and H. Tsoukas (eds), *Process, Sensemaking, and Organizing* (pp. 1–26). Oxford: Oxford University Press.

Leitch, C.M., McMullan, C. and Harrison, R.T. (2013). The development of entrepreneurial leadership: The role of human, social and institutional capital. *British Journal of Management*, 24, 347–66.

Lévi-Strauss, C. (1966). *The Savage Mind*. Chicago, IL: University of Chicago Press.

Lewin, K. (1945). The research center for group dynamics at Massachusetts Institute of Technology. *Sociometry*, 8(2), 126–36.

Leybourne, S.A. (2007). Improvisation within management: Oxymoron, paradox, or legitimate way of achieving?. *International Journal of Management Concepts and Philosophy*, 2, 224–39.

Lok, J. and De Rond, M. (2012). On the plasticity of institutions: Containing and restoring practice breakdowns at the Cambridge University Boat Club. *Academy of Management Journal*, 56, 185–207.

Low, M.B. and MacMillan, I.C. (1988). Entrepreneurship: Past research and future challenges. *Journal of Management*, 14, 139–61.

Luhmann, N. (1995). *Social Systems*. Stanford, CA: Stanford University Press.

Mainemelis, C. (2001). When the muse takes it all: A model for the experience of timelessness in organizations. *Academy of Management Review*, 26, 548–65.

Mainemelis, C. (2010). Stealing fire: Creative deviance in the evolution of new ideas. *Academy of Management Review*, 35, 558–78.

Mair, J. and Marti, I. (2006). Social entrepreneurship research: A source of explanation, prediction, and delight. *Journal of World Business*, 41, 36–44.

Mair, J. and Marti, I. (2009). Entrepreneurship in and around institutional voids: A case study from Bangladesh. *Journal of Business Venturing*, 24, 419–35.

Mangham, I.L. and Pye, A. (1991). *The Doing of Managing: A Study in Executive Process*. Oxford: Blackwell.

McMullen, J.S. and Dimov, D. (2013). Time and the entrepreneurial journey: The problems and promise of studying entrepreneurship as a process. *Journal of Management Studies*, 50, 1481–512.

McMullen, J.S., Plummer, L.A. and Acs, Z.J. (2007). What is an entrepreneurial opportunity?. *Small Business Economics*, 28, 273–83.

McMullen, J.S. and Shepherd, D.A. (2006). Entrepreneurial action and the role of uncertainty in the theory of the entrepreneur. *Academy of Management Review*, 31, 132–52.

Meindl, J.R. (1995). The romance of leadership as a follower-centric theory: A social constructionist approach. *Leadership Quarterly*, 6, 329–41.

Meindl, J.R., Ehrlich, S.B. and Dukerich, J.M. (1985). The romance of leadership. *Administrative Science Quarterly*, 30, 78–102.

Metcalf, L. and Benn, S. (2013). Leadership for sustainability: An evolution of leadership ability. *Journal of Business Ethics*, 112, 369–84.

Millar, R. and Hall, K. (2013). Social return on investment (SROI) and performance measurement: The opportunities and barriers for social enterprises in health and social care. *Public Management Review*, 15, 923–41.

Mintzberg, H. and Waters, J.A. (1985). Of strategies, deliberate and emergent. *Strategic Management Journal*, 6, 257–72.

Mitchell, T.R. and James, L.R. (2001). Building better theory: Time and the specification of when things happen. *Academy of Management Review*, 26, 530–547.

Montuori, A. (2003). The complexity of improvisation and the improvisation of complexity: Social science, art and creativity. *Human Relations*, 56, 237–55.

Morris, M.H., Avila, R.A. and Allen, J. (1993). Individualism and the modern corporation: Implications for innovation and entrepreneurship. *Journal of Management*, 19, 595–612.

Munro, I. (2014). Organizational ethics and Foucault's 'Art of Living': Lessons from social movement organizations. *Organization Studies*, 35 (8), 1127–48.

Nayak, A. (2008). On the way to theory: A processual approach. *Organization Studies*, 29, 173–90.

Nayak, A. and Chia, R. (2011). Thinking becoming and emergence: Process philosophy and organisation studies. In H. Tsoukas and R. Chia (eds), *Research in the Sociology of Organizations, Volume 32: Philosophy and Organization Theory* (pp. 281–310). Bingley: Emerald.

Nicholls, A. and Cho, A.H. (2006). Social entrepreneurship: The structuration of a field. In A. Nicholls (ed.), *Social Entrepreneurship: New Models of Sustainable Social Change* (pp. 99–118). Oxford: Oxford University Press.

Northouse, P.G. (2004). *Leadership: Theory and Practice*, 3rd edn. London: SAGE Publications.

OED Online (2014). Kairos. *Oxford English Dictionary*. Oxford University Press.

Orlikowski, W.J. and Yates, J. (2002). It's about time: Temporal structuring in organizations. *Organization Science*, 13, 684–700.

Orton, J.D. and Weick, K.E. (1990). Loosely coupled systems: A reconceptualization. *Academy of Management Review*, 15, 203–23.

Pastakia, A. (1998). Grassroots ecopreneurs: Change agents for a sustainable society. *Journal of Organizational Change Management*, 11, 157–73.

Pearce, C.L. and Conger, J.A. (2003). *Shared Leadership: Reframing the How's and Why's of Leadership.* Thousand Oaks, CA: SAGE Publications.

Pentland, B.T. (1999). Building process theory with narrative: From description to explanation. *Academy of Management Review*, 24, 711–24.

Peplowski, K. (1998). The process of improvisation. *Organization Science*, 9, 560–561.

Peredo, A.M. and McLean, M. (2006). Social entrepreneurship: A critical review of the concept. *Journal of World Business*, 41, 56–65.

Perrini, F. and Vurro, C. (2006). Social entrepreneurship: Innovation and social change across theory and practice. In J. Mair, J. Robinson and K. Hockerts (eds), *Social Entrepreneurship* (pp. 57–85). New York, NY: Palgrave MacMillan.

Pettigrew, A.M. (1997). What is a processual analysis?. *Scandinavian Journal of Management*, 13, 337–48.

Polletta, F. and Jasper, J.M. (2001). Collective identity and social movements. *Annual Review of Sociology*, 27 (1), 283–305.

Pozzebon, M. and Pinsonneault, A. (2005). Challenges in conducting empirical work using structuration theory: Learning from IT research. *Organization Studies*, 26, 1353–76.

Putnam, L.L. and Nicotera, A.M. (2008). *Building Theories of Organization: The Constitutive Role of Communication*. New York, NY: Routledge.

Ramoglou, S. (2013). Who is a 'non-entrepreneur'? Taking the 'others' of entrepreneurship seriously. *International Small Business Journal*, 31, 432–53.
Rost, J.C. (1993). *Leadership for the Twenty-first Century*. Westport, CT: Praeger.
Ruvio, A., Rosenblatt, Z. and Hertz-Lazarowitz, R. (2010). Entrepreneurial leadership vision in nonprofit vs. for-profit organizations. *Leadership Quarterly*, 21, 144–58.
Ryan, P.W. and Lyne, I. (2008). Social enterprise and the measurement of social value: Methodological issues with the calculation and application of the social return on investment. *Education, Knowledge and Economy*, 2, 223–37.
Sandberg, J. and Tsoukas, H. (2011). Grasping the logic of practice: Theorizing through practical rationality. *Academy of Management Review*, 36, 338–60.
Schatzki, T.R., Cetina, K.K. and von Savigny, E. (2001). *The Practice Turn in Contemporary Theory*. New York, NY: Routledge.
Schumpeter, J.A. (1934). *The Theory of Economic Development: An Inquiry into Profits, Capital, Credit, Interest, and the Business Cycle*. Cambridge, MA: Harvard University Press.
Schumpeter, J.A. (1947). The creative response in economic history. *Journal of Economic History*, 7, 149–59.
Shane, S.A. (2012). Reflections on the 2010 AMT Decade award: Delivering on the promise of entrepreneurship as a field of research. *Academy of Management Review*, 37, 10–20.
Shane, S.A. and Nicolaou, N. (2013). The genetics of entrepreneurial performance. *International Small Business Journal*, 31, 473–95.
Shane, S.A. and Venkataraman, S. (2000). The promise of entrepreneurship as a field of research. *Academy of Management Review*, 25, 217–26.
Sharir, M., and Lerner, M. (2006). Gauging the success of social ventures initiated by individual social entrepreneurs. *Journal of World Business*, 41, 6–20.
Short, J.C., Ketchen, D.J., Shook, C.L. and Ireland, R.D. (2010). The concept of 'opportunity' in entrepreneurship research: Past accomplishments and future challenges. *Journal of Management*, 36, 40–65.
Shotter, J. (2005). 'Inside the moment of managing': Wittgenstein and the everyday dynamics of our expressive-responsive activities. *Organization Studies*, 26, 113–35.
Shotter, J. (2008). Dialogism and polyphony in organizing theorizing in organization studies: Action guiding anticipations and the continuous creation of novelty. *Organization Studies*, 29, 501–24.
Somers, M.R. (1994). The narrative constitution of identity: A relational and network approach. *Theory and Society*, 23, 605–49.
Steyaert, C. and Hjorth, D. (2008). *Entrepreneurship as Social Change*. Movements in Entrepreneurship series. Cheltenham, UK and Northampton, MA: Edward Elgar Publishing.
Sullivan Mort, G., Weerawardena, J. and Carnegie, K. (2003). Social entrepreneurship: Towards conceptualisation. *International Journal of Nonprofit and Voluntary Sector Marketing*, 8, 76–88.
Tsoukas, H. (2008). Towards the ecological idea: Notes for a complex understanding of complex organisations. In D. Barry and H. Hansen (eds), *The SAGE Handbook of New Approaches in Management and Organization* (pp. 195–8). London: SAGE Publications.
Tsoukas, H. and Chia, R. (2002). On organizational becoming: Rethinking organizational change. *Organization Science*, 13, 567–82.
Tsoukas, H. and Knudsen, C. (2003). *The Oxford Handbook of Organization Theory: Meta-Theoretical Perspectives*. New York, NY: Oxford University Press.
Uhl-Bien, M. (2006). Relational leadership theory: Exploring the social processes of leadership and organizing. *Leadership Quarterly*, 17, 654–76.
Urbano, D., Toledano, N. and Soriano, D.R. (2010). Analyzing social entrepreneurship from an institutional perspective: Evidence from Spain. *Journal of Social Entrepreneurship*, 1, 54–69.
Vecchio, R.P. (2003). Entrepreneurship and leadership: Common trends and common threads. *Human Resource Management Review*, 13, 303–27.

Warren, L. (2004). Negotiating entrepreneurial identity: Communities of practice and changing discourses. *International Journal of Entrepreneurship and Innovation*, 5, 25–35.

Wartick, S.L. and Cochran, P.L. (1985). The evolution of the corporate social performance model. *Academy of Management Review*, 10, 758–69.

Weaver, G.R. and Agle, B.R. (2002). Religiosity and ethical behavior in organizations: A symbolic interactionist perspective. *Academy of Management Review*, 27, 77–97.

Weerawardena, J. and Mort, G.S. (2006). Investigating social entrepreneurship: A multidimensional model. *Journal of World Business*, 41, 21–35.

Weick, K.E. (1995). *Sensemaking in Organizations*. Thousand Oaks, CA: SAGE Publications.

Weick, K.E. (1998). Improvisation as a mindset for organizational analysis. *Organization Science*, 9, 543–55.

Weick, K.E. (2000). Emergent change as a universal in organizations. In M. Beer and N. Nohria (eds), *Breaking the Code of Change* (pp. 223–41). Boston: Harvard Business School Press.

Weick, K.E., Sutcliffe, K.M. and Obstfeld, D. (1999). Organizing for high reliability: Processes of collective mindfulness. In R.I. Sutton and B.M. Staw (eds), *Research in Organizational Behavior*, Vol. 21 (pp. 81–123). Stanford: JAI Press.

Weiskopf, R. and Willmott, H. (2013). Ethics as critical practice: The 'Pentagon Papers', deciding responsibly, truth-telling, and the unsettling of organizational morality. *Organization Studies*, 34, 469–93.

Wenger, E. (2000). Communities of practice and social learning systems. *Organization*, 7, 225–46.

Wood, M. (2005). The fallacy of misplaced leadership. *Journal of Management Studies*, 42, 1101–21.

Wood, M. and Case, P. (2006). Leadership refrains – again, again and again. *Leadership*, 2, 139–45.

Zahra, S.A. and Dess, G.G. (2001). Entrepreneurship as a field of research: Encouraging dialogue and debate. *Academy of Management Review*, 26, 8–10.

Zahra, S.A., Gedajlovic, E., Neubaum, D.O. and Shulman, J.M. (2009). A typology of social entrepreneurs: Motives, search processes and ethical challenges. *Journal of Business Venturing*, 24, 519–32.

12. Entrepreneurial distributed leadership in the emergence and development of high-growth internationalizing firms
Omaima M. Hatem

INTRODUCTION

This chapter examines the actions, processes and attributes of entrepreneurial distributed leadership in the high growth and rapid internationalization of emerging multinationals. Entrepreneurial leadership is a distinctive style of leadership that can be present in an organization of any size, type or age (Renko et al., 2013). Although leadership is the resource most distinctive to a specific organization, effective leadership processes are fundamental to the development and growth of new international ventures and to the provision of entrepreneurial leadership in established corporations (Hatem, 2012).

Entrepreneurial leadership is emerging as a critical issue in our understanding of the dynamics of economic development in the twenty-first century (Leitch et al., 2013; Kuratko, 2007). It is important because it recognizes the importance of different individuals in the entrepreneurial process. However, there has been very limited research on the emergent theme of entrepreneurial distributed leadership (Cope et al., 2011) and the role played by entrepreneurial teams in the growth of firms. Although recent research has explored numerous entrepreneurial leadership styles (Leitch et al., 2013; Kuratko, 2007), progress has been hindered by the lack of conceptual development of distributed leadership entrepreneurial characteristics and behaviours. The purpose of this chapter is to explore and understand this emergent leadership approach.

Most successful new ventures are started by teams (Watson et al., 1995; Cope et al., 2011). Reich (1987) argued that economic growth comes through collective entrepreneurship in which talent, energy and skills are integrated into a team, and this collective capacity to innovate becomes greater than the sum of individual contributions (Chen, 2007). The development of leadership, to build company resources and capabilities, rests on the availability of both human capital (the repository of valuable knowledge and skills) and social capital (the relationships between individuals and organizations that facilitate action and create value) (Hitt and Ireland, 2002).

A leader's role can vary in different stages (gestation, development and growth) and in different types of business, such as partnerships, family businesses and social enterprises (Leitch et al., 2013). The context of this research focuses on high-growth and rapid internationalizing (HGRI) entrepreneurial firms from the Middle East and North Africa (MENA) region. It is based on a unique data set of 108 entrepreneurial firms from the MENA region. All 108 firms attributed an important factor of their success as world leaders of their respective industries to the distributed leadership style they adopted in their journey from local small and medium-sized enterprises (SMEs) to emerging multinational enterprises (MNEs) operating all over the world. In this chapter, we focus on the examination and discussion of 18 interpretivist, abductive and qualitatively analysed case studies from the data set context of the Middle East and North Africa.

Based on the initial analysis of the data, an interesting finding on the theme of strategic entrepreneurial leadership emerged and is explored further here: the entrepreneurs' perspective of success in internationally diversifying their business activities to create companies in different parts of the world was attributed by them to the fact that they had capable managers to whom they could delegate and entrust with major tasks. As one chief executive officer (CEO) suggested, they rely upon members' teamwork, commitment and leadership to grow rapidly across the globe and become world leaders in their field. This belief was shared by almost all case companies during the interviews and participant field observation enquiries. In other words, a common theme from these case companies was that as leaders of entrepreneurial firms they highlighted the importance of 'distributed leadership'; this meant that they as founders drove, encouraged, motivated and worked with entrepreneurial team members to initiate viable initiatives for the future of their internationally diversified companies. As a result, the development of entrepreneurial teams for distributed leadership was what these leaders concluded to be an exceptional element in their respective diversified firms' superior performances as they rapidly internationalized.

The context for the analysis in this chapter draws on Wiklund and Shepherd's (2008) investigation into aspects of human and social capital relevant to portfolio entrepreneurship, and specifically their classification of them in terms of whether they are generic or embedded resources. Business founders with more education were more likely to engage in portfolio entrepreneurship and are probably better at interpreting information and judging whether it is suitable or not to pursue a new entry (Cooper and Daily, 1997). Portfolio entrepreneurs also have the knowledge to assess what resources are needed and how they should be assembled when pursuing a new entry (Davidsson and Honig, 2003). Business network membership had a positive association with the pursuit of portfolio entrepreneurship, suggesting that these founders leverage their business contacts to access the resources needed for new entry (Davidsson and Honig, 2003). Thus, frameworks of human capital (Becker, 1964; Schultz, 1961) and social capital (Bourdieu, 1986; Coleman, 1988, 1990; Lin, 2001; Putnam, 2000) can illuminate both the entrepreneurship (Debrulle et al., 2010) and leadership (Day, 2000; Iles and Preece, 2006) domains (Leitch et al., 2013).

This chapter therefore examines distributed leadership from the MENA region entrepreneurs' perspective that illuminates an interesting organizational development pattern, and potentially illustrates the movement from entrepreneurial control to other team members in the business taking the lead, and the connectivity with international diversification and growth triggering this outcome. This research contributes to knowledge in three significant ways. First, it contributes to the entrepreneurial distributed leadership development literature (Bolden, 2011). This study extends the descriptive and normative perspectives (Youngs, 2009; Gordon, 2010) which dominate the literature, by developing a more critical account. This recognizes the rhetorical and discursive significance of distributed leadership (Gronn, 2010) in (re)constructing leader–follower identities and mobilizing collective engagement by challenging and reinforcing traditional forms of organization (Bolden, 2011). Second, the research extends the entrepreneurial teams' literature through the analysis of the role of distributed leadership development as the enhancement of human capital, knowledge and abilities in response to challenges facing the business' entrepreneurial and managerial growth processes (Kempster and Cope, 2010; Cope et al., 2011). Additionally, the research enhances the understanding of business group formation through international diversification and the enactment of portfolio entrepreneurship through the development of the social capital of distributed leadership. Third, this research makes a contribution to the concept of distributed leadership as it connects in a meaningful way with the experiences and aspirations of leadership practitioners (Harris and Spillane, 2008) from the HGRI MENA region firms. It also explicitly recognizes the inherently political nature of leadership within organizations (Gordon, 2010) during the different stages of growth of the rapidly internationalizing multinational firms from the emerging markets of the MENA region.

The chapter is structured as follows. An initial brief review of the distributed leadership literature is followed by a discussion of the methodology used in the empirical investigation. This explains how, by adopting Bolden's (2011) method, this study presents a methodological approach that supports a shift in focus from simply studying how leadership is 'distributed' to a contextually situated exploration of how distributed and focused forms of leadership interact with one another within a 'hybrid configuration' of practice (Gronn, 2008, 2010). Such an approach required detailed ethnographic studies of leadership practices and discourses in situ, as well as a multilevel approach to research (Yammarino and Dansereau, 2008). The chapter then presents the analysis and discussion of findings from the empirical investigation of the field study and triangulates with the existing literature to elucidate theoretical and empirical contributions, and concludes with implications for future research and managerial practice.

DISTRIBUTED LEADERSHIP LITERATURE

Cope et al. (2011) have argued that:

> there is a dearth of research that explores leadership in context generally (Currie et al. 2009; Liden and Antonakis 2009) and in particular within the SME context; and even less in regard to notions of distributed leadership and entrepreneurial teams within established small businesses (Sapienza et al. 1991). We have very little empirical understanding of how the transition from 'heroic' lone entrepreneur to entrepreneurial team occurs: in essence, how is the crisis of leadership addressed?

Edwards (2011) claims that the review of the literature on community and distributed leadership marks out the potential for a more context-rich understanding of the nature of leadership. However, the mainstay of the literature regarding distributed leadership appears to have a heavy emphasis on the education sector and was published mainly in education management journals (e.g. Currie et al., 2009; Gosling et al., 2009; Harris, 2007, 2009; Leithwood et al., 2009; Spillane, 2006; Thurston and Clift, 1996).

Even Bolden's (2011) seminal work, 'Distributed leadership in organizations: a review of theory and research', drew mainly on previous research undertaken by education scholars such as Peter Gronn (2002, 2006, 2008, 2009, 2010), Spillane (2006), Spillane and Diamond (2007a, 2007b) and Harris (2005, 2007, 2009). Bolden (2011) considers a number of different concepts relating to the distribution of leadership within organizations, and the manner in which they tend to be used. He asserts that Leithwood et al. (2009: 1) suggest that, for the majority of authors, distributed leadership (DL) can be considered to incorporate shared, democratic, dispersed and other related forms of leadership. From this perspective, DL tends to be considered from a normative perspective, as a means for enhancing the effectiveness of, and engagement with, leadership processes. For such authors, the key question is how leadership should be distributed in order to have the most beneficial effect in terms of student learning outcomes for research within schools.

He also maintains that a number of other authors (including Spillane and Gronn), however, take an explicitly descriptive approach, in which they argue that DL offers an analytical framework through which one can assess and articulate the manner in which leadership is (and is not) distributed throughout organizations. Additionally, Bolden (2011) declares that such authors go to great lengths to argue that, while leadership may be shared and/or democratic in certain situations, this is not a necessary or sufficient requirement for it to be considered 'distributed'. Furthermore, they suggest that DL is not an alternative or replacement for individual or focused leadership and that distribution per se is not necessarily related to more effective or efficient leadership.

Bolden (2011) concludes his study by drawing on authors such as James et al. (2007) and Ross et al. (2005a, 2005b) who outline the need for a more systemic approach to leadership development that situates this activity as part of a wider change process. He argues that the reviewed literature poses some serious challenges to traditional management and leadership development processes, and calls for far greater investment in the development of interpersonal networks and shared understandings both within and beyond organizations; what Day (2000) refers to as 'leadership development' as opposed to 'leader development'. Bolden (2011) argues that elaboration on how this might be done effectively remains an important area for further research, which is the gap that this chapter addresses through a theoretical and empirical stance.

EMPIRICAL INVESTIGATION

The primary aim of the main study from which the material drawn on in this chapter was derived was to understand the phenomenon of the high growth and rapid internationalization of firms from the emerging market of the MENA region. More specifically, the main research questions focused on why, where and how some emerging market enterprises grow fast and internationalize early and rapidly. Particular attention was paid to entrepreneurs, entrepreneurial teams and the entrepreneurial process in the discovery, evaluation and exploitation of new business opportunities. The study adopted an interpretivist stance which recognized that reality is socially constructed, rather than objectively determined, and appreciated the different constructions and meanings that people placed on their experience (Easterby-Smith et al., 1991). It followed a qualitative approach based on extended, multiple selected case studies of internationalizing firms. Data collection involved in-depth interviews with the entrepreneurs/founders/CEOs and other key leaders/managers of internationalizing firms over three years. Access to archival data and expertise within the emerging market of the MENA region and other secondary information provided triangulation of the data.

Constructing a comprehensive data set for the sampled firms was a lengthy and extensive procedure. The process of compiling this data employed several sources of financial data. These sources included the stock markets of each of the 16 MENA countries: Bahrain, Egypt, Iraq, Jordan, Kuwait, Lebanon, Libya, Morocco, Oman, Palestine, Qatar, Saudi Arabia, Syria, Tunisia and the United Arab Emirates (Dubai and Abu Dhabi).[1] Further, the sources included a number of the world's renowned international financial business newspapers (published and online sources).[2] Other Arabic-language newspapers[3] and financial reports were also used for this study. The criteria of selection was based on being a multinational company from the MENA region, with the number of employees above 1000, a high percentage of sales generated through international business, exhibiting high growth rates in the last three to four years due to the internationalization process, being a listed public company or a privately owned, partially state-owned or family business. Most of these entrepreneurs and families are members of the World's Billionaires list. To the best of the author's knowledge, this is the first comprehensive set of data on high-growth and rapidly internationalizing firms from the MENA region emerging market. Triangulation was performed during both phases of data collection and data analysis. Thus, it was important to obtain reports, independent of the participants of the field study, regarding the broader research context. In addition to the field interviews, context interviews were conducted with relevant financial and international bodies and professionals who were directly associated with the firms in the field site (Kvale, 1996). This was intended to evaluate the field participant's perspective, to allow an outside view to assess the information and data collected by the author (Kirk and Miller, 1986). The author conducted context interviews with different professional figures over a period of two years. The interviews undertaken included: World Bank and United Nations officials, members of central and commercial banks in more than one country, and staff members of Moody's investment service responsible for the MENA region. These interviews were helpful during data analysis. The companies gave their permission for the use of these documents, which are not normally available to the public.

This study adopted theoretical sampling to select cases that have the potential to offer theoretical insights by capturing the interrelationships in the data collected (Eisenhardt and Graebner, 2007). The theoretical reasons for selection included the revelation of an unusual phenomenon (HGRI of MENA firms), replication of findings from other cases, contrary replication, elimination of alternative explanations, and elaboration of the emergent theory (Eisenhardt and Graebner, 2007). As Yin (2009) summarizes, cases are chosen because they are unusually revelatory, extreme exemplars or represent opportunities for unusual research access. As is common in qualitative analysis, purposive theoretical sampling rather than statistical sampling was used (Silverman, 2000: 104). This sampling strategy complied with the arguments that qualitative sampling is 'purposive' and 'theory-driven' (Miles and Huberman, 1994: 27).

The sample of respondent entrepreneurs in this study were purposefully selected following recommendations from business contacts, because they were founding entrepreneurs who continued to be the major owners and managing directors of their ventures; some of their customer base was within the MENA region, while others were globally spread. They had significant international growth ambitions and their product and service offerings were knowledge-intensive. The sectoral coverage of the selected firms was wide: telecommunications, pharmaceutical industries, construction and engineering, electrical and fibre-optic cables, auto assembling, consultancies, retail, real estate development, fast food franchisee chains, agro-clean cultivation and exporting, software programming, tourism, hotels, new town developments and resorts creation. Case firms were selected from within the MENA region based on some conditions, namely that they: (1) fit the sample frame definition of founder-owned and managed firms; and (2) achieve at least $1 billion turnover within four years of foundation. Those conditions were assessed via secondary sources such as financial media and internet searches, and through networking processes. In the Middle East, successful entrepreneurs are typically well known to one another through social and family connections, or through business ties. Of the 108 firms initially identified, access and agreement to participate in the research process was secured from 18 firms in addition to the pilot case study.

ANALYSIS AND TRIANGULATION WITH LITERATURE

The main aim of the study was to understand why, where and how the MENA region emerging market firms have attained their high growth and rapid internationalization in an average span of four to six years. To address the objective of this chapter of how the theme of distributed leadership played an important role in the phenomenon of high growth and rapid internationalization, this section explains how the analysis and discussion of findings from empirical investigation and the triangulation with existing literature are presented.

The analysis of the entrepreneurs' interviews and case studies revealed that entrepreneurial and managerial processes were interrelated and firmly interconnected in the study of HGRI MENA firms. These firms exhibited advantage and opportunity-seeking behaviours that resulted in creating value for the entrepreneurs, their organizations and society as a whole. The behaviour of these firms involved actions taken to exploit advantages while concurrently exploring new opportunities that sustained their natural ability to create value across time. The HGRI MENA firms were unique as they possessed the characteristics of international new ventures (INVs) and MNEs at the same time. They were INVs as they started their international operations and expansion, yet they became MNEs through their high growth and rapid internationalization within short periods of time. That said, they continued to exhibit the international entrepreneurial nature of young firms while displaying the superior performances of large established firms in strategic management. In the subsequent sections, this chapter presents the underpinning argument of the research, explaining how those international new ventures achieved and sustained success and became large established firms, and their exploitation of competitive advantages, whilst maintaining their entrepreneurial nature. The HGRIs' international entrepreneurial processes of discovery, enactment and evaluation were analysed simultaneously with their strategic management processes of exploitation of competitive advantages.

The full study has presented the analysis and discussion of the resources and capabilities of the HGRI MENA firms (Hatem, 2012). However, how these resources were internationally mobilized and utilized to manage the firms' operations are discussed through analysing the various effecting processes. The international mobilizing of tangible and intangible resources through the utilization and management of human (knowledge), social (network) and financial capitals are further discussed to explain how these factors facilitated the acquisition of resources and helped to identify opportunities as well as exploiting these resources and opportunities to create competitive advantage. As noted above, the theme that stood out from the inductive research was the process of distributed leadership as entrepreneurs led, drove and motivated team members to fulfil an international vision, and as leaders anticipated and worked with entrepreneurial team members to initiate change in their firms. In terms of process, there is a particular focus on portfolio entrepreneurship, international diversification and the formation of business groups through management processes undergone by entrepreneurial team members to achieve rapid internationalization and sustain high growth. The ensuing sections present entrepreneurial teams and business groups, the role of human and social capital in distributed leadership and entrepreneurial strategy and distributed leadership.

ENTREPRENEURIAL TEAMS AND BUSINESS GROUPS

An entrepreneurial leader is central to the entrepreneurial team. It has been suggested that such a leader has to create visionary scenarios that are necessary for selecting and mobilizing a supporting cast of interdependent members who commit to and enact the vision to achieve strategic value creation (Gupta et al., 2004; Rickards and Moger, 2006). The ability and skill in attracting other key management members and then building the team is one of the most valued capabilities for lead entrepreneurs. In addition to the critical role of entrepreneurial leader, the quality of the entrepreneurial team is strongly connected with the growth potential of a new venture (MacMillan et al., 1987; Watson et al., 1995). There are numerous qualities that the team needs to have, including relevant experience and skill (Long, 1983; Ibrahim and Goodwin, 1986), creativity (Amabile, 1997), opportunity obsession (Ardichvili et al., 2003) and interpersonal skills (Watson et al., 1995). Entrepreneurial teams lead ventures which have better financial performance than firms led by individual entrepreneurs (Ensley et al., 1998). Beckman et al. (2007) argue that more diverse founding teams are associated with higher performance, particularly in more complex environments.

In the context of the emerging multinationals in the MENA region, the most critical aspect of leadership was developing and inculcating a vision for the organization. This was even more critical for an entrepreneurial venture in which the operation was little more than the embodiment of the vision of the entrepreneur or the entrepreneurial team members. Entrepreneurial teams make better decisions than individuals (West, 2007). Carland and Carland (2012) conceptualize that understanding how a vision evolves leads us to better understand how shared vision works.

The growth process of entrepreneurial firms is frequently achieved through the formation of business groups (that is, a set of companies run by the same entrepreneur or entrepreneurial team). Iacobucci and Rosa (2005) hypothesized that business group formation was a result of an entrepreneurial growth process through diversification of the original activity. This entrepreneurial growth process offers an alternative explanation for the formation of business groups to that arising from managerial efficiency and expediency. Running a group of companies by the same entrepreneur is not only initiated by geographical extension of their operation and by diversification, but also by the differentiation policy aimed at serving different market segments within the same sector (Iacobucci and Rosa, 2005: 65). Growth is the result of an entrepreneurial process 'in which the entrepreneur is constantly identifying and evaluating new opportunities; and over time, a significant "portfolio" of surviving ventures (acquired or founded) can be built up' (Rosa, 1998: 44). Iacobucci and Rosa (2005) describe entrepreneurial firms as 'characterized by ownership concentration and the direct involvement of the entrepreneur or entrepreneurial team in the effective control of the firm'. Entrepreneurial teams are 'persons controlling a company or a group (through ownership) and directly involved in its management' (Iacobucci and Rosa, 2005).

The analysis of the findings from the empirical investigation showed that business groups' formation led to the formation of entrepreneurial teams to manage their companies' growth and international diversification. It was this restructuring that led to the emergence of distributed entrepreneurial leadership to enable the high growth and rapid internationalization of the firms. To be able to diversify into different international markets, business founders depended on their internal entrepreneurial team members of managers to run these new entities. Additionally, it was evident in all case companies that were investigated in the study that the formation of entrepreneurial teams was crucial to the international growth, diversification and success of their business groups. For example, the interview with Mr C3, the CEO of Case Company in Africa West, who was responsible for Cameroon, Guinea, Ghana and Sierra Leone, revealed that it was of paramount importance that the entrepreneurial team member – that is, himself – was not only the manager of businesses in four different countries in Africa but also a shareholder in the group and a dynamic member of the strategic executive committee that was responsible for major strategic decision-making for the whole business group. He had the authority not only to identify and locate business opportunities, but also to enact these opportunities through financing the different contracts, and to exploit these opportunities via initiating relationships and governmental contacts that required the expenditures and 'gifts' that are a feature of doing business with some African governmental agencies.

Similar patterns were identified with Mr P2, the CEO of Case Company P in Egypt who was similarly responsible for identifying, enacting and exploiting new international business opportunities in the field of poultry farming, tourism, real estate and construction projects; this highly diversified set of activities entitled him to create new international firms in different industrial sectors. Thus Mr P2 was responsible for the creation of new firms and new business groups within the holding company of Case Company L business group. As a further example, Mr A2 was an entrepreneur who worked with the founder of Case Company A for two years before it was decided to internationalize into Italy and form the new company of Weather International. According to A's CEO, it was evident that without Mr A2 the formation of Weather Company, which later on became Weather Holding Group, would not have been possible. His entrepreneurial team leader role was pivotal in overseeing the management and execution of this company's formation and, later, of the activities of the business group. For Case Company E's CEO to be able to operate resorts in six different countries in the world across Africa, Asia and Europe, he had to depend on his entrepreneurial teams of managers to run, organize and control the management of these resorts that constituted his business group. Similarly, the founder of Case Company Q's Group who had 120 000 employees spread over 42 countries in a number of miscellaneous business activities, emphasized the obvious importance of his entrepreneurial teams in the successful international management of his operations. These findings are in agreement with Loane et al.'s (2004) study that supports similar impacts that internationalizing teams had in creating the core internal capabilities and leveraging the external resources required for rapid internationalization.

By growing through international diversification and setting up new companies, responsibility fell upon trusted entrepreneurial team members from within their companies to continue the management and control of these new entities. This confirms attention drawn by Iacobucci and Rosa (2010) to the vital function of entrepreneurial teams in managing and sustaining the growth and profitability of their respective companies and groups, and that is why the lead entrepreneur ensures that the entrepreneurial teams have shareholding stakes in their companies. Analysis of the findings also supports Wright's (2009: 13) emphasis that the significance of 'the nature of compensation for management poses important issues for strategic entrepreneurship since it can influence their time horizons and hence their strategic behaviour', especially in relation to 'ownership rights'; this is 'crucial for entrepreneurship since they permit the entrepreneur to make decisions about the coordination of resources to gain entrepreneurial rents, in return for bearing the uncertainty associated with owning those resources'.

The portfolio entrepreneurship literature focuses on how business group formation leads to the formation of entrepreneurial teams. However, emergent findings from this study suggest that entrepreneurial teams enabled the founders to form new internationally diverse companies due to the existence of entrepreneurial managers within their original companies. This indicates that the formation of business groups can lead to the formation of entrepreneurial teams, as much as entrepreneurial teams can lead to the formation of business groups, thus portraying a two-way driving force for international growth. This is an additional emergent theme that the case companies exhibited, as the lead entrepreneurs clearly highlighted the crucial role of what they called 'distributed leadership'.

It was evident that Case Company J's new way of giving shareholding ownerships to some of Mr J's employees was one of the main motivating forces driving his new international company formations. In the year 2000, it was not a very common management style, in the MENA region, for a lead entrepreneur/founder to make his employees part-owners of his company. However, by doing so, Mr J ensured that the regular employee turned shareholder had an incentive to lead the company's international growth successfully. Other case companies exhibited a similar fit with the literature when they demonstrated the possibility of business group formations through entrepreneurial teams. In addition, the findings extended the theory by offering this new perspective on the strategic behaviour of lead entrepreneurs to legitimate some of their team members from their original businesses to become effective partners with shareholding ownership. Lead entrepreneurs/founders considered this strategic decision to be a crucial element of their international diversification and hence business group formation, and thus successful sustained growth via portfolio entrepreneurship.

Resource-based view theory sees networks as an embedded social capital that is an inherent firm-specific intangible resource which is difficult to replicate, thus providing competitive advantage (Peng and Luo, 2000). Wernerfelt (1984) recognized that international contacts as networks are valuable resources. Loane and Bell (2006) postulate the importance of networks in the internationalization of entrepreneurial firms. However, while they confirm that firms tend to use their existing networks, they illustrate that many rapid internationalizers have to build new networks as they expand into new foreign markets. This research shares Loane and Bell's (2006) perspective and shows how the case companies have continued to build new networks at different stages of their internationalization processes. Examples below will illustrate how the entrepreneurs and their entrepreneurial teams drew upon more than one type of the networks discussed above, at different stages of their high growth and rapid internationalization.

Case Company B's entrepreneur explains that the social capital of networks differed according to the stage of the company's growth. Initially, to start his pharmaceutical business, he drew upon his educational relationship to help initiate his new venture. As his firm started expanding in new international markets he focused on building new networks with governmental authorities. He strengthened the firm ties and positive communications with his connections in the government of Jordan, and built new resources of networks with the USA, Portuguese and British authorities. Networking with these governmental authorities was to ensure ease of his firm's operation in these new foreign markets. He also drew on his business connections to expand his businesses into both the USA and Portugal to ensure that he attained appropriate strategic alliances and partnerships. When Case Company B decided to go to the MENA region, Mr B had to enact political networks to overcome bureaucratic barriers to this very lucrative market. The last stage, according to Case Company B's entrepreneur, was to underline the importance of having the resource of networking with customers. Customer needs were what drove him to innovate and come up with new ideas for injectables, diabetes and different medication approved by the Food and Drug Administration for different international markets.

The HGRI firms' entrepreneurs believed that empowerment in entrepreneurship was a management practice of sharing information, rewards and power with employees so that they could take initiatives and make decisions to solve problems and improve service and performance. Empowerment, to the entrepreneurs, was based on the idea that giving employees skills, resources, authority, opportunity and motivation, as well as holding them responsible and accountable for the outcomes of their actions, would contribute to their competence and satisfaction. The entrepreneurial teams of different internationalizing firms were the entrepreneurs and manager team members of those companies that internationalized successfully. The entrepreneurial teams' capabilities were expressed in terms of their background, foreign work experience and international or global vision. The findings of this study revealed that new ventures led by managers with foreign work experience were able to internationalize rapidly and successfully.

HUMAN AND SOCIAL CAPITAL IN DISTRIBUTED LEADERSHIP

The development of leadership, to build company resources and capabilities, rests on the availability of both human capital (the repository of valuable knowledge and skills) and social capital (the relationships between individuals and organizations that facilitate action and create value) (Hitt and Ireland, 2002). Business founders pursue portfolio entrepreneurship through their human capital – education and start-up experience; and their social capital – business networks and links with government support agencies (Wiklund and Shepherd, 2008). Wiklund and Shepherd (2008) use human and social capital theory to hypothesize differences in entrepreneurial action based upon a founder's human and social capitals, as well as the implications of capital differences across portfolio founders in how these actions are organized.

Social capital is described as sets of resources embedded in relationships (Burt, 1992). The analysis and discussion of the social network supports Anderson and Jack's (2002) notion of a resource that fits neatly with the concept of entrepreneurial networks, because although entrepreneurship is a creative process, it operates in constrained circumstances. They explain that one way to overcome some of the constraints the entrepreneur may face is to acquire knowledge and resources by tapping into an extended pool, which exists outside the business. This network of resources and information may represent and offer a rich source of explicit and implicit knowledge, experience and privileged access to physical resources (Anderson and Jack, 2002). Networks are considered to be both a firm's resource as well as a process that facilitates firms' rapid internationalization and high growth.

Human capital indicates the principal founders' knowledge: background education, work experience and language proficiency. These indicators suggest the importance of the intangible resources that the entrepreneurs draw upon in their internationalization activities. Knowledge of international markets from innovative products and services as well as tacit knowledge were key skills that enabled the entrepreneurs to embark on an internationalization path that targeted hostile markets proactively (Hatem, 2012). The moderating force of knowledge influences the speed of internationalization. Bell et al. (2003) underlined the importance of knowledge in speeding up the internationalization of firms. Furthermore, networking is a powerful tool for the entrepreneur because it provides immediate access to knowledge (Dubini and Aldrich, 1991). Network analysis has been a powerful framework for international entrepreneurship researchers (Oviatt and McDougall, 1994; Bell, 1995; Coviello and Munro, 1995, 1997). Oviatt and McDougall (2005) specify that cross-national-border networks, in combination with different tacit knowledge types, help in moderating the speed with which international entrepreneurial opportunities are exploited.

The international growth of the case companies in this study happened very rapidly. Analysis of the case companies revealed heavy reliance on the distributed entrepreneurship leaders' deep knowledge of the industry and international markets. Analysis also disclosed firms' confidence in the knowledge that was deliberately accessed and resourced by means of strategically recruiting people. Nearly all firms in this study headhunted new managers with both deep technical knowledge and strategic management experience in their industrial sectors. Additionally, case companies formed business relationships that would fill gaps identified in industry or new markets. Most principal founders and entrepreneurial team members of case companies that internationalized successfully had received education abroad and had language proficiency. They had entrepreneurial and management competence that led to their HGRI. Their international experience and experimental or tacit knowledge, acquired during their personal development and work exposure, played an important role in their deep knowledge of new international markets and the industry they invested in. This research agrees with Bell et al. (2003) who proposed that the differences in the complexity and sophistication of knowledge used in a firm explain their speed of internationalization.

Networks of relationships were fundamental to the development in all businesses as currently found in all case companies in this study. These networks were developed in previous business activities or educational backgrounds, but in each case a proactive approach to develop further new networks was evident. Some companies used family networks; others used educational background networks; a third group of entrepreneurs used political networks; and some entrepreneurs used customer ties. The most important set of networks, as revealed by the findings, were internal networks, meaning entrepreneurs networking with their own employees and staff members to produce intrapreneurs with new ideas to identify, enact, evaluate and exploit opportunities internationally, which added to their success stories in terms of their high growth and rapid internationalization activities.

In addressing the rapidly changing environment, Case Companies A, C, D, E, J, Q and R managed to coordinate internal and external activities, resources and technologies to reconfigure the firms' asset structures. They did so through intensive training and development programmes, which enhanced the learning process capabilities as well as the tacit and experimental knowledge of the entrepreneurial team members. The author had an ethnographic participant observation experience in attending one of the in-house training and development workshops for staff members, in preparation for international assignments. The magnitude of preparation, as witnessed by the author, was emphasized by the lead entrepreneur to be 'our continuous investment to develop new skills and capabilities for our entrepreneurial team members'. Evidence from the analysis of findings supported what the entrepreneurs aspired to achieve. International training courses and regular field meetings with a diverse customer base as well as possible suppliers in new foreign markets were imperative, as they allowed the entrepreneurial team members to expand their vision and entrepreneurial orientation in terms of alertness, discovering, scanning and evaluating new opportunities as well as reconfiguring and coordinating resources and competences.

Most of the HGRI MENA firms have shown swiftness in developing, honing and exploiting their entrepreneurial capability to recognize, conceive, create and exploit opportunities for competitive advantage. However, as they continue their international expansion, the firms recognize their need to learn new skills that sustain profitable exploitation of their capabilities.

Similarly, operationalizing social capital by considering links only in business and political networks (Wiklund and Shepherd, 2008) seemed insufficient. This did not capture the diverse nature and scope of networking processes that supported the international diversification, business group formation and portfolio entrepreneurship of the HGRI MENA firms. Networking was not only a resource but also a continuous process that was vital in the HGRI MENA firms' rapid growth and international expansion.

Overall, evidence from the analysis of findings from the case companies supported Anderson and Jack's (2002) conceptualization that social capital is said to be both the glue that forms the structure of networks, and the lubricant that facilitates the operation of networks. HGRI MENA firms emerged from emerging economies and internationalized into developing and developed economies. Therefore the increasingly dynamic and turbulent environments in which they operated demanded strategic entrepreneurial flexibility to sustain international growth. Thus, firms were able to create and manage knowledge that was valuable, rare and difficult to substitute, were able to increase their value and strengthen their international competitive advantage as suggested by Kuivalainen and Bell (2004). In such evolutionary knowledge-based international markets the emphasis was not on the static nature of resources per se, but on the dynamically evolving, internationally acquired routines and capabilities through coordinating relationships and networking processes.

Case Companies B, D, E, F and J explained how the processes of networking went through different stages as their internationalization expanded. The lead entrepreneurs and different members of their entrepreneurial teams were actively leveraging their own social and business contact networks to gain knowledge of accelerated access to international markets. Many of these relationships had been formed in previous employment, and when studying, working or living in these target international markets. Firms were combating the dual liability of foreignness and newness by leveraging the social capital inherent in relationships with external parties. They were utilizing these networks to access foreign market knowledge, identifying key industries or major client bases. Thereby they also managed to enhance their efforts to access funding streams and venture capital, and identified other channels and networks. Indeed, such relationships often acted as links to other network resources for the firm, as in Case Companies I, M, O and R, when clients encouraged these firms to internationalize into new markets where they had strong relations. This is in agreement with Jack et al.'s (2008) argument that these networking processes depended on which stage of the life cycle the firm was in, as illustrated and detailed in the multifaceted networking process of Case Company B's entrepreneurial narrative and in the within-case analysis of Case Company C.

Findings also revealed that many of the firms actively sought to address perceived capability gaps via the acquisition of new team members. Such individuals often provided new technical capabilities, greater knowledge of international markets, new business contact networks and/or access to financial resources. Thus, the composition of management teams often changed over time. Loane and Bell's study (2006) conducted in Australia, Canada, Ireland and New Zealand demonstrated similar firms' network development activities to build international networking processes due to the advanced nature of their offering in the new markets.

Portfolio entrepreneurs protected their entrepreneurial activities by exploiting other sources of social capital such as their links with governmental support agencies, as suggested by Wiklund and Shepherd (2008). They did so by strengthening their relationship with different government bodies in different local and international markets. Government regulations differed in new international markets, and were sometimes an obstacle in the path of business opportunity exploitation as founders tried to establish their performance in these new markets. It was observed in the findings of the investigated case companies that most of the entrepreneurs and entrepreneurial teams kept an ongoing positive relationship with different governmental organizations that were instrumental in minimizing bureaucratic challenges facing their international growth process. Findings revealed that governments of the new international markets acknowledged these relationships as a means of partnering with the case companies in order to build their own economies. For example, Case Company C established a new division in Guinea to oversee the smooth construction of its cable plant and later on to maintain a trouble-free operation in this new international market, which sustained a regular high performance.

Later, with the help of the governmental agencies and bodies, it managed to export to other African countries. Case Company R's entrepreneur expressed the importance of regular free samples, promotions and gifts as a public relations tool that their company employed with government agencies in all international markets in which they operated. This was necessary to ensure the uninterrupted running of operations through keeping government agencies and members content. Entrepreneurs pursued and protected their international diversification activities through this 'social capital' of maintaining relationships with government agencies, as was highly exhibited in the case companies investigated in this study, which fits with the theoretical concepts of Wiklund and Shepherd's (2008) portfolio entrepreneurship literature.

ENTREPRENEURIAL STRATEGY AND DISTRIBUTED LEADERSHIP

Although leadership is the resource most distinctive to a specific organization, effective leadership processes are fundamental to the development and growth of new international ventures and to the provision of entrepreneurial leadership in established corporations. The findings from the case companies confirmed distributed leadership to be both a resource and a valuable process of management for the HGRI MENA firms. Distributed leadership ability revealed in the case studies by the founders, as they initiated their firms' internationalization and growth processes, was instrumental in leading and driving firms together with the entrepreneurial team members. All case companies in this study suggested that their lead entrepreneurs shared strong guidance approaches as they worked with entrepreneurial team members to initiate viable initiatives for the future of their companies. All entrepreneurs and founders of the case companies displayed distributed entrepreneurial features with high leadership qualities. Leaders of these companies exhibited the dual characteristics of being strategic entrepreneurs through their innovative and proactive behaviour, as well as their acceptance of calculated risk and nurturing an entrepreneurial culture.

The characteristic features of each of the case firms supported the notion that while the original entrepreneurial ideas and vision grew within the head of one person (that is, the leader/entrepreneur), the subsequent growth and enactment of the vision, as well as the further development of this vision, is equally attributed to the impetus and engagement of the entrepreneurial teams formed to lead and manage their companies. Distributed leadership in the HGRI MENA firms resulted in team efficiency and competence. This was a consequence of the lead entrepreneurs' valuable ability to envision, maintain flexibility and work with others to initiate changes that create a viable future for the firm. Interviews and participant observation at the HGRI MENA firms revealed how lead entrepreneurs established clear visions and developed strategies that focused on both opportunity and advantage within that visualization. That, in turn, enhanced opportunity identification and exploitation as well as the strategies formulated to achieve the firms' development. Case Company G's head explained his leadership role by explaining how he differentiated between leadership and management:

> To me, leadership was setting a new direction and vision for my group that they follow; I was the spearhead for that new direction . . . At the same time, I gave my team leaders management controls such that they directed people and resources in our group according to principles and values that have already been established.

Additionally, other lead entrepreneurs highlighted how by maintaining flexibility during their internationalization and growth processes, they managed to balance the structure of firm with freedom to implement and change strategy, which in turn facilitated quick response to change. The HGRI MENA firms' entrepreneurs/leaders and managers regularly assessed their firms' core resources and competencies to ensure they were developed and reconfigured. To many of them, maintaining flexibility guaranteed competitive and sustainable advantage. The continuous search for new sources of competitive advantage, whilst preserving a sense of unity and coherence in their firms' culture, was an outstanding attribute that HGRI MENA leaders grasped, mastered and shared with their team members, through their internationalization journeys. This was evident during the participant observation undertaken by the author, as it was the leaders' wish to emphasize that had it not been for the general entrepreneurial culture nurtured by these firms, none of the valuable initiatives to create and exploit new business opportunities would have been accomplished.

The strategic entrepreneurial leadership illuminated the entrepreneurs' success in diversifying their international business activities to create multinationals due to the capability of their entrepreneurial teams. The belief shared among all case companies during the interviews and participant field observation enquiries was that the high growth and rapid internationalization was only possible because of what they constantly labelled 'distributed leadership'. The development of entrepreneurial teams for distributed leadership was what leaders concluded to be an exceptional element in their respective firms' superior performances as they rapidly internationalized. More than one leader agreed with Case Company Q's entrepreneur that:

> the characteristic features of each of our companies was [as follows]: while the original entrepreneurial ideas and vision grew within the head of one person [that is, the founder/entrepreneur], the subsequent growth and enactment of the vision, as well as the further reinvigoration of and development of this vision, is equally attributed to the impetus and engagement of the entrepreneurial teams formed to lead their companies.

Other examples from Case Company H's interview excerpt confirm this notion, as he elaborated:

> Leadership is not about a one man operation; it is leadership by entrepreneurial teams that are constituted of individuals that are well educated, carefully selected and meticulously trained and importantly also possess entrepreneurial traits. These entrepreneurial team members share their firm's vision because they have been integral in building this vision.

Other case companies' entrepreneurs deemed their support of this emergent theme of distributed leadership to be instrumental in their respective firms' high growth and rapid internationalization. While the lead entrepreneurs of these firms acknowledge their central role in the creation of their firms, most of them claim that their firms could not continue to survive and operate without their presence, as they are managed efficiently by capable entrepreneurially minded team members. Another viewpoint that supported the distributed leadership was made by Case Company J's entrepreneur, who added a crucial point in the understanding of the essence of distributed leadership: 'As all members of these entrepreneurial teams are shareholders, the teams' bonds are strong and that strength is based on trust and mutual interest in growing profitable businesses.'

Thus, the findings of this research agree with Covin and Slevin's (2002) notion that entrepreneurial leadership is the ability to influence others to emphasize opportunity-seeking and advantage-seeking behaviours. Interpretation of the findings agrees with Gupta et al. (2004) that entrepreneurial leaders create visionary scenarios that can be used to assemble and mobilize a supporting group in the firm that is committed to opportunity discovery and exploitation. As presented by the analysis of the findings, entrepreneurial leadership constitutes leaders with strategic vision and managerial talent, which confirms Kuratko's (2007) conceptualization. Entrepreneurial leaders in this study exhibited combinations of managerial and visionary leadership; they had strong, positive expectations of performance; they formulated and implemented strategies that enhanced their organizational growth and success. This is in agreement with Ireland et al. (2001) and Kuratko (2009) who advocate that growth-orientated firms need to adopt a competitive mindset in which they display flexibility, speed, innovation and strategic leadership. Through effective application of entrepreneurial strategic leadership, MENA growing firms adapted their behaviours and exploited new business opportunities. The concept of entrepreneurial leadership fits well with the behaviour of case companies in this study. As for distributed leadership, it is a theme that emerged from the findings in this study and has not been addressed by the strategic entrepreneurship or leadership literature so far. To this extent, the theme may contribute to the development of new knowledge in both literatures.

These findings are also in line with Ghoshal and Bartlett (1995), who have pointed to the example of a few successful companies such as GE, ABB and Toyota which have broken the mould and rejected the principles of the multidivisional doctrine. These companies employed an emerging management model which, the authors argued, was not a new organizational structure, but a new set of key management processes, as well as new roles and tasks of managers at different levels needed to carry out these processes. The core processes were entrepreneurial (encouraging initiatives), integrative (linking and leveraging competence) and renewal (managing rationalization and revitalization). Each process needed a new management mindset to carry it out.

There are a number of entrepreneurial and managerial processes that explain how the HGRI MENA firms grow and internationalize rapidly. The elements included the international identification processes that have an overarching effect that constituted the activities of discovery, creation and evaluation of international business opportunities through managerial processes. All case companies of this study revealed the international strategic entrepreneurial process behaviour in all stages of start-up, growth, high performance and sustained high growth as they strategically internationalized into new markets. The identification of new international business opportunities, followed by the creation of new firms and the international diversification, followed by formation of international business groups, through an exploitation stage, constituted the ongoing entrepreneurial and managerial process identified in all case companies.

The international mobilization and strategic deployment of resources constituted another element in the growth process. The learning and networking processes represent international utilization of resources. The dynamic capabilities represent the resource orchestration through structuring, bundling and leveraging of firms' resources to craft competitive advantages in the face of changing international business environments. The deployment and management of resources also explains how the distributed leadership of the international entrepreneur and his entrepreneurial team reconfigure and renew the firm's resources and skills through their strategic entrepreneurial leadership abilities, as well as their entrepreneurial characteristics of innovativeness, proactiveness and acceptance of risk. This is achieved through maintaining flexibility of decision-making processes within firms to ensure a high level of dynamism without sacrificing the structural integrity of organizations. Portfolio entrepreneurship explains how international diversification enhanced the formation of entrepreneurial business groups, led by entrepreneurial teams. Case companies of this study exhibited how they turned the identification of unusual opportunities into means of competitive advantage as they employed deficiencies to their own benefit through exploiting the availability – or rather, the non-availability – of infrastructures to construct and introduce new systems, services and products. The exploitation of these opportunities was an important element of the firm's high growth and rapid internationalization performance, through an acknowledged, enacted and empowered distributed leadership process.

CONCLUSION

This chapter has examined how distributed leadership development can be seen as a managerial and entrepreneurial process, and the role of human and social capital in its enactment. This was investigated in the context of high-growth, rapidly internationalizing MNEs from the emerging market of the MENA region. Thus, this study contributes to the literature on leadership development in entrepreneurial firms (Anderson and Gold, 2009; Leitch et al., 2009, 2010; Pittaway et al., 2009; Rae, 2009). In the context of the entrepreneurial teams' distributed leadership development, this research recognizes the role of human capital of skills, knowledge and abilities in response to challenges facing the business's entrepreneurial and managerial growth processes (Zahra and George, 2002). Additionally, the research adds to the literature on business group formation (Iacobucci and Rosa, 2005, 2010) through international diversification and the enactment of portfolio entrepreneurship (Rosa and Scott, 1999) via the development of the social capital of distributed leadership.

This research illustrates how distributed leadership operates through a constant exchange of ideas, insights, perspectives, opinions, values and concepts, about both the vision of and for the entrepreneurial firm, and the command and control of the venture (Eisenhardt and Schoonhoven, 1990). That results in a continuously evolving and growing firm which embodies the concept of a team of leaders of potential entrepreneurial minds (Ensley et al., 1998; Carland and Carland, 2012). This research examined how entrepreneurial teams engaged in distributed leadership, and how the composition of that team had a significant impact on the financial performance of the venture. Distributed leadership was shown to be composed of the visioning process, which evolves the initial and ongoing vision or idea for the venture; and of the leading process, which involves the initial and ongoing command and control of the entrepreneurial firm. Thus, distributed leadership leads to improved entrepreneurial venture performance (Ensley et al., 2006).

Furthermore, the research illustrates how business group formation leads to the formation of entrepreneurial teams to manage their companies as they grow, diversify and internationalize. It also shows how entrepreneurial team members share responsibility for leading the different multinationals, thus allowing each member of the team to contribute their strengths to the team, and providing an opportunity for the members of the team to use each other's skills and abilities to produce a greater level of insight and knowledge. Analysis of case companies illustrates a contribution to the literature of strategic entrepreneurship and portfolio entrepreneurship through the addition of the new perspective of international business concepts of distributed leadership. Efficient leadership processes were fundamental in the development and growth of the new international ventures of this study. International entrepreneurial strategic leadership enabled the HGRI MENA firms to identify, manage and exploit international business opportunities. The distributed leadership approach adopted by the lead entrepreneurs empowered the entrepreneurial team members through the international growth process. This international element in distributed leadership extends the literature of strategic entrepreneurship.

International diversification of HGRI MENA firms was shown to enhance the formation of international entrepreneurial business groups in the entire population of 108 companies of this study. The high growth was sustained through international diversification and differentiation by entrepreneurs who introduced new business models and started new additional firms. This international element of distributed leadership in diversification and formation of business groups extends the literature of portfolio entrepreneurship. Findings from this study underlined the importance of the formation of entrepreneurial teams to the international growth, diversification and success of their business groups. This research revealed that international entrepreneurial teams enabled the founders to form, grow and sustain new internationally diverse companies due to their shareholding presence and distributed leadership in these HGRI firms. The international element of distributed leadership in entrepreneurial teams extends the literature of portfolio entrepreneurship.

This research makes a contribution to the concept of distributed leadership as it connects in a meaningful way with the experiences and aspirations of leadership practitioners (Harris and Spillane, 2008) from the HGRI MENA region firms. However, the key contribution of distributed leadership is not in offering a replacement for other accounts, but in enabling the recognition of a variety of forms of leadership in a more integrated and systemic manner (Bolden, 2011). This research on distributed leadership explicitly recognizes the inherently political nature of leadership within organizations (Gordon, 2010), and has demonstrated its applicability during the different stages of growth of the rapid internationalizing multinational firms from the emerging markets of the MENA region. However, it remains the case that the concept of distributed leadership needs to be explored in further empirical research in a wider range of entrepreneurial contexts.

NOTES

1. Other stock exchanges including London, New York, Zurich, Geneva and Berlin were also consulted.
2. The *Financial Times* (FT), the British international business newspaper, which specializes in international business and financial news. The FT provides full daily reports on the London Stock Exchange and world markets. *Fortune*, the global business magazine, known for its annual Fortune Global which features ranking the top corporations worldwide as measured by revenue. The flagship publication *Forbes*, the bi-weekly magazine, and its online source for the latest business and financial news and analysis, covers personal finance, lifestyle, technology and stock markets. The World's Billionaires list based on the annual ranking of the world's wealthiest people is compiled and published by *Forbes* magazine. The Forbes Global 2000 is an annual ranking of the top 2000 public companies in the world. The ranking is based on a mix of four metrics: sales, profit, assets and market value (in billion dollars). The Forbes Global 2000 companies are the biggest, most powerful listed companies in the world. *The Economist*: articles of the weekly newspaper focusing on international business news and opinion were yet another source of information.
3. *Al Ahram, Al Kudus, Al Shark, Al Awsat, Sout Al Mal.*

REFERENCES

Amabile, T.M. (1997). Motivating creativity in organizations: on doing what you love and loving what you do. *California Management Review*, 40: 39–58.
Anderson, A. and Jack, S. (2002). The articulation of social capital in entrepreneurial networks: a glue or a lubricant. *Entrepreneurship and Regional Development*, 14: 193–210.
Anderson, L. and Gold, J. (2009). Conversations outside the comfort zone: identity formation in SME manager action learning. *Action Learning: Research and Practice*, 6: 229–42.
Ardichvili, A., Cardozo, R. and Ray, S. (2003). A theory of entrepreneurial opportunity identification and development. *Journal of Business Venturing*, 18: 105–23.

Becker, G.S. (1964). *Human Capital*. Chicago, IL: University of Chicago Press.

Beckman, C., Burton, M.D. and O'Reilly, C. (2007). Early teams: the impact of entrepreneurial team demography on VC financing and going public. *Journal of Business Venturing*, 22: 147–73.

Bell, J. (1995). The internationalisation of small computer software firms: a further challenge to 'stage' theories. *European Journal of Marketing*, 29(8): 60–75.

Bell, J., McNaughton, J., Young, R. and Crick, D. (2003). Towards an integrative model of small firm internationalisation. *Journal of International Entrepreneurship*, 1: 339–62.

Bolden, R. (2011). Distributed leadership in organizations: a review of theory and research. *International Journal of Management Reviews*, 13, 251–69.

Bourdieu, P. (1986). The forms of capital. In J.G. Richardson (ed.), *Handbook of Theory and Research for Sociology of Education*. New York, NY: Greenwood, pp. 241–58.

Burt, R.S. (1992). *Structural Holes*. Cambridge, MA: Harvard University Press.

Carland, J.C. and Carland, J.W. (2012). A model of shared entrepreneurial leadership. *Academy of Entrepreneurship Journal*, 18(2): 71–81.

Chen, M-H. (2007). Entrepreneurial leadership and new ventures: creativity in entrepreneurial teams. *Creativity and Innovation Management*, 16: 239–49.

Coleman, J.S. (1988). Social capital in the creation of human capital. *American Journal of Sociology*, 94(Suppl.): 95–120.

Coleman, J.S. (1990). *Foundations of Social Theory*. Cambridge, MA: Belknap Press.

Cooper, A.C. and Daily, C.M. (1997). Entrepreneurial team. In D.L. Sexton and R.W. Smilor (eds), *Entrepreneurship*. Chicago, IL: Upstart Pub. Co., pp. 127–50.

Cope, J., Kempster, S. and Parry, K. (2011). Exploring distributed leadership in the small business context. *International Journal of Management Reviews*, 13: 270–285.

Coviello, N.E. and Munro, H.J. (1995). Growing the entrepreneurial firm: networking for international market development. *European Journal of Marketing*, 29: 49–61.

Coviello, N.E. and Munro, H.J. (1997). Network relationships and the internationalisation process of small software firms. *International Business Review*, 6: 361–86.

Covin, J.G. and Slevin, D.P. (2002). The entrepreneurial imperatives of strategic leadership. In M.A. Hitt, R.D. Ireland, S.M. Camp and D.L. Sexton (eds), *Strategic Entrepreneurship: Creating A New Mindset*. Oxford: Blackwell Publishers, pp. 309–27.

Currie, G., Lockett, A. and Suhomlinova, O. (2009). Leadership and institutional change in the public sector: the case of secondary schools. *Leadership Quarterly*, 20: 664–79.

Davidsson, P. and Honig, B. (2003). The role of social and human capital among nascent entrepreneurs. *Journal of Business Venturing*, 18: 301–31.

Day, D.V. (2000). Leadership development: a review in context. *Leadership Quarterly*, 11: 581–613.

Debrulle, J., Maes, J. and Sels, L. (2010). Organizational absorptive capacity: an empirical exploration of the role of the entrepreneur's human and social capital. Paper presented to 7th AGSE International Entrepreneurship Research Exchange Conference.

Dubini, P. and Aldrich, H. (1991). Personal and extended networks are central to the entrepreneurial process. *Journal of Business Venturing*, 6: 305–13.

Easterby-Smith, M., Thorpe, R. and Lowe, A. (1991). *Management Research: An Introduction*. London: Sage.

Edwards, G. (2011). Concepts of community: a framework for contextualizing distributed leadership. *International Journal of Management Reviews*, 13: 301–12.

Eisenhardt, K.M. and Graebner, M. (2007). Theory building from cases: opportunities and challenges. *Academy of Management Journal*, 50: 25–32.

Eisenhardt, K.M. and Schoonhoven, C.B. (1990). Organizational growth: linking founding team, strategy, environment, and growth among US semiconductor ventures, 1978–1988. *Administrative Science Quarterly*, 35: 504–29.

Ensley, M.D., Carland, J.A. and Carland, J.W. (1998). The effect of entrepreneurial team skill heterogeneity and functional diversity on new venture performance. *Journal of Business and Entrepreneurship*, 10(1): 1–14.

Ensley, M.D., Hmieleski, K.M. and Pearce, C.L. (2006). The importance of vertical and shared leadership within new venture top management teams: implications for the performance of startups. *Leadership Quarterly*, 17(3): 217–31.

Ghoshal, S. and Bartlett, C.A. (1995). Changing the role of top management: beyond structure to processes. *Harvard Business Review*, January–February 1995: 86–96.

Gordon, R.D. (2010). Dispersed leadership: exploring the impact of antecedent forms of power using a communicative framework. *Management Communication Quarterly*, 24: 260–287.

Gosling, J., Bolden, R. and Petrov, G. (2009). Distributed leadership in higher education: what does it accomplish?. *Leadership*, 5: 299–310.

Gronn, P. (2002). Distributed leadership as a unit of analysis. *Leadership Quarterly*, 13: 423–51.

Gronn, P. (2006). The significance of distributed leadership. *Educational Leadership Research*, 7 (30 October).

Gronn, P. (2008). Hybrid leadership. In K. Leithwood, B. Mascall and T. Strauss (eds), *Distributed Leadership According to the Evidence*. Abingdon: Routledge, pp. 17–40.

Gronn, P. (2009). Leadership configurations. *Leadership*, 5: 381–94.

Gronn, P. (2010). Hybrid configurations of leadership. In A. Bryman, D. Collinson, K. Grint, B. Jackson and M. Uhl-Bien (eds), *The SAGE Handbook of Leadership*. London: SAGE, pp. 435–52.

Gupta, V., MacMillan, I. and Surie, G. (2004). Entrepreneurial leadership: developing and measuring a cross-cultural construct. *Journal of Business Venturing*, 19: 241–60.

Harris, A. (2005). Leading or misleading? Distributed leadership and school improvement. *Journal of Curriculum Studies*, 37: 255–65.

Harris, A. (2007). Distributed leadership: conceptual confusion and empirical reticence. *International Journal of Leadership in Education*, 10(3): 315–25.

Harris, A. (2009). Distributed leadership: what we know. In A. Harris (ed.), *Distributed Leadership: Different Perspectives*. Dordrecht: Springer, pp. 11–21.

Harris, A. and Spillane, J. (2008). Distributed leadership through the looking glass. *Management in Education*, 22: 31–4.

Hatem, O. (2012). High growth and rapid internationalisation of firms from emerging markets: the case of the Middle East and North Africa. PhD Thesis, University of Edinburgh.

Hitt, M.A. and Ireland, R.D. (2002). The essence of strategic leadership: managing human and social capital. *Journal of Leadership and Organizational Studies*, 9: 3–14.

Iacobucci, D. and Rosa, P. (2005). Growth, diversification and business group formation in entrepreneurial firms. *Small Business Economics*, 25(1): 65–82.

Iacobucci, D. and Rosa, P. (2010). The growth of business groups by habitual entrepreneurs: the role of entrepreneurial teams. *Entrepreneurship Theory and Practice*, 34(2): 351–77.

Ibrahim, A.B. and Goodwin, J.R. (1986). Perceived causes of success in small business. *American Journal of Small Business*, Fall: 41–50.

Iles, P. and Preece, D. (2006). Developing leaders or developing leadership? The Academy of Chief Executives' programme in the North East of England. *Leadership*, 2: 317–40.

Ireland, R.D., Hitt, M.A., Camp, S.M. and Sexton, D.L. (2001). Integrating entrepreneurship and strategic management actions to create firm wealth. *Academy of Management Executive*, 15(1): 49–63.

Jack, S., Drakopoulou, S. and Anderson, A. (2008). Change and the development of entrepreneurial networks over time: A processual perspective. *Entrepreneurship and Regional Development*, 20(2): 125–59.

James, K.T., Mann, J. and Creasy, J. (2007). Leaders as lead learners: a case example of facilitating collaborative leadership learning for school leaders. *Management Learning*, 38: 79–94.

Kempster, S. and Cope, J. (2010). Learning to lead in the entrepreneurial context. *International Journal of Entrepreneurial Behaviour and Research*, 16: 5–34.

Kirk, J. and Miller, M. (1986). *Reliability and Validity in Qualitative Research*. Beverly Hills, CA: SAGE.

Kuivalainen, O. and Bell, J. (2004). Knowledge-based view of the firm and small firm interna-tionalisation. *Proceedings of the 7th McGill Conference on International Entrepreneurship*, Montreal, Canada, September.

Kuratko, D.F. (2007). Entrepreneurial leadership in the 21st century. *Journal of Leadership and Organizational Studies*, 13(4): 1–11.

Kuratko, D.F. (2009). *Entrepreneurship: Theory, Process, Practice*, 8th edition. Mason, OH: Southwestern/Cengage Publishers.

Kvale, S. (1996). *Interviews: An Introduction to Qualitative Research Interviewing.* Thousand Oaks, CA: SAGE.

Leitch, C., Hill, F. and Neergaard, H. (2010). Entrepreneurial and business growth and the quest for a 'comprehensive theory': tilting at windmills. *Entrepreneurship: Theory and Practice*, 34: 249–60.

Leitch, C.M., McMullan, C. and Harrison, R.T. (2009). Leadership development in SMEs: an action learning approach. *Action Learning: Research and Practice*, 6: 243–64.

Leitch, C., McMullan, C. and Harrison, R. (2013). The development of entrepreneurial lead-ership: the role of human, social and institutional capital. *British Journal of Management*, 24: 347–66.

Leithwood, K., Mascall, B. and Strauss, T. (2009). New perspectives on an old idea: a short history of the old idea. In K. Leithwood, B. Mascall and T. Strauss (eds), *Distributed Leadership According to the Evidence.* Abingdon: Routledge, pp. 1–14.

Liden, R.C. and Antonakis, J. (2009). Considering context in psychological leadership research. *Human Relations*, 62: 1587–605.

Lin, N. (2001). *Social Capital: A Theory of Social Structure and Action.* New York, NY: Cambridge University Press.

Loane, S. and Bell, J. (2006). Rapid internationalisation among entrepreneurial firms in Australia, Canada, Ireland and New Zealand: an extension to the network approach. *International Marketing Review*, 23(5): 467–45.

Loane, S., McNaughton, R. and Bell, J. (2004). The internationalization trajectories of entre-preneurial Internet start-ups: evidence from Europe and North America. *Canadian Journal of Administrative Science*, 21(1): 1–18.

Long, W. (1983). The meaning of entrepreneurship. *American Journal of Small Business*, 8: 47–59.

MacMillan, I.C., Zeemann, L. and Narasimha, P.N.S. (1987). Criteria distinguishing suc-cessful from unsuccessful ventures in the venture screening process. *Journal of Business Venturing*, 2: 123–37.

Miles, M.B. and Huberman, A.M. (1994). *Qualitative Data Analysis: An Expanded Sourcebook*, 2nd edition. Thousand Oaks, CA: SAGE.

Oviatt, B. and McDougall, P. (1994). Toward a theory of international new ventures. *Journal of International Business Studies*, 25(1): 45–64.

Oviatt, B.M. and McDougall, P.P. (2005). Defining international entrepreneurship and modelling the speed of internationalization. *Entrepreneurship Theory and Practice*, 29(5): 537–53.

Peng, M. and Luo, Y. (2000). Managerial ties and firm performance in a transition economy: the nature of a micro-macro link. *Academy of Management Journal*, 43(3): 486–501.

Pittaway, L., Missing, C., Hudson, N. and Maragh, D. (2009). Entrepreneurial learning through action: a case study of the Six-Squared program. *Action Learning: Research and Practice*, 6: 265–88.

Putnam, R.D. (2000). *Bowling Alone. The Collapse and Revival of American Community.* New York, NY: Simon & Schuster.

Rae, D. (2009). Connecting entrepreneurial and action learning in student-initiated new business ventures: the case of SPEED. *Action Learning: Research and Practice*, 6: 289–304.

Reich, R.B. (1987). Entrepreneurship reconsidered: the team as hero. *Harvard Business Review*, May–June: 1–8.

Renko, M., El Tarabishy, A., Carsrud, A. and Brännback, M. (2013). Understanding and measuring entrepreneurial leadership style. *Journal of Small Business Management*, 53(1), 54–74. doi: 10.1111/jsbm.1208.

Rickards, T. and Moger, S. (2006). Creative leaders: a decade of contributions from *Creativity and Innovation Management Journal*. *Creativity and Management Journal*, 15: 4–18.

Rosa, P. (1998). Entrepreneurial processes of business cluster formation and growth by 'habitual' entrepreneurs. *Entrepreneurship Theory and Practice*, 22 (4): 43–62.

Rosa, P. and Scott, M. (1999). The prevalence of multiple owners and directors in the SME sector: implications for our understanding of start-up and growth. *Entrepreneurship and Regional Development*, 11(1): 21–38.

Ross, L., Rix, M. and Gold, J. (2005a). Learning distributed leadership: Part 1. *Industrial and Commercial Training*, 37: 130–137.

Ross, L., Rix, M. and Gold, J. (2005b). Learning distributed leadership: Part 2. *Industrial and Commercial Training*, 37: 224–31.

Sapienza, H.J., Herron, L. and Menendez, J. (1991). Strategic management's potential contributions to a theory of entrepreneurship. *Entrepreneurship Theory and Practice*, 6: 73–90.

Schultz, T.W. (1961). Investment in human capital. *American Economic Review*, 51: 1–17.

Silverman, D. (2000). *Doing qualitative research: A practical handbook*. Thousand Oaks, CA and London: Sage.

Silverman, D. (2006). *Interpreting Qualitative Data: Methods for Analyzing Talk, Text and Interaction*, 6th edition. Thousand Oaks, CA and London: SAGE.

Spillane, J.P. (2006). *Distributed Leadership*. San Francisco, CA: Jossey-Bass.

Spillane, J. and Diamond, J.B. (2007a). *Distributed Leadership in Practice*. New York, NY: Teachers College Press.

Spillane, J.P. and Diamond, J.B. (2007b). Taking a distributed perspective. In J.P. Spillane and J.B. Diamond (eds), *Distributed Leadership in Practice*. New York, NY: Teachers College Press, pp. 1–15.

Thurston, P.W. and Clift, R.T. (1996). *Distributed Leadership: School Improvement through Collaboration*. Greenwich, CT: JAI Press.

Watson, W.E., Ponthieu, L.D. and Critelli, J.W. (1995). Team interpersonal process effectiveness in venture partnerships and its connection to perceived success. *Journal of Business Venturing*, 10: 393–411.

Wernerfelt, B. (1984). A resource-based view of the firm. *Strategic Management Journal*, 5(2): 171–80.

West, G.P. (2007). Collective cognition: when entrepreneurial teams, not individuals, make decisions. *Entrepreneurship Theory and Practice*, 31(1): 77–102.

Wiklund, J. and Shepherd, D. (2003). Knowledge-based resources, entrepreneurial orientation, and the performance of small and medium-sized business. *Strategic Management Journal*, 24: 1307–14.

Wiklund, J. and Shepherd, D.A. (2008). Portfolio entrepreneurship: habitual and novice founders, new entry, and mode of organizing. *Entrepreneurship Theory and Practice*, 32: 701–25.

Wright, M. (2009). Strategic entrepreneurship, Cited in D.F. Kuratko and D.B. Audretsch, Strategic Entrepreneurship: Exploring Different Perspectives of an Emerging Concept. *Entrepreneurship, Theory and Practice*, 33(1): 13–14.

Yammarino, F. and Dansereau, F. (2008). Multi-level nature of and multi-level approaches to leadership. *Leadership Quarterly*, 19: 135–41.

Yin, R. (2009). *Case Study Research: Design and Methods*, 2nd edition. Thousand Oaks, CA: SAGE.

Youngs, H. (2009). (Un)critical times? Situating distributed leadership in the field. *Journal of Educational Administration and History*, 41: 377–89.

Zahra, S.A. and George, G. (2002). International entrepreneurship: the current status of the field and future research agenda. In M. Hitt, D. Ireland, D. Sexton and M. Camp (eds), *Strategic Entrepreneurship: Creating an Integrated Mindset*, Strategic Management Series. Oxford: Blackwell, pp. 255–88.

13. Gender differences in leadership and collective entrepreneurship behaviour of Nigerian entrepreneurs
Adebimpe Adesua-Lincoln and Jane Croad

INTRODUCTION

It is becoming increasingly important to study the difference between male and female entrepreneurs due to the soaring influx of Nigerian women into entrepreneurship witnessed in recent decades (Woldie and Adersua, 2004). A 2012 study conducted by the Global Entrepreneurship Monitor (GEM) Women's Report shows that there are about equal levels of entrepreneurial engagement between Nigerian men and women. The study shows that almost 40 per cent of women in Nigeria are engaged in entrepreneurial activity (GEM, 2012). The influx of women into entrepreneurship is also reported on a global scale. The Women's Report carried out by the Global Entrepreneurship Monitor shows that an estimated 98 million women were running established businesses and 126 million were starting or running new businesses, in 67 economies around the world (GEM, 2012). The impact of such studies is of significant importance to countries such as Nigeria where lack of credible research makes any meaningful comparison challenging. In Nigeria, entrepreneurship is often the only option for those seeking an income to overcome poverty and unemployment. For example, the unemployment rate in Nigeria is a staggering 23.90 per cent (National Bureau of Statistics, 2014).

Despite the importance of entrepreneurship in overcoming poverty and unemployment and in enabling sustainable economic growth and development, the Nigerian small and medium-sized enterprise (SME) sector is plagued with challenges. It is characterised by low productivity, inability to compete with imports, lack of diversification, unfavourable business environment, infrastructural deficiencies, corruption, low access to and high cost of finance, and weak institutions (OECD, 2005). Although many of these constraints are shared by both female and male entrepreneurs, women entrepreneurs face additional obstacles rooted in discriminatory socio-cultural values and traditions (UNIDO, 2001; Woldie and Adersua, 2004). Nigeria is a patriarchal society and entrepreneurship in Nigeria remains a traditionally male-dominated activity, and consequently women encounter significant obstacles compared to their male counterparts. Women often lack the skills, education and support systems that can expedite their business pursuits. A report published by GEM (2012) shows that the level of education for women entrepreneurs is lower than that of their male counterparts. Women's inferior education and lack of training puts them at a disadvantage, and women are regarded as subordinate to men regardless of their age or educational status (Woldie and Adersua, 2004). Gender roles are still prevalent in many countries around the world (GEM, 2012), and Nigeria is no exception. Traditional female roles are still highly regarded, and such qualities as subservience, supportiveness and submissiveness meet with approval. Socio-cultural practices in many parts of Nigeria relegate women to secondary positions as wives and mothers, and in many instances women are unable to occupy comparable positions to men. Furthermore, women's prevalent position within the family makes it challenging for them to combine their various roles, and female entrepreneurs often juggle both family needs and entrepreneurship demands (Woldie and Adersua, 2004; GEM, 2012).

In a developing country such as Nigeria, the concern for increasing women's economic participation can be seen within the wider general concern to alleviate the socio-economic conditions of poor households. The growth and prosperity of any economy is highly dependent on dynamic entrepreneurial activity. In order to stimulate this activity, an economy needs individuals with the abilities and motivations to start businesses, and people participating at every phase of this process (GEM, 2012). Furthermore, entrepreneurial activities provide a unique avenue for many women to thrive economically, thereby rising above many of the socio-cultural obstacles (Woldie and Adersua, 2004; Lincoln, 2012). Entrepreneurship is a dynamic field, particularly as it relates to the process of change creation and vision. The entrepreneurs' vision to recognise opportunities and willingness to take calculated risks and formulate an effective venture team are critical factors needed for success (Kuratko and Hodgetts, 2007). In light of recent economic downturns there is now recognition that the ability to increase global wealth is dependent to an extent on the development of successful entrepreneurship in transition economies. Transition economies such as the MINT economies (a neologism which refers to the economies of Mexico, Indonesia, Nigeria and Turkey) are predicted to become substantial contributors to the global economy and gross domestic product (GDP). The importance of the SME sector to these economies has also been recognised. The prominence of the sector is matched by the appreciation of its unique role as one of the most vital contributors to people's income and to economic development and innovation. SMEs are perceived to be the seedbed for indigenous entrepreneurship and are known to generate many small investments; thus encouraging entrepreneurship is a key policy instrument for promoting economic growth and employment creation in Africa (Lincoln, 2012).

This chapter explores gender differences in Nigerian men and women's leadership practices and collective entrepreneurial behaviour. The rationale for this study stems from the fact that very little is known about the leadership practices and collective entrepreneurial behaviour of Nigerian entrepreneurs. Research generalising empirical findings from other countries within the Nigerian entrepreneurship context is lacking; the current study aims to redress this deficiency in the literature. Furthermore, in spite of the importance of the leader in entrepreneurial activities, very little research has been carried out which combines the two concepts (Patterson et al., 2012; Leitch et al., 2013). Writers such as Miller and Friesen (1984) and Gartner et al. (1992) call for convergence of the twin concepts of entrepreneurship and leadership in a bid to achieve better understanding of theoretical developments in the field (Cogliser and Brigham, 2004; Patterson et al., 2012). Kuratko (2007) notes that entrepreneurial leadership is becoming a global necessity; however, he calls for more understanding of the elements that comprise the concept in order that we can obtain more clarity and advance the concept.

Additionally, limited attention has been devoted to the gendered nature of entrepreneurial leadership (Gupta et al., 2004; Kuratko, 2007). In fact there is a dearth of such research in the Nigerian context, and a large number of questions remain unanswered. Patterson et al. (2012) call for detailed examination of women's entrepreneurial leadership practices in light of society's expectation of their role. There is also evidence of a gendered perspective in both the entrepreneurship and leadership literatures (Cogliser and Brigham, 2004; Marlow et al., 2009; Mavin, 2009). In recent times, academic literature has witnessed an increase in studies focusing on the existence or otherwise of gender differences in the leadership behaviour of men and women, and there are calls for more studies to gain insights into gender-based leadership across cultures, and the importance of leadership practices of male and female entrepreneurs in fostering work teams and collective entrepreneurship. For example, researchers such as Pounder and Coleman (2002), Cole (2004) and Andersen and Hansson (2011) argue that gender does not determine leadership behaviour, while a range of other studies posit that there are more commonalities than differences between men and women. In addition, Eagly and Johnson (1990) suggest that leadership research provides an excellent opportunity to determine whether the behaviour of leaders is gender-stereotypic. However, there is now a considerable body of evidence which demonstrates that women leaders have unique characteristics which differ from those possessed by their male counterparts (Eagly and Johnson, 1990; Helgesen, 1990a; Bass and Avolio, 1994; Rosener, 1995; Bass et al., 1996; Maher, 1997; Butterfield and Grinnell, 1999; Book, 2000; Casimir, 2001; Eagly et al., 2003; Trinidad and Normore, 2005; Northouse, 2007).

Eagly et al. (2003) assert that the possibility that women and men differ in their typical leadership behaviour is important, because leaders' own behaviour is a major determinant of their effectiveness and chances for advancement. Furthermore, a study carried out by Park (1996) demonstrated that gender is related to leadership behaviour, which in turn influences the decision style of the leader. Studies which argue for gender differences include the argument that women possess a transformational leadership style and are seen to display collaborative leadership behaviour, are considered to be more democratic, display relationship-oriented behaviour described as communal, and embrace interpersonal qualities such as sensitivity, generosity, being compassionate and showing understanding towards subordinates. On the other hand, men are considered to be more authoritarian and task-oriented and instrumental in their leadership approach (Eagly and Johnson, 1990). Women's feminine qualities such as interpersonal dexterity, malleability to conflict resolution, empathic nature and their heightened communication skills put them in an advantageous leadership position (Helgesen, 1990b; Cantor and Bernay, 1992; Rosener, 1995; Maher, 1997; Eagly et al., 2003; Patterson et al., 2012).

Our chapter explores gender differences between Nigerian men and women entrepreneurs' leadership and collective entrepreneurial behaviour. It makes two primary contributions to the leadership and entrepreneurship literature. First, we contribute to the call for more empirical research on entrepreneurship as a gendered process (Powell and Eddleston, 2008, 2013). Second, we contribute to the theoretical understanding of leadership and entrepreneurship upon which future research within the Nigerian context can be developed. This study is the first of its kind in the Nigerian context to align research on entrepreneurship leadership and collective entrepreneurial behaviour. It seeks to provide answers to two main research questions, namely:

1. Are there differences and/or similarities in the leadership behaviour of male and female entrepreneurs in Nigeria?
2. Are there differences and/or similarities in the collective entrepreneurial behaviour of male and female entrepreneurs?

LEADERSHIP CONCEPT

Leadership is conceptualised from different perspectives. Some scholars consider leadership as a transformational process, which views leaders as instrumental in moving their followers to accomplish more than is expected of them; the leader is also considered to be strategic in group change and activity, and embodies the will of the groups (Northouse, 2010). The leadership process is interactive in nature, involving the leader's ability to influence their followers or a group of people who have a shared purpose. Consequently, the importance of a dynamic group in the leadership milieu is of strategic significance, with emphasis placed on the leader's ability to work with followers to achieve mutual goals (Rost, 1991; Northouse, 2010). Other scholars address leadership as a power relationship, or from a personality or skill-based perspective. The personality perspective embodies traits or characteristics possessed by some individuals which enable them to influence their followers to accomplish set tasks (Bass, 1990; Northouse, 2010). The skills perspective, on the other hand, views the leader as having requisite capabilities, knowledge and skills which bring about effective leadership (Northouse, 2010). The power relationship perspective views leaders as having the power and ability to effect change in their followers, by wielding their power (French and Raven, 1959). This view is supported by Burns (1978), who views leadership as an aspect of power which is also a separate and vital process in itself. Power-wielders exercise influence by mobilising their own power base in such a way as to establish direct physical control over the behaviour of others. Leadership is exercised when persons with certain motives and purpose mobilise institutional, political, psychological and other resources so as to arouse, engage and satisfy the motives of followers (Burns, 1978). Edwards et al. (2002) view leadership as the ability to use personal power to win the hearts and minds of people in order to achieve a common purpose. It also involves giving people a clear understanding of what they have to do, why and how it might be done, and generating feelings of challenge, involvement, ownership and commitment. Consequently Gill (2011) asserts that this definition implies a directive style of leadership which embodies three important principles of leadership. First, there must be a common shared mission or purpose, and clear strategies for pursuing it. Second, the hearts and minds have to be won, in the sense that the vision, mission and strategies must make sense intellectually, appeal to or create a positive emotion, and motivate or inspire followers. Third, the use of position power is abrogated in favour of gaining commitment through the use of one's personal power.

Burns (1978) defines leadership as a mobilisation process by individuals with certain motives, values and access to resources, in a context of competition and conflict in the pursuit of goals. Grint (2000) considers leaders as those in the forefront who pull followers after them whilst at the same time sharing the way rather than showing the way. As such, leadership should involve influencing others through the personality or actions of the individual leader (Lincoln, 2012). Northouse (2010: 3) defines leadership as 'a process whereby an individual influences a group of individuals to achieve a common goal'. His assertion stems from the notion that defining leadership as a process is rooted in the belief that leadership is a transactional event which exists in the exchange that occurs between the leader and their followers. Vroom (2000) states that defining leadership style requires an analysis of several factors such as the relevance of decisions, the importance of commitment, success probability, leader and group experience, group support to goal achievement, and team competency. Often-cited competencies include being enthusiastic, a champion of change and a good communicator. Furthermore, Kouzes and Posner (2002) postulate that the four most consistent characteristics of admired leaders are that they are honest, forward-looking, competent and inspiring. Rost (1991) defines leadership as a multidirectional relationship exerting influence on the followers, concerned with developing mutual purpose. Gronn (2003) is of the view that leadership is about doing the right thing. Grint (2005) states that while there is little consensus on what counts as leadership, whether it can be taught, or even how effective it might be, the recent plethora of publications of all kinds of leadership extols the need for excellence.

Leadership theories in recent years have become more vibrant and holistic by distinguishing between transformational, transactional and laissez-faire leadership styles (Burns, 1978; Bass, 1985; Bass and Avolio, 1994; Bass et al., 1996; Lowe et al., 1996; Powell and Graves, 2003; Bush, 2003). Transformational and transactional leadership dimensions are the most influential leadership theories in recent times. These dimensions of leadership also serve as the foundation upon which female and male leadership styles are distinguished (Lincoln, 2012). Rosener (1990), for example, notes that men are more likely than women to describe themselves in ways that represent transactional leadership. The perceived differences in leadership style could to a large extent explain preconceptions about women's leadership efficacy and their advancement within organisations. Transformational leadership was first devised by Downton (1973) in his *Rebel Leadership* study. This concept was revisited and extended by Burns in his seminal work titled *Leadership* in 1978. Transformational leadership, which is similar to democratic or charismatic leadership (House, 1976; Cole, 2004; Storey, 2011), involves heightened motivational levels of both the leader and followers through the leader's active engagement and connection with their followers (Northouse, 2007; Yukl, 2012). Transformational leadership involves engagement with others and the formation of connections which inspire followers and raise mutual morality levels in both the leader and followers (Burns, 1978). There is some support in academic literature that transformational leadership is the most effective, with close association to enhanced job performance and a positive mindset in followers (Lowe et al., 1996; Ehrhart and Klein, 2001).

The transformational leader is said to focus on the mission of the organisation and strategies for achieving them, and uses vision to create symbols for subordinates, thereby instigating and achieving change through communication and expressiveness (Fairhurst, 2001). This leadership style is held to be participative and relationship-oriented, involving mobilising subordinates to want to struggle for mutual aspirations, thus increasing collaboration and teamwork (Bass, 1985; Bass and Avolio, 1994; Kouzes and Posner, 2002; Bass and Riggio, 2006; Bass and Bass, 2008). Transformational leaders motivate subordinates to surpass individual self-interests for the good of the organisation by setting high performance standards and putting mechanisms in place for subordinates to achieve those standards (Powell and Graves, 2003). The need for values, morals and ethics, and long-term goal orientation is essential in aligning internal structures and systems to reinforce values and goals. Avolio (2011: 51) identifies some global distinguishing characteristics of transformational leadership. According to Avolio (2011), transformational leaders develop followers into leaders. Such leaders are said to stimulate challenge in their followers, and are moral agents who focus themselves and their followers on achieving higher-level missions and purpose. Transformational leaders however may be transactional leaders when necessary to attain their objectives (McWhinney et al., 1997; Powell and Graves, 2003; Lincoln, 2012).

Transactional leadership is often referred to as authoritative leadership (Storey, 2011). It is task-oriented, and involves a preoccupation with power and position, and a need for achievement and to get the job done (McClelland, 1961). This leadership style involves a work-for-reward attitude, with an emphasis on good performance and productivity (Cruz et al., 1999; Adesua-Lincoln, 2010). Transactional leaders focus on clarifying the responsibilities of subordinates and responding to how well subordinates execute those responsibilities (Powell and Graves, 2003). Avolio (2011) states that transactional leaders induce their followers to move in the direction they desire, and exchange promises of reward for cooperation and compliance to get the tasks done. This leadership style is dependent upon laying out contingencies through two main methods, that is, contingent rewards, or management by exception (Avolio, 2011). In relation to contingent rewards, the leader secures agreement on what needs to be done by setting work objectives and performance standards, and providing financial or psychological rewards to the followers in exchange for being able to carry out the task in a satisfactory manner. Management by exception involves a form of corrective transaction, and is said to be ineffective when used in excess. The corrective transaction may be passive or active. Where the transaction is active, the leader actively keeps track of tasks performed and monitors deviation from standards so as to take any corrective action. This involves the leader being attentive and vigilant in terms of how tasks are being performed. When passive, the leader waits for deviations or mistakes to be made and takes the necessary corrective steps to rectify the situation.

COLLECTIVE ENTREPRENEURSHIP BEHAVIOUR

Entrepreneurship is a process whereby entrepreneurs as individuals exploit market opportunity through technical and organisational innovation (Schumpeter, 1965). According to various writers such as Knight (1921) and Drucker (1970), entrepreneurship is about taking calculated risks. Collective entrepreneurship, on the other hand, involves economic relations between the entrepreneur who provides resources such as labour, skills, knowledge, experience and capital to subordinates in exchange for some share of the return in the enterprise. In addition, collective entrepreneurship involves interpersonal relationships among team members involved in the business venture. Collective entrepreneurship is thus said to encompass taking the initiative, consolidation of resources to accomplish set objectives, effective management, and autonomy and risk-taking (Mourdoukoutas, 1999). Lounsbury (1998) posits that the entrepreneur as a leader is in a unique position to affect the attitude and behaviour of their subordinates, consequently creating a condition where collective entrepreneurship can flourish. Diverse leadership styles have different influences on entrepreneurship and the manner in which entrepreneurial spirit is transmitted.

Collective entrepreneurship is said to emerge from voluntary collaboration of subordinates and work teams involved in the formation, ownership and management of a business venture (Cooney, 2005; Cruz et al., 2012). Collective entrepreneurship thus redirects attention from the commonly held perception of the entrepreneur as the hero (Reich, 1987; Soriano and Martínez, 2007) and transforms conventional business enterprises into entrepreneurial networks. To be effective, collective entrepreneurship requires a less rigid organisational structure that cultivates and nourishes individual team member creativity and imagination, rather than the imposition of a bureaucratic conformity (Mourdoukoutas, 1999). Human capital embedded in professionals is the ultimate source of sustainable competitive advantage. Collective entrepreneurship is about structures that afford the opportunity and the incentive to individuals both inside and outside conventional corporations, as well as individuals across corporations, to share and integrate technical and market information for the discovery and the exploitation of new business. As a network the team members share both the risks and the rewards associated with the discovery and exploitation of business opportunities, and are accountable for any failures (Mourdoukoutas, 1999).

In essence, the entrepreneurial networks can be seen as fluid organisational structures enjoying both economies of scale and economies of scope. Jack et al. (2008) posit that networks are essential to the entrepreneurial process; they are a 'vital living organisms, changing, growing and developing over time'. Consequently, the involvement of entrepreneurial teams in identifying, exploiting and evaluating opportunities is fundamental to their existence (Cooney, 2005; Wright and Vanaelst, 2009; Cruz et al., 2012). Entrepreneurial teams are task-oriented, creative and innovative (Beckman, 2006; Soriano and Martínez, 2007). Team members bring diverse skills such as entrepreneurial, technological and managerial skill sets proven to be essential to entrepreneurial teams. Incubator organisations and prior experience also provide entrepreneurial teams with access to ideas, opportunities and resources (Beckman, 2006; Wright and Vanaelst, 2009; Cruz et al., 2012). Through effective collaboration, individuals within the team are therefore able to work together for the mutual benefit of the team and contribute to creativity and innovation (Scott, 1999). It is also essential that entrepreneurial leaders give more consideration to leadership styles which contribute to creative collaboration and innovative firm performance (Yukl, 2002, 2012), thus enhancing the transmission of collaborative entrepreneurship and the work team (Soriano and Martínez, 2007). Using subordinates as a source of innovation requires that they are motivated to communicate their ideas and are provided with a channel for this communication (Burt, 2004; Santos and Spann, 2012).

Previous studies on leadership have produced findings consistent with the belief that diverse leadership styles have an impact on various aspects of the decision-making process such as flexibility, accountability, values and remuneration, and on organisational climate (Goleman, 2000; Appelbaum et al., 2003). A fundamental fact is that leadership behaviour influences employee attitudes in the organisation (Shamir et al., 1993; Lincoln, 2012). This is not surprising, as the entrepreneur is the single most important person who carries the responsibility for running and directing the business and ensuring day-to-day functionality is achieved (Adesua-Lincoln, 2010). In so doing, the entrepreneur is not alone, they are charged with ensuring that those employed in the business are delegated efficiently in achieving the overall vision of the business. Strong evidence exists in the entrepreneurship literature to suggest a correlation between SME performance and the individual entrepreneur. Several studies, in a bid to identify the various factors that influence SME performance, emphasise the importance of leadership behaviour of the entrepreneur in enhancing firm performance (Cogliser and Brigham, 2004). As early as the 1980s, the academic literature on leadership practices has focused to a large extent on the human factor of the leader and their effect on the organisation (Bass, 1985). Research in this area is, however, still a long way from being simplified and researchers have yet to arrive at a consensus. A common identifiable thread is that the leadership style adopted by the individual entrepreneur is integral to the growth and development of the firm (O'Farrell and Hitchens, 1989; Lincoln, 2012). For example, Jusko (2003) posits that leadership mistake is an important factor leading to business failure. This view is supported by Birley and Niktari (1996), who suggest that the causes of failure include the inflexibility or autocratic nature of the individual entrepreneur. An earlier work by Berryman (1983) reviews factors that influence small firm failure and places greater emphasis upon the managerial and personal characteristics of the owner. Berryman (1983) argues that small firms generally reflect the personalities of the entrepreneurs who created them. Berryman draws upon the work of Argenti (1976), who observes that a key defect of small firms is an autocratic chief executive who is unwilling to take advice. The present chapter seeks to explore the leadership styles of Nigerian male and female entrepreneurs in enhancing collaborative entrepreneurship, and their ability to increase team interaction within their enterprises.

RESEARCH DESIGN AND METHODOLOGY

Data for the study were collected through the use of a face-to-face questionnaire survey. The questionnaire uses a combination of closed-ended and Likert scale questions. Closed-ended questions were adopted in relation to the demographic characteristics of the male and female entrepreneurs. A five-point Likert scale was used to capture data on task-, relationship- and participative-oriented leadership practices as well as collective entrepreneurship. The five-point Likert scale questions were based on theoretical underpinnings derived from the leadership and entrepreneurship literature. The advantage of these types of questions rests on the fact that they are easier and relatively quicker to administer. Questions can be answered within a short time, and the respondents can perform with greater reliability the task of answering the questions (Oppenhiem, 1992). As a result of a lack of established data sets and records from which meaningful random sampling could be drawn, convenience sampling was used to identify the entrepreneurs who participated in the study. Convenience sampling involves the use of those readily available to participate in the study (MacNealy, 1999). Malhotra (2010) notes that the basic principle of sampling is that by selecting some of the elements in a population, a researcher can draw their own conclusion about the entire population. Consequently, the test of sample design is how well the sample structure represents the characteristics of the population it purports to be representative of (Cooper and Schindler, 2011); bias inevitably occurs where the number of subjects is too small. Babbie (2010) states that the larger a sample, the more representative of the population it becomes, and so the more reliable and valid the results based on it will become. This view is supported by Saunders et al. (2009), who note that the larger the sample size, the lower the likely error in generalising to the population. The decision was therefore made to adopt a larger sample size in order to minimise the potential bias which can often arise through convenience sampling. Consequently, a sample size of 400 was considered as an adequate and workable sample. Indeed, several studies have worked with smaller samples and have achieved satisfactory results.

From previous research conducted in Nigeria, the highest concentrations of SMEs are thought to be in Lagos state, and this state is considered as the commercial nerve centre of the country; it is also the most populated and diverse state in the country. The sample target was set in Lagos in order to make the sample more representative. In order to ensure that the sample was representative of the general population, the decision was made to focus the study in areas with a large cluster of SMEs. The sample includes male- and female-owned firms in different industries, different trading companies and companies in different geographical locations throughout Lagos in order to ensure diversity. In order to ensure validity and reliability, no leading questions were posed to the entrepreneurs. Furthermore, we based our questionnaire questions on stable sources of theory in the literature. As Gill and Johnson (2010) rightly put it, in the case of questionnaires, reliability derives from the clear formulation of questions, which facilitates understanding and hence correct answering. The Cronbach's Alpha test was also used to statistically test the internal consistency of various parts of the questionnaire (Bryman and Bell, 2011). The Cronbach Alpha coefficient in the questionnaire is 0.90. As the internal reliability value is above 0.80, the study has a satisfactory level of internal consistency.

RESULT AND ANALYSIS OF FINDINGS

The analysis of findings is divided into three subsections. The first of these provides descriptive statistics in the form of percentages and mean scores. Descriptive statistics were used to provide a general description of the demographic characteristics of the male and female entrepreneurs. The second section involves the use of exploratory factor analysis as a reduction mechanism in order to focus on the most significant correlations. Factor analysis is used in this study for a variety of reasons. It enables effective exploration of the differences between male and female entrepreneurs on an entire scale, and it serves as a reduction mechanism in order to focus on the most significant correlations. The reduced number of factors obtained from the analysis and the underlying dimensions between measured variables and latent constructs enables the formation and refinement of theoretical perspective on gender differences within the Nigerian entrepreneurial context (Thompson, 2004; Henson and Roberts, 2006). The third section of the analysis involves the use of the Mann–Whitney non-parametric test. The Mann–Whitney test was used to draw statistical inference and identify the significance of the leadership variables between the male and female entrepreneurs identified from the factor analysis carried out. In addition, mean and standard deviation were used in order to examine gender differences and similarities between the responses provided.

Demographic Characteristics of the Male and Female Entrepreneurs

As shown in Table 13.1, 53.9 percent of the entrepreneurs who took part in the study were male and 46.1 percent were female. The average entrepreneur was 31–40 and married. The finding also shows that the majority of the male and female entrepreneurs were very well educated and had previous professional experience. Many of the businesses were run as sole proprietorship businesses, and were based predominantly in the service and wholesale/commerce sector. The finding also shows that a high proportion of the businesses were between 11 and 20 years old, employing 11–20 employees. A high majority of the entrepreneurs obtained their sources of finance from family and friends and their own savings, and many were driven to self-employment as a result of financial motivation and the desire to be independent.

Factor Analysis

Exploratory factor analysis was used to establish composite variables representing elements of the leadership and collaborative entrepreneurship

Table 13.1   Demographic characteristics of male and female entrepreneurs

Demographic characteristics	%	Mean
Gender		
Male	53.9	1.46
Female	46.1	
Age		
Below 20	5.0	3.42
21–30	12.2	
31–40	38.1	
41–50	25.6	
Above 50	19.2	
Marital status		
Single	13.3	2.09
Married	73.9	
Divorced	2.8	
Widowed	10.0	
Previous working experience		
Prior SME experience	17.2	2.41
Professional (lawyers, accountants, teachers, etc.)	44.2	
Skilled manual (hairdressers, tailors, etc.)	24.7	
Unskilled manual	7.8	
Unemployed	6.1	
Academic qualifications		
Postgraduate degree (Master's, PhD)	6.9	3.43
Professional qualifications	11.9	
Bachelor's degree	24.7	
Diploma	45.6	
Secondary school qualifications	9.7	
Primary school qualifications	1.1	
Business structures		
Sole trader	60.0	1.75
Partnership	5.3	
Company	34.7	
Firm sector		
Agriculture	5.8	4.58
Mining and quarrying	4.4	
Manufacturing	7.8	

Table 13.1 (continued)

Demographic characteristics	%	Mean
Wholesale and commerce	29.7	
Construction	11.9	
Service	40.3	
Firm age		
1–5	11.9	2.45
6–10	38.3	
11–20	42.5	
Above 20	7.2	
Number of employees		
1–5	6.7	3.05
6–10	26.4	
11–20	39.4	
21–50	10.6	
Above 50	16.9	
Sources of capital		
Family and friends	40.0	2.03
Savings	38.1	
Informal sources of finance	0.8	
Formal sources of finance	21.1	
Motivation for firm set-up		
Desire to be independent	27.2	2.74
Threat of unemployment	9.2	
Financial motivation	48.1	
Job satisfaction	6.7	
Self-fulfilment	0.8	
Attractive lifestyle	3.3	
Helping to create employment in Nigeria	4.7	

scale. All the assumptions for exploratory factor analysis were met (see Table 13.2). The Bartlett's test of sphericity = 27788.613, $p < 0.00$. The Kaiser–Meyer–Olkin value (KMO = 0.75) also suggests that the data can be used appropriately for factor analysis.

Principal axis of extraction with non-orthogonal rotation, that is, direct oblimin, was conducted in order to determine construct validity. The exploratory factor analysis yielded a three-factor solution accounting for 64 per cent of the variance with eigenvalues greater than 1. The scree plot in Figure 13.1 also shows a clear inflection at three factors.

Table 13.2   KMO and Bartlett's test

Kaiser–Meyer–Olkin measure of sampling adequacy		0.751
Bartlett's test of sphericity	Approx. chi-square	27788.613
	Df	903
	Sig.	0.000

Scree Plot

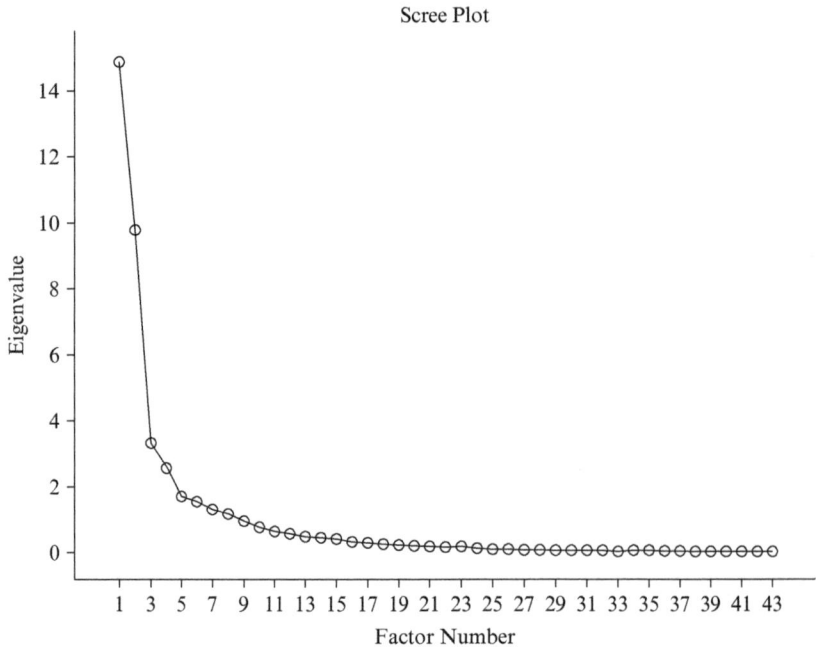

Figure 13.1   Scree plot of leadership factors

The initial eigenvalue total score for Factor 1 is 34.179, Factor 2 is 22.326, and Factor 3 is 7.253. Table 13.3 shows the final rotated factors. The variables loaded mainly on one factor each, and as such are distinguishable when considering the specific variables. Factor 2 loaded more items compared to Factor 1 and Factor 3.

The items retained for each factor show that six items measuring relationship-oriented leadership practices loaded on Factor 1 labelled RTL1–6. The items relate to a keen interest in fostering a relationship of support and collaboration with subordinates and teams, and increased collaboration through communication. In addition, Factor 2 contained nine items

Table 13.3   Factor loading

Leadership variables	Factor		
	1	2	3
RTL1: Members of the team should identify themselves with the organisation and the team	0.887		
RTL2: I often put satisfactory work above my own needs	0.857		
RTL3: I believe that my behaviour as a leader allows subordinates to be more satisfied and willing to contribute to the team	0.817		
RTL4: I attempt to increase collaboration and work teams and group tasks	0.792		
RTL5: My behaviour includes support, development, recognition and consultation with my subordinates and team members	0.766		
RTL6: My attitude demonstrates a keen interest in people and their relationships	0.678		
TTL1: Only the leader is in the position to offer a new approach or solution to problems		0.937	
TTL2: The leader should always keep his/her distance from subordinates		0.926	
TTL3: The leader should define the regulations of their subordinates, explaining what to do, why and how tasks should be performed		0.902	
TTL4: The function of the leader is to supervise subordinates closely in order to attain formally pre-established goals and objectives		0.874	
TTL5: As a leader I often encourage my subordinates to carry out work or tasks in line with standard procedures and regulations		0.861	
TTL6: As a leader I often criticise unsatisfactory work and I always focus on the failings of my subordinates		0.815	

Table 13.3 (continued)

Leadership variables	Factor		
	1	2	3
TTL7: I believe that subordinates and group members should have a feeling of dependency towards the leader		0.790	
TTL8: I am task oriented and I often define and structure my own rules and those of my subordinates		0.758	
TTL9: The leader is the individual hero that contributes to reaching a certain level of entrepreneurship in teams as an individual business person		0.717	
PTLCE1: I believe that when the leader backs up the actions of the subordinate it increases motivation in the work place			-0.893
PTLCE2: I believe that if the leader were to stimulate positive attitude towards the firm, work and personal relationships in their daily attitudes and behaviour, this would produce an increase in collaborative entrepreneurship			-0.840
PTLCE3: I believe that when the leader backs up the actions of the subordinates it improves commitment within the team and encourages a positive attitude towards the leader			-0.831
PTLCE4: I believe that when the leader modifies his/her behaviour and attitude towards a more personal relationship, it would improve subordinate behaviour and attitude towards work and teams			-0.807
PTLCE5: The leader should constantly back up the actions of subordinates and work teams			-0.775
PTLCE6: When a collaborative attitude is adopted, communication is improved and problem solving encouraged	0.519		-0.610

Table 13.3   (continued)

Leadership variables	Factor		
	1	2	3
PTLCE7: The leader should enhance the team through their own collaborative attitude and behaviour	0.570		-0.599
PTLCE8: I use the daily activity of my team/subordinates to help increase mutual obligation and responsibility and personal interaction between team members			-0.598

measuring tasks-oriented leadership practices. The items labelled TTL1–9 focus on the leader and their role in defining tasks, goals and objectives. The items in Factor 2 also include the leader actively supervising employees and criticising unsatisfactory work. Finally, Factor 3 contains eight items measuring participation leadership practices and collaborative entrepreneurship. This factor was labelled PTLCE1–8, related to a keen interest in promoting a close relationship between the leader and their subordinates, and also the need to foster subordinate participation in key organisation functions. The items in Factor 3 include the leader's attitude and behaviour in fostering collaborative entrepreneurship, enhanced subordinate motivation through the leader's support, collaborative attitude in ensuring effective communication and problem-solving, and using daily work activities in increasing team interaction within the organisation.

Descriptive and Inferential Analysis

Assessment of the mean value in Table 13.4 shows that both the male and female entrepreneurs agree with all of the items in Factor 1. The items in Factor 1 relate to transformational leadership, building a relationship of support and collaboration with subordinates and teams, and increased collaboration through communication. The finding obtained from the Mann–Whitney (M-W) test shows that the responses provided by female entrepreneurs differ to an extent from responses emphasised by the male entrepreneurs. The finding confirms that there are gender differences in relation to the following statements: RTL2: 'I often put satisfactory work above my own needs'; RTL3: 'I believe that my behaviour as a leader allows subordinates to be more satisfied and willing to contribute to the

Table 13.4   Mean score of responses obtained from the male and female entrepreneurs in relation to Factor 1

Leadership response (1 = strongly disagree, 2 = disagree, 3 = neutral, 4 = agree, 5 = strongly agree)	M-W asymp. sig. (two-tailed)	Gender	N	Group mean	Std.	Mean rank
Members of the team should identify themselves with the organisation and the team	0.57	Male	194	3.84	1.02	183.25
		Female	166	3.80	0.96	177.29
I often put satisfactory work above my own needs	0.00	Male	194	3.92	0.98	158.25
		Female	166	4.33	0.93	206.51
I believe that my behaviour as a leader allows subordinates to be more satisfied and willing to contribute to the team	0.00	Male	194	3.72	0.94	164.08
		Female	166	4.01	0.86	199.69
I attempt to increase collaboration and work teams and group tasks	0.47	Male	194	3.68	0.93	177.10
		Female	166	3.75	0.88	184.47
My behaviour includes support, development, recognition and consultation with my subordinates and team members	0.02	Male	194	3.45	0.94	169.83
		Female	166	3.72	0.90	192.97
My attitude demonstrates a keen interest in people and their relationships	0.00	Male	194	3.74	0.99	156.10
		Female	166	4.20	1.05	209.02

team'; and RTL6: 'My attitude demonstrates a keen interest in people and their relationships'. The three statements are very significant at (0.00). Statement RTL5: 'My behaviour includes support, development, recognition and consultation with my subordinates and team members', is also significant at (0.02). The test results indicate that there was no significant difference in the responses provided by the male and female entrepreneurs in relation to statement RTL1: 'Members of the team should identify themselves with the organisation and the team'; and RTL4: 'I attempt to increase collaboration and work teams and group tasks'. A close examination of the group mean shows that female entrepreneurs adopt a more transformational leadership style, are more supportive and have a stronger desire for building a close relationship with their subordinate and work teams than male entrepreneurs.

Table 13.5 reveals notable differences and similarities between the male and female entrepreneurs. The items in the table reflect tasks and transactional leadership practices. The M-W results indicate that there are no statistically significant differences between male and female entrepreneurs in relation to the following statements: TTL1: 'Only the leader is in the position to offer a new approach or solution to problems'; TTL2: 'The leader should always keep his/her distance from subordinates'; TTL4: 'The function of the leader is to supervise subordinates closely in order to attain formally pre-established goals and objectives'; TTL6: 'As a leader I often criticise unsatisfactory work and I always focus on the failings of my subordinates'; and TTL9: 'The leader is the individual hero that contributes to reaching a certain level of entrepreneurship in teams as an individual business person'. However, the M-W test shows significant differences in relation to the following statements: TTL3: 'The leader should define the regulations of their subordinates, explaining what to do, why and how tasks should be performed'; TTL5: 'As a leader I often encourage my subordinates to carry out work or tasks in line with standard procedures and regulations'; TTL7: 'I believe that subordinates and group members should have a feeling of dependency towards the leader'; and TTL8: 'I am task oriented and I often define and structure my own rules and those of my subordinates'. TTL3, TTL5 and TTL8 are very significant at (0.00); item TTL7 is also significant at (0.02). The result of the mean rank shows that male entrepreneurs had a higher mean rank than female entrepreneurs in relation to items TTL3, TTL5 and TTL7. Female entrepreneurs had a higher mean rank in relation to item TTL8, indicating that the female entrepreneurs are task-oriented.

An overall male advantage can be seen in relation to many of the items in Factor 3, as shown in Table 13.6. The result of the M-W test shows statistically significant differences (0.00) in the responses provided by the

*Table 13.5   Mean score of responses obtained from the male and female
entrepreneurs in relation to Factor 2*

Leadership response (1 = strongly disagree, 2 = disagree, 3 = neutral, 4 = agree, 5 = strongly agree)	M-W asymp. sig. (two-tailed)	Gender	N	Group mean	Std.	Mean rank
Only the leader is in the position to offer a new approach or solution to problems	0.10	Male	194	4.07	1.07	188.12
		Female	166	3.89	1.18	171.59
The leader should always keep his/ her distance from subordinates	0.71	Male	194	3.80	1.21	178.71
		Female	166	3.88	1.19	182.59
The leader should define the regulations of their subordinates, explaining what to do, why and how tasks should be performed	0.00	Male	194	3.97	1.14	196.29
		Female	166	3.61	1.12	162.05
The function of the leader is to supervise subordinates closely in order to attain formally pre-established goals and objectives	0.38	Male	194	3.86	1.20	176.32
		Female	166	4.06	0.83	185.38
As a leader I often encourage my subordinates to carry out work or tasks in line with standard procedures and regulations	0.00	Male	194	4.11	1.04	196.14
		Female	166	3.78	1.09	162.23
As a leader I often criticise unsatisfactory work and I always focus on the failings of my subordinates	0.17	Male	194	3.74	1.15	187.11
		Female	166	3.61	0.98	172.77
I believe that subordinates and group members should have a feeling of dependency towards the leader	0.02	Male	194	3.85	1.31	191.67
		Female	166	3.73	0.97	167.45

Table 13.5   (continued)

Leadership response (1 = strongly disagree, 2 = disagree, 3 = neutral, 4 = agree, 5 = strongly agree)	M-W asymp. sig. (two-tailed)	Gender	N	Group mean	Std.	Mean rank
I am task oriented and I often define and structure my own rules and those of my subordinates	0.00	Male	194	3.58	1.43	167.93
		Female	166	3.89	1.39	195.19
The leader is the individual hero that contributes to reaching a certain level of entrepreneurship in teams as an individual business person	0.42	Male	194	3.75	1.17	176.59
		Female	166	3.91	0.73	185.07

male and female entrepreneurs in relation to the following statements: PTLCE1: 'I believe that when the leader backs up the actions of the subordinate it increases motivation in the work place'; PTLCE5: 'The leader should constantly back up the actions of subordinates and work teams'; PTLCE6: 'When a collaborative attitude is adopted, communication is improved and problem solving encouraged'; PTLCE7: 'The leader should enhance the team through their own collaborative attitude and behaviour'; and PTLCE8: 'I use the daily activity of my team/subordinates to help increase mutual obligation and responsibility and personal interaction between team members'. The group mean values show that male entrepreneurs scored higher than female entrepreneurs in all the statistically significant items. This finding shows that male entrepreneurs are more likely to adopt practices which increase interaction in work teams compared to female entrepreneurs.

DISCUSSION

Research on leadership has produced conflicting findings as to whether gender is a determinant of leadership behaviour. The findings obtained in this study differ from previous research which posits little or no difference

Table 13.6   Mean score of responses obtained from the male and female entrepreneurs in relation to Factor 3

Leadership response (1= strongly disagree, 2 = disagree, 3 = neutral, 4 = agree, 5 = strongly agree)	M-W asymp. sig. (two-tailed)	Gender	N	Group mean	Std.	Mean rank
I believe that when the leader backs up the actions of the subordinate it increases motivation in the workplace	0.00	Male	194	4.05	1.19	204.58
		Female	166	3.33	1.44	152.36
I believe that if the leader were to stimulate positive attitude towards the firm, work and personal relationships in their daily attitudes and behaviour, this would produce an increase in collaborative entrepreneurship	0.96	Male	194	3.26	0.94	180.27
		Female	166	3.25	1.32	180.77
I believe that when the leader backs up the actions of the subordinates it improves commitment within the team and encourages a positive attitude towards the leader	0.13	Male	194	3.21	1.00	173.08
		Female	166	3.40	1.41	189.17
I believe that when the leader modifies his/her behaviour and attitude towards a more personal relationship, it would improve subordinate behaviour and attitude towards work and teams	0.17	Male	194	3.69	1.35	187.20
		Female	166	3.42	1.51	172.67
The leader should constantly back up the actions of subordinates and work teams	0.00	Male	194	3.05	1.09	196.26
		Female	166	2.58	0.81	162.08
When a collaborative attitude is adopted, communication is improved and problem solving encouraged	0.00	Male	194	4.15	0.97	201.80
		Female	166	3.75	0.98	155.60
The leader should enhance the team through their own collaborative attitude and behaviour	0.00	Male	194	4.22	0.98	204.93
		Female	166	3.73	0.99	151.95
I use the daily activity of my team/subordinates to help increase mutual obligation and responsibility and personal interaction between team members	0.00	Male	194	4.02	1.09	193.23
		Female	166	3.81	0.97	165.62

in leadership behaviour of men and women (see, e.g., Dobbins and Platz, 1986; Van Engen et al., 2001; Vecchio, 2002). Our findings support previous research which suggests that: (1) male leaders adopt a more directive leadership style (Eagly and Johnson, 1990); and (2) female leaders are inclined to adopt a more democratic and participative leadership style and focus on interactive and transformational leadership qualities, and are more likely to develop close relationships with their employees compared to their male counterparts. For example, a study by Rosener (1990) confirms that female leaders actively work to ensure interactions with their subordinates. In addition, various writers such as Grant (1988), Eagly and Johnson (1990) and Trinidad and Normore (2005) suggest that female leaders adopt participative leadership styles and behaviour which promote more communication, cooperation, intimacy and nurturing when compared to their male counterparts. Many of the male entrepreneurs involved in the study were observed to be more transactional, task-oriented and more authoritarian than women in their leadership practices. This finding finds support in the study conducted by Park (1996), who suggests a relationship between men and task-oriented leadership style, and between women and relations-oriented leadership style. The finding is also in line with research carried out by Eagly and Johnson (1990) on gender differences which highlights that men were more directive and autocratic. However, female entrepreneurs were also observed as being task-oriented. The finding is in line with previous research carried out by Eagly et al. (1992) who concluded that female leaders can also be task-oriented in order to achieve set objectives. The research carried out by Eagly and Johnson (1990) did not report any difference in task-oriented styles of men and women.

The finding also shows that male entrepreneurs were more likely to focus on the failings of their employees rather than caring about them as individuals. The finding is in line with empirical literature which suggests that men often like to clarify responsibilities, task and objectives, and reward good performance and productivity or criticise unsatisfactory work. For example, Gibson (1995) notes that male leaders were more likely to be goal-oriented and controlling. The findings obtained from the study also show that women leaders can sometimes display transactional leadership qualities, and male leaders display transformational leadership qualities when needed to achieve their objective. This view finds support in the study conducted by Andersen and Hansson (2011), who state that the decoupling of gender from sex recognises that female leaders can exhibit male gender qualities, and vice versa. Furthermore, Clark et al. (1999) suggest that male leaders are sometimes perceived to demonstrate transformational leadership practices. In addition, Miles (1985) states that, when necessary, women would emulate masculine leadership practices in order to earn respect and get the job done.

The results obtained confirm a gendered distinction in collective entrepreneurship of male and female entrepreneurs in Nigeria. The research suggests that male entrepreneurs are more likely to communicate effectively to their employees in enhancing collaborative entrepreneurship and problem-solving, and use daily work activities to increase team interaction within their enterprise. One explanation for this finding could be as a result of the fact that societies such as Nigeria are heavily male-dominated and women are considered to be subordinate to men. Davies (1994) is of the view that male dominance is built into the socio-cultural systems, as such prevalent socio-cultural practices to a large extent determine the practices adopted by the women as they interact across different societal and cultural lines (Ojong and Moodley, 2005). Our finding supports the view posited by De la Rey (2005) who suggests that it is very difficult for women leaders to adopt a team-based approach, and possess entrepreneurial vision and effective communication skills, in light of the fact that women are often isolated. The finding is unique within the Nigerian context as it supports the view that male entrepreneurs are more likely than female entrepreneurs to foster collective entrepreneurship and subordinate participation in key organisation functions, thus allowing employees to follow the entrepreneur's guidance, encouraging transfer of knowledge and helping to foster creative and innovative thinking.

CONCLUSION

This chapter has sought to explore gender differences between the leadership and collective entrepreneurial behaviour of Nigerian men and women. The first research question sought to ascertain whether there are differences and/or similarities in the leadership behaviour of male and female entrepreneurs in Nigeria. Our findings to a large extent have helped to confirm a gendered distinction in leadership practices of male and female entrepreneurs in Nigeria, thus supporting previous research which advocates for gender differences between men and women. The finding shows that the average female entrepreneur is more transformational in her leadership approach, relationship-oriented and more supportive when compared to her male counterpart. Male entrepreneurs were observed to be more transactional, task- and goal-oriented in their leadership practices. Our second question sought to address differences and/or similarities in collective entrepreneurship behaviour of male and female entrepreneurs, in order to identify which gender adopts more collaborative entrepreneurship behaviour. Our finding shows Nigerian male entrepreneurs are more collective in their entrepreneurship behaviour compared to female entrepreneurs. Male entrepreneurs involved in the study were observed to collaborate with their subordinates and use daily work routines to increase interaction between work teams.

This study has several limitations. First, it utilised convenience sampling in identifying the male and female entrepreneurs who took part in this study, due to the lack of data upon which to draw any meaningful sample frame for the study. Second, the study focus is on Lagos state and may not be representative of other states in Nigeria. Finally, the research focuses on the perceptions of the leader, and does not incorporate responses from subordinates in order to assess the wider impact of the leadership style and collaborative entrepreneurial behaviour of the male and female entrepreneurs who took part in the study. Future research may focus on subordinates' perceptions of leadership qualities and collaborative behaviour of the entrepreneur, and also compare the leadership practices of entrepreneurs across different states in Nigeria.

REFERENCES

Adesua-Lincoln, A. (2010), Gender-based differences in leadership style of small and medium-sized enterprises in Nigeria. In G. Papanikos (ed.), *International Essays on Small and Medium Sized Enterprises*. Athens: Athens Institute of Education and Research, pp. 339–48.

Andersen, J. and Hansson, P.H. (2011), At the end of the road? On differences between women and men in leadership behaviour. *Leadership and Organization Development Journal* 32 (5), 428–41.

Appelbaum, S.H., Audet, L. and Miller, J.C. (2003), Gender and leadership? Leadership and gender? A journey through the landscape of theories. *Leadership and Organization Development Journal* 24 (1), 43–51.

Argenti, J. (1976), *Corporate Collapse: The Cause and Symptoms*. Maidenhead: McGraw-Hill.

Avolio, B.J. (2011), *Full Range Leadership Development*. Thousand Oaks, CA: SAGE Publications.

Babbie, E. (2010), *The Basics of Social Research*, 5th edn. Belmont, CA: CENGAGE Learning, Wadsworth Publishing Company.

Bass, B.M. (1985), *Leadership and Performance beyond Expectation*. New York, NY: Free Press.

Bass, B. (1990), From transactional to transformational leadership: learning to share the vision. *Organizational Dynamics* 18 (3), 19–31.

Bass, B.M. and Avolio, B.J. (1994), *Improving Organizational Effectiveness through Transformational Leadership*. Thousand Oaks, CA: SAGE Publications.

Bass, B.M., Avolio, B.J. and Atwater, L. (1996), The transformational and transactional leadership of men and women. *International Review of Applied Psychology* 45, 5–34.

Bass, B. and Bass, R. (2008), *The Bass Handbook of Leadership: Theory, Research, and Managerial Applications*. New York, NY: Free Press.

Bass, B.M and Riggio, R.E. (2006), *Transformational Leadership*, 2nd edn. Mahwah, NJ: Lawrence Erlbaum Associates.

316   *Research handbook on entrepreneurship and leadership*

Beckman, C.M. (2006), The influence of founding team company affiliations on firm behaviour. *Academy of Management Journal* 49 (4), 741–58.

Berryman, J. (1983), Small business failure and bankruptcy: a survey of the literature. *International Small Business Journal* 1 (4), 47–59.

Birley, S. and Niktari, N. (1996), Reasons for business failure. *Leadership and Organisational Development Journal* 17 (2), 52.

Book, E.W. (2000), *Why the Best Man for the Job is a Woman*. New York, NY: Harper Collins Publishers.

Bryman, A. and Bell, E. (2011), *Business Research Methods*, 3rd edn. Oxford: Oxford University Press.

Burns, J.M. (1978), *Leadership*. New York, NY: Harper & Row Publishers.

Burt, R.S. (2004), Structural holes and good ideas. *American Journal of Sociology* 110 (2), 349–99.

Bush, T. (2003), *Theories of Educational Leadership and Management*, 3rd edn. London: SAGE Publications.

Butterfield, D.A. and Grinnell, J.P. (1999), Re-viewing gender, leadership, and managerial behavior: do three decades of research tell us anything?. In G.N. Powell (ed.), *Handbook of Gender and Work*. Thousand Oaks, CA: SAGE Publications, pp. 223–38.

Cantor, D. and Bernay, T. (1992), *Women in Power*. New York, NY: Houghton Mifflin Publishers.

Casimir, G. (2001), Combinative aspects of leadership style: the ordering and temporal spacing of leadership behaviors. *Leadership Quarterly* 12, 245–78.

Clark, H., Chandler, J. and Barry, J. (1999), Gender and managerialism. In P. Fogelberg, J. Hearn, L. Husu and T. Mankkinen (eds), *Hard Work in the Academy*. Helsinki: Helsinki University Press, pp. 177–83.

Cogliser, C. and Brigham, K. (2004), The intersection of leadership and entrepreneurship: mutual lessons to be learned. *Leadership Quarterly* 15, 771–99.

Cole, G. (2004), *Management Theory and Practice*, 6th edn. London: Thomston Publishers.

Cooney, T.M. (2005), Editorial: What is an entrepreneurial team?. *International Small Business Journal* 23 (3), 226–35.

Cooper, D.R. and Schindler, P.S. (2011), *Business Research Methods*, 11th edn. New York, NY: Irwin Publishers.

Cruz, A., Howorth, C. and Hamilton, E. (2012), Intrafamily entrepreneurship: the formation and membership of family entrepreneurial teams. *Entrepreneurship Theory and Practice. Entrepreneurial and Family Business Teams* 37 (1), 17–46.

Cruz, M.A., Henningsen, D.D. and Smith, B.A. (1999), The impact of directive leadership on group information sampling, decisions, perceptions of the leader. *Communication Research* 26, 349–70.

Davies, M. (1994), *Women and Violence*. London and New Jersey: Zed Books.

De la Rey, C. (2005), Gender, women and leadership. *Women and Leadership* 65, 4–11.

Dobbins, G. and Platz, S (1986), Sex differences in leadership – how real are they?. *Academy of Management Review* 11, 118–34.

Downton, J.V. (1973), *Rebel Leadership: Commitment and Charisma in the Revolutionary Process*. New York, NY: Free Press.

Drucker, P. (1970), Entrepreneurship in business enterprise. *Journal of Business Policy*, 1 (1).

Eagly, A.H., Johannesen-Schmidt, M.C. and Van Engen, M.L. (2003), Transformational, transactional and laissez-faire leadership styles: a meta-analysis comparing men and women. *Psychological Bulletin* 129 (4), 569–91.

Eagly, A.H. and Johnson, B.T. (1990), Gender and leadership style: a meta-analysis. *Psychological Bulletin* 108, 233–56.

Eagly, A.H., Makhijani, M. and Klonsky, B. (1992), Gender and effectiveness of leaders: a meta-analysis. *Psychological Bulletin* 117, 125–45.

Edwards, G.P., Winter, P.K. and Bailey, J. (2002), *Leadership in Management*. Ross-on-Wye: Leadership Trust Foundation.

Ehrhart, M.G. and Klein, K.J (2001), Predicting followers' preferences for charismatic leadership: the influence of follower values and personality. *Leadership Quarterly* 12, 153–79.

Fairhurst, G.T. (2001), Dualisms in leadership research. In F.M Jablin and L.L Putnam (eds), *Organizational Communication*. Thousand Oaks, CA: SAGE Publications, pp. 379–439.

French, J. and Raven, B.H. (1959), The bases of social power. In D. Cartwright (ed.), *Studies of Social Power*. Ann Arbor, MI: Institute for Social Research, pp. 150–67.

Gartner, W.B., Bird, B.J. and Starr, J.A. (1992), Acting as if: Differentiating entrepreneurial from organizational behavior. *Entrepreneurship Theory and Practice* 16 (3), 13–32.

GEM (2012), Global Entrepreneurship Monitor Women's Report. Global Entrepreneurship Research Association. Available at http://www.babson.edu/Academics/centers/blank-center/global-research/gem/Documents/GEM%202012%20Womens%20Report.pdf.

Gibson, C. (1995), An investigation of gender differences in leadership across four countries. *Journal of International Business Studies* 26 (2), 225–79.

Gill, J. and Johnson, P. (2010). *Research Methods for Managers*, 4th edn. London: Paul Chapman.

Gill, R. (2011), *Theory and Practice of Leadership*, 2nd edn. Thousand Oaks, CA: SAGE Publications.

Goleman, D. (2000), Leadership that gets results. *Harvard Business Review* March–April, 78–90.

Grant, J. (1988), Women as managers: what they can offer to organizations. *Organisational Dynamics* 16 (3), 56–63.

Grint, K. (2000), *The Arts of Leadership*. Oxford: Oxford University Press.

Grint, K. (2005), Problems, problems, problems: the social construction of leadership. *Human Relations* 58 (11), 1467–94.

Gronn, P. (2003), *The New Work of Educational Leaders: Changing Leadership Practice In An Era Of School Reform*. London: Paul Chapman Publishers.

Gupta, V., MacMillan, I.C. and Suriec, G. (2004), Entrepreneurial leadership: developing and measuring a cross-cultural construct. *Journal of Business Venturing* 19 (2), 241–60.

Helgesen, S. (1990a), *The Female Advantage: Women's Ways of Leadership*. New York, NY: Doubleday Press.

Helgesen, S. (1990b), *Women's Way of Leading*. New York, NY: Doubleday Press.

Henson, R. and Roberts, J. (2006), Use of exploratory factor analysis in published research: common errors and some comment on improved practice. *Educational and Psychological Measurement* 66 (3), 393–416.

House, R.J. (1976), Theory of charismatic leadership. In J.G. Hunt and L.L. Larson (eds), *Leadership: The Cutting Edge*. Carbondale, IL: Southern Illinois University Press.

Jack, S., Dodd, S.D. and Anderson, A.R. (2008), Change and the development of entrepreneurial networks over time: a processual perspective. *Entrepreneurship and Regional Development* 20 (2), 125–59.

Jusko, J. (2003), Secrets of longevity. *Industry Week* 252, 24–7.

Knight, F.H. (1921), *Risk, Uncertainty, and Profit*. Boston, MA: Hart, Schaffner & Marx / Houghton Mifflin Company.

Kouzes, J.M. and Posner, B.Z. (2002), *The Leadership Challenge*. San Francisco CA: Jossey-Bass.

Kuratko, D.F. (2007), Entrepreneurial leadership in the 21st century. *Journal of Leadership and Organizational Studies* 13 (4), 1–11.

Kuratko, D.F. and Hodgetts, R.M. (2007), *Entrepreneurship: Theory and Process, Practice*, 7th edn. Mason, OH: Thompson South Western Publishing.

Leitch, C., McMullan, C. and Harrison, R. (2013), The development of entrepreneurial leadership: the role of human, social and institutional capital. *British Journal of Management* 24 (3), 347–66.

Lincoln, A. (2012), Nature of leadership practices of Nigerian female entrepreneurs. *International Journal of Business and Social Science* 3 (10), 50–59.

Lounsbury, M. (1998), Collective entrepreneurship: the mobilization of college and university recycling coordinators. *Journal of Organizational Change Management* 11 (1), 50–69.

Lowe, K.B., Kroeck, K.G. and Sivasubramaniam, N. (1996), Effectiveness correlates of transformation and transactional leadership: a meta-analytic review of the MLQ literature. *Leadership Quarterly* 7, 385–425.

MacNealy, M. (1999), *Strategies for Empirical Research in Writing*. New York, NY: Longman.

Maher, K. (1997), Gender-related stereotype of transformational and transactional leadership. *Sex Roles* 37, 209–25.

Malhotra, N.K. (2010), *Marketing Research: An Applied Orientation*, 6th edn. Upper Saddle River, NJ: Pearson.

Marlow, S., Henry, C. and Carter, S. (2009), Exploring the impact of gender upon women's business ownership: introduction. *International Small Business Journal* 27, 139–48.

Mavin, S. (2009), Navigating the labyrinth: senior women managing emotion. *International Journal of Work Organisation and Emotion* 3 (1), 81–3.

McClelland, D.C. (1961), *The Achieving Society*. New York, NY: Free Press.

McWhinney, W., Webber, J.B., Smith, D.M. and Novokowsky, B.J. (1997), *Creating Paths of Change: Managing Issues and Resolving Problems in Organizations*, 2nd edn. Thousand Oaks, CA: SAGE Publications.

Miles, R. (1985), *Women and Power*. London: Macdonald.

Miller, D. and Friesen, P. (1984), *Organizations: A Quantum View*. Englewood Cliffs, NJ: Prentice-Hall.

Mourdoukoutas, P. (1999), *Collective Entrepreneurship in a Global Economy*. Westport, CT: Greenwood Publishing / Quorum Books.

National Bureau of Statistics (2014), Nigerian unemployment rate. Available at http://www.tradingeconomics.com/nigeria/unemployment-rate.

Northouse, P.G. (2007), *Leadership: Theory and Practice*, 3rd edn. Thousand Oaks, CA and London: SAGE Publications.

Northouse, P.G. (2010), *Leadership: Theory and Practice*, 5th edn. Thousand Oaks, CA: SAGE Publications.

OECD (2005), Financing SMEs in Africa. Policy Insights No. 7, African Economic Outlook 2004/2005. A joint publication of the African Development Bank and the OECD Development Centre, France.

O'Farrell, P.N. and Hitchens, D.M. (1989), *Small Firm Competitiveness and Performance*. Dublin: Gill & Macmillan Publishers.

Ojong, V. and Moodley, V. (2005), Leadership and issues affecting the productivity of women entrepreneurs in KwaZulu-Natal. *Women and Leadership* 65, 76–82.

Oppenhiem, A.N. (1992), *Questionnaire Design and Attitude Measurement*. London: Heinemann Publishers.

Park, D. (1996), Gender role, decision style and leadership style. *Women In Management Review* 11 (8), 13–17.

Patterson, N., Mavin, S. and Turner, J. (2012), Envisioning female entrepreneur: leaders anew from a gender perspective. *Gender in Management: An International Journal* 27 (6), 395–416.

Pounder, J. and Coleman, M. (2002), Women – better leaders than men? In general and educational management it still 'all depends'. *Leadership and Organization Development Journal* 23 (3), 122–33.

Powell, G.N. and Eddleston, K.A. (2008), The paradox of the contented female business owner. *Journal of Vocational Behavior*, 73, 24–36.

Powell, G.N and Eddleston, K.A. (2013), Linking family-to-business enrichment and support to entrepreneurial success: do female and male entrepreneurs experience different outcomes?. *Journal of Business Venturing* 28, 261–80.

Powell, G. and Graves, L. (2003), *Women and Men in Management*, 3rd edn. Thousand Oaks, CA: SAGE Publications.

Reich, R.B. (1987), Entrepreneurship reconsidered: the team as hero. *Harvard Business Review* 65 (3), 77–83.

Rosener, J.B. (1990), Ways women lead. *Harvard Business Review* Nov–Dec, 119–25.

Rosener, J.B. (1995), *America's Competitive Secret: Utilizing Women as a Management Strategy*. New York, NY: Oxford University Press.

Rost, J.C. (1991), *Leadership in the 21st Century*. New York, NY: Praeger Publishers.

Santos, R. and Spann, M. (2012), Collective entrepreneurship at Qualcomm: combining collective and entrepreneurial practices to turn employee ideas into action. *R&D Management* 41 (5), 2011.

Saunders, M., Lewis, P. and Thornhill, A. (2009), *Research Methods for Business Students*, 5th edn. London: Pitman.

Schumpeter, J.A. (1965), Economic theory and entrepreneurial history. In H.G. Aitken (ed.), *Explorations in Enterprise*. Cambridge, MA: Harvard University Press, pp. 45–64.

Scott, H. (1999), Our future requires collaboration leadership. *Workforces* 78 (12), 30–34.

Shamir, B., House, R.J. and Arthur, M.B. (1993), The motivational effects of charismatic leadership: a self-concept based theory. *Organization Science* 4, 577–93.

Soriano, D. and Martínez, J. (2007), Transmitting the entrepreneurial spirit to the work team in SMEs: the importance of leadership. *Management Decision* 45 (7), 1102–22.

Storey, J. (2011), Changing theories of leadership and leadership development. In J. Storey (ed.), *Leadership in Organizations: Current Issues and Key Trends*. London: Routledge, pp. 11–37.

Thompson, B. (2004), Exploratory and confirmatory factor analysis: understanding concepts and applications. Washington, DC: American Psychological Association.

Trinidad, C. and Normore, A.H. (2005), Leadership and gender: a dangerous liaison. *Leadership and Organization Development Journal* 26 (7), 574–90.

UNIDO (2001), Women entrepreneurship development in selected African countries. Working Paper No. 7, UNIDO, Vienna.

Van Engen, M., Van der Leeden, R. and Willemsen, T. (2001), Gender context and leadership styles: a field of study. *Journal of Occupational and Organisational Psychology* 74, 58–98.

Vecchio, R.P. (2002), Leadership and gender advantage. *Leadership Quarterly* 13 (6), 643–71.

Vroom, V.H. (2000), Leadership and the decision making process. *Organizational Dynamics* 28 (4), 82–94.

Woldie, A. and Adersua, A. (2004), Female entrepreneurs in a transitional economy: businesswomen in Nigeria. *International Journal of Social Economics* 31 (1/2), 78–93.

Wright, M. and Vanaelst, I. (2009), Introduction. In M. Wright and I. Vanaelst (eds), *Entrepreneurial Teams and New Business Creation*, Vol. 13. Cheltenham, UK and Northampton, MA: Edward Elgar Publishing.

Yukl, G.A. (2002), *Leadership in Organizations*, 5th edn. Upper Saddle River, NJ: Prentice Hall.

Yukl, G. (2012), Effective leadership behavior: what we know and what questions need more attention. *Academy of Management Perspectives* 26 (4), 66–85.

PART V

ENTREPRENEURIAL LEADERSHIP AND LEARNING

14. A review of entrepreneurial leadership learning: an exploration that draws on human, social and institutional capitals
Steve Kempster, Sue Smith and Stewart Barnes

INTRODUCTION

This chapter explores entrepreneurial leadership learning: what it is, and how it is different to leadership learning within employed contexts. We use communities of practice (CoP) theory as a lens for understanding how owner-managers of small and medium-sized enterprises (SMEs) learn entrepreneurial leadership. Drawing upon an empirical case study of an SME leadership development programme and an autoethnographic account of one of the owner-managers (Barnes et al., 2015), we explore how entrepreneurial leadership learning becomes evident in the entrepreneurial context and how it can be developed within a CoP. Developing this further we use the notions of human, social and institutional capitals to illustrate how such learning becomes manifest: the connect between individual skills, knowledge and attitudes within social relationships supported through an organised structure with guiding informal rules of collective engagement.

The organisation of the chapter is as follows. First, we provide an overview of debates and research evidence to delineate the nature of entrepreneurial leadership learning. Recent discussions in the field of leadership have begun to assert an ontological orientation towards relational dynamics rather than essentialist qualities of individuals; that is an emphasis on relational practices and identities formed within specific contexts of both leaders and followers (DeRue and Ashford, 2010). The chapter next explores formative leadership learning and the differences in the employed and the SME and entrepreneurial contexts. We continue looking at the SME context using the lens of CoP theory to examine how a leadership programme helps owner-managers of SMEs develop their entrepreneurial leadership capabilities. We highlight a particular case through an autoethnographic account of an owner-manager which examines the lived experience of entrepreneurial leadership learning. The account is used to show how Leitch et al.'s (2013) three capitals – human, social and institutional – provide an in-depth rich sense of verisimilitude of the experience of all three dimensions. We conclude the chapter by exploring opportunities for the development of research into entrepreneurial leadership learning.

WHAT IS ENTREPRENEURIAL LEADERSHIP LEARNING?

The field of entrepreneurial leadership is 'in the very early stages of conceptual and theoretical development' (Bagheri and Pihie, 2011: 449; similarly argued in Cogliser and Brigham, 2004; Jensen and Luthans, 2006; Leitch et al., 2013). Gupta et al. (2004: 242) offer a useful definition: 'entrepreneurial leadership that creates visionary scenarios that are used to mobilise a supporting cast of participants who become committed by the vision to the discovery of exploitation of strategic value'. In a recent article, Renko et al. (2015: 2) summarised a range of definitions; the essence of these is to suggest a relational influence process that focuses on vision and exploiting opportunities. They believe this phenomenon can occur in organisations of all sizes. Bagheri and Pihie (2011) suggest that it is a dynamic occurring most prominently during new venture creation and early stages of the development of the venture. Vecchio (2003) places emphasis on taking advantage of opportunities, similar to Surie and Ashley (2008) who extend opportunity recognition to innovation and adaptation.

These definitions are not significantly different to the debates in the leadership field. Leadership is generally considered to be a situated and relational process of influence oriented toward goals, directions, purposes and vision (for a useful review, see Drath et al., 2008). The notion of vision or future-oriented activity is similarly suggested to be an important element of entrepreneurship (Ruvio et al., 2010; Jensen and Luthans, 2005). As such, Vecchio (2003: 304) argues that entrepreneurship should not be considered a distinct field, and learning from the field of leadership might be most useful in the context of business growth and individual development. The orientation of Vecchio's (2003) review of both phenomena was to an (understandable) ontological assumption of leadership as an individual. A similar orientation is adopted by Gupta et al. (2004: 242–5) who sought to fuse the notion of the entrepreneurial emphasis of individuality – self-interest, innovative combinations of available resources, tolerance of uncertainty and risk-bearing, and a proactive, opportunity orientation – with an essentialist perspective of leadership anchored in models of charismatic, transformational and authentic leadership: an individual who can influence followers towards achieving greater performance through appealing to their implicit motivations, often centred on articulating an appealing vision anchored to an ethical basis to decisions and actions centred on participation and involvement.

However, debates in the leadership field suggest that the idealised qualities highlighted as essential for the 'leader' are mostly rare, romanticised (Meindl, 1995) or sacred (Grint, 2010). Alvesson and Sveningsson (2003) have suggested that as they searched for leadership, it disappeared; people were unable to point to it, yet people were mostly accepting that it has significant influence in their lives. Through a critical interpretation of leadership, Kelly (2014) has suggested a negative ontology placing emphasis on the notion of it as an empty signifier: a rarefied phenomenon that we would be better to accept as fluid and under continual social (re)construction. In this way individuals (re)create the desire for leadership and connect it to people in perceived leadership roles with an anticipatory identity attribution.

If leadership is seen as rarefied and a floating signifier (Kelly, 2014) then this speaks to the importance of leadership being socially constructed, rather than having a concrete or essentialist quality. Debates in the field of leadership are beginning to take this view. There has been an increasing assertion of an ontological orientation towards relational dynamics rather than essentialist qualities of individuals (Uhl-Bien, 2006), and an increasing attention to relational practices and identities of leaders and followers within a specific context (DeRue and Ashford, 2010) emerging as leadership as practice (Carroll et al., 2008; Raelin, 2011). The importance for us of this discussion is to position entrepreneurial leadership as a socially constructed relational practice. The focus of the practice is toward vision and exploiting opportunity; not centred singularly on an individual's skills, but rather a learnt dynamic that emerges as a consequence of interaction of individuals within leadership relationships situated in particular contexts, such as the SME. The plurality of people undertaking leadership leans towards a distributed, shared and collective notion of leading, vis-à-vis the leader with followers. In the field of entrepreneurship, similar conclusions have been drawn. For example, Gartner et al. (1994: 6) assert: 'the entrepreneur in entrepreneurship is more likely to be plural rather than singular. The locus of entrepreneurial activity often resides not in one person but many'. Similarly, Cooney (2005: 226) states: 'It is arguable that despite the romantic notion of the entrepreneur as lone hero, the reality is that successful entrepreneurs either built teams about them or were part of a team throughout'.

In a review of literature exploring distributed leadership in SMEs, Cope et al. (2011) suggested entrepreneurial teams are more successful than lone entrepreneurs in surviving and growing. They sought to explore how to develop the SME and the entrepreneur, which we discuss below. The connection of the entrepreneur and their development and the development of the business are fundamentally interconnected through relationships. Leitch et al. (2013) helpfully 'join the dots' together, providing a useful summary of entrepreneurial leadership. They describe it as 'a social process enacted through everyday active encounters as a practice of relational learning'. That is, focused on identifying and exploiting opportunities guided through the 'presence of an entrepreneurial vision' that align to the need for 'processes that nurture innovation through generating and securing resources. All of these aspects enable capacity to undertake continuous exploration and idea generation' (ibid.: 348). The focus of Leitch et al.'s (2013) argument is towards Cope's (2005) notion of a learning dynamic of entrepreneurial leadership; that is, a move from a sole focus on human capital (the entrepreneur) to one including social capital, in essence seeing entrepreneurial leadership as an outcome: the consequence of social interaction. Again, the crossover to debates in leadership is striking. Recently, Drath et al. (2008) have suggested the same: a reorientation of the ontology of leadership to be seen as an outcome. They suggested higher-order outcomes of direction, alignment and commitment. In terms of entrepreneurial leadership these outcomes would be seen to provide an integrative frame to Leitch et al.'s (2013) definition above. Drath et al. (2008) and Leitch et al. (2013) broadly reach similar conclusions with regard to the nature of entrepreneurship, leadership and entrepreneurial leadership. It is best seen as an emergent property of a relational learning dynamic (see also Cope and Watts, 2000; Thorpe et al., 2009; Kempster and Cope, 2010; Cope et al., 2011; and Bagheri and Pihie, 2011). This is important due to the emphasis in terms of social learning that shapes how we learn the practice of leading within a specific context. We shall return to social learning shortly. First, we outline the foundations of leadership learning that inform entrepreneurial leadership and highlight structural limitations of the SME context that limit its manifestation.

FORMATIVE LEADERSHIP LEARNING: THE EMPLOYED AND ENTREPRENEURIAL CONTEXT

Understandings of entrepreneurial leadership, and to an extent entrepreneurial learning, are embryonic but growing. In contrast, the field of leadership learning is well established. It is broadly accepted that leadership learning occurs through the milieu of lived experience (Davies and Easterby-Smith, 1984; Cox and Cooper, 1989; Jackson and Parry, 2001; Bennis and Thomas, 2002; Hill, 2003; Janson, 2008; Kempster, 2006; McCall, 2004). Earliest reports of such learning have been traced back to the age of four: the experience of the playground and being collected by the teacher to start class; 'leadership is the person in front' (Kempster, 2009). As we travel through our life course the experiences shape our understanding of leadership, and such experiences become manifest in our practice of leading (Kempster, 2006). The experiences and the context in which such experiences occur become all-important to leadership learning.

Drawing on both extant literature and empirical work, Kempster (2009) outlines a model of relational leadership learning that is centred on both intra- and interpersonal dynamics. 'Intra' in the sense of identity, self-efficacy and leadership salience; and 'inter' related to three learning processes: observed, enacted and situated. Kempster suggests the intra- and interpersonal combine to create an emergent and ongoing process of becoming that is centred on relational and participative social learning. Drawing on Bennis and Thomas's (2002) notion of crucibles of learning, the dynamics within contexts are all-important. The contexts of the familial environment, education and first and subsequent employment opportunities, provide a variety of roles and a variety of people to engage with (McCall et al., 1988; McCall, 2004). Within the employed context, leadership is highly valued and as a phenomenon is most salient. The consequence is a deepening relationship with leadership; the aspiring leader's closer identification and continual testing (in terms of self-efficacy). The empirical data in Kempster and Cope (2010) also resonate with Avolio's (2005) suggestion of trigger events (similar to Cope and Watts, 2000, on critical incidents in the business venture) acting as catalysts to stimulate learning reorientation.

Kempster (2009) explored how managers have learnt to lead, comparing employed managers with owner-managers, highlighting similarities and differences. The similarities were associated with the formative influences such as familial context, education and first and subsequent employment contexts. The differences related to how owner-managers related to the phenomenon of leadership compared to their employed counterparts. For employed managers, leadership was a highly valued identity. It was a prominent career aspiration. Success in career related to being seen and acknowledged as a 'leader'. The career pathway was an important mechanism that carried these managers through leadership learning experiences. With regard to the owner-managers, however, the relationship with leadership was much more problematic. For many the leadership career pathway was restricted by factors such as a poor boss, a constraining environment, a lack of freedom and a hunger to do their own thing.

Kempster and Cope (2010) show how the entrepreneurial context has a marked impact on entrepreneurial leadership learning. In many ways the entrepreneurial context stifles leadership learning. This does not mean that the entrepreneur is not leading – far from it. Their leadership has a very powerful impact on their employees and the business. Rather, the context limits the stimuli of leadership learning. The outcome is often a form of leadership that draws heavily on early formative experiences, most notably the familial, educational and first employment context. In essence, 'the small business is the dominant situated crucible in which entrepreneurs learn to lead . . . [the] relationship between the entrepreneur and his/her business reflects a reinforcing and arguably limiting situation with regard to [entrepreneurial] leadership learning' (Kempster and Cope, 2010: 21–2).

The leadership learning lifeblood of varieties of context, roles and participative relationships is severely limited within the developing business. We outline how this can be addressed later on, in terms of entrepreneurial leadership learning. First, we explore the process of social learning, through the lens of CoP theory, to highlight dynamics of entrepreneurial leadership learning in the SME context.

SOCIAL LEARNING THEORY AND ITS APPLICATION TO ENTREPRENEURIAL LEADERSHIP LEARNING

We have argued that entrepreneurial leadership learning needs an ontological orientation towards a relational dynamic whereby relational practices, context and identity are paramount. Social learning theories can provide a useful lens for understanding identity and the relational dynamic of entrepreneurial leadership learning. Crucially, these theories adopt a social constructionist perspective which argues that learning (and knowledge) occurs through social participation that takes place in everyday activities, through conversations and interactions between people (Lave and Wenger, 1991; Brown and Duguid, 1991; Gherardi, 1995; Gherardi et al., 1998). This challenges the traditional view of learning as something to be acquired cognitively from a knowledgeable source. Gherardi et al. (1998: 277) argue that if one applies a social perspective to learning, attention shifts from the processing of information and the modifying of cognitive structure to the processes of participation and interaction that provide and sustain the proper context for learning. Learning is seen as a collective activity, a product of and engagement through social activities with people, rather than as an individual phenomenon. For Gherardi et al. (1998), learning is not conceived as a way of coming to know the world, but as a way of becoming part of the social world. Such a view of learning sees knowledge as socially constructed, where learning takes place through engagement.

Recent debates on leadership development share this social view of learning, focusing on it as a socially situated process (Iles and Preece, 2006; Kempster and Stewart, 2010; Raelin, 2011) with activity situated in a collective practice. Entrepreneurial leadership development is also seen as a social process emphasising the relational nature of learning through everyday action (Taylor and Thorpe, 2004; Cope, 2005; Pittaway and Thorpe, 2012). Theorists call for the need to better understand entrepreneurial leadership learning in the context of smaller firms (see Leitch et al., 2013). In response to this call, we argue that CoP theory (as a social learning theory) can act as a useful analytical tool for more fully understanding the entrepreneurial leadership learning process and its relation between identity and context in the small firm. The crux of CoP theory lies in the significance of shifting the analytic focus from the individual as learner, to learning as participation in the social world (Lave and Wenger, 1991; Wenger, 1998). The premise is of learning through participation in social, situated activity, achieved through participation with other people, in a social context. The focus is on the practices of communities, with identity a key feature of the learning process. In this sense, CoP theory is a heuristic, a way of understanding learning in practice, whereby learning is an integral and inseparable aspect of social practice. The practice of leading within a specific context, that is, the CoP, is an emergent property of a relational learning dynamic whereby the engagement and participation in the community is the basis for learning.

So, what does this mean in the context of the small firm and entrepreneurial leadership development? It is commonly understood that individuals alone do not create successful firms (Thorpe et al., 2009), and there is a move in entrepreneurial leadership development beyond the skills development of the entrepreneur to the development of their human capital (Leitch et al., 2013). Equally, CoPs do not exist in isolation; their effectiveness is not a matter of their internal development alone, but also a matter of how well they connect with other communities and constituencies inside and outside the organisation (Wenger, 2000). It has been shown that using CoP theory to understand entrepreneurial leadership development involves identity work (Smith, 2011; Smith and Smith, 2013). Smith (2011) argues that the identity of the entrepreneur shifts as leadership becomes increasingly salient to them. Kempster (2009) presents a model of relational leadership learning which highlights the importance of becoming. With a reorientation of the ontology of leadership to be seen as an outcome, the process of becoming through identity work is the consequence of social interaction in leadership contexts.

HOW CAN ENTREPRENEURIAL LEADERSHIP LEARNING BE DEVELOPED?

Building on the previous argument that entrepreneurial leadership needs to be viewed as an ongoing outcome that is generated from a collective relational process, the development approach needs to be a focus on human and social capitals. Cope et al. (2011) suggest a focus on the entrepreneur (the human capital) and the context in which the entrepreneur is being developed. Leitch et al. (2013: 360) suggest the necessity for entrepreneurial leadership development to connect human capital and social capital with what they describe as 'institutional capital' (Anderson, 2010).

We provide a brief examination of human, social and institutional capitals. When we speak here of human capital we are giving emphasis to the skills, knowledge, attitudes and talents of an individual (Fernandez and Castilla, 2001, cited in Leitch et al., 2013: 350); capital that an individual is able to acquire and develop and use in an exchange process to extract value for their own benefit (Zhu et al., 2005). Social capital is a relational form of capital (Adler and Kwon, 2014). It is formed through resources (actual and potential) that are embedded in a network of relationships, and 'thus comprises both the network and the assets that may be mobilised through the network' (Nahapiet and Ghoshal, 1998: 243). The capital exchange process fundamentally works through notions of trust and reciprocity. By investing in the network, individuals can draw on the social capital and 'thereby gain the benefits in the form of superior access to information, power, and solidarity . . . and augment their capacity for collective action' (Adler and Kwon, 2014: 21). Social capital is interconnected with human capital. The strength of reciprocation and trust is related with the individual's skills, knowledge and attitudes, such as integrity. If someone has little of value to the network (or *in extremis* is corrosive to the solidarity of the network), then the ability to draw on the social capital over the medium term is restricted. Institutional capital is less developed than human and social capitals. Leitch et al. helpfully elaborated the concept, drawing on the work of Anderson (2013). It draws from the existence of both human and social capital; without these it would not exist, as it requires something of value for an institution to become developed around (Leitch et al., 2013: 349). Institutional capital exists in institutions (perhaps rather self-evidently). The nature of an institution is centred on notions of organising, rules and governance. Organising around a common purpose, rules that help understand what is allowed, governance structures to enforce/regulate what is allowed and thereby reduce uncertainty. Institutional capital allows individuals to come together and enable social capital to be generated as it allows enhanced trust and solidarity with reduced risk (ibid.:

361). Drawing on empirical research, Leitch et al. (2013: 360) identified how activities within an executive development programme constituted an institution in terms of being governed by a set of rules and norms that are accepted by all the members. Additionally, they showed the emergence of strong organisational structures – such as agendas and procedures – and the beginnings of governance approaches to handle sharing, collaboration and learning: 'In other words, the emergence of a strong resilient institution that can provide space and support for its members' (ibid.: 360).

The earlier discussion on social learning gives emphasis to the process of 'being' active members of CoPs. We describe how institutional capital can be developed through the establishment of a CoP that can enable the development of entrepreneurial leadership through enhancing human, social and institutional capitals. In developing this argument we address two questions:

1. How can a CoP develop entrepreneurial leadership?
2. How does a CoP impact on human, social and institutional capital?

HOW CAN A COMMUNITY OF PRACTICE DEVELOP ENTREPRENEURIAL LEADERSHIP?

The authors have been involved developing entrepreneurs through a leadership development programme (LEAD) for more than ten years. More than 2000 businesses have participated across the United Kingdom. It has been demonstrated that the programme develops entrepreneurial leadership (see Wren and Jones, 2006, 2012) and that using a CoP approach enables the owner-manager to undertake identity work, shifting their identity to that of leader (see Smith, 2011). Over the course of ten months, LEAD engages owner-managers in a process through learning interventions including masterclasses, coaching, action learning, business shadowing, and exchanges and critical reflection. Rather than a taught programme, the focus is on building a CoP whereby the delegates become co-learners, who all have a valid contribution to make to the community. Learning arises from participation in the CoP and gaining recognised membership within that community (see Lave and Wenger, 1991). The activity for the delegates on the programme is their own work practices as owner-managers of SMEs. In other words, the learning they experience as a result of LEAD is situated back into their own contexts with the aspiration of developing entrepreneurial leadership. In this way, the negotiation of meaning is around the competence of being an entrepreneurial leader. In other words, a pedagogical context is created to increase the salience of leadership for owner-managers, thus enabling entrepreneurial leadership learning.

Using CoP theory as an analytical tool provides a pedagogical heuristic for entrepreneurial leadership learning, which helps the owner-managers to view themselves as leaders without explicitly 'teaching' them leadership. This pedagogy is based on constructionist views of knowledge which require the delegates to engage with the ideas that come from the different elements of LEAD and to develop skills and capabilities relevant to their own situations in their businesses. In CoP terms it enables them to address problems and share knowledge (Wenger, 2004). The circulation of knowledge within LEAD comes largely from the delegates and their experiences of running small businesses. This pedagogy includes learner-directed styles of learning and interactive approaches for the delegates to learn from each other and the knowledge they have about running small businesses. The learning is naturalistic through a continual process of participating in the CoP (and experiencing the learning interventions) and embedding their learning back in their own contexts, that is, their businesses. This loop and the trajectory back and forth between the CoP and the workplace is very important in the development of an entrepreneurial leadership identity, and it requires time for this to have an effect.

Conceptualising the programme as a CoP, Smith (2011) uses the term 'enablers' to show how the programme team and the facilitators create the environment for learning and for a CoP to emerge. The enablers are part of the construction of a situated curriculum which Gherardi et al. (1998: 275) have described as the 'pattern of activities that instruct the process socialization of novices in a context of ongoing work activities'. The enablers engage with the delegates in a form of a co-constructed situated curriculum. The delegates bring a language and meanings from their own businesses and blend these together through activities to form a unique CoP. This is a co-construction between the delegates and the enablers which results in a CoP with a central focus on entrepreneurial leadership learning.

HOW DOES A COMMUNITY OF PRACTICE IMPACT ON HUMAN, SOCIAL AND INSTITUTIONAL CAPITAL?

We are beginning to understand how a CoP can be created in an entrepreneurial leadership development programme. In essence, we suggest, building a programme CoP enables a three-dimensional perspective to developing entrepreneurial leadership. Evaluation of the LEAD programme has shown that a significant impact occurs on the first two dimensions: first, the owner-managers' acquisition of human capital; and second, on the business through social capital (Wren and Jones, 2006). Additionally, in the third dimension, a programme CoP develops akin to Leitch et al.'s (2013) notion of institutional capital. While Leitch et al. (2013: 360) do not explore how this capital is developed, they acknowledge the need for social trust, which is itself developed from individuals having already learnt to cooperate. Our argument in this chapter is to assert that exploring how a programme CoP can be developed is central to explaining the interrelationship of social and institutional capital.

DEVELOPING HUMAN, SOCIAL AND INSTITUTIONAL CAPITAL

The penultimate section of this chapter illustrates the development of all three dimensions of human, social and institutional capital. We do this through a co-constructed autoethnographic approach that has been shown to enable the granular detail of leader becoming to be illuminated (Kempster and Stewart, 2010). Autoethnography 'does not merely require us to explore the interface between culture and self, it requires us to write about ourselves. It is the conscious experiencing of the self as both inquirer and respondent, as teacher and learner . . . coming to know the self within the process of research' (ibid.: 210). The co-constructed aspect is a partnered process of a researcher pursuing an in-depth examination of a particular phenomenon experienced by the respondent. The outcome of co-constructed autoethnography is an aesthetic narrative that manifests as a 'theory sandwich' (Ellis, 2004: 198). The 'tasty' filling is the partner respondent; the 'ethno' cultured subject (Watson, 2011) with the 'graphy' as the spatial and temporal aspects of the experience. The 'dry' bread represents theory being developed through examining the partner respondent's lived experience. The next section outlines such an aesthetic narrative: a co-constructed autoethnographic examination of entrepreneurial leadership learning that draws on the preceding literature discussion of this chapter.

Applying the Principles: The Case of Freddie Porter

Barnes et al. (2015) provide a research based examination of entrepreneurial leadership learning in the SME context through a real-life narrative encapsulating the development of three business people on a leadership programme, whilst explaining the key theories, models and techniques that underpin the leadership methods and approaches deployed. The learning journey of three SME business leaders was explored through a series of in-depth, semi-structured interviews aided by formal outputs of LEAD produced by the interviewees during and after the programme. Data was collected through access to more than 150 pages of transcripts generated from interviews with three participants, and was used in the narrative to describe their unfolding stories. Additionally, the meta-reflections of the three business leaders, captured in the 7000-word work-based learning submissions submitted as part of their Master's qualification, were accessed. The case of Freddie was selected to further explore the three different types of capital, as it was representative of entrepreneurial leadership learning in an established family business in a traditional industry, indicating that positive change is achievable.

Freddie Porter was one year into the Managing Director role of a century-old, medium-sized, family-owned, building materials company. He worked alongside his two brothers, his wife and his retired father who remained as Chairman. The company had laboured through the last ten years, led by an autocratic and highly directive board with poor leadership and ineffective communication. Communication was one way: top-down. Managers felt battered and bruised and the 80 employees were disengaged. Freddie's father had ruled with an iron glove, controlling all aspects of the business, and his sheer will and determination drove the organisation. Freddie not only had inherited the business but he had also unknowingly inherited some of his father's rather direct ways, though he was trying his best to adopt a more empowering style.

Freddie was concerned about the performance of his company as sales had ceased to grow. Old business methods and models had remained unchanged over past decades, with personnel and systems left to stagnate. The mentality embedded within the business was one of 'the company can run itself, we don't really need director intervention'. There was a severe lack of communication and planning.

Freddie was full of trepidation and scared of the responsibility of the role of Managing Director. Although it said 'Managing Director' on his business card, he did not feel like one. While he held the title he had the job responsibility, but he did not know how to do the role. It felt like the blind leading the blind. The management team were not up to standard and the family were all on top of each other, resulting in ill feeling. Freddie's enthusiasm and confidence were privately waning under his self-doubts.

The following are extracts from an interview with Freddie after he had completed the LEAD programme, in which he reflects on aspects of the programme. We have selected from his reflections extracts that resonate with entrepreneurial leadership learning focusing on human, social and institutional capitals.

Human Capital: Leadership Learning

One of the first learning experiences was from my leadership timeline, which I populated with incidents and experiences from an early age. This was an invaluable exercise as I quickly discovered that the majority of my leadership experiences were based from negative memories. I now understand that I developed my own leadership from learning from the mistakes of other leaders that I have worked with in the past, thus creating my own style. This is why I believe that I sometimes come across too placid and not as authoritarian as I should be as a leader, as I have seen very aggressive styles of this leadership not working.

What also was quite startling to realise was how little support I had received from my family that were involved in the business. My father and directors had never taken me to one side to coach, nurture, praise, or reprimand when required.

Social Capital: Communications and Employee Engagement

[The] exercise involved four of us standing on a chess board with a manager directing us around the board via a radio linked through to directors. We were faced with pawn like pieces on the board and a competitor moving the pieces trying to win the game. At first my chess board colleagues and I were very jovial, appreciating the stress free nature of our job. However, when we seemed to be going nowhere and colleagues were getting taken out of the game, frustration started to occur. We questioned the manager's direction but she was only taking instruction from her director. We had worked out a way to win the game ourselves but the manager wasn't listening. We then started to argue amongst ourselves with two of my peers wanting to walk off and the other being a model employee. I was undecided on whether to depart or remain in the game with both sides trying to influence me. The manager could not control the situation. Morale and engagement were at a low.

This whole exercise provided me with a very steep learning curve and a realisation of my own business. I posed several questions to myself: How do the 'shop floor workers' feel in my organisation? Are we carrying out mushroom management? Do we ask them for their ideas? Do we communicate with them effectively or indeed at all? Are they bitter towards management due to a negative response to the questions posed above? The answer to this last question was yes which was a bolt out of the blue as I did not realise that was happening.

I connected this learning with that from the Employee Engagement Masterclass to build a new communication structure within our business. An employee newsletter is now completed bi-monthly and sent to the employees' home (to curtail negativity amongst partners where the employee could make out an inaccurate image and description of the work place). Conducting a leadership questionnaire has helped to let the employees anonymously have their say on their manager's performance. The newly formed employee committee has allowed the 'voice' of the workforce to be heard and provided some very valid points, issues and ideas for the Company.

Directors have encouraged managers to relay essential information back to their teams after the key decision makers meeting, this wasn't happening before and information channels were blocked. These action plans have all been brought on by the realisation that communication wasn't working at all in our organisation. The Company endured a strict hierarchy with major barriers to cross-organisational communication with former long standing directors struggling to communicate between themselves meaning any interaction and exchange with staff at any level was minimal.

Both Human and Social Capitals: Leading In- and Out-Groups

From a leadership masterclass, I linked Leader Member Exchange [LMX] Theory with my organisation. We had very distinct sub groups. The financial controller and sales manager with access to a wide range of information were the 'in-group'. A sales office manager, interiors manager and operations manager were in the 'out-group'.

I have heavily relied on the information provided to me by the 'in-group' and made big decisions based on their knowledge and facts. Although I would listen to the 'out-group', they were on the periphery. This however has been to the detriment of the business and the two members of the 'in-group' no longer are at the company due to inaccurate information being provided.

I have learnt a harsh but very valuable lesson from this experience, and on reflection, I spent too much time relying and listening to the 'in-group' when the 'out-group' were holding key operational information which hadn't been tapped into. After my recent encounter with the LMX theory I realise being too close to an 'in-group' alienates the 'out-group' and does not promote employee relationships. For future reference, I will be extremely careful not to harbour strong links with certain managers who are on the same level as each other to avoid creating groups which would not be beneficial for relationships within the Company.

Institutional and Human Capitals: Personal Responsibility

I recognise that I cannot do it all and that I need a capable management team around me. Leaving managers to manage on their own is not suitable either. During the course of LEAD I have discussed replacing poor performing senior managers with my peers inside and outside of Action Learning Sets as well as with my coach. This is something that has never happened in our company's history, but because peers that I respect said it was the correct course of action, I have changed most of the senior team.

Due to LEAD, I have found myself constantly reflecting on every meeting that I have, which in turn, has aided me to evolve in my role as Managing Director. An example of this is a key decision makers meeting which I chair. I ensure that I am well prepared going into the meeting with a set agenda and forward this to members of staff to add content/points before the meet. As this is an important meeting, it is important that I listen intently and answer succinctly any questions posed. Prior to LEAD, I was a poor listener. I also asked closed questions rather than the open questions I have been coached to use in Action Learning.

Institutional, Social and Human Capitals: The Journey

My LEAD journey has provided me with the basis to form a new structure within the organisation. Before I started the programme I had certainly approached a cliff and realised I needed further learning, knowledge and peer support to help increase my skill level as a Managing Director in my company. I felt isolated in my environment and required an added impetus to help change my organisation. After obtaining new knowledge from some very beneficial Masterclasses, I was able to reflect on my learning from the Overnight Experiential and contextualised it opening my eyes to what was not working in my organisation. This helped me enormously in putting my new learning into practice to 'fix' what was being run poorly within the business.

Shadowing and Exchange helped increase my confidence further by 'living' in another business for two days, realising that my new knowledge and learning could also help another organisation.

The peer group that has been part of the LEAD programme have been a huge aid to my development . . . having access to such a network is immeasurably important and I have learnt a wealth of information from just listening to other owner-managers. This has been the greatest support group I could have hoped for and I continue to network/socialise with my peers post-LEAD with continued personal and business gain for us all.

I now feel that I have arrived at a major crossroads in my working career with implementation of key strategies being the future heartbeat of the organisation, with growth and expansion of the business not just a pipe dream but a reality. I have gained much experience, knowledge and learning over the past year and will be putting this further into practice over the coming years.

Reflections

We hope the case study helps to demonstrate the interrelatedness of human, social and institutional capital. Leitch et al. (2013: 360) suggest such integration is needed for the development of entrepreneurial leadership within the small business relational context. We demonstrate the interrelatedness between each element below.

First, Freddie has developed his human capital; that is, improving his knowledge, skills and capabilities. This is evident through the acquisition of new knowledge he says he has gained from the learning interventions and the other owner-managers, which he has put into practice and plans to continue to do so. He has developed his practice to embrace open questions and active listening alongside, an increasing accent on reflection, for example reflecting back on events, during meetings, and reflecting forwards to prepare himself and his staff for when they meet. He highlights how his confidence has increased and identifies with aspiring to become a particular leader identity. A sense of a narrative identity (Ezzy, 1998) has emerged in that Freddie sees himself as central to developing his business, through establishing a business plan for the first time in the company's 100-year history, creating a new business unit and growing sales.

Second, Freddie has developed notions of internally oriented social capital (Adler and Kwon, 2014) with a particular orientation to relationships between individuals and organisations that facilitate action and create value (Hitt and Ireland, 2002). He recognised the need for a capable management team around him, resulting in a change of most of the senior team, in a sense implicitly taking the view that social capital development was limited by role incumbents. We see a mindfulness of Freddie toward his future behaviour and relationships with managers to seek to maximise social capital through being careful to create beneficial internal networks. More broadly, aspects of social cohesion and solidarity have been advanced with attention to communications. This is illustrated by the implementation of an employee engagement strategy. The consequence has been an overt change to Freddie's previous highly directive leadership practice. In a sense, giving a 'voice' to the workforce in turn has enabled issues and ideas to be circulated. Blockages have been addressed and communication has been encouraged between directors and managers to relay essential information back to their teams after the key decision-makers' meeting.

Third, institutional capital was developed through the creation of the LEAD CoP, that is, the formal structures and organisations which enhance the role of social capital and go beyond enriching the human capital stock of individual leaders (Anderson, 2010). This has been enabled through the expanded network of Freddie's LEAD peers, the business leaders who did not know each other previously coming together to create a CoP. Freddie's comments give clear recognition that this peer group has been a huge aid to his development. Leitch et al. (2013: 358) argue that the development of the reservoir of social capital (in our case, the LEAD peers) transcends the boundaries of each individual firm which provides the platform for the development of institutional capital. The structures and informal governance approaches, pedagogy and the rules of engagement within the LEAD CoP have enabled the creation of an institution. Comments from Freddie illustrate him drawing from the institutional capital in terms of its effect on his own entrepreneurial leadership development and his business. He recognises that his peers have been a most valuable support group. The ongoing presence of the institution is reflected in his continuing to network and socialise with them after the programme officially finished. The informal structures and governing rules of engagement have persisted. An example of this is where Freddie highlights how, through his engagement and investment in the CoP, he can see the benefit to himself, his own organisation, his peers and their organisation from 'his peers'. He cites how the process of 'shadowing' another business has added institutional value to the community as well as the participating businesses. The risks associated with the process are mitigated through the accepted governance of the relationships within the institution.

The case study brings together human, social and institutional capitals, showing how institutional capital can be developed through the establishment of a CoP (as in the above example of LEAD) that can enable the development of entrepreneurial leadership through nurturing and enhancing human, social and institutional capitals.

NEXT STAGES FOR RESEARCH AND DEVELOPMENT IN ENTREPRENEURIAL LEADERSHIP LEARNING

It has been our intention in this chapter to summarise what is known about entrepreneurial leadership learning. We have sought to elaborate the phenomenon in the context of emerging debates in the leadership field. In particular, we have highlighted how leadership is seen as a relational social process focusing on practices and identities vis-à-vis the essentialist qualities and characteristics of an individual; leadership as relational rather than individual. In terms of leadership learning the corollary is to look to social learning theory to give insight. In this chapter we have outlined social learning theory and its constituent, legitimate peripheral participation and communities of practice (CoP) theory. Together, they provide a relational frame to understand notions of becoming in terms of practices and identities that are developed within particular situations through processes of legitimate peripheral participation. Knowing, being and doing become learned as a shared dynamic; a community of shared understanding. In the context of entrepreneurial leadership learning the relationship is between the owner-manager(s) and the employee(s). The practice of leading is the knowing, being and doing that emerges and is continually becoming and ongoing within this community of leadership practice. It is a form of learned occupational practice of leading.

The case of Freddie gives insight into the lived experience of entrepreneurial leadership learning as a collective and integrative process of human, social and institutional capital development. For us, this insight suggests a range of questions and avenues for researching entrepreneurial leadership learning. Our argument has proposed that this phenomenon is relational and that situated learning theory has much to offer in terms of what is occurring within entrepreneurial leadership learning. As such, our first research agenda is focused on learning. We suggest that this would need to be qualitative to understand the situated social learning processes. The focus on in-depth, thick descriptions (Orr, 1996) is needed to illuminate something of the emergent and opaque phenomenon that is situated learning. For example, how does an individual entrepreneur become an active member of a CoP? What stages of transition might be evident? How does the language and meaning become shared? Where is the language and meaning drawn from? How does this impact upon the individual and their businesses? How do the shared meanings and the shared repertoire of practices and identities within this CoP migrate across to the individual and their practice (human capital) within the entrepreneurial context (social capital)? How does a CoP emerge within a leadership development programme?

Our second research agenda is related to the first and is associated with the development of human, social and institutional capital. We have suggested that these three capitals are interrelated through the relational learning process of situated learning. In particular, notions of leader becoming (human capital) are informed by shared being, doing and knowing that occurs in the CoP – the programme cohort. Questions that follow this assertion are: What is the relationship of a CoP and the development of human, social and institutional capital? How do the three capitals operate inside a CoP? Can a CoP emerge without the presence of all three capitals?

The third research agenda is more specifically oriented to the three capitals. Leitch et al. (2013) have suggested that little is known of how these capitals interrelate, and comment that social capital and institutional capital reinforce each other. However, we need to know how. Further, we need to understand the tripartite relationship of all three. How does social and human capital development, as emergent and ongoing in the entrepreneurial context, shape the institutional capital? What happens when the LEAD CoP ends? We are assuming that all three capitals malleably interact, but is this so? Are there significant time lags between these? Does one capital have greater influence than the others? Final big question: how valuable are the three capitals to business survival and growth?

These three connected research agendas would point towards important policy issues related to the efficacy and effectiveness of leadership development designs for the development of entrepreneurial leadership and for the development of the small business.

To address these three research agendas and the policy aspect of business survival and growth, we suggest a comprehensive research programme that is centred on a longitudinal design: a study which tracks LEAD participants and their businesses over time (see Barnes et al., 2015, for an illustration of such longitudinal research). Although we have suggested above the need for qualitative research to address the range of research questions we have outlined, this should not mean that quantitative research should be ignored. Rather, we suggest that a mixed-methods approach (Bryman, 2006) would usefully allow detailed examination of the interrelated issues. The range and number of businesses that have undertaken the LEAD programme provide a data set that would enable complementary quantitative and qualitative examination. For example, more than 2000 owner-managers have engaged on the LEAD programme. Although this has been helpfully evaluated, it has not sought to attend to an understanding of the development of entrepreneurial leadership learning and the related aspects of situated learning, CoP and the three capitals. First, this data set could be base-lined through qualitative and quantitative approaches to understand, for example, whether the manifestation of the three capitals has occurred, whether they have been sustained and what impact is evident. This may reflect questionnaires and interviews, but also other possible approaches such as repertory grid, critical incidents and narrative analysis. Subsequently, LEAD cohorts could be followed to address the research agenda. Respondents might include the owner-managers, of course, but also colleagues in their organisations (to explore internal social capital), possibly other business stakeholders (customers, suppliers), as well as leadership development practitioners. Approaches additional to interview might include ethnography, autoethnographies, critical incidents and possibly questionnaires. By undertaking a complementary mixed-methods approach this would allow for a robust elaboration of the development of entrepreneurial leadership learning through a relational lens and its relationship with and between the three capitals.

CONCLUSION

Although the phenomenon of entrepreneurial leadership learning is at the very early stages of construction and understanding, our chapter has provided an illumination of the salient aspects that can help further research and development to occur. In this way we hope we have been able to build upon Leitch et al.'s (2013: 361) call for more research and theory development for the integration of institutional capital with social and human capitals. We hope the exploration we have outlined, of a social learning dynamic of entrepreneurial leadership learning incorporating the three capitals, has embraced such integration and provides a platform for future theory-building and complementary empirical research. The need for understanding the development of entrepreneurial leadership interconnected with the three capitals is most important for the growth of businesses and the societies in which they are embedded; in a sense, generating a fourth capital: economic capital.

REFERENCES

Adler, P.S. and Kwon, S.-W. (2014) Social capital: Prospects for a new concept. *Academy of Management Review*, 27(1): 17–40.
Alvesson, M. and Sveningsson, S. (2003) The great disappearing act: Difficulties in doing 'leadership'. *Leadership Quarterly*, 14(3): 359–81.
Anderson, L.E. (2010) *Social Capital in Developing Democracies: Nicaragua and Argentina Compared.* Cambridge: Cambridge University Press.
Avolio, B.J. (2005) *Leadership Development in Balance: Made/Born.* Hillsdale, NJ: Erlbaum.
Bagheri, A. and Pihie, Z.A.L. (2011) Entrepreneurial leadership: Towards a model for learning and development. *Human Resource Development International*, 14(4): 447–63.
Barnes, S., Kempster, S. and Smith, S. (2015) *LEADing Small Business: Business Growth through Leadership Development.* Cheltenham, UK and Northampton, MA: Edward Elgar Publishing.
Bennis, W.G. and Thomas, R.G. (2002) Crucibles of leadership. *Harvard Business Review*, 80(9): 39–46.
Brown, J.S. and Duguid, P. (1991) Organizational learning and communities of practice: Toward a unified view of working, learning and innovation. *Organization Science*, 2: 40–57.
Bryman, A. (2006) Integrating quantitative and qualitative research: How is it done?. *Qualitative Research*, 6: 97–113.
Carroll, B., Levy, L. and Richmond, D. (2008) Leadership as practice: Challenging the competency paradigm. *Leadership*, 4(4): 363–79.
Cogliser, C.C. and Brigham, K.H. (2004) The intersection of leadership and entrepreneurship: Mutual lessons to be learned. *Leadership Quarterly*, 15: 771–99.
Cooney, T.M. (2005) Editorial: What is an entrepreneurial team?. *International Small Business Journal*, 23(3): 226–35.
Cope, J. (2005) Toward a dynamic learning perspective of entrepreneurship. *Entrepreneurship Theory and Practice*, 29(4): 373–97.
Cope, J., Kempster, S. and Parry, K. (2011) Exploring distributed leadership in the small business context. *International Journal of Management Reviews*, 13(3): 270–285.
Cope, J. and Watts, G. (2000) Learning by doing: An exploration of experience, critical incidents and reflection in entrepreneurial learning. *International Journal of Entrepreneurship Behaviour and Research*, 6(3): 104–24.
Cox, C.J. and Cooper, C.L. (1989) The making of the British CEO: Childhood, work experience, personality, and management style. *Academy of Management Executive*, 3(3): 241–45.
Davies, J. and Easterby-Smith, M. (1984) Learning and developing from managerial work experience. *Journal of Management Studies*, 21(2): 169–83.
DeRue, D.S. and Ashford, S.J. (2010) Who will lead and who will follow? A social process of leadership identity construction in organizations. *Academy of Management Review*, 35: 627–47.
Drath, W.H., McCauley, C.D., Palus, C.J., Van Velsor, E., O'Connor, P.M.G. and McGuire, J.B. (2008) Direction, alignment, commitment: Toward a more integrative ontology of leadership. *Leadership Quarterly*, 19(6): 635–53.
Ellis, C. (2004) *The Ethnographic I: A Methodological Novel about Autoethnography.* Walnut Creek, CA: AltaMira Press.
Ezzy, D. (1998) Theorizing narrative identity: Symbolic interactionism and hermeneutics. *Sociological Quarterly*, 39(2): 239–52.

Fernadez, R.M. and Castilla, E.J. (2001) How much is that network worth? Social capital in employee referral networks. In K. Cook, N. Lin and R.S. Burt (eds), *Social Capital: Theory and Research*. Chicago, IL: Aldine-de-Gruyter, pp. 85–103.

Gartner, W.B., Shaver, K.G., Gatewood, E. and Katz, J.A. (1994) Finding the entrepreneur in entrepreneurship. *Entrepreneurship Theory and Practice*, 18(3): 5–9.

Gherardi, S. (1995) Organizational learning. In Warner, H. (ed.), *International Encyclopaedia of Business and Management*. London: Routledge & Kegan Paul, pp. 3934–42.

Gherardi, S., Nicolini, D. and Odella, F. (1998) Towards a social understanding of how people learn in organizations: The notion of a situated curriculum. *Management Learning*, 29(3): 273–97.

Grint, K. (2010) The sacred in leadership: Separation, sacrifice and silence. *Organizations Studies*, 31(1), 89–107.

Gupta, V., MacMillan, I.C. and Surie, G. (2004) Entrepreneurial leadership: Developing and measuring a cross-cultural construct. *Journal of Business Venturing*, 19: 241–60.

Hill, L.A. (2003) *Becoming a Manager: How New Managers Master the Challenges of Leadership*. Boston, MA: Harvard Business School Press.

Hitt, M.A. and Ireland, R.D. (2002) The essence of strategic leadership: Managing human and social capital. *Journal of Leadership and Organization Studies*, 9(1): 3–14.

Iles, P. and Preece, D. (2006) Developing leaders or developing leadership? The Academy of Chief Executives' programme in the North East of England. *Leadership*, 2: 317–40.

Jackson, B. and Parry, K. (2001) *The Hero Manager: Learning from New Zealand's Top Chief Executives*. Auckland: Penguin Books.

Janson, A. (2008) Extracting leadership knowledge from formative experiences. *Leadership*, 4(1): 73–94.

Jensen, S.M. and Luthans, F. (2006) Entrepreneurs as authentic leaders: Impact on employees' attitudes. *Leadership and Organization Development Journal*, 27(8): 646–66.

Kelly, S. (2014) A negative ontology of leadership. *Human Relations*, 67(8): 905–22.

Kempster, S.J. (2006) Leadership learning through lived experience: a process of apprenticeship?. *Journal of Management and Organization*, 12(1): 4–22.

Kempster, S.J. (2009) *How Managers Have Learnt to Lead: Exploring the Development of Leadership Practice*. Basingstoke: Palgrave Macmillan.

Kempster, S. and Cope, J. (2010) Learning to lead in the entrepreneurial context. *International Journal of Entrepreneurial Behaviour and Research*, 16(1): 5–34.

Kempster, S. and Stewart, J. (2010) Becoming a leader: A co-produced autoethnographic exploration of situated learning of leadership practice. *Management Learning*, 41(5): 205–19.

Lave, J. and Wenger, E. (1991) *Situated Learning: Legitimate Peripheral Participation*. Cambridge: Cambridge University Press.

Leitch, C.M., McMullan, C. and Harrison, R.T. (2013) The development of entrepreneurial leadership: The role of human, social and institutional capital. *British Journal of Management*, 24: 347–66.

McCall, M.W. (2004) Leadership development through experience, *Academy of Management Executive*. 18(3): 127–30.

McCall, M.W., Lombardo, M.M. and Morrison, A.M. (1988) *The Lessons of Experience: How Successful Executives Develop on the Job*. Lexington, MA: Lexington Books.

Meindl, J. (1995) The romance of leadership as a follower-centric theory: A social constructionist approach. *Leadership Quarterly*, 6(3): 329–41.

Nahapiet, J. and Ghoshal, S. (1998) Social capital, intellectual capital, and organizational advantage. *Academy of Management Review*, 23: 242–66.

Orr, J.E. (1996) *Talking about Machines: An Ethnography of a Modern Job*. Ithaca, NY: Cornell University Press.

Pittaway, L. and Thorpe, R. (2012) A theory of entrepreneurial learning: A tribute to Jason Cope. *Entrepreneurship and Regional Development*, 24(9/10): 837–59.

Raelin, J. (2011) From leadership-as-practice to leaderful practice. *Leadership*, 7(2): 195–211.

Renko, M., Tarabishy, A.E., Carsud, A.L. and Brannback, M. (2015) Understanding and measuring entrepreneurial leadership style. *Journal of Small Business Management*, 53(1): 54–74.

Ruvio, A., Rosenblatt, Z. and Hertz-Lazarowitz, R. (2010) Entrepreneurial leadership vision in non-profit vs. for profit organizations. *Leadership Quarterly*, 21: 144–58.

Smith, S. (2011) How do small business owner-managers learn leadership through networked learning?. In Dirckinck-Holmfeld, L., Hodgson, V. and McConnell, D. (eds), *Exploring the Theory, Pedagogy and Practice of Networked Learning*. New York, NY: Springer, pp. 221–36.

Smith, S. and Smith, L. (2013) 'I am therefore I think': Exploring the complexities of identity within action learning for entrepreneurs. Paper presented at the British Academy of Management Conference, September, Liverpool.

Surie, G. and Ashley, A. (2008) Integrating pragmatism and ethics in entrepreneurial leadership for sustainable value creation. *Journal of Business Ethics*, 81(1): 235–46.

Taylor, D.W. and Thorpe, R. (2004) Entrepreneurial learning: A process of co-participation. *Journal of Small Business and Enterprise Development*, 11: 203–11.

Thorpe, R., Cope, J., Ram, M. and Pedler, M. (2009) Leadership development in small- and medium-sized enterprises: The case for action learning. *Action Learning: Research and Practice*, 6(3): 201–8.

Uhl-Bien, M. (2006) Relational leadership theory: Exploring the social processes of leadership and organizing. *Leadership Quarterly*, 17: 654–76.

Vecchio, R.P. (2003) Entrepreneurship and leadership: Common trends and common threads. *Human Resource Management Review*, 13: 303–27.

Watson, T.J. (2011) Ethnography, reality, and truth: The vital need for studies of 'how things work' in organizations and management. *Journal of Management Studies*, 48: 202–17.

Wenger, E. (1998) *Communities of Practice: Learning, Meaning, and Identity*. Cambridge: Cambridge University Press.

Wenger, E. (2000) Communities of practice: The key of knowledge strategy. In Lesser, E.L., Fontaine, M.A. and Slusher, J.A. (eds), *Knowledge and Communities*. Woburn, MA: Butterworth-Heinemann, pp. 3–20.

Wenger, E. (2004) Learning for a small planet: A research agenda. Paper presented at the annual meeting of the American Educational Research Association, San Diego, CA, April.

Wren, C. and Jones, J. (2006) Ex-post evaluation of the LEAD Programme. Unpublished report, University of Newcastle Upon Tyne. Available at http://www.lums.ac.uk/leaddeval.

Wren, C. and Jones, J. (2012) Quantitative evaluation of the LEAD Programme, 2004–11. University of Newcastle Upon Tyne. Available at http://www.ncl.ac.uk/nubs/research/publication/192709.

Zhu, W., Chew, I.K.H. and Spangler, W.D. (2005) CEO transformational leadership and organizational outcomes: The mediating role of human-capital-enhancing human resource management. *Leadership Quarterly*, 16: 39–52.

15. Entrepreneurial leadership competencies and motivation to learn: a focus on student entrepreneurial leaders
Afsaneh Bagheri and Zaidatol Akmaliah Lope Pihie

INTRODUCTION

Entrepreneurial leadership has recently emerged as a specific leadership style at the interface of entrepreneurship and organizational leadership (e.g., Renko et al., 2013; Fernald et al., 2005; Gupta et al., 2004). As a distinctive leadership style, its historical evolution begins with a focus on the exceptional characteristics of entrepreneurial leaders, the situational and contextual factors affecting them as they step into leading entrepreneurial activities, and their behaviors in facing the complexities and difficulties of the activities (Gupta et al., 2004). Recent research has explored the social process of learning through which entrepreneurial leaders not only develop their knowledge, capabilities and attributes to face the inherited challenges of leadership in entrepreneurial contexts (Leitch et al., 2013; Kempster and Cope, 2010; Gupta et al., 2004), but also improve their capacity to influence and regulate their group members' performance toward exploring and exploiting entrepreneurial opportunities (Renko et al., 2013). These studies have mostly examined the entrepreneurial leadership practices of organizational leaders (Gupta et al., 2004; Vecchio, 2003; Swiercz and Lydon, 2002). Research on competencies of such leaders in contexts other than established organizations and entrepreneurial firms is scarce (Leitch et al., 2013; Young and Sexton, 2003). More specifically, only a few studies have examined entrepreneurial leadership among university students (Mattare, 2008; Okudan and Rzasa, 2006). Furthermore, prior research has investigated the factors that motivate entrepreneurs to learn how to develop their business (Young and Sexton, 2003). As far as we know there is no published work on the factors that drive university students to learn and develop their entrepreneurial leadership competencies.

In this chapter, we explore the entrepreneurial leadership competencies and the factors that motivate students in student entrepreneurship clubs in universities to learn and develop their entrepreneurial leadership competencies. In particular, we consider the specific challenges they face in creating entrepreneurial ideas, recognizing entrepreneurial opportunities, marshaling resources, and mobilizing and inspiring a group of students to successfully fulfill the objectives of entrepreneurship clubs and projects. In accordance with prior research, we define entrepreneurship clubs as the 'informal, non-accredited student-led' communities whose key objective is to improve entrepreneurial knowledge and capabilities of interested students by involving them in entrepreneurial tasks and roles such as leading student entrepreneurship projects and activities (Pittaway et al., 2010).

Using a qualitative research method, we sought to address two main questions: (1) What are the entrepreneurial leadership competencies of students leading student entrepreneurship clubs and projects? (2) What are the factors that motivate them to learn how to lead the clubs and projects and develop these competencies? We present the experience of 14 students as entrepreneurial leaders to explore their constant practices in developing leadership competencies and their motives to learn and develop these competencies. This study contributes to the scarce research on entrepreneurial leadership in the context of entrepreneurship education where the individuals intentionally participate in programs to improve their knowledge, skills and competencies of entrepreneurial leadership (Leitch et al., 2013; Okudan and Rzasa, 2006). The remainder of this chapter is organized in six sections. The first section reviews the definitions of entrepreneurial leadership and the most frequently cited competencies and characteristics of entrepreneurial leaders. Then, we present an overview of prior studies on motivation to learn in entrepreneurial ventures. Subsequently, we describe the research methodology and findings. Finally, we conclude with a discussion of the findings, their implications for entrepreneurial leadership education and research, and present an agenda for future research.

ENTREPRENEURIAL LEADERSHIP DEFINITION AND COMPETENCIES

Despite the promising role that entrepreneurial leadership can play in new venture creation, performance and development, as well as in addressing the challenges faced in the current organizational environment (Frey, 2010; Murali et al., 2009; Baron, 2006; Gupta et al., 2004), there is no commonly accepted definition and theory for this type of leadership. Early definitions of the concept focused on the personal traits and attributes of entrepreneurial leaders and the competencies that enable them to lead entrepreneurial organizations toward growth and development (Surie and Ashley, 2008; Chen, 2007; Kuratko, 2007; Gupta et al., 2004; Swiercz and

Lydon, 2002). While entrepreneurial traits are innate and static characteristics of entrepreneurial leaders, 'entrepreneurial competencies are considered a higher-level characteristic encompassing personality traits, skills and knowledge' and 'have long-term effects and closer links to organizational performance' (Man et al., 2002: 124). Empirical research has also revealed the importance of some characteristics of entrepreneurial leaders over other factors at different stages of entrepreneurial companies' performance and growth (Vecchio, 2003; Swiercz and Lydon, 2002). More recent definitions include the process through which entrepreneurial leadership occurs, and how it is learned and developed (Leitch et al., 2013; Renko et al., 2013; Kempster and Cope, 2010; Gupta et al., 2004). Based on an organizational leadership perspective, Renko et al. (2013: 2) defined the notion as a process of 'influencing and directing the performance of group members toward the achievement of organizational goals that involve recognizing and exploiting opportunities'.

Gupta et al. (2004) have emphasized the critical roles that entrepreneurial leaders play in influencing, inspiring and regulating their group members' behavior and paving the way for them to enact their entrepreneurial vision. However, for them to be able to overcome this challenge, entrepreneurial leaders require to improve their personal capabilities. Therefore, such leaders need to develop their personal knowledge, attributes and capabilities through different stages of their organization growth and development (Swiercz and Lydon, 2002). Specifically, during the early stage of a new venture, entrepreneurial leaders need to possess certain personal competencies that enable them to successfully achieve the goals of the entrepreneurial companies. These include accepting the responsibility of leading entrepreneurial activities, exploring and evaluating the entrepreneurial opportunities, marshaling the required resources and creating a group to exploit the opportunities (Vecchio, 2003; Swiercz and Lydon, 2002). Drawing on human capital and social capital theories, Leitch et al. (2013) have described entrepreneurial leadership development as a social interactive process through which the personal knowledge, traits and capabilities of the leader and their leadership capacity develop at the same time.

Entrepreneurship scholars have reached a relative consensus on the distinctive competencies of entrepreneurial leaders that motivate and enable them to successfully lead entrepreneurial activities (Nicholson, 1998). Three key personal competencies of entrepreneurial leaders have been most cited by previous studies: proactiveness, innovativeness and risk-taking (Surie and Ashley, 2008; Chen, 2007; Kuratko, 2007; Fernald et al., 2005; Gupta et al., 2004). Entrepreneurial leaders are distinguished from other types of leaders by being proactive, which is their capability to envision and create a successful future for their companies by exploring entrepreneurial opportunities and anticipating the future challenges and problems (Hannah et al., 2008; Okudan and Rzasa, 2006; Kuratko et al., 2007). Entrepreneurial leaders also have a high capability to think of creative and novel entrepreneurial ideas and develop them to work in practice (Mattare, 2008; Chen, 2007; Okudan and Rzasa, 2006; Rae, 2007; Gupta et al., 2004). Therefore, entrepreneurial leaders are creative innovators who are committed to action and value creation (Surie and Ashley, 2008).

Prior research has also identified calculated and prudent risk-taking as a personal capability of entrepreneurial leaders (Chen, 2007). This trait reflects the leaders' propensity and ability to absorb the uncertainties and ambiguities inherited in entrepreneurial activities, and take the burden of responsibility for the future and outcomes of the activities (Chen, 2007; Zhao et al., 2005; Mueller and Thomas, 2000). Although necessary, possessing personal traits does not guarantee the success of entrepreneurial leaders in facing the challenges and problems of entrepreneurial activities (Gupta et al., 2004). Therefore, entrepreneurial leaders should also develop their competencies to perform the specific roles and tasks of the leader in entrepreneurial organizations (Vecchio, 2003; Swiercz and Lydon, 2002). While Swiercz and Lydon (2002) related these leadership competencies to more managerial activities and performances of entrepreneurial leaders such as operations, finance, marketing and human resources, more recent research has focused on the capabilities of these leaders to influence, inspire and regulate their group members' behavior and performance toward fulfilling the goals which have been set (Leitch et al., 2013; Renko et al., 2013; Gupta et al., 2004).

Gupta et al. (2004) have developed a theoretical foundation for entrepreneurial leadership based on both the personal and functional challenges of entrepreneurial leaders in organizational settings. According to the theory, the personal competencies of such leaders enable them to envision a successful future by exploring an innovative vision. Furthermore, the leaders have the capacity to: (1) influence and inspire their group members to abandon their current conventional activities and extend their energy and efforts to perform creative and entrepreneurial actions; (2) reshape their perceptions of their capabilities through involving them in developing creative ideas; and (3) build their confidence and commitment to achieve the entrepreneurial vision. These interpersonal competencies enable entrepreneurial leaders to intentionally influence and regulate their followers' behavior and performance, and direct activities and interactions in an entrepreneurial group or company (Leitch et al., 2013).

Previous research has emphasized the influential impact of entrepreneurship education and training (Kempster and Cope, 2010; Gupta et al., 2004), and specifically student entrepreneurship clubs, in developing entrepreneurial leadership competencies by involving students in leading real entrepreneurial activities (Pittaway et al., 2010). Building on Leitch et al.'s (2013) definition, we have defined student entrepreneurial leadership as a process of social interaction and influence that develops students' entrepreneurial knowledge and competencies as well as their capabilities to successfully perform the tasks and roles of the leader in university entrepreneurship clubs and projects. However, empirical research on this notion of leadership in educational settings is scarce (Leitch et al., 2013; Okudan and Rzasa, 2006).

MOTIVATION TO LEARN ENTREPRENEURIAL LEADERSHIP

Literature on the motivation factors of entrepreneurship has evolved through three main streams. The first body of literature examined the factors that drive individuals to select entrepreneurship as their career path (McMullen et al., 2008; Matlay, 2005; Shane et al., 2003; Aldrich, 2000), enhance their commitment to entrepreneurial activities, and improve their business ventures' performance and success (Raposo et al., 2008; Cardon et al., 2005; Shane et al., 2003; Alstete, 2002). Despite the influential impact of personal motivation factors on individuals' entrepreneurial intentions, efforts and behavior (Renko et al., 2012; Carsrud and Brännback, 2011), prior research has mostly concentrated on the environmental factors, and particularly economic constraints, that influence people to step into business venturing (Carsrud and Brännback, 2011; Aldrich, 2000). This focus on the economic and environmental motives of entrepreneurs has led to our greater understanding and knowledge of the entrepreneurship process rather than the various personal motivation factors that drive individuals to initiate and lead the process (Shane et al., 2003; Alstete, 2002). Scholars argue that only very highly motivated individuals, who have developed their entrepreneurial capabilities over a long period of time, step into entrepreneurship and are capable of coping with the inherent challenges of the complex entrepreneurial tasks and roles (Schjoedt and Shaver, 2007; Stewart and Roth, 2007; Segal et al., 2005).

Through an integrated approach, research has provided empirical evidence for the impact of both personal and environmental factors that drive individuals' decision to engage in the process of entrepreneurship (Segal et al., 2005; Shane et al., 2003). While negative factors such as joblessness or job dissatisfaction push some to choose entrepreneurship as their career path, others are attracted by 'pull' factors such as personal development to engage in entrepreneurial activities (Stewart and Roth, 2007). Interestingly, people become entrepreneurs mostly because they are drawn or 'pulled' to entrepreneurship (Schjoedt and Shaver, 2007; Segal et al., 2005). McMullen et al. (2008) examined people's motivation to become entrepreneurs among different countries, and classified entrepreneurial motives as the opportunities and necessities that attract or push people to launch their entrepreneurial venture. Carsrud and Brännback (2011) grouped entrepreneurial motivations into 'intrinsic' factors (for example, personal interest in entrepreneurial roles) and 'extrinsic' factors (for example, external consequences and rewards of performing the roles), and argued that a combination of the two factors drives entrepreneurial behavior.

The second stream of research explored the factors that motivate entrepreneurs to learn how to grow and develop their entrepreneurial ventures. In a longitudinal study over ten years, Wiklund et al. (2003) showed how small business managers' positive attitudes toward growth, and their expectations of the outcomes of the growth, motivated them to expand their businesses. Young and Sexton (2003) specifically focused on entrepreneurs' motivation to learn and expand their entrepreneurial ventures, and argued that their motivation to learn is a function of the changes and challenges in the environment of entrepreneurial companies. Accordingly, entrepreneurs engage in learning and developmental activities in order to prevent or deal with the challenges and problems. They identified two sources that motivate entrepreneurs' learning and development opportunities – internal (originating from inside the business) and external sources (factors in the organizational environment) – and concluded that a combination of both is necessary. Although previous research has shed some light on entrepreneurs' motivation to learn, research on the factors that motivate entrepreneurs to learn and develop their personal capabilities, and the effects of these factors on driving entrepreneurial behavior, has only recently emerged in the literature (Block and Landgraf, 2014).

Finally, our knowledge on motivation to learn and develop entrepreneurial capabilities specifically in educational settings is limited to those empirical studies that examine the factors that drive students to learn about entrepreneurship. Anderson and Jack (2008) classified students' impetuses to learn about entrepreneurship into their personal desire for self-development that attracts them to seek out learning experiences, and economic necessities that push them to do so. Previous research has also emphasized the impact of economic necessities such as recessions and problems that push students toward learning about entrepreneurship (Tan et al., 1995). Entrepreneurship education is one of the most significant environmental factors that motivates students to learn and develop their entrepreneurial capabilities and impacts on their intentions to become an entrepreneur (e.g., Guerrero et al., 2008; Pittaway and Cope, 2007a; Fayolle et al., 2006). In fact, without the desire to become an entrepreneur, there is no reason for learning and developing entrepreneurial competencies (Rae and Carswell, 2000). Positive experiences in entrepreneurship education, such as interactions with team members, act to increase students' affection and desire toward entrepreneurial activities (Man and Yu, 2007; Peterman and Kennedy, 2003). However, compulsory and ineffective entrepreneurship education can also reduce students' motivation and ambition to become entrepreneurs (Oosterbeek et al., 2010; Fuchs et al., 2008). This chapter attempts to explore those factors that encourage students to learn how to lead student entrepreneurship clubs and projects and develop their entrepreneurial leadership competencies, to design and implement more effective entrepreneurship education and training.

METHOD

This study examined the everyday leadership experiences and reflections of university students who deliberately choose to lead university entrepreneurship clubs, including the projects and activities organized by the clubs. Also, we examined the particular challenges which they faced, including recognizing an entrepreneurial opportunity, convincing stakeholders of its value, gathering limited resources and inspiring a group of students to achieve the goals of the club, projects and activities. We were particularly interested in how these shaped, and how students learned and developed, their entrepreneurial leadership competencies (Leitch et al., 2013; Okudan and Rzasa, 2006; Shank, 2002).

In Malaysia, entrepreneurship clubs are communities which are embedded in co-curricular university programs and led by the students. The main goal of these clubs is to enhance students' entrepreneurship knowledge and skills by engaging them in leading the clubs and/or in entrepreneurship projects from inception through to launch, including creating a new entrepreneurial idea, exploring an opportunity to do a new business, mobilizing the essential resources, and starting and leading a real business with the help and support of the university.

Data for this study were collected during the academic year of 2010–2011. Both public and private universities were included in the study in order to capture the variety of the universities in terms of their students and their entrepreneurship programs (Matlay, 2006). From the six public universities and 15 private colleges and universities located in the central zone of Malaysia, two public and two private universities were chosen as the data

Table 15.1   Participants' background information

Pseudonym	Age	Gender	Field of study	University	Parents as entrepreneurs
Zakaria	23	Male	Computer Science	Public	No
Eza	21	Female	Accounting	Public	No
Muaz	22	Male	Business Administration	Public	Mother
Nadiah	22	Female	Landscape Architecture	Public	Father
Farhad	23	Male	Business Management	Public	No
Hakim	21	Male	Accounting	Public	No
Firdaus	22	Male	Business Administration	Public	Mother
Clive	21	Male	Computer Science	Public	No
Akhyar	22	Male	IT Business	Private	Father
Ariz	25	Male	Networking System	Private	No
Hisyam	23	Male	Software Engineering	Private	Mother
Saif	22	Male	Creative Multimedia	Private	Mother
Zahid	22	Male	Accounting	Private	No
Ariif	24	Male	Telecommunication Engineering	Private	Father

collection sites for this study. The participants included student entrepreneurial leaders (Table 15.1), defined as those who had successfully led student entrepreneurship clubs, projects and activities for more than one year. This ensured that the students had attempted to learn and develop their entrepreneurial leadership capabilities by being actively involved in leading various projects and activities, compared with those who had recently joined clubs, and those who had just been appointed to leadership positions but had not had an opportunity to practice leadership roles and tasks (Pittaway et al., 2009; Plumly et al., 2008; Fayolle et al., 2006). A sample of 14 student entrepreneurial leaders was selected using a purposive sampling strategy (Patton, 1990). The sample size reflects the in-depth understanding of the students' entrepreneurial leadership competencies and the factors that motivated them to learn and develop these competencies (Onwuegbuzie and Leech, 2007; Mason, 2002; Patton, 1990). The students were selected by university entrepreneurship program coordinators and their friends, to avoid sample selection biases. All of the students were undergraduates, because at the time of this research only undergraduates in Malaysia were provided with the opportunity to join entrepreneurship clubs, projects and activities (Cheng et al., 2009).

In line with previous research into entrepreneurial leadership, the data collection method chosen was the in-depth, qualitative interview (Leitch et al., 2013; Kempster and Cope, 2010; Swiercz and Lydon, 2002). According to Fernald et al. (2005), the existence of entrepreneurial leadership competencies in an individual can be most reliably determined by an in-depth interview. Moreover, in-depth interviews were utilized to gain a better insight of each student's views and experiences regarding their entrepreneurial leadership learning and development (Hoepfl, 1997). All of the participants were interviewed at their respective university. The interviews lasted between 50 and 110 minutes and were audio-recorded for later transcription and analysis.

A list of questions on personal competencies of entrepreneurial leaders and the reasons for developing their entrepreneurial capabilities was developed, based on the literature review. The list included but was not limited to questions such as: What do you think makes you capable of leading entrepreneurship clubs and projects? What are your tasks and responsibilities in leading the clubs and projects? Why are you engaged in leading the clubs and projects? The list of interview questions was submitted to a panel of experts including three local university entrepreneurship and qualitative research lecturers to ensure the content validity of the questions.

Data analysis was performed using NVIVO 8 software to assist in transcription, organization, coding and analysis of the data. Two phases of data analysis were conducted. In the first phase, the data were initially analyzed during and after each interview had been conducted. Through reading the transcripts over and over, the emerging issues, potential themes, gaps in the data and future research directions were identified. This ongoing process enhanced the quality of the data and helped in revising the questions asked, to better identify students' entrepreneurial leadership competencies and their motivations to learn and develop those competencies (Denzin, 1994). The second phase was performed after the interviews had been conducted and was concerned with reducing the data into manageable and meaningful groups, categories and themes, based on the research questions. Using the constant comparative method (Merriam, 1998), the responses to the same questions were read and the similarities and differences in the competencies of the students and their motivation to learn entrepreneurial leadership were explored.

The trustworthiness of the findings was ensured through employing several techniques. First, the data were coded independently by the authors to guard against biases in coding. We also provided detailed transcriptions and field notes and checked the findings against biasness by presenting the codes, themes and findings to some of the lecturers involved in entrepreneurship researches at our faculty (Bogden and Biklen, 2003). Furthermore, we triangulated the data collection methods in two ways: we employed member checking with the participants, where we sent the transcribed interviews to the students for content validity confirmation; and we presented the findings to a group of entrepreneurship researchers for peer review (Creswell, 2007). The results of the data analysis and the emerging themes are detailed in the following sections.

ENTREPRENEURIAL LEADERSHIP COMPETENCIES

In this section, we concentrate on addressing the first research question: What are the entrepreneurial leadership competencies of the students? To answer this, the analysis was constructed from previous research on personal competencies of entrepreneurial leaders, including less tangible capabilities (Swiercz and Lydon, 2002), as well as their leadership competencies, that enable them to successfully influence, inspire and regulate their group members' behavior and performance toward the fulfillment of the objectives of the entrepreneurship clubs and projects (Leitch et al., 2013; Renko et al., 2013).

Personal Competencies of Students as Entrepreneurial Leaders

Entrepreneurial leadership self-efficacy, love of challenges and versatility emerged as the personal competencies of the students as entrepreneurial leaders (Table 15.2). These represent a set of prominent capabilities that separate the students from the average entrepreneurship students, and enable them to successfully lead student entrepreneurship clubs and projects. For the students in our study, these competencies emerged as dynamic because they contained different dimensions that some students may have and some may not.

Entrepreneurial leadership self-efficacy
We structure our findings in this subsection based on Hannah et al.'s (2008) conceptualization of leaders' self-efficacy (leaders' perceived capabilities in successfully performing the specific leadership tasks and roles) and Barbosa et al.'s (2007) dimensions of entrepreneurial self-efficacy (perceived abilities in management, opportunity identification, relationship and tolerance). Most of the students perceived themselves as highly confident in their abilities to successfully establish and lead a new business; for example: 'If I want to envision myself as a leader of my business, I can . . . because I have the capability [and] the confidence to do so' (Zahid).

Specifically, the participants perceived themselves as capable of gathering a group of their friends and 'motivating them to put efforts [into] and achieve the vision of [the entrepreneurship] projects' (Farhad). This

Table 15.2   Competencies of students as entrepreneurial leaders

Personal competencies

A: Entrepreneurial leadership self-efficacy

A1: 'I can do everything now, when they have problems, they will ask me, I instantly tell them . . . what we need to do' (Zakaria)

A2: 'I think I have [the] skills, the strategic mindset on management and [setting] the vision of the company' (Farhad)

A3: 'The opportunities I can see around me, I can say that I am capable of developing a company, because now I am dealing with a group of companies and there are many ideas in them' (Akhyar)

A4: 'I think I have the ability [to become a] wedding planner because I can organize [that]. In western countries, they have these businesses and I think, why not open it in Malaysia? So I want to grab the opportunity' (Eza)

A5: 'I can confidently say that I have the skill to convince people to buy my products. Because I know how to influence people in what they need' (Saif)

A6: 'I have the communication skills to talk and convince customers on things, and also because of my networks' (Farhad)

A7: 'When I come across failure, it will not slow me down from wanting to be an entrepreneur. But I have to just slow down and focus on the problem and try to solve it. So I think that I can overcome whatever comes to me' (Muaz)

A8: 'I don't think anything is a problem for me. Because risk is like a game actually and how we overcome the risk is the most important thing' (Muaz)

A9: 'Other students don't want to get involved because they [say]: I cannot learn it. It's really hard for me, [it is] too difficult for me. Actually when I joined this club, I didn't feel learning the [entrepreneurship] projects is like stressful [and] hard' (Zakaria)

B: Love of challenges

B1: 'I don't believe in playing safe. Like we just sit there and do nothing. Rather than drawing lines, I want to cross the lines. If you just keep drawing lines, you won't go anywhere. But I like to cross the lines. Because I like challenges to develop' (Eza)

B2: 'I tried to start something on my own and then moved on to a bigger project and slowly asked for a bigger project to put myself to a more challenging area where I challenged myself to develop' (Farhad)

B3: 'Students, in my opinion . . . don't want to challenge themselves. They don't want to [become] involved in more problems. But for me I want to join these activities, I want to put myself [in] difficult situations, I need to work hard, I need to think a lot. So, it makes me . . . learn from it' (Saif)

C: Versatility

C1: 'I am the accountant of the group and the leader. I am also the leader of another club at the faculty. Sometimes, I also help in designing the banners for the seminars. Doing all these helped me to learn different skills more' (Zahid)

C2: 'I am a person who is flexible. You can put me at the lowest level of management to work, and also to the strategic management where I could think of creative and innovative projects or business plans or business ventures' (Farhad)

C3: 'It actually put a lot of ideas in me by doing a lot of different things at the same time. Somehow after a while I can connect all the dots, and next time new problem or there is another business venture . . . I can make it more creative and more innovative' (Farhad) highlights self-efficacy as one of the core personal attributes in entrepreneurial contexts that highly affects individuals' efforts and persistence in successfully performing entrepreneurial roles and tasks (Carsrud and Brännback, 2011; De Pillis and Reardon, 2007; Wilson et al., 2007), and suggests that it is one of the influential factors in leadership in entrepreneurial contexts. Furthermore, entrepreneurial leadership self-efficacy that has not yet been formally identified as a competency of entrepreneurial leaders emerged as a multidimensional concept incorporating entrepreneurial self-efficacy (Barbosa et al., 2007) and leadership self-efficacy (Hannah et al., 2008).

The students' entrepreneurial leadership self-efficacy is also grounded in different sources including management, opportunity identification, relationship and influencing, tolerance and learning self-efficacy. While some students perceived themselves as highly efficacious in some areas, others were highly capable in other areas. In some cases, the strong perception and feeling of entrepreneurial leadership self-efficacy was rooted in students' beliefs about their capabilities in strategic planning, decision-making, organizing and management (Table 15.2, A1, A2). In others, it originated from their ability to search for and explore opportunities to establish and lead a new business (Table 15.2, A3, A4) as well as effectively influence, communicate and create strong relationships and networks with various people inside and outside the university (Table 15.2, A5, A6).

Most of the students also expressed a high capability and persistence in dealing with the challenges and problems involved in leading the entrepreneurial activities. They asserted that they put in their 'full efforts' and work hard and 'will never [become] disappointed' (Muaz) even if they face serious challenges and problems (Table 15.2, A7). This sense of high entrepreneurial leadership self-efficacy enhances the students' confidence in and capacity to perceive themselves as capable of overcoming the challenges and problems that entrepreneurial leaders may face, and to look at the risks and difficulties involved in leading a new business as learning opportunities that develop their capabilities (Table 15.2, A8). More importantly, the participants strongly perceived themselves as capable of acquiring the knowledge and skills required for leading their own business: 'you just [need] to believe in yourself that you can do it, that you came here to learn business' (Zahid). Some of the students also expressed their high perseverance in the face of the challenges and difficulties they encountered in their entrepreneurial leadership learning and development: 'we want to learn it, whatever it is, how difficult it is, we can learn it, it is not simple but we can learn' (Hisyam). For some students, involvement in leading the university entrepreneurship clubs and projects was the manifestation of their high self-efficacy in learning entrepreneurial leadership: 'By being entrepreneurial and leading [the entrepreneurial projects] we are actually . . . say[ing] that we can learn it, we can do it' (Farhad). On the other hand, the lack of efficacy in learning entrepreneurship competencies hindered other students from getting involved in the university entrepreneurship clubs and projects and acquiring the entrepreneurial knowledge and competencies (Table 15.2, A9).

Leadership learning self-efficacy, which was perceived as the ability to learn the complex and challenging skills of leadership (Anderson et al., 2008; Hannah et al., 2008), applying efforts and persevering in learning and developing the capabilities required for leading entrepreneurial activities and addressing the challenges of leadership practices in university entrepreneurship clubs and projects, emerged as influential in entrepreneurial leadership development for the students.

Love of challenges
Participants had a strong desire and propensity to seek, take on and frequently engage in challenging and difficult tasks in order to learn how to lead the entrepreneurship clubs and projects and develop their entrepreneurial leadership competencies (Table 15.2, B1). They described themselves as individuals who '[love] challenges' and '[enjoy] to go to a problem, solve the problem and learn it and do something that people don't want to do' (Ariz), because 'You won't learn from something which is easy. You have to put yourself in a challenging situation and then you will learn' (Firdaus). This strong desire is not limited to just a positive feeling toward challenges and problems involved in leading entrepreneurial activities, but also includes seeking out challenges to develop their entrepreneurial leadership (Table 15.2, B2). Compared with other students, the participants stated a stronger propensity to take on challenges, seek out difficult situations and problems, and cross boundaries that others do not want to (Table 15.2, B3). This is an emergent competency that has not yet been formally identified among entrepreneurial leaders, although previous research has identified 'love challenges' as one of the personal characteristics of entrepreneurs (Dvir et al., 2010), which highlighted it as a key personal competency in entrepreneurial contexts and an important capability required for successfully leading entrepreneurial activities.

Love of challenges creates in students the courage, passion and ability to face the often daunting tests associated with leading entrepreneurship projects and activities. It may be a starting point for the participants' propensity for risk-taking in educational settings. Students' love of challenge can be developed into calculated and prudent risk-taking, which is one of the crucial competencies of entrepreneurial leaders (Chen, 2007; Fuller and Marler, 2009), by being engaged in challenging and project-based entrepreneurial leadership learning opportunities (Pittaway and Cope, 2007a; Okudan and Rzasa, 2006). This capability can also be improved by students engaging in leading entrepreneurship clubs and societies where they have various learning opportunities to practice and experience the real roles and tasks of the leader, reflect on their leadership practices and interact with various people involved in entrepreneurial activities (Pittaway et al., 2010; Fayolle et al., 2006).

Versatility
The students had also a strong capability to perform various tasks and play multiple complex roles simultaneously, and cope with the problems and challenges of their task performances through learning different forms of knowledge, skills and behaviors. In other words, they had the capacity to perform various roles and tasks in their club, or in other clubs, projects and activities, because to be successful 'one of the leadership skills you need is that you must be a multi-tasker' (Saif). The challenging nature of the roles and tasks of the leader in the entrepreneurship clubs and projects encouraged the students 'to learn many skills and perform different roles' (Saif) simultaneously. For entrepreneurs, the ability to play different roles and carry out many tasks at the same time is vital, specifically at the early stages of new venture creation where the tasks are very demanding and challenging (Kempster and Cope, 2010; Mattare, 2008). For entrepreneurial leaders in particular, 'stretched multifunctional management and overlapping roles' have been recently identified as one of the critical challenges (Leitch et al., 2013: 348). Therefore, this versatility plays an influential role in developing the students' entrepreneurial leadership through acquiring various types of knowledge and skills by performing different roles and tasks, which enables them to cope with the complexities and challenges of their leadership task performances (Table 15.2, C1). The students' capacity to lead various entrepreneurial tasks and activities was grounded in their different competencies, including 'communication and [the ability to] easily engage with people' (Hakim) as well as their flexibility to work in different managerial positions (Table 15.2, C2). Versatility also played a critical role in enhancing the students' creativity and problem-solving skills (Table 15.2, C3).

Leadership Competencies of Students as Entrepreneurial Leaders

In addition to personal competencies, this study revealed students' competencies in creating caring interpersonal relationships and productive teams, as well as the ability to delegate tasks and build group members' self-efficacy. These enabled the participants to mobilize and inspire their group members, enhance their engagement in their task performance, and improve their commitment to achieve the objectives of the entrepreneurship clubs and projects. In effect, developing these 'social capital' (Leitch et al., 2013) competencies enabled the student entrepreneurial leaders to cope with one of the critical challenges of leaders in entrepreneurial organizations: lack of followers' commitment to entrepreneurial activities (Gupta et al., 2004).

Caring interpersonal relationships and teamwork
Most of the participants expressed their capability to create close and friendly relationships with and among their group members in order to successfully influence and guide them. In other words, the students had the ability to build a sense of caring, affiliation and belongingness with and among their group members through being friends with them, breaking down communication barriers, improving mutual understanding, building informal communication channels to recognize and solve problems on time, and providing an environment to work as a family (Table 15.3, D1). This interpersonal relationship competency is crucial for successfully leading an entrepreneurial group because of the specific entrepreneurial leadership task challenges and demands (Anderson and Jack, 2008) in improving the passion of the followers to abandon their current conventional activities (such as concentrating only on their studies) and to execute the challenging tasks in the entrepreneurship projects. Indeed, in an entrepreneurial group one cannot be the 'leader and control everything' because all of the group members 'have their own ideas' (Clive) and they need to feel free to express their ideas. Therefore, the leader plays the role of a facilitator and guides the group toward achieving the goals of the entrepreneurship projects and activities (Table 15.3, D2).

Creating such caring, friendly and close interpersonal relationships improves the group members' belongingness and commitment to their tasks and enables the group to achieve the objectives of the entrepreneurial projects and activities (Table 15.3, D3, D4) in three ways. First, it helped the students, as entrepreneurial leaders, to develop a common entrepreneurship vision and business venturing objectives that all of the group members were committed to achieving (Table 15.3, D5). Second, it enabled the students to improve their group members' self-confidence in proposing their new ideas (Table 15.3, D6), and their motivation and commitment to realize the objectives of the projects (Table 15.3, D7). Third, it assisted the students to inspire their group members to stay with the project, improve their performance and, consequently, achieve better results (Table 15.3, D8).

Table 15.3 Competencies of students as entrepreneurial leaders

Entrepreneurial leadership competencies

D: Caring interpersonal relationship and teamwork	*E: Enabling task delegation*
D1: 'We are doing [the projects] as friends. After work we can spend our time together talking about the business that we want to do. We can always have meeting every time. This got problem here, we just say. We discuss outside not only formal[ly], because if I as a boss and others as employees, I only know the problem when it comes to meetings. If no people bring it to the meeting then I don't know others' problems . . . and it can become bigger and more serious' (Zakaria)	E1: 'To bring out the best on others, [for example] I put Anita to approach a company, because I think she is good at communication and she wants to learn more on it. So by doing that she is exposing herself to the real thing' (Clive)
D2: 'It is not the case of leading actually, because in the group we are friends. I am assisting [them]. Through assisting I can also lead. Assisting is not like giving commands. I give them my opinion' (Zakaria)	E2: 'For example, some students love to do marketing, some love to do management . . . So, first we must know in a group of students, what are their interests, because based on their capabilities [we] know how to capture them and develop their potentials' (Akhyar)
D3: 'To improve their commitment you don't really have to lecture them like small kids. Because I don't think they listen if you keep talking and lecturing for hours. But if you have good relationships with them, you can always build your members so that they will actually listen to you, [they] don't leave the project and they achieve the goals better' (Eza)	E3: 'In my multimedia company they don't really love managing a business. So I don't want to force them. Because they have the interest in multimedia, they love to do multimedia jobs. So I am trying to just guide them, asking them what they want to learn' (Akhyar)
D4: 'Basically my style of leadership is I am friend with them. Because I like to work as a group. In a group, all are equal. There is not one who knows more or everything. I slowly talk to them can you do this? If not talk to me sooner. Maybe we can work on it together' (Ariif)	E4: 'When we bring out the best in them, they will try to do it day and night and we can produce more excellent results' (Clive)
	E5: 'To engage them I need [to] find their interest. How I do this? I ask them what they like to learn, what can I provide them? So when they see this relationship, they will be more willing and try more' (Hakim)
	E6: 'Someone just now wanted to learn about making financial budget for the event. She wanted to learn about how to make budget. So I said I have this kind of activities that we need budget, you can learn from this by doing it' (Hakim)

F: Building self-confidence of the group members

F1: 'The problem is there are many shy [students]. Some of them have the idea, but [they] lack confidence, they are really scared to speak up. So I have to encourage them to talk more and I ask them what do you think we should do to encourage them to talk more and give their ideas' (Zahid)

D5: 'We were thinking [about] what type of business we could make. Then, we went to a restaurant. We were eating and drinking together and were thinking. I suggested something, [it was] not really reliable for us as students. We thought of a smaller one. This one all agreed. So we all try to make it true' (Hisyam)

D6: 'Because of [this] close relationship . . . it will build up their commitment to the project. They [say] I like this project, why not we come up with these ideas. Then I in the group provoke them to suggest their own ideas' (Eza)

D7: 'By giving them motivation and telling them we are from different background[s], but we are all friends. Let's put our heads together and make sure that . . . this company will change from a small company that nobody knows it to a big multi-national company in near future' (Farhad)

D8: 'Usually I tell them very friendly that we cannot do alone all these things. So we must do it together and we need your knowledge and experience to do them. That I think motivate them not to leave it, to be better, and we get better results' (Zahid)

F2: 'Some people have less confidence. They can do it, but they don't have the confidence. So I need to motivate them and give them support. I tell them [by] doing this they are contributing to the results. When people do something and know [what] they are doing will help others to achieve this, they will be more willing to do [it], they will try more' (Hakim)

F3: 'I slowly put them into leading [the] projects. For example, we have this client who didn't pay the money. I will constantly call them . . . have you contact the client? If they don't know [something], they can always come to me. So, I give them a small piece of responsibility so that they will learn how to be more responsible and develop their confidence' (Farhad)

F4: 'They all have the capability to do so. It is just lack of confidence. So by asking them to give [their] opinion when we want to decide on the idea . . . they can develop themselves to become a very confident person' (Zahid)

F5: 'I have to convince them. Even though there is a risk in entrepreneurship, but once you overcome the risk you get more rewards. If you fall down, get up again. Do it again. If you want to become successful, you need to become brave. You need to become very confident in your abilities. You have to believe yourself' (Farhad)

361

Enabling task delegation and building self-efficacy of the group members
Some of the participants expressed that they employed an enabling approach to delegating tasks because entrepreneurial leaders need to develop group members' capabilities to come up with 'creative and innovative ideas for a business or overcoming the problems' (Hakim). The students applied an approach to learning and development by assigning tasks to their group to build their entrepreneurial competencies and enhance their commitment to the projects' objectives (Table 15.3, E1, E5, E6). Accordingly, the students considered their group members' interests, strengths and, most importantly, what they would learn from performing the tasks in order 'to bring out the best in them and develop them to go beyond what they are' (Zahid). By employing this approach, therefore, the student leaders could bring out the best potential in their group members and encourage their entrepreneurial creativity to flourish. This also helped to enhance the group's belongingness and engagement in performing their tasks, and improved their commitment to the project's objectives (Table 15.3, E2, E3, E4). By this enabling approach to task entrustment, therefore, the student entrepreneurial leaders coped with the lack of commitment among the group, and developed their abilities to think creatively and constantly create new business ideas, which are the critical challenges of entrepreneurial leaders in organizational settings (Mumford et al., 2008; Chen, 2007; Gupta et al., 2004).

We also recognized the important role that some of the participants played in constructing and improving group members' self-efficacy in performing their tasks and ensuring their commitment and contributions to attaining the objectives of the entrepreneurial projects. This finding confirms the importance of an entrepreneurial leader's ability to influence and to build group members' efficacy by reshaping their perceptions of their capabilities, eliminating their self-imposed limitations and improving their commitment to their task performance (Gupta et al., 2004). The students improved their group members' entrepreneurial self-efficacy in three ways. First, some of the participants not only motivated and encouraged their group members to believe in their abilities, but they also supported their creative thinking and generation and proposals of new business ideas (Table 15.3, F1). Second, others improved their group members' self-efficacy by appreciating and highlighting their contributions to achieve the results (Table 15.3, F2), and supporting them to perform their tasks under their close supervision (Table 15.3, F3). Third, some involved their group members in the process of recognizing entrepreneurial opportunities, making decisions and exploiting the opportunities (Table 15.3, F4), and enhanced their perseverance in facing the challenges and solving the problems involved in the entrepreneurship projects (Table 15.3, F5).

MOTIVATIONS TO ENGAGE IN ENTREPRENEURIAL LEADERSHIP LEARNING AND DEVELOPMENT

We structure our findings in this section around the second research question: What motivates the students to learn and develop their entrepreneurial leadership competencies? Indeed, motivation is the first block in learning and developing entrepreneurial competencies (Souitaris et al., 2007). Following Carsrud and Brännback's (2011) classification of entrepreneurial motivation, we grouped the students' motivation to learn and develop their entrepreneurial leadership around 'intrinsic' factors (personal interest in entrepreneurial roles) and 'extrinsic' factors (the external consequences of performing these roles). We also explored the factors in the environment that motivated the students to engage in learning and development. This study confirmed that a combination of personal and external factors motivated participants. The intrinsic factors that emerged were personal interest and self-development; and the extrinsic factors included entrepreneurial leadership task demands and challenges, entrepreneurial learning opportunities and programs.

Intrinsic Motivation Factors: Interest and Self-Development

Intrinsic factors reflect the personal impetuses originating from within the participants that drive and enable them to regulate their thoughts, goals and behavior toward learning how to lead student entrepreneurship clubs and projects, and develop their entrepreneurial leadership. In most cases, personal interest and passion to lead their own business were the strongest factors that attracted the students to learn: 'it emerge[d] with my interest … and I love manage[ing] a business. I love to learn about managing my own business' (Akhyar). This personal interest and passion drove the students to envision themselves as successful entrepreneurial leaders, and highly inspired them to do whatever it took to enact their vision and develop their entrepreneurial leadership competencies (Table 15.4, G1, G2). This supports previous research findings that individual interest in entrepreneurship is the most influential factor that motivates students to get involved in entrepreneurial activities, and affects their entrepreneurial intentions (Bagheri and Lope Pihie, 2014; Anderson and Jack, 2008; Jaafar and Abdul Aziz, 2008).

For others, self-development emerged as the dominant factor that encouraged them to seek and acquire entrepreneurial leadership knowledge and competencies. These students expressed their strong desire to discover their entrepreneurial potential and capabilities by leading university

Table 15.4   Factors motivating students to learn EL and develop their EL competencies

---

Intrinsic motivation factors

G: Interest in entrepreneurship

G1: 'I believe it comes from my heart. When it comes from my heart, the passion is there. I just need to improve it. I think I am not interested in any other things, actually. For me, I think . . . I have an eager for business' (Hisyam)

G2: 'I am pretty much interested in marketing, selling and business. Because it more involves business and [I am] not . . . [interested] in tasks on desk. Because accounting is more to deskwork, it is just like figures but I like to go out and meet people and talk. So I want to open up a business. I have the interest, the desire within my heart. That's why I am joining this' (Eza)

H: Self-development

H1: 'When you learn about entrepreneurship, it is about developing yourself to become more than what you are. It is like creating a different side of you that you have not known it before' (Eza)

H2: 'What motivates me is basically discovering [my] new abilities and developing [my] skills. That's why I am interested and joined these activities' (Hakim)

H3: 'Because I think it is best for me. It is all about myself. I want to improve my skills [to] open my own company' (Saif)

H4: 'Because we actually doing it first and most important freely. When you do something free of charge, then it means there must be something that capture[s] your interest. I want to learn, I want to develop my skills' (Akhyar)

---

entrepreneurship clubs and projects, and acquiring the knowledge and skills needed to lead their own businesses (Table 15.4, H1, H2, H3). This highlights that exploring their personal potential, along with self-actualization, is an influential factor that motivates students to step into entrepreneurial activities (Anderson and Jack, 2008; Stewart and Roth, 2007). Specifically, learning and developing entrepreneurial leadership competencies was one of the main reasons for the students to accept the responsibility and various challenges of leading university entrepreneurship clubs and activities (Table 15.4, H4). Therefore, personal interest and developing their capabilities play critical roles in driving individuals to engage in entrepreneurial activities and to persist in the face of challenges and difficulties (Block and Landgraf, 2014; Carsrud and Brännback, 2011).

Extrinsic Motivation Factors

External sources of motivation for the students included the environment that attracted or compelled them to learn about and to develop their entrepreneurial leadership competencies. These motivating environmental factors included entrepreneurial task demands and challenges, and entrepreneurial learning opportunities and programs. Importantly, entrepreneurial learning opportunities acted as incentives to engage in learning, while entrepreneurial leadership task demands and challenges were disincentives.

Entrepreneurial Leadership Task Demands and Challenges

The leadership task demands and challenges were also major motivating factors for some of the participants to learn how to lead the student entrepreneurship clubs and projects. Thus, by performing the tasks and roles of an entrepreneurial leader, the students encountered specific challenges and difficulties (such as creating new business ideas, exploring entrepreneurial opportunities, gathering essential resources, mobilizing a group of students and convincing sponsors) that improved their awareness of the gaps in their knowledge and skills and stimulated their entrepreneurial leadership learning and development (Table 15.5, J1, J2). Specifically, being responsible for the outcomes of the clubs and projects resulted in some students exploring their learning needs, and acquiring the essential knowledge and skills to successfully perform the leadership tasks and roles in the clubs and projects (Table 15.5, J3). Therefore, leadership task demands and challenges emerged as influential factors that develop individuals' leadership capacity in entrepreneurial contexts (Kempster and Cope, 2010; Gupta et al., 2004; Swiercz and Lydon, 2002).

Entrepreneurial Learning Opportunities and Programs

The university entrepreneurship learning opportunities and programs – such as entrepreneurship courses, seminars, workshops and, particularly, the entrepreneurship clubs and projects – attracted and motivated some of the participants to learn entrepreneurial leadership. The opportunity to lead university entrepreneurship clubs and projects was a strong motivator for some of the students to join the activities and develop their competencies through practicing the real tasks and roles of an entrepreneurial leader, with fewer risks and expenses (Table 15.5, I1). The universities also provided the required facilities and funds for students to establish a business that attracted some of the participants to learn how to lead entrepreneurial

Table 15.5   Factors motivating students to learn EL and develop their EL competencies

---

Extrinsic motivation factors

I: Entrepreneurial learning opportunities and programs	*J: Entrepreneurial leadership task demands and expectations*
I1: 'This club teaches me [to] improve my leadership skills to be an excellent entrepreneur. [It] teaches me how to connect to others and also improves my self-esteem. So I wanted to join this club to learn about leadership skills' (Saif)	J1: 'During that time, this club had a problem, an internal problem. A lot of my seniors were not involved in this club anymore. So, it was something like I created it by my own. All the people left and I needed to fix all foundation back. It was really a hard work. In one year, I needed to maintain my club. So, I thought I need to learn more' (Hisyam)
I2: 'They promote the students to do a business, and they provide [entrepreneurship] subjects for students of all faculties, either the students are from Multimedia or networking or business like me. They offer a subject called a small business and technopreneur development . . . all these encourage the students to learn' (Akhyar)	
I3: 'Because here in university entrepreneurship center, they provide us with printers, PCs also meeting rooms. So when we finish the work, we can study together here, so you feel comfort' (Zakaria)	J2: 'They actually made me work harder and study harder on entrepreneurship. For example, if I didn't know something, I actually went back home and turn on my computer and search online to get knowledge about entrepreneurship. I got some business books and learned from there. So next time [if] I face the same problem . . . I would know about it' (Farhad)
I4: 'I entered this club. I went to [the] national competition as one of the speakers. I saw the spirit of students there. I was encouraged [by] how they developed themselves. So, that's why I am into this club' (Ariif)	
I5: 'During my years here, I went to the world cup competition. When I came back, I was inspired by all the students all around the world doing entrepreneurial activities and [finding] solutions for all the problems [in] their communities. I looked at them, they were just at my age. What [is] stopping me from doing it. So, I started going around all these networking, business talks, seminars, conferences, [and] learned the knowledge' (Farhad)	J3: 'I am the leader. So, I have to decide on everything. I am responsible for that if it fails . . . this made me to understand my weaknesses, what I have to know more' (Zakaria)

activities (Table 15.5, I2, I3). For others, the university entrepreneurship clubs provided the opportunity to participate in national and international entrepreneurship competitions which highly motivated them to learn how to lead entrepreneurial projects and activities at these levels (Table 15.5, I4, I5). This finding supports the encouraging role of entrepreneurship education in developing students' entrepreneurial capabilities (Souitaris et al., 2007; Hynes and Richardson, 2007; Hannon, 2006) and highlights the critical role that university entrepreneurship clubs and projects play in developing entrepreneurial leadership competencies in students.

CONCLUSION

This chapter has attempted to provide a better understanding of entre-preneurial leadership competencies, including those factors that influence their development. In particular, we focused on leadership competencies, as these are the constant capabilities of the leaders which strongly affect the ability to lead and successfully perform entrepreneurial tasks and activities (Frey, 2010; Murali et al., 2009; Lans et al., 2008; Baron, 2006; Man et al., 2002). We concentrated on exploring those competencies that enabled the students as entrepreneurial leaders to successfully lead their university entrepreneurship clubs and projects. In so doing, we contribute to the scarce literature on entrepreneurial leadership competencies in a context other than an entrepreneurial organization and a small business (e.g., Gupta et al., 2004; Swiercz and Lydon, 2002; Leitch et al., 2013). Specifically, our study contributed insights into entrepreneurial leader-ship self-efficacy (management, opportunity identification, relationship and influence, tolerance and entrepreneurial leadership learning self-efficacy), love of challenges (desire to accept challenges, seek challenges and engage in challenging tasks) and versatility (capability to perform various complex and challenging tasks), which emerged as the personal competencies of the student entrepreneurial leaders. Furthermore, we explored three leadership competencies of the students that enabled them to mobilize and inspire their group members to enhance their engage-ment in and commitment to their task performance and attainment of entrepreneurship projects' objectives. In this, we have contributed highly to the research on interpersonal and interactive capabilities of entrepre-neurial leaders (Leitch et al., 2013). By engaging in the roles and tasks of a leader and facing the challenges and difficulties of leadership in student entrepreneurship clubs and projects, the students concentrated on learning and developing the personal and leadership competencies required for a specific entrepreneurial context (Leitch et al., 2013; Kempster and Cope,

2010). This highlights the influential role that university entrepreneurship clubs and projects play in developing both dimensions of students' entrepreneurial leadership competencies, and it contributes to the literature on the influential effects of university entrepreneurship in doing so (Pittaway et al., 2010; Okudan and Rzasa, 2006). Aligned with previous research, we can conclude from this study that entrepreneurial leaders require typical personal and leadership competencies, which will vary in different contexts, to enable them to successfully face the specific challenges of those contexts (e.g., Leitch et al., 2013; Gupta et al., 2004; Swiercz and Lydon, 2002). Furthermore, both personal and environmental factors motivate entrepreneurial leadership learning and development.

Implications

This study assists entrepreneurship educators, particularly in Malaysia, to provide the opportunities for students to learn and develop their entrepreneurial leadership by practicing the real roles and tasks of an entrepreneurial leader, if the number and quality of the future entrepreneurial leaders and the possibility of their success in leading entrepreneurial endeavors are to be improved. More specifically, our findings highlight the importance and necessity of learning self-efficacy in acquiring the multifaceted knowledge and skills of leadership in entrepreneurial contexts, and of exposing students to learning opportunities that develop such competencies in them (Kempster and Cope, 2010; Hannah et al., 2008). Entrepreneurship educators need to consider differences among students regarding their entrepreneurial leadership self-efficacy, and to develop entrepreneurship education and training programs that improve their strengths and weaknesses in different areas (Chen et al., 1998). Additionally, entrepreneurship education can provide students with leadership opportunities in entrepreneurship clubs, associations and projects where they can improve their entrepreneurial leadership self-efficacy through mastery of various leadership tasks and roles (Mattare, 2008; Okudan and Rzasa, 2006). Leading clubs and projects also improves students' confidence in learning through performing the real roles and tasks of an entrepreneurial leader and interacting with other students involved in entrepreneurial activities, and removes the barriers and complexities that students perceive for learning entrepreneurial leadership (Kempster and Cope, 2010; Mattare, 2008; Okudan and Rzasa, 2006). Introducing successful entrepreneurial leaders and providing an encouraging and supporting environment that persuades students to take the leadership position in entrepreneurship teams and projects can also be influential in improving their entrepreneurial leadership self-efficacy (Kickul et al., 2008; Pittaway and Cope, 2007b; Okudan and Rzasa, 2006).

This chapter also explored versatility as a competency of entrepreneurial leaders in educational settings, and suggested that it is required for successfully leading entrepreneurial activities. As such, it enhances our knowledge about personal entrepreneurial leadership competencies (Swiercz and Lydon, 2002). In order to develop versatility in students and thereby improve their entrepreneurial leadership competencies, educators may need to engage them in different entrepreneurship projects where they can learn various leadership knowledge and skills in different contexts. Furthermore, this study explored the combination of personal factors (personal interest and self-development) and environmental factors (entrepreneurial learning opportunities and programs, and entrepreneurial leadership task demands and challenges) which motivate students to develop their entrepreneurial leadership. Accordingly, entrepreneurship educators need to consider both the personal and the environmental factors which emerged from this study, and concentrate on those factors which encourage students to learn. Specifically, entrepreneurship education should focus more on personal motivation factors and develop entrepreneurship programs based on students' interests, rather than only focusing on theories and compulsory entrepreneurship education (Cheng et al., 2009), the effectiveness of which has recently been questioned (Oosterbeek et al., 2010).

Future Research

In this chapter, we examined the personal and leadership competencies of entrepreneurial leaders in a particular context, that of students as entrepreneurial leaders facing significant challenges and problems in leading university entrepreneurship clubs and projects. Further research could investigate whether the emerging competencies of students as entrepreneurial leaders are common among entrepreneurs and organizational leaders; and if they are different, what makes them so. Furthermore, different aspects of entrepreneurial leadership self-efficacy and, specifically, influence efficacy and entrepreneurial leadership learning self-efficacy, have great potential for further research on entrepreneurial leadership in small businesses and organizations. Future research can also develop a specific instrument to measure the dimensions of entrepreneurial leadership self-efficacy identified in this study, to investigate it in other contexts, and to examine its effects on the entrepreneurial behavior of students and nascent entrepreneurs as well as established entrepreneurs' performance and success. Further studies might also identify the specific forms of entrepreneurship education that can develop different aspects of entrepreneurial leadership competencies, particularly the entrepreneurial leadership self-efficacy of university students which might impact their entrepreneurial intentions and behavior. Future quantitative research with larger sample sizes and more diverse samples could also investigate the sources of entrepreneurial leadership self-efficacy and motivation to develop the competencies which emerged from this research. Finally, this chapter examined individual leadership learning and development of the student entrepreneurial leaders. Further research on the impact of collective and organizational learning on entrepreneurial leadership learning could provide better insights on how to develop it (Wang and Chugh, 2014).

REFERENCES

Aldrich, H. (2000), *Organizations Evolving*, Beverly Hills, CA: SAGE.

Alstete, W.J. (2002), 'On becoming an entrepreneur: An evolving typology', *International Journal of Entrepreneurial Behavior and Research*, 8 (4), 222–34.

Anderson, A.R. and Jack, S.L. (2008), 'Role typology for enterprising education: The professional artisan?', *Journal of Small Business and Enterprise Development*, 15 (2), 256–73.

Anderson, D.W., Krajewski, H.T., Goffin, R.D. and Jackson, D.N. (2008), 'A leadership self-efficacy taxonomy and its relation to effective leadership', *Leadership Quarterly*, 19, 595–608.

Bagheri, A. and Lope Pihie, Z.A. (2014), 'The moderating role of gender in shaping entrepreneurial intentions: Implications for vocational guidance', *International Journal for Educational and Vocational Guidance*, 14, 255–73.

Barbosa, S.D., Gerhardt, M.W. and Kickul, J.R. (2007), 'The role of cognitive style and risk preference on entrepreneurial self-efficacy and entrepreneurial intentions', *Journal of Leadership and Organizational Studies*, 13 (4), 86–104.

Baron, R.A. (2006), 'Opportunity recognition as pattern recognition: How entrepreneurs "connect the dots" to identify new opportunities', *Academy of Management Perspectives*, 20 (1), 104–19.

Block, J.H. and Landgraf, A. (2014), 'Transition from part-time entrepreneurship to full-time entrepreneurship: The role of financial and non-financial motives', *International Entrepreneurship Management Journal*, 12 (1), 259–82.

Bogden, R.C. and Biklen, S.K. (2003), *Qualitative Research for Education: An Introduction to Theories and Methods*, 4th edn, Boston, MA: Allyn & Bacon.

Cardon, M.S., Zietsma, C., Saparito, P., Matherne, B.P. and Davis, C. (2005), 'A tale of passion: New insights into entrepreneurship from a parenthood metaphor', *Journal of Business Venturing*, 20, 23–45.

Carsrud, A. and Brännback, M. (2011), 'Entrepreneurial motivations: What do we still need to know?', *Journal of Small Business Management*, 49 (1), 9–26.

Chen, C., Greene, P. and Crick, A. (1998), 'Does entrepreneurial self-efficacy distinguish entrepreneurs from managers?', *Journal of Business Venturing*, 13, 295–316.

Chen, M.H. (2007), 'Entrepreneurial leadership and new ventures: Creativity in entrepreneurial teams', *Creativity and Innovation Management*, 16 (3), 239–49.

Cheng, M.Y., Chan, W.S. and Mahmood, A. (2009), 'The effectiveness of entrepreneurship education in Malaysia', *Education + Training*, 51 (7), 555–66.

Creswell, J.W. (2007), *Qualitative Inquiry and Research Design: Choosing Among Five Approaches*, 2nd edn, Thousand Oaks, CA: SAGE.

Denzin, N. (1994), The arts and politics of interpretation. In N. Denzin and Y. Lincoln (eds), *Handbook of Qualitative Research* (pp. 500–515), Thousand Oaks, CA: SAGE.

De Pillis, E. and Reardon, K.K. (2007), 'The influence of personality traits and persuasive messages on entrepreneurial intention: A cross-cultural comparison', *Career Development International*, 12 (4), 382–96.

Dvir, D., Sadeh, A. and Malach-Pines, A. (2010), 'The fit between entrepreneurs' personalities and the profile of the ventures they manage and business success: An exploratory study', *Journal of High Technology Management Research*, 21 (1), 43–51.

Fayolle, A., Gailly, B. and Lassas-Clerc, N. (2006), 'Assessing the impact of entrepreneurship education programs: A new methodology', *Journal of European Industrial Training*, 30 (9), 701–20.

Fernald, L.W., Jr, Solomon, G.T. and Tarabishy, A. (2005), 'A new paradigm: Entrepreneurial leadership', *Southern Business Review*, 30 (2), 1–10.

Frey, R.S. (2010), 'Leader self-efficacy and resource allocation decisions: A study of small business contractors in the federal marketspace', *Proceedings of USASBE*, 781–810.

Fuchs, K., Werner, A. and Wallau, F. (2008), 'Entrepreneurship education in Germany and Sweden: What role do different school systems play?', *Journal of Small Business and Enterprise Development*, 15 (2), 365–81.

Fuller, B., Jr and Marler, L.E. (2009), 'Change driven by nature: A meta-analytic review of the proactive personality literature', *Journal of Vocational Behavior*, 75, 329–45.

Guerrero, M., Rialp, J. and Urbano, D. (2008), 'The impact of desirability and feasibility on entrepreneurial intentions: A structural equation model', *International Entrepreneurship Management Journal*, 4, 35–50.

Gupta, V., MacMillan, I.C. and Surie, G. (2004), 'Entrepreneurial leadership: Developing and measuring a cross-cultural construct', *Journal of Business Venturing*, 19, 241–60.

Hannah, S.T., Avolio, B.J., Luthans, F. and Harms, P.D. (2008), 'Leadership efficacy: Review and future directions', *Leadership Quarterly*, 19, 669–92.

Hannon, P.D. (2006), 'Teaching pigeons to dance: Sense and meaning in entrepreneurship education', *Education + Training*, 48 (5), 296–308.

Hoepfl, M.C. (1997), 'Choosing qualitative research: A primer for technology education researchers', *Journal of Technology Education*, 19 (1), 47–63.

Hynes, B. and Richardson, I. (2007), 'Entrepreneurship education: A mechanism for engaging and exchanging with the small business sector', *Education + Training*, 49 (8/9), 732–44.

Jaafar, M. and Abdul Aziz, A.R. (2008), 'Entrepreneurship education in developing country: Exploration on its necessity in the construction program', *Journal of Engineering, Design and Technology*, 6 (2), 178–89.

Kempster, S.J. and Cope, J. (2010), 'Learning to lead in the entrepreneurial context', *Journal of Entrepreneurial Behavior and Research*, 16 (6), 5–34.

Kickul, J., Wilson, F. and Marlino, D. (2008), 'Are misalignments of perceptions and self-efficacy causing gender gaps in entrepreneurial intentions among our nation's teens?', *Journal of Small Business and Enterprise Development*, 15 (2), 321–35.

Kuratko, D.F. (2007), 'Entrepreneurial leadership in the 21st century', *Journal of Leadership and Organizational Studies*, 13 (4), 1–11.

Kuratko, D.F., Hornsby, J.S. and Goldsby, M.G. (2007), 'The relationship of stakeholder salience, organizational posture, and entrepreneurial intensity to corporate entrepreneurship', *Journal of Leadership and Organizational Studies*, 13 (4), 56–72.

Lans, T., Hulsink, W., Baert, H. and Mulder, M. (2008), 'Entrepreneurship education and training in a small business context: Insights from the competence-based approach', *Journal of Enterprising Culture*, 16 (4), 363–83.

Leitch, C.M., McMullan, C. and Harrison, R.T. (2013), 'The development of entrepreneurial leadership: The role of human, social and institutional capital', *British Journal of Management*, 24, 347–66.

Man, T.W.Y., Lau, T. and Chan, K.F. (2002), 'The competitiveness of small and medium enterprises: A conceptualization with focus on entrepreneurial competencies', *Journal of Business Venturing*, 17, 123–42.

Man, T.W.Y. and Yu, C.W.M. (2007), 'Social interaction and adolescent's learning in enterprise education: An empirical study', *Education + Training*, 49 (8/9), 620–633.

Mason, J. (2002), *Qualitative Researching*, London: SAGE.

Matlay, H. (2005), 'Researching entrepreneurship and education. Part 1: What is entrepreneurship and does it matter?', *Education + Training*, 47 (8/9), 665–77.

Matlay, H. (2006), 'Researching entrepreneurship and education. Part 2: What is entrepreneurship education and does it matter?', *Education + Training*, 48 (8/9), 704–18.

Mattare, M. (2008), 'Teaching entrepreneurship: The case for an EL course', *Proceedings of USASBE conference*, 78–93.

McMullen, J.S., Bagby, D.R. and Palich, L.E. (2008), 'Economic freedom and the motivation to engage in entrepreneurial action', *Entrepreneurship Theory and Practice*, 32 (5), 875–95.

Merriam, S.B. (1998), *Qualitative Research and Case Study Applications in Education*, San Francisco, CA: Jossey-Bass.

Mueller, S.L. and Thomas, A.S. (2000), 'Culture and entrepreneurial potential: A nine country study of locus of control and innovativeness', *Journal of Business Venturing*, 16, 51–75.

Mumford, M.D., Bedell-Avers, K.E. and Hunter, S.T. (2008), 'Planning for innovation: A multi-level perspective', *Research in Multi-Level Issues*, 7, 107–54.

Murali, S., Mohani, A. and Yuzliani, Y. (2009), 'Impact of personal qualities and management skills of entrepreneurs on venture performance in Malaysia: Opportunity recognition skills as a mediating factor', *Technovation*, 29, 798–805.

Nicholson, N. (1998), 'Personality and entrepreneurial leadership: A study of the heads of the UK's most successful independent companies', *European Management Journal*, 16 (5), 529–39.

Okudan, G.E. and Rzasa, S.E. (2006), 'A project-based approach to EL education', *Technovation*, 26, 195–210.

Onwuegbuzie, A.J. and Leech, N.L. (2007), 'Sampling designs in qualitative research: Making the sampling process more public', *Qualitative Report*, 12 (2), 238–54.

Oosterbeek, H., van Praag, M. and Auke Ijsselstein, A. (2010), 'The impact of entrepreneurship education on entrepreneurship skills and motivation', *European Economic Review*, 54, 442–54.

Patton, M.Q. (1990), *Qualitative Evaluation and Research Methods*, 2nd edn, Newbury Park, CA: SAGE Publications.

Peterman, N.E. and Kennedy, J. (2003), 'Enterprise education: Influencing students' perceptions of entrepreneurship', *Entrepreneurship Theory and Practice*, 28 (2), 129–45.

Pittaway, L. and Cope, J. (2007a), 'Entrepreneurship education: A systematic review of the evidence', *International Small Business Journal*, 25 (5), 479–510.

Pittaway, L. and Cope, J. (2007b), 'Simulating entrepreneurial learning: Integrating experiential and collaborative approaches to learning', *Management Learning*, 38 (2), 211–33.

Pittaway, L., Hannon, P., Gibb, A. and Thompson, J. (2009), 'Assessment practice in enterprise education', *International Journal of Entrepreneurial Behaviour and Research*, 15 (1), 71–93.

Pittaway, L., Rodriguez-Falcon, E., Aiyegbayo, O. and King, A. (2010), 'The role of entrepreneurship clubs and societies in entrepreneurial learning', *International Small Business Journal*, 29 (1), 37–57.

Plumly, L.W., Marshall, L.L., Eastman, J., Iyer, R., Stanley, K.L. and Boatwright, J. (2008), 'Developing entrepreneurial competencies: A student business', *Journal of Entrepreneurship Education*, 11, 17–28.

Rae, D. (2007), 'Connecting enterprise and graduate employability: Challenges to the higher education culture and curriculum?', *Education + Training*, 49 (8/9), 605–19.

Rae, D. and Carswell, M. (2000), 'Using a life-story approach in entrepreneurial learning: The development of a conceptual model and its implications in the design of learning experiences', *Education + Training*, 42 (4/5), 220–227.

Raposo, M., Paço, A. and Ferreira, J. (2008), 'Entrepreneur's profile: A taxonomy of attributes and motivations of university students', *Journal of Small Business and Enterprise Development*, 15 (2), 405–18.

Renko, M., Kroeck, K.G. and Bullough, A. (2012), 'Expectancy theory and nascent entrepreneurship', *Small Business Economy*, 39, 667–84.

Renko, M., Tarabishy, A., Carsurd, A. and Brännback, M. (2013), 'Understanding and measuring entrepreneurial leadership', *Journal of Small Business Management*, 53 (1), 54–74.

Schjoedt, L. and Shaver, K.G. (2007), 'Deciding on an entrepreneurial career: A test of the pull and push hypotheses using the panel study of entrepreneurial dynamics data', *Entrepreneurship Theory and Practice*, 31 (5), 733–52.

Segal, G., Borgia, D. and Schoenfeld, J. (2005), 'The motivation to become an entrepreneur', *International Journal of Entrepreneurial Behaviour and Research*, 11 (1), 42–57.

Shane, S., Locke, E.A. and Collins, C.J. (2003), 'Entrepreneurial motivation', *Human Resource Management Review*, 13, 257–79.

Shank, G. (2002), *Qualitative Research. A Personal Skills Approach*, Upper Saddle River, NJ: Merril Prentice Hall.

Souitaris, V., Zerbinati, S. and Al-Laham, A. (2007), 'Do entrepreneurship programmes raise entrepreneurial intention of science and engineering students? The effect of learning, inspiration and resources', *Journal of Business Venturing*, 22, 566–91.

Stewart, W.H., Jr and Roth, P.L. (2007), 'A meta-analysis of achievement motivation differences between entrepreneurs and managers', *Journal of Small Business Management*, 45 (4), 401–21.

Surie, G. and Ashley, A. (2008), 'Integrating pragmatism and ethics in entrepreneurial leadership for sustainable value creation', *Journal of Business Ethics*, 81, 235–46.

Swiercz, P.M. and Lydon, S.R. (2002), 'Entrepreneurial leadership in high-tech firms: A field study', *Leadership and Organization Development Journal*, 23 (7), 380–386.

Tan, W.L., Tan, L.K., Tan, W.H. and Wong, S.C. (1995), 'Entrepreneurial spirit amongst tertiary students in Singapore', *Journal of Enterprise Culture*, 3 (2), 211–27.

Vecchio, R.P. (2003), 'Entrepreneurship and leadership: Common trends and common threads', *Human Resource Management Review*, 13, 303–27.

Wang, C.L. and Chugh, H. (2014), 'Entrepreneurial learning: Past research and future challenges', *International Journal of Management Reviews*, 16, 24–61.

Wiklund, J., Davidsson, P. and Delmar, F. (2003), 'What do they think and feel about growth? An expectancy-value approach to small business managers' attitudes toward growth', *Entrepreneurship Theory and Practice*, 27 (3), 247–71.

Wilson, F., Kickul, J. and Marlino, D. (2007), 'Gender, entrepreneurial self-efficacy, and entrepreneurial career intentions: Implications for entrepreneurship education', *Entrepreneurship Theory and Practice*, 31 (3), 387–401.

Young, J.E. and Sexton, D.L. (2003), 'What makes entrepreneurs learn and how do they do it?', *Journal of Entrepreneurship*, 12, 155–82.

Zampetakis, L.A. (2008), 'The role of creativity and proactivity on perceived entrepreneurial desirability', *Thinking Skills and Creativity*, 3, 154–62.

Zhao, H., Seibert, S.E. and Hills, G.E. (2005), 'The mediating role of self-efficacy in the development of entrepreneurial intentions', *Journal of Applied Psychology*, 90 (6), 1265–72.

16. Developing entrepreneurial leadership for sustainable organisations
David Rae

INTRODUCTION

The concept of entrepreneurship has developed significantly in recent years and, especially since the financial crisis of 2008, there has been increasing critique of the more extreme forms of entrepreneurial behaviour (Rae, 2010). This has been accompanied by continuing interest in socially and ecologically sustainable and responsible forms of entrepreneurship, including, but not limited to, social entrepreneurship (Shepherd and Patzelt, 2011).

These rapidly emerging new forms of entrepreneurship can demonstrate influence at community, societal and cultural levels, whilst engaging interest and support in different ways than most conventional entrepreneur-driven firms (Underwood et al., 2012). The roles of founders, entrepreneurs and leaders of such organisations can give them a public profile, yet little is known about the development of leadership in the field of sustainable entrepreneurship. There is increasing interest in understanding the points of convergence between the ideas of sustainable entrepreneurship as a social movement, and leadership as a distributed concept, in the economic and cultural context of such organisations. The connections between leadership, entrepreneurship and sustainability can be dynamic and powerful in their potential for educational, economic and social change, but there is not yet a conceptualisation of leadership in a sustainable enterprise, and how this can be developed. The emerging literature on sustainable entrepreneurship arguably lacks new insights into the human dynamics through which it can be realised, referring for example to 'institutional entrepreneurs' (Shepherd and Patzelt, 2011) and 'ecopreneurs' (Dixon and Clifford, 2007), suggesting that more development is required.

The aim of this chapter is to explore the field of leadership development and its emerging contribution to sustainable entrepreneurship, why there is a need to develop research and effective practices in this area, and how this might be achieved. In particular, it studies the question of how such organisations can generate entrepreneurial leadership for their longer-term sustainability, by developing a culture of entrepreneurship and facilitating people into leadership roles, to enable continuing innovation, development and growth. It considers four cases of leadership in different types of enterprises.

The chapter proposes the need for leadership in sustainable entrepreneurship. It then summarises a review of relevant literature in the fields of entrepreneurial leadership, social and sustainable entrepreneurship, and identifies relevant themes from this work for the study presented. The approach used in researching the four case studies is described, and the cases themselves are presented. A cross-case comparison is employed to elicit a set of themes and insights in relation to the questions posed on leadership development and organisational sustainability. From these, a conceptual model of leadership for organisational sustainability is proposed, followed by conclusions. The exploration of these cases of organisations suggests that achieving an organisationally sustainable approach, in particular related to succession management, can be problematic in developing new leadership in such organisations. Knowledge of how such organisations can generate new leadership to achieve sustainability beyond the first generation of founders is not well established, and this study aims to contribute to this emerging knowledge base.

THE PROBLEM

Entrepreneurship, in the context of sustainable and social operation, can be taken as the recognition and enaction of opportunities for creating and sharing multiple forms of value (QAA, 2012). This includes the application of ideas and innovations which enact opportunities for social, economic and environmental change, both in immediate, practical situations and in future-oriented scenarios which transform new thinking into realities. Such entrepreneurial opportunities create value, which is broader in scope than purely financial and economic, important as those metrics are. Social, environmental and ecological, technological, cultural, heritage and aesthetic dimensions must be valued alongside financial and economic metrics. Financial returns remain important, but are reinvested, in whole or in part, back into the venture or the community.

The conventional, 'free-enterprise' model of entrepreneurship is based on individual action and risk-taking in a competitive market for personal financial reward, or, as it can be termed, 'old-era' entrepreneurship. At its most extreme this becomes, to paraphrase Stevenson and Jarillo (1990), 'the pursuit of opportunities regardless of the consequences'. The old model is not going to disappear, but it is problematic and increasingly challenged by emerging concerns about the social, ethical and ecological consequences of unrestrained exploitation of finite resources. Sustainable entrepreneurship incorporates values gathered from a much wider range of sources than free-market economics alone. Sustainability is defined here consistently with the International Union for Conservation of Nature (IUCN) summarised by Adams (2006) as development being sustainable in relation to the interdependent pillars of economic growth, environmental protection and social progress: 'Sustainability needs to be made the basis of a new understanding of human aspiration and achievement' (Adams, 2006: 12).

There are strong connections between sustainable entrepreneurship and the related, but distinct, fields of social enterprise, entrepreneurship and innovation (Underwood et al., 2012), and with ecopreneurship (Dixon and Clifford, 2007; Moon, 2013). It can also be expressed as 'new-era' entrepreneurship (Rae, 2010) and includes aspects of, for example, social justice and inclusion, ecological and environmental awareness, communitarianism, feminism and political economy.

Sustainable, new-era and ecopreneurship challenge the link between entrepreneurship and Western capitalist economic growth models which was more generally accepted prior to the 2008 financial crisis. Capitalist and corporate models tend to prioritise the exploitation of short-term opportunities in the interests of financial and economic value capture and maximisation, rewarding principally the managers and investors, to the exclusion of longer-term community, social and especially environmental sustainability, which is limited at the margins by legal frameworks and the salve of corporate social responsibility (Baumol, 1990). Sustainable entrepreneurship is based on long-term values, but as an approach it is unlikely to succeed if it relies solely on myriads of unconnected individual actions. Rather, sustainable entrepreneurship must become a collective movement for systemic cultural, social and economic transformation, progressing from the foundations of community and social enterprise. Its scale has to be both local and immediate, but also global, ultimately seeking change at corporate, governmental and international levels (CBI, 2012).

To succeed, it is proposed that sustainable entrepreneurship depends on the development of three interconnected aspects: leadership, learning, and a supportive cultural, political and economic context. Leadership is required at the levels of the individual enterprise, institutions, communities, and on a broader scale at intellectual and political levels. The vision and ambition for change is an essential characteristic. Yet leadership for sustainable entrepreneurship should be seen as a socially responsive, shared responsibility. This is not a new idea: the notion of distributed leadership (Ancona, 2005) is one where people at all levels and in all roles within an organisation assume and demonstrate leadership towards a common set of goals. Greanleaf (1977) long ago espoused the practice of servant leadership. Such forms of leadership are inclusive and enabling of others to develop and to themselves become leaders. The lack of leadership capacity and capability can be a constraint on the development of sustainable enterprises, yet the development of entrepreneurial leadership unlocks the potential for wider-scale ambition and impact of sustainable entrepreneurship (Greenberg et al., 2013).

The term 'leadership' is used to denote an organisational process for leading, rather than the role description of leader, in just the same way as we refer to entrepreneurship as distinct from entrepreneurs. Individuals will at various times respond to the perceived needs and opportunities to act as leaders, entrepreneurs and a combination of both roles, as illustrated by the case studies in this chapter. However, the requirement for organisational sustainability means that these processes need to become culturally embedded and practised at a collective, as distinct from purely individual, level. The promotion of the individual can be problematic, since both leadership and entrepreneurship can carry implicit meanings of exceptional performance, exclusivity, power and more, often perpetuated by social and media stereotypes.

Entrepreneurial learning assumes that any person can enhance their capacity for entrepreneurship and for leadership, if they choose to do so, within the limits of their known abilities (Kempster and Cope, 2010). As all individuals are in some respects limited and flawed, it is essential that they learn to interact with others who have complementary strengths. Entrepreneurial leadership is a social and connected practice, involving trust, shared values and reciprocity. Learning is integral and essential within sustainable entrepreneurship. Within education, and more broadly at a societal level, people need to learn why and how entrepreneurship can and must be sustainable, and what that means in understanding and dismantling the effects of unsustainable entrepreneurship, and moving this from being a norm to an outmoded practice. Entrepreneurial learning is a process of social emergence and identity construction, in which the individual learns and comes to fulfil their potential (Rae, 2015).

Campbell (2014) proposes that governance is an essential aspect of the accountability of leadership to communities. He offers a conception of social leadership based on foundations of sociology, philosophy, servant leadership, social interactionism and sustainability. A supportive cultural, political and economic context is essential for the growth of sustainable entrepreneurship. If the ambient social and economic values reward only individual self-enrichment regardless of its wider costs and consequences, the task is much harder. Educating society, policy-makers and decision-makers is therefore essential to inform and influence changes in policy, norms and practices (DEFRA, 2011).

SUMMARY OF PRIOR LITERATURE

This section summarises relevant contributions from the literature on entrepreneurial leadership, and explores the relationships with leadership in social enterprise, entrepreneurship and sustainable entrepreneurship. Roomi and Harrison (2011) made a valuable contribution to the field in both defining entrepreneurial leadership and reviewing approaches to its teaching in higher education. Their definition is cited below:

> we develop the notion that entrepreneurial leadership involves running an organisation through a variety of means – through relationships and culture, for example, in addition to command and control. This requires understanding how to handle and deal with the risk, uncertainty and ambiguity that face all entrepreneurial organisations – and, arguably, all organisations in an increasingly risky, uncertain and ambiguous world. Entrepreneurial leadership education should, therefore, aim to provide students with a mind-set that encourages and teaches them to lead in an entrepreneurial way. (Roomi and Harrison, 2011: 2)

They discussed the lack of prior research on entrepreneurial leadership, and deficient understanding of the topic, with little attention paid to how entrepreneurial leadership behaviours are learnt and how they can be taught. Highlighting significant prior contributions, they compared contextual, situation-specific leadership (Vecchio, 2003) and holistic approaches to entrepreneurial leadership in the literature, noting a lack of definition based on conflicting models. They observed that the teaching of entrepreneurial leadership is perceived as more orientated towards entrepreneurship than leadership, whilst there is little explicit teaching of entrepreneurial leadership. Their overall conclusion was that: 'entrepreneurial leadership education should teach students how to cultivate their entrepreneurial capability in leadership roles and their leadership capability in entrepreneurial contexts' (Roomi and Harrison, 2011: 29). They commented further on the need to develop entrepreneurial teams which used both the leaders' and co-workers' mindsets, and to balance creativity, influence, risk and access to resources.

Their review highlighted other contributors, including Gupta et al. (2004), who explored entrepreneurial leadership as a set of active behaviours, suggesting that entrepreneurial leaders enact the challenges of communicating a vision and of influencing others to help them realise it. The active and experiential nature of learning was also noted by Gibb (1993) in the context of the small business.

Kuratko (2007), introducing a special issue on the topic, addressed the role of entrepreneurial leadership primarily as economic leadership, operating entirely within the paradigm of Western capitalist economies and celebrated rather than questioned this approach, other than a brief consideration of 'the dark side of entrepreneurship' and the ethical role of the entrepreneurial leader. In contrast, Greenberg et al. (2013: 56) proposed an explicitly values-based approach to entrepreneurial leadership, for which they viewed leaders as relying more on action than analysis to create new opportunities. 'By taking action, leaders can use situational learning to guide future action, whilst inspiring others in co-creating solutions to seemingly intractable problems'.

They differentiated entrepreneurship as new value creation from entrepreneurial leadership, as: innovating; enacting new strategic directions; solving complex business, social and environmental problems; and starting new companies. Three principles for entrepreneurial leadership and related developmental actions for leaders are presented:

1. Cognitive ambidexterity: integrating two diverse ways of making decisions into a single approach to pursuing opportunity, using both predictive and creative logic.
2. A commitment to social, environmental and economic value creation as a different way of framing opportunities. Leaders are driven by their commitment to social, environmental and economic responsibility and sustainability, and finding new ways to relate organisational performance to society and seeking opportunities to simultaneously create shared value.
3. Self-awareness, starting from 'who I am'; entrepreneurial leaders start from a deep understanding and self-awareness of who they are which guides their actions: 'reflect on who you are and connect your passion to your profession' (Greenberg et al., 2013: 57–61).

Harrison, Leitch and McMullan have made several substantive contributions to the field, posing implications for education and development and addressing the design of a team-based approach to learning for team leadership (Harrison and Leitch, 1994; also Henry et al., 2005). Leitch et al. (2009) addressed the application of action learning to leadership in the small firm context, focusing on the effectiveness of learning outcomes and proposing the integrated development of personal identity, social interaction and organisational development in the learning process. Leitch et al. (2013) explored the roles of human, social and institutional capital in developing entrepreneurial leadership through a relational perspective. As individuals learned how to lead, the processes of peer interaction and trust-building were formative experiences.

Kempster and Cope (2010) brought prior research perspectives to bear on entrepreneurial learning, introducing a conceptual framework of four themes for restricted leadership learning in the entrepreneurial context, with limited opportunity and the variety of social interactions, roles, low salience and development of leadership practice. They found limited experiential forms of social interactive and reflective learning to develop entrepreneurial and leadership capabilities. Parent-dominated family businesses tended to limit leadership ambition, and there were few other references to significant individuals as influences on leadership learning. Again drawing on the entrepreneurial learning literature, Bagheri and Pihie (2011) proposed a model defining entrepreneurial leadership development, based on a dynamic process of experiential, social interactive, observational and reflective learning. This offered a foundation for entrepreneurial leadership practice, education and research to recognise entrepreneurial opportunities, create novel solutions for challenges and address crises of leading entrepreneurial ventures. They advanced useful sets of personal and functional competencies of entrepreneurial leaders, whilst highlighting experiential learning, social interaction and reflection as learning processes.

Other contributors such as Baron and Ensley (2006) and Lans et al. (2008) have also argued that entrepreneurial competencies and leadership can be learned. In the domain of Taiwanese high-technology practice rather than education, Ming-Huei Chen (2007) concluded that leadership effectiveness is very strongly determined by the ability to interact with a team's creativity, and that lead entrepreneurs who are risk-taking, proactive and innovative can stimulate their entrepreneurial team members' creativity.

In relation to social entrepreneurs, Smith et al. (2011) addressed leadership skills and pedagogical tools, developing a theory about how leaders of social enterprises can cultivate skills for managing competing social and financial demands. They addressed the questions of the leadership challenges posed by attending to the competing demands of social enterprises; the skills leaders need to respond to these challenges; and the pedagogical tools available. They proposed a paradoxical leadership theory to address the inherent conflicts between social and economic missions, and to enable social entrepreneurs to accept, differentiate and integrate competing demands.

Gravells (2012) examined the factors determining leadership success in United Kingdom social enterprises. Through a series of interviews, a range of success factors were identified, including both behaviours and traits, or 'ways of being' in which personality, values and beliefs interacted with formative experiences; whilst competence frameworks alone were seen as insufficient indicators of success. The proposed model includes 'ways of being' of self-awareness: courage and calmness, strong values, and caring for others. Contraindicators and behaviours were also identified as required for successful leadership in social enterprises.

In relation to sustainable entrepreneurship, there has been some development of the concept and definitions, but arguably less attention has been paid to the human agency required and to the requirement for leadership in this field. Shepherd and Patzelt (2011) developed a conceptual framework for sustainable entrepreneurship, which is helpful in setting boundaries for inclusion and exclusion. They advanced an institutional perspective and future research agenda for the field, and considered psychological aspects of the motivation for sustainable entrepreneurship and the role of personal values. Schaltegger and Wagner (2011) proposed a framework to position sustainable entrepreneurship in relation to sustainability innovation, building on a typology of sustainable entrepreneurship:

> The core motivation and main goals mentioned with ecopreneurship are to earn money through contributing to solving environmental problems. Economic goals are the ends of the business, whereas environmental goals are considered as an integrated part of the economic logic of the business. The organizational challenge of entrepreneurship is to better integrate environmental performance into the economic business logic. (ibid.: 223)

This useful typology tends to view entrepreneurship from an institutional and structural perspective, and there is again little exploration of the human agency of entrepreneurial leadership.

Overall, the extant literature cited on entrepreneurial leadership includes a number of theoretical perspectives and conceptual models. There is more evidence of work situated in educational initiatives in leadership development within higher education than on the study of actual cases of leadership in entrepreneurial organisations. There is, so far, little consensus on the nature of entrepreneurial leadership beyond the notion of the individual, and little convergence between the study of entrepreneurial leadership and of leadership in sustainable entrepreneurship. However, the development of sustainable enterprises is clearly reliant on the formation of effective leadership in the long term. This can be considered as a new area of knowledge, and it is appropriate for this study to explore it further.

METHODOLOGY

The aim of the study was to develop understanding of entrepreneurial leadership within sustainable organisations. The chosen approach was inductive and interpretive, specifically to research a small number of organisations, to develop case studies of leadership from these, and to compare them in order to identify any distinctive or shared themes or characteristics. The subject of the case study was the organisation, with the leader being a key informant in its development. The challenge for these organisations was their ongoing sustainability rather than their current leadership, hence consideration of leadership within their wider context, culture and community was essential.

This methodology was informed by a number of sources including Eisenhardt (1989) and Yin (2003) on case study research, and Leitch et al. (2010) on conducting interpretive research in a social context. The method was qualitative, with information being gathered in a range of ways. These include an arranged interview with the leader; collection of documents including strategic plans and marketing information; presentations; attendance at meetings and site visits; informal conversations with employees and members in the community; observation within the organisation; and website-related information. The collection, analysis and editing of this information enabled a descriptive case study to be prepared for each organisation, whilst using a consistent approach overall.

In terms of selecting organisations for inclusion in the study, the criteria were that the organisation should be a pre-existing body with at least five years' history to demonstrate its own sustainability, and that the leader would have a track record of leadership. Further, it should be an entrepreneurial organisation, as demonstrated by a track record of innovation and growth in its activities. It should have some form of social or community mission, and a commitment to environmental sustainability, ideally with evidence of reviewing or reporting on these aspects. Within the group of case studies, it was desirable to include a mix of different organisational types, activities and community relationships. Coverage of more than one country, and inclusion of both male and female genders in leadership roles, was also desirable. Finally, it was desirable for the organisations to be prepared to be named, and for information in the cases to be in the public domain. Although anonymous cases are commonly used and may allow more sensitive information to be revealed, the advantage of using named organisations is that readers are free to form their own interpretations from the case data as well as other information they may collect. Also, the use of named organisations allows the use of a more 'authentic' and realistic approach.

Table 16.1   Case study organisations

Organisation	Year established	Location	Type	Main activity	Founder/ leader
Hill Holt Wood	1997	Lincolnshire, UK	Social enterprise	Woodland enterprise	Nigel and Karen Lowthrop
Genesis Social Enterprise	1991	Derbyshire, UK	Social enterprise	Social and community enterprise	Steve Holmes
Cool Milk Group	1998	Lincolnshire, UK	Private limited company	School milk supply	Jon Thornes
Membertou First Nation	1959	Cape Breton, Canada	Corpo- ration	Community economic development	Chief Terry Paul

A range of organisations were considered, from which four were selected and contacted, and agreed to participate in the study. Their characteristics are shown in Table 16.1.

Each of the founders was contacted and an interview was arranged, lasting between 60 and 90 minutes. The conversation covered the background to the organisation, and explored questions, responses and practices relating to a range of themes, including:

- organisational strategy (purpose, values, goals);
- community (culture, responsibility, reciprocity, engagement);
- entrepreneurial development (opportunities, innovation);
- leadership development (management, learning, staffing, selection);
- power (decision-making, resources and rewards).

The conversations were not audio-recorded, but notes were taken by the researcher. Further material was gathered in the course of the researcher's involvement with each organisation, which in three of the cases occurred over a period of several years. To prepare the case studies, the material gathered was analysed, coded to identify concepts and categories arising from the material, and a narrative case was drafted, edited and checked. The draft cases were shared with the founder for accuracy prior to publication.

The cases follow in the next section. Each of these summarises the background of the organisation in its community, its development, its approach to community and sustainability, and leadership issues relating to the case. The cases are then compared at a thematic level and a conceptual model is developed from this analysis.

THE CASES

Hill Holt Wood: A Case of Social Innovation

Background and development

The story of Hill Holt Wood (HHW) began with the ambition of Nigel Lowthrop, a biologist, to own and bring into active use an area of ancient woodland. Nigel saw that many small and old woods were neglected and unproductive, too small for commercial forestry, yet had the potential to become community assets. Aided by his wife, Karen, in 1995 he purchased Hill Holt Wood, a 14-hectare envelope of mixed woodland between Lincoln and Newark in the East Midlands of the UK. He recognised that putting the wood to active use could create a resource for social enterprise and community development. Guided by three interdependent principles of environmental, economic and social sustainability, an organisation was established to include an education and training charity and a community-based subsidiary trading arm. There was an ambition to make a social difference, but it took ten years to build trust with communities, decision-makers and organisations such as local authority district and county councils. Representation was vital to create the connections and contacts for this. An open and transparent approach, based on justice and honesty, was practised even when the openness resulted in other agencies taking ideas and running with them. The ethical business model was to gather problems and create new solutions which made innovative uses of available resources.

Community and sustainability

Initially a management committee was established, with community representation welcoming people to meetings to become involved in running the business. From this the board of directors of the social enterprise developed, trading as a charity, in 2002. Engaging closely with the local communities, HHW diversified from the original mission to conserve the woodland into becoming a resource base of environmental, social and therapeutic health activities. The strategy developed into not being reliant on any individual or family, and to balance economic, environmental, and social and community value creation equally. Generating revenue and profit is necessary, but profit maximisation is not the goal.

The woodland is managed actively, being conserved and maintained for public use, whilst promoting environmental sustainability. Young people experience a learning environment in which they can develop skills and realise their potential, and as an enterprise it provides useful products and services for the community. The educational arm provides an alternative curriculum for young people who may be at risk and excluded from mainstream education. The woodland management service provides ranger and countryside management across other woodland, employing around 40 rangers. The environment provides ecotherapy woodland activities for adults with mental distress to improve their well-being. An events and café business have developed as commercial services including weddings, tree planting to celebrate births, and green burials.

Creating buildings within the woodland required a mix of new and old skills which led to the formation of a design team for sustainable buildings, providing work experience for architecture students. This specialises in creating sustainable buildings using traditional methods and natural materials including timber framing, rammed earth, straw bales and limecrete. Many projects have been created, including a spectacular Woodland Community Hall. Hill Holt Wood has won many awards, but also attracted recognition from policy-makers and community groups, environmentalists and social enterprises for developing innovative approaches to tackle social and environmental problems through the principles of sustainable, environmental and local action in economically viable ways: creating jobs; providing valued services; and maintaining woodland as a community asset.

In the nearby town of Gainsborough, a project to refurbish derelict housing for homeless young people by employing local people showed that a community-based approach to regeneration in a challenged environment can work. However the dynamics of urban regeneration are different from woodland enterprise, although the community-based approach is transferable to this context. Urban areas such as Gainsborough have economic and employment needs, together with potential resources and property available for development at low cost. There is a need for leadership to bring community development about, by 'bonding' within but also 'bridging' between communities (Putnam, 2000). In such communities, the professional middle classes have often migrated, leaving an absence of articulate people able to bid for and manage resources and projects. This community capacity requires the voice and business skills needed for governance.

Leadership
Nigel's perspective on leadership was expressed as:

> If you have vision, viable ideas and leadership skills, then lead or it probably will not happen. Develop communication skills to ensure you can explain your vision, inspire and enthuse communities to support the development, and not be seen as imposing your model but providing solutions to multiple problems. For local community enterprises, adding value is key to success and survival.

Although he founded HHW, he stepped down as chief executive officer (CEO) when it was remarked that 'it's all about you'. Nigel sees himself as the visionary and creative thinker, initiating change and problem-solving. He described this as a missing element in the organisation. His wife Karen moved from the corporate sector to become active in the enterprise, replacing him as CEO. She also announced her intention to stand down, giving the board and management team two years' notice. This created a challenge in terms of the future leadership of the organisation.

At HHW there is a senior management team covering operations, finance, project director and training roles. They became settled and comfortable in their roles, managerial rather than entrepreneurial, with little interest in expansion beyond the Wood, whilst the board members have limited understanding of the potential of the organisation to achieve lasting change. There was a continuing need for ambition, vision and creative thinking, together with the drive to realise this. Social enterprise needs vision and ideas. HHW is assured about its ethos, values and purpose, but lacked clarity about its future strategy and ambitions for growth.

Talent development is a vital issue, yet the organisation did not attract or develop the people with the motivation and vision to lead it in the future. This made succession a live issue, which was resolved by the external appointment of a new leader.

Nigel feels entrepreneurs are 'not normal', and his own experience has been to initiate opportunities and to innovate where others see risks but he does not. Recruiting and mentoring potential talent is a vital area for entrepreneurial development in social enterprise. Nowhere is this truer than in the leadership of the organisation.

Genesis Social Enterprise

Background and development
The Genesis Enterprise Foundation was formed in 1991 from a vision of four Christian couples to make a difference in their community of Alfreton, a Derbyshire former mining town. Steve Holmes, a corporate banker and entrepreneur, was part of this group, who were concerned about the social fabric of the community and the limited opportunities for young people.

The first years saw the development of several building projects to accommodate and support teenage expectant mothers as a refuge to avoid abortion, and disaffected young teenagers, and a youth hostel foyer scheme. These projects were delivered with minimal capital grant support and sustained by a mixture of grants and income generation with personal contributions from the board and staff. The learning curves were significant but the need for funding meant projects faltered once grant support had ended. In 1999, taking part in a study group to examine the story and structure of Mondragon in northern Spain, Steve Holmes was inspired by how the region had been transformed by a Catholic priest and local entrepreneur working together, 'combining heart and mind'. But he saw the ex-drug addicts running a hostel in Madrid and a food bank as more attainable ideas: social enterprise could be a 'prophetic pendulum' which 'causes the conscience of the nation to respond'.

Community and sustainability
The challenge was how to grow the organisation to serve its community objectives, whilst producing wealth and social capital, such that ethical business could work within the community:

> I moved from banking in the private sector into social enterprise, taking social responsibility as an entrepreneur. My psyche is meeting challenges with enterprising thoughts. I see making money as an enabler for sustainability. When we started in the early 2000's, charities and voluntary organisations were told to become social enterprises. They did not have entrepreneurial people running them or as trustees, it was a bear trap. (Steve)

During the next few years the organisation grew into childcare and youth delivery, acquiring a derelict coach house in the town which became a restaurant, and a free range chicken farm to provide revenue and job opportunities, and several other ventures. The organisation offered training days for churches and established a network of organisations building community projects. The organisation applied to use a dilapidated bus garage in the town centre as an impromptu five-a-side football facility for local youths. They were offered the entire site at a time when regional funding was available to deliver sustainable community projects. This was ideal to build a centre to produce wealth and also serve the community. They submitted a proposal for the redevelopment of the bus depot into a Centre for Social Enterprise and Incubation Unit. This attracted matching funding from the Coalfield Regeneration Trust and a rental deal to purchase the building, creating the Genesis Centre for Social Enterprise. This created more than 40 new jobs plus training places, investing in community work, and has developed a net asset base of £2.2 million. It includes a family leisure centre, business incubation unit, Vocational Academy and Adult Education Centre.

Other ventures included acquiring Alfreton Hall, an eighteenth-century manor house refurbished for use as a wedding and conference venue. This and the coach house are projects which maintain community heritage by creating new uses for historic buildings. Genesis Dental Care identified access to NHS dentistry as an opportunity. After a research study showed a correlation between deprived communities with high indices for multiple deprivation and lack of access to dentists, a business with 13 dental practices, generating over £8 million pa in revenue and £400 000 profit was established. This was sold for £1.7 million and the funds were reinvested.

Genesis Social Enterprise is 90 per cent self-funding, but its financial sustainability is fragile as it has public sector tenants and contracts which could be cut or withdrawn, putting the organisation at risk. It employs 260 people, and faces sustainability challenges over the coming years. Sustainability can be achieved, says Holmes, through creating profit which can be reinvested, and through a cyclical approach to continual innovation. Rather than stasis, they flip problems into opportunities, find latent resources, and put them to work.

Leadership
Steve Holmes described his approach as a social entrepreneur:

> being entrepreneurial is different to being a manager. I am motivated by a start-up challenge, building a team. I've seen it before I've touched it. I have managers in my business, they organise and do the detail. It's about turning dreams into reality, 'I can see it' into 'I can do it'. You have to be able to connect opportunity spotting with people . . . I am a serial entrepreneur, the challenge is to find who could succeed and take over from myself, it's how to get freed up.

Cool Milk Group

Background and development
Jon Thornes, founder of the Cool Milk Group, grew up on a dairy farm in West Yorkshire and went to agricultural college after leaving school. Over the next 30 years he worked in many roles in the dairy industry, from milking cows to selling milk to consumers. In this period he saw many changes and much concentration in the milk supply industry, which brought not only challenges for farmers but also a long-term decline in milk consumption by schoolchildren, who lost the health benefits of daily fresh milk. He saw an opportunity to reverse this trend by creating a business which connected farm-fresh milk with schools more efficiently, and

marketed milk to schools, parents and children more effectively. Jon has a determined and sales-focused approach to building a business:

> My skillset is innovation. I started with 50 clients as schools in 1988, we had to reach 200 to get to breakeven. We took it to 24 000 schools. You have to sell, it took 7–8 years to find ways in. Cool Milk is efficient and focussed. Cool Milk has acquired 1.5 million customers, from the start it was about client acquisition. You have to go and see people, build relationships, make them part of your business and let them help you.

Cool Milk at School was established in 1998, and works in partnership with local authorities to supply free and subsidised milk for children in primary, infant, junior and special schools. Building on this success, Cool Milk Ltd was established in 2001, to work in partnership with local authorities to supply free milk for children aged under five in pre-school childcare. The mission of these businesses was to supply the government-recommended 189 ml of fresh, chilled milk daily, either free or subsidised, to hundreds of thousands of children in many locations, through a network of local and regional dairy partners. A national organisation, Cool Milk National Contracts, was formed to allow national groups to supply fresh local dairy products to their customers. Together they form the Cool Milk Group.

Community and sustainability
The aim is for the businesses to operate through an economically and environmentally sustainable business model. The businesses hold ISO 14000 accreditation for compliance with environmental standards. They buy from local and regional farmers and independent milk producers who meet quality standards. The businesses have to be economically sustainable to pay the milk producers a competitive rate whilst making the price charged to customers affordable, with government subsidy where applicable. The British milk industry in recent years has experienced volatility, with plunging prices paid to dairy farmers, concentration of control in a few small groups, and aggressive price-setting by powerful supermarket groups. Growing an ethical and independent business in this context is a challenge. The companies in the Cool Milk Group are privately owned, profit-making businesses. Ownership rests mainly with Jon and his family; it is not a social enterprise or co-operative, though community and partnership are significant driving values for the business. Cool Milk can be seen as a private sector business which behaves responsibly towards its stakeholders and invests back in children, schools and communities.

Leadership

Jon explained that:

> I have a personalised approach, I pick people. It's finding the right people for the culture and stage the business is at, the right people for the type of business. I approach people to get them to come and work in the business. Sometimes they just work in the village here in Lincolnshire and it's never occurred to them that they would want to work here, so you have to get them through the door and plant the idea in their mind.

Jon resigned as managing director and took on the role of chairman in 2008. 'I realised I couldn't do it all myself,' he says. 'It was difficult to accept, but I couldn't lead the team. I didn't have the right skills, or understand big business. I am very much a hands-on person and good at starting things up. But I'm a fiddler; I'm not good at running a team. I'm an individual player.'

He appointed a new managing director, and set up a board, as well as bringing in an experienced non-executive director. 'It was challenging to take the plunge,' he says, 'but as chairman I spend more time than ever on the company, focusing on strategy, acting as a figurehead and looking to Europe for new business':

> My model with Cool Milk was to look for someone who had done it before, and find the right guy to run it. In running the business, I give authority and a direction. We create the story of how we got here, and what's the gap from the present, and avoid shocks. It's a story, not a plan. You visualise and explain. I take people for a walk and get to know them, how they will work.

Jon relies on mentors:

> I have multiple mentors as experts and on problem areas. International business was an example. I was advised to go into Hungary but the economic, cultural and language differences were just too great and we closed it . . . What's important to me is my time and money, my family and enjoyment, making a difference. My time is planned around holidays, working at Cranfield and Stanford Universities on their business programmes, meetings and visits. With Stanford and Cranfield, it's about developing case studies and peer learning, opening up ideas, understanding and the social side.

Jon is highly entrepreneurial and focused on business results of client acquisition and revenue growth. He is both strategic and relational. 'With startups I have about ten key factors. I look at them and say, in six months, "Can it make you rich?" I lose money on most of the startups I invest in, I enjoy backing them and try to learn from what I'm doing.' Business development at Cool Milk centres on finding the right people and putting them in place, and managing relationships with them, making them feel a sense of 'it's their business' whilst Jon holds most of the equity. But there is also a strong sense of his motivation to return value to the community, by investing time and money in new businesses and staying involved with several universities on entrepreneurial growth programmes.

Membertou First Nation: Canadian Leadership in Community Entrepreneurship

Background and development

Sydney in Cape Breton, Nova Scotia was an industrial centre of coal and steel production which brought prosperity and economic development from the nineteenth to the mid-twentieth century. The decline of these heavy industries left a void which many similar communities struggle to fill. But one group of people who had never been allowed to share in its prosperity were the First Nation Mi'kmaq tribe, who for generations had been excluded from mainstream opportunities and deprived of their Reserve lands. They occupied the Membertou district at the edge of the city, named after Grand Chief Henri Membertou. Small-scale entrepreneurship, in traditional crafts, then retailing and services, became part of their way of life. The Membertou First Nation organisation dates back to 1959, but until the 1990s it operated as a grant-aided reserve community under the Indian Act with very little self-generated income. It is included here as a pioneering reserve in Atlantic Canada which has become a highly successful business organisation.

The tribe's Chief, Terry Paul, had been exposed to economic development ideas in the early days of the Harvard Project on American Indian Economic Development, while he was living in Boston. He was elected Chief in 1984, and started to apply those principles from the 1990s to create business activity and employment for the Membertou community. After a few false starts an approach, developed through experience, was to create a 'First Nations progression model' of initial capacity-building to develop leadership, management and systems for financial accountability and governance, whilst being based on principles of conservation, sustainability, innovation and success. This enabled preparation for strategic planning, resource allocation and investment in business opportunities. The result was economic development through partnerships, agreements and new ventures, creating income streams and employment. Over 20 years, a series of businesses were established, based on the Membertou Reserve, including a trade and convention centre, a major hotel, a restaurant, a gaming commission, a business centre, entrepreneur centre and other businesses including seafoods, retailing and a corporate division which develops services to address corporate client needs.

Community and sustainability

Chief Paul developed a management team which expanded to run a range of service divisions and businesses. Long-term commitment to education and human capital development is enabling young people to progress into higher education and then into responsible roles in the organisation. The community continues to expand its land ownership, population, business activities and rate of employment. The total revenue has grown to $57 million, with more than 698 employees. Membertou was able to borrow $10 million for long-term infrastructure investment and to build a new junction for the Reserve on Highway 125, enabling more land to be acquired for retail, residential and business development (Membertou, 2015). Membertou has become one of the fastest-growing parts of the Cape Breton economy. Its success demonstrates that a community-led, collective approach to strategic entrepreneurial development can inspire the regeneration of the wider and still struggling regional economy.

Leadership

A decade ago, Scott (2004) attributed the success of Membertou's business growth to its leadership and human capital development, 'using a business approach to achieve social objectives'. This was reinforced in 2014 when Membertou First Nation won the Canadian Aboriginal Economic Development Corporation's inaugural award for excellence in aboriginal economic development. Chief Terry Paul commented: 'We must envision the future for all Aboriginal communities, a future of self-governance, self-determination and economic independence.' In June 2014, 62-year-old Chief Paul was re-elected for his sixteenth consecutive term as chief of Membertou First Nation. He won 341 of 672 total votes cast, defeating the next candidate with 314 votes in the close race.

Paul's winning campaign was based on jobs, housing, community and youth. He also pointed to hard work and going door-to-door to speak with residents. 'I got a lot of insight from the people of the community from the elders and other concerns that people had,' he said. 'The youth were really very impressive to me. I was pleasantly surprised. I didn't realize they knew so much about the issues concerning the community and their concern about the future of Membertou.'

The youth, he said, offered good advice on how he could better relate to the community, be more open and have better lines of communication with them, particularly when major decisions were being made. The Youth Chief, together with the Junior Chief and their respective Councils, offer an important insight into how young people's leadership ability is being fostered by the community. Though winning a sixteenth consecutive two-year term as Chief was an impressive feat, Paul was happy to have another opportunity to move his community into the future. 'I believe we can have a very good relationship with the whole community. The best way to move forward in a positive manner is for all of us to work together' (*Cape Breton Post*, 2014). In the wings is a mooted constitutional change that would enable the Membertou Chief and Council to assume governance of the Reserve lands from the federal government. The contribution of other Council members is increasingly evident in this move.

Discussion and Cross-Case Comparison

Since the four cases presented are diverse in many respects, this comparison highlights broad themes whilst noting a few specifics.

The leaders, identity and community

All four organisations have been led on a long-term basis by people with undoubted qualities of entrepreneurial vision and ability to create innovative projects by drawing in underused resources. They have been able to gain followership and to build trust within and around their organisations. Leadership in this way can be seen as a co-created relationship between the leader and the organisation and broader community, rather than a power- or role-based relationship. McKeever et al. (2012) explored the relationship between the entrepreneur and the community in which they are embedded, referring to Barth's (1969) exploration of the interaction between community membership and entrepreneurial activities, with their identity being influenced by their community origin and background: 'If entrepreneurs are embedded in and committed to the welfare of their communities, then the developments which emerge are more likely to be in a form which is co-created by the community and the entrepreneur' (McKeever et al., 2012: 13).

Anderson and Jack (2002) had previously explored the significance of social capital and embeddedness in entrepreneurial networks, and this study aligns with the conclusions of their prior work that entrepreneurial contributions to community development are identified and shaped by being embedded, as suggested by Granovetter (1985). Extending this to the role of the leader, it suggests that the identity of entrepreneurial leaders in such organisations and communities can be, and is strengthened by being, co-created.

In terms of gender, whilst four are men, in the case of Hill Holt Wood organisational leadership has been practised by a dyad of Karen as CEO, who gained acclaim as a social entrepreneur and leader in her own right, and Nigel as founder. There is more research to be done in exploring the growing contributions of female leaders in social and sustainable enterprises. Each of these leaders had effectively either founded the organisation or, in the case of Terry Paul in Membertou, become leader of the aboriginal people on the Reserve in 1984 when it was highly reliant on government funding and had a growing debt. In all four cases, the leaders became highly identified with the enterprises they led. Even in the cases of Hill Holt Wood and Cool Milk Group, where the founders stepped down from executive roles and appointed others to run them, this strong identification continues, and can make the transition to new leadership problematic. One factor can be ownership, where founding families retain ownership of a vital business asset.

In all four cases, the appointment and succession of new leaders to replace the founders and incumbents at some point is both inevitable and the subject of speculation in the respective communities. Arguably, this is little different from the perennial succession issue which most family businesses face. Indeed, there is a close association between all four of the enterprises and the founding or controlling families, and family succession could conceivably play a role in the leadership of some of the organisations. In the case of Membertou, the families of Paul but also of others are well represented in the governance of the organisation and the community. Partly as a result of the India Act which requires periodic elections of a Chief and Council, Membertou has the most structured and democratic form of leadership of the four cases. This engages the leader with the community as a mechanism for renewal.

The conventional social and private enterprise models are more dependent on the development or appointment of new leadership. It is suggested that this process is best viewed as a reasonably long-term process, in which the attraction and development of younger talent who can move into increasingly responsible leadership roles over a period, and gain confidence and trust within the organisation, is necessary and needs to be planned.

Direction
The direction, or strategic path, taken by the leader and their team is also a critical factor. A main reason for loss of confidence in leaders is as a result of poor judgements. The leaders of these organisations have been relatively successful over time in taking and implementing decisions. In most cases, they would claim to be innovators and ambassadors, rather than detail-oriented managers; as Steve Holmes commented, he relies on others to look after this. The strategies adopted have been entrepreneurial,

emergent and to some extent iterative; both Genesis and Membertou had periods of struggle and some failures prior to being able to consolidate and grow by investment. There is a divide perpetuated here between 'leaders' as strategic pioneers and communicators, who disclaim the role of 'managers' who are more administratively and practically oriented, as in the distinction between entrepreneurs and managers (Rae, 2015).

Entrepreneurial innovation and value creation
A distinguishing characteristic of the direction pursued by all four cases is growth through entrepreneurship. In the case of Cool Milk, this was an orthodox business strategy of identifying a market opportunity and focusing on the development and exploitation of this with determined efficiency. The other cases conceived of the opportunities in community-centred ways. HHW and Genesis both identified social problems and developed creative ways to address these, using or attracting latent resources in the community to achieve this. Social innovation can also describe projects such as the mental well-being work at HHW and the family entertainment centre at the heart of Genesis, which create social value through applying latent resources in new ways. Membertou has transformed its identity as a community, from a disadvantaged native reserve to one which on its strapline 'welcomes the world' to its world-class hotel, conference centre and other amenities. This reflects a transformation of identity and of aspiration and orientation to the wider world as visitor and destination. McKeever et al. (2012: 12) reinforce this notion of creating value from latent community resources, as 'the entrepreneurs described seemed to share an understanding of latent value, and how to transform it into an appropriate form for harvesting benefit for the local community'. Lyons et al. (2012) also found examples of communities and local entrepreneurs co-developing opportunities to promote sustainable community-centred growth.

Community
The relationships between entrepreneurship, community and value creation are increasingly recognised as significant (Lyons et al., 2012). These four organisations assert that their relationship with their communities is a defining value, but this takes quite different forms. For Cool Milk, the communities of dairy suppliers and school and childcare organisations are much closer to being supplier and customer networks, in which the enterprise promotes and communicates a discourse of community. The organisation itself is located in and has a close relationship with its village community, in the sense that a reasonably significant and well-oriented employer can demonstrate by growing a social capital network through its employees and their families.

Both Genesis and Membertou set out to be for, and increasingly of, their communities. Membertou's community is both ethnic, of the Mi'kmaq families, and geographic, of those who live on the reserve. This is distinctive, but not unique, as there are examples of community enterprise organisations situated in and for ethnic minority areas in the UK. Genesis started with a Christian faith-based motivation to help young people in a community with limited opportunities to develop more meaningful lives. By locating itself in the centre of its small town, it has become one of two focal points, the other being an oversized Tesco supermarket across the main road. Both these organisations have been able to attract resources and to create physical facilities, amenities and opportunities for their communities which make them a daily part of many residents' lives.

Leadership has played an enabling role to engage their communities in the governance and running of the organisations; the enterprise is an integral part of, and has helped to regenerate, the community, in a reflexive relationship. The case of Hill Holt Wood is perhaps different, in that it regenerated a woodland asset that was largely forgotten by the rural villages in its proximity, and the enterprise reached out to engage those communities and to offer them participation in the development, governance and use of an amenity. This has been successful, and has been adapted and translated into an urban outreach strategy in Gainsborough.

Culture

An organisation's culture can be conceived of as the collective resource of normative values, discourses, practices and behaviours which are enacted in it (Watson and Harris, 1999). All organisations will, in time, develop a culture organically. The culture of the new and small enterprise often tends to reflect the personality, values and behaviours of the founder-entrepreneur, whilst the cultural values which are espoused may be at odds with those that are practised; few organisations would claim to be unethical or unsustainable, for example. There is a relationship between the approach, personality and behaviours of a leader of an organisation, especially a founder, and its culture. So we see reified in Cool Milk, for example, Jon Thornes' guiding priorities for customer acquisition, being valued, efficiency and financial performance. However, as organisational cultures grow, being organic, they can be notoriously slow and resistant to change, which is itself an issue for leaders, especially new leaders, to reflect on.

Organisations such as those in this study aim to change, challenge and improve the status quo, rather than to accept it, being formed and led by people discontent with an unsatisfactory stasis. Hence the cultural values they espouse and practise (and the gaps between these need to be minimised) are also likely to be ones which prompt their communities to take note and to change. Promoting and practising a culture of sustainability is a prime example of this. However, in organisations which are 'of and for' their communities, the culture of the community is also likely to infuse the organisation. This may be positive, but in the case of declining communities with little shared tradition of entrepreneurship, changing deep-set attitudes of dependency can be a challenging endeavour.

Sustainability
'Sustainability', like many intangible nouns, has a broad range of meanings. Referring back to Adams (2006) and Scott Cato (2009), sustainable development can be defined by social, economic and environmental renewability and having positive or neutral effects. Enterprises define sustainability in their own terms and those they deem acceptable to their consciences and communities. Thus, in the case of Cool Milk for example, compliance with the ISO 14000 standard and having sustainable procurement practices which also make commercial sense in the interests of economic sustainability may be sufficient. Hill Holt Wood would go further, and is the most developed of the four organisations in terms of sustainability, in seeking to promote societal awareness and change at a more wide-ranging level. There is a danger, as Steve Holmes expressed, that the perceptions of being green, fairtrade and ethical have been hijacked by organisations as part of their marketing, as distinct from their core values. A passive and compliant approach to sustainability may be evidence of good corporate citizenship, but does not really qualify an organisation to be described as 'sustainable'.

The case of Membertou again has a distinctive contribution to this discussion. The First Nations peoples in Canada increasingly act as stewards of the natural environment, with a longer-term perspective towards their land heritage than corporate organisations which can seek to extract maximum value with minimal financial costs and a disregard for the environmental consequences, as seen in the concerns over mineral extraction and the effects on First Nations' territories. This is an increasingly contested issue in Canada, set to become more so following the Tsilhqot'in First Nation's legal ruling in June 2014, which required legal consent to be obtained from indigenous peoples for development on lands to which they can assert title. However, Membertou itself does not comment on environmental sustainability in its Annual Report.

All of the case organisations have adopted different stances on sustainability, with greater emphasis being given to economic and social sustainability than environmental sustainability in three of the four cases. Further movement would be likely to depend on changing expectations from the communities or external stakeholders. Public grant-awarding bodies are increasingly concerned with environmental performance, so this will become a growing issue.

Conceptualisation: sustainability as an outcome of entrepreneurial leadership

A conceptual framework can be proposed from these themes. Essentially, the organisation has to define its own meaning of sustainability, based on its own goals and values. External standards and measures can of course inform this decision-making, for which Adams's (2006) framework of social, economic and environmental sustainability provides a normative approach. Leadership is clearly a critical factor in the pursuit of sustainability. The strategic direction and goals which are set out and pursued by the organisational leadership can make more or less specific reference to different aspects of sustainability. In following this strategic direction towards sustainable goals, four aspects and the connections between them appear significant:

1. Identity: the identification of the leader with the organisation and community in a co-constructed relationship.
2. Culture: the values, practices, discourse and behaviours manifested by the organisation, being consistent with the strategic direction and prioritisation of sustainability.
3. Community: the active engagement and participation of the organisation's community (internal staff and external stakeholders) in its governance and operations, consistent with the culture and aligned with the strategy.
4. Entrepreneurial innovation: a continual process of identifying problems, reconfiguring these as opportunities, developing innovative solutions, attracting and using resources in new ways.

The interaction between these four aspects can both generate energy to achieve the strategic direction, and result in progress towards sustainable goals (see Figure 16.1). The model presented is relatively simple; however, it can make a contribution to the need for knowledge of leadership in relation to the development of sustainable, yet entrepreneurial organisations. It is important to recognise that the qualities referred to are discursive, with contextual meanings, so that rather than 'culture' or 'sustainability' being reified, they are labels applied to fluid concepts, the meanings of which are co-created and contextual in the case of each organisation. However, it can also be argued that organisational progress towards sustainability, however defined, is unlikely to be achieved without awareness, development and connections between these aspects.

Leadership

Identity: co-constructed between individual, organisation & community	**Culture:** values, discourse, practices & behaviours	**Community:** participation in governance & operations	**Innovation:** combining entrepreneurial opportunity, resources & solution

Sustainability:
Economic growth & viability
Social gain to community
Environmental benefit & impact

Strategic direction

Figure 16.1   Leadership for sustainability in entrepreneurial organisations

CONCLUSIONS

This chapter makes a small contribution to understanding leadership for organisations which are both sustainable and entrepreneurial. The growth of interest in this field, and in the related ones of social entrepreneurship and innovation, community development and sustainability per se, means that more research and practitioner and organisational development will occur internationally in the coming years. It is to be hoped that research and practitioner development can increasingly be linked together to become mutually reinforcing.

There has been quite extensive exploration of entrepreneurial leadership development, but much of this has been in the context of structured programmes often based in higher education, and there has been less research centred in organisations. Thus research contributes to the latter, and suggests that the dimensions of identity, community engagement and innovation can be explored in more depth in the organisation–community context. The significant role of communities (and within these, of families), and the interactions between community and value creation from latent resources, were surprising and interesting perspectives which would not have surfaced in an educationally oriented study.

The chapter has focused on the practice of leadership in the context of entrepreneurial organisations and their communities, aiming to explore how leadership can further sustainability, both organisationally and more generally. There is no clear or simple answer, since the variables of how sustainability is expressed in the context of the organisational and community culture are significant. The comparison of research cases suggests ways in which the personal and ethical values of the leader, and their expression of shared cultural values, contribute to this, together with the openness and motivation to change of the leader, organisation and community. Deep community engagement and relations forged between the leader, individuals, families and groups are fundamental factors. However, this engagement itself can be a barrier to succession and to allowing the founding leaders to step down. Further study of leadership development, adopting a longer-term approach to follow the development of emergent entrepreneurial leaders in organisations aiming for sustainability, could provide valuable insights.

REFERENCES

Adams, W.M. (2006), The future of sustainability: re-thinking environment and development in the twenty-first century. Report of the IUCN Renowned Thinkers Meeting, World Conservation Union, 29–31 January, www.iucn.org.

Ancona, D. (2005), Leadership in an age of uncertainty. MIT Leadership Center Research Brief. Cambridge, MA: MIT.

Anderson, A. and Jack, S. (2002), The articulation of social capital in entrepreneurial networks: a glue or a lubricant?. *Entrepreneurship and Regional Development*, 14, 193–210.

Bagheri, A. and Pihie, Z. (2011), Entrepreneurial leadership: towards a model for learning and development. *Human Resource Development International*, 14(4), 447–63.

Baron, R.A. and Ensley, M.D. (2006), Opportunity recognition as the detection of meaningful patterns: evidence from the comparison of novice and experienced entrepreneurs. *Management Science*, 52(9), 1331–44.

Barth, F. (1969), *Ethnic Groups and Boundaries*. Boston, MA: Little, Brown.

Baumol, W. (1990), Entrepreneurship: productive, unproductive, and destructive. *Journal of Political Economy*, 98(5), 893–921.

Campbell, R. (2014), *Governance and Social Leadership*. Cape Breton, Canada: Cape Breton University Press.

Cape Breton Post (2014), Terry Paul gets 16th term as Membertou chief. http://www.cape-bretonpost.com/News/Local/2014-06-21/article-3771894/Terry-Paul-gets-16th-term-as-Membertou-chief/1 (accessed 21 June 2014).

CBI (2012), The colour of growth. Maximising the potential of green business. London: CBI.

Chen, M. (2007), Entrepreneurial leadership and new ventures: creativity in entrepreneurial teams. *Creativity and Innovation Management*, 16(3): 239–49.

DEFRA (2011), Skills for a green economy. London: DEFRA. https://www.gov.uk/gov ernment/uploads/system/uploads/attachment_data/file/32373/11-1315-skills-for-agreen-economy.pdf (accessed 1 July 2014).

Dixon, S.E.A. and Clifford, A. (2007), Ecopreneurship – a new approach to managing the triple bottom line. *Journal of Organizational Change Management*, 20(3), 326–45.

Eisenhardt, K. (1989), Building theories from case study research. *Academy of Management Review*, 14(4), 488–511.

Gibb, A. (1993), The enterprise culture and education. *Entrepreneurship Theory and Practice*, 11(3), 11–34.

Granovetter, M. (1985), Economic action and social structure: the problem of embeddedness. *American Journal of Sociology*, 91(3), 481–510.

Gravells, J. (2012), Leaders who care – the chief executives' view of leadership in social enterprises: natural aptitude versus learning and development. *Human Resource Development International*, 15(2), 227–38.

Greenberg, D., McKone-Sweet, K. and Wilson, H. (2013), Entrepreneurial leaders: creating opportunity in an unknowable world. *Leader to Leader: Executive Forum*, 2013(67), 56–62.

Greenleaf, R.K. (1977), *Servant Leadership: A Journey into the Nature of Legitimate Power and Greatness*. New York, NY: Paulist Press.

Gupta, V., MacMillan, I.C. and Surie, G. (2004), Entrepreneurial leadership: developing and measuring a cross-cultural construct. *Journal of Business Venturing*, 19, 241–60.

Harrison, R.T. and Leitch, C.M. (1994), Entrepreneurship and leadership: the implications for education and development. *Entrepreneurship and Regional Development*, 6(2), 111–25.

Henry, C., Hill, F. and Leitch, C. (2005), Entrepreneurship education and training: can entrepreneurship be taught?. *Education and Training*, 47(2), 98–111.

Kempster, S.J. and Cope, J. (2010), Learning to lead in the entrepreneurial context. *International Journal of Entrepreneurial Behaviour and Research*, 16(1), 6–35.

Kuratko, D. (2007), Entrepreneurial leadership in the 21st century. *Journal of Leadership and Organizational Studies*, 13(4), 1–12.

Lans, T., Hulsink, W., Baert, H. and Mulder, M. (2008), Entrepreneurship education and training in a small business context: insights from the competence-based approach. *Journal of Enterprising Culture*, 16(4), 363–83.

Leitch, C.M., Hill, F.M. and Harrison, R.T. (2010), The philosophy and practice of interpretivist research in entrepreneurship: quality, validation, and trust. *Organizational Research Methods*, 13(1), 67–84.

Leitch, C.M., McMullan, C. and Harrison, R.T. (2009), Leadership development in SMEs: an action learning approach. *Action Learning: Research and Practice*, 6, 243–64.

Leitch, C.M., McMullan, C. and Harrison, R. (2013), The development of entrepreneurial leadership: the role of human, social and institutional capital. *British Journal of Management*, 24, 347–66.

Lyons, T., Alter, T., Audretsch, D. and Augustine, D. (2012), Entrepreneurship and community: the next frontier of entrepreneurship inquiry. *Entrepreneurship Research Journal*, 2(1), 1–24.

McKeever, E., Jack, S. and Anderson, A. (2012), Entrepreneurs in their communities: their role and impact. Paper presented at ISBE Conference, Dublin, November.

Membertou (2015), Developing a healthy mind, body and community spirit: 2014–2015 Annual Report, Membertou Inc., Membertou, Nova Scotia, Canada.

Moon, C. (2013), Where are all the ecopreneurs? The development of a construct for eco-entrepreneurship. Paper presented at ISBE Conference, Cardiff, November.

Putnam, R. (2000), *Bowling Alone: The Collapse and Revival of American Community*. New York, NY: Simon & Schuster.

Quality Assurance Agency for Higher Education (QAA) (2012), Enterprise and entrepreneurship education: guidance for higher education providers in England Wales and Northern Ireland. Gloucester: QAA.

Rae, D. (2010), Universities and enterprise education: responding to the challenges of the new era. *Journal of Small Business and Enterprise Development*, 17(4), 591–60.

Rae, D. (2015), *Opportunity-Centred Entrepreneurship*. London: Palgrave Macmillan.

Roomi, M.A. and Harrison, P. (2011), Entrepreneurial leadership: what is it and how should it be taught?. *International Review of Entrepreneurship*, 9(3), 1–44.

Schaltegger, S. and Wagner, M. (2011), Sustainable entrepreneurship and sustainability innovation: categories and interactions. *Business Strategy and the Environment*, 20(4), 222–37.

Scott, J.T. (2004), Doing business with the devil: land, sovereignty, and corporate partnerships in Membertou Inc. Halifax, CA: Atlantic Institute for Market Studies.

Scott Cato, M. (2009), *Green Economics: An Introduction to Theory, Policy and Practice*. London: Earthscan.

Shepherd, D. and Patzelt, H. (2011), The new field of sustainable entrepreneurship: studying entrepreneurial action linking 'what is to be sustained' with 'what is to be developed'. *Entrepreneurship Theory and Practice*, 35(1), 128–62.

Smith, W., Besharov, M., Wessels, A. and Chertok, M. (2011), Paradoxical leadership model for social entrepreneurs: challenges, leadership skills, and pedagogical tools for managing social and commercial demands. *Academy of Management Learning and Education*, 11(3), 463–78.

Stevenson, H. and Jarillo, C. (1990), A paradigm of entrepreneurship: entrepreneurial management. *Strategic Management Journal*, 11, 17–27.

Underwood, S., Blundel, R.K., Lyon, F. and Schaefer, A. (eds) (2012), Introduction to *Social and Sustainable Enterprise: Changing the Nature of Business* (pp. xi–xv). Contemporary Issues in Entrepreneurship Research book series, Vol. 2. Bingley: Emerald.

UNEP (2011), Towards a green economy. https://sustainabledevelopment.un.org/content/documents/126GER_synthesis_en.pdf (accessed 24 November 2011).

Vecchio, R.P. (2003), Entrepreneurship and leadership: common trends and common threads. *Human Resource Management Review*, 13(2), 303–27.

Watson, T.J. and Harris, P. (1999), *The Emergent Manager*. London: SAGE.

Yin, R. (2003), *Case Study Research: Design and Methods*, 3rd edn. Thousand Oaks, CA: SAGE.

17. The rise of the underdogs: situating and storying 'entrepreneurial leadership' in the BrewDog business story
*Robert Smith**

INTRODUCTION

It is accepted that 'leadership' is a situated context (Stewart and Smith, 2009). By 'situated context', I mean that it often occurs in particular contexts, regimes or settings such as in industries, or work settings, which influence how the entrepreneurial leadership manifests itself and is operationalised, and how this manifests in the small and medium-sized enterprise (SME) context investigated. In this context, entrepreneurs and small business owners may be called upon to perform many types of leadership actions and activities, not all of which could be classified as entrepreneurial or as entrepreneurial leadership. To be classified as the latter there must be a specific characteristic or quality relating to newness, novelty or difference. Also, we often unintentionally bring our own situated understandings of theoretical concepts such as entrepreneurial leadership to our readings of other scenarios. This is of particular interest in relation to our understanding of entrepreneurship or entrepreneurial leaders because, to date, most of our knowledge has been derived from small-scale case studies of corporate leaders and is heavily situated in corporate contexts (Burns, 2008). From a teaching perspective, my personal corporate entrepreneurial heroes are John DeLorean, the chief executive officer (CEO) of the ill-fated DeLorean cars; Tony O'Reilly of Heinz and Waterford Crystal fame; Michael O'Leary of Ryan Air; Richard Branson of Virgin; the iconic Steve Jobs of Apple; and of course Jack Welch of GE. Most of these men need no introduction because their entrepreneurial storied capitals are so well narrated in the media. What these inspirational examples have in common is that they are unquestionably charismatic, successful entrepreneurs as well as being acknowledged as great leaders of men – perhaps even Great Men themselves (after the Great Man thesis; Stewart and Smith, 2009). They are all corporate heroes, but flawed too because their leadership styles have been heavily criticised in the press and in academic journals for their lively, voluble, vociferous, didactic, authoritarian and often brusque leadership styles. For example, John DeLorean self-styled himself the 'maverick CEO'; Tony O'Reilly, Steve Jobs and Jack Welch are famous for their aggressive management styles; and Richard Branson and Michael O'Leary are exceptional communicators in authoring their own legends by fabricating entrepreneurial fable (Smith, 2005). Whilst this may not make them flawed leaders per se, it does influence public perceptions of their leadership style because of the self-serving and self-aggrandising nature of their stories. All are '*über*' males who conform to the accepted template of the heroic masculine entrepreneur (Anderson and Smith, 2007), and are 'alpha male' entrepreneurs (Burns, 2010). They are first and foremost entrepreneurs. However, as Burns appreciates, being an entrepreneur imbues one with the mantle of leader by the very nature of entrepreneuring. Nevertheless, not all entrepreneurs are natural leaders, but in performing an entrepreneurial role they must on occasion perform the role and function of a leader, whether they are comfortable with it or not. However, as entrepreneurship scholars we know many female entrepreneurial leaders and it is one of the problems with so-called Great Man theories that they often do not resonate with women. Nevertheless, they are theoretical products of their time despite the rise of new theories of shared and distributed leadership and the regendering of entrepreneurship and entrepreneurial identity. We acknowledge Great Woman stories too as a legitimate genre of business stories, albeit an individualistic, heroic story.

Yet, these iconic examples are only part of the construct about experienced corporate warriors such as Fred Goodwin and Stephen Hester who are first and foremost leaders, but who have been tagged as entrepreneurial by the media. This presents the interesting dichotomy of leaders who are entrepreneurial by nature, and entrepreneurs who are consummate leaders too. Ideologically, ontologically and epistemologically they are very different actors, despite both being accommodated under the rubric of entrepreneurial leadership. From a gendered perspective my favourite example of an entrepreneurial leader is Edel Harris of Aberdeen Foyer.[1] The reader may have their own personal list of leading entrepreneurial heroes, villains and fools (Aldrich, 2011). Context is therefore extremely important. Much less attention has been given to issues of leadership, and leadership development, in the context of entrepreneurial and small and medium-sized enterprises. This chapter addresses this.

I am not so much concerned with entrepreneurship simply as a type of leadership that occurs in a specific setting, but rather with understanding how leadership can be exercised situationally as an abstract and thus abstracted concept. It is abstract because it illustrates a particular quality, or characteristic, of BrewDog's self-expression of their own unique style of entrepreneurial leadership as opposed to a concrete, applied but potentially abstruse theoretical instance enacted within an entrepreneurial small business setting. In seeking *Verstehen*, I apply leadership theory to make sense of the stories used herein. I make a contribution by exploring the entrepreneurial actions and antics of two founders and entrepreneurs, James Watt and Martin Dickie, who have taken a small brewing company, BrewDog, on an incredible journey of success and expansion. This chapter discusses how leadership occurs in entrepreneurial contexts, and demonstrates related insights by drawing on the BrewDog story. In doing so, the powerful story fills a gap in the literatures of entrepreneurship and leadership, and demonstrates the impact of James Watt and Martin Dickie as business and product leaders. This plays a crucial factor in the success of their venture and has implications for our understanding of new venture viability and growth. Thus, understanding leadership in this context is particularly pertinent, given the importance attached to entrepreneurship as an agent of economic development and restructuring (Harrison and Leitch, 2013). The gaps, and limitations in the protean literature, are worth explicating. The emerging literature of entrepreneurial leadership is often descriptive, and comparative in nature. It spans two established literatures, and those who invoke the theoretical label do not always make explicit what they mean by its use, nor do they always contextualise it properly. The literature presently privileges examples of heroic men in corporate settings, or those with established reputations as maverick tycoons. It describes entrepreneurs and leaders in a variety of situated contexts. There are numerous individual case studies but few theoretically informed empirical studies. Contexts such as gender, marginality, ethnicity, the informal and SMEs are under-represented in the literature. This illustrative case study of informal entrepreneurial leadership in an SME context expands the conceptual and theoretical coverage in practical everyday contexts. I begin by examining the theoretical underpinning to the concept, before considering methodological issues. The BrewDog story is told, and thereafter a series of layered, storied contexts are presented to illuminate entrepreneurial leadership interventions.

THEORETICAL UNDERPINNING

The concept of entrepreneurial leadership is topical and is a conflation of two of the most powerful conceptual metaphors of our age: entrepreneurship and leadership. It has been suggested by leadership commentators that the term is an oxymoron, since the concepts of leadership and entrepreneurship are so distinct. Entrepreneurship is usually associated with the creation of a new business venture but virtually all business leaders face the challenges of entrepreneurship.[2] In many respects the literatures of entrepreneurship and leadership are germane and cognate with much crossover and many commonalities. For example, Kuratko (2007) positions successful growth-oriented entrepreneurs as entrepreneurial leaders, albeit the term is used to describe individuals and actions in traditional entrepreneurial contexts, new ventures, and traditional leadership contexts corporations and public sector organisations. In Western societies we have come to revere the entrepreneur and the leader in equal measure and entrepreneurs achieve a double dose of legitimacy (Burns, 2013). Thus those identified as entrepreneurial leaders benefit from the cult-like status attributed to entrepreneurs and leaders.

Defining Entrepreneurial Leadership

The earliest definition of entrepreneurial leadership appears to be from Lippitt (1987). Since then a small but steady stream of studies have investigated the topic. It is an exciting protean stream of literature which forms the basis of a 'competitive advantage' in today's dynamic, competitive, global economy (Bettis and Hitt, 1995; Brown and Eisenhardt, 1998; McGrath and MacMillan, 2000; Gupta et al., 2004). As a concept it spans both public and private sectors (Morris and Jones, 1999; Eyal and Kark, 2004). Gupta et al. (2004) list three areas of entrepreneurship research relevant to leadership. These are: entrepreneurship (Schumpeter, 1934), entrepreneurial orientation (Miller, 1983; Covin and Slevin, 1988) and entrepreneurial management (Stevenson, 1983). They also suggest that leadership involves taking a strategic approach to entrepreneurship, making strategic entrepreneurship a potentially fruitful field of inquiry.

Cogliser and Brigham (2004) identified similarities in the models and constructs examined in leadership and entrepreneurship research. Both have moved on from a focus on traits and characteristics (individual) to content (What do entrepreneurs/leaders actually do?) to context (How do they interact with the environment?). Both literatures have progressed through distinct phases and it is agreed that both entrepreneurship and leadership are activities accessible to all. The 'born versus made' arguments pervade both literatures. Consequentially, both literatures have resonance and transferability to the extent that if one reads a passage about leadership and substitutes the word 'leader' for the word 'entrepreneur', the passage usually makes perfect sense.

Czariawska-Joerges and Wolff (1991) differentiate between leadership and entrepreneurship, articulating the former as responsible for clarifying causality, simplifying reality and strengthening control over it, whilst they viewed the latter as an action related to generating new realities. At a semiotic level, leadership involves influencing a subject's symbolic realm in order to move them towards certain actions, and determining the time and scope of these actions (Leavy, 1996; Shamir et al., 1993); whereas entrepreneurship represents the operational translation of symbols and behaviours into actions.

Researchers distinguish between entrepreneurs and leaders through observable attributes (Perren, 2000) such as belief in control of events, ambiguity tolerance, need for independence and identification of market opportunities. This is in line with Stewart et al. (1998), who suggested that entrepreneurs demonstrate a greater need for achievement, a greater risk-taking propensity and a greater preference for innovation than corporate managers and leaders. Vecchio (2003) suggests that research into the attributes and behaviours of entrepreneurs (as opposed to leaders) has been inconclusive and often contradictory, thus small firm creation is just another context in which we can study leadership. Fernald et al. (2005) conclude that both leaders and entrepreneurs are successful largely to the extent that they provide: strategic leadership (vision and long-term goals); problem solving skills; timely decision making; a willingness to accept risk; and good negotiating skills.

There are numerous attributes and behaviours common to leadership and entrepreneurship. Studies by Cogliser and Brigham (2004), Perren (2000) and Fernald et al. (2005) identified overlapping constructs or characteristics that define this interface; see Table 17.1.

These characteristics were chosen at random from the dual literatures as representative examples of common shared traits. Innovation, creativity and vision are characteristics common to both entrepreneurs and leaders, but this offers an overly simplistic viewpoint because most entrepreneurs innovate, create and are visionary, although not all leaders do so.

Table 17.1   Characteristics shared between leaders and entrepreneurs

Authors	Perren (2000)	Cogliser and Brigham (2004)	Fernald et al. (2005)
Characteristics identified as common to leaders and entrepreneurs	Innovation and vision Personal drive Risk acceptance	Vision Innovation/ creativity Influence Planning	Visionary Creative Ability to motivate Risk-taker Achievement-oriented Flexible Patient Persistent

Source: Stewart and Smith (2009).

Obviously, the preceding sentence is indicative and not all-encompassing, but illustrates the point. Innovation is the ability to implement newly designed services and/or products (Eyal and Kark, 2004) and proactivity is one's inclination to shape the environment, rather than merely react to it passively. It is initiated action to which competitors respond (Covin and Slevin, 1991; Slevin and Covin, 1990). Definitions of entrepreneurial leadership may thus privilege the entrepreneurial elements of the make up. There has been a trend towards compiling lists and taxonomies of cognate behaviours. Emerging themes are detailed in Table 17.2.

The contents of Table 17.2 help us to tease out the ramifications of the themes. When analysing common characteristics of both entrepreneurship and leadership there is a tendency to concentrate on the characteristics, and not context and setting; therefore we miss important nuances. In drawing parallels from other literatures and examples there is a danger that we misinterpret or overextend the examples. In relation to innovative combinations of leadership and entrepreneurship theory being used to define entrepreneurial leadership as a term, there is a further danger that such examples which occur in a mundane, everyday setting such as SMEs are overlooked. Also, because 'entrepreneurial leadership' is a new term that still has to be adequately defined, there is a danger that we consider it anachronistic to use examples which predate the first use of the theory. In terms of the masculine dominance and hegemonic masculinity arguments, the heroic metaphors skew the term so that we are more likely to associate heroic males with being entrepreneurial leaders rather than other gendered or ethnic exemplars.

Leadership and Entrepreneurial Leadership

Trait theorists such as Stogdill (1974) attribute good leadership to characteristics, qualities and attributes that are inherent in an individual and cannot be learnt. This is at odds with the prior findings of Tannenbaum and Schmidt (1958) and Blake and Mouton (1964), who concluded that good leadership consists of particular behaviours or 'styles', including entrepreneurial leadership, which can be learnt. Chell (1985) suggests that entrepreneurial leaders can utilise different personality characteristics in different ways at different times, dependent on the specific demands of that context. Thus entrepreneurial leaders may switch heuristics or 'gears', dependent on their situation. As situation and context change, the entrepreneur may have to switch between entrepreneurial traits and actions to those associated with leadership. It is not known whether this change in heuristic gearing is a conscious or subconscious shifting. This interchange between 'leader' and 'entrepreneur' is sometimes confusing, and it is

Table 17.2   Approaches to defining and discussing entrepreneurial leadership

Approaches and themes	Meaning
Analysis of common characteristics between entrepreneurs and leaders, or identifying leadership characteristics thought to identify entrepreneurial leadership.	This pushes us down the traits route, which is analogous to the Great Man route, but there is still mileage in this route for researchers (Nicholson, 1998).
Drawing parallels with existing concepts in leadership or entrepreneurship, that is, leadership as form of entrepreneurship or entrepreneurship as form of leadership, for example transformational leadership.	This suggests that transformational leadership is difficult to tie down in terms of how the leader can achieve the necessary behaviours. Mentions concepts such as charisma that no one can define let alone teach, but which take on a life of their own in narrative.
Innovative combinations of different strands of research in leadership and entrepreneurship, for example Gupta et al. (2004) combine entrepreneurship, entrepreneurial orientation, entrepreneurial management and leadership (transformational leadership, team-oriented leadership and value-based leadership).	Entrepreneurial orientation is a little more concrete than transformational leadership, but is this about the firm or the individual? Does this indicate, or define entrepreneurial leadership? We believe not. Transformation, innovation and charisma emerge as themes. This alludes to entrepreneurial leadership as a form of adaptability (or 'shape-shifting' in mythic terms), with common terminology used including words such as volatility, visionary, dynamic, superior performance, moving fast, proactivity and adaptation.
No definition as a default position that leadership infers modern leadership of a kind required in today's dynamic environment.	The qualities of a successful leader in contemporary times of change differ substantially from those popular in the conditions of former times (Nicholson, 1998).
Male dominance and hegemonic masculinity as continuing themes. This narrative is reminiscent of Burns's (2010) argument of the entrepreneur as super-hero.	Kuratko (2007) viewed entrepreneurs as 'aggressive catalysts for change in the world of business; individuals who recognise opportunities where others see chaos, contradiction of confusion'. Entrepreneurs are compared to Olympic athletes breaking new barriers, to long-distance runners, to symphony orchestra conductors who balance the different skills and sounds into a cohesive whole, or to *Top Gun* pilots who continually push the envelope of speed and daring.

Source: Stewart and Smith (2009).

not always clear how comment about leadership becomes an argument about the entrepreneur, making context and situation vital. In real time, the entrepreneurial leader or the leader being entrepreneurial will both operate intuitively or experientially and may not know when they change heuristics.

Drawing on the significance of temporal context, Gupta et al. (2004) identify three modern leadership perspectives 'capable of sustaining innovation and adaptation in high-velocity and uncertain environments'. These are neocharismatic or transformational leadership (House, 1977; Conger and Kanungo, 1987; Yukl and Van Fleet, 1982), team-oriented leadership and value-based leadership. Charisma is an important characteristic of the transformational leader's toolkit (Bass, 1985) and is central to many new leadership theories denoting a leader's behaviours and followers' emotions (Bass and Avolio, 1993). It facilitates the development of an extraordinary level of influence over followers and enables leaders to transform the nature of work by making it appear more heroic, morally correct and meaningful (Conger and Kanungo, 1998). Organ (1996) suggests that transformational leaders achieve success by being magnetic, charming and visionary, but context and situation determine whether this is necessarily a good thing. Also of interest to this discussion are visionary leadership (Bennis and Nanus, 1985; Sashkin, 1988) and transformational leadership (Bass, 1985; Organ, 1996). These so-called 'post-heroic' leadership theories (Parry and Hansen, 2007: 293) describe exceptional leaders, who have extraordinary effects on the people and systems around them.[3] The roles of manager and leader as change agents is of interest (Schein, 1996; Spreitzer et al., 1999; Work, 1996) because the entrepreneurial leader is not always the business owner.

Entrepreneurial leaders manipulate the emotional and spiritual resources of the organisation, such as values commitment and aspiration (Bennis and Nanus, 1985), to manage meaning, infuse ideological values, construct lofty goals and visions, and inspire. They inspire followers by meeting higher-order needs. They transform constructive or adaptive change (Kotter, 1998) instead of merely manipulating physical resources (Bennis and Nanus, 1985) to produce consistency and order (Kotter, 1998). It may well be that these new, aspirational forms of leadership lend themselves towards being aligned to entrepreneurial leadership. Entrepreneurial leaders are capable of facilitating proactive transformation (Venkataraman and Van de Ven, 1998). The entrepreneurial leader creates scenarios of possible opportunities and assembles resources to enact transformation (Gupta et al., 2004). Thus, leadership in general, but specifically entrepreneurial leadership, can be viewed as a dramaturgical performance or performed role (Gardner and Avolio, 1998). Eyal and Kark state that charismatic (transformational) leaders 'are by nature entrepreneurial and change oriented' (Conger and Kanungo, 1998), and transformational leaders promote change and innovation in organisations (Bass, 1985; Howell and Avolio, 1993).

Tarabishy et al. (2002) position the entrepreneurial leader as an 'enterprising, transformational leader who operates in a dynamic market that offers lucrative opportunities'. Entrepreneurial leaders have high levels of communication skills, consistency, self-confidence and vision. For them, part of entrepreneurship is the ability to recognise opportunities in a dynamic market. McGrath and MacMillan (2000) identify five key leadership roles:

- framing the challenge (tempering ambitious goals within limitations);
- absorbing uncertainty (the leader shoulders responsibility if things go wrong);
- path-clearing role (gaining support, eliminating obstacles);
- building commitment (motivating the team); and
- specifying limits (defining constraints to eliminate self-imposed ideas of limitation).

These key principles illuminate our understanding of entrepreneurial leadership, because practising it necessitates dealing with ambiguity, risk and uncertainty, and operating in new markets and ways rather than issuing orders and following established practices. Gupta et al. (2004) further identify skills that entrepreneurial leaders possess, including bargaining, team-building, foresight, intuition and creativity. Whilst traditional leaders may also practise these skills, they suggest that the entrepreneurial leader achieves this through personal modelling. Kirby (2003) suggests that entrepreneurial leaders do so (lead) by example, and setting direction to empower their followers to be creative in reaching end goals. They initiate and model a culture for employees and followers to follow.

Entrepreneurship and Entrepreneurial Leadership

One would expect entrepreneurs to possess leadership characteristics. To build, or even start, a business the entrepreneur must exert influence (over their banker, their customers, their team) to achieve their goals, and influencing is at the heart of leadership (Stewart and Smith, 2009). One also associates entrepreneurs with leadership functions such as providing vision to the development of a new product, service or organisation (Fernald and Solomon, 1996). Eggers et al. (1994) identified management and leadership skills that help in determining the growth rate of a small business:

- seeing and clearly communicating a clear direction for the future;
- leading and motivating others;
- recognising shortcomings in the team and supplementing those skills; and
- having the business skills from an educational and experience viewpoint.

Nevertheless, the type and extent of leadership displayed is perhaps dependent on the business size, stage and growth. Nicholson (1998) argues that entrepreneurial leaders differ from managers in seven dimensions: higher conscientiousness, higher assertiveness, higher dutifulness, lower depression, lower self-consciousness, lower actions and lower compliance. He viewed leadership as a form of character armour. The entrepreneurial leader appears to be more stress-resistant, unselfconscious, assertive and competitive than the traditional stereotypical leader. Again, these characteristics can be found in traditional leaders but particularly relate to the intensity of presence in entrepreneurial leaders.

Interestingly, Nicholson's study was conducted among independent, successful, 'growth-orientated' United Kingdom firms operating in a traditional SME entrepreneurial environment, but scholars of leadership may not be familiar with the concepts and nuances of business and the SME sector. Nicholson affirms that entrepreneurial leadership is achievable in traditional entrepreneurial environments and can be enacted by entrepreneurs or leaders. The entrepreneurial leaders must 'reconcile the impatience of the entrepreneur with the constraints imposed by an organisation in its desire to control events' (Burns, 2008). This raises an interesting suggestion that entrepreneurial leadership is a stage of evolution of the entrepreneur, coincident with the growth and maturation of the firm.

Entrepreneurship, the Great Man Thesis and Idolatry

Great Man theory was posited by the historian Thomas Carlyle (1888) who commented that, 'The history of the world is but the biography of great men'. Thus it is embedded in a storied 'masculinised' construct and brought to us via stories and biographies which play an important part in our education and development as leaders. We go in search of opportunities to narrate compelling stories which illustrate our leadership ability. This thesis spans the literatures of entrepreneurship and leadership and introduces the narrative-based subjects of heroism and hero-worship into play (Stewart and Smith, 2009). Carlyle argued that the study of Great Men was 'profitable' to one's own heroic side. By examining the lives of such heroes, one could uncover one's true nature. It has elements of active voyeurism and boyish hero-worship. However, the theory has been criticised as a hopelessly primitive, childish and unscientific position, in that so-called 'Great Men' were merely products of their time and social environment (Stewart and Smith, 2009). Yet, Cawthon (1996) argued that situational forces and leadership theories cannot always account for the emergence of great leaders, and that we cannot ignore Great Man theory as a heuristic device, because it helps to illuminate and penetrate the mystery of leadership as it is based on everyday observation and common sense by weaving innate qualities, distinctive experiences, or a combination of both, into convincing narratives of leadership. When coupled with trait-based characteristics such as charisma, the thesis restories people as 'Great Leaders' made of the 'right stuff' required for leadership (Organ, 1996; Stewart and Smith, 2009). Charisma is central to both leadership and entrepreneurial narrative. Nevertheless, it must be borne in mind that the essence of Carlyle's Great Man perspective is accounts of men destined to lead on the basis of their exceptional qualities, and this naturally sets up a strong narrative element, but it only complements the position of the leader and in this respect such narratives are not based on everyday observation. Also, in such narratives, the 'leader' is determined a priori, meaning that leadership is their product. Obviously, this depends upon how leadership is defined. Another problematic with the Great Man thesis is that narratives do not go looking for the leader; the leader is already there and therefore the leader (or followers or biographers) must story the narrative as a Great Man story. This assumes that this is a positive thing. Also, the narrative is constructed around the leader. Finally, there is an assumption that narratives of great men do not start from the practical doing of leadership but from the biology and social circumstances of the leader, said to be gifted with extraordinary qualities (such as charisma), making it a self-reinforcing construct. This is not necessarily a contradiction, because such stories are a product and a genre.

Although best operated at a storied level, the Great Man thesis is also capable of enactment as a leadership style or dramaturgical performance (Gardner and Avolio, 1998). The thesis is the embodiment of heroic leadership, and heroic leaders can adopt the Great Man persona via performing male-centric characteristics and traits such as charisma, courage, risk-taking propensity and stoicism. These are the very traits which characterise the entrepreneurial personality, and from which entrepreneur stories are fashioned (Stewart and Smith, 2009). Great Men as a general rule exude legitimacy and authenticity, because being seen to be an authentic leader is a vital component of leadership success (Sparrowe, 2005). Thus, if one is not seen as being an authentic leader then one is unlikely to be seen as a Great Man; although this need not follow. Conversely, many Great Men, although they are successful leaders, may not be viewed as authentic.

For Parry and Hansen (2007: 290) it is necessary to be storied as a leader by others. They suggest that followers follow, and are influenced by organisational stories which mirror shared leadership values. Thus story-making is a leadership activity, as stories have the potential to inspire followers and are an excellent medium through which to enact leadership and story a compelling vision towards its fulfillment. For Parry and Hansen the stories themselves operate as leaders, because followers follow a story as much as the leader. This is particularly so of entrepreneurial leaders such as Richard Branson and Steve Jobs. Thus entrepreneurial leadership is an exciting and vibrant narrative, making it an easy-to-follow script. It is necessary for entrepreneurial leaders to develop leadership narratives which resonate both within organisations and the customer base. For Parry and Hansen (2007: 283), organisations have, tell and are stories. The storied entrepreneurial elements help to reinvigorate the leadership elements. Yet, there is always a danger of Great Man stories reifying the charismatic, entrepreneurial hero as a false god, and of academics committing the sin of worshipping false idols. This applies to policy-makers, practitioners and journalists as well as to academics. To understand the BrewDog story 'as told' in this chapter, it is necessary to consider issues of methodology.

METHODOLOGY

This chapter is grounded in theories of entrepreneurship and leadership but draws examples from my personal observations of the BrewDog story and from close readings (Amernic and Craig, 2006) of the BrewDog website (www.brewdog.com), and also of press and media coverage of the company using documentary research methodology (Scott, 2006). I thus consciously gathered stories and scenarios which (to me) illustrated some diverse examples of the type of 'abstract' or 'abstracted' entrepreneurial leadership displayed by James Watt and Martin Dickie. This personal apercus influenced the methodology and the narration of the story. The BrewDog website and the media coverage are easily accessible; and the former is updated regularly, while the latter are constant. This methodology is justified because the two founders seldom give press interviews or engage with academia. They have an active policy of media engagement, but on their terms. They are very internet-savvy and disseminate

BrewDog stories and news via their website and blogs. They release material to the press but do not actively court personal publicity. Moreover, neither James nor Martin engage in what Amernic and Craig (2006) refer to as CEO 'double-speak' because of its dual meaning, nor do they appear to engage with or tell entrepreneur stories. What they do well, is tell BrewDog stories. It is difficult to disentangle the different story types. Nevertheless, they are widely recognised within the industry as entrepreneurs; for instance, wine industry expert Richard Halstead (2013) has challenged the wine industry to 'marshal its mavericks' and think outside traditional industry norms, and presented BrewDog as a classic example of the outcome of maverick entrepreneurial proactivity.

To gain a deeper insight into the narratives and semiotics of the BrewDog story I employ the 'cultural web' model as posited by Johnson et al. (2012). This is composed of six interrelated elements that in organisational culture (in this instance) form the emerging paradigm of entrepreneurial leadership, albeit as a fluid, fuzzy paradigm. The model is accepted in the management literature as a useful framework for analysing organisations and patterns of doing things, especially identifying political, symbolic and structural issues within an organisation. The model allows us to analyse the factors in turn, enabling a bigger picture to emerge. I use it as an analytical tool to demonstrate the shared semiotics of entrepreneurship, leadership and entrepreneurial leadership. The six elements are:

1. Stories: or past events and people talked about inside and outside the organisation. The focus is upon who and what the organisation chooses to immortalise. These embed values and behaviours which are cherished.
2. Rituals and routines: these are the behaviours and actions of staff that signal acceptable behaviour. This in turn influences what is expected to happen in given situations and, more importantly, what is valued by management.
3. Symbols: the visual representations of the organisation including insignia, logos, status symbols such as offices, cars and dress codes.
4. Organisational structure: including the structure defined by the organisation chart, the unwritten lines of power or influences that followers value.
5. Control systems: these are how an organisation is controlled, and traditionally include financial systems, quality systems, disciplinary systems and rewards.
6. Power structures: relate to where the real power lies in the organisation; that is, key senior executives and middle management with the ability to influence decisions, operations and strategic direction.

It is of note that issues of organisational structure, control systems and power structures are elements of leadership. Johnson and Scholes present these elements graphically as six semi-overlapping circles which combine to influence the cultural paradigm or web. I used the model to build cultural webs for entrepreneurial leadership drawing on the BrewDog example. This entailed trawling the website for storied examples and, through a process of coding and constant comparative analysis, populating the chosen themes with the examples. Because of space constraints I discuss only three of the categories: stories, symbols, and rituals and routines.[4] There is also a semiotic aspect to the methodology in that I made use of photographic images of BrewDog which I downloaded from their website and Google Images. However, because of copyright issues I have not presented these here. Instead, when I discuss a semiotic phenomenon I direct readers to the appropriate hosted pages.

ENTREPRENEURIAL LEADERSHIP THE BREWDOG WAY

This section presents the storied context as understood and narrated by me, the author. As such, it is difficult to separate narrator from story. It is necessary to present storied context for readers unfamiliar with the story before applying the cultural web. In the storied examples which follow I concentrate on telling the story descriptively to align the story with the theme from the cultural web. BrewDog are currently Scotland's largest independently owned brewery, producing about 120 000 bottles per month for export all over the world.[5] The company was founded in 2006 by two childhood friends James Watt and Martin Dickie from Fraserburgh in the north-east of Scotland (see Smith et al., 2010 for the founding story and case study).[6] They produced their first brew in April 2007 and have had an exciting and at times controversial business story to tell since then. From the outset BrewDog had problems with the brewing industry establishment. For example, the Portman Group controversy is typical of the company stories which underpin their Punk ethos of 'gleefully cheeking the industry's big players'.[7] This anti-establishment spirit is summed up by a quote from James Watt: 'This [UK] market is dominated by multinational, faceless mega-corporations, making the lowest common denominator, homogenized, bland product, spending millions on advertising to convince people that's what good beer is'.[8]

The ethos is derived from their desire to challenge industry giants such as Stella, Budweiser and Tennents. Martin appreciated that the craft and real ale markets were niche markets and that stereotypical representation of a real ale buff was a middle-aged man with sandals and a cardigan. They set out to be different, and instead of selling their beers in a typical larger bottle wanted to sell them in smaller bottles to set them apart from their competitors. They deliberately stood out by engaging in publicity stunts. This was clever entrepreneurial marketing, because they did not have a marketing budget like their competitors and so, as will be demonstrated below, manufacturing stories deliberately designed to cause controversy is part of their ethos. Stories and storytelling are therefore part of their avowed Punk ethos and leadership style, to the extent that they have become rituals and routine.

The Portman Group and Storying Controversy

In 2008 the Portman Group, the industry watchdog, challenged BrewDog publically in the press, criticising them for selling high-strength beers, linking them to fears over underage drinking and binge drinking. Portman claimed BrewDog were in breach of their Codes of Practice and wanted the company to change the labelling on the beers. BrewDog denied the allegations, claiming that Portman was impeding the development of smaller brewing companies, leading to an eight-month dispute. A preliminary adjudication ruled against the company but in December 2008 BrewDog were cleared of all breaches. This allowed them to continue marketing their brands without making changes to the packaging. This was quite a victory for a small new venture, but the case could have jeopardised the fledgling brewery. The story positions BrewDog as an industry champion and giant-killer challenging authority.

In 2009, the BrewDog beer Tokyo caused further controversy when the Portman Group criticised the availability of a beer of that strength in 330 ml bottles with traditional crown caps. In response, BrewDog brewed progressively stronger high-strength beers, laying claim to the title 'strongest beer ever brewed' on more than one occasion. One of their beers was provocatively branded as Sink The Bismarck and another, Speedball, was marketed with the quip, 'we thought we would give them something worth banning us for'. It was controversial because the term 'speedball' has connotations with drugs. The Portman Group responded by promptly banning the product, giving BrewDog the publicity they sought. BrewDog rebranded the product as Dogma. They also brewed a 32 per cent Tactical Nuclear Penguin and a 55 per cent throat-burner branded The End of History.[9] This is typical of BrewDog storytelling practices in which the product becomes the story, and has come to symbolise their irreverent Punk ethos. We have come to expect BrewDog stories to routinely be rituals of entrepreneurial differentiation.

The Diageo controversy is yet another example of BrewDog flouting the establishment. On 9 May 2012, BrewDog revealed that Diageo had threatened to withdraw funding from BII Scotland's annual awards if BrewDog was named winner of the Best Bar Operator award. A panel of judges had apparently voted for BrewDog, but a Diageo representative overruled them and the award was presented to another bar. Diageo was forced to issue an apology, blaming a 'serious misjudgment' by a staff member. This increased BrewDog's anti-establishment credibility.[10] This is a classic David-versus-Goliath underdog story which has become part of company legend.

In 2013, it was reported that a counterfeit BrewDog bar was operating in China without their knowledge. The pragmatic response was to initiate a media story about imitation being the best form of flattery. BrewDog stories are usually stories told with a commercial purpose to sell products or 'big up' the brand. Other examples relate to James and Martin going clay pigeon shooting with cans of Tennent's, ten-pin bowling with bottles of Budweiser, and playing golf with cans of Stella; or to hiring a 'dwarf' to lobby outside the Houses of Parliament, successfully, for the right to serve beer in a two-thirds pint glass. Another storied advertising stunt involved placing big brewers' logos on BrewDog posters in a rather unflattering light. BrewDog fell foul of the Advertising Standards Authority for their use of profane language in their advertising. This produced a string of expletives from James. These stories illustrate a form of entrepreneurial leadership achieved through 'offensive' entrepreneurial marketing practices which corporations could not countenance.

Offensive Marketing and Going on the Offensive

BrewDog's provocative, proactive marketing strategy is a key aspect of their entrepreneurial business practices and has leveraged them substantial international press and media coverage. The Portman Group's response is an example of establishment moral outrage. The BrewDog response is an example of what I term 'deliberately offensive marketing', to differentiate it from the literature of offensive marketing or 'perverse marketing'.[11] This guerrilla marketing tactic (Gruber, 2004; Ay et al., 2010) is a conscious, aggressive technique of being deliberately offensive to gain free publicity, thereby raising one's product profile in marketing terms. BrewDog, as a brand, benefits on account of their representatives' offensive comments and anti-establishmentism. There is a clear distinction between being deliberately offensive and simply being aggressive. It is also a form of 'ego-based' entrepreneurial marketing (Chaston, 2000; Stokes, 2000) as a marketing strategy which challenges convention. Another storied example occurred in July 2010, when BrewDog produced their The End of History range. The bottles were packaged in small stuffed animals (from roadkill victims) and were priced at £500 and £700 each. Only 12 bottles were produced, 11 being sold for retail and one auctioned via the internet. The stunt raised a storm of publicity, being criticised by the charity Advocates for Animals as a perverse gimmick.[12] Another example of ego-based marketing was the Vladimir Putin stunt in which BrewDog marketed a beer provocatively labelled 'Hello, My Name is Vladimir' with a pink label to signify their protest against the anti-gay policies of the Russian leader. The beer was labelled as the world's first protest beer.[13] The photograph on the bottle's label shows James and Martin posing as Vladimir Putin.[14] These stories situate BrewDog in contemporary social narratives.

BrewDog's maverick approach to marketing extends to their idiosyncratic approach to finance, with their Equity for Punks fundraising scheme which offers beer lovers the chance to 'buy shares at £95 a pop'. This innovative funding stream was a UK first, raising nearly £6 million from 12 500 investors. All these storied examples illustrate an entrepreneurial approach by the company's leaders and thus, by extension, are examples of entrepreneurial leadership. In the examples, the stories are the context and the medium.

BrewDog Rituals and Routines as Storying Opportunities

BrewDog regularly win industry awards and this has become an established routine born out of the ritual (or ritualistic practice) of defying the establishment. In 2007, their beer Physics won World's Best Strong Pale Ale and another, Rip Tide, won the World's Best Imperial Stout at the World Beer Awards.[15] In 2008, BrewDog won the Prince's Scottish Youth Business Trust Young Entrepreneur of the Year award and an Entrepreneur of the Year award for demonstrating exceptional vision and leadership at the National Business Awards for Scotland. In 2008, BrewDog won a Gold Medal at the World Beer Cup for their beer Paradox. In 2010, their Hardcore IPA won Gold at the World Beer Cup. In September 2013, a TV show titled *Brew Dogs* premiered on the US television channel Esquire Network, where James and Martin travel across America visiting different American beer towns, celebrating distinctive craft beers and creating their own locally inspired brews.[16] These stories demonstrate that BrewDog have a reputation for being industry leaders, which is in itself a form of abstract entrepreneurial leadership in that it is the storied context which denotes leadership position and not the individual observed actions and behaviours of the leaders.

BrewDog small business stories are characterised by themes of growth, of expansion, of winning prizes and awards and of taking on the establishment, as illustrated by their growth strategy of opening up BrewDog bars in the recession when other brewing chains were divesting bars from their portfolio. In October 2010 they opened their first bar in Aberdeen. Further bars opened in Edinburgh, Glasgow and Camden in London during 2011; and 2012 was a busy year for BrewDog, seeing bars open in Nottingham, Newcastle, Manchester, Bristol and Birmingham. A further three opened in 2013 in Leeds, Stockholm and another in London in Shepherd's Bush. In 2014, they opened a bar in São Paulo, Brazil and another in Dundee. These examples illustrate an entrepreneurial leadership approach not normally associated with SME leadership.

Symbols, Symbolism and Symbollocks

The semiotics and iconology of the company's Punk image and imagery are of note. Punk iconology has been linked to the practice of entrepreneurship by Drakopoulou-Dodd (2014), and in particular how artefacts, interviews and videos are used to create countercultural, alternative, entrepreneurial identities. The most obvious example of the use of symbols by BrewDog is their iconic logo and the story behind it. See their website for the iconic visual representation of the logo of the masculine, wolf-like image of a dog. The story behind the company name is fascinating. It came from an attachment between James Watt and his dog Sweep. He liked brewing, and his dog too. The conjoined words are now part of brewing industry history and the BrewDog story. However, the dog on the logo is more wolverine than family pet. The company name is printed as 'BrewDog', thus forming an instantly recognisable trademark to accompany the logo. From a marketing perspective this is clever, because the words 'Brew' and 'Dog' seldom appear anywhere else in print, making it unusually distinctive and valuable. The logo is now on products and merchandise, raising additional income for the company. Stickers bearing the iconic logo can now be found adhering to buildings in far-flung places, testament to the power of guerrilla marketing in providing free publicity. Guerrilla marketing works by attempting to reach 'private worlds' of consumers to give them a memorable experience with their brands (Chaston, 2000). Guerrilla advertising works by placing advertisement material in unusual (and usually unauthorised) places, thus attracting the attention of consumers whilst irritating and annoying the consumers. It may be unethical, or break the law (Ay et al., 2010). However, this makes shrewd business sense. In 2013, the firm which grew from humble beginnings posted an impressive £2.5 million profit on a turnover of £20 million. BrewDog iconology is not so much symbolism, but an exercise in 'symbollocks', as the ethos of their advertising is to 'take off' or 'send up' competitors by making fun of them.

On a visit to the company brewery in January 2013, I came across an interesting aspect, or example, of their Punk ethos and imagery of 'conforming nonconformity' (see Smith and Anderson, 2003).[17] BrewDog broadcasts an image associated with being a nonconformist organisation which baits the establishment, and in particular Diageo. This is epitomised by the masculine company imagery adopted by the brewers. The brewing team adopt a manly dress code, wearing BrewDog brand T-shirts, and most are heavily tattooed on the arms and upper body. This form of self-publicity is shrewd marketing for BrewDog but obviously runs deeper than that, being a form of hegemonic masculinity (Connell, 2005; Connell and Messerschmidt, 2005). At the time, Martin Dickie was sporting a beard and ponytail, and the look adopted by the brewers may be an example of 'mimetic leadership' (Pink, 2008). Mimetic leadership is a relatively new theory based on the human propensity for mimesis. We copy what works for us culturally, socially and organisationally. We often mimic the images, artefacts and behaviours of others who are in our social peer group, and this is how we learn and progress. As effective leaders Martin (and James) channel their 'mimetic desires' into shared goals, values and outcomes that can be perceived as having a wide benefit. Thus in a small firm setting (for example, BrewDog) if we want to become a leader it is common to emulate or copy the traits, characteristics, actions and attitudes of company leaders. Ambitious employees thus mould themselves in the form of a successful leader and try to become them by acting and looking as if they were them. Thus, if they look like and behave like their leading role model, then they are more likely to be socialised into the company ethic.

Moreover, the senior brewer and others also sported long, forked-tail beards similar to those worn by heavy metal rock bands, creating an iconic counter-image.[18] For BrewDog, Punk is the ethos and style, but it performs a very similar role to that of a corporate uniform. This whole imagining is reflected in their practices, their financing and marketing, and even their product is in itself non-conforming, but equally conforms functionally. So it is about style and substance too, and it ties in conceptually with the emotional and rational engagement that Michael O'Leary of Ryanair broadcasts (Anderson and Warren, 2011). Several younger employees sport new beards. So even with an SME culture of an anticorporate company, the culture and ideology of non-conformism demonstrates a strong need to conform and to copy, to imitate cultural motifs. It illustrates mimetic replication in action. As a small business or collective entrepreneurial identity it is very powerful. In stark contrast, James Watt looks like a positively civilised small businessman.

James Watt and Martin Dickie operate on a daily basis as both entrepreneurs and leaders, by being entrepreneurial leaders in their industry and by leading by example within the company. Moreover, they have taken the company out of its traditional confines and have brought their boardroom to the customers, new and old. They typify the successful growth-orientated entrepreneurs described by Kuratko (2007). Their enacted, situational leadership interventions exemplify and clarify causality as understood by Czariawska-Joerges and Wolff (1991). The situated stories are 'initiated action' in the sense understood by Covin and Slevin (1991). James and Martin as entrepreneurial leaders manipulate the emotional and spiritual resources of their organisation as understood by Bennis and Nanus (1985), to manage meaning, infuse ideological values, construct lofty goals and visions and inspire. Their performances are dramaturgical performances, or performed roles, as envisaged by Gardner and Avolio (1998). BrewDog stories help to craft an entrepreneurial culture (Kirby, 2003), and the BrewDog story perhaps introduces the concept of 'Great Company' stories, thus extending the situational forces vision of Cawthon (1996). Importantly, James and Martin self-story themselves as entrepreneurial leaders (Parry and Hansen, 2007). Whilst BrewDog stories are classic entrepreneur stories, they are also stories denoting entrepreneurial leadership.

DISCUSSION

Like many small companies, BrewDog operates in an entrepreneurial setting which provides a venue characterised by highly organic, non-formalised simple structures, where the impact of leadership is likely to be most pronounced (Harrison and Leitch, 2013). Individual leadership roles are obviously important. James Watt appears to lead the business, and Martin Dickie product development. They lead entrepreneurially by example, taking decisions as they face them. There is no apparent external sign of conflict between leadership development and the entrepreneurial situational context, as one may expect. James and Martin may be dominant individuals, but they do not dominate each situation and context, spreading their company message and vision via digital storytelling and blogging on their interactive website. They appear to practise authentic, charismatic leadership (Turner and Mavin, 2008) and actively engage with their employees and followers at company events, annual general meetings, corporate beer tastings, and by patronising their growing establishments to meet the customers. This infers that there is something more to the leadership story, because if they do not dominate everything then how does their leadership or charisma reach their audiences? This is an interesting issue. Communication is a big part of this, and the unusual empirical material is only the beginning of the research needed. Irreverence for normal corporate practice lies at the heart of the BrewDog way, as discussed by James Watt in his biographical business book, *Business For Punks: Break All the Rules* (Watt, 2015).

They do not appear to lack flexibility, engagement, openness and responsiveness, which are often associated with SME leadership (Harrison and Leitch, 2013). They have created their own safe company environment. James and Martin (both university graduates) have conceptualised their own brand of Punk leadership in an entrepreneurial and SME context, albeit very differently from that in the corporate context, but like their beers they are maturing by the week, the month and the year, paradoxically becoming brewing Leviathans with a corporate status and structure. James Watt wrote, in a now deleted blog post that, 'It would go against everything we believe in. I could think of nothing worse than sitting by and watching a big company destroy everything we've worked so hard for', and, 'We love beer . . . everyone here lives and dies by what's in the glass'.

James and Martin continue to espouse their counter-cultural Punk ethos through their use of staged promotional 'vimeos'[19] which Brewdoggers can access via the company website. In these staged performances, James and Martin broadcast their well-articulated anti-establishment BrewDog personas, and tell leadership stories to an appreciative audience of loyal followers. James and Martin do not follow a conventional leadership script in business, but despite their apparent immaturity they run a very successful small business. One could question whether or not there is such an entity as a conventional leadership script, but there are accepted scripts associated with all leadership styles and theories. Perhaps James and Martin's strength is that they question the labels attached to them by industry insiders and resist them in their own inimitable manner.

BrewDog have around 210 staff, making them major employers, and will fast outstrip the SME definition of having 1–250 employees. So what do underdogs do when they mature and grow up? The dilemma will be to retain their entrepreneurial flair and not sell out, albeit that entrepreneurially oriented firms are capable of corporate transformation (Ghoshal and Bartlett, 1996). For a firm to be entrepreneurially orientated, its leaders and top managers must be orientated towards risk-taking, innovation and proactivity (Covin and Slevin, 1991). There is no sign of BrewDog slowing down on these fronts. But how long can they maintain a Punk ethos and story themselves as underdogs, when as entrepreneurial leaders and industry leaders they influence the industry norm? Nevertheless, BrewDog is a storytelling organisation (as defined by Boje, 1991: 111), so perhaps the story told may simply change with the times and context, if and when underdog becomes top dog.

CONCLUSION

This chapter has helped to consolidate existing theory on entrepreneurship and its development, and may stimulate new conceptual thinking via its path-breaking empirical exploration of entrepreneurial leadership as an abstract and abstracted concept which has to be storied in multiple contexts. It provides worked examples of situated entrepreneurial leadership whilst offering different theoretical, methodological and philosophical perspectives. The BrewDog story and the examples of situated entrepreneurial leadership are entrepreneur stories, but tell stories of leadership. These stories articulate a very different perspective on entrepreneurship and leadership as applied in an entrepreneurial and SME context. Nevertheless, the BrewDog scenario is an interesting research setting, but for all the irreverence, the philosophical grounding still follows mainstream leadership thinking. The novel aspect of this research is that in examining the nature and role of leadership in an entrepreneurial firm which is rapidly expanding and growing exponentially both in the UK and internationally, we see an accelerated form of entrepreneurship and entrepreneurial leadership. This was not apparent until the research was conducted, but acts as a rationale and justification for the research. It is a story of emotion, passion, cognition, effectuation and trust which demonstrates that entrepreneurship need not be focused on the individual entrepreneurs, but on the company and the product, as in the case of BrewDog. The product can itself be a form of entrepreneurial leadership. The story is not about James Watt and Martin Dickie but about BrewDog, its ethos and its marketing antics, albeit that these are authored and orchestrated by James and Martin and their employees. They do not consciously dwell on the 'humble beginnings' storyline, but the overriding BrewDog storyline is of a small company leading entrepreneurially and taking on the establishment. It is not a storyline spun by James or Martin. Instead, they concentrate on the Punk ethos. There is no conflict here between the storylines, but merely a refusal to trade on the traditional entrepreneur label.

This chapter contributes by demonstrating that both entrepreneurs and leaders can switch heuristics or gears dependent on their situation (Chell, 1985), to operate at an entrepreneurial level whilst enacting personal acts of leadership. They operate as both entrepreneur and leader separately or simultaneously as the situation requires, drawing on the same pool of concepts, traits, skills and behaviours when performing certain actions. This means that entrepreneurial leadership is both a philosophy and a situated, storied practice. Entrepreneurship can be differentiated in narrative, but leaders and entrepreneurs must be free to exercise leadership and entrepreneurship fluidly, as interpreted by them in context. It is about acting and reacting to circumstances. Both entrepreneurship and leadership are socially constructed cognitive activities enacted and articulated within the same semiotic system, using a shared framework of common linguistic and symbolic artefacts (Anderson and Smith, 2007). Entrepreneurs and leaders share so much in common, telling similar stories, recounting similar experiences, attitudes, emotions and feelings; and when called upon to 'lead' they do so, and when required to be entrepreneurial they do so with ease. Entrepreneurs like James and Martin do not stop to contextualise the activity as being exclusively entrepreneurship or leadership; and why should they? Their story, as told in this chapter, is being used to demonstrate an abstract idea. In 'shifting up a gear' they intuitively perform and enact in an individuated 'stream of consciousness' effect. It is us who observe, categorise and articulate their deeds and actions as entrepreneurial, or an example of leadership, dependent upon the situation (Stewart and Smith, 2009). Leaders and entrepreneurs are generally revered in society, thus the entrepreneurial leader has an added value attached to the use of the label. However, there is a danger that in eulogising them, and the concept of entrepreneurship, we place both the individual and the concept on a pedestal by overusing the very term itself to define a style of leadership that can succeed in competitive environments (the SME sector) where others have failed. This conceptual elusivity makes it appealing, but why should we grace it with the heroic label of 'entrepreneurship' instead of 'situated leadership'?[20]

It is important to ground the discussion in this chapter in terms of its contribution to conceptualising our understanding of entrepreneurship and leadership from a theoretical and conceptual position, and how it differs from the literature. This critical review of literature has identified interesting areas of convergence and divergence, and engages in an academic discussion of the similarities between leadership and entrepreneurship, identifying entrepreneurship as the common ground between both paradigms. They share a common ontological and epistemological development. However, we must question why we as entrepreneurship scholars are so obsessed with labels, because in real life entrepreneurs can be leaders, and leaders can be entrepreneurs. From a pedagogical perspective we can teach entrepreneurship by illustrating the concept with theory and examples, but the entrepreneurial elements in play must remain the prerogative of the individual enacting them. Perhaps the true definition of entrepreneurial leadership lies in society's perception of entrepreneurship as the embodiment of what society feels is needed to face the challenges of a fast-paced competitive business environment. The BrewDog saga continues.

NOTES

*   This chapter builds upon and develops the ideas first articulated in an earlier conference paper by Victoria Stewart and myself. See Stewart and Smith (2009) for full details. Victoria, a former Doctoral student of mine, is no longer in academia, but my thinking on entrepreneurial leadership was shaped through supervision of her thesis, and it is only fitting and right to acknowledge this. Her literature review influenced this work.

1.   Aberdeen Foyer is a very successful social enterprise based in Aberdeen, Scotland. Harris's entrepreneurial leadership skills transformed the venture into a thriving business.

2.   Part of the answer to the question, 'What is entrepreneurial leadership?' (Arthur M. Spiro Institute for Entrepreneurial Leadership, n.d.).

3.   Again, it is context and situation which will determine whether the styles are post-heroic or not.

4.   The rationale behind this is that the three elements chosen lent themselves to such analysis, whereas the other three elements would have required personal interviews. The level of detail required was simply not available from the website, and the structure of the company frequently changes. There is an acknowledged danger that this may limit the level of our understanding of the construct, but this cannot be helped. In any case, the BrewDog company structure and leadership style is too fluid and protean to write sensibly about. The company is like an early version of Virgin.

5.   From 'Brewdog – About', brewdog.com (accessed 8 August 2014).

6.   See also Smith (2011) and Smith (2013) for a discussion of BrewDogs Marketing and Internationalization strategies.

7.   See http://www.thisismoney.co.uk/money/smallbusiness/article-2399209/JAMES-WATT-INTERVIEW-BrewDog-biting-drinks-giants.html.

8.   From 'Profile of James Watt, Managing Director of BrewDog', brewdog.com (accessed 10 August 2014).

9.   'The end of history', brewdog.com, 22 July 2010 (accessed 9 August 2014). See also '"Perverse" animal beer bottles sell out in hours'. *BBC News*, 23 July 2010, http://www.bbc.co.uk/news/uk-scotland-north-east-orkney-shetland-10737787 (accessed 10 August 2014). See also Brian Lilley (22 July 2010). 'Scottish brewer offers beer packed in roadkill'. *Toronto Sun*, www.torontosun.com/news/canada/2010/07/22/14794821.html (accessed 9 August 2014).

10.   'Diageo screw BrewDog', brewdog.com, 9 May 2012 (accessed 9 August 2014). 'Statement regarding the 2012 BII Scotland Annual Awards', Diageo, 9 May 2012, https://www.diageo.com/en/news-and-media/ (accessed 9 August 2014). Nathalie Thomas, 'Scottish beer company BrewDog forces Diageo to apologise over "dirty tricks" at awards', *Telegraph*, 9 May 2012, http://www.telegraph.co.uk/finance/news-bysector/retailandconsumer/9255369/Scottish-beer-company-BrewDog-forces-Diageo-to-apologise-over-dirty-tricks-at-awards.html (accessed 9 August 2014).

11.   It is not offensive marketing in the accepted sense of being proactive and going on the offensive, which is an accepted corporate strategy. However, it is more than a mere play on words between 'going on the offensive' and 'being offensive'. I have spoken to other

academics and industry insiders who are genuinely offended by the offensive nature of stories, comments and the use of expletives by BrewDog, hence being controversial and engaging in offensive marketing may cause unintended consequences for a company. Nevertheless, it is a novel marketing strategy, and is not dissimilar to the style of marketing Michael O'Leary engages in to market Ryan Air whereby he uses expletives and 'tells it as he sees it'. Both Michael O'Leary and Richard Branson use offensive marketing but in a charming, humorous way. However, this behaviour may also result from a 'devil may care' attitude.

12.   See the image at the 'The End of History' at www.BrewDog.com.
13.   H. Kenny (2014), 'BrewDog sparks global debate with worlds first protest beer – Hello My name is Vladimir', http://prexamples.com/2014/02/brewdog-hello-my-name-is-vladimir/ (accessed 11 August 2014).
14.   See the images at brewdog.com. Alternatively, conduct your own search of Google Images.
15.   Run annually by *Beers of the World* magazine.
16.   From http://tv.esquire.com/shows/brew-dogs (accessed 10 August 2014).
17.   In Smith and Anderson (2003) I discussed the semiotics of entrepreneurial identity and established that entrepreneurs convey imagery paradoxically associated with 'conforming non-conformists'.
18.   The beards have a mythic Scandinavian or Germanic aura. The overall hegemonic appearance is quite stunning and striking. I do not know what the average brewer looks like, or if this is an industry-wide phenomenon, but it is certainly interesting.
19.   A trademark for a short video clip.
20.   Whilst the archetypal 'Great Man' and the 'entrepreneurial leader' stereotypes (or ideal-types) are both undoubtedly the 'darlings of the establishment', I do not get a sense that James Watt and Martin Dickie court the establishment; certainly not the Portman Group, Diageo nor the brewing industry establishment.

REFERENCES

Aldrich, H. (2011). Heroes, villains and fools: institutional entrepreneurship *not* institutional entrepreneurs. *Entrepreneurship Research Journal*, 1(2), 1–6.

Amernic, J., Craig, R. (2006). *CEO Speak: The Language of Corporate Leadership*. McGill Queens University Press, London.

Anderson, A.R., Smith, R. (2007). The moral space in entrepreneurship: ethical imperatives and moral legitimacy. *Entrepreneurship and Regional Development*, Special Edition – Pioneering New Fields of Entrepreneurship Research, 19(6), 479–97.

Anderson, A.R., Warren, L. (2011). The entrepreneur as hero and jester: enacting the entrepreneurial discourse. *International Small Business Journal*, 29(6), 589–609.

Arthur M. Spiro Institute for Entrepreneurial Leadership (n.d.). What is entrepreneurial leadership?. https://www.clemson.edu/centers-institutes/spiro/ (accessed 15 July 2014).

Ay, C., Aytekin, P., Nardali, S. (2010). Guerrilla marketing communication tools and ethical problems in guerilla advertising. *American Journal of Economics and Business Administration*, 2(3), 280–286.

Bass, B.M. (1985). *Leadership and Performance beyond Expectation*. Free Press, New York, NY.

Bass, B.M., Avolio, B.J. (1993). Transformational leadership: a response to critiques. In M.M. Chemers and R. Ayman (eds), *Leadership Theory and Research: Perspectives and Directions* (pp. 49–80). Academic Press, San Diego, CA.

Bennis, W., Nanus, B. (1985). *Leaders: The Strategies for Taking Charge*. Harper & Row, New York, NY.

Bettis, R.A., Hitt, M.A. (1995). The new competitive landscape. *Strategic Management Journal*, 16, 7–19.

428   *Research handbook on entrepreneurship and leadership*

Blake, R., Mouton, J. (1964). *The Managerial Grid: The Key to Leadership Excellence*. Gulf Publishing Co., Houston, TX.
Boje, D.M. (1991). The storytelling organization: a study of story performance in an office-supply firm. *Administrative Science Quarterly*, 36(1), 106–26.
Brown, S.L., Eisenhardt, K.M. (1998). *Competing on the Edge: Strategy and Structured Chaos*. Harvard Business School Press, Boston, MA.
Burns, P. (2008). *Corporate Entrepreneurship: Building an Entrepreneurial Organization*. Palgrave Macmillan, London.
Burns, P. (2010). *Entrepreneurship and Small Business: Start Up-Growth and Maturity*. Palgrave Macmillan, London.
Burns, P. (2013). *Corporate Entrepreneurship*. Palgrave Macmillan, London.
Carlyle, T. (1888). *On Heroes, Hero Worship and the Heroic in History*. Fredrick A. Stokes & Brother, New York, NY.
Cawthon, D.L. (1996). Leadership: the Great Man theory revisited. *Business Horizons*, 39(3), 1–4.
Chaston, I. (2000). *Entrepreneurial Marketing: Competing by Challenging Convention*. Purdue University Press, West Lafayette, IN.
Chell, E. (1985). The entrepreneurial personality: a few ghosts laid to rest?. *International Small Business Journal*, 3, 43–54.
Cogliser, C.C., Brigham, K.H. (2004). The intersection of leadership and entrepreneurship: mutual lesson to be learned. *Leadership Quarterly*, 15, 771–99.
Conger, J.A., Kanungo, R.N. (1987). Toward a behavioral theory of charismatic leadership in organizational settings. *Academy of Management Review*, 12, 637–47.
Conger, J.A., Kanungo, R.N. (1998). *Charismatic Leadership in Organizations*. SAGE, Thousand Oaks, CA.
Connell, R.W. (2005). *Masculinities*, 2nd edition. University of California Press, Berkeley, CA.
Connell, R.W., Messerschmidt, J.W. (2005). Hegemonic masculinity: rethinking the concept. *Gender and Society*, 19(6), 829–59.
Covin, J.G., Slevin, D.P. (1988). The influence of organization structure on the utility of an entrepreneurial top management style. *Journal of Management Studies*, 25(3), 217–59.
Covin, J.G., Slevin, D.P. (1991). A conceptual model of entrepreneurship as firm behavior. *Entrepreneurship Theory and Practice*, 16, 7–25.
Czariawska-Joerges, B., Wolff, R. (1991). Leaders, managers and entrepreneurs on and off the organizational stage. *Organizational Studies*, 12(4), 529–46.
Drakopoulou-Dodd, S.L. (2014). Roots radical – place, power and practice in punk entrepreneurship. *Entrepreneurship and Regional Development*, 26(1/2), 165–205.
Eggers, J.H., Leahy, K.T., Churchill, N.C. (1994). Entrepreneurial leadership in the development of small business. 14th Annual Entrepreneurial Research Conference, Babson College, MA.
Eyal, O., Kark, R. (2004). How do transformational leaders transform organisations? A study of the relationship between leadership and entrepreneurship. *Leadership and Policy in Schools*, 3(3), 211–35.
Fernald, L.W., Solomon, G.T. (1996). Entrepreneurial leadership: oxymoron or new paradigm? *Journal of Management Systems*, 8, 2–16.
Fernald, L.W., Soloman, G.T., Tarabishy, A. (2005). A new paradigm: entrepreneurial leadership. *Southern Business Review*, Spring, 1–10.
Gardner, W.L., Avolio, B.J. (1998). The charismatic relationship: a dramaturgical perspective. *Academy of Management Review*, 23, 32–58.
Ghoshal, S., Barlett, C.A. (1996). Rebuilding behavioural context: a blueprint for corporate renewal. *Sloan Management Review*, 37(2), 23–36.
Gruber, M. (2004). Marketing in new ventures theory and empirical evidence. *Schmalenbach Business Review*, 56, 164–99.
Gupta, V., MacMillan, I.C., Surie, G. (2004). Entrepreneurial leadership: developing and measuring a cross cultural construct. *Journal of Business Venturing*, 19, 241–60.

Halstead, R. (2013). Time for the wine industry to marshal its mavericks to target consumers. *Wine and Viticulture Journal*, 28(4), 73–4.

Harrison, R. and Leitch, C. (2013). Call for papers.

House, R.J. (1977). A 1976 theory of charismatic leadership. In J.G. Hunt and L.L. Larson (eds), *Leadership: The Cutting Edge* (pp. 189–207). Southern Illinois University Press, Carbondale, IL.

Howell, J.M., Avolio, B.J. (1993). Transformational leadership, transactional leadership, loss of control and support for innovation: key predictors of consolidated business unit performance. *Journal of Applied Psychology*, 78, 891–902.

Johnson, A. and Scholes, K. (1999). *Exploring Corporate Strategy*, 5th edition. Prentice Hall, London.

Johnson, G., Whittington, R., Scholes, K. (2012). *Fundamentals of Strategy*. Pearson Education, London.

Kirby, D.A. (2003). *Entrepreneurship*. McGraw Hill Educational, Maidenhead.

Kotter, J.P. (1998). Winning at change. *Leader to Leader*, 10, 27–33.

Kuratko, D.F. (2007). Entrepreneurial leadership in the 21st century: Guest editor's perspective. *Journal of Leadership and Organizational Studies*, 13(4), 1–11.

Leavy, B. (1996). On studying leadership in the strategy field. *Leadership Quarterly*, 7(4), 435–54.

Lippitt, G.L. (1987). Entrepreneurial leadership: a performing art. *Journal of Creative Behavior*, 21(3), 264–70.

McGrath, R.G., MacMillan, I.C. (2000). *The Entrepreneurial Mindset*. Harvard Business School Press, Boston, MA.

Miller, D. (1983). The correlates of entrepreneurship in three types of firms. *Management Science*, 29(7), 770–791.

Morris, M.H., Jones, F.F. (1999). Entrepreneurship in established organisations: the case of the public sector. *Entrepreneurship Theory and Practice,* 24(1), 71–91.

Nicholson, N. (1998). Personality and entrepreneurship: a study of the heads of the UK's most successful independent companies. *European Management Journal*, 16(5), 529–39.

Organ, D. (1996). The Editor's Chair: leadership: the Great Man theory revisited. *Business Horizons*, May–June, 1–4.

Parry, K.W., Hansen, H. (2007). The organizational story as leadership. *Leadership*, 3, 3, 281–300.

Perren, L. (2000). Comparing entrepreneurship and leadership: a textual analysis. Working Paper, Council for Excellence in Management and Leadership.

Pink, C. (2008). Leadership through the lens of mimetic desire. *International Journal of Leadership in Public Services*, 4(2), 10–14.

Sashkin, M. (1988). The visionary leader. In J.A. Conger and R.A. Kanungo (eds), *Charismatic Leadership: The Elusive Factor in Organizational Effectiveness* (pp. 122–60). Jossey-Bass, San Francisco, CA.

Schein, E.H. (1996). Leadership and organisational culture. In F. Hesselbein, M. Goldsmith and R. Beckhard (eds), *The Leadership of the Future: New Visions, Strategies and Practices for the Next Era* (pp. 59–70). Peter Drucker Foundation for Nonprofit Management, New York, NY.

Schumpeter, J. (1934). *The Theory of Economic Development*. Irwin University Books, New York, NY.

Scott, J. (2006). *Documentary Research*. SAGE, London.

Shamir, B., House, R.J., Arthur, M.B. (1993). The motivational effects of charismatic leadership: a self-concept based theory. *Organization Science*, 4, 577–93.

Slevin, D.P., Covin, J.G. (1990). Juggling entrepreneurial style and organizational structure: how to get your act together. *Sloan Management Review*, 31(2), 43–53.

Smith, R. (2005). The fabrication of entrepreneurial fable: a biographical analysis. *Journal Private Equity*, 8(4), 8–19.

Smith, R. (2011). Entrepreneurial genius or marketing madness?. *ISBE Enterprising Matters Magazine*, http://www.isbe.org.uk/geniusormadness (accessed 17 November 2017).

Smith, R. (2013). Brewing up a storm: internationalization, the BrewDog way!. http://www. isbe.org.uk/EMBrewDog (accessed 17 November 2017).

Smith, R., Anderson, A.R. (2003). Conforming non-conformists: a semiotic analysis of entrepreneurial identity. Paper presented at the Babson-Kauffman Entrepreneurship Research Conference, Boston, June.

Smith, R., Moult, S., Burge, P., Turnbull, A. (2010). The BrewDog crew: business growth for Punks!*** A teaching case. *International Journal of Entrepreneurship and Innovation*, 11(2), 161–8.

Sparrowe, R.T. (2005). Authentic leadership and the narrative self. *Leadership Quarterly*, 16(3), 419–39.

Spreitzer, G.M., Janasz, S.C., Quinn, R.E. (1999). Empowered to lead: the role of psychological empowerment in leadership. *Journal of Organizational Behaviour*, 20, 511–26.

Stevenson, H. (1983). A perspective on entrepreneurship. Harvard Business School Working Paper 9, 384–391.

Stewart, V., Smith, R. (2009). Entrepreneurial leadership: reinventing the Great Man thesis?. Presented at ISBE Conference 2009.

Stewart, W.H., Watson, W.E., Carland, J.C., Carland, J.W. (1998). A proclivity for entrepreneurship: a comparison of entrepreneurs, small business owners and corporate managers. *Journal of Business Venturing*, 14, 189–214.

Stogdill, R.M. (1974). *Handbook of Leadership: A Survey of the Literature*. Free Press, New York, NY.

Stokes, D. (2000). Entrepreneurial marketing: a conceptualisation from qualitative research. *Qualitative Market Research: An International Journal*, 3(1), 47–54.

Tannenbaum, A.S., Schmidt, W.H. (1958). How to choose a leadership pattern. *Harvard Business Review*, 36, 95–101.

Tarabishy, A., Fernald, L.W., Solomon, G.T. (2002). Understanding entrepreneurial leadership in today's dynamic markets. https://www.academia.edu/1287765/Understanding_ Entrepreneurial_Leadership_in_todays_Dynamic_Markets (accessed 9 August 2017).

Turner, J., Mavin, S. (2008). What can we learn from senior leader narratives? The strutting and fretting of becoming a leader. *Leadership and Organization*, 29(4), 376–91.

Vecchio, R.P. (2003). Entrepreneurship and leadership: common trends and common threads. *Human Resource Management Review*, 13, 303–27.

Venkataraman, S., Van de Ven, A.H. (1998). Hostile environmental jolts, transaction sets and new business development. *Journal of Business Venturing*, 13(3), 231–55.

Watt, J. (2015). *Business for Punks: Break All the Rules – the BrewDog Way*. Penguin Books, London.

Work, J.W. (1996). Leading a diverse workforce. In F. Hesselbein, M. Goldsmith and R. Beckhard (eds), *The Leadership of the Future; New Visions, Strategies and Practices for the Next Era* (pp. 71–80). Peter Drucker Foundation for Nonprofit Management, New York, NY.

Yukl, G.A., Van Fleet, D.D. (1982). Cross-situational, multi-method research on military leader effectiveness. *Organizational Behavior and Human Performance*, 30, 87–108.

18. Key issues in the development of the entrepreneurial university of the future: challenges, opportunities and responses

Allan A. Gibb and Gay Haskins

INTRODUCTION

The overall objective of this chapter is to explore key issues in the design and development of the entrepreneurial university in both concept and practice. It aims to be of value not only to members of the academic community who wish to explore this issue but also to policy-makers and the wide range of international stakeholders, public and private, who are demonstrating a growing interest in this development. It seeks to capture the not inconsiderable experiment in organisational design of universities, across the world, as they attempt to adjust to an environment growing in complexity and uncertainty (Kwiek, 2001, 2005b; Lazzeroni and Piccaluga, 2003; Higher Education in Europe, 2004; UNESCO, 2004, 2007; OECD, 2001, 2003, 2005, 2011; Bernasconi, 2005; Williams and Kitaev, 2005; Kirby, 2006; Wissema, 2008; Pilbeam, 2008; Shattock, 2009; Chan and Lo, 2007; Ernst & Young, 2012). The argument is also considerably influenced by the practice of engagement with senior university staff over several years via the UK-based Entrepreneurial University Leaders Programme.[1]

The discourse moves beyond a focus upon entrepreneurship and enterprise education in universities. This has been the subject of considerable practical development and academic publication over the past two decades (Kristensen, 1999; Cherwitz, 2002; EU Directorate-General for Enterprise, 2004; Volkmann, 2004; NIRAS, 2007; Papayannakis et al., 2008; Masri et al., 2010; EU Commission of the European Communities, 2008a; European Commission, 1998, 2013; OECD, 2011), and the key remaining challenges in this area will be noted. It will also go beyond what has almost become a 'traditional' entrepreneurial focus upon the technology transfer role of universities, although it will deal with this issue.

THE RELEVANCE OF THE ENTERPRISE AND ENTREPRENEURSHIP CONCEPT TO FUTURE UNIVERSITY DEVELOPMENT

Finding Appropriate Definitions

The word 'entrepreneurship', for many, is wholly associated with business, and with the pursuit of commercial 'for profit' opportunity. In the university context it is therefore commonly linked with the now wide range of institutional activities designed to facilitate the commercial exploitation of academic intellectual property (Ranga, 2002; Cook et al., 2008; Hofer and Potter, 2010). It also carries with it an ideological underpinning of certain forms of capitalism that sit uneasily with many academics more concerned with their discipline and the nurturing of discovery and learning, whatever their ideological or cultural roots (Slaughter and Leslie, 1997; Evans, 2004; Olssen and Peters, 2005; Schuetze, 2007; Berglund, 2008). It therefore easily translates into the notion of the university becoming a corporate business (Maunter, 2005), more 'managerialistic' (Deem, 2007) and/or more 'business like' (Chan and Lo, 2007). Weighty academic attacks and discussions on the notion of universities becoming more entrepreneurial frequently build from these roots (Maunter, 2005; Armbruster, 2008; Collini, 2012).

A broader conception of entrepreneurship is therefore proposed in this chapter, building on Gibb's (2002, 2005) work which underpin the notions of enterprise and entrepreneurship used in the Entrepreneurial University Leaders Programme. As part of this conception there is a need to characterise the development of the 'enterprising' individual acting in a wide range of different contexts. In the English language the expression 'enterprising person' can clearly be distinguished from 'entrepreneur': the former being a person demonstrating behaviours, attitudes and attributes often associated with the entrepreneur, but which can be observed in any context. Unfortunately the word 'enterprise' in the above sense does not translate easily in many languages. But it is nevertheless increasingly used by the European Union (EU) in the context of argument about the need for 'enterprising' young people in all walks of life (EU Directorate-General for Enterprise, 2004).

Notwithstanding difficulties in interpretation, the definitions proposed in this chapter and that are used in practice in working with high-level staff of universities are as follows: 'The Enterprise Concept focuses upon the development of the "enterprising person and entrepreneurial mindset"'.[2] The former constitutes a set of personal skills, attributes, behavioural and motivational capacities associated with those of the entrepreneur, but which can be used in any context (social, work, leisure, and so on). Prominent among these are: intuitive decision-making, capacity to make things happen autonomously, networking, initiative-taking, opportunity identification, creative problem-solving, strategic thinking and self-efficacy. The 'mindset' concept focuses not just upon the notion of 'being your own boss' in a business context, but also upon the ability of an individual to empathise with the life-world of the person operating in an entrepreneurial environment and the associated entre-preneurial ways of doing, thinking, feeling, communicating, organising and learning.

The Entrepreneurship Concept focuses upon the application of these personal enterprising skills, attributes and mindsets to the context of setting up a new venture or initiative of any kind, developing or growing an existing venture or initiative, and designing an entrepreneurial organi-sation (one in which the capacity for effective use of enterprising skills will be enhanced). This concept also embraces the development of appropriate business and organisation development skills. The application of many of these skills is not, however, confined to business but is equally applicable to social enterprise, education, health, non-governmental organisations and mainstream public and autonomous organisations (for example, uni-versities and governments).

UNCERTAINTIES, COMPLEXITIES, PRESSURES FOR CHANGE AND THE EMERGING RESPONSE

Interest in, and approaches to, the development of an entrepreneurial university model are not confined to Europe. Since the turn of the century examples of such approaches can be observed throughout Asia, Latin America, Africa and Eastern Europe (Davies, 2001; Currie, 2002; Lazzeroni and Piccaluga, 2003; Jacob et al., 2003; Ka Ho Mok, 2005; Thorn and Soo, 2006; Wong et al., 2007; EUEREK, 2008; Guerrero-Cano, 2008; Oberman Peterka, 2011; Farsi et al., 2012; Fayolle and Redford, 2014). In North America there has long been much debate relat-ing to entrepreneurial models of higher education institutions, and there are outstanding examples of highly innovative approaches in Arizona State University (Crow, 2008), the University of North Carolina (Thorp and Goldstein, 2010) and the University of Texas (Cherwitz, 2002). The success of Massachusetts Institute of Technology (MIT) is also widely quoted, but mainly in the context of business creation (O'Shea et al., 2007). Much of the focus in North America has traditionally been upon the university as a promoter of innovation, business entrepreneurship, and local and regional social and economic development (Shane, 2004), and it is this emphasis that has been substantially modelled elsewhere.

Universities throughout the world are facing distinctive, wide-ranging challenges which question the long-run viability of many traditional university models (Chan and Lo, 2007; Chen, 2007; Ernst & Young, 2012; Barber et al., 2013). In particular, they are increasingly being judged by the way in which they are responding directly to the social and economic needs of society; how well they are meeting the demands of the emerging middle classes around the world; how they are funding the substantial growth of demand for higher education; how they are contributing to economic growth; how they are dealing with graduate unemployment and creating highly employable, educated and motivated young graduates; how they are acting as a hub for local and regional social and economic development; how they are contributing to social mobility; to what degree they are helping societies to respond to global competitive and cultural pressures; how they are contributing to issues of sustainability;[3] and to what degree they are stimulating new entrepreneurial businesses and social enterprises. These issues constitute major challenges as to how universities in the future will 'situate' themselves (Vaira, 2004). These challenges can be broadly grouped into those that follow from national and international public policies, and those that are part of an overlapping but wider environmental change scenario.

In terms of public policy there are five key challenges. First, the 'massification' (Guri-Rosenblit et al., 2007) of demand in both developed and developing economies carries with it the problem of how it can best be funded, requiring some combination of revenue-raising and cost-cutting (Hearn, 2003; Chiang, 2004; Standard & Poor's, 2008; Williams, 2009; Estermann and Pruvot, 2011). Second, universities are increasingly seen as 'engines of growth', and a source of economic value-added (European Commission, 1998; Hayrinen-Alestalo, 1999; European Commission, 2005; Corbett, 2006), with a focus on, for example, university engagement with business (Owen-Smith et al., 2002; Dooley and Kirk, 2007; EU Commission of the European Communities, 2008a; EU European Commission, 2009) and real knowledge exchange (EU Commission of the European Communities, 2008b), learning alongside and from industry and external stakeholders, moving away from the hitherto narrower focus upon knowledge transfer out of the university (EUEREK, 2008). Third, increasingly the 'engines of growth' metaphor has been translated into a local and regional development context (Ropke, 1998; OECD, 2005; Charles, 2006; Woollard et al., 2007; Smith, 2007; Braun and Diensberg, 2007; Potter, 2008; Arbo and Benneworth, 2008; Goddard and Kempton, 2011). In both, there remains a considerable focus upon mechanisms by which universities can contribute to high-tech and knowledge-based commercial development (Roos et al., 2005; Wong et al., 2007; Mittelstadt and Cerri, 2008; OECD, 2008, 2009, 2010), with a continued strong emphasis upon spin-outs, spin-offs, incubators, technology and science parks, and the role of technology transfer offices (Ylinenpää, 2001; LERU, 2006; Link, 2006; Collier and Gray, 2007; Cook et al., 2008; Hudson, 2009). Increasingly attention is being focused upon how this process can be better managed (Lee, 1996; Roos et al., 2005; Geuna and Muscio, 2008; Kwiek, 2008) in the light of evidence of limited impact and often negative cost–benefit returns from university efforts (Hughes, 2003). Fourth, there are growing concerns about the employability, employment and subsequent career paths and rewards of graduates and postgraduates as supply grows, seemingly, in many countries beyond the capacity of the economy to absorb them (Moreland, 2007; Artess et al., 2011; Pavlin, 2012; Green and Saridakis, 2008). Fifth and finally, and a major leadership challenge for the entrepreneurial university, is its role in enhancing greater social mobility in society, in particular ensuring how it is facilitating wider access to disadvantaged or low- and middle-income sectors of the community (AUQA, 2005; Asean University Network, 2011; University of Dar es Salaam, 2007; Nikolai and Ebner, 2011).

Together, these public policy imperatives can be seen as challenging the concept of the university as a focus for independent discovery and the creation of knowledge for its own sake (Haggis, 2006), often referred to as the traditional European Bologna and Humboldt models. Although different models of universities in Europe have emerged over time, these two Italian and German models with their strong research focus have had considerable influence upon university development worldwide. Yet not only in many parts of Europe, but also in the developing world, the failure of the economy to absorb the graduate population is seen as a source of future social and political instability and is leading to a questioning of this model. Some developing countries are seeking to review what might be labelled the 'colonial' model of a university in favour of one where scarce resources are channelled into research, discovery and teaching that links much more directly into contributing to key areas of specific national, cultural, economic and social development.[4]

In terms of the wider environment within which the contemporary university operates, there are six key challenges. First, universities are increasingly operating in a highly competitive national, regional and global marketplace in which the traditional flow of students from the developing world to Western European and North American institutions is increasingly under threat by the growth of provision in the newly emerging economies themselves (Noir sur Blanc, 1999; Kwiek, 2001; Knight, 2003;

OECD, 2004; International Association of Universities, 2005; Maringe and Foskett, 2010; Bone, 2011; Barber et al., 2013; Middlehurst and Woodfield, 2007; King et al., 2010). As a result there is increasing positive pressure for Western institutions themselves to be more sensitive to the cultures, ways of learning and doing of emerging economies (Toakley, 2004; Bourn et al., 2006; Nivesjö et al., 2011), and universities are increasingly responding to this scenario via the creation of international partnerships. Second, advances in technology and the boundary-less knowledge society have stimulated the emergence of 'borderless education' (Observatory on Borderless Education, 2011; Barnett, 2000; Green and Baer, 2000), and the adoption of practice-oriented Mode 2 forms of learning (Nowotny et al., 2003; National Academy of Science USA, 2005; Sa, 2008), becoming continuous translators of knowledge from all sources (Kristensen, 1999). Third, the rise of open and big data[5] brings with it a major pedagogical challenge, reflected in the growth of massive open online courses (MOOCS) (Department for Business Innovation and Skills UK, 2013) and the creation and development of 'virtual' academic institutions (D'Antoni, 2006). Fourth, social media are of growing significance in academic and student communication, and therefore learning (Selwyn, 2012; Institute of Educational Technology, 2012), questioning traditional teaching and learning pedagogies and encouraging staff to move towards the notion of the flipped classroom and indeed the flipped academic. In this scenario, students are charged with 'discovering' more of their learning, and the academic teacher becomes more of a facilitator of learning. This neoliberal marketisation has been challenged by Leisner (2006) as endangering the democratic character of the university and trivialising education. Fifth, the global information technology revolution is also challenging the way that academe conventionally reaches its audience and gains reputation through the mechanism of the academic journal, as open access, author pay and self-publication initiatives challenge the hegemony of the traditional academic publishers. Finally, funding constraints in the public sector and the growth of the private sector provide new opportunities for competition and cooperation (Kwiek, 2005a; Lane and Kinser, 2011; The Programme for Research in Private Higher Education PROPHE website (http://www.albany.edu/dept/eaps/prophe/index.html)).

PATHWAYS TO CHANGE: REMOVING BARRIERS AND CLARIFYING OBJECTIVES

This section of the chapter focuses upon key issues relating to the management of change. It first confronts the challenge, articulated powerfully by some academics, that the entrepreneurship concept threatens the essential 'idea' of a university. It then explores the challenge to teaching and learning posed by the concepts of enterprise and entrepreneurship education, and the means by which this offer, hitherto often narrowly confined to business schools, can be extended right across the university as a central component of teaching and learning strategy.

The 'Idea' of a University

The tradition of academe, following Bologna, has been that of the independence of academic discovery and teaching processes (Furedi, 2001), and the associated notion that the institution is sustained by a mode of thought shared by all its members yet underpinned by the detachment of their members' motivations from the goals and functions of the organisation (Habermas and Blazek, 1987). Excellence is viewed through the lens of peer review processes, and particularly through the prism of publication in learned journals. The direction of the pursuit of knowledge lies with the individual academics and their peers (Anderson, 2010). Such independence has in many countries traditionally been underpinned by state funding channelled through autonomous agencies applying agreed academic criteria to the funding of excellence (Bridgman, 2007). The quality and extent of research and publication has been a key determinant of the attraction of funds and judgement of excellence. This narrow focus is being challenged. Mohrman et al. (2008) identify a number of key additional determinants, including global mission, new roles for professors, research intensity, worldwide recruitment, diversification of funding, partnerships with business and government, and global partnerships.

In reality the perfect world of university autonomy, if it ever existed, has been increasingly eroded by the flows of public and private funding being channelled into fields of apparently useful knowledge often linked to key strategic economic and social goals of society, a process underpinned by policy rhetoric (Henkel, 2004; European Commission, 1998, 2005). It is argued that this process threatens the blue skies research through which unforeseen long-term benefits to society may emerge (Collini, 2012). Yet, given the changes in the way in which knowledge is becoming widely available, combined with the strategies of funding organisations (Chiang, 2004) noted above, there has been, for some considerable time, pressure upon academics, even in blue skies research, to collaborate with public and private institutions and businesses.

The reality is, therefore, throughout the world, independence is a state negotiated by academic institutions and individuals, much in the same way as the individual entrepreneur, by managing interdependence, has to negotiate their personal and organisational autonomy through a web of external stakeholder pressures and demands (Gibb and Haskins, 2014). As demonstrated above, this pressure is growing, and will increasingly demand an enterprising and entrepreneurial approach to managing autonomy (Pan, 2007; Armbruster, 2008).

The idea of a university is also being challenged in other ways. A key issue is whether universities should be judged as predominantly research institutions, as opposed to teaching and learning institutions (Willets, 2013). The link between good teaching and research performance is not always clear, and there is a traditional philosophical school that argues that universities should be primarily teaching and scholastic learning institutions (Whitehead, 1927; Newman, 1852 [1917]). Backing up this argument is the evidence of the substantial growth of academic journals worldwide, the research-based contents of which are read thoroughly by very few people. The changing knowledge scenarios, painted earlier in this chapter, also challenge the universities to broaden their teaching function to engage more substantially in translation of their knowledge for wider consumption, rather than leaving this to consultant groups, the press or independent research bodies and think tanks.

The growing demands on the sector in most countries (see, e.g., Volkmann, 2004; Wong et al., 2012) have led to new institutions entering the field, public and private (IHEP, 2009), which are essentially focused on teaching only. In addition, many universities offer professional vocational degrees and qualifications, increasingly involving industrial and commercial partners. Given the competitive environment, there is a move towards specialisation in disciplines and cross-disciplinary areas targeted at different student groups (Sa, 2008).

Enterprise and Entrepreneurship in Teaching and Learning

The pressure for universities to respond to the employment and employability needs of students has for some time been driving efforts to take enterprising and entrepreneurial learning across the whole university (Fatt and Ang, 1995; Blenker et al., 2006; Penaluna et al., 2012). To date, most of the surveys of entrepreneurship education in universities show delivery concentrated mainly in business schools (see, for example, the NIRAS, 2007 EU study). This creates a number of barriers to the development of a wider offering across the whole university. The business school treatment of the entrepreneurship concept is naturally focused upon the business context of new venturing or business growth, and this is reflected in courses provided across the university which may be less embedded in, or related to, the context of departmental disciplines. As business school entrepreneurship modules are mainly conventional award-driven pro-grammes, there is also often a substantial focus upon teaching 'about' entrepreneurship, with a strong emphasis upon concept and theory, as opposed to 'for' entrepreneurship. Moreover, much of the pedagogy is limited to case material, conventional project work and presentations from entrepreneurs (NIRAS, 2007). Teaching, to stimulate enterprising behaviours and attributes 'through' highly enterprising pedagogies, is growing (Rae and Carswell, 2001; Politis, 2005) but it is as yet difficult to assess the impact. Akola and Heinonen (2006) provide a more detailed review of these issues.

There is growing evidence of attempts to take entrepreneurship teaching across the university. In the US the Kauffmann Foundation's Cross Campus Entrepreneurship Initiative (Mendes et al., 2006; http://www.kauffman.org/entrepreneurship/kauffman-campuses.aspx) provided a major thrust in this direction. This initiative was founded upon its own research in the US showing that proportionately more entrepreneurs ultimately emerge from non-business school departments. The initiative had mixed results and was not extended, although good examples of impact remain. There are also increasing examples, across the globe, of entrepreneurship teaching (Klofsten, 2000) and learning initiatives embedded in different disciplinary contexts (see, e.g., Papayannakis et al., 2008) although there is less evidence of the degree to which these, by using an 'enterprising' pedagogy, focus upon and measure impact on different mindsets, attributes and competencies. The 2013 European Commission study of Entrepreneurship Education, for example, contains many interesting case studies of pedagogies used, but does not set out the detailed impact of each of these. It is perfectly possible to build into conventional mainstream disciplinary offers a greater focus upon opportunity-seeking, initiative-taking, creative problem-solving, intuitive decision-making and a range of other enterprising attributes, without a focus upon business venturing; but this requires very careful pedagogical design. There are examples of university staff development programmes that focus upon this issue.[6]

Recognising Different Objectives and Outcomes

A major barrier to progress is often the failure to recognise the very different approaches that might be pursued under the entrepreneurship or enterprise education label, and the different delivery agents that may be involved. For example, it is often difficult in practice to clearly distinguish between use of the currently much debated tripartite concept of teaching 'for', 'about' and 'through' enterprise, first set out by Jamieson

(1984): 'for' entrepreneurship is focused upon the 'how to' of starting and developing a venture; 'about' entrepreneurship is concerned with a more academic exploration of the concept and literature; and 'through' focuses upon highly student centred pedagogy in any disciplinary context aimed at practising and stimulating enterprising behaviours and attributes. Failure to fully recognise the mix can lead to weak results from evaluations. Among the mix in any university may appear:

- Short promotional and awareness-raising courses offered usually on a non-accredited basis. Such programmes, often of a day, weekend or evening duration, may be delivered by student societies or by external agencies.
- Programmes more specifically targeted to those students and staff who have a business idea and a motivation, while at university, to pursue it. These are often of greater length and may be offered by student groups or staff–student partnerships with external agencies. They are most likely to be organised to recruit from across the university.
- More in-depth simulation programmes aimed at providing students with a greater 'feel' for what it would be like to own and run a business or venture. Some aim to develop the self-efficacy and intentionality of participants (feelings of confidence and perceived ability, and intention to start, at some future time, a business or new venture of any kind). Whether or not they deliver the necessary 'how to' is unknown, as results are often measured by end-of-programme self-reporting assessments. Such programmes may be offered by university staff or in partnership with external agencies.
- Programmes often run by business schools as academic modules within the school or offered as accredited modules to other departments. These are usually of standard module duration and are usually examined. They may or may not focus upon new venturing and may vary as to whether they teach the 'how to' and 'for' as opposed to the 'about'.
- Programmes often embedded in the context or discipline of different departments, offered as accredited or non-accredited modules. These may focus upon business or social enterprise venturing in the context of the discipline, or may solely focus upon pedagogy aimed at stimulating the development of enterprising attributes, as noted above, in the context of the department's core discipline courses.
- Full or part-time entrepreneurship degree programmes for undergraduates or postgraduates. The number of such programmes is

growing and may be widely differentiated in their focus upon the 'for', 'through' or 'about' approaches.

- There are also programmes focused upon European doctoral students involving collaboration between different universities.
- Programmes offering placements and work experience in small businesses, social enterprises and entrepreneurial firms. These may be part of an accredited programme or offered as a non-accredited vacation course. They may or may not be funded in partnership with businesses or other organisations, and may or may not be tied to ultimate employment.
- Programmes embodied in university approaches to technology transfer or exchange, efforts at stimulating spin-offs and spin-outs, and incubation facilities.

The precise shape of the above menu in each country is also considerably influenced by government, private sector and international agency-funded programmes. It is also being influenced by some universities in Europe now branding themselves as entrepreneurial,[7] with a strong curriculum focus upon entrepreneurial engagement with external stakeholders, both business and social enterprise. There is therefore a very rich programme mix across Europe (Fayolle and Redford, 2014) and indeed the world, and surveys of entrepreneurship education rarely unpick and portray the very different offers and intended outcomes. This constitutes a major challenge, particularly to measuring the ultimate impact on the quality and numbers of new ventures and/or business growth. This search for ultimate impact evaluation is complicated by the research that demonstrates that most graduates will start their own business in their thirties (although the new technologies may shorten this time span). Tracing such impact over long periods of time is a formidable task, if not impossible, bearing in mind the wide range of other factors that will shape ultimate motivation and success.

UNIVERSITIES AS ENTREPRENEURIAL STAKEHOLDER ORGANISATIONS

The Engaged University

It was demonstrated earlier that the thrust towards the development of the entrepreneurial university stems not only from the need to cope with high levels of uncertainty and complexity but also from the resultant need to manage a process of often complex interdependence with a wide and growing range of national and international stakeholders (UNESCO, 2003; Moses, 2005; Weerts, 2007; Watson, 2010).

This challenges the notion of university excellence being judged solely through the eyes of peer institutions, moving it to one of excellence as perceived by the wide range of stakeholders with whom the institution engages. It has been argued that the excellence of any independent entrepreneurial organisation can be most appropriately judged through the prism of its many stakeholders (Gibb, 2000). It is by this means and the creation of social capital that the organisation builds up its intangible asset base to ensure its survival and growth. This model seems to fit the university environment as described above.

The dominant governance and organisational pressure (Kogan and Blieklie, 2007) therefore is to engage in partnership, as an entrepreneurial strategy to harvest resources, find opportunities and negotiate independence through the building of trust-based relationships. By this means universities are moving towards a model of public value creation which is influencing not only the focus of their research and teaching but also, particularly, the processes of university engagement with a wide range of stakeholders in society in knowledge creation and utilisation. The concept of public value, first espoused by Moore (1995), provides a framework within which an organisation seeks to create its legitimacy and value from its interface with its key stakeholders, and builds its organisation capacity around this focus. It thus approaches the issue of value creation via a process rather than an input–output model.

Beyond the Triple Helix Model

Much of the academic and wider public debate surrounding the notion of the engaged university has focused upon the triple helix model of university partnership with business and government (Shinn, 2002; Etzkowitz, 2008; Zhou, 2008), latterly also embracing the wider culture of society. The initial focus of this model was upon technology transfer and exchange, and although this has broadened over time much of the thrust still seems to be in this direction. It has been extremely well promoted and has had considerable influence on debate about the role of universities, particularly in the sphere of science and engineering-based innovation through technology development.

The model's emphasis on the science base of universities can, however, lead to neglect of the role of the humanities in external relationship development and a belief that they lie outside of the entrepreneurial paradigm. In practice many humanities departments, and their students, are heavily engaged with external stakeholders in enterprising and entrepreneurial activity (for example, in the arts, music, drama, divinity). Universities are complex pluralistic organisations, with each department and discipline facing different stakeholder environments, with different degrees of relationship and with different degrees of complexity. These relationships provide different opportunities and indeed imperatives for engagement in pursuit of research and teaching.

Combining the concept of Mode 2 forms of learning and the public value model, noted earlier, the challenge to the university of becoming an organisation for learning through partnership engagement becomes clear. This notion moves the triple helix model away from a triple or indeed quadruple focus of partnership to one of a multi-stakeholder dimension, the context of which will be differentiated between departments. The challenge to the university is that of becoming a learning as opposed to solely a learned organisation (Senge, 1990; Senges, 2007). Such an organisation is porous to learning at all levels and in all forms both within and outside the institution.[8]

EXPLORING THE CHANGE POTENTIAL

The pressures, responses and challenges described above are impacting upon many aspects of university life and organisation, including: governance (Kohler and Huber, 2006) and management (OECD, 2005); student recruitment procedures; the organisation of knowledge within the university and the breakdown of disciplinary boundaries; relationships and partnerships with external stakeholders; alumni relationships; international cooperation; staff recruitment and development; attitudes to funding, revenue-raising and leverage of public with private finance; development from research and measures of its impact; pedagogical innovation in teaching and learning; experimentation in finding new ways of engaging in true knowledge exchange and technology transfer; and, importantly, student ownership of learning. Many of the responses noted earlier are being embraced piecemeal within the silos of established university departments or professional services. Yet they all impact upon each other. This raises the potential for bringing them together into a holistic approach for exploring the entrepreneurial potential of the university, and as the basis for future strategy development.

The Potential for Bringing Things Together

Tracing the impact of change across different areas of the university can provide the platform for reviewing areas of potential entrepreneurial synergy, necessary for creating a strategic approach in moving the university to an entrepreneurial model (Gibb, 2012). Key areas for review, as set out in Figure 18.1, include:

- changes in governance, leadership and organisation structures made in response to pressures and opportunities;
- changes in teaching and learning, and particularly enterprise and entrepreneurship education;
- changes in research, knowledge transfer and exchange processes;
- changes relating to international competition and cooperation;
- changes in stakeholder relationships.

There can be major advantages to exploring interdependencies, in revealing that the whole sum of the piecemeal parts is greater than might be initially recognised. As shown in Figure 18.1, the process of strategically bringing things together can then be evaluated in terms of their contribution to the overriding objectives of the university, described in detail in Gibb (2012). Two brief examples of exploring interdependency and the potential for synergy are described below.

A review of enterprise and entrepreneurship education can reveal its scope for contributing to many other areas of university activity. Entrepreneurial and enterprising educational approaches can be built into: action research and problem-solving development agendas; finding innovative forms of dissemination and translation of research findings; the discovery of research partners and resources; doctoral and postdoctoral training and employability; technology transfer processes; knowledge exchange activities, particularly with small and medium-sized enterprises (SMEs); and local and social enterprise development initiatives. Many of the entrepreneurial programme approaches, described earlier, demand partnership with stakeholder organisations, will link with local development opportunities, will cut across disciplinary boundaries, will raise potential for working with alumni groups and with global technology reach-out, and will cross international boundaries. They may provoke changes in assessment and accreditation procedures and offer opportunities for staff development linked to creating more innovative pedagogical learning approaches. They may also involve change in senior staff responsibilities, organisation and rewards to facilitate the development of appropriate capacities (McInnis, 2001). Almost certainly such a 'whole' campus approach to entrepreneurship and enterprise education will also demand strong leadership (Miclea, 2004).

Similarly, a strong strategic thrust in external and internal stakeholder partnership and relationship development cannot be separated from its

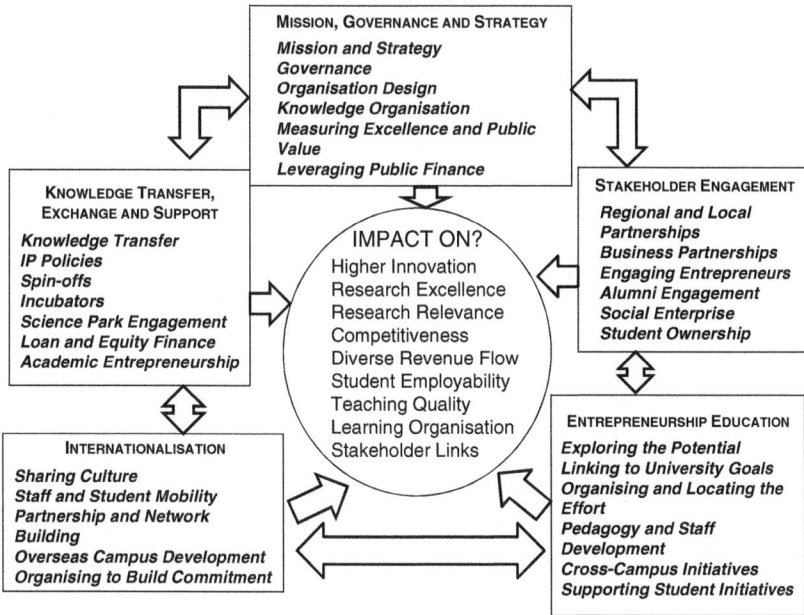

Source: Gibb (2012).

Figure 18.1 *Exploring synergies in entrepreneurial university development: the potential contribution to key strategic goals*

potential to add considerable value to: technology transfer and exchange processes; the creation of partnerships in research and development; the enhancement of entrepreneurial learning by the engagement of a wide range of external personnel in the process (Massey, 2010); the enhancement of the capacity of the university to engage with local and regional social and economic development issues; and a strengthening of international ties and alumni engagement. Such a strategy of engagement will almost certainly demand change in organisation and governance structures to reflect the true involvement of wider stakeholder groups in university life and work. In summary, exploring existing and future scenarios in each of the areas shown in Figure 18.1 will reveal overlapping opportunities, exploited and underexploited, and perhaps areas where opportunity is neglected.

The Potential for Change

It should be clear from the earlier discussion that there are a wide range of different institutions operating globally under the higher education banner. Legal frameworks differ between and even within countries, although there is growing harmonisation to facilitate student mobility and award recognition. In almost every country there is also a hierarchy of institutions, often based upon age, but increasingly upon resources. Within the hierarchy there are also different organisation cultures, particularly relating to the research versus teaching status of the university. There is also differentiation in disciplinary focus, with specialist institutions for industry sectors in some countries, for professions such as law and accountancy, different emphases upon vocational subjects, and with different links back into primary, secondary and further education. The pressures noted earlier in this chapter will therefore impact in different ways, provide different threats and opportunities, and invoke highly differentiated responses to change (Navarro and Gallardo, 2003). There is therefore no standard recipe for entrepreneurial development. Each institution will find its own way, often from a very different base. The older, venerable and frequently well-resourced and culturally embedded institutions will be able to maintain their current position and culture more easily than others. For the others there is the probability that they will increasingly seek to differentiate themselves into educational and professional niches.

Universities will also differ in their degree of 'change readiness' (Rafferty et al., 2013). This can be defined as a collection of individual 'beliefs, attitudes, and intentions regarding the extent to which changes are needed and the organization's capacity to successfully undertake those changes' (Armenakis et al., 1993: 681). It is argued by Rafferty et al. that change readiness has two major elements, cognitive and affective, the latter being focused upon the emotional response. Within each university there will be those who resist change, and particularly the entrepreneurial notion in both of the above respects, and those who find it challenging and exciting once the fears noted earlier have been assuaged. Different departments will have different views, dependent upon the degree to which they are threatened by, or see opportunity in, their existing exposure to a wider stakeholder environment (Todorovic et al., 2005). Much will also depend upon the leadership of the university and the strength and values of its top management team. Internally there will also be challenges to the existing relationships between professional and academic staff, with the growth of subcontracting and the challenge to academic staff to 'engage' with the wider world rather than have this done for them by professionals. Professional staff may therefore become even more 'engagement facilitators' in assisting academics to actively cross boundaries, and will be judged by their success in this respect.

Strategies for Supporting Change

The above scenario has major implications for the way in which the wider entrepreneurial agenda as set out in this chapter might be supported. Change is continuously influenced by public policy, most often by financial incentives. Such inducements include efforts to: encourage universities to leverage public money with private; engage in local development initiatives; undertake joint degree ventures with business; and establish new technology transfer initiatives. Much of the direction of this effort has been stimulated in Europe by European Union programmes and is covered in EU and Organisation for Economic Co-operation and Development (OECD) papers. Most of these are focused upon business and social and economic infrastructure development. They are highly important in identifying and stimulating avenues for change, and facilitate responses in key areas identified above. They therefore offer opportunities for wider institutional refocusing.

In the Entrepreneurial University Leaders Programme (EULP), attempts have been made to introduce a profiling instrument to create awareness by senior staff of universities in reviewing their own institutions with the aim of developing strategies for entrepreneurial development.[9] The use of an instrument that has intellectual rigour can assist in approaching the cognitive element of change management and can be adapted and owned by those academic and sometimes senior professional staff with strong motivations for exploring and driving change. It does not, however, deal with the affective aspect of change management, or with the wider cognitive aspects relating to the levels of comprehensive understanding needed. Limited experience suggests that a scoring system is best replaced by informal discussion with a range of staff throughout the institution in a process of continuous dialogue. There are a number of lessons from this experience and from staff development programmes. The first is that change within a university needs senior champions to own the initiative and manage the process. Second, such champions will often start from their own area of interest and their own position of responsibility in the university. Most pro or deputy vice-chancellors who have participated in the EULP have specific areas of responsibility within their universities, for example for research and development; teaching and learning; knowledge exchange; local and regional development; and internationalisation. Professional staff on the programme will similarly carry more specific responsibilities, for example for employment and employability; for internal operations and human resources; for technology transfer; for internationalisation; for revenue-raising; and for alumni and external relationships. Each person will most commonly develop their strategies starting from their own key focus area, and may look for synergies with other areas of university activity as described earlier (Gibb, 2012). A few, with responsibility for overall university strategy development, will attempt a more holistic approach.[10]

One advantage of a programme approach is that it can attempt to deal with both cognitive and affective components of change. It can explore and seek to remove some of the misunderstandings of the entrepreneurial concept; bring in vice-chancellors and eminent academics who can contribute key aspects of concept and practice; facilitate investigations in universities that have won awards for being entrepreneurial;[11] through a strong alumni organisation, offer peer support and create confidence through peer group work throughout the programme; and offer opportunity to debate with key public and private stakeholders. This breaks down barriers, but the ultimate success of this route will depend substantially upon the leadership of the university and the degree to which the head of the institution and their senior team are committed to a culture of creating public value by entrepreneurial processes of wide stakeholder engagement.

Adding Real Value to University Goals

Experience dictates that the key to success in progressing the entrepreneurial concept through the university is the degree to which it is seen to add value to the overriding goals of the institution, which may include:

- the quality, funding, relevance and impact of its research (see Kauffman Foundation, 2008);
- the quality of teaching and learning across the university;
- the reputation of the university with key stakeholders, public and private, local, regional, national and international;
- the attraction of students and their ultimate satisfaction;
- student employability and employment;
- the funding of the university;
- the quality and range of its partners; and
- overall, a reputation for creativity and innovation in creating public value.

These form the hub of the synergy approach highlighted by Gibb (2012). The strength and specific focus upon each of these 'outcomes' will depend upon the priorities as seen by the particular university. For example, if a university brands itself as business-facing then this will be a dominant criterion. If its overriding target is high student employability then the thrust may be different. If a major goal is for the university to position itself successfully in an international marketplace and/or as a research-based institution, then the focus will again be different.

THE FUTURE ENTREPRENEURIAL UNIVERSITY

This chapter aimed to map out the ways in which the concept and practice of the entrepreneurial university is emerging. In pursuit of this objective it has sought to clarify relevant concepts; explored the uncertainties and complexities facing universities and briefly summarised the response; reviewed major challenges to the acceptance of the concept in general, and particularly in the context of teaching and learning; explored the notion of the university as a broader stakeholder relationship institution; and identified key issues in the management and promotion of change (see Gibb et al., 2009). This final section of the chapter takes a speculative and more normative look at what might be the broad profile of an entrepreneurial university.

A Broad Definition

It should be clear from the above argument that it is not possible to have a standard, 'branded' view of what constitutes an entrepreneurial university. Individual universities that do indeed brand themselves as such may place very different weights of emphasis upon business, local/regional/ national and international, knowledge exchange, teaching and learning, and research and development relationships, and will differentiate in their strategies for crossing boundaries internally and externally in order to further their goals of excellence. Moreover, just as there is much enterprising and entrepreneurial activity in universities that may not be branded as such, it might equally follow that formal strategic declarations may not constitute the reality in practice. It has been pointed out above that universities are highly pluralistic organisations; individuals and departments enjoy wide degrees of freedom, and very different views and approaches to many of the issues described earlier in this chapter may prevail across the institution. It follows from this point that individuals in a university may view its entrepreneurial status in very different ways.

Recognising that it is not possible or desirable to produce a 'recipe' for an entrepreneurial university, the definition offered below is deliberately broad-based enough to allow considerable scope for differentiation in approach. It focuses upon the emerging practice of how universities seem to be responding to an increasingly dynamic, complex and uncertain environment.

It is proposed that an entrepreneurial university is: an academic organisation designed to contribute effectively to the enhancement of learning in a societal environment characterised by high levels of uncertainty and complexity; empowering its staff and students to demonstrate enterprise, innovation and creativity in research, teaching and pursuit and use of knowledge across boundaries; and dedicated to creating public value via a process of open engagement, mutual learning, debate, discovery and exchange with all stakeholders in society, local, national and international.

Key Characteristics

It follows from the above definition and the preceding arguments that the entrepreneurial university organisation would need to embody a number of key characteristics, as follows:

- designed to be supportive of learning from all sources external or internal to the organisation;
- partnered in many of its activities with external stakeholders; importantly, in strategic alliances;
- designed to stimulate innovation of all kinds through support of individual and collective enterprising behaviour;
- designed to empower individuals throughout the organisation to own their own initiatives, engage in innovation and build personal trust-based stakeholder relationships across external and internal boundaries in search of synergy;
- engaging enterprising staff with appropriate reward and promotional systems for personal enterprise and innovation;
- striving to create trust-based partnerships between professional and academic members of its community;
- demonstrating entrepreneurial and enterprising leadership in an organisation that is constantly adapting to uncertainty and complexity;
- judging its excellence through the eyes of all of its stakeholders in pursuit of a shared vision and culture, not overloaded with managerial systems and focused upon the creation of public value;
- prepared to constantly strive for its autonomy via the entrepreneurial management of its various interdependencies with stakeholders;
- constantly evaluating its entrepreneurial and enterprise efforts against the degree to which they add value to its overriding objectives as an academic institution.

Organisation Design

Meeting such objectives has major implications for organisation design. Governance structures and processes may need to be re-examined to open up external engagement with wider representation of entrepreneurs and social enterprise organisations on the council or board (Miller and Katz, 2004; Mora and Vieira, 2009). There may need to be closer active working relationships between the chair of the council or board and the vice-chancellor or chief executive. The leadership team would ideally clearly share an appropriate entrepreneurial vision, be flexible in strategy in pursuing this, and be substantially networked with the stakeholder community as role models for staff throughout the organisation (Gupta et al., 2004; Goffee and Jones, 2007; Coyle et al., 2013). If innovation is to be pursued across boundaries, bottom-up, then faculty and departmental heads may have to take responsibility for performance in this respect and be prepared to defend risk-taking behaviour and, at times, associated failure. Borrowing from the best of practice in other large organisations, pursuit of change may be managed by carefully selected and balanced project teams rather than committees, with responsibility for carrying things through.

Overall organisation design may be structured in such a way to facilitate cross-disciplinary teaching and research not only focused upon current problems and issues but also with a vision of the longer-term issues of strategic importance and relevance to the particular society or region. It has been shown that whole universities or faculties may be organised in this way, breaking down traditional disciplinary silos. Entrepreneurial education programmes will be contextually embedded in all disciplines in the university with clear targeted personal enterprise development agendas with associated pedagogies. The entrepreneurial university will also be strong as a translator of knowledge for the wider public, and have a strong presence in social media throughout the organisation. This will demand close relationships between academic staff and internal and external professional personnel, as many of the traditional internalised services may be outsourced. Responsibilities relating to employment, employability, building alumni relationships, revenue-raising, development from research and entrepreneurship, and enterprise education may be placed with departments in recognition of the fact that each department faces many distinctly different stakeholder, employment and research pathways for its students and staff. Reward and promotion systems may need to be geared to this scenario so that 'routes to innovation' of all kinds, as set out earlier in this chapter, can lead to professorial status.

Entrepreneurial Leadership

The leadership role in universities has been extensively debated (US Department of Education, 2006; Bryman, 2007; Greenhalgh, 2008; Herrmann, 2008). Leadership in managing change under conditions of uncertainty and complexity is of critical, transformational importance (Bass and Riggio, 2008; Epitropaki, 2001) in several key respects:

- presenting a strong intellectual and passionate vision of the entrepreneurial role for the university and the rationale for entrepreneurial behaviours;
- establishing a culture of supporting innovation and some risk-taking across the university;
- building a team of shared values;
- presenting a clear and convincing vision of organisation design aimed at bottom-up empowerment across the university;
- identifying, supporting and rewarding the key change agents at the faculty and departmental level;
- demonstrating strong network and relationship management skills both externally and internally;
- demonstrating a strong strategic orientation allowing flexibility for initiative-taking across the university via a process of informal culture trust-based development.

These attributes will be of particular importance in guiding relationship management of the council or board of the university and shaping the organisation culture (Schein, 1992).

The Student Experience

In a competitive and employment environment, the student experience will be increasingly important, with the entrepreneurial university offering, in each programme, more opportunity for exposure to tacit knowledge; and allowing students more ownership, direction and assessment of their learning. Much of student new venture programmes may be managed by student societies. In mainstream education, the flipped classroom model will become increasingly important, challenging students to research and find their own solutions to issues, making sense of 'big data' with guidance from staff. There will be more degree and professional qualification offers in partnership with external organisations, and much greater use of adjunct, associate and visiting staff for both teaching and research purposes. There will be a closer relationship between concept, theory and practice.

A Future Rich Mix

As noted at the beginning of this chapter, some universities already brand themselves as entrepreneurial and exhibit a growing number of the characteristics noted above. Others will select and focus upon particular aspects of the entrepreneurial model, and over time may reach out beyond an initial narrow focus in search of broader synergy. As the higher education sector expands around the world to cater in particular for burgeoning middle-class populations, and as competition becomes acute and staff and student mobility increases, so many of the pressures identified in this chapter will change in nature, demanding an ever more entrepreneurial approach to managing the environment. A rich mix of experience may therefore emerge, creating numerous future learning opportunities (Pratt, 2001; Neubauer, 2011). Finally, it is important to again underline that the scenarios portrayed in this chapter will differ in relevance, weight of emphasis, and priority within individual countries and indeed individual universities, in many respects. The university sector worldwide offers strong but varied cultures, each with different propensity for change (Vukasovic et al., 2012), yet with common threads (Sporn, 1996). This chapter has not therefore offered a recipe, but a framework within which readers may create their own vision as to priorities and response.

NOTES

1. The Entrepreneurial University Leaders Programme (EULP), now in its tenth cohort, explores the development of the entrepreneurial university with senior academic and professional staff from UK and European universities and beyond. Key partners are the National Centre for Entrepreneurship Education, Universities UK and Oxford University (see www.eulp.co.uk for programme details and associated academic papers). This UK-based programme aimed at senior university staff was initially designed and co-directed by the authors.
2. While 'mindset' is an expression increasingly used in the context of entrepreneurship education it is often without clear definition. It can best be described as attitudes fuelled by beliefs and values which, when hardened through repeat experience, create a predisposition to think, believe, act and see things in particular ways (Duffy, 2009).
3. See for example Asean University Network (2011) and Australian Universities Quality Forum (AUQA, 2005).
4. This issue, provoked by the Minister for Higher Education, was debated at the Policy Dialogue Higher Education in Sri Lanka and the UK on the theme of the entrepreneurial university (2008). See the report by Eranda Ginige available from the British Council, Sri Lanka.
5. 'Open data' refers to widening access to non-sensitive, publicly available information; 'big data' to the challenges in crossing boundaries and accessing and making sense of the sheer volume of information on the web. See McAuley et al. (2012) for a review.

6. The NCEE International Entrepreneurship Educators Programme (IEEP) and the European partnership-funded version 3EEP seek to focus pedagogy on distinctive aspects of entrepreneurial behaviour support and attribute development by the use of more than 40 pedagogical techniques. See Gibb (2011) for a review of the programme, and the website www.allangibb.com for details of each of the pedagogies.
7. See, for example, the University of Wismar Germany (http://ec.europa.eu/education/higher-education/doc/business/forum09/prause_en.pdf) and the Estonian Entrepreneurship University of Applied Sciences (www.euas.eu).
8. This model, however, is not without criticism in terms of its learning focus. Haggis (2006) argues that the major issue is not that of 'learning' but, within the existing higher education system, one of educational practices and the possible effects of cultural values, assumptions and practices. These include: personal and institutional processes involved in study and assessment; lack of acceptance of a wide range of different motives and types of engagement; weakness in exploring key assumptions and principles of a discipline; and opaqueness in use of language.
9. NCEE, 'The Entrepreneurial University Scorecard. Reviewing the entrepreneurial potential of the university' (http://www.ncee.org.uk/publication/Entrepreneurial_University_SCORE_CARD.pdf). A simpler and differently weighted guide has recently been produced by the OECD/EU (op cit) and is being backed by a promotional and awareness campaign.
10. See case examples of different university approaches in Coyle et al. (2013).
11. For example in the UK the winner of the previous year's, NCEE sponsored, *Times Higher Education Supplement* 'Entrepreneurial University of the Year' award is explored in depth as an exemplar in the EULP.

REFERENCES

Akola, E. and Heinonen, J. (2006) 'Does Training of Entrepreneurs Support Entrepreneurial Learning? A Study of Training Programmes for Existing and Potential Entrepreneurs in Seven European Countries'. Paper presented in the 51st ICSB World Conference, 18–21 June, Melbourne, Australia.
Anderson, R. (2010) 'The Idea of a University Today'. History and Policy. Available at: http://www.historyandpolicy.org/papers/policy-paper-98.html.
Arbo, P. and Benneworth, P. (2008) 'Understanding the regional contribution of higher education institutions: A literature review'. A research report prepared for the OECD Institutional Management in Higher Education Programme: 'The contribution of higher education to regional development', Paris.
Armbruster, C. (2008) 'Research universities: autonomy and self-reliance after the Entrepreneurial University'. *Policy Futures in Education*, 6(4), pp. 372–89.
Armenakis, A.A., Harris, S.G. and Mossholder, K.W. (1993) 'Creating readiness for organizational change'. *Human Relations*, 46(6), pp. 681–703.
Artess, J., Forbes, P. and Ripmeester, N. (2011) 'Supporting Graduate Employability: HEI Practice in Other Countries'. Department for Business, Innovation and Skills, UK.
Asean University Network (2011) 'University Social Responsibility and Sustainability. A Collection of Good Practices'. Asean University Network and Japan Foundation, Bangkok, Thailand.
AUQA (2005) 'Proceedings of the 2005 Australian Universities Quality Forum. Engaging Communities: Sydney, Australia 6-8 July 2005'. AUQA Occasional Publications, 5, The Australian Universities Quality Agency, Melbourne, Australia.
Barber, M., Donnelly, K. and Rizvi, S. (2013) 'An Avalanche is Coming. Higher Education and the Revolution Ahead'. Institute of Public Policy Research, London, UK.
Barnett, R. (2000) 'University knowledge in an age of supercomplexity'. *Higher Education*, 40, pp. 409–22.

Bass, B. and Riggio, R.E. (2008) *Transformational Leadership*. Taylor and Francis, New York, NY.

Berglund, E. (2008) 'I wanted to be an academic, not "a creative": Notes on universities and the new capitalism'. *Ephemera: Theory and Politics in Organization*, 8(3), pp. 322–30.

Bernasconi, A. (2005) 'University entrepreneurship in a developing country: The case of the P. Universidad Católica de Chile, 1985-2000'. *Higher Education*, 50(2), pp. 247–74.

Blenker, P., Dreisler, P. and Kjeldsen, J. (2006) 'Entrepreneurship Education – the New Challenge Facing the Universities'. Working Paper 2006-02, Department of Management, Aarhus School of Business, Aarhus, Denmark.

Bone, D. (2011) 'Internationalization 2011: An overview'. *Higher Learning Research Communications*, 1(1), pp. 4–9.

Bourn, D., McKenzie, A. and Shiel, C. (2006) 'The Global University: The Role of the Curriculum', October, Development Education Association, London.

Braun, G. and Diensberg, C. (2007) 'Cultivating Entrepreneurial Regions – Cases and Studies from the Network Project'. Baltic Entrepreneurship Partners, *Rostock Contributions to Regional Science*, 19, Rostock: Universität Rostock, Wirtschafts- und Sozialwissenschaftliche Fakultät.

Bridgman, T. (2007) 'Freedom and autonomy in the university enterprise'. *Journal of Organizational Change Management*, 20(4), pp. 478–90.

Bryman, A. (2007) 'Effective leadership in higher education: A literature review'. *Studies in Higher Education*, 32(6), pp. 693–710.

Chan, D. and Lo, W. (2007) 'Running universities as enterprises: University governance changes in Hong Kong'. *Asia Pacific Journal of Education*, 27, pp. 305–22.

Charles, D.R. (2006) 'Universities as key knowledge infrastructures in regional innovation systems'. *Innovation: the European Journal of Social Science Research*, 19(1), pp. 117–30.

Chen, S. (2007) 'The features and trends of university development in Australia and China'. *Higher Education Policy*, 20(2), pp. 207–16.

Cherwitz, A.R. (2002) 'Intellectual entrepreneurship. A vision for graduate education'. *Change: The Magazine of Higher Learning*, 34(6), pp. 22–7.

Chiang, L.-C. (2004) 'The Relationship between university autonomy and funding in England and Taiwan'. *Higher Education*, 48(2), pp. 189–212.

Collier, A. and Gray, B. (2007) 'The Commercialisation of University Innovations'. Centre for Entrepreneurship, School of Business, University of Otago, NZ.

Collini, S. (2012) *What are Universities for?*. Penguin Books, London, UK.

Cook, T., Dwek, T.R., Blumberg, B. and Hockaday, T. (2008) 'Commercialising university research: Threats and opportunities–The Oxford Model'. *Capitalism and Society*, 3(1), pp. 1–17.

Corbett, A. (2006) *Universities and the Europe of Knowledge: Ideas, Institutions and Policy Entrepreneurship in European Union Higher Education Policy, 1955-2005*. Palgrave Macmillan, London, UK.

Coyle, P., Gibb, A. and Haskins, G. (2013) 'The Entrepreneurial University: from Concept to Action. (Key Questions and Cases)'. National Centre for Entrepreneurship in Education, UK. Available at: www.ncee.org.uk and Entrepreneurial University Leaders Programme: www.eulp.co.uk.

Crow, M.M. (2008) 'Building an Entrepreneurial University' in 'The Future of the Research University: Meeting the Global Challenges of the 21st Century'. Paper to 2008 Kauffman-Planck Summit on Entrepreneurship Research and Policy, June 8–11, Bavaria, Germany, pp. 31–41.

Currie, J. (2002) 'Australian Universities as Enterprise Universities: Transformed Players on a Global Stage' in 'Globalisation: What Issues are at Stake for Universities?' An IAU international Conference hosted by the Université Laval, Québec Canada.

D'Antoni, S. (ed.) (2006) 'The Virtual University: Models and Messages. Lessons from Case Studies'. UNESCO, France.

Davies, J.L. (2001) 'The emergence of entrepreneurial cultures in European universities'. *Higher Education Management*, 13(2), pp. 25–45.

Deem, R. (2007) 'Managing contemporary UK universities – Manager-academics and new managerialism'. *Academic Leadership*, Empirical Research, pp.1–14. Available at: www.academicleadership.org/empirical_research/Managing_Contemporary_UK.

Department for Business Innovation and Skills UK (2013) 'The Maturing of the MOOC. A Literature Review of Massive Open Online Courses and other Forms of Online Distance Learning'. BIS Research Paper, 130.

Dooley, L. and Kirk, D. (2007) 'University-industry collaboration: Grafting the entrepreneurial paradigm onto academic structures'. *European Journal of Innovation Management*, 10(3), pp. 316–32.

Duffy, F.M. (2009) 'Paradigms, mental models, and mindsets: Triple barriers to transformational change in school systems'. *International Journal of Educational Leadership Preparation*, 4(3). Available at: http://cnx.org/content/col10723/1.1/.

Epitropaki, O. (2001) 'What is Transformational Leadership'. Institute of Work Psychology, Sheffield, UK.

Ernst & Young (2012) 'University of the Future'. Ernst & Young, Australia.

Estermann, T. and Pruvot, E.B. (2011) 'Financially Sustainable Universities II: European Universities Diversifying Income Streams'. European University Association, EU DG Education and Culture.

Etzkowitz, H. (2008) *The Triple Helix. University-Industry-Government: Innovation in Action*. Routledge, Oxford, UK and New York, NY.

EU Commission of the European Communities (2005) 'Mobilising the Brainpower of Europe: Enabling Universities to Make their Full Contribution to the Lisbon Strategy'. Communication from the Commission, COM, Brussels.

EU Commission of the European Communities (2006) 'Implementing the Community Lisbon Programme: Fostering Entrepreneurial Mindsets through Education and Learning'. EU, COM(2006) 33 final, Brussels.

EU Commission of the European Communities (2008a) 'Towards More Knowledge-based Policy and Practice in Education and Training'. EU, SEC(2007), 1098, Brussels.

EU Commission of the European Communities (2008b) 'Entrepreneurship in Higher Education, Especially within Non-business Studies'. Final Report of the Expert Group, Directorate-General for Enterprise and Industry, EU, Unit B.1: Entrepreneurship, Brussels.

EU Directorate-General for Enterprise (2004) 'Helping to Create an Entrepreneurial Culture. A Guide on Good Practices in Promoting Entrepreneurial Attitudes and Skills through Education'. Directorate-General for Enterprise and Industry, EU, Unit B.1: Entrepreneurship (SC27 3/4), Brussels.

EU European Commission (2009) '30 Good Practice Case Studies in University-Business Cooperation'. Directorate-General for Education and Culture, Science-to-Business Marketing Research Centre.

EUEREK (2008) 'European Universities for Entrepreneurship: their Role in the Europe of Knowledge'. Sixth Framework Programme, Citizens and Governance in Knowledge-based Society, Final review.

European Commission (1998) 'Promoting Entrepreneurship and Competitiveness'. COM(1998) 550 final, September, Brussels.

European Commission (2005) 'The Competitiveness Challenge'. *Enterprise Europe*, January–March.

European Commission (2013) 'Entrepreneurship Education: A Guide for Educators'. European Commission, DG Enterprise and Industry, June, Brussels.

Evans, M. (2004) *Killing Thinking. The Death of the Universities*. Bloomsbury, London.

Farsi, J.Y., Imanipour, N. and Salamzadeh, A. (2012) 'Entrepreneurial university conceptualization: Case of developing countries'. *Global Business and Management Research: An International Journal*, 4(2), pp. 193–204.

Fatt, J.P.T. and Ang, T.H. (1995) 'Enhancing entrepreneurial spirit: A resolve for university graduates'. *Management Research News*, 18(1/2), pp. 31–52.

Fayolle, A. and Redford, D.T. (2014) *Handbook on the Entrepreneurial University*. Edward Elgar Publishing, Cheltenham, UK and Northampton, MA.

Furedi, F. (2001) 'An intellectual vacuum'. *Times Higher Education Supplement*, 5 October, UK.

Geuna, A. and Muscio, A. (2008) 'The Governance of University Knowledge Transfer'. SPRU Electronic Working Paper Series, paper 173, September.

Gibb, A.A. (2000) 'Corporate restructuring and entrepreneurship: What can large organisations learn from small?'. *Enterprise and Innovation Management Studies*, 1(1), pp.19–35.

Gibb, A.A. (2002) 'Creative destruction, new values, new ways of doing things and new combinations of knowledge. In pursuit of a new enterprise and entrepreneurship paradigm'. *International Journal of Management Reviews,* 4(3), pp.233–68.

Gibb, A.A. (2005) 'Towards the Entrepreneurial University. Entrepreneurship Education as a Lever for Change'. National Council for Graduate Entrepreneurship (NCGE) Policy Paper. Available at: www.ncee.org.uk.

Gibb, A.A. (2011) 'Concepts into practice: Meeting the challenge of development of entrepreneurship educators around an innovative paradigm. The case of the International Entrepreneurship Educators' Programme (IEEP)', *International Journal of Entrepreneurial Behaviour and Research*, 17(2), pp.146–65.

Gibb, A.A. (2012) 'Exploring the synergistic potential in entrepreneurial university development: Towards the building of a strategic framework'. *Annals of Innovation & Entrepreneurship*, 3, pp.1–24.

Gibb, A.A. and Haskins, G. (2014) 'The Entrepreneurial University of the Future. An Entrepreneurial Stakeholder Learning Organisation' in Fayolle, A. and Redford, D.T. (eds) *Handbook on the Entrepreneurial University*. Edward Elgar Publishing, Cheltenham, UK and Northampton, MA, pp.25–64.

Gibb, A.A., Haskins, G. and Robertson, I. (2009) 'Leading the Entrepreneurial University. Meeting the Entrepreneurial Development Needs of Higher Education Institutions'. A National Council for Graduate Entrepreneurship (NCEE) Policy Paper. Available at: www.ncge.org.uk.

Goddard, J. and Kempton, L. (2011) 'Connecting Universities to Regional Growth. A Practical Guide'. European Union DG Regional Policy, Brussels.

Goffee, R. and Jones, G. (2007) 'Leading clever people'. *Harvard Business Review*, Reprint R0703D.

Green, F.J. and Saridakis, G. (2008) 'The role of higher education skills and support in graduate self-employment'. *Studies in Higher Education*, 33(6), pp.653–72.

Green, M. and Baer, M. (2000) 'What does globalisation mean for teaching and learning?' CHET Transformation Debates, 21 July.

Greenhalgh, R. (2008) 'Perspectives on Management and Leadership from HE and Industry' in Herrmann, K. (ed.) *Leadership in an Age of Supercomplexity*. Council for Industry in Higher Education, UK, pp.17–21.

Guerrero-Cano, M. (2008) 'The Creation and Development of Entrepreneurial Universities in Spain. An Institutional Approach', Doctoral Thesis Universitat Automona, Barcelona, Spain.

Gupta, V., MacMillan, I.C. and Surie, G. (2004) 'Entrepreneurial leadership: developing and measuring a cross-cultural construct'. *Journal of Business Venturing*, 19, pp.241–60.

Guri-Rosenblit, S., Sebcova, H. and Teichler, U. (2007) 'Massification and Diversity of Higher Education Systems: Interplay of Complex Dimensions'. UNESCO.

Habermas, J. and Blazek, J.R. (1987) 'The idea of the university: Learning processes'. *New German Critique*, 41(Spring/Summer), pp.3–22.

Haggis, T. (2006) 'Pedagogies for diversity: Retaining critical challenges amidst fears of dumbing down'. *Studies in Higher Education*, 31(5), pp.521–35.

Hayrinen-Alestalo, M. (1999) 'The university under the pressure of innovation policy – Reflecting on European and Finnish experiences'. *Science Studies*, 12(1), pp.44–69.

Hearn, J.C. (2003) 'Diversifying Campus Revenue Streams. Opportunities and Risks'. American Council of Education, Center for Policy Analysis, USA.

Henkel, M. (2004) 'Current science policies and their implications for the formation and maintenance of academic identity'. *Higher Education Policy*, 17, pp.167–82.

Herrmann, K. (ed.) (2008) *Leadership in an Age of Supercomplexity*. Council for Industry in Higher Education, UK.
Higher Education in Europe (2004) 'Entrepreneurship in Europe'. XXIX(2), Carfax Publishing.
Hofer, A.R. and Potter, J. (2010) 'Universities, Innovation and Entrepreneurship: Criteria and Examples of Good Practice'. OECD Local Economic and Employment Development (LEED) Working Papers.
Hudson, A. (2009) 'New Professionals and New Technologies in New Higher Education? Conceptualising Struggles in the Field', Doctoral Thesis. Department of Interactive Media and Learning (IML), Umeå University, Sweden.
Hughes, A. (2003) 'Knowledge Transfer, Entrepreneurship and Economic Growth'. ESRC Centre for Business Research Working Paper 273, University of Cambridge, Small Business and Entrepreneurship, UK.
IHEP (2009) 'Privatization in Higher Education: Cross-Country Analysis of Trends, Policies, Problems, and Solutions'. Issue Brief, IHEP, Washington, DC.
Institute of Educational Technology (2012) 'Future Learning Systems'. Open University, UK.
International Association of Universities (2005) 'Key results: 2005 IAU Global Survey on Internationalisation of Higher Education'. Available at: www.unesco.org.
Jacob, M., Lundqvist, M. and Hellsmark, H. (2003) 'Entrepreneurial transformations in the Swedish university system: the case of Chalmers University of Technology'. *Research Policy*, 32(2003), pp.1555–68.
Jamieson, I. (1984) 'Schools and Enterprise' in Watts, A.G., and Moran, P. (eds) *Education for Enterprise*. CRAC, Ballinger, Cambridge, MA, pp.19–27.
Ka Ho Mok (2005) 'Fostering entrepreneurship: Changing role of government and higher education governance in Hong Kong'. *Research Policy*, 34(2005), pp.537–54.
Kauffman Foundation (2008) 'The Future of the Research University. Meeting the Global Challenges of the 21st Century'. Conference papers from the Kauffmann-Max Planck Annual Summit, 'Rethinking the Role of the University and Public Research for the Entrepreneurial Age', 8–11 June, Bavaria, Germany.
King, R., Findlay, A. and Ahrens, J. (2010) 'International Student Mobility literature Review'. Report to HEFCE and co-funded by the British Council, UK National Agency for Erasmus.
Kirby, D. (2006) 'Creating entrepreneurial universities in the UK. Applying entrepreneurship theory in practice'. *Journal of Technology Transfer*, 31, pp.599–603.
Klofsten, M. (2000) 'Training entrepreneurship at universities: A Swedish case'. *Journal of European Industrial Training*, 24(6), pp.337–44.
Knight, J. (2003) 'Internationalization of Higher Education Practices and Priorities'. 2003 IAU Survey Report, IAU. Available at: http://www.unesco.org/iau.
Kogan, M. and Bliek lie, I. (2007) 'Organisation and governance of universities'. *Higher Education Policy*, 20, pp.477–93.
Kohler, J. and Huber, J. (eds) (2006) *Higher Education Governance Between Democratic Culture, Academic Aspirations and Market Forces*. Council of Europe Publishing, Strasbourg.
Kristensen, B. (1999) 'The entrepreneurial university as a learning university'. *Higher Education in Europe*, 24(1), pp.35–46.
Kwiek, M. (2001) 'Globalization and higher education'. *Higher Education in Europe*, 26(1), pp.27–38.
Kwiek, M. (2005a) 'Academic Entrepreneurship and Private Higher Education in Europe (in a Comparative Perspective)'. Center for Public Policy, Poznan University, Poland.
Kwiek, M. (2005b) 'The university and the state in a global age: Renegotiating the traditional social contract?' *European Educational Research Journal*, 4(4), pp.324–41.
Kwiek, M. (2008) 'Academic entrepreneurship vs. changing governance and institutional management structures at European universities'. *Policy Futures in Education*, 6(6), pp.757–70.

Lane, J. and Kinser, K. (2011) 'Reconsidering privatization in cross-border engagements: The sometimes public nature of private activity'. *Higher Education Policy*, 24, pp. 255–73.

Lazzeroni, M. and Piccaluga, A. (2003) 'Towards the entrepreneurial university'. *Local Economy*, 18(1), pp. 38–48.

Lee, Y.S. (1996) 'Technology transfer and the research university: A search for the boundaries of university-industry collaboration'. *Research Policy*, 25, pp. 843–63.

Leisner, A. (2006) 'Education or service? Remarks on teaching and learning in the entrepreneurial university'. *Educational Philosophy and Theory*, 38(4), pp. 483–95.

LERU (2006) 'Universities and Innovation: The Challenge for Europe'. League of European Research Universities, Belgium.

Link, A.N. (2006) 'An Empirical Analysis of the Propensity of Academics to Engage in Informal University Technology Transfer'. Department of Economics, Rensselaer Polytechnic Institute. Working Papers in Economics, No. 0610 from Phan, P.H., Siegel, D.S. 2006 'The Effectiveness of University Technology Transfer. Foundations and Trends in Entrepreneurship', 2(2), pp. 77–144. Available at: http://www.rpi.edu/dept/economics/www/workingpapers/.

Maringe, F. and Foskett, N. (eds) (2010) *Globalization and Internationalization in Higher Education. Theoretical, Strategic and Management Perspectives.* Continuum International Publishing Group, London.

Masri, M., Jemri, M., Al-Ghassani, A. and Badawi, A.A. (2010) 'Entrepreneurship Education in the Arab States. Case Studies on the Arab States (Jordan, Tunisia, Oman, and Egypt) and Regional Synthesis Report'. UNESCO LB/2010/ED/PI/34.

Massey, A. (2010) 'Higher Education in the Age of Austerity. Part Two: Shared Services, Outsourcing and Entrepreneurship'. Policy Exchange Research Note.

Maunter, G. (2005) 'The entrepreneurial university. A discursive profile of a higher education profile'. *Critical Discourse Studies*, 2(2), pp. 95–120.

McAuley, D., Rahemtulla, H., Goulding, J. and Souch, C. (2012) 'How Open Data, Data Literacy and Linked Data will Revolutionise Higher Education' in Coiffait, L. and Hill, J. (eds) *Blue Skies: New Thinking about the Future of Higher Education in the Asia Pacific Region.* Pearson, Hong Kong, pp. 88–93. Available at: http://pearsonblueskies.com/category/editions/2012-asia-pacific/.

McInnis, C. (2001) 'Promoting academic expertise and authority in an entrepreneurial culture'. *Higher Education Management*, 13(2), pp 45–57.

Mendes, T., Estabrook, L., Magelli, P., and Conlin, K. (2006) 'How Academics Really View Entrepreneurship and Entrepreneurial Behavior: A Study of 2,000 Faculty, 10,000 Graduate Students and 100 Academic Administrators at the University of Illinois at Urbana-Champaign'. University of Illinois, USA.

Miclea, M. (2004) '"Learning to do" as a pillar of education and its links to entrepreneurial studies in higher education: European contexts and approaches'. *Higher Education in Europe*, 29(2), pp. 221–31.

Middlehurst, R. and Woodfield, S. (2007) 'Responding to the Internationalisation Agenda: Implications for Institutional Strategy'. Research Report 05/06. Higher Education Academy UK.

Miller, M.T. and Katz, M. (2004) 'Effective Shared Governance: Academic Governance as a Win-Win Proposition' in *The NEA 2004 Almanac of Higher Education*. NEA, Washington, DC.

Mittelstädt, A. and Cerri, F. (2008) 'Fostering Entrepreneurship for Innovation'. OECD Science, Technology and Industry Working Papers, 2008/5. OECD publishing, 10.1787/227624785873.

Mohrman, K., Wanhua, M. and Baker, D. (2008) 'The research university in transition: The emerging global model'. *Higher Education Policy*, 21, pp. 5–27.

Moore, M.H. (1995) *Creating Public Value: Strategic Management in Government.* Harvard University Press, Cambridge, MA.

Mora, J.-G. and Vieira, M.-J. (2009) 'Governance, Organisation Change and Entrepreneurialism: Is there a Connection' in Shattock, M. (ed.) *Entrepreneurialism in*

Universities and the Knowledge Economy. Open University Press, Maidenhead, UK and New York, NY, pp. 74–100.

Moreland, N. (2007) 'Entrepreneurship and higher education: An employability perspective'. Higher Education Academy, Heslington, UK.

Moses, I. (2005) 'Institutional Autonomy Revisited: Autonomy Justified and Accounted'. *Higher Education Policy*, 19, pp. 411–31.

National Academy of Science USA (2005) 'Facilitating Interdisciplinary Research'. National Academies Press, Washington, DC.

Navarro, J.R. and Gallardo, F.O. (2003) 'A model of strategic change: Universities and dynamic capabilities'. *Higher Education Policy*, 16(2), pp. 199–212.

Neubauer, D.E. (ed.) (2011) *The Emergent Knowledge Society and the Future of Higher Education: Asian Perspectives*. Routledge, London.

Newman, J.H. (1852 [1917]) 'Knowledge, Learning and Professional Skill' in Alden, R.M. (ed.) *Readings in English Prose of the Nineteenth Century*. Houghton Mifflin Company, Cambridge, MA, pp. 418–39.

Nikolai, R. and Ebner, C. (2011) 'The Links between Vocational Training and Higher Education in Switzerland, Austria and Germany'. Presentation at the ECER Conference in Berlin.

NIRAS Consultants (2007) 'Survey of Entrepreneurship in Higher Education in Europe', FORA, ECON Pöyry.

Nivesjö, S., Winzer, R. and Brassell, L. (2011) 'Strategies and Trends in the Internationalisation of Universities'. Policy Report 1994 Group's Strategic Planning and Resources Policy Group.

Noir sur Blanc (1999) 'Survey. Internationalisation of Universities' Development Strategies'. Noir sur Blanc, Paris.

Nowotny, H., Scott, P., Gibbons, M. (2003) '"Mode 2" Revisited: The New Production of Knowledge'. *Minerva*, 41, pp. 179–94.

Oberman Peterka, S. (2011) 'Entrepreneurial university as the most important leverage in achieving knowledge-based society'. pp. 547–67 in Proceedings of 9th International Conference: 'Challenges of Europe: Growth and Competitiveness – Reversing the Trends'. University of Split, Croatia.

Observatory on Borderless Education (2011) 'Perspectives on the Future'. Available at: www.obhe.org.

OECD (2001) *Higher Education Management: Journal of the Programme on Institutional Management in Higher Education*, 13(2), Special Issue: Education and Skills. OECD Publishing, Paris.

OECD (2003) 'Changing Patterns of Governance in Higher Education' in *Education Policy Analysis*, 2003 Edition, OECD Publishing, Paris, pp. 59–78.

OECD (2004) 'The Internationalisation of Higher Education'. Policy Brief, August, OECD Publishing.

OECD (2005) *Higher Education Management and Policy*, 17(3), Special Issue: Entrepreneurship. OECD Publishing, Paris. In particular 'Entrepreneurial Universities and the Development of Regional Societies: A Spatial View of the Europe of Knowledge', pp. 59–86.

OECD (2008) 'Innovating to Learn, Learning to Innovate'. Centre for Educational Research and Innovation (CERI), OECD Publishing, Paris.

OECD (2009) 'Universities, Innovation and Entrepreneurship: Criteria and Examples of Good Practice'. OECD, Paris.

OECD (2010) 'The Nature of Learning: Using Research to Inspire Practice'. Centre for Educational Research and Innovation (CERI), OECD Publishing, Paris.

OECD (2011) 'Partnership for Success in Fostering Graduate Entrepreneurship'. OECD Local Economic and Employment Development (LEED) Programme.

Olssen, M. and Peters, M.A. (2005) 'Neoliberalism, higher education and the knowledge economy: From the free market to knowledge capitalism'. *Journal of Education Policy*. 20(3), pp. 313–45.

O'Shea, R.P., Allen, T.J., Morse, K.P., O'Gorman, C. and Roche, F. (2007) 'Delineating the anatomy of an entrepreneurial university: the Massachusetts Institute of Technology experience'. *R&D Management*, 37(1), pp. 1–16.

Owen-Smith, J., Riccaboni, M., Pammolli, F. and Powell, W.W. (2002) 'A comparison of U.S. and European university-industry relations in the life sciences'. *Management Science*, 48(1), pp. 24–43.

Pan, S.-Y. (2007) 'Intertwining of academia and officialdom and university autonomy: Experience from Tsinghua University in China'. *Higher Education Policy*, 20(2), pp. 121–44.

Papayannakis, L., Kastelli, I., Damigos, D. and Mavrotas, G. (2008) 'Fostering entrepreneurship education in engineering curricula in Greece. Experiences and challenges for a technical university'. *European Journal of Engineering Education*, 33(2), pp. 199–210.

Pavlin, S. (2012) 'Employability of Graduates and Higher Education Management Systems'. (Final report of DEHEMS project) Faculty of Social Sciences, University of Ljubljana.

Penaluna, K., Penaluna, A. and Jones, C. (2012) 'The context of enterprise education: Insights into current practices'. *Industry and Higher Education*, 26(3), pp. 163–75.

Pilbeam, C. (2008) 'Designing an entrepreneurial university in an institutional setting'. *Higher Education Policy*, 21(3), pp. 393–404.

Politis, D. (2005) 'The process of entrepreneurial learning: A conceptual framework'. *Entrepreneurship Theory and Practice*, 29, pp. 399–424.

Potter, J. (2008) 'Entrepreneurship and Higher Education'. OECD Local Economic and Employment Development (LEED) Programme.

Pratt, J. (2001) 'Changing patterns of diversity in Europe. Lessons from an OECD study tour'. *Higher Education Management*, 13(2), pp. 93–105.

Rae, D. and Carswell, M. (2001) 'Towards a conceptual understanding of entrepreneurial learning'. *Journal of Small Business and Enterprise Development*, 8(2), pp. 150–158.

Rafferty, A.E., Jimmieson, N.L. and Armenakis, A.A. (2013) 'Change readiness. A multilevel review'. *Journal of Management*, 39(1), pp. 110–135.

Ranga, L.M. (2002) '"Entrepreneurial Universities" and the Impact of University-Industry Collaboration on Academic Research Performance and Management of Academic Research Groups'. Centre for Managerial Economics and Strategy, Catholic University of Leuven, Namsestraat 69, Leuven 3000, Belgium.

Roos, G., Fernstrom, F. and Gupta, O. (2005) 'National Innovation Systems: Finland, Sweden and Australia Compared. Learnings for Australia'. Report for the Australian Business Foundation. Intellectual Capital Service.

Ropke, J. (1998) 'The Entrepreneurial University. Innovation, Academic Knowledge Creation and Regional Development in a Globalized Economy'. Department of Economics, Philipps-Universität Marburg, Germany.

Sa, C.M. (2008) 'Interdisciplinary strategies in US research universities'. *Higher Education* 55, pp. 537–52.

Schein, E.H. (1992) *Organisational Culture and Leadership*. Jossey Bass Publishers, San Francisco, CA.

Schuetze, H.G. (2007) 'Research universities and the spectre of academic capitalism'. *Minerva*, 45, pp. 435–43.

Selwyn, N. (2012) 'Social Media in Higher Education' in *The Europa World of Learning 2012*, 62nd edition, Routledge, London, pp. 3–7. Available at: www.worldoflearning.com.

Senge, P.M. (1990) *The Fifth Discipline. The Art and Practice of the Learning Organization*. Random House, London.

Senges, M. (2007) 'Knowledge Entrepreneurship in Universities. Practice and Strategy in the case of Internet Based Innovation Appropriation', Doctoral Thesis. Universitat Oberta de Catalunya, Barcelona Spain.

Shane, S. (2004) 'Encouraging university entrepreneurship? The effect of the Bayh-Dole Act on university patenting in the United States'. *Journal of Business Venturing*, 19(2004), pp. 127–51.

Shattock, M. (ed.) (2009) *Entrepreneurialism in Universities and the Knowledge Economy*. Open University Press, Maidenhead, UK and New York, NY.

Shinn, T. (2002) 'The triple helix and new production of knowledge: Prepackaged thinking on science and technology'. *Social Studies of Science*, 32(4), pp. 599–614.

Slaughter, S. and Leslie, L.L. (1997) *Academic Capitalism: Politics, Policies and the Entrepreneurial University*. John Hopkins University Press, Baltimore, MD.

Smith, H.L. (2007) 'Universities, innovation, and territorial development: A review of the evidence'. *Environment and Planning C: Government and Policy*, 25(1), pp. 98–114.

Sporn, B. (1996) 'Managing university culture: An analysis of the relationship between institutional culture and management approaches'. *Higher Education*, 32(1), pp. 41–61.

Standard & Poor's Performance Evaluation Services (2008) 'Revenue Diversification and Sustainability: A Comparison of Trends in Public Higher Education in the UK and US'. Council for Industry and Higher Education, London.

Thorn, K. and Soo, M. (2006) 'Latin American Universities and the Third Mission. Trends, Challenges and Policy Options'. World Bank Policy Research Working Paper 4002, August.

Thorp, H. and Goldstein, B. (2010) *Engines of Innovation: The Entrepreneurial University in the 21st Century*. University of North Carolina Press, Chapel Hill, NC.

Toakley, A.R. (2004) 'Globalization, Sustainable Development and Universities'. *Higher Education Policy*, 17(3), pp. 311–24.

Todorovic, W.Z., McNaughton, R.B. and Guild, P.D. (2005) 'Making university departments more entrepreneurial. The perspective from within'. *International Journal of Entrepreneurship and Innovation*, 6(2), pp. 115–22.

UNESCO (2003) 'Internationalisation of Higher Education: Trends and Developments since 1998'. Meeting of Higher Education Partners, Background paper prepared by The International Association of Universities. UNESCO, Paris.

UNESCO (2004) 'Higher Education in a Globalized Society'. UNESCO Education Position Paper. UNESCO, Paris.

UNESCO (2007) 'Main Transformations, Challenges and Emerging Patterns in Higher Education Systems'. UNESCO Forum on Higher Education, Research and Knowledge Occasional Paper Series Paper no. 16. UNESCO, Paris.

University of Dar es Salaam (2007) 'Institutional Self-Assessment of the University's Mission in Relation to the Civic Role in and Social Responsibility to Society, with a Special Focus on Two Self-Initiated Global Projects'. An Institutional Assessment Report. Prepared for The Talloires Network.

US Department of Education (2006) 'A Test of leadership. Charting the Future of U.S. Higher Education. A Report of the Commission Appointed by Secretary of Education Margaret Spellings'. US Department of Education, Washington, D.C. Available at: www.ed.gov/about/bdscomm/list/hiedfuture/index.html.

Vaira, M. (2004) 'Globalization and higher education organizational change: A framework for analysis'. *Higher Education*, 48(4), pp. 483–510.

Volkmann, C. (2004) 'Entrepreneurial studies in higher education'. *Higher Education in Europe*, 29(2), pp. 177–85.

Vukasovic, M., Maasen, P., Nerand, M., Stensker, B., Pineiro, R. and Vabo, A. (eds) (2012) *Effects of Higher Education Reforms: Change Dynamics*. Sense Publishers, Rotterdam.

Watson, D. (2010) 'Universities' Engagement with Society' in Peterson, P., Baker, E. and McGaw, B. (eds) *The International Encyclopedia of Education,* 3rd Edition. Elsevier, Amsterdam.

Weerts, D.J. (2007) 'Toward an engagement model of institutional advancement at public colleges and universities'. *International Journal of Educational Advancement*, 7(2), pp. 79–103.

Whitehead, A.N. (1927) 'Universities and their Function'. Address to the American Association of the Collegiate Schools of Business.

Willets, D. (2013) 'Robins Revisited. Bigger and Better Higher Education'. Social Market Foundation, London, UK.

Williams, G. (2009) 'Finance and Entrepreneurial Activity in Higher Education in the Knowledge Society' in Shattock, M. (ed.) *Entrepreneurialism in Universities and the*

Knowledge Economy. Open University Press, Maidenhead, UK and New York, NY, pp. 9–33.

Williams, G. and Kitaev, I. (2005) 'Overview of national policy contexts for entrepreneurialism in higher education institutions'. *Higher Education Management and Policy*, 17(3), pp. 125–41.

Wissema, J.G. (2008) *Towards the Third Generation University: Managing the University in Transition.* Edward Elgar Publishing, Cheltenham, UK and Northampton, MA.

Wong, P.-K., Ho, Y.-P. and Singh, A. (2007) 'Towards an "entrepreneurial university" model to support knowledge-based economic development: The case of the National University of Singapore'. *World Development*, 35(6), pp. 941–58.

Wong, P.-K., Ho, Y.-P. and Low, P.-C. (2012) 'Global University Entrepreneurial Spirit Students' Survey: 2011 Singapore Report'. NUS Entrepreneurship Centre, University of Singapore.

Woollard, D., Zhang, M. and Jones, O. (2007) 'Academic enterprise and regional economic growth. Towards an enterprising university'. *Industry and Higher Education*, 21(6), pp. 387–403.

Ylinenpää, H. (2001) 'Science Parks, Clusters and Regional Development'. Luleå University of Technology, Department of Business Administration and Social Sciences, Division of Industrial Organization & Small Business Academy. Luleå University of Technology: AR 2001:48. Paper presented at 31st European Small Business Seminar in Dublin, Sept 12–14.

Zhou, C. (2008) 'Emergence of the entrepreneurial university in evolution of the triple helix'. *Journal of Technology Management in China*, 3(1), pp. 109–26.

PART VI

FUTURE DIRECTIONS

19. Breaking glass: towards a gendered analysis of entrepreneurial leadership*

Richard T. Harrison, Claire M. Leitch and Maura McAdam

INTRODUCTION

Glass, transparent yet impermeable, whether as ceiling (Morrison et al., 1987; Mattis, 2004) or walls (Wellington et al., 2003; Weidenfeller, 2012), is one of the most powerful and resonant metaphors of contemporary feminist discourse. Breaking glass encapsulates the call for action, the practice of critique against the orthodoxy, the overthrow of the structures and constraints that preclude gender – and other – equality in both leadership (Reger, 2007) and entrepreneurship. Within the emerging domain of entrepreneurial leadership research, our argument in this chapter is that gender issues have been rarely acknowledged. Our aim therefore is to highlight the role of gender in entrepreneurial leadership by building upon the more extensive gender debates in the entrepreneurship and leadership disciplines. In developing a research agenda for a gendered analysis of entrepreneurial leadership, we review the definition and conceptualisation of the term, before summarising the elements of a gendered perspective which highlights the embedded masculinity of the entrepreneurial leadership domain. Further, we follow Patterson et al.'s (2012) argument that due to this embedded masculinity, entrepreneurial leadership is gender blind, gender defensive and gender neutral: gender blind, in that mainstream management theory is more accurately labelled 'male stream', because it fails to recognise the relationship between management and gender (Wilson, 1996); gender neutral, in that 'the sex of the actor is irrelevant in how the behaviour is understood, perceived and experienced by leaders and followers' (Fletcher, 2004: 654); and gender defensive, in behaving in a way such as to protect gender identity (maleness and/or femaleness) (Goldberg, 1987).

It is important to challenge prevailing gendered assumptions and conceptions (Broadbridge and Simpson, 2011; Orser et al., 2011), 'to understand how gendered language has permeated constructions of entrepreneurial leadership providing a gender consciousness to this developing area' (Patterson et al., 2012: 396). In so doing, we make three contributions in this chapter. First, from an intellectual perspective, we demonstrate that the adoption of a gendered lens addresses issues concerning diversity, the generalisability of findings and the inclusivity of theories (Ayman and Korabik, 2010). Second, we highlight the danger that entrepreneurial leadership, like other new post-heroic models of leadership (which emphasise collaborative, relational and interdependent behaviours), may be co-opted into the mainstream discourse due to an incongruence with the prevailing individualistic, meritocratic perspective which underpins traditional approaches (Fletcher, 2004; Collinson, 2005). Third, in practical terms, we illustrate that this understanding of how women experience entrepreneurial leadership can inform the design and delivery of initiatives to support the development of female entrepreneurial leaders (Eagly et al., 2003).

In the remainder of this chapter, we review the entrepreneurial leadership literature, summarise key themes in the gendered analysis of leadership not yet acknowledged in the entrepreneurship-based literature, and develop a research agenda for the gendered analysis of the rapidly expanding interface arena between leadership and entrepreneurship.

ENTREPRENEURIAL LEADERSHIP

Entrepreneurial leadership is at the nexus of entrepreneurship and leadership (Cogliser and Brigham, 2004). Even though 20 years has passed since commentators first advocated integrating the two domains (Miller and Friesen, 1984; Gartner et al., 1992; Harrison and Leitch, 1995; Patterson et al., 2012), entrepreneurial leadership remains atheoretical, and lacks definitional clarity and appropriate tools to assess its characteristics and behaviours (Leitch et al., 2013; Renko et al., 2015). There are two diametrically opposed views of what entrepreneurial leadership is. For Vecchio (2003) there is nothing distinctive about the small entrepreneurial firm context and it is appropriate to simply extend existing leadership research into entrepreneurship, whereby entrepreneurship is a subdomain of leadership. By contrast, Kuratko (2007) has suggested that leadership should be considered a constituent of entrepreneurship, in that an entrepreneurial mindset and behaviours are essential for effective leadership.

It is possible to categorise the entrepreneurial leadership literature along two dimensions. The first is the internal/external orientation, which distinguishes between studies focused on the traits, characteristics and behaviours of entrepreneurial leaders, and those focused on the broader external domains within which entrepreneurial leadership is observed. The second is the fragmented/integrated disciplinary basis, distinguishing between studies which are grounded explicitly in one or other disciplinary tradition, and those which emphasise a more integrated perspective. Following Roomi and Harrison (2011), we can map four different approaches to entrepreneurial leadership, while at the same time recognising that these categories are not completely mutually exclusive (Figure 19.1).

The first of these comprises a set of disciplinary studies, which are descriptive rather than analytical or explanatory, and look at entrepreneurship and leadership as separate constructs. Second, there is an extensive body of literature that builds on the psychological approach to entrepreneurship, focusing in particular on the traits and behaviours of 'entrepreneurial leaders'. Moving towards a more integrated disciplinary basis for entrepreneurial leadership research, two closely related themes can be identified. The first of these is the contextual approach, which looks more at the process through which entrepreneurial leadership develops and at the circumstances associated with its emergence. The second is the holistic approach, which focuses more on the internal, intrinsic elements of the phenomenon.

For us, as in entrepreneurship more generally, it is impossible to discuss entrepreneurial leadership separate from the context within which it is demonstrated (Welter, 2011). If psychological entrepreneurial leadership research asks, 'Who are you?' (traits) and disciplinary research asks, 'What do you do?' (behaviours), contextual research asks, 'Where do you do it?' and recognises that the nature of entrepreneurial leadership itself is constituted by, not independent of, its context (Due Billing and Alvesson, 2000; Leitch et al., 2013). This diversity of approaches is reflected in the absence of any agreed definition of entrepreneurial leadership (Table 19.1). We define entrepreneurial leadership as 'the leadership role performed in entrepreneurial ventures, rather than in the more general sense of an entrepreneurial style of leadership' (Leitch et al., 2013: 2). This definition aligns with others, the majority of which explicitly or implicitly identify that there is something distinctive about the entrepreneurial context, in terms of ambiguity, risk, uncertainty, innovation, environmental dynamism and volatility, organisational size and newness (Chen, 2007; Surie and Ashley, 2007; Autio, 2013).

Across all of these definitions of entrepreneurial leadership, the one common theme that unites them is the absence of a substantive engagement with gender. Accordingly, in the remainder of this chapter we focus on how approaches to the analysis and practice of leadership in an entrepreneurial domain can be developed in light of contemporary discussions of the role of gender in leadership research.

ORIENTATION

Internal

HOLISTIC
(Yang, 2008; Nahavandi, 2002; Surie and Ashley, 2007; Robinson et al., 2006; Kuratko, 2007; Greenberg et al., 2011; Thornberry, 2006)

DISCIPLINARY
BASIS

Integrated

CONTEXTUAL
(Antonakis and Autio, 2007; Eyal and Kark, 2004; Swiercz and Lydon, 2002; Chen, 2007; Harrison and Leitch, 1995; Henry et al., 2003; Autio, 2013; Cohen, 2004; Gibb, 1993; Jensen and Luthans, 2006; Leitch et al., 2013)

PSYCHOLOGICAL
(Brockhaus, 1982; Nicholson, 1988; Ensley et al., 2006a; Ensley et al., 2006b; Gupta et al., 2004; Antonakis and Autio, 2007; Renko et al., 2015; Covin and Slevin, 2002; Daily et al., 2002)

Fragmented

DISCIPLINARY
(Cogliser and Brigham, 2004; Fernald et al., 2005; Vecchio, 2003; Renko et al., 2015; Roomi and Harrison, 2011; Patterson et al., 2012; Miller and Friesen, 1984; Gartner et al., 1992; Ireland et al., 2003; Baum et al., 1998; Cunningham and Lischeron, 1991; Darling et al., 2007)

External

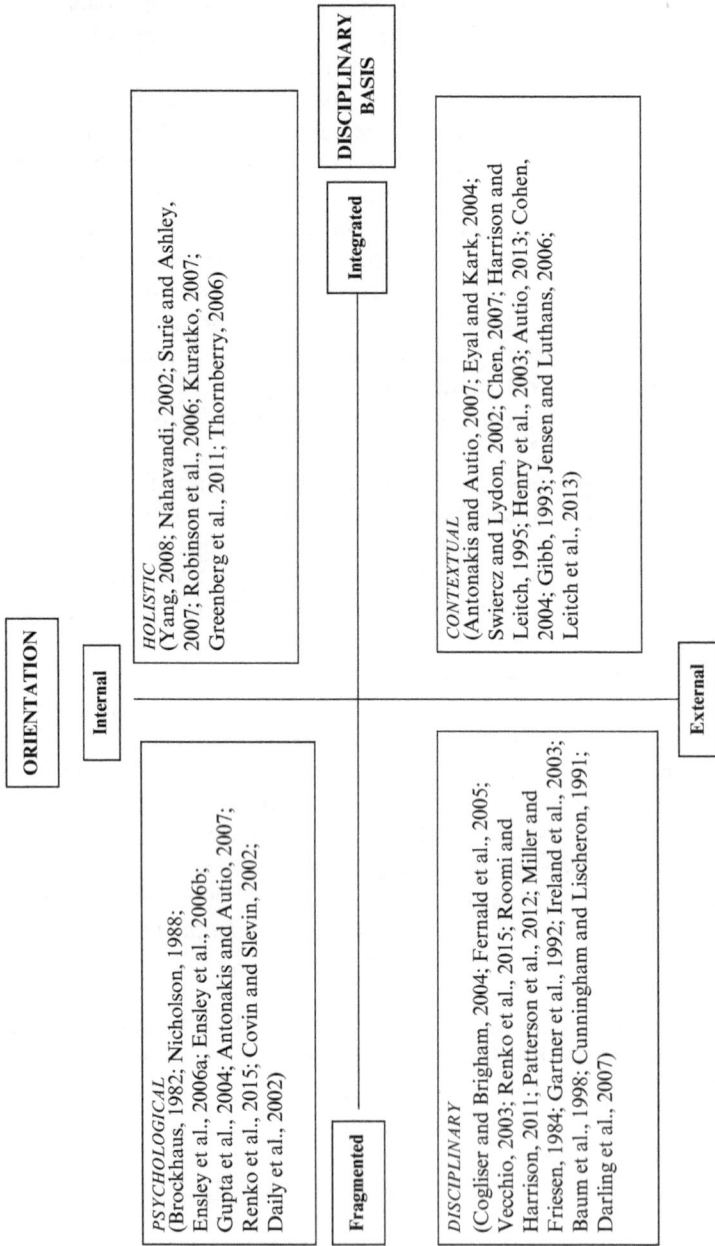

Source: Adapted and extended from Roomi and Harrison (2011).

Figure 19.1   A typology of the literature on entrepreneurial leadership

Table 19.1   Evolving definitions of entrepreneurial leadership

Authors	Definitions
Cunningham and Lischeron (1991)	Entrepreneurial leadership involves setting clear goals, creating opportunities, empowering people, preserving organizational intimacy, and developing a human resource system.
Cogliser and Brigham (2004)	Entrepreneurial leadership involve vision, influence (on both followers and a wider constituency) leadership of innovative and creative planning and planning.
Ireland et al. (2003)	Entrepreneurial leadership entails the ability to influence others to manage resources strategically in order to emphasize both opportunity-seeking and advantage-seeking behaviours.
Gupta et al. (2004)	Leadership that creates visionary scenarios that are used to assemble and mobilize a supporting cast of participants who become committed by the vision to the discovery and exploitation of strategic value creation.
Thornberry (2006)	Leadership requires passion, vision, focus, and the ability to inspire others. Entrepreneurial leadership requires all these, plus a mind-set and skill set that helps entrepreneurial leaders identify, develop, and capture new business opportunities.
Antonakis and Autio (2007)	Gives explicit consideration to the context as a mediator between entrepreneurial leadership behaviours and task entrepreneurial task outcomes.
Chen (2007)	Greater response to new market opportunities through new business creation.
Kuratko (2007)	Entrepreneurial leadership is a unique concept combining the identification of opportunities, risk taking beyond security and being resolute enough to follow through.
Darling et al. (2007)	Attention through vision, meaning through communication and trust through positioning, confidence through respect.
Surie and Ashley (2007)	Leadership capable of sustaining innovation and adaptation in high velocity and uncertain environments.
Roomi and Harrison (2011)	Entrepreneurial leadership is a fusion of two constructs; having and communicating the vision to engage teams to identify, develop and take advantage of opportunity in order to gain competitive advantage.
Greenberg et al. (2011)	Entrepreneurial leaders are individuals who, through an understanding of themselves and the contexts in which they work, act on and shape opportunities that create value for their organizations, their stakeholders, and the wider society.
Leitch et al. (2013)	Entrepreneurial leadership is the leadership role performed in entrepreneurial ventures, rather than in the more general sense of an entrepreneurial style of leadership.
Renko et al. (2015)	Entrepreneurial leadership entails influencing and directing the performance of group members toward the achievement of organisational goals that involve recognizing and exploring entrepreneurial opportunities.

Source: Adapted from Renko et al. (2015: 41).

LEADERSHIP, MASCULINITY AND FEMININITY

We view gender as socially constructed and actively produced through participation in social activities such as entrepreneurial leadership (Patterson et al., 2012). Nevertheless, reflecting broader debates such as those within critical management studies, we recognise that gender stands as a proxy for femininity (Ashcraft, 2011). As Kelan (2009: 166) remarks, gender 'sticks' to women in a very specific, and indeed gendered, manner supporting the notion that masculinity is the default, needing no explanation or rational defence. Oakley (1972) is credited with first drawing distinctions between sex as a biological category, and gender as a social construction of feminine and masculine characteristics which are then crudely mapped onto males and females (Holmes, 2007). Through the separation of biological sex and socially ascribed gendered roles, Oakley (1972) demonstrated how the latter acts as a socio-economic valorisation process which devalues characteristics associated with the feminine. Accordingly, those associated with masculinity are afforded greater respect, legitimacy and authority, while those associated with femininity are subordinated within this hierarchical binary (Hirdman, 2001; Bowden and Mummery, 2009).

However, although there is no essential femininity or masculinity, gender makes us culturally intelligible (Butler, 2004; Holmes, 2007). As social actors we make sense of others in terms of their ascribed gender. Thus, the notion of gendered identities is critical in order to understand the ontology of the constructed subject positions ascribed to men and women through ascribed masculinities and femininities (Bowden and Mummery, 2009), and this provides the basis for a gendered analysis of entrepreneurial leadership. In recent years, the field of leadership has shifted focus in three significant ways, as it has moved from a positivist or post-positivist mindset emphasising command, control and hierarchy, towards newer models more reflective of the economic, demographic and competitive changes characterising the modern workplace (Kanter, 2001; Johanson, 2008). First, there has been a shift in interest away from the personal characteristics of the leader towards the role of leadership per se; from an individualised heroic conceptualisation of leadership towards leadership as a role incorporating interaction with the social and organisational context (Thorpe et al., 2009; Leitch et al., 2013). Second, there has been a shift from leadership as a set of individual traits, towards leadership as a collective social activity (Bolden, 2011). Third, there has been a shift away from leadership as generic, to a focus that recognises its diversity in terms of gender, ethnicity and situational context.

Given these shifts it is clear that organisations and practices built on 'a nineteenth-century mixture of beliefs from patriarchal visions of the world, militarism, theories of social Darwinism and the metaphor of the machine bequeathed by Newtonian physics' (Rao and Kelleher, 2000: 74–75) are no longer applicable. However, in practice it remains the case that the symbolic universe of masculinity (Patterson et al., 2012) has so significantly influenced the development of leadership that it is difficult to separate leadership and men (Eagly and Carli, 2007), to the extent that the language of masculinity and leadership are so intertwined that they have become synonymous (Hearn and Parkin, 1988; Schnurr, 2008). Our understandings of organisations, leaders and individual roles are grounded on gendered expectations (Patterson et al., 2012: 398), where masculinity and men are normalised (Calás and Smircich, 1996) and where women learn to become leaders against a male background (Elliott and Stead, 2008). Furthermore, the practice of leadership has been compounded by the fact that the majority of research has mainly tended to be conducted in the context of Western industrialised culture, which expounds these masculine ideals (Stelter, 2002; Elliott and Stead, 2008).

Gender, however, is neither fixed nor stable, but is constructed through daily interactions with others; as a result individuals learn how to play the part of man or woman depending on what a given context demands or what is considered appropriate (Goffman, 1987). As a result of this gender socialisation process, 'we learn what it means to be an adult human being within our society' (Holmes, 2007: 41). In fact, if an individual does not behave appropriately with regards to their gender, this may result in them being rejected or sanctioned (West and Zimmerman, 1987). Moreover, challenging gender conformity creates 'gender trouble' (Jagose, 1996; Roseneil, 2000), as disputing the alleged 'natural order' results in uncertainty and suspicion (Fiske, 1989; Keltner, 1995). There is considerable social, hetero-normative pressure to observe gender conformity and convention. So, despite the complexity of the debate surrounding articulations of gender, value-laden social assumptions actively shape normative behaviours and social expectations (McRobbie, 2009). Thus, women as a biological category are subordinated by gendered ascription (Holmes, 2007; Bowden and Mummery, 2009), but the manner in which such subordination is experienced and articulated is experienced in relation to, and in reflection of, particular socio-economic contexts.

As in entrepreneurship, the male/female and masculine/feminine dichotomy is evident, where the male or masculine is regarded as the universal, neutral subject against which the woman or female is judged (Ahl, 2006). From a role-congruity theory perspective, which considers how consistent behaviour is with socially accepted gender roles, this can clearly range from positive to negative assessments (Dahlvig and Longman, 2010). Indeed, much leadership research to date seems to have been 'constrained by its own fundamental dualism' (Bowring, 2004: 383), not only in employing the categories man/woman and masculine/feminine, but also because of the distinction drawn between leaders and followers. Such a perspective reinforces social relations based on hierarchy underpinned by 'a world view that sees power as a limited commodity, held by the few to control the behaviour of many' (Rao and Kelleher, 2000: 75). Nevertheless, there are growing arguments that, as far as the global professional elite are concerned, the 'fracturing of sisterhood' means that the highly educated professional minority now have careers increasingly like those of successful men (Wolf, 2013): the real divide is less one of gender and more a matter of education, profession and position. However, while new, post-heroic models of leadership emphasising a collaborative, relational process 'are often presented as gender and, to a lesser degree, power neutral', Fletcher (2004: 648) suggests instead that they can be considered to be 'rooted in a set of social relations in which doing gender, doing power and doing leadership are linked in complex ways'. In essence, as gender has visible and invisible components which can impact upon identity, group cohesion and interpersonal interactions as well as access to power and resources (Ayman and Korabik, 2010), it remains necessary to challenge the dominant, masculinised frameworks and power structures underpinning leadership research and practice (Chin, 2004).

Contemporaneous with the post-heroic models of leadership is the notion of feminine leadership, which emphasises apparently feminine attributes, attitudes and behaviours such as an interpersonal orientation, collaboration, empathy, kindness, and more participatory and relational leadership styles (Lipman-Blumen, 1996; Due Billing and Alvesson, 2000; Eagly, 2007; Goleman and Boyatzis, 2008; Mortimer, 2009; Hanold, 2013). Perhaps unsurprisingly, this has been defined in 'complementary and corresponding terms to masculinity' (Due Billing and Alvesson, 2000: 147). In part this challenge to contemporary leadership thinking reflects a postmodern sensibility to 'uncertainty, movement, multiplicity of meaning, fragmentation and indeterminancy' (Hatcher, 2003: 392), the very conditions held to justify the distinctiveness of entrepreneurial leadership. However, while an alternative to the prevailing perspective has been advanced, focusing solely on a feminist approach can continue to limit our understanding by potentially perpetuating a superficial analysis of leadership which reinforces dualisms and stereotypes. Indeed, despite the calls for or identification of the feminisation of leadership (Gerzema and D'Antonio, 2013; Wolf, 2013), 'leadership positions remain populated by white males and . . . leadership is predominantly tied to masculine attributes' (Hanold, 2013: 91–92). Instead, it would be more helpful to view feminine leadership as a 'critical concept' which acts as a foil to the dominant masculine way in which leadership is currently conceptualised (Due Billing and Alvesson, 2000: 155), permitting a more nuanced appreciation of a complex construct. Nevertheless, although masculine leadership has shown some signs of decline in recent years (Koenig et al., 2011), aspiring leaders still appear to hold feminine leadership skills in low esteem (Holt and Marques, 2012).

Accordingly, although contemporary leadership theory has progressed from traditional masculine constructs to draw upon femininities through, for example, self-awareness, empathy and capacity for listening (Fletcher, 2004), it fails to help move beyond dualistic thinking, leaving women leaders trapped within their sex role stereotype, reproducing the inequalities of the binary (Patterson et al., 2012). However, despite the rhetoric surrounding such new leadership styles, which have been around for nearly two decades, very few organisations actually use them; this is reflected in little or no change in the number of women in senior leadership positions. Indeed, the lack of fit (Heilman, 2001) and role incongruity (Eagly and Karau, 2002; Heilman and Eagly, 2008; Eagly and Chin, 2010) arising from this binary privileging the masculine continue to perpetuate diversity-based discrimination in leadership practice. Despite post-heroic leadership being presented as gender neutral, this is not the case (Fletcher, 2004). In other words, the so-called feminisation of leadership is reflected in increased attention to authenticity in its practice, to the social context in which it is exercised in terms of the inextricable engagement between leaders and followers, and to the elaboration of multiple models of post-heroic leadership.

EXTENDING THE GENDERED ANALYSIS OF ENTREPRENEURIAL LEADERSHIP

Gender in entrepreneurial leadership cannot be considered in isolation or as generic (Ashcraft, 2011), but sits as part of a wider discourse of diversity (Ayman and Korabik, 2010; Metcalfe and Woodhams, 2012). This debate introduces notions of intersectionality, which suggests that previous work has been embedded in generic racist and heteronormative assumptions that uncritically position gender subordination as universal and dominant within the hierarchy of disadvantageous social ascriptions. 'Intersectionality' as a term originated from the work of Crenshaw (1997), who criticised mainstream feminist discourse for being white in origin and association. Intersectionality continues to be at the centre of debates looking at power dynamics from the perspective that argues interdependence between intersecting inequalities of gender, race, sexuality, age, disability, social class, religion and nationality, in relation to subject positions and identities (Adib and Guerrier, 2003; Holvino, 2010).

In considering how to extend gender research in the emerging area of entrepreneurial leadership it is helpful to situate this in the context of the history of the discussion of gender in management theory more generally. This can be considered as a trajectory in which themes have risen to prominence and been supplanted by new emphases through the process of critique and reconstruction. Table 19.2 shows seven key themes in the evolution of theorising gender, feminism and diversity in management and organisation theory. As discussed above, much of the extant literature on entrepreneurial leadership is still set within the traditional gender-as-variable (GAV) approach. More recently there has been a growing recognition of the potential contribution of feminist theory-based analyses in the tradition of the gender and organisation theory theme, and of the importance of diversity in shaping individual entrepreneurial identities. However, as in entrepreneurship research more generally, there has to date been little engagement with the rest of these themes in the entrepreneurial leadership literature. In the remainder of this chapter we recommend a research agenda, at three levels of abstraction, for the gendered analysis of entrepreneurial leadership informed by these wider contemporary discussions. At the micro level, we build on current gender research on social constructionism, critical management studies and intersectionality to identify a number of issues which extend contemporary entrepreneurial leadership research. At the meso level, we apply the critical social science literature on men's studies and race studies to examine more comprehensively the implications of diversity for entrepreneurial leadership. Finally, at the macro level, we draw on contemporary debates in critical social science to identify three pillars that can provide a foundation for theoretically advancing the knowledge domain of entrepreneurial leadership research.

Micro Level: Social Constructionism

Arising out of the masculinity/femininity literature reviewed above there are three current topics in management and leadership that are not reflected in entrepreneurship. First, situated within the argument that the gender problem within organisations has been solved (Lewis and Simpson, 2011) (in)visibility refers to the revealing and concealing of gender. We can distinguish between surface (in)visibility, the exclusion or marginalisation due to belonging to a minority group; and deep (in)visibility, the ways in which power is maintained through in(visibility) and taken-for-granted male norms (Simpson and Lewis, 2005). Indeed, as we have already shown, masculinity is taken to be the normative standard, 'against which

Table 19.2   Themes in the treatment of gender in management theory and their application in entrepreneurial leadership

Theme	Description	Key references
Current approaches		
Women in management	Gender as a variable approach which is descriptive and reflects inequalities due to sex difference and gender stereotypes	Kanter (1977, 2001), Eagly (1987), Wajcman (1998)
Gender and organisation theory	A move away from biological essentialism to acknowledge gender as a socially constituted ongoing social process	Calás and Smircich (1992, 1996), Acker (1990, 1992), Gherardi (1995)
Diversity	Recognises that individual identities are shaped by a multitude of difference characteristics such as race, disability, culture, sexuality, class and location	Cox (1994), Kandola and Fullerton (1994), West and Zimmerman (1987)
Emerging approaches		
Micro Social constructionism and critical management studies	Exploring how gender relations and heteronormative sexuality, ethnicity and class relations intertwine in society's structural and institutional fabric	Alvesson (1998), Alvesson and Due Billing (1999), Calás and Smircich (1999), Crenshaw (1997), Puar (2005)
Meso A Men's studies	Focuses on the principles of hegemonic masculinity underpinning management and organisation theory and marginalises both women and men who do not meet this ideal	Collinson and Hearn (1994, 1996), Connell (1995), Martin (2001), Kerfoot and Knights (1993)
Meso B Race studies	Within the context of the civil rights movement challenges the predominance of neoliberal governance regimes	Ahmed (1998, 2000), Collins (1990), bell hooks (2000)
Macro Emerging research directions: post-colonialism, transnationalism, space and place	Based on critiques drawing on social theory and community development of the broader organisation processes and power relations in the development of global capitalism	Castells (2009), Escobar (1998, 1995), Featherstone (1990), Nader (1989), Spivak (1989)

Source: Based on Metcalfe and Woodhams (2012).

difference is constructed . . . [it] never has to speak its name, never has to acknowledge its role as an organising principle in social and cultural relations' (Lipsitz, cited in Lewis, 2006: 455). Failure to fit in with such norms results in the process of 'othering' (Hearn, 1996), and as 'other', women become visible in the workplace (Lewis and Simpson, 2011). Women in male-dominated domains are highly visible as a result of their gender (Stead, 2013) and are often awarded token status; however, they are frequently invisible with regard to the authority and credibility required by the position (Lewis and Simpson, 2011). In other words, concerns about such invisibility are grounded in lack of worth, reputation and credibility (Tyler and Cohen, 2010). Women entrepreneurial leaders have to straddle their visibility and invisibility (that is, their in-group/out-group status; Kanter, 1977) which can result in gender switching (Bruni and Gherardi, 2002) between a male and a female identity to advance their entrepreneurial leadership positions (Stead, 2013). If the behaviours associated with visibility reflect gender defensiveness, 'queen bee' syndrome is a quest for invisibility, where women seek to blend into the masculinised world (Lewis, 2006) and so distance themselves from any practices, especially feminine ones, that might exclude them (Lewis and Simpson, 2011).

Second, as women progress up the corporate ladder the barriers they encounter intensify relative to those faced by their male counterparts (Baxter and Wright, 2000). For example, the 'glass ceiling' refers to a metaphorical barrier encountered by suitably qualified women trying to advance within their chosen occupations (Gupta et al., 2008; Gupta et al., 2009). Though similar, the 'glass wall' refers to 'functional segregation that prevents women from obtaining line and general management experience' (Mattis, 2004: 159). So, instead of simply blocking potential ascent, the glass wall effect works laterally, preventing a woman from moving to a position that has a promotional ladder (Wellington et al., 2003; Weidenfeller, 2012). Several features have been attributed to the make-up of this metaphorical glass wall, with similar traits being found within the concept of the glass ceiling (Weidenfeller, 2012), including a gender pay gap, exclusion from networks and groups, and harassment within the workplace. Indeed both the glass ceiling and the glass wall are believed to be responsible for women's lack of advancement to senior leadership positions and their premature exit from organisations (Mattis, 2004), thus reducing organisations' ability to retain suitably qualified leaders. For the gendered analysis of entrepreneurial leadership this suggests that more attention needs to be paid to the career dynamics (in both organisational and entrepreneurial contexts) of women leaders as they seek to accumulate, or are prevented from accumulating, the human and social capital necessary for entrepreneurial leadership.

Third, there is a growing argument from individuals (male and female) in the workplace that they work in a gender-neutral environment, that they do not register gender and, accordingly, that they believe gender does not matter. However, there is emergent evidence of gender fatigue in the relations between individuals and their working environment: women, and indeed men, are tiring of constructing the workplace over and over again as gender neutral in spite of evidence that gender discrimination exists (Kelan, 2009). Despite the complexity of the debate surrounding articulations of gender, therefore, value-laden social assumptions based upon the binary divide actively shape normative behaviours (McRobbie, 2009). Indeed, there is an assumption that women have somehow reached a state of equality. Apart from the pay gap between men and women, it is argued, they are no longer discriminated against and hence women can be more like men in the workplace; that is, more competitive, individualistic in outlook, less concerned with caring for others and more concerned with the care of self (Powell et al., 2002; Eagly and Chin, 2010). One of the implications of this is that gender fatigue reinforces the perception that entrepreneurial leadership is predominately tied to masculine attributes (Fondas, 1997; Hearn, 2000; Guthey, 2001). As such, any attempt to activate 'cultural stereotypes inconsistent with widely accepted ideals of leadership . . . can undermine leadership opportunity . . . by eliciting doubts about stereotyped individuals' leadership abilities . . . [and] by making them personally anxious about confirming these doubts and, therefore, wary about taking on leadership roles' (Eagly and Chin, 2010: 218).

Meso Level: Diversity – Critical Men's Studies and Race and Ethnicity Studies

There has been increasing recognition, in the gender literature and elsewhere, of the need to acknowledge the implications of diversity for our understanding of leadership (Ayman and Korabik, 2010). While intersectionality is becoming more recognised in entrepreneurship, there is still little acknowledgement of how the markers of differences (Essers and Benschop, 2009) – such as ethnicity, religion, education, location – intersect with gender to limit women's engagement with entrepreneurial leadership. These markers represent the diverse contexts in which male privilege is and can be hidden and protected; an emerging research agenda, therefore, should address how gender power in these contexts is preserved and revealed through processes of conceiving, exposure and erasure (Fletcher, 2004; Patterson et al., 2012). Given recent calls for gender research in entrepreneurship to more specifically acknowledge masculinity (Jennings and Brush, 2013), this suggests that entrepreneurial leadership research should recognise that gender is not just something that sticks to women. In so doing, this will draw more explicitly on the critical men's studies literature that recognises that men were being ignored in social science and development debates (Kerfoot and Knights, 1993; Collinson and Hearn, 1994, 1996; Connell, 1995; Martin, 2001). Equally, the emergence of the critical turn in social sciences with respect to race studies and ethnicity points to additional research opportunities.

While entrepreneurship research more generally has a long tradition of research into ethnic entrepreneurship, as with much of the gender research discussed above, this has adopted an 'ethnicity as a variable' approach, where 'ethnic' becomes a marker to define and isolate a community for study (Ram and Jones, 2008). However, from an intersectionality perspective the social construction processes of gender are complex, multifaceted and heterogeneous and will vary by age, race, ethnicity, sex, life history, culture and location. Entrepreneurial leadership research that takes gender seriously, therefore, needs to take into consideration these changing contexts and changing perceptions of male and female, of masculinity and femininity, as these are not fixed temporally or spatially. Accordingly, researchers will have to address a fundamental limitation of entrepreneurship scholarship. James (2012) has recently argued that entrepreneurship scholars have a long history of approaching the phenomena through the lens of problems requiring solutions, and suggests that in the case of women's entrepreneurship this problem-oriented focus has stunted our understanding of the factors that contribute to the flourishing of women's entrepreneurial activity. Furthermore, this focus has emerged at the expense of alternative views of women's entrepreneurship and the insights these perspectives might offer (Calás et al., 2009).

Macro Level: Emerging Research Directions

We have already shown that there have been calls for entrepreneurial leadership to be based on a different business logic, maximising the common good and minimising social injustice (Greenberg et al., 2011). In responding to this call, and adopting a genuinely global perspective, entrepreneurial leadership research will need to move beyond the micro- and meso-level extensions that we have discussed and engage with the macro-level analysis of the structures producing inequality on the basis of difference. Given the marginalisation of gender and diversity in academic discourse, and the limitations of Western perspectives on gender and diversity in evaluating contemporary global, social and organisational change (Metcalfe and Woodhams, 2012: 124), a point hinted at, but not developed, by Hughes et al. (2012), it is necessary to develop a holistic interpretation of gender, diversity and difference based around the themes of social justice and inequality agendas as they play out in both the Global North and the Global South. Metcalfe and Woodhams (2012) do so by focusing on three areas – feminist post-colonial studies, transnationalism and the geographies of space and place – that have implications for theorising and analysis in diverse territories and with diverse populations. Each of these areas is concerned with 'critiques of broader organization processes and power relations in the development of contemporary global capitalism' (Metcalfe and Woodhams, 2012: 130): as well as social justice, rights and equality, they focus on understanding the relationship of the global to the local through multilayered social enquiry; they address the relationships of organisations from grassroots activism to international non-governmental organisations and transnational corporations; and they are concerned with the relations of power among these actors as they shape culture and identity.

For post-colonial scholars the key focus is on the interdisciplinary analysis of how processes of decolonisation have transformed and reconfigured the global social, economic, political and cultural world order (McEwan, 2001). Feminist post-colonial theory, in particular, has at its core the racialisation of mainstream feminist theory on the one hand, and the insertion of feminist concerns into the conceptualisation of colonialism and post-colonialism on the other (Lewis and Mills, 2003). In exploring the intersectionality of race and gender against the backdrop of challenges to Western ethnocentrism in research, policy and practice, feminist post-colonial theory develops a critique of the women of the 'other' (Nader, 1989; Hale, 2005). This raises two questions (Hale, 2005), both of which will shape the conduct of globally aware entrepreneurial leadership research: how does critique of the 'other' function as a process through which women are controlled by cultures and states? And how are masculine signifiers represented in ideas about the place of women versus men as a civilisation develops?

Transnationalism has become the focus of a significant literature in the social sciences (Vertovec, 2009). At its core it refers to the emergence of a new global space where individuals, groups, institutions, firms and states interact with each other, and where the cultural and political characteristics of societies defined at the level of the nation combine with emerging multinational or multi-level activities. In this focus on the multiple ties and interactions linking institutions and individuals across state borders, transnationalism complements intersectionality (Metcalfe and Woodhams, 2012). As such, it addresses social and economic restructuring, the production of hybrid dynamic cultures and identities, the growing power of global capital in shaping the macro and micro structures of organising, the role of voluntary organising and capacity-building in state development, and the variability of organisational and social identities across space and time (Vertovec, 2009). Within these emerging transnational spaces, multiple points of reference redefine the way in which people identify and do gender, and reinforce the relationships of gender, ethnicity, class, age, ability and skills and national or citizenship status. In so doing, we need to recognise the tension between the global, specifically the imposition of Western culture and capitalism, and the local, where there is scope for the emergence of new ways of doing gender in the context of entrepreneurial leadership.

Recent research in entrepreneurship is developing a sensitivity to the role that geography plays, both as a contextual space within which entrepreneurial activity takes place and as an influence on the nature, shape and extent of that activity (Aldrich, 2000; Welter, 2011; McCann and Oxley, 2012). In developing a research agenda for entrepreneurial leadership, and in particular for the role of gender in that, there is scope to incorporate insights from the analysis of the gendered geographies of space and place within which uneven patterns of development, opportunity and access to resources shape the choices and identity positions of individuals (Massey, 1994). If gender operates on different spatial scales and across transnational spaces, then the geographies of power, the countless processes of domination and resistance that are the myriad entanglements integral to the workings of power as it plays out in, across and through the many spaces of the world (Paddison et al., 2000: 1), constitute the various domains within which gendered entrepreneurial leadership can be observed. In essence, the 'geographies of power remind us of the need to consider space and place as signifiers in discriminatory regimes and consider conditions of post-modernity in diverse geographical territories' (Metcalfe and Woodhams, 2012: 134).

CONCLUSION

Entrepreneurial leadership is emerging as something distinctive, whether because of the contextual specificities of the exercise of leadership in new and small, rather than large, corporations, or in the light of the changing context within which all organisations and institutions find themselves, characterised by non-calculable uncertainty rather than measureable risk (Alvarez and Barney, 2005). While the topic is still evolving, there is growing agreement that given the disruptive conditions leaders now face, a new mindset for understanding leader and leadership development is required (Holzmer, 2013). For scholars approaching entrepreneurial leadership from a base in entrepreneurship, and with a particular interest in the development of a robust and nuanced analysis of the role of gender in entrepreneurial leadership, it is necessary to become more aware of the recent evolution of both gender-based research (Ahl, 2006) and leadership research in general (Harrison and Leitch, 1995; Antonakis and Autio, 2007). Doing so opens the opportunity to develop new research into gendered entrepreneurial leadership incorporating new frameworks and perspectives at the micro level (the (in)visibility issue, the role of glass walls, and the implications of individual and organisational gender fatigue), the meso level (the critical intersectional study of masculinities as a gendered experience, and of race and ethnicity) and the macro level (feminist postcolonialism, transnationalism, and the emerging and shifting geographies of power, space and place). Accordingly, this will provide the basis for the development of new ways to think about gender and entrepreneurial leadership, and through this to think more generally afresh about both leadership and entrepreneurship. This adoption of a gendered lens allows entrepreneurial leadership scholars to address wider issues concerning diversity, the generalisability of their findings and the inclusivity of the theories they develop.

As our thinking and conceptualisation develops, and in particular as we respond to the challenge of developing and implementing a research agenda sensitive to the issues of intersectionality with respect to gender as one of many interdependent bases for difference playing out in emerging transnational spaces and manifest in distinctively different ways across space and time, this will in turn pose challenges for how we approach the practical process of leadership development. It is increasingly clear that leaders require significant personal, especially psychological, development to develop and use more complex and inclusive worldviews (Torbert, 2004). As Holzmer (2013: 59) has commented, this development will only be possible to the extent that leaders, male and female, 'surrender traditional worldviews and deeply reflect on their beliefs about both leadership and themselves'. In so doing, this introspection can support a shift to new and more complex ways of thinking and to more inclusive and multi-perspective worldviews.

The challenge, for both research and practice, is to recognise that the nature and basis of leadership is changing, moving away from the recognised limitations of models viewing leaders as omniscient heroic (male) exemplars rooted in an industrial-era command and control mindset of heroic rationality (Crevani et al., 2007; Küpers and Weibler, 2008; Grint, 2010) to a broader, more complex and inclusive view where 'a new leadership paradigm seems to be emerging that is marked by an inexorable shift away from one-way, hierarchical, organization-centric communication toward two-way, network-centric, participatory and collaborative leadership styles' (McGonagill and Dörffer, 2010: 3; see also Mabey and Morrell, 2011). In responding to this so-called feminisation of leadership (Fletcher, 2004), the challenge for research and practice is to continue to avoid the dangers of adopting a stance which is gender blind, gender neutral and gender defensive, and to help leaders, women and men, 'walk on the path enlightening . . . walk on beyond the broken glass'.

NOTE

*   This chapter was previously published as Harrison, R.T., Leitch, C.M. and McAdam, M. (2015). 'Breaking glass: Towards a gendered analysis of entrepreneurial leadership'. *Journal of Small Business Management*, 53 (3), 693–713. Reproduced by permission of John Wiley and Sons. © John Wiley and Sons.

REFERENCES

Acker, J. (1990). 'Hierarchies, jobs, bodies: A theory of gendered organizations'. *Gender and Society*, 4, 139–58.
Acker, J. (1992). 'Gendering organizational theory'. In A.J. Mills and P. Tancred (eds), *Gendering Organizational Analysis* (pp. 248–60). London: SAGE.
Adib, A. and Guerrier, Y. (2003). 'The interlocking of gender with nationality, race, ethnicity and class: The narratives of women in hotel work'. *Gender Work and Organization*, 10 (4), 413–32.
Ahl, H.J. (2006). 'Why research on women entrepreneurs needs new directions'. *Entrepreneurship Theory and Practice*, 30 (5), 595–621.
Ahmed, S. (1998). *Differences that Matter: Feminist Theory and Postmodernism*. Cambridge: Cambridge University Press.
Ahmed, S. (2000). *Strange Encounters: Embodied Others in Post-coloniality*. London: Routledge.
Aldrich, H.E. (2000). 'Learning together: National differences in entrepreneurship research'. In D. Sexton and H. Landström (eds), *The Blackwell Handbook of Entrepreneurship* (pp. 5–25). London: Blackwell.
Alvarez, S.A. and Barney, J.B. (2005). 'How do entrepreneurs organize firms under conditions of uncertainty?'. *Journal of Management*, 31 (5), 776–93.
Alvesson, M. (1998). 'Gender relation and identity at work: a case study of masculinities and felinities in an advertising agency'. *Human Relations*, 51 (8), 969–1005.
Alvesson, M. and Due Billing, Y. (1999). *Kon och organisation* [Gender and organization]. Lund: Studentlitteratur.
Antonakis, J. and Autio, E. (2007). 'Entrepreneurship and leadership'. In J.R. Baum, M. Frese and R. Baron (eds), *The Psychology of Entrepreneurship* (pp.189–208). London: Routledge.
Ashcraft, K.L. (2011). 'Knowing work through the communication of difference: A revised agenda for difference studies'. In D.K. Mumby (ed.), *Reframing Difference in Organizational Communication Studies: Research, Pedagogy, Practice* (pp. 3–29). Thousand Oaks, CA: SAGE Publications.
Autio, E. (2013). 'Promoting leadership development in high-growth new ventures'. Discussion paper. Paris: OECD.

Ayman, R. and Korabik, K. (2010). 'Leadership: Why gender and culture matter'. *American Psychologist*, 65 (3), 157–70.

Baum, J.R., Locke, E.A. and Kirkpatrick, S.A. (1998). 'Longitudinal study of the relation of vision and vision communication to venture growth'. *Journal of Applied Psychology*, 83, 43–54.

Baxter, J. and Wright, E.O. (2000). 'The glass ceiling hypothesis: A comparative study of the United States, Sweden and Australia'. *Gender and Society*, 14 (2), 275–94.

bell hooks (2000). *Feminist Theory: From Margin to Center*. Cambridge, MA: South End Press.

Bolden, R. (2011). 'Distributed leadership in organizations: A review of theory and research'. *International Journal of Management Reviews*, 13, 251–69.

Bowden, P. and Mummery, J. (2009). *Understanding Feminism*. New York, NY: Acumen.

Bowring, M.A. (2004). 'Resistance is *not* futile: Liberating Captain Janeway from the masculine–feminine dualism of leadership'. *Gender, Work and Organization*, 11 (4), 381–405.

Broadbridge, R. and Simpson, R. (2011). '25 years on: reflecting the past and looking to the future in gender and management research'. *British Journal of Management*, 22, 470–483.

Brockhaus, R.H. (1982). 'The psychology of an entrepreneur'. In C. Kent, D. Sexton and K. Vesper (eds), *Encyclopaedia of Entrepreneurship* (pp. 39–56). Englewood Cliffs, NJ: Prentice Hall.

Bruni, A. and Gherardi, S. (2002). 'Omega's story: The heterogeneous engineering of a gendered professional self'. In M.D. Dent and S. Whitehead (eds), *Managing Professional Identities: Knowledge, Performativity and the 'New' Professional* (pp. 174–201). London: Routledge.

Butler, J. (2004). *Undoing Gender*. London: Routledge.

Calás, M. and Smircich, L. (1992). 'Using the F word: Feminist theories and the social consequences of organisational research'. In A.J. Mills and P. Trancred (eds), *Gendering Organizational Analysis* (pp. 222–32). Newbury Park, CA: SAGE.

Calás, M. and Smircich, L. (1996). 'From the woman's point of view: Feminist approaches to organization studies'. In S. Clegg, C. Hardy and W.L. Nord (eds), *Handbook of Organization Studies* (pp. 218–57). London and Thousand Oaks, CA: SAGE.

Calás, M. and Smircich, L. (1999). 'Past postmodernism? Reflections and tentative directions'. *Academy of Management Review*, 24, 649–71.

Calás, M., Smircich, L. and Bourne, K.A. (2009). 'Extending the boundaries: Reframing "entrepreneurship as social change" through feminist perspectives'. *Academy of Management Review*, 34 (4), 552–69.

Castells, M. (2009). *Communication Power*. Oxford: Oxford University Press.

Chen, M.H. (2007). 'Entrepreneurial leadership and new ventures: Creativity in entrepreneurial teams'. *Creativity and Innovation Management*, 16 (3), 239–49.

Chin, J.L. (2004). 'Feminist leadership: Feminist visions and diverse voices'. *Psychology of Women Quarterly*, 28, 1–8.

Cogliser, C.C. and Brigham, K.H. (2004). 'The intersection of leadership and entrepreneurship: Mutual lessons to be learned'. *Leadership Quarterly*, 15, 771–9.

Cohen, A.R. (2004). 'Building a company of leaders'. *Leader to Leader*, 34, 16–20.

Collins, P. (1990). *Black Feminist Thought: Knowledge, Consciousness and the Politics of Empowerment*. Boston, MA: Unwin Hyman.

Collinson, D. (2005). 'Dialectics of leadership'. *Human Relations*, 58, 1419–42.

Collinson, D.L. and Hearn, J. (1994). 'Naming men as men: Implications for work, organization and management'. *Gender, Work and Organization*, 1, 2–22.

Collinson, D.L. and Hearn, J. (1996). *Men as Managers, Managers as Men: Critical Perspectives on Men, Masculinities and Management*. London: SAGE Publications.

Connell, R. (1995). *Masculinities*. Berkeley, CA: University of California Press.

Covin, J.G. and Slevin, D.P. (2002). *The Entrepreneurial Imperatives of Strategic Leadership*. Oxford: Blackwell.

Cox, T. (1994). *Cultural Diversity in Organizations: Theory, Research and Practice*. San Francisco, CA: Berrett-Koehler.

Crenshaw, K. (1997). 'Intersectionality and identity politics: Learning from violence against women of colour'. In M. Lyndon Shanaey and U. Narayan (eds), *Reconstructing Political Identity* (pp. 178–93). University Park, PA: Pennsylvania State University Press.

Crevani, L. Lindgren, M. and Packendorff, J. (2007). 'Shared leadership: A post-heroic perspective on leadership as a collective construction'. *International Journal of Leadership Studies*, 3, 40–67.

Cunningham, J.B. and Lischeron, J. (1991). 'Defining entrepreneurship'. *Journal of Small Business Management*, 29 (1), 45–62.

Dahlvig, J.E. and Longman, K.A. (2010). 'Women's leadership development: A study of defining moments'. *Christian Higher Education*, 9 (3), 238–58.

Daily, C.M., McDougall, P.P. and Covin, J.G. (2002). 'Governance and strategic leadership in entrepreneurial firms'. *Journal of Management*, 28 (3), 387–412.

Darling, J., Gabrielsson, M. and Seristo, H. (2007). 'Enhancing contemporary entrepreneurship: A focus on management leadership'. *European Business Review*, 19 (1), 4–21.

Due Billing, Y. and Alvesson, M. (2000). 'Questioning the notion of feminine leadership: A critical perspective on the gender labelling of leadership'. *Gender, Work and Organization*, 7 (3), 144–57.

Eagly, A. (1987). *Sex Differences in Social Behaviour: A Social Role Interpretation*. Hove: Psychology Press.

Eagly, A.H. (2005). 'Achieving relational authenticity in leadership: Does gender matter?'. *Leadership Quarterly*, 16, 459–74.

Eagly, A.H. (2007). 'Female leadership advantage and disadvantage: Resolving the contradictions'. *Psychology of Women Quarterly*, 31, 1–12.

Eagly, A.H. and Carli, L.L. (2007). *Through the Labyrinth: The Truth about How Women Become Leaders*. Boston, MA: Harvard University Press.

Eagly, A.H. and Chin, J. (2010). 'Diversity and leadership in a changing world'. *American Psychologist*, 63, 216–24.

Eagly, A.H. and Karau, S.J. (2002). 'Role congruity theory of prejudice toward female leaders'. *Psychological Review*, 109, 573–98.

Eagly, A.H., Johannesen-Schmidt, M.C. and van Engen, M.C. (2003). 'Transformational, transactional and laissez-faire leadership styles: A meta-analysis comparing women and men'. *Psychological Bulletin*, 129, 569–91.

Elliott, C. and Stead, V. (2008). 'Learning for leading women's experience: Towards a sociological understanding'. *Leadership*, 4 (2), 159–80.

Ensley, M.D., Hmieleski, K.M. and Pearce, C.L. (2006a). 'The importance of vertical and shared leadership within new venture top management teams'. *Leadership Quarterly*, 17 (3), 217–31.

Ensley, M.D., Pearce, C.L. and Hmieleski, K.M. (2006b). 'The moderating effect of environmental dynamism on the relationship between entrepreneur leadership behaviour and new venture performance'. *Journal of Business Venturing*, 21 (2), 243–63.

Escobar, A. (1988). 'Power and visibility: The invention and management of development in the Third World'. *Cultural Anthropology*, 4, 428–43.

Escobar, A. (1995). 'Imagining a post-development era'. In Crush, J. (ed.), *Power of Development* (pp. 211–27). London: Routledge.

Essers, C. and Benschop, Y. (2009). 'Muslim businesswomen doing boundary work: The negotiation of Islam, gender and ethnicity within entrepreneurial context'. *Human Relations*, 62 (3), 403–23.

Eyal, O. and Kark, R. (2004). 'How do transformational leaders transform organisations? A study of the relationship between leadership and entrepreneurship'. *Leadership and Policy in Schools*, 3 (3), 211–36.

Featherstone, M. (1990). *Global Culture: Nationalism, Globalization, and Modernity*. London: Sage.

Fernald, L., Solomon, G. and Tarabishy, A. (2005). 'A new paradigm: Entrepreneurial leadership'. *Southern Business Review*, 30 (2), 1–10.

Fiske, S.T. (1989). 'Examining the role of intent: Toward understanding its role in stereotyping and prejudice'. In J.S. Uleman and J.A. Bargh (eds), *Unintended Thought* (pp. 253–86). New York, NY: Guilford.

Fletcher, J. (2004). 'The paradox of post-heroic leadership: An essay on gender, power and transformational change'. *Leadership Quarterly*, 15, 647–61.

Fondas, N. (1997). 'Feminization unveiled: Management qualities in contemporary writings'. *Academy of Management Review*, 22, 257–83.

Gartner, W.B., Bird, B.J. and Starr, J.A. (1992). 'Acting as if: Differentiating entrepreneurial from organizational behavior'. *Entrepreneurship, Theory and Practice*, 16 (3), 13–31.

Gerzema, J. and D'Antonio, M. (2013). *The Athena Doctrine: How Women (And the Men Who Think Like Them) Will Rule the Future.* San Francisco, CA: Jossey-Bass.

Gherardi, S. (1995). *Gender, Symbolism and Organizational Cultures.* London: SAGE Publications.

Gibb, A. (1993). 'Enterprise culture and education: Understanding enterprise education and its links with small business, entrepreneurship and wider educational goals'. *International Small Business Journal*, 11 (3), 11–34.

Goffman, E. (1987). *Gender Advertisements.* New York, NY: Harper & Row.

Goldberg, H. (1987). *The Inner Male: Overcoming Roadblocks to Intimacy.* Gretna, LA: Wellness Institute.

Goleman, D. and Boyatzis, R. (2008). 'Social intelligence and the biology of leadership'. *Harvard Business Review*, September, 74–81.

Greenberg, D., McKone-Sweet, K. and Wilson, H.J. (2011). *The New Entrepreneurial Leaders: Developing Leaders who Shape Social and Economic Opportunity.* San Francisco, CA: Berrett-Koehler.

Grint, K. (2010). 'The sacred in leadership: Separation, sacrifice and silence'. *Organization Studies*, 31, 89–107.

Gupta, V., McMillan, I. and Surie, G. (2004). 'Entrepreneurial leadership: Developing and measuring a cross-cultural construct'. *Journal of Business Venturing*, 19 (92), 241–60.

Gupta, V.K., Turban, D.B. and Bhawe, N.M. (2008). 'The effect of gender stereotype activation on entrepreneurial intentions'. *Journal of Applied Psychology*, 93 (5), 1053–61.

Gupta, V.K., Turban, D.B., Wasti, S.A. and Sikdar, A. (2009). 'The role of gender types in perceptions of entrepreneurs and intentions to become an entrepreneur'. *Entrepreneurship Theory and Practice*, 33 (2), 397–417.

Guthey, E. (2001). 'Ted Turner's corporate cross-dressing and the shifting images of American business leadership'. *International Journal of Business History*, 2, 111–42.

Hale, S. (2005). 'Transnational gender studies and the mitigating concept of gender in the Middle East and North Africa'. *Cultural Dynamics*, 21, 133–52.

Hanold, M. (2013). '(De/Re)constructing leading bodies: Developing critical attitudes and somaesthetic practices'. In Melina, L.R., Burgess, G.J., Falkman, L.L. and Marturano, A. (eds), *The Embodiment of Leadership* (pp. 89–107). San Francisco, CA: Jossey-Bass.

Harrison, R. and Leitch, C. (1995). 'Entrepreneurship and leadership: The implications for education and development'. *Entrepreneurship and Regional Development*, 6, 112–25.

Hatcher, C. (2003). 'Refashioning a passionate manager: Gender at work'. *Gender, Work and Organization*, 10, 391–412.

Hearn, J. (1996). 'Deconstructing the dominant: Making the one(s) the other(s)'. *Organization*, 3 (4), 611–26.

Hearn, J. (2000). 'On the complexity of feminist intervention in organization'. *Organization*, 7, 609–24.

Hearn, J. and Parkin, P.W. (1988). 'Women, men and leadership: A critical review of assumptions, practices and change in industrialized nations'. In N. Alder and D. Izrali (eds), *Women in Management Worldwide* (pp. 17–40). Armonk, NY: M.E. Sharpe.

Heilman, M.E. (2001). 'Description and prescription: How gender stereotypes prevent women's ascent up the organizational ladder'. *Journal of Social Issues*, 57, 657–74.

Heilman, M.E. and Eagly, A.H. (2008). 'Gender stereotypes are alive, well, and busy producing workplace discrimination'. *Industrial and Organizational Psychology*, 1, 393–8.

Henry, C., Hill, F.M. and Leitch, C.M. (2003). *Entrepreneurship Education and Training*. Aldershot: Ashgate Publishing.
Hirdman, Y. (2001). *Genus – om det stabilas foranderliga*. Stockholm: Liber AB.
Holmes, M. (2007). *What is Gender?*. London: SAGE.
Holt, S. and Marques, J. (2012). 'Empathy in leadership: Appropriate or misplaced? An empirical study on a topic that is asking for attention'. *Journal of Business Ethics*, 105, 95–105.
Holvino, E. (2010). 'Intersections: The simultaneity of race, gender and social class in organizations studies'. *Gender, Work and Organization*, 17, 248–77.
Holzmer, D. (2013). 'Leadership in the time of liminality: A framework for leadership in an era of deep transformation'. In L.R. Melina, G.J. Burgess, L.L. Faulkman and A. Marturno (eds), *The Embodiment of Leadership* (pp. 43–64). San Francisco, CA: Jossey-Bass.
Hughes, K.D., Jennings, J.E., Brush, C., Carter, S. and Welter, F. (2012). Extending women's entrepreneurship research in new directions. *Entrepreneurship Theory and Practice*, 36 (3), 429–42.
Ireland, R.D., Hitt, M.A. and Sirmon, D.G. (2003). 'A model of strategic entrepreneurship: The construct and its dimensions'. *Journal of Management Development*, 29 (6), 963–89.
Jagose, A. (1996). *Queer Theory: An Introduction*. New York, NY: New York University Books.
James, A.E. (2012). 'Conceptualising "woman" as an entrepreneurial advantage: A reflexive approach'. In K.D. Hughes and J.E Jennings (eds), *Global Women's Entrepreneurship Research: Diverse Settings, Questions and Approaches* (pp. 226–40). Cheltenham, UK and Northampton, MA: Edward Elgar Publishing.
Jennings, J.E. and Brush, C.G. (2013). 'Research on women entrepreneurs: Challenges to (and from) the broader entrepreneurship literature?'. *Academy of Management Annals*, 7, 663–715.
Jensen, S.M. and Luthans, F. (2006). 'Entrepreneurs as authentic leaders: Impact on employees' attitudes'. *Leadership and Organizational Development Journal*, 27 (7/8), 646–66.
Johanson, J.C. (2008). 'Perceptions of femininity in leadership: Modern trend or classic component?'. *Sex Roles*, 58, 784–9.
Kandola, R. and Fullerton, J. (1994). *Managing the Mosaic*. London: IPD.
Kanter, R.M. (1977). *Men and Women of the Corporation*. New York, NY: Basic Books.
Kanter, R.M. (2001). *E-volve!*. Cambridge, MA: Harvard Business School Press.
Kelan, E.K. (2009). 'Gender fatigue: The ideological dilemma of gender neutrality and discrimination in organizations'. *Canadian Journal of Administrative Sciences*, 26 (3), 197–210.
Keltner, D. (1995). 'Signs of appeasement: Evidence for the distinct displays of embarrassment, amusement and shame'. *Journal of Personality and Social Psychology*, 68, 441–54.
Kerfoot, D. and Knights, D. (1993). 'Management, masculinity and manipulation: From paternalism to corporate strategy in financial services in Britain'. *Journal of Management Studies*, 30, 679–97.
Koenig, A.M., Mitchell, A.A., Eagly, A.H. and Ristikari, T. (2011). 'Are leader stereotypes masculine? A meta-analysis of three research paradigms'. *Psychological Bulletin*, 137, 616–42.
Küpers, W. and Weibler, J. (2008). 'Inter-leadership: Why and how should we think of leadership and followership integrally?'. *Leadership*, 4, 443–75.
Kuratko, D.F. (2007). 'Entrepreneurial leadership in the 21st century: Guest Editor's perspective'. *Journal of Leadership and Organizational Studies*, 13(4), 1–11.
Leitch, C.M., McMullan, C. and Harrison, R.T. (2013). 'The development of entrepreneurial leadership: The role of human, social and institutional capital'. *British Journal of Management*, 24 (3), 347–66. DOI: 10.1111/j.1467-8551.2011.00808.x.
Lewis, P. (2006). 'The quest for invisibility: Female entrepreneurs and their masculine norm of entrepreneurship'. *Gender, Work and Organization*, 13 (5), 453–69.
Lewis, P. and Simpson, R. (2011). 'Kanter revisited: Gender, power and (in)visibility'. *International Journal of Management Reviews*, 14, 141–58.

Lewis, R. and Mills, S. (2003). *Feminist Postcolonial Theory: A Reader*. London: Routledge.
Lipman-Blumen, J. (1996). *The Connective Edge: Leading in an Interdependent World*. San Francisco, CA: Jossey-Bass.
Mabey, C. and Morrell, K. (2011). 'Leadership in crisis: "Events, my dear boy, events"'. *Leadership*, 7, 105–17.
Martin, L. (2001). 'Are women better at organisational learning? An SME perspective'. *Women in Management Review*, 16 (5/6), 287–96.
Massey, D. (1994). *Space, Place and Gender*. Minneapolis, MN: University of Minnesota Press.
Mattis, M.C. (2004). 'Women entrepreneurs: Out from under the glass ceiling'. *Women in Management Review*, 19 (3), 153–63.
McCann, P. and Oxley, L. (eds) (2012). *Innovation, Entrepreneurship, Geography and Growth*. Chichester: John Wiley & Sons.
McEwan, C. (2001). 'Postcolonialism, feminism and development: Intersections and dilemmas'. *Progress in Development Studies*, 1, 93–111.
McGonagill, G. and Dörffer, T. (2010). *Leadership and Web 2.0: The Leadership Implications of the Evolving Web*. Gütersloh, Germany: Bertelsmann-Stiftung.
McRobbie, A. (2009). *The Aftermath of Feminism*. London: SAGE.
Metcalfe, B.D. and Woodhams, C. (2012). 'Introduction: New directions in gender, diversity and organization theorizing – re-imagining feminist post-colonialism, transnationalism and geographies of power'. *International Journal of Management Review*, 14, 123–40.
Miller, D. and Friesen, P.H. (1984). 'A longitudinal study of the corporate life cycle'. *Management Science*, 30 (10), 1161–83.
Morrison, A.M., White, R.P. and Van Velsor, E. (1987). *Breaking the Glass Ceiling: Can Women Reach the Top of America's Largest Corporations?*. Reading, MA: Addison-Wesley.
Mortimer, C. (2009). 'Developing a new perspective on leadership theory: From a tree of knowledge to a rhizome of contingencies'. *Electronic Journal of Business Research Methods*, 7, 55–65.
Nader, L. (1989). 'Orientalism, Occidentalism and the control of women'. *Cultural Dynamics*, 2, 323–55.
Nahavandi, A. (2002). *The Art and Science of Leadership*, 3rd edn. Upper Saddle River, NJ: Prentice Hall.
Nicholson, N. (1988). 'Personality and entrepreneurial leadership: A study of the heads of the UK's most successful independent companies'. *European Management Journal*, 16 (5), 529–39.
Oakley, A. (1972). *Sex, Gender and Society*. London: Temple Smith.
Orser, B.J., Elliott, C. and Leck, J. (2011). 'Feminist attributes and entrepreneurial identity'. *Gender in Management: An International Journal*, 26 (8), 561–89.
Paddison, R., Philo, C., Routledge, P. and Sharp, J. (2000). 'Entanglements of power: Geographies of domination/ resistance'. In J.P. Sharp, P. Routledge, C. Philo and R. Paddison (eds), *Entanglements of Power: Geographies of Domination/ Resistance* (pp. 1–42). London: Routledge.
Patterson, N., Mavin, S. and Turner, J. (2012). 'Envisioning female entrepreneur: Leaders anew from a gender perspective'. *Gender in Management: An International Journal*, 27 (6), 395–416.
Powell, G.N., Butterfield, D.A. and Parent J.D. (2002). 'Gender and managerial stereotypes: Have the times changed?'. *Journal of Management*, 28, 177–93.
Puar, J. (2005). 'Queer times, queer assemblages'. *Social Text*, 23, 121–38.
Ram, M. and Jones, T. (2008). *Ethnic Minorities in Britain*. Milton Keynes: Small Business Research Trust.
Rao, A. and Kelleher, D. (2000). 'Leadership for social transformation: Some ideas and questions on institutions and feminist leadership'. *Gender and Development*, 8 (3), 74–9.
Reger, J. (2007). 'Where are the leaders? Music, culture, and contemporary feminism'. *American Behavioral Scientist*, 50, 1350–1369.
Renko, M., El Tarabishy, A., Carsrud, A. and Brännback, M. (2015). 'Understanding and

measuring entrepreneurial leadership style'. *Journal of Small Business Management*, 53, 54–74.

Robinson, D.A., Goleby, M. and Hosgood, N. (2006). 'Entrepreneurship as a Values and Leadership Paradigm'. Australia: Bond Business School Publication 11-10-2006. Available at: http://epublications.bond.edu.au/cgi/viewcontent.cgi?article=1009&context=business_pubs.

Roomi, M.A. and Harrison, P. (2011). 'Entrepreneurial leadership: What is it and how should it be taught?'. *International Review of Entrepreneurship*, 9 (3), 1–44.

Roseneil, S. (2000). 'Queer frameworks and queer tendencies: Towards an understanding of post-modern transformations of sexuality'. *Sociological Research Online*, 5 (3), http://www.socresonline.org.uk/5/3roseneil.html.

Schnurr, S. (2008). 'Surviving in a man's world with a sense of humour: An analysis of women leaders' use of humour at work'. *Leadership*, 4 (3), 299–319.

Simpson, R. and Lewis, P. (2005). 'An investigation of silence and a scrutiny of transparency: Re-examining gender in organization literature through the concepts of voice and visibility'. *Human Relations*, 58 (10), 1253–75.

Spivak, G.C. (1999). *A Critique of Postcolonial Reason*. Cambridge, MA: Harvard University Press.

Stead, V. (2013). 'Learning to deploy (invisibility): An examination of women leaders' lived experiences'. *Management Learning*, 44 (1), 63–79.

Stelter, N.Z. (2002). 'Gender differences in leadership: Current social issues and future organizational implications'. *Journal of Leadership and Organizational Studies*, 8 (4), 88–99.

Surie, G. and Ashley, A. (2007). 'Integrating pragmatism and ethics in entrepreneurial leadership for sustainable value creation'. *Journal of Business Ethics*, 81, 235–46.

Swiercz, P. and Lydon, S. (2002). 'Entrepreneurial leadership in high-tech firms: A field study'. *Leadership and Organization Development Journal*, 23 (7), 380–389.

Thornberry, N. (2006). *Lead like an Entrepreneur: Keeping the Entrepreneurial Spirit Alive within the Corporation*. New York, NY: McGraw-Hill.

Thorpe, R., Cope, J., Ram, M. and Pedler, M. (2009). 'Editorial: Leadership development in small- and medium-sized enterprises: The case for action learning'. *Action Learning: Research and Practice*, 6, 201–8.

Torbert, W.R. (2004). *Action Inquiry: The Secret of Timely and Transforming Leadership*. San Francisco, CA: Berrett-Koehler.

Tyler, M. and Cohen, L. (2010). 'Living and working in grey areas: Gender (in)visibility and organisational space'. In P. Lewis and R. Simpson (eds), *Revealing and Concealing Gender: Issues of Visibility in Organizations*, 27th International Congress of Applied Psychology, pp. 23–38.

Vecchio, R.P. (2003). 'Entrepreneurship and leadership: Common trends and common threads'. *Human Resource Management*, 13 (2), 303–28.

Vertovec, S. (2009). *Transnationalism*. London: Routledge.

Wajcman, J. (1998). *Managing Like a Man: Women and Men in Corporate Management*. Cambridge: Polity Press.

Weidenfeller, N.K. (2012). 'Breaking through the glass wall: The experience of being a woman enterprise leader'. *Human Resource Development International*, 15 (3), 365–74.

Wellington, S., Kropf, M. and Gerkovich, P. (2003). 'What's holding women back'. *Harvard Business Review*, 81, 18–19.

Welter, F. (2011). 'Contextualising entrepreneurship – conceptual challenges and ways forward'. *Entrepreneurship Theory and Practice*, 35 (1), 165–84.

West, C. and Zimmerman, D.H. (1987). 'Doing gender'. *Gender and Society*, 1 (2), 125–51.

Wilson, F.M. (1996). 'Research note: Organisation theory: Blind and deaf to gender?'. *Organization Studies*, 17, 825–42.

Wolf, A. (2013). *The XX Factor: How Working Women are Creating a New Society*. London: Profile Books.

Yang, C. (2008). 'The relationships among leadership styles, entrepreneurial orientation and business performance'. *Managing Global Transitions*, 6 (3), 257–75.

Index

action learning 93–6
active entrepreneurship 118
Adams, W.M. 376, 397, 398
Adas, E. 120, 121
Adizes, I. 180, 182
Agle, B.R. 249
Akola, E. 439
Aldrich, H. 110
Alford, R. 119
'alpha male' entrepreneurs 404
Alvesson, M. 16, 88, 96, 99, 342
Amernic, J. 415
Andersen, J. 292, 313
Anderson, A. 110, 275, 277, 350, 393
Anderson, L.E. 330
Andriopoulos, C. 150
Anglo cultures 113
Angus, D. 44
Arabic-language newspapers 267
Argenti, J. 299
Armour, J. 118
Ashley, A. 324
assemblage concept 73, 74
Audretsch, D.B. 221
authentic leadership 51
authors, articles 54–7
Avolio, B.J. 19, 176, 200, 296, 327, 422

Babbie, E. 300
Badawi, J. 114
Bagheri, A. 324, 380
Barbosa, S.D. 354
Barnes, S. 333
Baron, R.A. 162–3
Barth, F. 393
Bartlett, C.A. 282
Bartlett's test of sphericity 303, 304
Bass, B.M. 176, 200
Baumol, W.J. 199
Becherer, R.C. 56
Beckman, C. 270
becoming-realism 67
Beekun, R. 114

being-realism 67
Bell, J. 273, 275–8
Bennis, W.G. 188, 327, 422
Berryman, J. 299
bibliometric analysis 37–61
    future research 60–61
    Leximancer overall concept map 47–53
    limitations 60–61
    methodology 41–7
Bird, B.J. 134, 142
Birley, S. 299
Blake, R. 408
Bolden, R. 69, 264–6
borderless education 436
Brännback, M. 198, 210, 350, 363
BrewDog business story 403–27
bricolage 73
Bridge, S. 181
Brigham, K.H. 40, 54, 136, 197, 206, 406, 407
Brundin, E. 227
Bruni, A. 92
Burgelman, R.A. 226
Burns, J.M. 174, 176, 200, 294
Business For Punks: Break All the Rules (Watt) 423
business venture 133, 134, 136

Calas, M.B. 90, 92, 98
Campbell, R. 377
Cantillon, R. 195
capital exchange process 330
career pathway 327
Carland, J.C. 270
Carland, J.W. 270
Carlyle, Thomas 412, 413
Carroll, B. 69
Carsrud, A.L. 198, 210, 350, 363
case study organisations 383
Casson, M. 115
cause and effect concept 74
Cawthon, D.L. 413, 422

491